THE
DO-IT-YOURSELF
AND HOME IMPROVEMENT MANUAL

© 1985, 1986 Orbis Publishing Ltd
© 1989 Macdonald & Co (Publishers) Ltd

This edition specially produced for CEEPI Ltd/Dealerfield Ltd in
1989

ISBN 0 907305 25 3

Printed and bound in Yugoslavia by Mladinska Knjiga, Ljubljana

THE
DO-IT-YOURSELF
AND HOME IMPROVEMENT MANUAL

EDITED BY MIKE LAWRENCE

CAXTON

CONTENTS

PART 1

BASIC BUILDING

BRICKS AND BRICKWORK

Successful bricklaying relies on three easily-mastered elements.
The first is mixing mortar properly – like a cook's recipe,
sloppy measuring and mixing spells disaster, while a correctly-mixed mortar
will be as strong and long lasting as the bricks or blocks
it bonds together. The second is laying a brick squarely and level.
The third – and arguably the hardest – is laying all the other bricks square
and true with their neighbours, yet provided you can lay one properly
and you're prepared to check your work regularly as you proceed,
a perfect wall will be the end result.

BASIC BRICKLAYING TECHNIQUES

There's a lot in bricklaying that you only really pick up with practice. But there are some rules which can guide you every step of the way. Understanding bricks themselves, the right way to mix mortar and how to use the trowel correctly will help you achieve a result to be proud of.

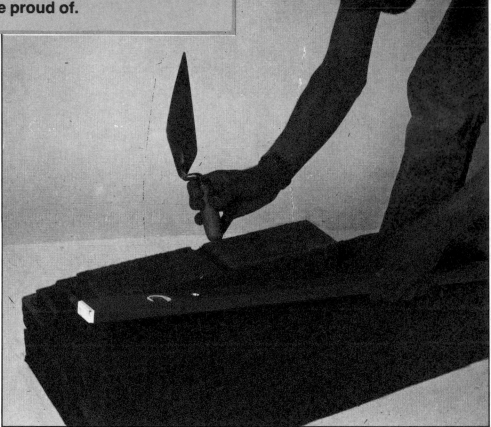

Brickwork is made up of two things: the bricks, and the mortar which forms the joints. Building a wall that's going to last needs careful attention to both, and the first thing is to choose the right bricks for the job.

Know your bricks

There are three groups of clay bricks:

1 Common bricks have no special finish because they are made to be used where they will not be seen or be subjected to major stress or load. They are mostly used in situations where they will be covered by paint, plaster, cladding, rendering etc. They are a relatively inexpensive brick and are usually a rather patchy pink in colour.

2 Facing bricks come in a variety of colours and textures for they are made to be displayed indoors and out. Also called *stocks,* they are capable of bearing heavy loads. If classed as *ordinary quality,* it means they can be used for most projects, but in very exposed conditions outdoors will need to be protected by a damp proof course at ground level (either a course of engineering bricks, see below, or a layer of bituminous felt) or with a coping above to prevent the bricks becoming saturated with rain. Without this protection they are liable to be affected by frost which would cause disintegration. *Special quality* facing bricks are suitable for use in exposed places or where great strength is needed, eg, for paving, retaining walls, garden walls and steps.

3 Engineering bricks are smooth and dense, designed to be used where strength and low water absorption is essential – for example in foundation courses (thus providing a damp proof course for a wall or planter) and load bearing walls.

Another type of bricks completely are the *calcium silicate bricks.* These are flint/lime bricks which are whitish when steam-hardened in an autoclave (they aren't fired like clay), but these are available in many colours because they take pigment well. They absorb moisture easily, so must never be laid with a mortar that doesn't contain a plasticiser. They can be used in just the same way as clay bricks. Like engineering bricks, they are also more regular in shape and vary less in size than ordinary bricks.

Brick types

Bricks also vary in their character as well as their composition: they may be solid, perforated or hollow, but most fall into the solid category. Even bricks with small or large holes in them (these are also known as cellular) are classed as solid so long as the perforations do not exceed 25% of the total volume. The same is true of bricks with a shallow or deep indentation known as a *frog.* As well as making the bricks lighter, perforations and frogs give bricks a better key (ie, the mortar is better able to bond them together).

Bricks are measured in two ways: when they come from the works the actual size is 215mm long, 102.5mm wide and 65mm deep; the format size, however, is the one used for calculating the number of bricks you need. This needs an allowance of about 10mm added to each of these dimensions for the mortar joints – ie, 225mm long, 113mm wide and 75mm deep. Bricks are also made in special shapes and sizes for particular uses (copings, bullnose and angles are some

examples). For information about these see pages 112–113.

Storing bricks

As all bricks (except engineering bricks) are porous, they should be stacked on a level area away from damp, otherwise long after you've used them the mineral salts inside the clay will stain the surface with an unsightly powdery white deposit (known as *efflorescence*). In the garden, put bricks on planks or a metal sheet and cover them with plastic sheeting. Apart from anything else, bricks which are saturated with water (as opposed to just being wet) are hard to lay and will prevent a satisfactory bond between bricks and mortar.

Mortar for bricklaying

Cement and sand made into mortar with water will set quickly, but is liable to create a crack between the mortar and the brick if it shrinks during drying. The ideal mortar, in fact, doesn't set too quickly, doesn't shrink

8

much and can take up settling movements without cracking. There are two ways of making a mortar like this:

● The first way is by adding hydrated lime to the mix. This makes the mortar more workable and smooth (or 'buttery' as the experts say).

● The second is by adding a plasticiser – a proprietary liquid or powder. Air bubbles are formed which provide spaces for the water to expand into, thus preventing cracks.

● Basic to mortar is cement. This acts as the adhesive, binding the particles of sand together. Ordinary portland cement is the one most commonly used.

● Fine sand is used for mortar to give it its correct strength. Use clean builder's sand (also known as 'soft' sand) which does not contain clay, earth or soluble salts (these can lead to efflorescence).

Buying the materials

Cement is usually sold in 50kg (112lb) bags, although you may also find smaller sizes. Sand is sold by the cu metre (1⅓ cu yd) and in parts of a cu metre. To give you a sense of scale, a cu metre of sand weighs about 1,500kg (1½ tons) — a very large heap. Both are usually bought from builders merchants, where you can also buy lime or

MIXING MORTAR

1 Unless you're using dry ready-mix (most suitable for small jobs) carefully proportion 1 part cement to 6 parts builders sand.

2 Thoroughly mix the cement into the sand so that you end up with an entirely consistent colour. Turn the mix over at least three times.

3 Adding a little plasticiser to the water (the amount will be specified on the container) will make the mortar easier to work with.

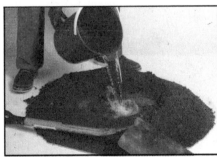

4 Form a crater and pour in half the water. In total you'll need about the same amount of water (by volume) as cement — but add the rest gradually.

5 Mix in the dry mortar from the inside walls of the crater. As the water is absorbed, add a little more. Turn the whole mix over several times.

6 The final mix should look like this. Check it by stepping the shovel back — the ridges should be firm and smooth, holding the impression of the shovel.

READY REFERENCE

BRICKLAYING GLOSSARY

Frog: the identation in the top of a brick. Generally bricks are laid frog up except on the top course of a free-standing wall.

Header face: the small end of the brick. Bricks laid so this end shows on the face of the wall are called headers.

Stretcher face: the long side of a brick. Bricks laid lengthways are called stretchers.

Bed face: the underside of the brick which is set into a mortar bed.

Bonds: the patterns of bricklaying to give walls strength. Vertical joints (called perpends) in one course must be overlapped by bricks in the next so the joint doesn't run through.

Course: name for a single row of bricks. A course of stretchers is known as ½ brick thick, a course of headers 1 brick thick.

Joints: the average of 10mm of mortar between bricks.

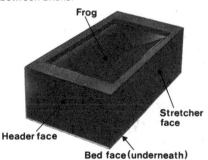

BRICK SIZES

A standard brick is 215mm (8½in) long, 102.5mm (4in) wide and 65mm (2⅝in) deep. For estimating purposes the 'format size' is used instead. This includes 10mm in each dimension to allow for one mortar joint. Format size is 225 x 113 x 75mm (8⅞ x 4⅜ x 3in).

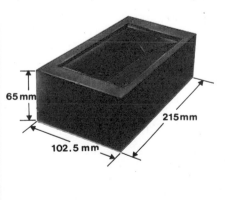

USING THE TROWEL

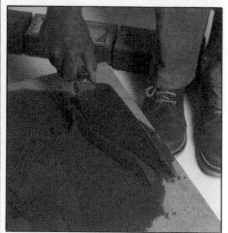

1 *Use the trowel to chop off a section of mortar (about the same size as the trowel) and separate it from the rest with a clean slicing action.*

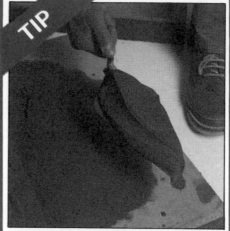

2 *Shape the back of the mortar slice into a curve — so that it's pear-shaped. Sweep the trowel underneath to lift the mortar off the board.*

3 *Slide the trowel sharply backwards to lay the mortar in a 'sausage' shape. Spread it out by stepping the tip of the trowel down the middle.*

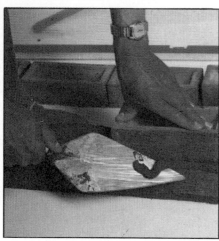

4 *When you've laid a brick in position, remove the mortar that squeezes out of the joint by sweeping the trowel upwards with its edge just scraping the brick.*

5 *To create the vertical joints between bricks, you 'butter' one end before you lay it. Scrape the mortar on by sliding the trowel backwards.*

6 *Hold the brick upright and scrape down all four edges. Finally spread out the mortar evenly to a thickness of 10mm-12mm (about ½in).*

proprietary plasticisers. Alternatively you can buy special masonry cement which has a plasticiser already in it and only needs to be mixed with sand and water.

Proprietary plasticisers are available in 5kg containers and you will have more than you need if you're only doing a small job — only a capful or two for each bucket of cement. But always follow manufacturer's instructions for use. Hydrated lime is a powder bought in 25kg bags.

Dry ready-mix mortars are also available with all the necessary ingredients ready mixed — so you just add water. Although more expensive than buying the sand and cement separately, it's a convenient way of buying for small projects. Bags usually come in

10kg, 25kg, 40kg and 50kg sizes. Alternatively, you can buy bags in which the cement is packaged separately from the sand.

Remember that it's always better to have a little more than you need — so be generous in estimating (see *Ready Reference).* Also make sure that any surplus cement or dry-mix is well sealed. This is vital to prevent it going off.

Rules to remember

● When filling the cement bucket (proportions are by volume, not weight), tap it frequently to disperse any trapped air.
● Mortar that has begun to set is no use. Any not used within 2 hours of the wetting of the cement should be discarded – if used it would

dry too quickly and would not give the required strength to the brickwork.
● The sand and cement have to be thoroughly mixed before any water is added. Turn mixture over and over with the shovel until the pile is a consistent colour all through. The same rule applies to dry-mix mortar.
● When mixing in water, make crater on top of the pile, add some water and bring dry materials from sides to centre. Turn over whole pile several times, make another crater and repeat until mixture has a consistency which will hold the impression of the fingers when squeezed, or the impression of the trowel point.
● As builders' sand is rarely dry it is not possible to know how much water will be

needed to achieve the right consistency. Using a small container such as an empty tin will give you more control than using a bucket – and add water bit by bit.

The vital bricklaying tool

The trowel is the tool which makes the job, and no other tool can be substituted for it. A bricklayer's trowel is heavier and less flexible than any other trowel, and can be used to pick up and smooth down a required amount of mortar. Brick trowels can be bought in various blades sizes (from 225 to 350mm, or 9in to 14in) but the easiest to handle is the 250mm/10in one.

Brick trowels are roughly diamond shaped with a sharp point at the end opposite to the handle. The left side has a straight edge for scooping up mortar; the right side has a slight curve used for cleaning up the edges of bricks and for tapping the brick down into the mortar to level it. These are reversed in left-handed trowels.

Professional bricklayers use the curved edge of the trowel to cut bricks, but a more accurate and cleaner cut can be made with a brick hammer and bolster chisel. The trowel has a wooden handle raised slightly above the diamond, and at an angle to it to prevent you brushing your knuckles on the bricks as you are working. Getting the feel of the trowel and handling it properly is the key to good brickwork.

The trowel must be manipulated so that the mortar is scooped up in what's called a 'pear' or 'sausage' shape (see left) and placed on the bricks. This action is one that needs a lot of practice, for mortar that isn't compact is hard to manoeuvre and won't go where you want it to.

Practice routines

Make up a small amount of mortar (or 1 part of lime to 6 of sand, plus water to make it pliable) and practise combining it with bricks before you undertake a bricklaying project. The bricks can be scraped off within 2 hours (before the mortar sets). You have longer with

BRICK JOINTS

1 The simplest brick joint is a 'struck' joint — do the vertical joints first, drawing the trowel upwards or downwards with a firm action.

2 Next do the horizontal joints — use the full length of the trowel and drawing it firmly backwards with a sliding action.

Types of pointing

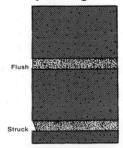
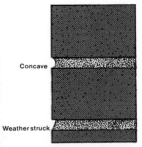
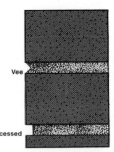

There are lots of ways of finishing off the joints in brickwork. Above is a selection of six of the most common. The flush joint is finished flush with the brick surface, while struck, weatherstruck and vee joints are all formed with the point of the trowel. Concave or rounded pointing is formed by running the edge of a bucket handle or a piece of hose pipe along the joints, while recessed pointing is pressed back with a piece of wood planed to the same size as the brick joints.

LAYING AND LEVELLING

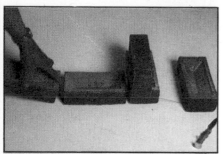

1 Check layout by 'dry laying' the bricks, setting them a finger-width apart. Use string and pegs as a guide, fixing the ends with bricks, as shown.

2 Use your gauge rod — see **8** — to check that a corner is square. Measure 3 marks along one side, 4 along the other; if square, the diagonal will be 5 marks.

3 With the line and pegs still in position, lay the mortar on the base by drawing the trowel sharply backwards. Lay enough for at least 2 bricks at a time.

4 Tap the first brick into position, using the string as your guide. The mortar should make a joint 10mm (just under ½in) thick.

5 Lay the next 4 or 5 bricks, still following the line, making sure all mortar joints are the same thickness. Carefully scrape off the excess mortar.

6 Use the spirit level to check that the bricks are sitting perfectly level. If one is too high, tap it down. If too low, remove it and add mortar.

7 Each brick for the next course should straddle two on the first course. This creates the 'stretcher bond', evenly distributing the weight of bricks.

8 Check that the courses are rising correctly with a 'gauge rod'. The rod is marked at 75mm intervals — brick height plus a 10mm mortar joint.

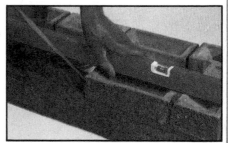

9 With string and pegs removed, check each brick with the spirit level as you lay it. Tap the bricks gently with the trowel handle.

10 With each new course, check the corner with the gauge rod. With the first brick correctly positioned, other bricks are aligned with it.

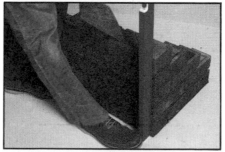

11 Check that the faces of the bricks are vertical and aligned with each other. If not tap bricks back into position with the trowel.

12 Also check diagonally across the face of the bricks. Lay the bricks frog (the indentation in the top of the brick) down only on the final course.

lime mortar. The 'sausage' or 'pear' is the basic shape of mortar lifted onto the trowel. The following sequence is worth practising over and over until it becomes easy to do. Chop down into the mortar and draw a slice of it towards the edge of the board. Move the trowel to and fro, along the length of the slice, pressing the body of the trowel on to the mortar till you have shaped the back of the slice into a curve – the mortar should be smooth and have no cracks.

Now sweep the trowel underneath the curved slice and load it on to the trowel, it will either look like a sausage or a pear, hence the name. Put it back on the spot board, shape it again, then sweep it up ready for placing. This amount of mortar should give you a 10mm thick bed for two stretchers. Hold the trowel parallel to the course, then, as you draw it back towards you, lift and jerk it slightly so the mortar rolls off gradually in a smooth elongated sausage. Press the mortar along the middle with the point of the trowel so a furrow is made in the mortar. When you place a brick on it a small amount of mortar should ooze out.

Joints in brickwork
Bricks are laid with both horizontal and vertical joints to keep the bricks apart. After the excess mortar has been removed from the face of the bricks (and behind), the joints can be finished in various ways – for an attractive effect as well as for protection against the weather. Coloured mortar is a specially prepared dry mix to which only water needs to be added. Pigment can be bought to colour your own mix of mortar but it can be difficult to obtain the same colour for each batch.

Making a cross joint
Sometimes 'buttering' is used to describe the technique of coating the end of a brick with mortar to form the vertical joint. Sweep up enough mortar to cover about a third of the trowel. Now sharply flick the trowel so the mortar lifts up, then falls back onto the trowel, (this squashes out air and makes the mortar 'sticky'). Hold the brick at a slight angle, then scrape the trowel against the bottom edge. Use the trowel point to flatten and level the mortar on the header – it should be 10mm thick.

Cleaning off
The other important trowel action is removing excess mortar from the side of the bricks as you lay them. Cut the mortar off cleanly by firmly lifting the trowel upwards (if you do it horizontally it will smudge the bricks). This leaves a flush joint.

Tricks or bad habits?
Bricklayers will often add a few squirts of washing-up liquid to the water when mixing mortar. This on-site plasticiser, used instead of lime or a proprietary plasticiser, is not added in any precise manner. Although it might make the mortar more pliable it could also weaken it. And how much is a squirt anyway? If you want a pliable mix, buy a proprietary plasticiser additive, or ready-mix with it already added.

● The shovel is frequently used as a measuring stick when mixing mortar, and there's no doubt it's an easy way of proportioning the ingredients. It can, however, give wildly inaccurate results. A mound of powdery cement won't sit on a shovel in the same way as sand will. Measurement should always be by volume. A bucket is ideal for most quantities – although if you're only making a very small amount use a small metal container instead.

● The curved edge of the bricklayer's trowel will effectively cut bricks when wielded by a professional. Apart from doing a great deal of damage to the trowel (the edge of which is needed for the upward sweep required to remove mortar from brickwork), it is easier to cut bricks on a sandy or soft ground with a bolster chisel and a hammer.

Protecting brickwork from damage
As soon as you have finished bricklaying, and you've cleaned off and finished all the joints, it's worth taking a few simple precautions to protect your work until the mortar has set and it is able to take care of itself.

The biggest enemy is rain. A heavy downpour could wash mortar out of freshly-pointed joints – which you would then have to re-point – and stain the face of the brickwork. Such stains are particularly difficult to remove except by hosing and scrubbing. Furthermore, if your brickwork is set on a hard surround – a patio, for example, or alongside a path – rain could splash up from the surface onto your brickwork, again causing staining and erosion of mortar joints at or near ground level.

So on small projects it's a good idea to cover your work, at least for 24 hours or so, until the mortar has had time to set to something like its final hardness. Drape polythene or similar water-proof sheeting over the brickwork, anchoring it on top with several loose bricks, and drawing the sides of the sheeting away from the face of the brickwork before anchoring them at ground level a foot or so away from the wall. In windy weather, lay a continuous line of bricks, or use lengths of timber, to prevent the wind from whipping underneath the sheeting.

Remember that until the mortar has hardened any knocks will displace bricks and break mortar joints. Corners are particularly prone to knocks and accidental collisions. So it's well worth erecting some kind of simple barricade in front of the new work for a day or two.

FORMING CORNERS & PIERS

The techniques involved in making a brick wall turn a corner or to finish with a pier require an understanding of bonding and how cut bricks might have to be used to keep a design symmetrical.

Building walls isn't simply a matter of arranging bricks in straight lines. You may have to include corners and, when you come to the end of the wall, it must be finished off properly. The techniques for doing this effectively are relatively easy once you know the basis of brick bonding.

Brick bonds are crucial to bricklaying; simply stacking bricks one above the other without any kind of interlocking would neither distribute the weight of the wall evenly nor provide the wall with any kind of strength, however strong the mortar between the bricks. And because the joints line up they would provide a perfect channel for water to get in and wash out the mortar.

The simplest way of bonding is to overlap the bricks, with no vertical joints continuing through adjacent courses. This kind of bonding can create numerous different patterns — some very simple, such as the stretcher bond used on pages 8 -13, others much more complicated and requiring advance planning.

Exactly the same principle applies whether you're building a wall a half-brick thick (a single line of bricks) or one that needs to be one brick thick (two adjacent lines of bricks or one line laid header on). The difference is that instead of only overlapping the bricks lengthways as in a *stretcher bond* you can also overlap them widthways. With the *header bond*, for instance, all of the bricks are arranged header on to the face of the wall — and again the vertical joints only line up in alternate courses. In effect, the bricks overlap by half their width.

With any bonding pattern, there may be a need for cut bricks to maintain the bond. This may happen at the end of a wall built in stretcher bond where half bricks (called ½ bats) are needed in alternate courses. It may also occur where a new wall is being tied in to an existing wall (see below).

Similarly, with a wall built in header bond the ends need two three-quarter bricks (called ¾ bats) laid side by side in alternate courses to maintain the symmetry, the overlap and wall thickness. With other types of bond, the number and variety of cut bricks increases. The *English bond*, for instance, alternates a course of bricks laid stretcher face on with a course header face on to make a one-brick thick wall — and it needs a brick cut in half lengthways (called a queen closer) in each header course or two ¾ bats laid side by side in the stretcher course.

Corners in brickwork

When it comes to turning a corner in brickwork (known as a *quoin*) the importance of correct bonding is even more apparent. Without it, you'd be building two walls which weren't interlocked and so lacking in real strength. In a half-brick thick wall in stretcher bond the corner is easy to make. Instead of cutting ½ bats for alternate courses, a whole brick is placed header face on at right angles to the front face of the wall.

The necessary 'tying in' of bricks with other bonding patterns, however, usually requires additional cut bricks and careful planning. In effect, the bond may change when you turn a corner. In header bond for example, which has alternate courses starting with ¾ bats, ¾ bats must be placed header on as well to create the corner. In English bond the stretcher course on one side of the quoin becomes the header course on the other.

MARKING OUT FOR A CORNER

1 Bricks can be used to hold the string lines on already laid concrete but use profile boards if a trench has to be dug. Check with a builders square that all the lines cross at right angles.

2 Laying the bricks dry is the best way of checking your calculations after setting out is completed, the width of your finger being a good guide to the eventual thickness of the joint.

3 After the first course is laid there are two things to check: the bricks must be horizontal (you can tap down any out of alignment) and their faces must be truly perpendicular.

4 From the first course onwards, the squareness of the corner must be checked so that any adjustments can be made immediately to prevent the wall leaning out (called an overhang).

A bond may also have to be altered if the bricks don't fit the actual length of the wall. When this happens you have to break the bond as close as possible to the centre of the wall. If the length differs by 56mm or less don't use a ¼ bat (this is considered bad building practice) but use ½ and ¾ bats instead, making sure you place them so that no straight joints occur.

PROFILE BOARDS

These are placed to give accurate lines when digging the trench for the foundation. Strings attached to nails in the top of the boards define the width of the trench and must cross at perfect right angles where the corner is to be built.

Craig Warwick

Keith Morris

The end of the wall

If you're building a wall as a boundary, or enclosing a corner of your garden, it may have to meet existing walls at one or even both ends. In such situations you have to tie in the bricks with the other wall(s), so this may affect your choice of bond for the new wall — it's always better if the new matches the old. It also means you have to match levels, and before you lay your first new brick you have to chip out bricks from alternate courses of the existing wall to provide for 'toothing-in'. Even if you can satisfactorily match the bond pattern, the old bricks may be a different size, so to make a proper connection expect to cut bricks to odd lengths to tooth in. More about this in another section.

If your wall comes to a free-standing end you must create what's called a *stopped end*. This requires careful checking for vertical alignment, and needs to be finished off to make a clean, neat face. But it is important to make sure the end is strong enough — and to do this you actually increase the width by a half brick to create a 'pier'. In effect, instead of cutting a ½ bat to finish off each alternate course, you lay the last brick in alternate courses at right angles to the wall face. By adding a ½ bat next to it you create a squared-off end — a simple pier.

Piers for support

It's not just at the end of a wall that you may need the added strength of a pier. To give a wall extra support, particularly on a long run, you need piers at regular intervals. For instance, walls of half-brick thickness need piers that project by at least half a brick every 1.8m (6ft). To do this in a wall built in stretcher bond, you will have to alter the bonding pattern to accommodate the pier, and add cut bricks to ensure the correct overlapping is maintained. For how to do this see pictures page 95. If the wall is over 12 courses high, a more substantial pier is needed: three bricks are placed header on in the first course, and ¾ bats are used on the pier and either side of the middle stretcher in the second course.

One brick thick walls need piers at less frequent intervals — in fact every 2.8m (9ft) — but the pier has only to project by half a brick (see diagram).

Where piers occur, the foundation must be dug slightly wider at that point (about half a brick wider on both sides and beyond the end of the pier).

Method of building

Planning how you're going to lay the bricks is, of course, only the theoretical side of bricklaying. In practice, to make sure the wall stands completely perpendicular and the corners and ends are vertical it's most important to follow a certain order of work. Lay at least the first course of bricks dry so that you're sure they all fit in (see also pages

TURNING A CORNER

1 On each face of the wall check that it is perpendicular by holding the level at an angle. Tap bricks in or out.

2 As each course is laid use the gauge rod to check that the wall is rising evenly, with equal horizontal joints.

3 Check that the corner is vertical by using the spirit level straight. Hold it steady with your foot.

4 Lay the first course from the corner to the stopped end following a line and cutting bricks as needed.

5 Build up the stopped end so the courses are stepped by the correct overlap. This is called 'racking back'.

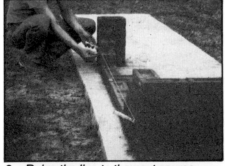

6 Raise the line to the next course between the racked corner and stopped end and fill in between.

7 To make sure you get vertical joints in line, mark the position of each one on the whole brick above it.

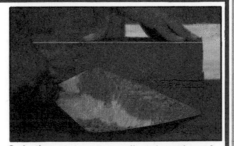

8 In the next course, align the edge of the brick with the mark. The joints will then be the right width too.

READY REFERENCE

A BUILDERS SQUARE

Essential for checking that corners are 90°, this is simply three pieces of wood cut in the proportions of 3:4:5 (ie, a right-angled triangle). Nail them together with a half-lap at the right-angled corner and with the longest side nailed on top of the other two sides.

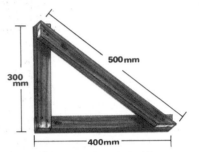

WHAT CAN GO WRONG

You can lose the horizontal because you didn't check often enough as the wall was rising. With every course
● use the spirit level
● use the gauge rod
The wall can lean out or in because you didn't check the vertical with the spirit level. Use it when
● racking back
● starting a new course
When laying to a line the last brick won't fit because the vertical joints further back along the course were not the same width. So make sure that in each course
● the joint width remains constant
● vertical joints line up in alternate courses – use the gauge rod for this.

LAYING TO A LINE

When you build up two corners at opposite ends of a wall, the process of laying bricks in between is called 'laying to a line'. To fix the line for each course use
● a bricklayers line and pins

● twine tied around two spare bricks

● triangular profile boards (good for beginners as you can see that the courses are rising evenly).

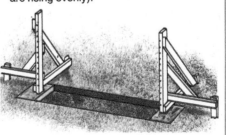

Keith Morris

A PIER IN STRETCHER BOND

1 *In order to prevent any straight joints you have to break the bond. On the first course place two bricks header on, then place a ½ bat so it spans the joint equally.*

2 *On the second course to get the pattern right you have to lose a quarter from each of the stretchers on either side of the ½ bat. So cut and place two ¾ bats.*

3 *On the pier itself, the second course is not tied on but is merely a stretcher laid across the projecting two headers. This gives a pier the same width as the wall.*

Keith Morris

8 -13). Another big problem is that it is difficult to lay a line of bricks with each vertical joint exactly the same width — an inaccuracy of just 1mm in each joint between a line of 10 bricks will mean that the last brick at the corner or end will project over the one underneath by 10mm. The best way to avoid this happening is by 'racking back' — build up each corner or end first, stepping the bricks upwards and checking the vertical each time. When the bricks reach the required height, start filling in. Any slight inaccuracies can be accommodated by the joints in the middle part of the wall where they'll be less noticeable as long as you make sure the bricks overlap each other by as close to half a brick as possible.

Making the corner square

Marking out the corner for the foundation is the first priority—and it's vital that it is square. Using profile boards and strings—explained in Foundations, pages 34–38—is the best way to start. Set the boards for each line of the corner about 1 metre (3ft) back from the actual building line (see diagram page 15). The strings must cross at right angles (90°) and to make sure that they do, use the 3:4:5 method (see *Ready Reference* page 16) to make yourself a builder's square. This is a large set-square made by nailing together three

75mm×38mm (3in×1½in) softwood battens cut into lengths of 450mm (18in), 600mm (2ft), and 750mm (2ft 6in) so that the sides are in the ratio 3:4:5. This is a manageable size but it can be made bigger if you prefer.

Laying out the corner

When you have the profile boards in position, dig the foundation trenches — see pages 30 - 34 — and lay the concrete. Allow it to 'cure' for at least 5 or 6 days before laying the first course of bricks. This gives it time to harden properly (although it needs about 3 weeks to reach its full strength). The next step is to mark out the actual building lines on the concrete, again using the profile boards and strings (see pages 34–38 again).

Lay the first course of the entire wall, starting at the corner and working outwards first along one wall line and then along the other. In building a half-brick thick wall in stretcher bond it is easy to turn the corner simply by laying two bricks to make a right angle. Check the angle using the builder's square.

Once the first course is laid, check again with the spirit level to make sure that all the bricks are sitting correctly. Add a little mortar or remove a little from underneath any bricks which are out of true. At the same time, check again that all the bricks follow your building line, and tap them into position if they don't.

CORNERS AND STOPPED ENDS

Left: At a stopped end in stretcher bond, the cut side of the ½ bats on alternate courses are hidden by the mortar joints.

Right: In a brick-thick wall in English bond, two ¼ bats or a queen closer are laid before the final header at a stopped end.

Below: At a corner in a stretcher bond wall, the header face is seen on one side while the stretcher shows on the other.

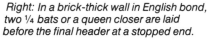

Below: The arrangement is the same at a corner, but to maintain the bonding the course on the other face becomes stretchers laid side by side.

Craig Warwick

Once this is done you can remove the lines and start building up the ends and corners.

Putting in the piers

If you're going to need piers at any point along the wall, don't forget to plan them in from the beginning. In a half-brick thick stretcher bond wall a pier is tied in by two bricks laid header on in alternate courses. The courses in between are not tied in but consist of a single stretcher laid parallel to the wall for the pier, and a ½ bat and two ¾ bats replacing two stretchers in the face of the wall.

A pier at a stopped end in a half-brick stretcher bond wall is made using a stretcher face at right angles at the end. The course is completed with a ½ bat and on the alternate course two stretchers are used parallel to the wall.

Checking as you build

One of the most useful checking tools you can make yourself is a gauge rod (see pages 8 - 13) and as you build up the corners and ends check each course with the rod to make sure the horizontal joints are consistent. If you're aiming for a wall of about 12 courses in total, build up the corners and ends to about 6 or 7 courses first before starting to fill in between them.

To step the bricks correctly, lay 3 bricks along the building line for every 5 courses you want to go up — so it's best to start by laying 4 bricks along each side of the corner and in from each end (see pictures 5 and 6 on page 16).

Filling in

Once you've built up corners and ends properly racked back (stepped with the correct overlap), the rest of the wall can be filled in course by course. Although you can lay the bricks normally, checking each time with the level and gauge, a good tip here is to string a line between bricks already laid at each end, then lay the bricks in between to this line. A bricklayer's line and pins (the pins are specially shaped to slip into a mortar joint) is ideal, but a string can be hooked around a brick at the correct height and then anchored under a loose brick to give a start line to follow.

If you over-mortar a brick and it protrudes above the level, gently tap it down with the end of the trowel handle and scrape off the excess mortar squeezed out of the joint. If a brick does not stand high enough, remove it and the mortar underneath, then replace it with fresh mortar.

Getting the last brick into the line can be quite tricky and a good tip is to scrape the mortar onto the end of bricks at each side — then squeeze the brick in.

(see pages 8 - 13)

(see pictures 5 and 6 on page 16).

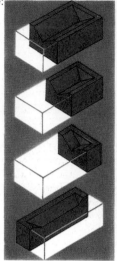

READY REFERENCE

BRICK CUTS

The most common cut bricks, used in different bonds, are:

¾ bat – cut widthways, ¼ removed

½ bat – brick cut widthways, ½ removed

¼ bat – brick cut widthways, ¾ removed (the same size as a ½ queen closer)

queen closer – brick cut in two lengthways

CUTTING BRICKS

Mark cutting line on each face with chalk

Nick the line all round; with hard bricks nick each face at least twice

Place brick bottom up on grass, sand or newspaper. Put bolster on nicked line, give sharp blow with hammer

DON'T use the edge of the trowel to cut bricks because
● it's an expensive tool
● it's rarely accurate

DID YOU KNOW?

A pig in a wall means the wall isn't level. *An overhang* means the corner leans out. *A batter* is when a corner leans back.

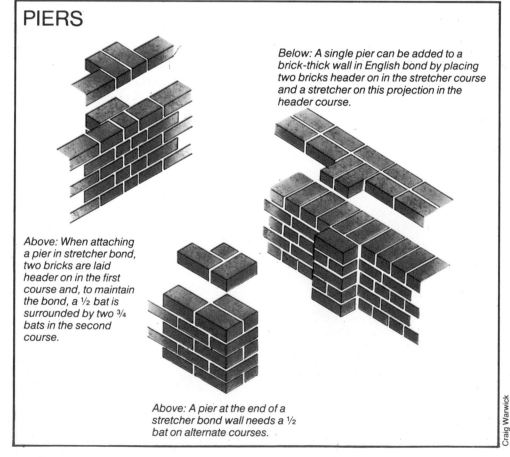

PIERS

Below: A single pier can be added to a brick-thick wall in English bond by placing two bricks header on in the stretcher course and a stretcher on this projection in the header course.

Above: When attaching a pier in stretcher bond, two bricks are laid header on in the first course and, to maintain the bond, a ½ bat is surrounded by two ¾ bats in the second course.

Above: A pier at the end of a stretcher bond wall needs a ½ bat on alternate courses.

Craig Warwick

LAYING SPECIAL BONDS

Brick bonds are crucial to the strength of a wall, and they also provide a decorative face. With careful planning, even complex patterns are easy to make.

When you're building a brick wall it's vital that you lay each brick so that it overlaps and interlocks with its neighbours. You can't simply stack the bricks, one on top of the other; this would create vertical planes of weakness and, under load, the wall would soon collapse.

Instead, the bricks must be arranged so that the vertical joints (called perpends) in one course don't coincide with those in the course above and below. This arrangement, called a 'bonding pattern', ensures mainly that the weight of the wall and any load bearing on it is evenly distributed, but it can also be a decorative feature.

Types of brick bond
There are many bonding arrangements you can use, depending on the type of wall you're building, how strong it's to be, and whether its appearance is a consideration. They're basically all variations on the 'half-lap' bond, in which all bricks lap half a brick over the bricks in the course below, but there's also 'quarter-lap' bond, in which the bricks lap over a quarter of a brick length.

Stretcher bond
The most straightforward and common arrangement is called 'stretcher' or 'running' bond, which is used mainly for 112mm (4½in) thick – or half-brick thick – walls. Each course is identical; the bricks are laid end to end and each overlaps the one below by half its length, presenting its long stretcher face to the front face of the wall.

Header bond
The simplest type of bonding for a 225mm (9in) thick – or single brick – wall is 'header' bond, in which all the bricks are laid side by side with their ends (again often decorative) presented to the front face of the wall, and each course overlapping its neighbours by half its width. This type of bonding pattern, although attractive, is wasteful of bricks.

English bond
The strongest brick bond for 225mm (9in) thick or thicker walls – particularly if they're loadbearing – is called English bond. It consists of one course of parallel stretchers – to give the wall thickness – alternated with a course of headers laid across the thickness of the wall. In this tough, criss-cross bonding arrangement no straight joints occur within the thickness of the wall, which could weaken the structure.

Flemish bond
Where a highly decorative effect is needed in a single or half-brick thick wall, Flemish bond is often regarded as one of the most popular. The pattern consists of alternate headers and stretchers in each course – and the decorative effect can be increased by using contrasting coloured and textured headers, or even by slightly recessing some of the headers in the face of the wall, or allowing them to protrude fractionally.

Garden Wall bonds
Other common brick bonds you can use, mainly for their attractive appearance, but also because they're more economical, are really just modified versions of English and Flemish bonds. Basically they reduce the number of headers used, and introduce more stretchers yet still maintain the basic bonding patterns.

English Garden Wall bond, for example, originally used for boundary walls of one brick thickness, is one bond that reduces the

19

ENGLISH BOND WALL WITH END PIER

1 *English bond consists of a course of stretchers alternated with one of headers. Mark out the shape of the wall and pier and dry lay the first course.*

2 *Remove the bricks then re-lay them on a mortar bed. Lay the first course of the pier and the return wall first and check the level between them.*

3 *Make sure the end pier is laid perfectly square by checking with a builder's square. Note the brick that 'ties' the pier to the wall.*

6 *Work towards the pier using stretcher bond over the first header course then return to the corner laying the second half of the course.*

7 *Complete the second course then start the third course, which is a repeat of the first course. The return wall is laid as a row of stretchers.*

8 *Bond the pier with alternate courses of stretchers and headers spaced with queen closers. Lay the corners first and fill in with cut bricks.*

number of bricks that you'll need for headers; it usually consists of three or five courses of stretchers to one of headers.

Flemish Garden Wall bond is another decorative yet durable bond that consists of an arrangement of three, four or five stretchers to one header per course – each course being identical – and is especially attractive as the outer skin of a cavity wall. You can introduce headers of constrasting colour or texture, either inset or projecting, for a greater decorative effect.

When you're using these bonds in a half-brick thick wall you'll have to use cut bricks, called half-bats (see below and *Ready Reference*) for the headers.

Open bonding

Where load-bearing capacity isn't a vital consideration in ycur wall you can use an economical form of 'open' bond. It's especially good for screen walls for your garden or patio, giving a fairly solid appearance yet still admitting light and air.

Each course is laid as stretchers and the bricks are separated by quarter-brick spaces.

Using cut bricks

Any bonding pattern – except open bond – will need to include cut bricks in order to maintain the bond.

In a stretcher bond wall you'll have to include half bricks (called half-bats) in alternate courses at the end of the wall, or where you're tying a new wall into an original wall.

In a header bond wall you must insert two three-quarter bricks (called three-quarter-bats) laid side by side in alternate courses to maintain the symmetry of the pattern.

With the more complicated bonds the number – and variety – of cut bricks increases. English bond, for example, needs a

brick cut in half lengthways (called a queen closer) in each header course, or two three-quarter-bats laid side by side in the stretcher course to maintain the bond.

You won't need to include cut bricks in an open-bond wall; you can maintain the symmetry by simply reducing the spaces between the bricks.

Turning corners

It's important to maintain the bonding arrangement throughout the wall for strength and symmetry, although when you come to turn a corner (called a quoin) you may have to vary the pattern over a small area (see pages 14 -18). The most crucial point is to ensure both sides of the corner are interlocked, otherwise you'd end up with two separate walls lacking rigidity.

With some bonds, corners are fairly straightforward to make. If you're building a

4 *Lay the bricks header on between pier and corner. The bond changes to stretchers on the return wall, with a queen closer spacer at the corner.*

5 *Start the second course at the corner; line up the first brick with the centre of the header next to the queen closer in the first course and the end brick.*

9 *Continue to lay alternate courses of stretchers and headers until you reach the finished height of your wall. Check the level frequently with a spirit level.*

10 *Check the 'plumb', or vertical level, of the wall, paying particular attention to the corners of the pier. Rack back the return wall if you're continuing next day.*

half-brick wall in stretcher bond, for example, you can simply turn a corner by placing a whole brick, header on, at the corner instead of filling in with half-bats at alternate courses. You can then continue to build the wall at the other side of the angle in exactly the same stretcher bond.

Other bonding arrangements, however, will require additional cut bricks so that you can tie-in the two leaves of the corner. In effect the pattern will change when you turn a corner, although it's re-established on the course above. In English bond, for example, the stretcher course on one side of the quoin becomes the header course on the other.

Piers for support
If you're building a particularly high or long wall you'll need to build in supporting columns called piers to give added strength to the structure. Build them at regular intervals throughout the wall ('attached' piers) and at the ends. For a half-brick thick wall you'll need a pier that projects from the wall by at least half a brick every 1.8m (6ft). In a stretcher bond wall you must alter the bonding pattern by adding cut bricks to give the necessary overlap, which ensures that the pier is correctly tied into the wall. To form a minimum-sized attached pier in this type of wall, you must lay two bricks header-on in the first course and, to maintain the bond, a half-bat flanked by two three-quarter-bats in the second course. Repeat this arrangement.

For one brick thick walls you'll need piers at only 2.8m (9ft) intervals, but the pier must still project from the wall by at least half a brick. To form an attached pier of this size in an English bond wall you should lay two bricks header on in the stretcher course and a stretcher on the projection in the header course.

BRICK CUTS
When you're building a brick wall you'll need to cut some bricks in order to maintain the bond. The most common cut bricks are:

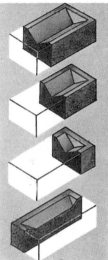

● ¾ bat, cut widthways, removing ¼ of the brick (A)

● ½ bat, cut widthways, removing ½ of the brick (B)

● ¼ bat, cut widthways, removing ¾ of the brick (C)

● queen closer, cut in two lengthways (the same width as a ¼ bat) (D).

CUTTING A BRICK

To cut a brick accurately:
● mark the cutting line on each face with chalk against a rule (A)

● nick the line all round with a club hammer and cold chisel (B)

● place the brick, frog down, on a soft surface (grass, sand or newspaper) and hit the chisel sharply on the nick with the hammer (C)

● use the side of your brick trowel to trim off irregularities in the brick (D).

FLEMISH BOND WALL WITH ATTACHED PIER

1 Flemish bond consists of alternate headers and stretchers in each course. Mark out the wall and dry lay the bricks, incorporating an 'attached pier'.

2 Lay the facing bricks of the first course on a mortar bed, including a queen closer at a stopped end. Fill in the second half of the course.

3 The first course of a single brick attached pier is bonded to the wall with headers for the sides and a stretcher brick between them for the back edge.

4 The second course is the same as the first, but the stretchers are laid over the headers and vice versa. Lay the facing bricks first.

5 The second course of the pier is laid using ³⁄₄-bats at the back corner to keep the shape of the pier, with a ¹⁄₄-bat to fill the gap that's left inside.

6 A stopped end – one without a pier – is formed by the inclusion of a queen closer and a brick header-on in alternate courses; then continue normally.

7 Build the wall as high as you'd like it, repeating the rows of headers and stretchers in alternate courses. Check the level across the face of the wall.

8 Check that the mortar joints are constant using a gauging rod marked off in 75mm (3in) intervals – brick height plus a 10mm (³⁄₈in) mortar joint.

9 If you leave the wall overnight, rack back the end in steps so that your continuation can be bonded correctly. Finally, check the plumb of the pier.

BUILDING ARCHES IN BRICKWORK

An arch can make a decorative feature of your door and window openings – or even give a grand treatment to your garden gate. Here's how to build a basic brick arch.

If you're making a large opening in a wall for a new door, window or serving hatch – or where you're knocking two rooms into one – you must include adequate support for the masonry above, and any load that bears on it. The usual way to span an opening such as this is to bridge it with a rigid horizontal beam called a lintel, or, for very large openings, a rolled steel joist, or RSJ. But this limits you to a square or rectangular opening, which you may not think is really suitable for a more decorative effect.

In the past, arches – although there were many complex, elegant variations on the basic shape – were used for more practical reasons: wider openings could be spanned than was possible with timber or stone lintels, and they were also used in conjunction with lintels or in long stretches of wall to relieve the pressures on the structures.

Nowadays, however, with the development of lightweight steel lintels, RSJs and reinforced concrete lintels – which can be used to span much wider openings – arches aren't a really practical or cost-effective proposition. Consequently they're used mainly for their decorative effect on smaller-scale structures.

How an arch works

An arch works in virtually the same way as a lintel, by transmitting the weight of the walling above, and its load, to solid masonry at each side of the opening.

The individual components of your arch – usually bricks, reconstituted stone or natural stone blocks – are laid on a curve, forming a compact, stable beam.

Types of arch

The type of arch you choose to build depends on whether you simply want a decorative effect or a load-bearing structure.

You can use arches on internal walls as conventional doorways, to create an open-plan scheme between two rooms, or as a serving hatch. On external walls you can form arches above doors and windows, and outdoors they can make an attractive feature of your garden gate, connected to your boundary walls or even to the house.

Decorative arches

If your arch is to be a purely aesthetic feature indoors you don't necessarily have to build a sturdy structure from masonry. Instead you can make a decorative arch to your own specification from plasterboard, hardboard or chipboard panels cut with a curved edge and fixed to the masonry at the sides of the opening underneath the lintel of a conventional doorway. You can use hardboard, which can be bent, for the underside of your arch. You don't need to alter the structure of the wall in any way.

To finish off your arch, if you're careful to conceal the join between it and the wall, you can simply decorate it with wallpaper or textured paint.

Prefabricated arch formers made of galvanised steel mesh offer a ready-made choice of arch profiles. They come in various widths of opening – and you can even buy simple corner pieces to turn an ordinary doorway into an arched opening. The preformed mesh frames are simply attached to the masonry, under the lintel, then they're plastered over to match the rest of the wall. You can even use them outdoors for a rendered arch finish.

Structural arches

However, where your arch is to form an integral and load-bearing part of a wall its construction is rather more complicated. Brick

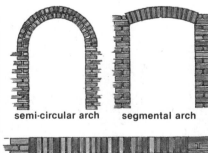

BUILDING INTEGRAL ARCHES

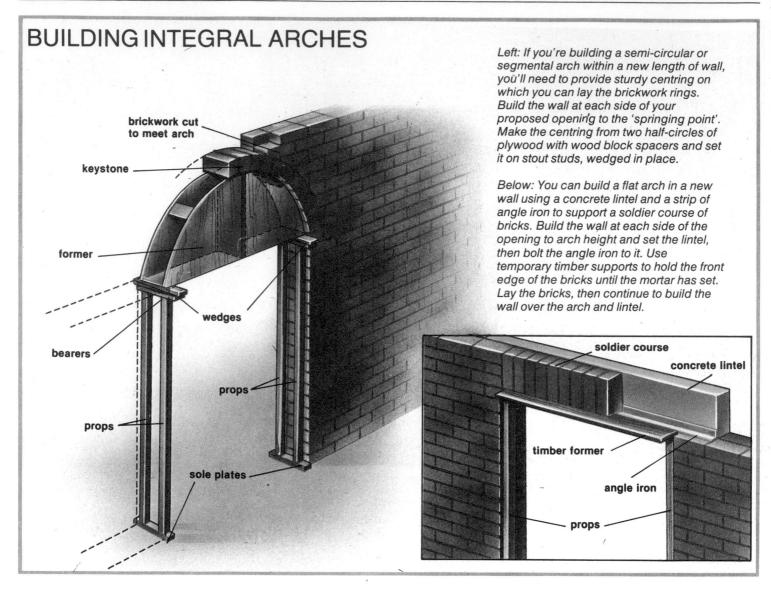

Left: If you're building a semi-circular or segmental arch within a new length of wall, you'll need to provide sturdy centring on which you can lay the brickwork rings. Build the wall at each side of your proposed opening to the 'springing point'. Make the centring from two half-circles of plywood with wood block spacers and set it on stout studs, wedged in place.

Below: You can build a flat arch in a new wall using a concrete lintel and a strip of angle iron to support a soldier course of bricks. Build the wall at each side of the opening to arch height and set the lintel, then bolt the angle iron to it. Use temporary timber supports to hold the front edge of the bricks until the mortar has set. Lay the bricks, then continue to build the wall over the arch and lintel.

Labels in upper illustration: brickwork cut to meet arch; keystone; former; bearers; wedges; props; props; sole plates

Labels in lower illustration: soldier course; concrete lintel; timber former; angle iron; props

is probably the best material to use for this type of arch; you can either leave it exposed as a feature or clad it with render outside or plaster inside for a smooth finish.

Arch profiles

There are various types of arch profiles you can make. One of the commonest is the 'flat' arch (see *Ready Reference*). It's suitable for narrow spans up to about 1.2m (4ft) and the bricks – usually special wedge-shaped types – are set to radiate from a central, vertical point, called the 'keystone' You can make large flat arches by laying conventional-shaped bricks vertically in a 'soldier' course on a steel or concrete boot lintel or resting on a length of angle iron used in conjunction with a concrete lintel (see 'Building integral arches', above).

On openings wider than about 1.8m (6ft) the brickwork may look as if it's sagging fractionally and you can remedy this optical illusion by laying the bricks so that the centre

of the arch is about 12mm (½in) higher than the ends. One way you can do this is to set the bricks on a curved strip of flat iron instead of the angle iron.

Simpler types of arch, which don't need the use of specially-shaped bricks, or the additional support of a lintel, are the 'semi-circular' (see *Ready Reference*) or 'segmental' types. Both of these arches form part of a circle. The centre of the circle in a semi-circular arch is on the imaginary line between the highest bricks on each side of the opening, from which the arch starts to curve inwards. Its diameter equals the distance between the sides of the opening. For a segmental arch the centre line of the much larger circle which the arch follows is some way below this point.

Because the bricks used for these arches are the conventional format the 'wedging' effect necessary to spread the load of the wall sideways is achieved by shaping the mortar joints between each brick. However, if you are contriving a solid wall above the arch,

you'll have to cut the bricks at each side to fit the arch shape.

Building piers

The base of your arch, called the 'springing point', or the point at which it starts to curve inwards, must be supported on sound brickwork at each side, for it's here that the load of the structure is transferred.

If you're building an arch into an existing wall, or if you're building a new wall containing an arch, the load will be taken on solid bearings at each side. But if you're building a freestanding arch between two walls, such as a surround for a garden gate, you'll have to build separate supporting columns called 'piers' at each side. Build up your piers from 225mm (9in) thick brickwork on concrete foundations (see pages 34–38) making sure that they're set perfectly vertical and that each course matches that of the opposite pier, (see step-by-step photographs on page 25).

BUILDING UP THE PIERS

1 Mark guide lines on the foundations to indicate the line of the arch, and start to build up the first pier – in this case measuring 1½ x 1 bricks.

2 As the first pier rises, check at intervals with your spirit level that it is rising vertically. Tap any out-of-line bricks gently into place.

3 Measure out precisely the separation of the two piers, and start to build up the second pier. Check continuously that the two piers align accurately.

4 When you have laid six to eight courses in each pier, go back and point up the mortar joints while the mortar is still soft.

5 Continue to build up the piers one course at a time, checking at every stage that the courses are level and the pier separation is constant.

6 When the piers have reached the desired height – about 1.5m (5ft) for a garden arch – check the measurements accurately on each pier.

MAKING THE FORMER

1 Using the pier separation to give the diameter of the semi-circular former, draw the curve out on plywood and cut it out with a jig-saw.

2 Nail the first semi-circle to a stout piece of softwood just narrower than the wall thickness, and cut a number of spacers to the same length.

3 Nail on the second semi-circle, and then add the spacers at intervals round the edge of the former to hold it rigid when it's in place.

BUILDING THE ARCH

1 Set timber props at each side of the arch opening. If the brickwork will be continued above the arch, use two props and wedges at each side.

2 Position the former on top of the props, and use a spirit level to check that it is level and that both its faces are truly vertical.

3 Lay the first brick of the inner ring on top of one of the piers, and bed it down so its inner face fits tightly against the former.

5 Measure the curve length at each side and divide this by the brick width to indicate how many whole bricks will fill the ring. Mark their positions.

6 Add bricks one by one to each side of the ring, tapping them gently into place and adjusting the mortar thickness as necessary for even joints.

7 Continue adding bricks until you reach the top of the inner ring. Then butter mortar onto both faces of the keystone and tap it into place.

9 Point the mortar joins between the bricks in the inner ring, and then carefully spread a mortar bed 10mm (³/₈in) thick on the top surface.

10 Build up the second ring in the same way as the first, trying to avoid aligning the mortar joins in the two rings. Add the second keystone.

11 Leave the former in place for at least 48 hours (and preferably longer) before carefully removing the props and allowing the former to drop out.

4 *Use the spirit level to draw a true vertical line on the face of the former, passing through the centre point of the semi-circle.*

8 *With the first ring complete, use the spirit level to check that all the bricks are accurately aligned and that the face of the arch is vertical.*

12 *Trim away excess mortar from the underside of the arch, and point up the joints carefully to match those on the rest of the arch.*

When you reach the arch height you should leave the piers for about 24 hours so that the mortar sets before continuing.

Supporting the arch

Semi-circular or segmental arches are usually built on a timber former or support called 'centring'.

If you're building a simple freestanding arch between two piers you can make a fairly lightweight frame from two sheets of plywood cut to the profile you want for your arch (see *Ready Reference* and step-by-step photographs, page 25). Set the former perfectly level at the springing point on timber studs wedged against the piers at each side. You can then build your arch over the former.

If you're building an arch within an existing wall – or if you're building a new wall – you'll have to provide much sturdier centring (see page 24). You'll also need temporary support for the existing walling above the opening You can do this by setting up adjustable metal props and timber needles which will support the masonry while you build the arch.

Building the arch

With your formwork in position you can start to lay the brickwork for your arch. The best way to do this accurately is to lay the bricks alternately from each side, finishing with the central, topmost, keystone brick.

So that you can keep the mortar joint thicknesses constant throughout the arch you'd be wise first to mark out the positions of each brick on the side of the plywood former as a guide to laying. When you're spacing out the bricks on your 'dry run', remember that the mortar joints will be thicker at the top than at the bottom and that the narrowest point shouldn't be less than 6mm (¼in) thick.

Your arch can have one, two or three 'rings', or courses, of bricks. But you must ensure that as few vertical joints as possible coincide with those on adjoining courses, or this will weaken the arch. Point the joints as you go, while the mortar is still soft.

Finishing the arch

Once you've laid the rings of the arch you can fill in the wall surrounding it, unless your arch is freestanding, and has a curved top. Follow the bonding pattern used for the rest of the wall, cutting the bricks next to the arch to fit the curve.

When you've completed the arch leave the structure for about one week so the mortar hardens then remove the centring. You'll have to rake out the joints underneath the arch and repoint them to match the rest of the brickwork.

(see page 24)

READY REFERENCE

TIP: MARKING CURVES

For a round arch, the diameter of the semi-circular former equals the pier separation. Use a pin, string and pencil to mark out the curve.

For a segmental arch, the curve centre is some distance from the edge of the former. Set the plywood from which the formwork will be cut on a flat floor, and mark out the curve as shown.

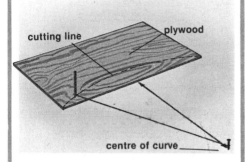

ARCHES IN CAVITY WALLS

If you are building an arch in a cavity wall, the bricks forming the arch must not bridge the cavity. For this reason arches in cavity walls are usually built with the bricks laid as stretchers rather than headers. Formwork is used as for arches in solid walls.

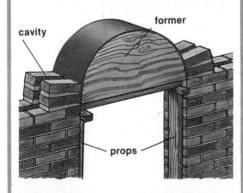

TIP: TILES FOR KEYSTONES

The dimensions of your arch may make it difficult to use a whole brick as the keystone without having very wide or very narrow mortar joints in the ring. In this case use pieces of flat roof tile – or even floor quarries – set in mortar instead.

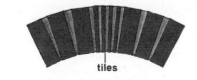

tiles

USING CONCRETE

Concrete is perhaps the do-it-yourselfer's most versatile building material.
It's cheap, easily mixed from readily available ingredients and capable
of forming floors, walls, paths and drives, bases for outbuildings
and many other things besides. As with mortar, half the skill
is in proper mixing of the correct ingredients for the job;
the other half is the laying, and different techniques are
used for different needs. Master these techniques and you'll have no problems,
whether you're working with a small bag of dry concrete mix
from the corner shop or a lorry-load of ready-mix from the local depot.

MIXING AND LAYING CONCRETE

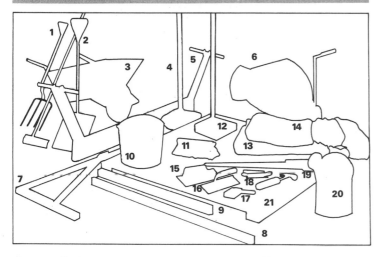

Mixing and laying concrete involves a surprising number of tools. Many of them you will have, some you can hire and others you can make. Always scrub tools well after each work session.

1 Fork For digging out foundations. You will also need a spade.

2 Shovel You will also need a rake to spread the concrete slightly proud of the formwork timbers.

3 Wheelbarrow

4 Ramming tool For compacting the subsoil or hardcore if a roller is unavailable. Fill a timer mould (about 200 x 150 x 100mm/8 x 6 x 4in) with concrete, insert a broom handle and keep it supported until the concrete has set.

5 Tamping beam. For levelling large areas. Make it from 150 x 50mm (6 x 2in) timber. Strong handles help you move the tamper more easily.

6 Hand-operated concrete mixer. The machine is pushed along a hard level surface to rotate the drum and mix the concrete.

7 Builder's square To check the corners of the form. Make one by joining three lengths of wood with sides in the proportions of 3:4:5. A good size is 450 x 600 x 750mm (18 x 24 x 30in). Use an L-shaped bracket and screws to make rigid joints.

8 Spirit level

9 Timber straight-edge For setting out fall of concrete if drainage is required. You can also use it for levelling: a 100 x 50mm (4 x 2in) straight-edge is sufficient.

10 Buckets You will need two for measuring and two shovels of equal size for mixing. Keep one bucket and shovel for measuring out and adding cement. The second set can be used for adding ballast and water and for mixing.

Using equal sized buckets gives an easy guide to quantities: a 1:5 mix needs one bucket of cement and five buckets of ballast.

11 Coarse brush You can give a textured finish to concrete by sweeping the surface with a coarse brush.

12 Punner For compacting concrete. Nail together several layers of timber and attach a broom handle.

13 Polythene sheeting Use to protect concrete from the elements.

14 Straw and sacking Either can be used to protect new concrete from frost.

15 Wood float For a textured finish.

16 Steel float For finishing concrete.

17 Measuring tape

18 Pegs and string For marking out the site.

19 General purpose saw and claw hammer For making formwork.

20 Watering can To control the rate at which water is added.

21 Mixing platform Use where there is no suitable solid area for mixing concrete. Nail boards together for the base and add side pieces to keep the concrete in place. Or fix sides to a larger sheet of 18 or 25mm (¾ or 1in) plywood.

BASIC CONCRETING TECHNIQUES

One of the most versatile of all building materials, concrete is also one of the easiest to work with. The techniques for laying anything from a garden path to a patio are much the same – once you know the basic rules for mixing up the ingredients, making formwork, laying and levelling.

Concrete is made of cement, aggregate and water. Cement itself is quite a complex chemical formed by burning chalk, limestone and clay at high temperatures and then grinding the resulting clinker to a fine powder. Added to the water it becomes an adhesive and coats and binds the aggregate (clean, washed particles of sand, crushed stone or gravel — never brick — for the clays can react against the cement).

The strength or hardness of any concrete simply depends on the proportions of these ingredients. Only a small part of the water you add is used up in the chemical reaction — the rest evaporates.

Ordinary portland cement is used for most concreting work. (The name doesn't refer to the manufacturer or where it is made, it's simply that when invented in the 1820s it was thought to resemble Portland stone.)

Aggregates are graded according to the size of sieve the particles can pass through — anything from 10-20mm. Coarse aggregate has the largest stones (20mm) while fine aggregate, often described as shingle, can be 10-15mm. Sand, the third part of concrete, is also considered aggregate. (The cement holds the sand together and the combination of sand and cement holds the stones together.) In concreting the sand used is known as 'sharp sand and graded by the sieve method. All-in aggregate is a combination of both sand and stones.

Choosing your mix

Different projects require different mixes of concrete. Three are most commonly used.

Mix A (see ESTIMATOR below and *Ready Reference* overleaf) is a general-purpose mix for surface slabs and bases where you want a minimum thickness of 75mm-100mm (3-4in) of concrete.

Mix B is a stronger mix and is used for light-duty strips and bases up to 75mm (3in) thick – garden paths and the like.

Mix C is a weaker mix useful for garden wall foundations, bedding in slabs and so on, where great strength is not needed.

The amount of water needed depends very much on how wet the sand and stones in the aggregate are. A rough guide is to use about half the amount (by volume) of cement. But add it gradually. Too much will ruin the mix and weaken the concrete.

How concrete works

New concrete hardens by chemical action and you can't stop it once it's started. The slower the set the better and it is important that after laying, exposed surfaces are covered with wet sacks, sand or polythene (and kept wet) for the first 4-6 days. Concrete also gives off heat as it sets — a useful property in very cold weather, although it would still need covering to protect it from frost.

Freshly mixed concrete will begin to set within 1-2 hours — in dry hot weather it will be faster. It takes 3-4 days to become properly hard — you can walk on it at this stage. To reach full strength, however, may take 28 days or more.

How to buy concrete

For small jobs it's best to buy the cement, sand and aggregate dry-mixed together, in

Estimator

What to buy for mixing concrete

The quantities given here for sand and aggregate are rounded up to the nearest fraction of a cu metre that can be ordered. The mixes are made up by volume (see **Ready Reference**) so some sand and aggregate may be left over.

To make 1 cu metre eg 10m x 1m x 100mm	Cement 50kg bags	Sharp sand plus aggregate	OR	All-in aggregate
MIX A (1:2½:4)	6 bags	½ cu metre + ¾ cu metre		1 cu metre
MIX B (1:2:3)	8 bags	½ cu metre + ¾ cu metre		1 cu metre
MIX C (1:3:6)	4 bags	½ cu metre + ¾ cu metre		1¼ cu metre

MIXING

1 *Unless you're using dry ready-mix, first spread the cement over the aggregate and gradually mix by heaping into a 'volcano'.*

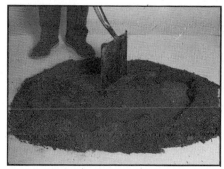

2 *Add about half the water to start with. Form a crater and mix in from the inside walls. Add the rest of the water gradually — not all at once.*

3 *When the concrete is about the right consistency shovel it into heaps again. Turn it into a new pile 3 times to ensure thorough mixing.*

4 *The finished concrete should look like this. When you draw the shovel back in steps, the ridges should be smooth and firm and not 'slump'.*

either 10kg, 25kg or 50kg bags. All you have to do is add water.

For larger projects, this can work out to be very expensive. Here it is better to buy the materials separately. The cement is normally sold in 50kg (just under 1 cwt) bags, though smaller (again more costly) quantities – 10kg and 25kg – are available. Both sand and aggregate are sold in 50kg bags, but it is more common to buy them loose by the cubic metre or fraction of a cubic metre. The combined or 'all-in' aggregate is available in the same way.

For really large work, however, (patios, long drives and the like) mixing the amount of concrete required by hand is extremely hard work. You could hire a powered mixer, but generally it is more convenient to buy it ready-mixed and have it delivered to the house. Check with the supplier on the minimum amount they are prepared to deliver — for quantities close to that minimum you could find it prohibitively expensive and you should consider sharing a load with a neighbour who is also carrying out building work. With ready-mix remember that you

have to be prepared to lay it fast and if there is no direct access to the site and the concrete can't be tipped directly into your prepared formwork, you must have plenty of able-bodied help with heavy-duty wheelbarrows (you can hire these) standing by.

Dry-mixes have the amounts that made-up concrete will cover printed on the bag. For mix-at-home quantities, see the ESTIMATOR.

How to store materials

Under normal conditions cement will start to harden after about 30 days simply because it'll be absorbing moisture from the air. However, older cement that's still powdery inside can still be used where great strength or a high quality finish is *not* essential – but mix in a higher proportion of cement than usual, ie 1:1:2.

Cement should always be stored under cover and raised well off the ground — on a platform of wood, for example. Stack the bags closely, keep them clear of other materials and cover them to help keep the

GETTING A LEVEL BASE

This is vital to avoid weak, thin spots in the concrete which will crack. These methods work on a reasonably flat site:
● drive 300mm (12in) pegs into the ground at 1 metre (3ft) intervals
● align their tops with batten and spirit level to match the final surface level of the concrete
● dig away soil to required depth, taking care not to disturb pegs. Use amount of peg exposed as your depth guide

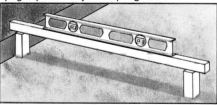

To level top of pegs over longer distances and round corners:
● tie a length of transparent hose between pegs
● fill the hose with water and drive in pegs so their tops match the water levels either end

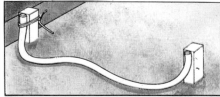

On long paths and drives:
use sighting rods made from sawn softwood – each is the same height (about 1.2 metres/4ft) and has a tee piece exactly at right angles across the top – you'll need three rods, and two helpers. Place rods on pegs and line up tops by adjusting pegs in ground.

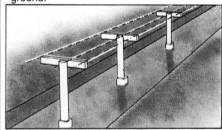

FOUNDATIONS FOR CONCRETE

● as a general rule lay rammed hardcore to the same depth as the final concrete
● on soft sub-soil excavate to twice the depth, filling soft pockets carefully with extra hardcore
● on clay, lay concrete quickly before the clay can dry out

Foundations for brickwork see pages 34–38.

moisture out. If a bag has been part used, the remainder can be stored for a while inside a well-sealed plastic bag.

Loose sand and aggregate should be piled on a flat, dry and hard area and covered with heavy-duty plastic sheeting. It's most important to avoid the aggregate being contaminated by soil or other foreign materials. Any organic matter would decompose in the concrete leaving 'voids' which weaken it.

Site preparation
This is a major stage before you begin to erect any formwork, mix or lay any concrete. For accurate marking out, use pegs and strings to give yourself guide lines to follow. The area should be dug out and made as level as possible (see *Ready Reference*).

The big question is, how deep should you dig and how thick should you lay the concrete? To some extent this depends on how firm the soil is. For a path or patio a 75-100mm/3-4in thickness of concrete is usually enough — add a layer of hardcore of the same depth if the soil is very soft. If, however, you're building a driveway where

there'll be a lot more weight on top, then 125-150mm/5-6in of concrete on top of hardcore would be advisable.

Some soils can lead to unsuccessful concreting. If your site is *clay* for example you have to concrete it as soon as possible after it has been revealed. The reason? Clay dries out quickly and then contracts. Because it will absorb water from the concrete mix, it makes an unreliable base.

Peaty and loamy soils will sink under a heavy load. Use good hardcore (see below) in the prepared area.

Made-up ground is another way of describing land that's been reclaimed. There's no knowing what was used as the in-fill, and it should always be assumed that it has minimal load-bearing capacity. Any concreting here will need good reinforcement such as hardcore, well compacted and the same thickness as the concrete you're laying on top.

Soft pockets
After you've prepared a site for laying a path or patio you could find pockets of soft soil which will cause any concrete to sink.

Large areas of soft pockets or made-up ground need something solid as a base — and this is where hardcore (broken concrete), rubble (broken brick) or a very coarse aggregate is essential. Tamp it into the ground until well consolidated — a must for areas such as drives or structural foundations taking a lot of weight.

If necessary small areas can be reinforced with a steel mesh set into the concrete. For most purposes 7mm diameter rods formed in a mesh of 150mm squares is quite adequate, and this is readily available at most builders' merchants. Rest the rods on small pieces of broken brick before you lay the concrete; make sure that the ends of the rods don't protrude from the area you're concreting, and that the mesh is completely covered.

Creating the work area
Using formwork boards to create a kind of box in which to lay your concrete has two big advantages. Firstly, it contains the concrete neatly, and secondly it gives you levels on either side to guide you in levelling the concrete itself. Although this is the most usual method of containing concrete, a brick

LAYING AND LEVELLING

1 *Shovel the concrete well into the corners and only lay as much as you can finish off in one go. It's important that there are no hollows.*

2 *Roughly level the concrete with your shovel to a height about 6mm/¼in above the sides of the formwork. This will allow for compaction.*

3 *The 'tamping' board fits neatly across the formwork. First use a sawing action to level the mix, then a firm chopping action to compact it.*

4 *With the surface level, tap sides of formwork with hammer. This helps to compact the concrete. Fill in any hollows that result and level off again.*

5 *For an expansion joint use a piece of softboard the same depth as the concrete you're laying. Support it with pegs on one side.*

6 *Finish the concrete off on one side before you start laying on the other. Once the board is supported, hammer the pegs in deeper.*

FINISHES

1 *Using a wooden 'float' gives you a smooth finish. Press the float down firmly as you 'scrub' the surface with circular movements.*

2 *A brushed finish leaves a much rougher surface by exposing the small stones in the aggregate. Use a stiff brush to create a pattern of straight lines.*

3 *For a polished finish, use a steel 'float' at a slight angle to the surface, drawing it towards you with a sweeping semi-circular action.*

surround can be used just as well — and this has the added advantage of not having to be pulled up. With bricks, however, it's more difficult to establish a completely straight and level line to follow.

For formwork use sawn (unplaned) softwood — it's called carcassing in the trade — for concrete that's to be placed below ground. It should be as wide as the depth of concrete you intend to lay and 25mm (1in) thick. Don't skimp on the thickness for it must be firm and rigid to support the weight of concrete.

Pegs are used to keep the formwork in place. They must be sturdy, not less than 50mm (2in) square and long enough to go well into the ground. Place pegs every 1 metre (3ft) against the *outside* face of the boards.

If building a raised path, formwork will give a finish to the concrete edge so you should use a timber that's planed. Unplaned timber can be used if the formwork is lined with 6mm (¼in) plywood, or if you intend finishing off the edges with more concrete after the formwork has been removed.

If you want to curve a corner in the formwork, use hardboard cut into strips as wide as the concrete is deep. This will need to be supported with pegs at more frequent intervals than softwood boards.

If you have difficulty driving the pegs into the ground (which may happen if you've put down hardcore) use lengths of angle iron instead. Alternatively drive the pegs in further away from the formwork and put timber blocks between the peg and formboard.

Expansion joints

Any large area of concrete needs expansion or movement joints to control cracking. A one-piece slab shouldn't be more than 3 metres (10ft) in any direction without a joint being included; a path should have joints at intervals of 1½ times the width of the path.

The simplest way of doing this is to incorporate a length of flexible plastic movement joint as you're laying the path. The material can be bought at most builders' merchants. Alternatively, use a piece of soft-board impregnated with bitumen — it should be the same depth as the concrete and about 12mm (½in) thick.

Drainage slopes

With a wide expanse you should have a gentle slope (1 in 60 is the general rule) so that rainwater can drain away. This is achieved by setting the forms on one side slightly deeper into the ground. To check that the slope is the same all along the formwork, set a small piece of wood (about 12mm/½in for a 1m/3ft wide path) thick on the lower side and use your spirit level to check across to the other side.

To keep the formwork on each side of a path rigid, place a length of softwood across the width at the peg points, but not so that it will make an impression on the concrete. This can be used as a guide for levelling as well.

Whether you are building a concrete path, a base for a shed or garage, a hardstanding for a car or even a large patio, the principle of formwork is the same — only the number of boxes or bays you divide the area into varies. With each stage of the job you should mix only enough concrete to fill one bay or box at a time.

As the concrete starts to dry (after 2 hours) cover the surface with plastic sheeting or damp sacking to stop it drying too quickly.

SETTING UP FORMWORK

You need:
● planks of sawn softwood 25mm (1in) thick and wide enough to match the concrete depth
● pegs of 50 x 50mm (2 x 2in) softwood at least 300mm (12in) long
● a string line to aid setting out

Position formwork along all edges to keep concrete in place until it's set, and provide a working edge for levelling the concrete:
● hammer pegs into the ground at 1 metre (3ft) intervals round the perimeter of the area to be concreted; use foot to hold peg in position

● place formwork against the pegs, aligning the boards accurately against a string line
● check levels between opposite lines of formwork with batten and spirit level, and allow for drainage slope if required
● nail the boards to the pegs

CONCRETE: WHAT TO MIX

MIX A for concrete over 75mm (3in) thick

    1 bucket cement
    2½ buckets sharp sand
    4 buckets washed aggregate

MIX B for concrete less than 75mm (3in) thick

    1 bucket cement
    2 buckets sharp sand
    3 buckets washed aggregate

MIX C for rough bedding concrete

    1 bucket cement
    3 buckets sharp sand
    6 buckets washed aggregate

All mixes need about ½ bucket water; exact amounts depend on the dampness of the sand.

FOUNDATIONS for garden walls

Even if it's only for a wall to grace the garden, building a solid foundation is a must. But how deep should you dig? How wide? And what's the right thickness of concrete? Here's an easy to follow explanation of why foundations are so important, how they differ and which one to choose.

All walls need foundations to give them stability, and free-standing garden walls are no exception. The foundation is like a platform, helping to spread the weight of the bricks in the wall onto the earth base below.

Most foundations are made of concrete laid in a trench, and for a garden wall where there's no additional weight for it to carry (unlike a structural wall, for example, which may also carry part of the weight of a roof) the concrete itself doesn't need to be very thick – between 100mm (4in) and 150mm (6in) of concrete is quite enough for a wall up to a metre in height. But the thickness of the concrete is not the only thing you have to consider. How deep in the ground you place it is just as important.

For a concrete foundation to provide an effective platform which won't allow the brick wall to crack, it has to be laid on firm 'subsoil'. And you won't find this until you get below the topsoil. The depth of topsoil varies enormously from place to place, so there can be no hard and fast rules about how deep you must dig – but expect anything between 100mm and 300mm (4-12in). Once you're through to the harder subsoil, you've then got to dig out enough for the depth of concrete – at least another 100-150mm (4-6in).

In practice the other big variable is the nature of your soil. Different subsoils have different load-bearing capacities – for instance hard chalky soils can support more weight than clay (see Choosing your foundation, page 38), but sandy soils can take less. The weaker the subsoil, the wider you have to build the foundation – consult your local building inspector for advice on soil conditions in your area.

There's another important reason for digging down so deep and that is the effect the weather has on soil. In clay subsoils, for example, a prolonged dry spell will cause the clay near the surface to shrink; then, when it rains, the clay will swell. All this causes considerable movement of the ground and

unless a concrete foundation has been laid deep enough it'll crack up under the stress of constant expansion and contraction. To counteract this, the foundation has to be laid *below* the point at which the weather can cause movement. Again, in different soils, this varies from 150mm (6in) to 500mm (20in) or more down, but it's advisable to consult your local building inspector to get a more precise figure for soil conditions in your area.

Foundation design

All foundations have to be designed so that they evenly transfer the weight of the wall above to the earth base below. Because of the way the wall's weight spreads out onto

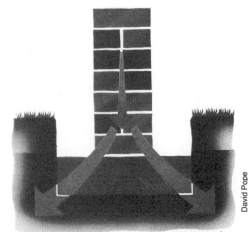

David Pope

The weight of a wall spreads at an angle of 45° from its base into the foundation and then on into the subsoil. This is called the angle of dispersion.

MARKING OUT

1 Set the pegs for the profile board outside the line the foundation will follow. First hammer the pegs in, then nail a cross-piece on top.

2 You'll need profile boards at each end of the foundation trench so that you can string guide lines for digging out between the two.

3 Fix nails in the cross-pieces to establish the width of the trench. Normally this is a minimum of 300mm (12in).

4 Tie the line to one of the nails, then string up to the others. Loop the line round each nail and keep it taut. Don't cut the line.

5 The lines now mark the edges of the trench. At a later stage the building line for the wall is marked out in the same way.

6 To give you an accurate line to follow for digging out, sprinkle sand beneath the lines. After this remove the strings, but not the profile boards.

the foundation — called the angle of dispersion — the foundation is built so that it is wider than the wall. In fact this 'load spreading' follows an angle of 45° (see page 41) and means that the width of the foundation on each side of the wall has to be at least equal to the depth of the concrete. This is a simple rule of thumb which will help you decide how wide your foundation has to be for different wall widths. Of course, if you're building on a relatively soft subsoil, your building inspector may recommend that you build a wider foundation. Like a raft floating on water, the bigger it is the more stable it will be.

Once you've dug your trench, you'll be faced with another decision: do you just lay the minimum thickness of concrete or lay enough concrete to fill up the trench so you have fewer bricks to lay? In fact, there can be quite a difference in the amount of work involved. If your trench is 500mm (20in) deep and you only lay a 150mm (6in) depth of concrete, it means that just to get back to ground level you've got to lay some 5 courses of bricks which ultimately won't even be seen. Nevertheless, it makes no difference to the strength of the foundation — it

LAYING THE CONCRETE

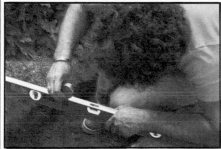

1 Once the trench is dug out, check the depth at 1 metre (3ft) intervals. The actual depth depends on the nature of the soil — see page 34.

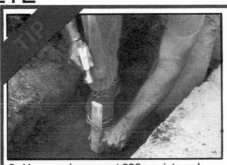

2 Hammer in pegs at 600mm intervals down the middle of the trench. These can be adjusted to act as an accurate depth guide for laying the concrete.

3 Use a spirit level to check that the tops of the pegs are level. This marks the top of the foundations, and accuracy is essential. (Continued overleaf)

Keith Morris

CHOOSING YOUR FOUNDATION

7 courses/ ½ brick thick

15 courses/ ½ brick thick

7 courses/ 1 brick thick

15 courses/ 1 brick thick

STRIP FOUNDATIONS

TRENCH FILL FOUNDATIONS

*The size of foundation you lay depends on the height and thickness of the wall you intend to build, and on the load-bearing capacity of the subsoil. The chart above gives recommended dimensions for strip and trench-fill foundations for half-brick and one-brick thick walls, below 7 courses or up to 15 courses high, on a typical clay subsoil. On crumbly, loose soils the recommended widths should be doubled. See also **Ready Reference.***

flower beds. In such cases the soil behind the wall is constantly trying to push outwards, completely changing the pattern of stress involved.

The simplest solution is to make the structure strong enough to withstand this extra pressure. With a 4 or 5 course wall this can usually be done by building the wall one brick thick (instead of ½ brick thick) and by providing 'weepholes' at regular intervals to drain excess water. These are made by removing mortar from a number of the vertical joints before it sets.

If you find that the surface of an earth-retaining wall is marked by white crusty deposits – called 'efflorescence', and caused by water carrying salts through the wall from the soil behind – dig away the earth

and coat the inner surface of the wall with bituminous emulsion to create a damp barrier.

Building on a slope

It is visually unsettling and structurally unde-sirable to lay bricks running parallel to a slope. So, to build a wall that 'steps' down a slope, the trench foundations also have to be stepped or 'benched' into the slope. Level-ling, pegging, pouring and finishing are all carried out in the same way as with a horizontal trench, but in stepped sections. You'll need form boards to frame the outer edge of each step, but otherwise the width and depth of the foundation is exactly the same as for an ordinary wall. Only the length of each step varies.

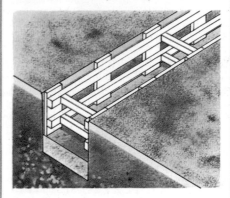
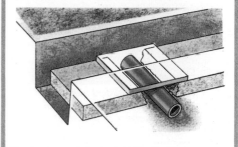

LAYING CONCRETE SLABS

Concrete is the ideal material for laying a slab for a shed, patio or driveway. Once you've mastered the techniques of mixing and casting it, you can provide a hard durable surface that will last for years.

A concrete slab can be a tough, hard-wearing base for a variety of uses in your garden, but its success is only as good as the preparation you've put into making it. Concrete consists of stone particles called 'aggregate', bonded with a Portland cement and water mix (see *Working with concrete*). You must mix the ingredients carefully, cast the slab on specially prepared foundations, apply a finishing texture, and allow the concrete to set properly, if your results are to be long-lasting.

Planning a concrete slab

After you've decided exactly where you want to put your square or rectangular slab, you'll have to mark out the ground accurately and prepare the foundations before laying the concrete. But if you're laying a more complex shape or a much larger concrete base, you'd be wise to make some preliminary sketches and transfer them to squared paper, to help in calculating the material required.

Before you start to lay your slab it's sensible to check with your local authority whether you're infringing any bye-laws. One of the main objections they might have is the position of your planned slab in relation to existing drains and pipe runs; as a result, you might have to re-route some of these to keep them out of harm's way.

Access to the site and the time you'll have available for laying your slab are important considerations, particularly if you're laying a large concrete drive or a garage floor, for example. With work on this scale you should use ready-mixed concrete, which is delivered in bulk ready for casting. If you go for this method, it's vital that you provide access for the lorry and space for the load to be dumped as close as possible to your site. You must have your foundations prepared so that you can cast the mix as soon as it's delivered. Any delay could mean that the mix starts to set rendering it useless.

Calculating the size of slab

Before you can mark out your slab on the ground and prepare its foundations you'll have to work out its dimensions and calculate how much concrete you're going to need. As a basic guide, the larger your slab the thicker it must be.

For an ordinary garden shed, for instance, you'll need a slab about 75mm (3in) thick, except where the ground is soft clay, when you should increase its depth to 100mm (4in). If your slab is to form the floor of a workshop, or a drive leading to your garage, a thickness of 100mm (4in) is appropriate on ordinary soils, 125mm (5in) on soft clay or other poor sub-soils.

Once you've decided on the dimensions of your slab you can estimate how much concrete you'll need and how you're going to mix it (see *Ready Reference*).

Marking out the slab

Before you start to mark out your slab on the ground, dig out and remove the top-soil, including any grass and the roots of shrubs, from the area you're going to concrete. Allow a margin of a few feet all round your proposed slab for working space.

Use strings stretched between wooden pegs driven into the ground just outside the area you're going to concrete to mark out the shape of your slab (although, for a very small slab it's possible simply to mark it out using planks positioned squarely on the ground – see photographs). Use a builder's square (see *Ready Reference*) to set the corners of your slab accurately. If you're

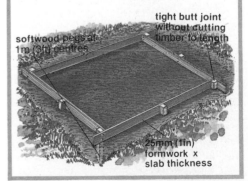

making strip foundations for a wall you can use 'profiles' to set the levels (see Working with concrete, pages 30–33).

Once you've positioned your string lines you can dig out the sub-soil to roughly the depth of your foundation, taking it about 150mm (6in) beyond the strings to leave space for setting up 'formwork', which moulds and retains the concrete while it's hardening.

Setting the levels

While the base for a shed should be virtually level, a concrete slab patio or garage drive should be laid with a slight slope to allow rainwater to run off quickly. And of course, if the slab is near a wall you'll have to ensure that the fall drains away from it. You must allow for the slope when you're preparing the base. A gradient across the site of about 1 in 60 is about right.

You'll also have to make sure when laying a drive leading to a garage that the drive doesn't drain into the garage. If the ground is naturally sloping in that direction take it to a level below the garage floor and lay a short section of slab sloping away from the garage. Where the two slopes meet you'll have to include a channel leading to a suitable drainage point.

To establish the level of your slab over its entire area hammer 50x25mm (2x1in) softwood pegs into the ground at about 1.5m (5ft) intervals. The first peg must be one that establishes the level of the others, and its called the 'prime datum'. If your slab is to adjoin a wall you can fix the level of this peg at the second course of brickwork below the dpc, (damp-proof course) or some other fixed point of reference.

Drive in some more pegs and check across their tops from the first peg with a spirit level on a straight-edged length of timber to check their level.

You can allow for a drainage fall by placing a wedge of timber called a 'shim' under one end of the straight edge.

Once you've set the datum pegs, measure down them whatever thickness of concrete you'll need for your slab and excavate the ground, or fill in, where necessary.

Fixing the formwork

Wet concrete tends to spread out as it sets and so you'll have to fix a timber frame called 'formwork' at the perimeter of the foundations to retain it and support its edges. It must be strong enough to withstand heavy tamping, which compacts and strengthens the mix. Use straight lengths of stout timber a minimum of 25mm (1in) thick, set on edge and nailed to pegs of 32x32mm (1¼x1¼in) timber driven into the ground at the perimeter of the slab at 1m (3ft) centres. Fix the pegs outside the area that's to be con-

PREPARING THE FOUNDATIONS

1 *You can mark out a small concrete slab on the ground with scaffold boards and pegs at the corners, then start to remove the topsoil or turfs.*

2 *Continue to dig out the topsoil or turfs until you've accurately marked out the shape of your slab. Then dig down to the depth you want the slab.*

3 *To fix formwork around your base butt joint four lengths at the corners. Nail battens at each corner to hold the angle; then saw off the waste.*

4 *Position the formwork within the foundations and check across the top with a long spirit level to ensure that it's level, or sloping for drainage.*

5 *Tamp or roll the base of the foundations firm. If the soil is soft, add some hardcore and compact this into the surface with a sledge hammer.*

6 *Add as much hardcore as you need to give a firm base for the concrete. You may need to add a layer of sand to fill any voids in the surface.*

creted, with their tops flush with, or slightly below, the top edge of the formwork.

You can use your string lines as a guide to positioning the formwork and a builder's square to ensure that the corners are set perfectly at right angles.

The top edge of the formwork must be set so that it's flush with the top of your finished slab; it's best to use timber that's the same thickness as your slab, otherwise you'll have to recess it into the ground. You can use your intermediate datum pegs as reference points when levelling the formwork with a builder's level, making sure you incorporate the drainage falls.

The corners of the formwork must be tightly butt-jointed (see *Ready Reference*) to prevent the wet concrete from seeping through. If you have to join two planks together end to end in order to make the required length you should again use butt joints, but back both planks at the joint with a short section of timber nailed in place and wedged with a peg at this point.

Movement joints
You can cast a slab in one piece if it's no longer than about 3m (10ft) in width or length. But if it's bigger than this, or if its length is greater than twice is width, it's usual to divide the overall slab into 'bays' that are as square as possible – or equal in size – and to include a gap called an 'expansion joint', which prevents the slab from cracking due to expansion or contraction. Fill the gap with a length of softwood 10 to 12mm (3/8in to 1/2in) thick, the depth of the slab, and cut to fit between the formwork at the sides of the slab. Treat the fillet with preservative before fitting it within the slab.

Each bay is cast separately so it's best to back up the jointing timber with a piece of formwork temporarily pegged in place for support. When you've cast and compacted the first bay, remove the formwork behind the jointing timber and cast the second bay, leaving it permanently in place.

Mixing the concrete
If your slab is too small to justify a load of ready-mixed concrete or you wish to lay it in stages over several weekends, you'll need to buy all the ingredients and mix them yourself. To decide on the volumes of cement and aggregates you'll need for your particular slab, you must first decide on the concrete mix proportions to use. *Ready Reference* gives a basic guide to proportioning, which you can relate to your own needs. Following these guidelines and using the example of the car port base given in *Ready Reference*, the volume of concrete you'd need is 1.8m³ (63 cu ft). Materials needed are therefore going to be in the order of 1.8mx6 = 10.8 bags of cement; 1.8x0.5 = 0.9m³ of sand; 1.8x0.8 = 1.44m³ of coarse aggregate.

1.8x0.8 = 1.44m³ of coarse aggregate.

Allow a 10 per cent margin for wastage to the cement to the nearest whole bag and buy 12 bags of cement. Round up quantities of aggregates to the nearest whole or half cubic metre and buy 1m³ (36 cu ft) of sand and 1.5m³ (53 cu ft) of coarse aggregate. Your calculations, though, should always be regarded as a guide only; exact amounts needed for a job will depend on the care you take in storage and handling and on the accuracy with which you prepare the base for the slab.

When you've an idea of the amounts of materials you'll need, you must decide on what method to use to mix them: by hand or by power mixer. Many different types of electric- petrol- and diesel-powered mixers are available for hire, and take much of the hard work out of mixing.

To get the correct consistency of concrete using a mixer, add half the coarse aggregate needed for the batch and half the water first. Then add all the sand and mix for a few minutes. Next you can add the cement and the remainder of the coarse aggregate. Finally add just enough water to achieve a workable mix. Most beginners add too much water; when it's of the right consistency the concrete should fall off the blade of your shovel cleanly without being too sloppy.

If you have to break off your work for a while, add the coarse aggregate and water you'll need for the next batch and leave the mixer running, while you are away, to keep the drum cleam.

For how to mix concrete by hand (although it's really only viable for small jobs), see pages 30–33.

If you're mixing the concrete yourself you can store the aggregates indefinitely on a hard surface covered with a polythene sheet to keep it clean. Cement, however, must be kept dry: moisture in the air can penetrate the paper sacks and cause it to harden. Stack the sacks,under cover if possible, flat on a raised platform of planks on bricks and cover them with polythene.

Using ready-mixed concrete
Ready-mixed concrete is delivered by mixer lorry, usually in minimum loads of 3m³ (105 cu ft). If you need this amount, or more, ready-mixed concrete is worth considering as it takes a lot of hard work out of concreting and enables you to complete fairly large projects quickly.

Your supplier will want to know the volume of concrete you'll need, at what time you want it delivered, what it'll be used for, and how you're going to use it on delivery. This information will enable him to determine an appropriate mix and give you a price. You'd be wise to seek several quotations and try to choose a depot close to your home: much of

READY REFERENCE

MAKING A BUILDER'S SQUARE
Set out square corners accurately with a builder's square, which you can make. To do this:
● nail together three strips of 50x25mm (2x1in) softwood in the proportion of 3:4:5, so that the angle between the two shorter sides is 90°.
A convenient size for the pieces is:
● 450, 600, 750mm (18, 24, 30in) respectively
● make a half-lap joint at the 90° corner and overlap the other two corners.

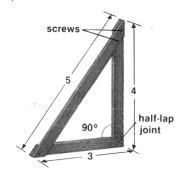

MAKING A TAMPING BEAM
To compact and level a concrete slab you'll need:
● a tamping beam made from a straight-edged length of 175x25mm (7x1in) softwood about 300mm (1ft) longer than the width of the slab
● or, for a very broad slab, a beam of 150x50mm (6x2in) timber with handles bolted on at each end so you can work standing up.

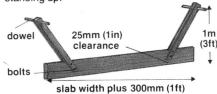

To use a tamping beam:
● lift the beam and drop it to compact the concrete as you work along the slab
● repeat this process a few times
● change to a sawing action, levelling the concrete flush with the top of the formwork.

CURING THE CONCRETE
Curing prevents the slab from drying out too quickly and becoming weak and cracking. To cure your slab:
● cover it with a large sheet of polythene
● weight down the edges – but not on the concrete – with bricks
● sprinkle sand on top to stop the sheet ballooning in the wind
● leave for 3 or 4 days before removing
● don't use the slab for 7 to 10 days.

CASTING THE CONCRETE

1 Lay a path of scaffold boards from the concrete mix to the slab so you can take the mix by wheelbarrow without harming the ground.

2 Spread out the first barrowload of concrete over your foundations, using a shovel to work it into the hardcore and to avoid air bubbles.

3 Continue to tip barrowloads of concrete into your foundations until you've half-filled the area, just proud of the tops of the formwork.

6 Compact the wet concrete by lifting and dropping the tamping beam onto the concrete as you work across the slab. Repeat using a sawing action.

7 When you've filled the entire slab and have tamped the mix thoroughly tap the outside edge of the formwork with a hammer to settle the concrete.

8 You can produce a non-slip finish of fine swirls on your slab by running the back of your shovel over the wet surface.

the cost of the concrete is in its transportation.

To receive your concrete you'd be wise to lay down a large polythene sheet to make clearing up easier afterwards. If you need to transport it any distance from the point of delivery get together as many wheelbarrows – heavy-duty ones, not light garden types – shovels and helpers as you can. It's sensible to lay a pathway of scaffold boards or planks from the pile to your site if you have to cross areas of lawn or go up or down steps.

Laying the concrete

When your formwork has been positioned you can remove the levelling pegs from within the areas, and the string lines from the perimeter, but if you're going to lay the concrete on a hardcore base you should add the ballast at this stage. Compact it well with a sledge hammer, fence post tamper or a garden roller, and leave the levelling pegs in

place until you've set the foundations at the correct level.

When the base is ready, tip in the concrete from a barrow, or by the bucketful: if you're making a big slab you might even be able to get the delivery lorry to tip the mix straight into your prepared base.

Spread the concrete evenly with a garden rake to level it to just above the tops of the formwork. This allows an excess for compacting the mix. When all the concrete has been cast, compact it, using a tamping beam (see *Ready Reference*) made from a straight-edged length of 175x25mm (7x1in) softwood about 300m (1ft) longer than the width of your slab. For very large slabs use 150x50mm (6x2in) timber to make the beam, with handles fitted at each end so that you can work from a standing position rather than crouching (see *Ready Reference*).

Use the beam with a chopping action, lifting

it then dropping it to compact the concrete and force out any air bubbles. Work along the slab in this way and, after a few passes, change to a sawing action, which levels any high spots and fills depressions as you move down the formwork. Continue to tamp until the concrete is even and flush with the top of the formwork.

Finishing the concrete

You can apply a variety of finishes to your concrete slab to suit its purpose. For a garage drive you can simply leave the fairly rough, non-slip, texture created by the tamping beam or you could brush the fresh concrete across its width with a stiff-bristled broom to give a more regular, but still non-slip, finish.

A smoother finish is easier to keep clean for a shed or garage floor, and you can produce this with a wooden float used in a wide, sweeping action. For a more polished effect,

4 Draw a stout timber tamping beam across the tops of the formwork to spread the concrete roughly and to flatten any high spots.

5 Fill any indents left behind after you've drawn the tamping beam over the top with shovelfuls of concrete, then draw the beam across again.

9 Run the blade of a steel trowel along the perimeter of the concrete to prevent the edges crumbling when you remove the formwork.

10 After about 24 hours, when the concrete has set, remove the formwork by tapping it away from the slab with a hammer.

READY REFERENCE

HOW MUCH CONCRETE?

To estimate the volume of concrete you'll need:
● first work out the area of your proposed slab by multiplying the length (A) by the width (B)
● then multiply the area by the slab thickness (C)

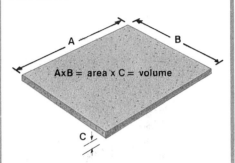

$A \times B =$ area $\times C =$ volume

For example: a car port base 6x3m (20x10ft) by 100mm (4in) thick needs 6x3x0.1m which equals 1.8m³ (63 cu ft) of concrete.

TIP: ROUND UP VOLUMES

For practical purposes always allow a margin for wastage, rounding up volumes to the nearest half or whole cubic metre.

CONCRETE MIX PROPORTIONS

To decide on the volumes of cement and aggregates you'll need, first decide on the mix proportions to use. For a general purpose mix suitable for a slab 75mm (3in) or over in thickness use the proportions of:
● 1 bucket of cement
● 2½ buckets of damp sand
● 4 buckets of coarse aggregate.

For 1m³ (36 cu ft) of concrete you'll need:
● 6 bags of cement
● 0.5m³ (17 cu ft) of damp sand
● 0.8m³ (28 cu ft) of coarse aggregate.

If you buy combined aggregates (sand is included with the coarse aggregate) use the proportions of:
● 1 bucket of cement
● 5 buckets of combined aggregates.

For 1m³ (36 cu ft) of concrete you'll need:
● 6 bags of cement
● 1m³ (36 cu ft) of combined aggregates.

TIP: IF THE SAND IS DRY

Sand is nearly always delivered damp but if it's dry, reduce the amount of sand at each mixing by about half a bucket.

you can smooth over the surface with a steel trowel after you've treated it with the wooden float, and once more when the concrete has almost set.

One of the simplest finishes to apply is to go over the surface with the back of a shovel, producing fine swirls.

Curing the concrete

After you've applied the finishing texture to your slab you should 'cure' the concrete by leaving it to set without drying out too quickly, which could cause it to crack.

Although you shouldn't attempt to lay concrete at all during frosty weather (as this can affect the strength of the slab) it's possible that a cold spell will strike when you're least expecting it. If this happens you can protect your freshly cast concrete by insulating it with a quilt of straw sandwiched between two layers of heavy gauge polythene, or you can shovel a layer of earth, sand or compost on top of your conventional curing sheet, which has the same effect.

Once you've cured the concrete properly, which normally takes about three or four days (ten in winter), you can remove the polythene. It's perfectly alright for you to walk on the slab, and you can even start to build onto it, but be very careful at the edges, which will still be weak and susceptible to chipping.

Don't put the base to full use for about ten days, when you can remove the formwork. To do this, tap it downwards with a hammer in order to release it from the slab, then knock it away from the face of the concrete edges by releasing the nails securing the butt joins at the corners.

Once you've removed the formwork you can fill in the gap it occupies with soil or lay turfs to continue your lawn.

LAYING READY-MIXED CONCRETE

Ready-mix concrete takes a lot of the hard work out of laying a large slab for a drive or patio, or as the base for a garage. It's delivered to your house and takes only a few hours to place.

Concrete is a tough, hardwearing material that is ideal for laying as a base for a shed or garage, or as a durable surface for a patio, path or driveway. Once you've mastered the basic techniques of mixing, casting and curing the concrete (see Laying concrete slabs, pages 39–43) it's quite straightforward to make a fairly small square or rectangular slab, mixing the ingredients by hand or portable mixer. But if you're covering a much larger area the amount of concrete you'll need makes mixing your own impractical – unless you plan to lay the base in stages over several weekends.

Ready-mix concrete, which is sold in bulk and delivered to your home by mixer truck ready for casting, takes a lot of the hard work out of mixing large quantities of concrete and enables you to complete substantial projects quickly. Ready-mix has a number of other advantages over mixing your own: because the cement, sand, coarse aggregates and water are all correctly proportioned by the supplier and mixed for you, there's less likelihood that your mix will be too weak or brittle, or that you'll run out before you complete the slab. Also, you don't need to store large quantities of materials or hire mixing equipment

Casting concrete in bulk

Laying a large area of ready-mixed concrete follows the same sequence of operations as laying a small slab – you simply have to spread the mix to an even thickness over prepared foundations (see 'Foundations and formwork' opposite), apply a finishing texture and leave it to harden.

But there are some important details you should be aware of before you go ahead and order your concrete. You must provide sufficient access for the mixer truck and space for the mix to be dumped (see *Ready Reference*). If you can't arrange for the concrete to be dumped direct onto your foundations, try to get it as close as possible to your site. You must be sure that you'll be able to handle such a large amount of concrete, as well as cast it, compact it and cure it in one session, because you won't have a second chance once it has set.

Slab dimensions

The first consideration is what your slab will be used for, as this helps you decide on the correct thickness of concrete and allows your supplier to determine the correct strength of mix you'll need. Basically, the greater the load on the slab the thicker it must be. If your slab is to form the floor of a workshop or garage, or a driveway, for instance, a thickness of about 100mm (4in) is appropriate on ordinary soils. But on soft clay or other poor soils allow 125mm (5in).

On normal soils you may be able to lay the concrete direct onto the well-compacted ground, but on loose or soft soils you should include a 75mm (3in) layer of well-rammed hardcore. This can be of broken bricks or concrete, and should be topped with a 'blinding' layer of sand to fill in any voids that would be wasteful of concrete.

When you've decided on the position of your slab, and its dimensions, draw a scale plan of it on squared paper to help you estimate how much concrete you'll need.

Planning a drive

If you're altering the position of an existing vehicle access on to your property to make a new drive, you'll have to apply for permission to do so from your local authority; they'll need to make a dropped kerb and a cross-over of the pavement from the road, for which there's usually a charge.

Pay particular attention to the slope of the ground when you're planning a drive. Acute changes from one gradient to another within the drive can cause your car to hit the ground at either end or underneath.

Check also that your proposed drive allows sufficient clearance for an up-and-over garage door or that there's plenty of room for side-hinged doors to open without binding on the ground.

Draining the slab

Your slab must incorporate a slight slope to allow rainwater to run off quickly and you must allow for this when you're preparing your base.

A minimum fall of 1 in 60 to one side is adequate for a large slab, although you can form a high point along the centre of the slab with falls to both sides.

If the ground slopes naturally and your slab would drain towards a garage or house wall you should excavate it to a level below that of the floor of the building, and make a short slope away from the wall, with a gully or gutter at the lowest point to ensure run-off of rainwater to a suitable drainage point (see *Ready Reference*, page 47).

Excavating and setting out

When you've decided where you're going to lay your slab you'll have to prepare the foundations (see Laying concrete slabs). Dig out and remove the top-soil and any grass or roots within this area. Allow a margin

FOUNDATIONS AND FORMWORK

Before you take delivery of your ready-mix you must prepare the base. On firm ground simply roll the surface and cast the concrete direct; on soft ground first add about 75mm (3in) of well-rammed hardcore topped with sand to fill any voids. Set up a frame of timber formwork to mould and retain the mix while it hardens.

hardcore

formwork to support expansion joint

expansion joint of 12mm (½in) softwood

softwood pegs 50x50x300mm (2x2x12in) at 1m (3ft) centres

75mm (3in)

softwood formwork 25mm (1in) x slab thickness

corners butt-jointed

pegs 1m (3ft) apart

A *Drive stout softwood pegs at the perimeter of the foundations and nail the form boards to them from inside.*

B *When joining two lengths of formwork, butt the ends together and nail them to two pegs placed side by side.*

C *Check levels with a spirit level on a straightedge; allow for a drainage fall with a small wedge under one end.*

D *To form an expansion joint, cast one bay to the wood fillet, remove the form board backing it and cast the second bay.*

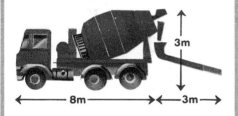

CASTING READY-MIX CONCRETE

1 Try to have your load of ready-mix concrete dumped direct onto your foundations. As soon as it's been unloaded, transfer it to barrows.

2 Transport the concrete to the far end of the slab, tip it onto the hardcore then spread it out. A sheet of hardboard will protect doors from splashes.

3 Spread out the concrete using a garden rake or a shovel. Work the mix well into the corners of the formwork and at the sides to avoid air pockets.

6 Fill any depressions in the concrete with shovelfuls of fresh mix, then pass over the area again with the tamping beam to level the surface.

7 Continue to tamp with a chopping action then work back with a sawing action to level the surface, drawing along a ridge of excess concrete.

8 When you've compacted the slab you can apply a finishing texture. For a polished surface, trowel over the concrete using a steel float.

of about 600mm (2ft) around your proposed slab so you've enough room to work.

Mark out the shape of your proposed slab on the ground with strings stretched between wooden pegs, and use a builder's square to set the corners accurately.

Next, dig out the sub-soil to roughly the depth of the foundation and take it about 150mm (6in) beyond the string lines to leave space for setting up the timber formwork, which you use to mould and retain the concrete while it's hardening.

To ensure that your finished slab will be perfectly level over its entire area use 50x25mm (2x1in) wooden 'datum' pegs, taken from a 'prime datum', or fixed point that establishes the level (see pages 39–43 and 68–71).

Drive the pegs into the ground at 1.5m (5ft) intervals and check across their tops from the prime datum with a spirit level on a straight-edged length of timber to check their level. Remember to incorporate a slight slope for drainage; you can allow for this by placing a 25mm (1in) wedge of timber called a 'shim' under one end of the straightedge (see 'Foundations and formwork', page 41).

Measure down the pegs whatever thickness of concrete you'll need for your slab, plus about 75mm (3in) for hardcore, and excavate or fill in the ground where necessary.

If there's a drainage pipe within the area of your proposed slab it must be at least 150mm (4in) below the underside of the concrete; if it isn't you'll either have to divert the pipe run or alter the level of your slab. If you don't need to move the pipe you should, nevertheless, dig out the soil about 150mm (6in) at each side of it and fill in with pea shingle. Lay shingle rather than hardcore directly over the pipe too.

Where there's a manhole within your slab you'll have to remove the frame and cover, then reset them at the new level, perhaps even raising the manhole brickwork itself by one or more courses (see also step-by-step photographs, page 48).

The original cover may be a lightweight one that's unsuitable for supporting heavy loads, such as your car, and you may have to buy a new, stronger one.

Fixing the formwork

A timber frame called 'formwork' (see 'Foundations and formwork', page 41) is used to retain and support the edges of the wet concrete, which tends to spread out as it sets. Use straight lengths of 25mm (1in) thick sawn timber as wide as the depth of the slab, set on edge and nailed to 50x50mm (2x2in) pegs driven into the ground at the perimeter of the slab at 1m (3ft) centres.

Position the formwork using your perimeter

4 If you're laying your slab adjoining the house you'll have to cast it in easily manageable 'bays' and compact the mix with a tamping beam as you work.

5 Work along the slab using the tamping beam in a chopping action to compact the concrete. This flattens high spots and reveals depressions in the surface.

9 The easiest finish to apply is to smooth over the surface of the fresh concrete with the back of a clean shovel, producing fine swirls.

10 For a more regular, yet still non-slip finish, draw a stiff-bristled broom gently across the slab to produce a finely ridged texture.

strings as a guide and make sure their tops are flush with the finished level of your proposed slab, using a spirit level and shim to incorporate a drainage fall, as previously described. Set the corners at right angles using a builder's square (see *Ready Reference*, page 39). All lengths of timber should be tightly butt-jointed to prevent the concrete seeping out.

Movement control joints

A slab that's longer than about 3m (10ft) in length or width must include a 'movement control' joint, which prevents the slab from cracking due to expansion or contraction.

To make the joints, divide the slab into equal-sized bays and fill the gap with a length of preservative-treated softwood fillet 10 to 12mm (⅜ to ½in) thick, matching the slab depth, and cut to fit between the formwork. Back up the fillet with temporary formwork and pegs and cast each bay separately: once you've cast and compacted the first bay, remove the temporary formwork and cast the second bay, leaving the fillet permanently in position, and so on along the slab.

If the slab is to abut a wall or existing paving use a length of bituminous felt as a dpc and movement joint instead of timber.

Estimating and ordering ready-mix

Ready-mix is usually sold and delivered in minimum loads of 3cu m (105cu ft) and in ¼cu m increments above that volume. To calculate how much concrete you'll need you must work out the volume of the proposed slab: multiply its length by its width (both in metres) to get the area; then multiply this figure by the slab thickness in mm, and divide the answer by 1000 to give the volume in cubic metres. For example a slab measuring 5x4m = 20sq m in area; at a thickness of 150mm the volume is 20x150 = 3000 ÷ 1000 = 3cu m.

Ordering ready-mix is straightforward: you can, in fact, leave most of the calculations to the supplier, although you should make sure you'll receive a little extra in case of miscalculations. He'll want to know the volume of concrete you'll need, at what time you want it delivered, what it'll be used for – hard standing for a car, for instance, or simply garden furniture or foot traffic – and how you're going to handle it on delivery. With this information he'll be able to determine an appropriate mix and give you a price. Obtain several quotations and try to choose a local depot because much of the cost of ready-mix is in its transportation.

You'll also need to discuss with the supplier access for the lorry and whether the load can be discharged directly into the formwork. If this isn't possible you'll have to arrange for a suitably sized space for dumping which won't cause an obstruction either to you or others. In this case you should lay a large sheet of thick-gauge polythene on the ground first to make clearing up easier afterwards.

Coping with delivery

If your ready-mix is going to be dumped some distance from the proposed site – or if the slab is very long – you'll need to gather as many helpers with heavy duty wheelbarrows as you can to transport the wet mix, (it takes 40 barrow loads to move 1 cu m). Lay down scaffold boards as runways for the barrows if you've to transport the mix up steps or across rough or soft ground. Wear old clothes or overalls, Wellington boots and gloves, when laying the concrete.

Placing and compacting concrete

Casting the concrete is a job for at least two people. But you'd be wise to enlist further aid as timing is critical.

Barrow the concrete to the furthest end of the foundations and tip it in. Work it well into the corners and around the edges with your boot or shovel to avoid air pockets. You can use your shovel or a garden rake to spread out the concrete to about 12mm (½in) above the level of the edge boards; this allows for settlement during compaction.

Try to organize your helpers as a team, using some to cast the concrete while two others follow along compacting the mix. Compaction is essential for the strength and durability of the mix; and it's done using a tamping beam (see *Ready Reference*). Position the beam so that it spans the edging formwork; and move along the slab about half the beam's thickness each time with a chopping action in a steady rhythm.

This tamping action will show up any high spots in the mix, which you can disperse by changing to a sawing action across the slab.

CASTING ROUND A MANHOLE

1 *If there's a manhole within your new slab you'll have to reset the lid at the new height. Remove its temporary cover when the mix has stiffened.*

2 *Build up the level of the manhole using bricks or, if the difference isn't too great, mortar. Set the lid frame in mortar, checking that it's level.*

3 *Once you've set the frame of the manhole lid accurately you can cement it into place so that it's flush with the new surface of your slab.*

4 *Remember to choose a manhole cover strong enough to support your loads. Apply a finishing texture to the slab and leave it to set hard.*

Use this excess to fill in any depressions that are left by the tamping beam, and go back over the surface to level it off. Repeat the tamping process until the concrete is level with the top of the formwork.

If you're unable to stand at each side of the slab to use the tamping beam – if it's against a wall, for example – you can cast and compact the concrete in narrow strips.

Finishing the concrete

There are a number of finishes you can apply to the concrete slab. The final pass with the tamping beam can, for example, make a slightly ridged non-slip surface texture for a drive. Alternatively, you could brush the fresh concrete across its width with a stiff bristled broom to give a finer, more regular but still non-slip, finish.

A smoother, polished effect is easier to keep clean for a shed, workshop or garage floor and you can achieve this texture by trowelling the surface with a wooden or steel float in a wide, sweeping action.

One of the simplest finishes, however, is to go over the surface with the back of your shovel, which produces a swirling pattern.

Curing the concrete

Together with thorough compaction, curing is essential for a durable concrete slab. This means that it shouldn't be allowed to dry out too quickly, when it could crack. As soon as the surface has set enough not to be marked easily, cover the entire slab with a polythene sheet, tarpaulins, wet hessian or sacking.

Curing will take about three to four days (ten in winter, though you shouldn't really attempt concreting then unless there is no risk of frost), after which you can remove the covering. You can remove the formwork and use your slab after about ten days.

PATHS, STEPS AND PATIOS

One of the best areas to practise your building skills
is in the garden. Absolute perfection won't matter so much,
it doesn't matter if you make a mess and to begin with
you only have to work in two dimensions. Garden paths and patios
can be laid extremely quickly using prefabricated slabs or bricks,
and once you've mastered the art of laying them level
you can move on to building simple freestanding or built-in steps.
From there it's a relatively short step to building garden walls
and creating exactly the garden you want.

LAYING PATHS WITH PAVING SLABS

Of all the materials you can use to build a path, slabs are among the simplest to lay. The large size of the individual units means a path should not take long to complete and the range of slabs available gives you a wide choice when deciding how your path will look.

Paths are made for going places and while their function might be to prevent mud being trampled into the house or to get a wheelbarrow to the garden shed without making furrows in the lawn, how they look in relation to the garden and your house is also important.

A wide range of attractive paving materials is available for you to choose from. This section deals with the techniques for laying pressed concrete slabs. Techniques for the smaller shapes such as bricks and concrete blocks (pavers) are covered on pages 54–57, and crazy paving on pages 65–67.

Planning a path

Any path should have a purpose. There's little point, for example, in laying a path that skirts the garden and then seeing it ignored as short cuts are taken across the lawn.

You should also make sure your choice of material blends with the surroundings. Concrete slabs, for instance, can look out of place if you have a lot of brick walls, whereas crazy paving might complement them. If the lawn is large and you want a path straight across it, an unbroken length of slabs might look too prominent and it might be preferable to use stepping stones with areas of grass in between (remember to relate the spacing of the stones to a normal walking pace or you will defeat the purpose of the path). If the garden is dotted with trees and shrubs it might be more eye catching to curve the path around them so that it doesn't dominate the setting.

When you're designing, think of the width as well as the length — a path that's too narrow to walk on easily will remain a source of irritation. If you make it too wide it might give the garden an unbalanced look, though a wide path can look very good if flanked on both sides with an array of shrubs or flowers.

PREPARING A HARDCORE BASE

1 Set up string lines to mark the trench edges about 50mm (2in) wider than the finished path.

2 Dig out the trench so it is just a little deeper than the thickness of the slabs you are going to use for paving.

3 Using a stout timber pole, tamp the dug-out area to compact the ground and provide a firm foundation on which the path can be built.

4 Use a timber straight-edge and a builder's level to check that the trench is flat. Inset: If the ground is still soft, dig down another 75mm (3in).

5 Fill the extra depth with a layer of broken brick (rubble) or concrete (hardcore) and compact this so it is firmly bedded down.

6 Fill gaps in hardcore with sand. You can then move string lines in to mark path edges. To lay slabs on sand, add an extra 25mm (1in) thick sand bed.

LAYING ON SAND

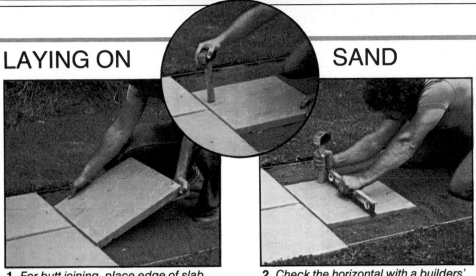

1 *For butt joining, place edge of slab against other slabs, lower it into place and tap it into position (inset) with the shaft of a club hammer.*

2 *Check the horizontal with a builders' level and make sure the slight drainage fall is even. Over several slabs use a timber straight-edge.*

3 *Fill the gaps left between the top surfaces of the slabs by carefully brushing a mixture of soil and sand into the cracks.*

4 *To complete the job, fill the gaps at the path sides with soil and let the grass grow back, or infill with soil and then replace turf on top.*

The best way to start planning is on paper. Use graph paper to make a scale plan of the garden, marking in any fixtures such as established trees and a shed or greenhouse and obvious targets for the path such as a gate or the washing line. Draw them in ink and use pencil to plan in path shapes — they can always be rubbed out if you change your mind.

The plan will give you something to work to as well as a method of calculating the number of slabs and the amount of sand and cement you'll need. But first you'll have to decide on the pattern you want and the type of slab (home-made or bought), whether you want grass to grow between the cracks or whether you prefer the overall look that formal pointing will give.

Paving shapes

The most common concrete paving slabs are square or rectangular in shape, though you can also buy them circular or as parts of a circle (called radius slabs). These are useful for curved or meandering paths which are difficult to make with formwork. Hexagon-shaped slabs look good, too, and these can be married up with half hexagons which give a straight edge for the path's borders.

Concrete slabs can be bought in a variety of colours — anything from red, green and yellow to brown and the ordinary 'cement' grey. Some concrete slabs which are patterned to look like brick or natural stone are finished with a blend of two colours — grey over deep red and grey over buff. But the important thing to remember about any coloured slabs is that the colours won't always last. The pigments are added to the concrete during manufacture, and in time they will fade with the effect of sun and rain. In damp shady spots under trees, lichen will grow on the surface and diminish the original colours. Some slabs may also show signs of staining as a result of efflorescence — white powdery deposits brought to the surface as water dries out of the concrete. Brushing will remove the deposits temporarily.

WHAT SIZE SLABS?

Square and oblong slabs come in a range of different sizes. The commonest are:
● 225 x 225mm (9 x 9in)
● 450 x 225mm (18 x 9in)
● 450 x 450mm (18 x 18in)
● 675 x 450mm (27 x 18in)

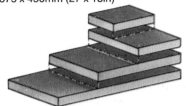

Some slabs are based on a 300mm (12in) unit, so squares are 300 x 300mm or 600 x 600mm (24 x 24in), and rectangles 600 x 300mm (24 x 12in) or 900 x 600mm (36 x 24in). Slabs over 450 x 450mm (18 x 18in) are very heavy.

Hexagonal slabs are usually 400mm (16in) or 450mm (18in) wide. Half slabs are also made, either cut side to side or point to point, and intended to be laid as shown in the sketch.

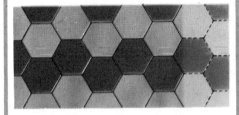

Both rectangular and hexagonal slabs are generally 38mm (1½in) thick.

LAYING METHODS

Light-duty paths – for walkers only – can be laid with slabs bedded on sand about 25mm (1in) thick. The joints should be filled with sand or soil, not pointed with mortar.

Heavy-duty paths – for wheelbarrows, rollers and heavy mowers – should have slabs bedded in stiff mortar (1 part cement to 5 parts sand) and mortared joints.

TIP: STACKING SLABS

To avoid chipping corners and edges and marking the slab faces, stack slabs on edge in pairs, face to face, against a wall, with their bottom edges on timber battens.

LAYING ON MORTAR

1 *For heavier duty use, lay slabs on pads of mortar. Place the fist-sized pads on the path bed ready to take the slab.*

2 *Lower the slab into place so there are 19mm (³⁄₄in) wide gaps between it and neighbouring slabs. Use timber spacers to give correct joint width.*

3 *Use the shaft of a club hammer to tap the slab into position – a builders' level will tell you if the surface is even or needs adjusting.*

4 *With a timber straight-edge and a builders' level check the level across the path, making sure the drainage fall is not too abrupt.*

5 *Brush a dry 1:5 cement:sand mix into the joints and sprinkle them with water, or* **6** *Mix up a crumbly mortar and use a pointing trowel to press this into the joints (inset). Then draw the trowel at an angle along the mortar surface.*

Patterns of laying

You may decide on a simple chequerboard pattern using one size of slabs or a pattern with staggered joints as in stretcher bond brickwork. Alternatively you can create a more decorative path using different sized slabs. Riven surfaced slabs can be particularly effective if two sizes of slabs are used with the larger slabs set to radiate around the smaller ones, producing a square which is repeated down the length of the path. For further suggestions on laying patterns see the slab manufacturers' literature.

Cutting slabs

If the pattern you've worked out requires cut slabs (it's helpful and certainly more easy if they're half sizes), the cutting is relatively easy. After you have marked the cutting line all round the slab you place it on a bed of soft sand or even on the lawn (anything to absorb the shock) and cut a groove along the cutting line, using a bolster chisel and a club hammer. You can then split the slab by tapping the bolster with the hammer along the groove.

Cutting sections out of paving slabs is not so easy. Chipping to shape is time consuming and cast slabs are likely to fracture anyway. It's worth considering filling L-shaped gaps with two separately cut pieces, or leaving out the paving slab altogether and infilling with pebbles, stones or even cobbles set in mortar, or simply finishing off with bricks.

If you want a perfect finish for cut pieces and have a lot of cutting to do, it is worth hiring a masonry saw from a plant hire shop. Although it's possible to fit masonry cutting discs to an ordinary drill, with a lot of cutting you run the risk of burning out the motor.

Buying paving slabs

Visit local garden centres and builders merchants to see what sizes, colours and textures they have in stock. It's always worth shopping around. Your supplier should be able to give you helpful information — for example, some coloured slabs are more colour-fast than others, and he should know which ones. If local suppliers don't have what you want, remember that the cost of transporting heavy slabs over a long distance is high, so it may be better (or at least cheaper) to choose from what is available.

Prices will obviously vary depending on the type of slab — for example, hydraulically pressed slabs are more expensive than cast slabs. And when ordering, allow for a few more than the exact number required for the path; you may crack one or two during laying so it's better to have spares handy.

Preparing the base

Making a flat base is the single most important step in laying the path. And to do this you will usually have to dig out a shallow trench along the line you want the path to follow.

Digging out the topsoil, roots and any organic matter needs to be done carefully

CUTTING SLABS

1 *Mark the cutting line right round the slab with chalk; use a straight-edge so you can mark a straight line the right distance from the sides of the slab.*

and you should dig the trench to a depth just a little deeper than the slab thickness. As well as being flat, the laying surface must be firm and compacted. At this stage, an easy way of checking that the trench is flat is to use a length of straight-edged timber — a plank or a fence post, for instance — to indicate hollows or bumps which might not be obvious to the eye.

Once the trench is dug you may find that because of the type of soil, the surface is still soft. The answer is to dig out another 75mm (3in) or so and then fill the extra depth with a layer of broken brick (rubble) or broken concrete (hardcore). This layer has to be well compacted before a layer of sand or fine ash (called a 'blinding' layer) is spread on it to provide a smooth surface. If you don't want anything to grow up through the path, saturate the trench with a powerful weed-killer.

Laying paving slabs

The easiest way to control the line of a path as you begin to lay the paving slabs is to set up string lines to mark out the edges. How the slabs are bedded — whether on sand or pads of mortar — depends on the weight of traffic the path will carry and whether you intend to point the gaps between the slabs with mortar.

As you lay the slabs, use a timber straight-edge to check that each slab sits flush with its neighbours across and along the path. On level ground, you must lay them so that there is a slight slope across the width of the path — a drop of about 25mm (1in) across 1 metre (just over 3ft) will be sufficient. Check the slope by placing a 25mm thick block of wood under one end of your spirit level or batten; the bubble should then be in the 'dead level' position. On sloping ground, the slabs can be laid dead level across the path width to achieve the same effect.

Slabs can sometimes be butt jointed tightly together. However, because there is often some slight variation in the sizes of slabs, it makes sense to allow for a joint of about 9mm to 12mm (3/8in to 1/2in) to take up these minor inaccuracies. It's important that the joints be kept even — for they act as a frame for the slab shape. Spacers cut from board will give you the desired joint thickness and will also prevent the newly laid slabs closing up as you lay adjacent ones.

Finishing off

When you have positioned all the slabs you can fill the joints. If you are not pointing them, simply brush a mixture of soil and sand into the gaps. Where you want a pointed finish there are two methods you can use — and both require care or mortar stains will mar the slabs.

One method is to mix the cement and sand dry — the sand needs to be very dry — and pour or brush this into the joints. You then sprinkle the joints with a watering can fitted with a fine rose, or wait until it rains.

A better method is to mix up dry crumbly mortar and press this into the joints with a pointing trowel. Any mortar crumbs falling onto the face of the slab can easily be brushed away without staining. You can also use a piece of wood or a trowel to finish the joint so it is slightly recessed.

After pointing is completed don't walk on the path for a few days — if you tread on an edge of a slab you may loosen it and you will have to lift it (using a spade) and lay it again on fresh mortar.

To finish off the gaps at the edges you can point them where they adjoin masonry or a flower bed; where they run alongside a lawn, fill them with soil and let the grass grow back, or fill space with gravel which will drain away excess water.

READY REFERENCE

HOW MUCH SAND?

For a 25mm (1in) thick sand bed, 1/2 cu metre (2/3 cu yd) of sand will cover about 20 sq metres (215 sq ft) – a path 20 metres long and 1 metre wide (22yd x 3ft 3in).

HOW MUCH MORTAR?

One 50kg bag of cement, mixed with 24 2-gallon buckets of damp sand will make enough mortar to lay about 30 slabs using the 'dab' method. One quarter of this mix will fill the joints between about 60 slabs measuring 450 x 450mm (18 x 18in).

GETTING THE RIGHT LEVEL

A path alongside the house should ideally be two courses of brickwork below the damp-proof course (dpc). If this is impossible, make a shallow, gravel-filled gutter about 150mm (6in) wide between the path and the wall to prevent rain from splashing the wall above the dpc.

If the path runs next to a lawn, the finished level should be below that of the grass so you can mow over the edge without the blades catching the masonry.

ALLOWING FOR DRAINAGE

Horizontal paths should have a slight slope across the path width to allow rainwater to drain off the surface. A fall of 25mm (1in) per 1 metre (3ft 3in) of path width should be sufficient: use a block of wood under your spirit level or batten to check that the fall is correct.

TIP: HANDLING SLABS

Slabs are heavy. To avoid injury
● grip the edges of the slab firmly
● lift them with your knees bent and back straight, or
● hold the top corners of the slab, and 'walk' it on its bottom corners
● wear heavy shoes to protect your feet in case you drop a slab on them
● wear gloves to protect your hands when handling slabs with a very rough surface.

2 *With the slab on a surface which will absorb the shock, use a bolster chisel and club hammer to cut a groove along the line, including the slab edges.*

3 *Place the slab face up and work the bolster back and forth along the groove, tapping it with the hammer as you go, until the slab splits in two.*

LAYING PATHS WITH BRICKS

Paths need to be functional but they should also contribute to the overall appearance of their surroundings. Brick and concrete pavers come in a variety of natural colours and can be laid in patterns to suit your style of garden.

Paul Forrester

When you want to build a path with a small-scale pattern you can use bricks or concrete block paving. They can also be used to break up the larger scale pattern of a slab path. Because they are small units you can lay them to gently rolling levels and in restricted spaces where it would be awkward to lay larger slab materials.

Buying bricks and concrete pavers

These materials should be obtainable from a good builders' merchant but, with such a variety on the market, they may have to be ordered. If you live near a brickmaker who makes paving bricks it may be worthwhile enquiring direct – be sure to make it clear you want bricks of paving quality.

Clay brick pavers are produced in a variety of colours from dark red through buff to dark blue/black and a range of finishes both smooth and textured. Calcium silicate are not recommended for paving as their edges are likely to chip. Concrete bricks come in a good range of colours with smooth and textured surfaces while concrete paving blocks tend to be light in tone. Colours include buffs, greys and light reds.

Planning the path

As with paths made from other types of materials, a path of brick or concrete pavers needs to meet functional and design requirements so it will serve its purpose and be an attractive feature of the garden.

Draw up a scale plan of the garden and work out where the path will go. You can also use this to assist you in working out the quantities of materials you will need. Work out patterns that will avoid unnecessary cutting of the pavers. For dry-laid paving, interlocking is an important feature and patterns which avoid continuous straight joint lines are preferable.

When deciding on your design remember that these small units of paving can be used on their own. You may feel, for example, that the bond pattern, colour and textural patterns of clay bricks give sufficient surface interest without recourse to mixing brick types – you might, in fact, find laying rather difficult if bricks were intermingled.

Preparing the base

The foundations on which the paving is laid must be properly prepared to ensure a long-lasting path. You will have to dig out grass, soil and roots – since there will be a granular sub-base topped with a bed of sand plus a layer of pavers, you should dig down to at least 225mm (9in) below the finished level to allow for the thickness of construction.

When you are calculating the depth, remember that if the path runs next to your house the finished level should ideally be two courses of brickwork below the dpc (damp proof course) in the wall. If it's alongside a lawn, make sure its surface is below that of the grass for convenient mowing. Don't forget that on a level path you will have to allow for a drainage fall to one side of the path. Where the path adjoins a wall, the slope should be away from the wall.

To set out the levels, slopes and edge lines you can use timber pegs and string lines. To work out slopes and levels you will need a length of straight-edged timber and a builder's level.

The sub-base should consist of hardcore, which is available through sand and gravel suppliers or builders' merchants. The levels and gradients should be formed in this material so the bed of sand in which the pavers or bricks are laid can be spread evenly over the whole area.

Laying paving dry

For an even, firm path you must take care when you lay the sand base to ensure consistent compaction and perfect level. To give a regular finished surface the sand should be exactly the same throughout the work so allow it to drain before use. Cover it over during storage to minimise variation in moisture content.

You'll also have to include edge restraints for dry-laid paving at both sides of the path. These can be of creosoted or preservative-

PREPARING THE BASE

1 *Stretch strings between pegs to mark the edges of the path. Include a margin for the timber edge restraints on dry-laid paths.*

2 *Cut along the string lines using a spade or, if making a path across a lawn, a turfing iron. Use this tool to lift thin rectangles of turf.*

3 *Dig down to a level that will take a 50mm (2in) sand bed and, if the soil is spongy, a hardcore base. Compact the base using a fence post tamper.*

4 *Set creosoted boards at the sides of the trench as edge restraints. On loosely packed earth, nail the boards to stakes driven into the ground.*

5 *Check the level of the boards across the path using a builder's level. On a lawn, lower the path slightly to make mowing the grass easier.*

6 *When you have levelled the base of the trench and set the edge restraints, shovel in washed sharp sand, which forms a level bed for the bricks.*

7 *Spread out the sand over the path using a garden rake. Work only a small area at a time to avoid walking on newly-levelled base.*

8 *Make a timber spreader to level the sand bed by drawing it along the path, resting on the edge restraints and fill any hollows and level again.*

Paul Forrester

READY REFERENCE

PAVING MATERIALS

Brick pavers are made in a variety of sizes up to 225mm (9in) square and up to 65mm (2½in) thick. Some are shaped to interlock; other have chamfered edges to reduce chipping.

Clay building bricks must be paving quality (frost-resistant when saturated). Standard size is 230 x 110 x 76mm (9 x 4½ x 3in).

Concrete building bricks are the same size as standard clay bricks.

Concrete paving blocks are rectangular (200 x 100 x 65mm) or square (225 x 225 x 65mm) and edges of face side are chamfered. Special interlocking shapes are about the same size overall.

LAYING METHODS

Dry-laid (without mortar) is best for interlocking brick and concrete pavers. Needs sub-base of hardcore 100mm (4in) thick and 50mm (2in) thick bed of sharp sand.

For 1 sq metre you'll need
● 40 brick-size units laid flat
● 60 brick-size units laid on edge
● 50 small concrete pavers

Mortar bed and jointed technique can be used for standard bricks. Needs a 75mm (3in) compacted hardcore sub-base, a blinding layer of sand or fine ash under 50mm (2in) thick mortar bed (1:4 cement and sand) with 10mm (⅜in) mortar joints. To lay and point 3 sq m (105 bricks laid flat) or 2.5 sq m (120 bricks on edge) you'll need:
● 40kg bag of cement
● 17 2-gallon buckets of damp sand

TIPS: STOPPING WEED GROWTH
● under bricks place plastic sheeting on top of the hardcore
● under concrete use a long-term weedkiller

LAYING BRICKS DRY

1 *Begin by laying the bricks in your chosen pattern – a* basketweave *design is shown here – butting up each brick to the next one.*

2 *Tap the bricks into place using the handle of your club hammer but don't exert too much pressure or you risk making the sand bed uneven.*

3 *If any of the bricks are bedded too low, remove them and pack more sand underneath, then level again.*

4 *Bed the bricks level using a stout timber batten held across the path, which you can tap with a club hammer, then check with a spirit level.*

5 *Hold your spirit level on top of the batten and check that the path is bedded evenly, incorporating a drainage fall to one side.*

6 *Brush sand over the surface of the path when fully laid, using a soft-bristled broom to fill the crevices between the bricks.*

Paul Forrester

treated timber, or of bricks or kerb stones set in mortar.

The base should be no less than 50mm (2in) thick. When the finished surface is bedded in some of the sand will be forced up into the joints from below so the depth of the sand layer will be effectively reduced. And to complicate matters, moist sand 'bulks' in volume – the moisture acts on the sand particles to give them a fluffy texture – so the thickness of the sand may seem more than it will, in fact, be when the bricks or blocks are firmly bedded down in place. In this case you may have too little sand and will have to compensate. However, you can have too much sand – a layer which is too thick may cause surface undulation.

It's a good idea to add an extra 6mm (1/4in) to 15mm (5/8in) of sand to the 50mm (2in) thickness to accommodate any unevenness. After you have levelled the first few metres of sand you can check to find out if you have added too much or too little and compensate if necessary. You should check again at frequent intervals as you continue levelling.

You will need a stout timber straight-edged board with notched ends to level the sand surface. The ends fit over the existing edge restraint and you draw the board along

over the sand so that it is evenly spread over the area to be paved. This also ensures that the surface is properly compacted.

You should find laying the paving units quite simple provided you take care how you position the first few pavers. Each paver should be placed so it touches its neighbour – be careful not to dislodge a laid paver from its position – accidental and unnoticed displacement will have a multiplying effect. Similarly, don't tilt any of the laid pavers by kneeling or standing on them as the depressed edge will distort the level of the sand.

Where whole bricks or pavers do not fit at the edges, fill the spaces by cutting whole units to the required size. Gulley entries and manholes can also be dealt with by cutting bricks or pavers to fit. Alternatively, very small areas with a dimension of less than 40mm (1 1/2in) can be filled with a 1:4 cement:sand mortar.

When all the bricks or pavers are in place you will have to bed them securely in the sand. For this you can use a stout timber straight-edge and a club hammer or, particularly useful where you are paving a large area, you can hire a mechanical plate vibrator. Once the bricks or pavers are bedded, you brush fine sand over the

paving and again go over the surface with the machine to vibrate sand into the joints or re-tamp the surface with the straight-edge to ensure settlement. Once all the joints are filled you can brush the surplus sand away. The path will be ready for immediate use.

Laying bricks on mortar
This method of laying bricks is more permanent than using a sand bed, and no edge restraint is needed. Again, when you are digging out the trench, remember to allow for the drainage fall and the level of the path in relation to the dpc or lawn, and dig down deep enough to allow for the thickness of construction.

The sub-base should be a layer of hardcore which is tamped down or rolled to provide a firm foundation for the path and topped with a blinding layer of fine sand or ash. The bricks are bedded in a fairly dry, crumbly mortar mix and with spaces between them to allow for grouting. Dry mortar is brushed into the joints and then the whole path is sprayed with water. With this method, you should not use the path until a week has passed after laying the pavers. In hot, dry weather the paving should be protected against drying out prematurely by covering it with polythene sheets or damp sacking.

LAYING BRICKS ON MORTAR

1 To bed bricks on a mortar base, trowel a fairly stiff mix in dabs onto the sand bed. No edge restraints will be needed when a mortar bed is used.

2 Press the bricks onto the mortar in your chosen design – here you can see a herringbone pattern – and adjust the mortar thickness so they are level.

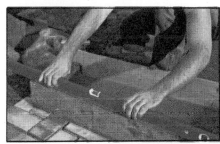

3 Leave a 10mm (³/₈in) gap between each brick to allow for a mortar joint, which is added afterwards. Use timber offcuts as spacers for the joints.

4 Check the level of the brickwork using a straight-edged length of timber and a spirit level. Adjust the thickness of the mortar if necessary.

5 Brush a dry mortar mix, in the same proportions as the bedding mix, into the joints until they are flush with the surface of the path.

6 Spray the path with clean water from a watering can fitted with a fine rose, then leave the path for about one week before using.

CUTTING A BRICK

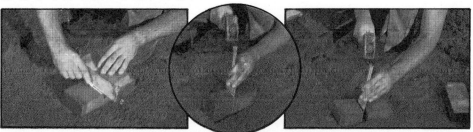

1 Mark a cutting line in chalk around the bricks to be cut; place them on a sand bed and mark the line by hitting it with a bolster chisel and club hammer.

2 Turn the brick over and score lines on each face (inset). Return to the first line and hit it sharply with the chisel until the brick breaks cleanly.

READY REFERENCE

PAVING PATTERNS

Here are three basic patterns you can use to lay rectangular bricks and pavers:

stretcher bond

herringbone

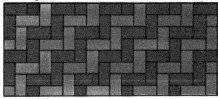

basketweave

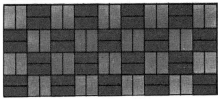

EDGE RESTRAINTS

With paths laid on a sand base, you need some form of restraint to stop the edge blocks from moving. You could choose
● pre-cast concrete kerb stones
● a band of bricks set in mortar (below)

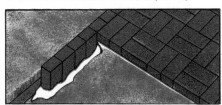

● a sloped mortar 'haunching' ending just under the brick edges (below)

● rot-proofed timber 25mm (1in) thick fixed with 50mm (2in) square wooden stakes. These will soon be hidden by grass overgrowing the path edges

Paul Forrester

BUILDING FREE-STANDING STEPS

A garden composed of different levels will look disjointed unless there is some visual link between parts. A flight of steps not only serves the practical purpose of providing access to the various levels but also gives a co-ordinated look to a scheme.

Cotswold paving and blocks by Mucklow

Paul Forrester

The main purpose of steps is to provide access from one level to another and they're an important factor in the landscaping of a garden, bringing otherwise detached areas into the overall scheme. Wide, shallow steps can, for example, double as seating for a terrace bordering a lawn, or as a display area for plants in containers, while narrow, angular steps will accentuate interesting changes of ground level.

This section deals with freestanding steps, which are designed to rise from flat ground level to a slightly higher level, such as a path to a terrace or raised lawn. Built-in garden steps describes how to construct steps which are not freestanding, but built into a bank or slope.

Types of materials

For a good visual effect, the steps should be constructed from materials that complement the style of the garden. If you've built a path, for instance, continue the run by using the same materials for the steps. Where you're building up to a wall, match the two structures, again by using the same materials.

For a formal flight, bricks can be used as risers (the vertical height of the step). Decorative walling blocks with 'riven' or split faces, or natural stone, used in the same way give a softer, more countrified look. You can top these materials with either smooth- or riven-faced slabs or even quarry tiles to form the treads (the horizontal part of the step on which you walk). Or, if you prefer, you can use other combinations of building materials for the steps; bricks and blocks, for example, make attractive treads as well as risers.

You can choose from a wide range of coloured bricks, blocks and slabs, mixing and matching them to best effect. Pre-cast or cast in situ concrete can be used as a firm base for these materials or makes a durable surface in its own right.

Planning the steps

There are no building regulations governing the construction of garden steps so you have a lot of flexibility in deciding how they will look. Sketch out possible routes – you can build them parallel to the side of the terrace so they don't extend too far into the garden. This is particularly suitable where the ground slope is steep. Decide whether the steps will be flanked by flower beds, rockeries or lawn, or linked at the sides to existing or new walls. You could build steps with double-skinned side walls and fill the gap between with soil to use as a planter.

Bear in mind the dimensions of the completed steps when choosing materials. Treads and risers should measure the same throughout the flight to ensure a constant, safe, walking rhythm. (If they are not constant the variations must be made

PREPARING THE BASE

1 Fix pairs of string lines so they are level and square over the centre of the concrete strip foundations to mark the height and width of the first riser.

2 Lay mortar along the front of the foundation and scribe a line parallel to the inside string to indicate the back of the first course of blocks.

3 Lay the first course of blocks on the mortar, checking the surface is even with a spirit level. Tap the blocks in place with the handle of a club hammer.

4 Position the first course of the side walls in the same way and check that the angle at the corners is at 90°, using a builder's square.

5 Start laying the second course of blocks at one corner, aligning them with the strings. Tap the blocks into place with the handle of your trowel.

6 When two courses of blocks are laid allow the mortar to set partially, then shovel in hardcore. Use a fence post to compact the hardcore.

Paul Forrester

visually obvious for safety reasons.) Make provision, also, for drainage of rainwater from the steps by sloping the treads slightly towards the front.

Steps should be neither too steep nor too gradual – steepness can cause strain and loss of balance while with too shallow a climb you run the danger of tripping on the steps. Steep steps, and those likely to be used by children and elderly people, require railings on one or both sides to aid balance. These can be of either tubular metal or wood and should be set at a height where your hand can rest on top comfortably – this usually

works out at about 850mm (2ft 9in) high measured from the nose of the steps. Alternatively, you can build small brick, block or stone walls at each side of the flight. There should be no hand obstructions along the length of the railings or walls, or other projections on which clothing could snag. Railings should also extend beyond both ends of the flight by about 300mm (1ft); they might, in fact, continue an existing run of railings along a path.

Treads should be non-slip for safety. However, this is difficult to achieve outdoors, where they are subjected to ice, rain

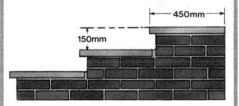

CONSTRUCTING THE STEPS

1 *Move the front strings back the depth of the tread to the second riser position, then lay the blocks on a mortar bed as described previously.*

2 *When the third and fourth courses are laid, in-fill with more hardcore and compact it thoroughly so it's flush with the top of the blocks.*

3 *After laying each course, you should check with a gauge rod at the corners that the mortar joints are of the same thickness throughout.*

4 *The slab treads can be laid on either a bed of mortar around their perimeter or on five dabs of mortar – one at each corner and one centrally.*

5 *Position the slabs squarely on the risers but projecting forward by about 25mm (1in) and sloping forward slightly to allow for drainage of rainwater.*

6 *When the slabs have been laid, fill the gap behind with a mortar fillet – but be sure not to spill wet mortar on the slabs, as this may stain them.*

Paul Forrester

and formation of moss. Proprietary liquids are available for painting on treads so they won't be slippery but a more practical solution is to use hydraulically-pressed slabs, which come with a variety of surface textures or relief designs that are both attractive and non-slip.

When you've decided on the basic appearance and route of the steps you must calculate the quantity of bricks, slabs or other material you'll need. It's best to work out your design taking into account the sizes of slabs, blocks or bricks available. Make a scale plan (bird's eye view) and a side view on graph paper to help in planning and construction.

Building methods

In order to support the steps, concrete trench foundations must be formed underneath the retaining walls. Mark out these foundations using strings stretched between pegs (see foundations. pages 34–38). Construct the flight one step at a time. When the first courses of the retaining walls have been built, a hardcore filling is used to provide a firm base for the treads. When this is rammed down, lay a blinding layer of sharp sand to fill

gaps and provide a level bed for the treads. Subsequent levels are built on top in the same way and the treads laid on mortar.

When tamping down the hardcore back-filling in each level take care not to dislodge any bricks or blocks. Concentrate on the areas that will support the next risers and the back edges of the treads because these parts are subject to the most pressure.

This method of construction is suitable only for freestanding units up to five steps high. If you want larger steps, you'll have to make substantial foundations in the form of a cast concrete slab about 75mm (3in) thick, covering the entire area of the steps, and build intermediate supporting walls the width of the flight under each riser – a hardcore back-filling alone is simply not firm enough to support the extra weight. These walls can be laid in a honeycomb fashion, with gaps between the bricks in each course; this allows for drainage through the structure and uses less bricks than a solid wall. Each section formed by the intermediate walls should contain a rammed-down hardcore back-filling topped with a blinding layer of sand.

Alternatively, you can cast a solid concrete flight in timber formwork and lay the surface materials on top, bedded in

mortar, but this will involve large quantities of concrete.

Larger flights built up to a wall should be joined to the wall or there's the risk of them parting company after time. 'Tooth-in' alternate courses to the brickwork or blockwork of the terrace by removing a brick from the terrace wall and slotting in the last whole brick from the side walls of the steps. On smaller flights you can tie in the steps by bedding a large 6in (150mm) nail in a mortar joint between the two structures for added rigidity.

Brick bonds

The type of brick bond you use in the construction of the retaining walls depends upon the size of the materials you use for the risers. You should, though, try to keep the perpends consistent throughout the flight for strength and for best visual effect.

It's wise to dry-lay bricks or blocks first to make sure you get the best – and strongest – bond; perpends that are very close together mean a weaker construction and you should try to avoid this if possible (see Bricklaying, pages 8 -13). When choosing materials, you should take note of typical, 'safe' tread/riser combinations (see *Ready Reference*).

ARRANGING THE BONDING

In this flight, which has one-and-a-half brick deep treads, the stretcher bond is reversed at the nosing bricks on courses three and four to maintain the bond throughout the rest of the flight.

1

2

This flight, which has two-brick deep treads, maintains the stretcher bond throughout, with bricks header-on at courses one, three and five.

TOOTHING IN

Large freestanding flights are connected to the side of the terrace at alternate courses by removing a brick from the wall and inserting the last whole brick of each course.

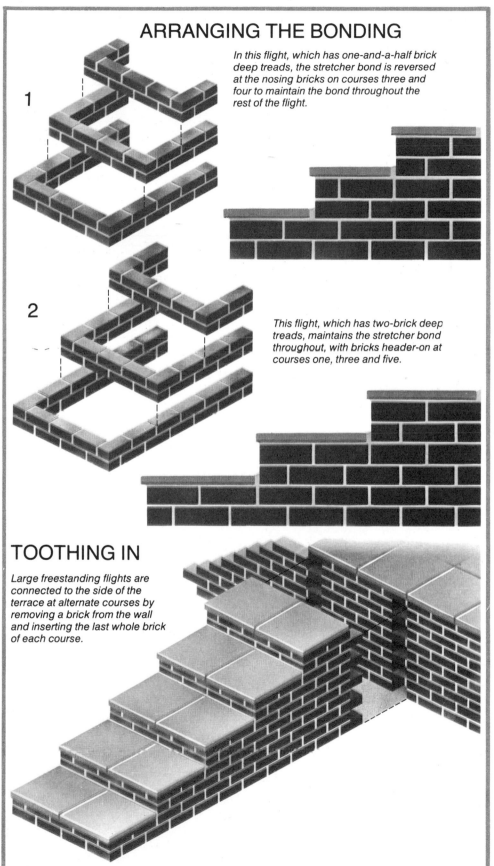

Nick Farmer

READY REFERENCE

MASONRY STEPS

A simple freestanding flight consisting of five treads requires:
● a concrete-filled trench about 100mm (4in) deep and twice as wide as each retaining wall
● broken brick or concrete back-filling
A flight larger than five treads requires:
● substantial foundations in the form of a cast concrete slab about 75mm (3in) thick, covering the entire area of the steps
● intermediate supporting walls the width of the flight under each riser
● rammed-down hardcore back-filling topped with a blinding layer of sand
● or a concrete base flight cast in timber formwork, on which the surface materials can be laid, bedded in mortar.

DRAINAGE

Rainwater must not be allowed to collect on the steps. Provide drainage by:
● allowing for a fall of about 12mm (½in) to the front of each tread or, where the steps abut a wall:
● make concrete gullies about 50mm (2in) deep by 75mm (3in) wide at each side of the flight to drain from the top.

If the flight drains towards a house wall:
● make a channel at the foot of the steps, parallel to the wall, to divert water to a suitable drainage point.

CREATING BUILT-IN STEPS

Steps can be used to great effect in the garden. They not only enable you to get from one level of the garden to another with ease, but draw together otherwise separated features of the landscape.

On pages 58–61 you'll find details of the techniques for freestanding unit steps, which lead from flat ground level to a slightly higher level and have their own support. It is also possible to incorporate steps into an existing slope or bank by using the shape and structure of the slope as the base.

The rough shape of the flight is dug into the bank and the steps are then bedded in mortar on a hardcore base. With some soils, well-compacted earth alone can make a firm enough base for the treads and risers. On a soft crumbly soil you may find it necessary to build low retaining walls at the sides of the flight before you lay the treads, to prevent the soil from spilling onto the treads.

Planning the site

When planning you should consider the site as a whole or the steps might end up looking out of place. You have a considerable amount of freedom in the design of your steps as construction rules are more relaxed outdoors than they are for buildings, but you should adhere to the design principle that the new element should fit into its setting. Because you're using the lie of the land as your foundations it's as well to plan the flight so that it traces existing gradients or skirts flower beds, trees or other features.

Make a sketch of the garden, plotting possible locations for the steps and transfer this information to a more detailed plan on graph paper, including a cross-section of the ground slope. With this plan you can calculate quantities of materials – always try to design the steps with particular sized bricks, slabs and blocks in mind to avoid having to cut them or alter the slope dimensions unduly.

Match materials that have been used elsewhere in the garden – as boundary walls or raised flower beds for instance – for a feeling of continuity. Also remember the basic rules of step design: although you should avoid creating steep steps, which can cause strain, shallow flights are also not recommended because you can easily trip on them.

Bricks, blocks and natural stone come in sizes that are suitable for building risers in one or more courses. Riven- or smooth-faced concrete slabs or quarry tiles make convenient, easy-to-use and non-slip treads for these materials. You can also use the smaller-scale materials such as bricks and blocks for the treads as well as the risers, although they'll need a much firmer base than slabs.

The colour of the steps is also important and most materials are available in a range of reds, greens, browns and greys.

Whatever combination of materials you choose, keep the dimensions of the steps constant throughout the flight – a jumble of sizes not only looks untidy but also upsets a comfortable walking rhythm and so can be dangerous.

Where your flight is larger than 10 steps it's wise to build in a landing. This will visually 'foreshorten' the flight, provide a broad resting place and more practically, will serve to 'catch' anyone accidentally falling from the flight above. You should also include a landing when changing the direction of a flight at an acute angle.

Include railings to aid balance on steep or twisting flights, or those likely to be used by children and elderly people. They can continue the run of existing fences or walls along a path for a sense of unity.

You should also allow for a slight fall towards the front of each tread so that rainwater will drain quickly away. Don't slope the

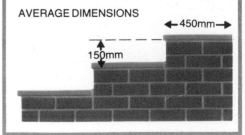

PREPARING THE SLOPE

1 To measure the vertical height of the slope stretch string between a peg at the top and a cane at the base; check that it's level with a spirit level.

2 Set string lines from the top to the bottom of the slope to indicate the sides of the flight, ensuring they are parallel and that the flight is straight.

3 Mark the nosing for each tread with string lines stretched across the slope; check that they are level and that the angle with the side strings is at 90°.

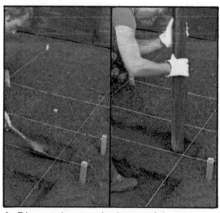

4 Dig out the rough shape of the steps, taking care not to dislodge the nosing markers and compact the earth using a fence post as a tamper.

5 Continue to dig out the steps, working up the slope. Use each cut-out as a standing base for excavating the next, but be careful not to crumble the edges.

6 Dig below and behind the nosing strings to allow for the depth of the slab treads and the thickness of the block risers, thus defining the step shape.

treads to one side as this can give the flight a lopsided look.

Planning awkward slopes

Your plans for building in steps will seldom run true, as your slope probably won't be regular in shape. If the riser height doesn't divide equally into the vertical height of the slope your steps will have inconsistent dimensions – not only unattractive but also likely to upset constant walking pace. One solution is to remodel the slope. Use earth from another part of the garden placed at the top to increase the slope's height; remove earth from the top to decrease its height. Any extra earth must be compacted before it can be 'stepped'.

You can often use any undulations to your advantage: because you're using the firmed ground as your foundations you're able to build much longer and twisting flights. So base your plan on the shape of the ground rather than vice versa.

Marking out the flight

Before you can mark out the flight on the slope you must calculate the number of steps you'll need by measuring the vertical height of the bank.

To mark out the steps stretch strings between pegs from the top to the bottom of the slope to indicate the width of the flight. You can then set other strings across the slope to indicate the top edges of each step's nosing. You should check the level of these nosing strings using a spirit level.

Constructing the flight

Starting at the base of the slope, excavate the rough shape of the first step, digging behind and below the nosing marker to a depth that will allow for a hardcore filling and the thickness of the tread and riser.

Compact the earth, then use the cut-out as a standing base for excavating the next step. Work in this way up the slope. When the whole flight has been excavated in this way, and compacted, lay a hardcore base (if necessary) followed by the treads and risers. Use the back of each tread as a base for the next riser and back-fill with hardcore, which should be well compacted with a fence post tamper, taking care not to dislodge the newly-laid riser.

The first riser should ideally be laid on a cast concrete footing to support the weight of of the flight, preventing it from 'slipping', although on small flights where the soil is firm this might not be necessary. The footing should be about 100mm (4in) deep and twice the thickness of the riser.

An alternative way to build steps into a slope is to cast a concrete slab flight in timber formwork and either face it with bricks, blocks, slabs or tiles, or leave it bare.

LAYING THE STEPS

1 Lay any slabs at ground level where a path run continues then add hardcore under the first riser position. Compact and lay mortar on top.

2 Lay the blocks for the first riser on the bed of mortar, making sure they're level and square. Tap down into place with the handle of your club hammer.

3 Fill the gap between the blocks and the soil with hardcore, then compact to the top level of the riser. Take care that you don't dislodge the blocks.

4 Shovel hardcore onto the first tread position and compact well using a fence post. Check the level of the foundation, incorporating a fall to the front.

5 Lay the first two slabs on mortar and check that they are level. Set them forward by about 25mm (1in); the nosing marker should align with their top edge.

6 Bed the next course of blocks for the second riser in mortar on the back of the first tread; try not to splash mortar on the slabs as this will stain.

7 Back-fill with hardcore and tamp down thoroughly, then lay the next two slabs; a bed of mortar at the perimeter of each slab makes a firm and level bed.

8 Continue in this way to the top of the flight, bedding each riser on the tread below it. Set the last tread level with the ground at the top of the slope.

9 Brush a dry mortar mix into the gaps between the slabs, point all the joints and brush off any debris. Leave the steps for 7 days before using.

LAYING CRAZY PAVING

Garden paving doesn't have to be all squares and rectangles. With crazy paving you can have a more informal look in any shape you fancy, and you can use it on wall surfaces too.

Crazy paving is a versatile material that can be used as a resilient and attractive surface for patios, driveways, garden paths or steps, or as a decorative feature in an otherwise plain paving scheme.

It's simply broken paving slabs and you can often buy it quite cheaply, by the tonne, from your local as demolition material. Slabs bought in this way will usually be a heavy duty variety used for pavements and have a rather dull grey colour and a relatively plain finish, but you can add interest in the way you lay the pieces. Local building contractors can often supply broken slabs of various textures in greens, pinks, reds and buff tones in sufficient quantities for use in paving. Natural stone can also be bought to make up crazy paving.

Planning crazy paving
Before you can begin to lay your paving, sketch out some ideas for its overall shape, size and, in the case of paths, its route through the garden. Transfer your final design to graph paper so that you can use this to estimate the total area to be covered and place an order for the correct quantity of paving. You can also use your plan as a blueprint for ordering and laying the slabs.

Because of its irregular profile crazy paving, unlike conventional square or rectangular slabs, can be used to form curves, such as a winding path, a decorative surround to a pond, or an unusual-shaped patio. Although you have a lot of freedom in your creative design you mustn't allow the paving to appear out of place with its surroundings. If your garden is strictly formal, for instance, avoid complex curves or too 'busy' a surface texture — the mix of angles could clash. Small areas of random paving can, on the other hand, give a plain scheme a visual 'lift'.

Although crazy paving has an overall random design, it must be placed with some precision to avoid an unbalanced look. The best way to plan out an area of paving when you've decided upon a basic site is to dry-lay it when the base is complete.

Separate the pieces that have one or more straight sides for use as edging and corners and lay these first, choosing only the largest pieces — small ones tend to break away.

You can lay the paving with a ragged outline to achieve an informal look, but you will still have to use the largest pieces for the edging. When plants have been introduced into the irregular edges and allowed to trail over the slabs you'll find that your path soon assumes an established air.

It's not important to make a regular joint width between the pieces — in fact, the paving will probably look much more natural if the joints vary. Fit the smaller inner pieces together like a jig-saw puzzle, mixing colours to best effect. When dry-laying the slabs avoid a continuous joint line across the path as this can be jarring to the eye and weakens the structure.

Laying the paving
The methods of laying crazy paving are similar to those using regular paving slabs (see pages 50–53 and 68–71) — with a firm base being the first requirement.

To prepare the base remove the topsoil and compact the area using a roller or tamper. If the ground is soft or crumbly add a layer of hardcore and compact this into the surface. A blinding layer of sand added to the top accommodates any unevenness in the hardcore base and acts as a firm bed for the slabs.

Lay the slabs on generous mortar dabs under each corner or, with smaller pieces, on an overall mortar bed.

Work your way across the dry-laid surface,

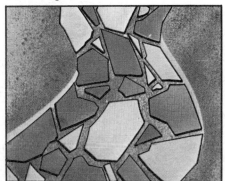

PREPARING THE BASE

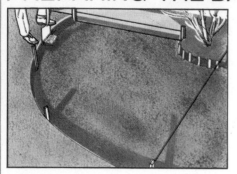

1 Mark out the area to be paved using pegs and string, and remove the topsoil (above). Then tamp the subsoil down all over (below), adding hardcore if needed.

2 Having thoroughly compacted the surface and filled any hollows, check that it is flat in both directions using a long timber straight edge. Allow for a slight drainage fall in one direction across the paved area by scraping away soil from the base so that your spirit level bubble is slightly off centre.

3 Spread a 50mm (2in) thick layer of sand across the area (above). Then use your long timber straight edge to tamp it down to a level, even bed (below).

bedding each stone in turn and checking the level frequently using a builder's level — don't forget to incorporate a slight drainage fall to one side of a path or to the front of a patio or step treads. Tap the paving in place using the handle of your club hammer: as you do this some mortar will be squeezed up into the joints, which can be anything up to 25mm (1in) wide. You needn't scrape out this mortar from the joints: it actually makes for a stronger bond.

After you've laid the slabs point between them with mortar (see *Ready Reference*). Be careful not to smear any on the faces of the slabs otherwise they will stain. Alternatively you can leave the joints mortar-free and brush in soil later in which to plant low growing plants or herbs.

If you have used crazy paving for patio or path surfaces, you may also want to give your garden a unified look by cladding steps and low walls.

On steps, start at the bottom of the flight and clad the lowest riser first. Build up the cladding from ground level, buttering mortar onto the back of each piece of paving and pressing it firmly into place against the riser. Finish cladding the riser with pieces that fit flush with the existing step surface, and then lay paving on the surface of the tread so that those at the front overlay the riser by about 25mm (1in). Clad all the risers and treads, then point between the pieces. Clad low walls in the same way as step risers.

DRY-LAYING THE SLABS

1 When you've marked out the shape of your paved area and dug out and prepared the foundations, start to dry-lay the slabs in one corner.

2 Separate the straight-edged slabs from the irregular-shaped ones and dry-lay the largest pieces at the perimeter of your marked-out area.

3 Fill in small gaps between the perimeter slabs with straight-edged fragments, but avoid a run of small pieces, as it makes a weaker edge.

4 When you've placed all of the perimeter slabs you'll be able to see what the overall effect will be: swap them about for the best-looking plan.

LAYING THE PAVING

1 When you're satisfied with the positions of the slabs you can start to bed them on a fairly stiff mortar mix; lay the large ones on five dabs of mortar.

2 You can lay smaller pieces on a continuous mortar bed. Trowel ridges in the mortar: this aids levelling and provides a stronger bond.

3 Bed each slab level with the ones next to it by tapping it gently with the handle of your club hammer. Allow mortar to squeeze out between the joints.

4 Mortar in the perimeter slabs first then start to in-fill with smaller irregular-shaped pieces, using different colours for a more varied pattern.

5 Check at intervals across the tops of the slabs with a builder's level to ensure they're bedded evenly. Tap them in place with the handle of a club hammer.

6 Mortar joints can be up to 25mm (1in) wide. Make the joint flush with the slabs but don't spill mortar on the slab faces, or it will stain them.

7 If you want to make a feature of the joints fill them with soil rather than mortar and add some low-growing plants to give a natural, established look.

8 After you've pointed the joints, or filled them with soil, brush over the surface of the paved area with a stiff-bristled broom to remove any debris.

READY REFERENCE

POINTING PAVING

There are three ways to treat the joints between crazy paving:
- Flush pointing — fill the joints with mortar flush with the tops of the slabs.
- Bevelled pointing — form bevels in the mortar about 9mm (³⁄₈in) deep at each side of the joint to outline the shape of each slab.
- Soil joints — fill the joints with soil and plant low-growing plants or herbs to blend in the paving with the rest of the garden.

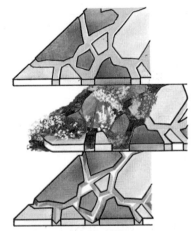

TIP: BREAKING LARGE SLABS

A delivery of crazy paving might include some pieces too large to lay. Break them by dropping them on any hard surface — easier than using a bolster chisel and club hammer. Use these tools for trimming smaller pieces.

COLOURED POINTING

Make a feature of the joints in crazy paving by colouring the mortar. Additives are available for adding to the mix but you should follow the maker's instructions precisely — too great a proportion of colouring can upset the strength of the mortar.

For more information on laying paving slabs see pages 50—53 and 68—71.

BUILDING A PAVED PATIO

Building a patio close to the house is one way of transforming a dull and featureless garden into a durable paved area that's geared especially for outdoor living.

A patio makes a versatile summertime extension to the house, providing space for dining, entertaining, or merely for relaxing and soaking-up the sun. You must plan your patio to take advantage of the best aspect and construct it from materials that are both in keeping with the house and garden and durable enough to withstand harsh weather conditions.

Siting the patio

Patios are usually sited as close to the house as possible – ideally adjoining it – or at least nearby for easy access. The best aspect is south-facing, but whichever way your garden faces, you should examine the proposed site at different times of the day during the summer to see how shadows fall. Neighbouring buildings, or your own house, might obscure the sun and this will severely limit the use of the patio. Unfortunately there's nothing you can do about this, but if the obstruction is just a tree or tall hedge you might be able to prune it.

Some shadows can be used to your advantage: although you might want to lie sun-bathing at certain times of the day, you'll appreciate the shade while you eat. If there's no natural shade, you could attach an awning to the house wall, which can be folded away when not needed. A pergola or trellis on which you can train climbing plants will also provide shade where you need it. Or you might prefer simply to allow enough space for a table with an umbrella or a swing seat with a canopy.

What size patio?

In theory a patio may be as large or small as you wish, but in practice you'll be limited by available space. Try to relate the dimensions of the patio to the needs – and size – of your household. Measure your garden furniture and allow enough space around it so that you won't be cramped: the patio must measure at least 2.4m (8ft) from front to back to enable you to position furniture and allow free passage. In general a patio measuring about 3.7m sq (12ft sq) is big enough to take a four-seater table or four loungers.

To work out the size and position of the patio make some preliminary sketches of the garden with the proposed patio in various locations. When you've decided upon a suitable scheme transfer your ideas to a scale plan on graph paper. Cut out a paper template of the patio and use it in conjunction with the plan to help you decide upon the best position.

What type of surface?

There is a wide range of paving materials available in various shapes, sizes and colours and you should choose those which blend with materials used around the house exterior and garden for a sense of unity. The main requisites are that the surface is reasonably smooth, level and free-draining. Whatever your choice of paving, avoid too great a mix – two types are usually sufficient to add interest without making the surface look cluttered. You can, however, include confined areas of small-scale materials such as cobblestones and granite setts to add a textural change to an otherwise flat scheme composed of larger slabs.

Cobblestones – oval pebbles – can be laid in three ways: on a continuous mortar bed over hardcore foundations; on a bed of dry mortar 'watered in' by watering can; or loosely piled on top of each other on compacted earth. Granite setts are durable square-shaped blocks with an uneven

PREPARING THE BASE

1 Set a long prime datum peg in a hole 300mm (1ft) deep at one side of the patio. Its top should be 150mm (6in) below the house dpc.

2 Set a second peg at the other side, level with the first. For a very wide patio use intermediate datum pegs set 1.5m (5ft) apart.

3 Use a string line to set timber pegs accurately in line with each other so that they outline the proposed perimeter of the patio.

4 Check with a builder's square to make sure that the corners of the patio are perfectly square. Adjust the peg positions if they are not.

5 Dig out the site to a depth of about 230mm (9in), saving the top-soil and turf. Then compact the earth with a garden roller.

6 Drive in pegs 1.5m (5ft) apart over the entire area. Check that they are level with the datum peg and each other using a spirit level.

7 Fill the hole with hardcore, then compact it thoroughly to a depth of about 125mm (5in) using a tamper. Don't disturb the pegs.

8 Rake out and roll a 50mm (2in) layer of sand over the hardcore. The peg tops should be level with the sand surface.

LAYING THE SLABS

1 Start to lay the slabs at the corner marked by the prime datum peg. You can lay them dry on the sand bed, without using any mortar.

2 As you progress across the patio you should check frequently with a builder's level that the slabs are bedded evenly on the sand.

3 Lift up any slabs that are unevenly bedded and trowel in some more sand until the bed is filled out and the slabs are flush with their neighbours.

4 Alternatively you can lay the slabs on dabs of fairly stiff mortar, one placed under each corner of the slab and one under the centre.

5 Position the slab carefully on top of the mortar dabs. Space out the slabs using offcuts of timber 9mm (³⁄₈in) thick for pointing later.

6 Bed down the slabs using the handle of your club hammer. If any of the slabs are too low, remove them and add more mortar to the dabs.

7 Stretch the string lines across the patio every second course to help you align the slabs accurately.

8 When all the slabs are laid, brush a dry mortar mix between the joins and remove any excess from their faces. This will form a bond when watered in.

9 Water in the dry mortar mix with clean water from a watering can fitted with a fine rose. Avoid over-watering or you'll wash away the mortar.

surface texture, and can be laid on sand or mortar.

Other small-scale paving materials that can be used in large or small areas include concrete blocks, brick pavers and paving-quality bricks. They're available in various colours and the blocks also come in a range of interlocking shapes. Lay these materials in patterns for best effect and use coloured mortar joints as a contrast.

You can also use special frost-proof ceramic tiles for a patio surface but they are very expensive and need a perfectly flat base if they are to be laid correctly. Consequently, they're really only suitable for very small patios.

Probably the simplest of surfaces is one made of a solid slab of cast concrete. Although the concrete can be coloured with pigments, many people find its surface appearance unattractive.

Concrete paving slabs are probably the best materials for a simple rectangular patio. Made with reconstituted stone, they're available in a range of reds, greens, yellows and buff tones with smooth, riven or patterned faces. Square, rectangular, hexagonal and half-hexagonal shapes are also made and they're easy to lay on a sand bed. Broken concrete slabs, known as crazy paving (see pages 61-63 for details), can also be used as a patio surface, laid on a mortar bed.

Link the patio to the rest of the garden by building walls, paths and steps (see pages 50–64 inclusive) in matching or complementary materials.

Marking out patterns

Whatever paving materials you choose you have enormous flexibility in the design of your patio. There's no reason why, for instance, it should be square or rectangular – most of the materials previously described can be laid in curves or can be cut to fit other shapes and angles.

Sketch out some patterns and dry-lay the paving in both width and length to test how the designs work in practice. Adjust the pattern or the dimensions of the patio to minimise the number of cut pieces you use. This will ensure the surface looks 'balanced'.

Concrete slabs can be laid in various grid and stretcher bond patterns but, for a more informal effect, whole and half slabs can be used together in a random fashion. Crazy paving should be laid with larger, straight-edged pieces at the borders and smaller fragments inside. You can lay bricks in herringbone or basket-weave designs.

Setting the levels

Draw your plan on graph paper, then use it to transfer the shape of the patio onto the site. Use strings stretched between pegs to mark out the perimeter of the patio. You must also drive pegs in to represent the surface level of the patio, so to ensure they're accurately placed you have to drive a 'prime datum' peg into the ground against the house wall (if the patio is to abut the house). The peg should indicate one corner of the patio and should be set in a hole about 300mm (1ft) deep with its top 150mm (6in) below the level of the house damp-proof course. If the soil is spongy you may have to dig deeper in order to obtain a firm enough surface on which to lay the foundations.

Set a second peg in the ground against the wall to mark the other side of the patio, and check that the level corresponds to that of the prime datum peg by holding a long timber straight-edge between the two and checking with a spirit level.

All other marking-out strings and pegs should be taken from the base line formed between these two datum pegs. Indicate squares and rectangles by stretching strings from the two pegs and checking the angle with a builder's square. Plot out curves by measuring from the base line at intervals and driving in pegs at the perimeter, or use lengths of string or a long hosepipe to mark the curves. Circles and half-circles can be marked out by taking a string from a peg placed as the centre of the circle: you place the first slabs or other paving along the string, then move it around the radius and set the next row.

If size permits, you could incorporate planting areas in your patio by leaving sections un-paved, or simply place tubs of plants on the perimeter.

Laying the paving

When you've marked out the shape of your patio, remove the topsoil (which you should save for use elsewhere in the garden) from within your guidelines and set intermediate datum pegs at 1.5m (5ft) intervals over the entire area of the excavation. These pegs have to be sunk to the level of the prime datum peg, using a spirit level on a batten between the pegs. Now is the time to set the drainage fall away from the house.

When you've set the levels, fill the hole with hardcore, which you must compact thoroughly by rolling and tamping. Then a layer of sand rolled out flat over the hardcore brings the level of the foundation up to that of the peg tops, and provides a flat base for the paving.

On a site that slopes away from the house you'll have to build a low retaining wall of bricks or blocks; the ground behind it can be filled with hardcore and then paved. However, where the ground slopes towards the house you must excavate the patio site in the bank (forming a drainage fall away from the house), and build a retaining wall.

PREPARING THE FOUNDATIONS

Patio paving requires foundations of compacted hardcore covered with a blinding layer of sand. The excavation should be:
● about 150 to 200mm (6 to 8in) deep to allow for 75 to 125mm (3 to 5in) of hardcore plus the sand and paving
● about 230mm (9in) deep if the patio is to be built up to a house wall, so the paving can be set 150mm (6in) below the dpc.

ALLOWING FOR DRAINAGE

To ensure run-off of rainwater the patio surface must slope by about 25mm in 3m (1in in 10ft) towards a suitable drainage point, which might be an existing drain or soakaway.

On ground sloping away from the house: construct perimeter walls for the patio from brick, block or stone, to form a 'stage'. Infill with hardcore and a blinding layer of sand and gravel, then pave. The walls must be set on 100mm (4in) deep concrete footings.

On ground sloping towards the house: excavate the site for the patio in the bank, forming a fall away from the house. Build a retaining wall to hold back the earth.

INSPECTION CHAMBERS

The patio must not interfere with access to drainage inspection chambers. If drain covers are within the patio area:
● build it up to the level of the new surface
● cover it with loose-laid slabs for access.

TIP: PAVING ROUND TREES

If you're paving around a tree or shrub to make a garden feature, keep the paving at least 300mm (1ft) from the trunk to allow rainwater to reach its roots.

For more information on laying paving slabs see pages 44–53.

ALTERATIONS

Once you've mastered the basic builder's skills, you can turn your attention to some more ambitious internal alterations. These may include replacing features such as doors and windows with new components, or even creating openings where none existed before. Fireplaces that have been gutted may need to be reinstated if you want to join the rush back to open fires; conversely, unwanted fire openings can be removed and blocked up to create much-needed living space. You can replace old, sagging ceilings with easy-to-handle plasterboard, and even sub-divide your living space exactly as you want it with partition walls.

MAKING A NEW DOORWAY I – the lintel

Making a new doorway or window can dramatically change the way you plan your rooms. The first part of the job, described here, is to insert the lintel.

The way some of the rooms of your house are laid out may not be suitable for all the activities and storage needs of your household, particularly if you have growing children. You may also feel that the existing layout of your house severely cramps your style when it comes to designing decorative schemes for your home. The problem may be a purely practical one: the position of doors and windows may be an obstacle when it comes to placing seating, wall-mounted cupboards, bookcases and other furniture exactly where you would like them. Life can be made very much easier if there is an uninterrupted flow of traffic between two rooms, such as the kitchen and dining room, but this is often not the case in an existing plan.

You might be able to solve some of your problems by changing the function of your rooms; for example, converting a living room to a dining room. You could even alter the shape and size of the rooms – or create an entirely new room – by building a partition wall (see pages 101–105). But, in addition, you may find it's necessary to reposition a door or window to improve an existing scheme or fit in with a new one.

It's a straightforward matter to block off a redundant window or doorway with bricks or plasterboard, but if you're making a new opening of this size in a wall you'll have to take into account some basic structural rules.

To cut out an area of wall you must support the masonry above, plus any additional load that bears upon it. The usual way to do this is to insert a rigid beam or 'lintel' made of wood, concrete or steel, directly above, which is recessed into the sides of the opening. Your choice of lintel depends on how your wall's been built and whether it's internal or external, load-bearing or non-load-bearing.

Planning the opening

Before you can make an opening in a wall – whether it's load-bearing or not – you must check with your local Building Department that what you plan is permissible under Building Regulations (see pages 129–133).

It's not always feasible to change the position of a window or a door in an external wall: your new location might infringe local bye-laws or, especially in the case of a window, it might simply have a poor outlook. But you can usually make a new opening in an internal wall wherever you want.

The first job in planning your new opening is to decide exactly where you'd like it to be. Your decision will be influenced by where you'd like to put your larger pieces of furniture, and particularly those which will stand against the wall, such as a sideboard or bookshelves. If, for instance, you're going to make a serving hatch between kitchen and dining room you might want to position it directly above your sideboard to make serving easier. Work and traffic flows are also important aspects of room scheming, particularly when you're making a new doorway.

Although you have a lot of flexibility in positioning your opening, it's best to keep the top a reasonable distance below the ceiling so you'll have ample access when fitting the lintel and making good the wall around it. You should also avoid making your opening too close to the corner of the room because you'll weaken the structure of the wall; leave a margin of at least two bricks' length to be safe.

It's best to site your opening away from electrical socket outlets, wall switches or wall lights, but if that's not possible you'll have to reposition the wiring, accessories

READY REFERENCE

SUPPORTING THE WALLS
If you're making a door or window-sized opening in a wall you must:
● temporaily support the walling above the proposed opening, and any load bearing upon it, with adjustable metal props and timber 'needles' (A)
● install a lintel (B), resting on suitable bearings (C) above the opening to support the walling permanently.

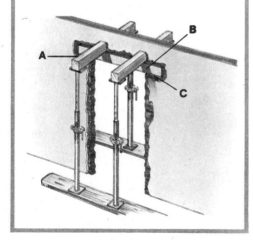

73

MARKING OUT A DOORWAY

1 *When you've decided where you want your doorway, mark one side on the wall then hold a spirit level against a timber straight edge at this point.*

2 *Adjust the straight edge so that it's vertical and draw along the edge using a pencil to mark one side of your proposed doorway.*

3 *Measure from your first guideline the width you want the doorway and mark the wall; extend the mark using the straight edge.*

6 *You'll also have to mark the lintel position on the wall: measure the length of the lintel and add on 25mm (1in) so it's easier to fit.*

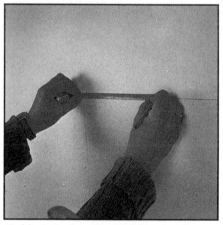

7 *Mark the length of the lintel on the wall; it should be central over the doorway and projecting beyond each side by about 150mm (6in).*

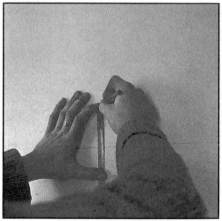

8 *Measure the depth of the lintel, add 25mm (1in) for fitting and transfer this dimension to the wall above the top of the door.*

and fittings. If there's enough slack in the cable you can simply move it further along the wall. Alternatively you'll have to extend or re-route the circuit to avoid the opening by joining in new lengths of cable.

You will also have to consider the dimensions of your opening and match them to the standard sizes of ready-made doors and window frames available from timber merchants unless you make the frames yourself to your own specifications.

Supporting the wall

It's possible to cut a door or window-sized hole in a non-load-bearing wall without supporting the wall above while you work. If it's properly bonded and the mortar joints are in good condition, the only area that's at risk from collapse is roughly in the shape of a

45° triangle directly above the opening Without a lintel the bricks or blocks within this area would tend to fall out, forming a stepped 'arch'; the walling that's left would, however be self-supporting – although weaker than it was – up to a span of about 1.2m (4ft).

So when you've marked out the position of your proposed opening it's quite safe to chop out the triangle of bricks or blocks above and insert your lintel. When that's in position, and you've filled in the triangle, you can remove the walling below to form your opening.

However, if you're going to cut an opening in a load-bearing wall you'll have to provide temporary supports not only for the walling above the opening but also for any load from floors or walls above, which bears upon the

wall. The weight imposed upon a wall is quite considerable and if it's not adequately supported the brickwork or blockwork could 'drop'. This type of structural damage is impossible to repair and the only remedy is to demolish the wall and rebuild it. To support the walling you'll need four adjustable metal props and two stout timber battens called 'needles'. The props work rather like a car jack, and to fit them you'll have to cut two holes through the wall directly above the lintel's position at each end, and slot in the needles. You can then use the props to support each end of the needles.

Rigging up the supports is a two-man job: you'll need one person of each side of the wall to tighten up the props simultaneously so that the needles can be fixed level.

4 *You can mark the height of the doorway in the same way using your straight edge and spirit level to get it truly horizontal.*

5 *Once you're satisfied that the straight edge is level, remove the spirit level and scribe along the top to mark the top of the doorway.*

9 *Position your straight edge at this point using your spirit level then draw a line on the wall to mark the top of the lintel slot.*

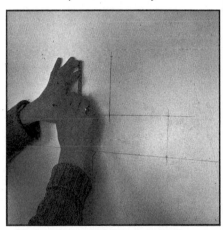

10 *Next you mark the slots for the needles directly above the lintel position, and centrally over the lines marking the sides of the door.*

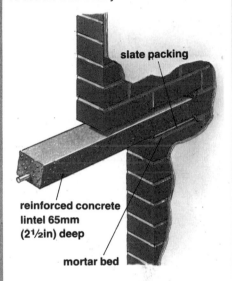
If floor joists from the rooms above are resting on your wall you'd be wise to provide extra support for the ceilings at each side of the wall. Again you can use adjustable metal props with stout battens at top and bottom.

With the wall supported in this way you can safely chop out a slot in the brickwork or blockwork directly below the needles and insert your lintel.

It's possible to cut an opening in a cavity wall by more or less the same process but only the inner leaf – usually blockwork – is load-bearing. Cutting into a timber frame wall involves a slightly different process and will be dealt with in a later issue.

Marking out the opening

When you've selected the best location for your opening you'll have to mark out its shape on the wall. Take the overall measurements of your frame and add on about 25mm (1in) to give fitting tolerance; then transfer these dimensions to the wall. You might have to move your proposed opening along the wall fractionally so that both its edges line up with a vertical mortar joint; this keeps the number of bricks or blocks you have to cut to a minimum.

If the wall is plastered you could chip away a section about 500mm (1ft 8in) square from the centre of your proposed opening to reveal the bricks or blocks beneath. With this small area uncovered you'll be able to measure from a mortar joint to your line marking the perimeter of the opening. If the lines at each side don't correspond with a mortar joint you'll have to move them over until they do.

CUTTING THE LINTEL SLOT

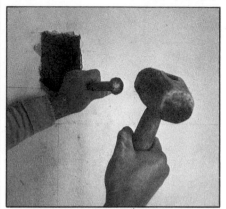

1 *Start to chop the first needle hole, using a bolster chisel and club hammer. If you're cutting into a thick wall use a 100mm (4in) cold chisel.*

2 *When you've cut your first hole through the wall you can slot in your needle. It should protrude equally on both sides of the wall.*

3 *With one man at each side of the wall, start to tighten up the adjustable metal props under both ends of the needles.*

4 *Once you've rigged up the supports you can chop around the lintel guidelines then start to remove the plaster from within the rectangle.*

5 *Hack out the brickwork carefully; if the walling above drops, chop a margin of plaster around the lintel slot and remove the loose bricks.*

6 *Continue to chop out the bricks to form the slot for the lintel. Try to keep the top surface inside the slot, and the bearings, as level as possible.*

When you're satisfied with the position of your opening you can draw its shape on both sides of the wall more accurately using a pencil held against a spirit level.

You'll also have to mark the position of the lintel on the wall directly above the line that marks the top of the opening. Make it wider than the opening by about 150 to 225mm (6 to 9in) to give a sufficiently sturdy bearing (see *Ready Reference*) plus an extra 25mm (1in) at each end and on top to make fitting the lintel easier.

Cutting the lintel slot

Before you can chop out any bricks or blocks you'll have to rig up your temporary supports for the walling.

If you're using a heavy concrete lintel you'd be wise to place it across two trestles in front of your proposed opening before you rig up the props and needles to save having to haul it in later.

Set up the adjustable props and needles first. If you're making a doorway or narrow window you'll need 100 x 75mm (4 x 3in) thick needles about 1800mm (6ft) long made of sawn timber. You'll have to chop out equivalent sized holes in the wall and feed the needles through. Support each end of the needles with an adjustable prop resting on a timber batten on the floor. The props mustn't be more than 600mm (2ft) from either side of the wall.

You may need to provide temporary supports for the ceiling, if it's necessary, by erecting three adjustable props between stout planks measuring about 100 x 50mm (4 x 2in) top and bottom and 1m (3ft) apart.

If you're working on a brick wall you can simply remove a single course of bricks in order to fit the lintel, but if the wall's made of blocks you'll have to remove a whole block and fill the gap above with a row of bricks. Start to cut out the bricks or blocks directly below the needles by chopping into the mortar joints with a bolster chisel and club hammer to loosen them.

When you've cut the slot for the lintel, trowel a bedding mortar mix of three parts soft sand to one of portland cement onto the bearings at each side and lift the lintel into place. If the walling and its load is to bear evenly on the lintel you'll have to make sure that it's bedded perfectly level. You can hold a spirit level below it and pack out where it rests on the bearings with squares of slate until it's level. Fill the 25mm (1in) fitting tolerance gap above and at each end of the lintel with mortar.

Wait for about 24 hours for the mortar to set before you move any of the bricks and blocks below the lintel.

See pages 78–81 for how to cut out your opening and fit a lining frame for your decorative architrave and door.

FITTING THE LINTEL

1 *Trowel mortar onto the bearing at each side of the doorway then lift the lintel into position and centre it carefully in its slot.*

2 *The lintel must sit firmly and perfectly level on its bearings; you can wedge small squares of slate underneath to pack it up.*

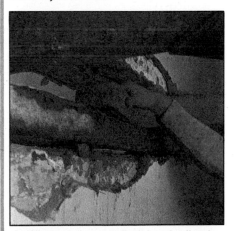

3 *When you're satisfied that the lintel is bedded evenly, start to replace the brickwork that's fallen out, bedding it in fresh mortar.*

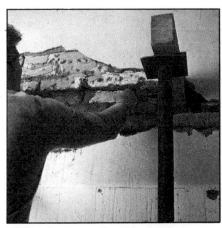

4 *Continue to replace the bricks on top of the lintel — at both sides of the wall if it's 224mm (9in) thick — and copy the original bond.*

5 *You can remove the needles and props about 24 hours later, when the mortar has set, and then fill in the gaps left with more bricks.*

6 *Point the mortar joints flush with the face of the brickwork and leave them about 24 hours for the mortar to set before cutting the walling below.*

READY REFERENCE

TIMBER STUD PARTITIONS

If you're making an opening in a load-bearing timber stud partition:
● temporarily support the floor or ceiling above with adjustable props and planks
● remove the plasterboard or lath and plaster cladding from each side of the wall
● cut through one of the vertical studs at the height you want your opening
● notch a timber lintel into the studs at each side of the cut one
● notch a new timber stud into the sole plate and the new lintel to give the opening width you want
● skew-nail additional timber noggins between the new stud and one next to it
● if you've making a hatch, notch in a sill at the required height within the opening
● fix new cladding around the opening.

timber lintel

notched half-way into the original framework

replacement noggins

original stud cut away

sill beam inserted for hatch; omitted for doorway

FIXING THE FRAME

To fix the frame in your opening:
● stand the frame temporarily in the opening
● cut recesses in the sides of the opening to take frame ties
● remove the frame and screw frame ties in position corresponding to the recesses
● return the frame to the opening and fill in the recesses over the ties with mortared in bricks
● fill the gap between the wall and frame with mortar and brick fillets before making good the wall.

MAKING A NEW DOORWAY II – the frame

You can change the layout of your rooms to suit your needs by making a new doorway. Part one of this job told you how to fit a lintel; the second part, described here, deals with cutting the opening and fitting a frame.

Making a new doorway or window in a masonry wall is a fairly straightforward job so long as you comply with some basic structural rules. These make sure that you carry out the work in safety and that your end result is sturdy, has no detrimental effect on the building, and is in keeping with the rest of your house.

The most important requirement is to provide some temporary means of support for the wall while you're cutting into it – usually adjustable metal props and stout beams called 'needles' – and the permanent support of a lintel above the opening.

If it's a non-load-bearing wall you'll only need to support the weight of masonry directly above the hole; if it's load-bearing however, you'll also have to support any load that bears on the wall higher up.

Pages 95-99 cover in detail what's involved in the first part of cutting a hole in a wall: planning and siting your opening, marking out its shape on the wall and finally cutting a slot for, and installing, a pre-stressed concrete lintel.

Cutting the opening

Once your lintel is in place and the mortar on which it's bedded has set, the next stage of the job is to chop away the masonry below to form the opening, within the guidelines that mark its perimeter.

If you're making a doorway you'll have to prise away the skirting board first, using an old chisel and a mallet if necessary. Alternatively, you might be able to chisel away just the section of skirting within your proposed doorway, although you'll probably find it easier to cut it with a saw when it's been removed, and then to re-fix the cut sections to the wall.

Next you should chop along your guidelines using a bolster chisel and club hammer. This gives you a fairly clean, straight, cutting edge through the plaster surface and minimises the amount of making good that will be necessary later.

When you're outlined your proposed opening you can hack off the plaster within this area to reveal the brickwork or blockwork beneath. From this stage on the job's very messy, producing a large amount of rubble and clouds of choking dust. For this reason you'd be wise to remove all of the furniture from your room, or at least to cover it completely with dust sheets. You'll also have to remove or roll back your floorcovering and you might find it useful to lay down large sheets of heavy gauge polythene to collect the debris. Work with the window open and the doors into adjoining rooms closed to keep the dust to a minimum: you can also

splash water onto the pile of rubble from time to time to help the dust to settle quickly.

Don't forget to wear old clothes, stout gloves and goggles to protect your eyes from flying fragments. You'll have to exert considerable pressure on your chisel when you're cutting masonry and it's easy for your hammer to slip off the top of the chisel onto your hand. It's a good idea to fit a special mushroom-shaped rubber sleeve, which has a guard at the top, onto the shank of your bolster chisel.

Start to remove the masonry just below the lintel. Cut into the mortar joints of the first brick or block, then lever it out with your chisel or wiggle it out by hand.

Once you're removed the first couple of bricks or blocks the rest shouldn't be too difficult to remove. The best way to work is to

CUTTING THE OPENING

1 When you've fitted the lintel, chop down the pencil line marking the perimeter of the doorway, using a club hammer and cold chisel.

2 Remove the skirting then hack off the plaster within your guidelines. Keep your chisel almost parallel to the wall and fit a knuckle guard.

3 Start to chop out the brickwork directly below the lintel. Loosen the first brick by chopping around its mortar joints and wiggle it out.

4 If the wall is 225mm (9in) thick you'll have to remove one leaf at a time. Working down the wall, lever out individual bricks.

5 To make a clean cut at the edges of your doorway chop at right angles into the half- or three-quarter bricks protruding into the opening.

6 Lever up the brick you've just cut and remove it. It's a good idea to save as many of the whole bricks as you can for use in other jobs.

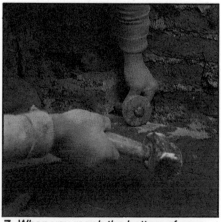

7 When you reach the bottom of your doorway you'll have to remove the brickwork to just below floor level so you can continue the flooring.

8 Go around to the other side of the wall and start to chop away the second leaf of brickwork, working from the top down in the same way.

9 When you've cut out all of the walling within your guidelines, return to the edges and trim off any uneven areas of brickwork.

FITTING THE FRAME

1 Your lining frame is fixed inside the doorway with six metal frame ties located in 'pockets'. Decide on their positions and screw them in place.

2 Chop out pockets in the sides of the opening on the face of the wall where the frame is to be flush and lift the frame into place.

3 Hold your spirit level at the sides and underside of the frame to check that it's square and level: pack it out with timber wedges if it's not.

4 Trowel mortar onto the base of the pockets into which the frame ties are slotted and cut brick fillets to fit the holes. Butter the bricks with mortar and insert them in the holes.

5 Secure all of the six frame ties in their pockets with fillets of brick, pack out the gap between the frame and the wall, then trowel a fairly wet mortar mix over the surface.

6 Trowel out the mortar as smoothly as you can over all the areas of exposed brickwork. Don't make it flush with the wall surface; leave about 6mm (¹/₄in) for plastering.

chop into the vertical joints first, followed by the horizontals you should then be able to lever the individual brick or block out. Some breakages are certain but you should try to keep whole bricks for use in other jobs.

Cut off the half or three-quarter size bricks that project into the opening on alternate courses as you come to them. Don't leave them until last to cut off or you could weaken their joints in the sides of the opening by hammering. It's always best to cut onto a solid surface. So chop into the wall opening at the side of the wall to ensure the brick splits vertically, then lever it out from below.

Your wall might be 225mm (9in) thick. Although this thickness of wall is usually external, you might come across one inside where an extension to the house has been added. One side – the original outer one – might be rendered and you'll find this

difficult to remove without damaging the masonry below. You'll have to remove one half of the wall first, then go around to the other side and remove the remaining skin to form the opening.

On a solid floor you'll simply have to level off the surface but on a suspended timber floor you should remove the walling to just below the level of the floorboards. Don't remove too much walling or you risk destroying the damp-proof course. Fix timber battens to the sides of the joists and then screw a length of replacement floorboard or a panel or chipboard to them.

Where there's a difference in floor levels between the two rooms you've connected you'll have to make a step with floorboards or by laying concrete inside simple formwork (see *Ready Reference*).

When you've formed your opening you can

tidy up the perimeter by filling any large cracks and voids at the edges with mortar. If you're making a doorway you'll have to fit a frame within the opening, to which you can attach a stop-bead, door and decorative architrave (see *Ready Reference*).

You can fix the lining frame to the sides of the opening with galvanised metal frame ties set into 'pockets' cut in the walling, or simply by screwing the frame to the masonry if it's fairly level.

You can fix a window frame with frame ties or by inserting timber wedges between the masonry and the frame and screwing through both.

With a 225mm (9in) thick wall, a door frame is set nearer the opening side of the doorway and the rest of the opening is plastered as a 'reveal': like the recess into which a window frame is fitted.

MAKING GOOD

1 To make good the area above your doorway spread a layer of Carlite Browning plaster onto the lintel and over the brickwork.

2 Make good the reveals flush with the frame: nail battens to the perimeter as thickness guides. Key the bricks with water for plastering.

3 Spread a layer of plaster onto the reveal and underside of the lintel using your steel trowel, filling any voids in the surface. Leave to stiffen.

4 When your first layer has stiffened you can spread on a second layer, bringing the surface of the reveal almost level with the thickness guide.

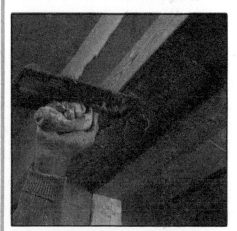

5 Fix a timber thickness guide to the face of the lintel and spread on a layer of plaster to the underside. Leave it to stiffen and apply another layer almost flush with the guide.

6 Use your trowel without any plaster to smooth the surface of the reveal. If you're going to fit a wide door stop to the reveal you needn't apply a thin coat of finishing plaster.

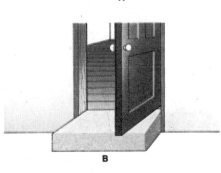
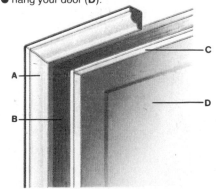

INSTALLING PATIO DOORS I – preparation

Aluminium-framed patio doors are the ideal replacement for old French windows. They offer greater insulation and are quick and easy to install. Part one of this article describes how to prepare the opening.

Traditional French windows or exterior glazed doors may provide convenient access to your garden – and they certainly admit more light to your room than a conventional window – but they're a notoriously easy way in for burglars. This is partly because they open outwards and so are difficult to look successfully, and partly because they usually consist of many small panes of glass, which don't offer much security. They tend to admit draughts, too, and if they're old and in poor condition they may well leak and rattle in bad weather.

Commonly, the frames used to be made of wood, which rots, or steel, which is prone to rust. Nowadays, however, patio doors with aluminium – or even plastic – frames, double glazing, and space-saving sliding action are made as replacements. The most readily available type will have a protective decorative grey, satin or 'anodised' finish, or a factory-applied coloured surface, normally just black or white.

You needn't, of course, stop at substituting aluminium doors for existing French windows or glazed doors: you can also make an entirely new opening in your wall to take your new frame, so long as you provide the necessary structural support for the walling above and any load that bears upon it by installing a new lintel to bridge the opening.

Although standard-sized doors are available from all the major door manufacturers, it's also possible for you to have them made to your own specification: this is especially useful if you're unable to – or you simply don't want to – modify the size of your existing opening to take an 'off-the-shelf' frame.

How the doors are made

Although there are small differences between models in the way modern patio doors are put together, they all consist of the same basic components (see *Ready Reference*). These are usually a main aluminium or UPVC frame screwed to a hardwood subframe or surround with an integral sill which is, in turn, screwed to the masonry at the perimeter of your opening.

The individual panels are supplied ready-made for you to insert in the frame. They have nylon or stainless steel rollers at the bottom, which you simply clip onto metal runners at the base of the outer frame. The top of the doors locates in a channel. All meeting faces – between adjoining doors and the frame – are sealed with weatherstrips to keep out draughts and to prevent moisture from penetrating.

The double-glazed panes usually comprise two factory-sealed sheets of 6mm (¼in) thick laminated or toughened glass – sometimes tinted – with a 12mm (½in) gap between giving an overall thickness of 24mm (1in). Some doors may even have a gap between panes of 20mm (¾in) for even greater heat and sound insulation.

Although aluminium is durable and never needs decorating, it's not a good insulator, so the hollow frames usually incorporate a thermal barrier, which stops condensation forming on the inside of the frame in cold weather.

If there aren't any other openable windows in your room, you'd be wise to install a ventilator into your new door frame; this is usually an unobtrusive panel with sliding vents, and a fly-screen which you fix at the top of the doors, just under the main frame. They allow fresh air to circulate in the room without you having to leave the door open.

Aluminium patio doors are also much more secure than conventional glazed doors; they incorporate tough locks and must have an 'anti-lift' device, without which any determined burglar would lift out a sliding panel easily.

Choosing patio doors

Visit the showrooms of local suppliers to see what styles are available, and to obtain price quotations. Your final choice should largely depend on the finish of other door or window frames in your house, especially those on the same elevation as your new doors. You should take care to maintain the overall appearance of your property; patio doors with, for example, a silvery-grey finish may look totally out of place in a house with other frames made of timber and painted white.

Aluminium patio doors are commonly made of two, three or four separate panels, and there are various combinations of positions you can have for the fixed and opening parts (see the *Ready Reference* column on page 110). Your choice depends on the position of furniture inside the house and access to your garden.

Ordering the doors

To calculate the size of the doors and frame you'll need, first measure accurately the height and width of your existing opening. But if you're altering the opening size, or your

REMOVING THE OLD FRAME

1 *To fit a new frame the same size as the old one, chop away some render at each side to expose the bricks, then measure for the new frame from here.*

2 *A metal unit has doors hinged to a surround. Unscrew from the timber frame and use a wood block and hammer to break the bond of the putty.*

3 *Get someone to help you to lift the doors away; then remove the smaller side windows and fanlights – if any – in the same way.*

4 *To remove the timber subframe, cut the verticals at an angle, about 150mm (6in) above the sills; then lever them away with a bolster.*

5 *You should then be able to pull away the main vertical frame jambs. They're held by cut nails; you'll need to exert some pressure to remove them.*

6 *The head piece of the timber frame is held by cut nails also, and you should remove this in two parts, by cutting it in half at the centre.*

READY REFERENCE

PATIO DOOR FORMAT

An aluminium-framed patio door usually consists of:
- a timber subframe with integral sill (A)
- an aluminium outer frame, incorporating the sliding track (B)
- one or more fixed double-glazed panels (C)
- one or more sliding double-glazed panels (D)
- a threshold strip (E)
- a head infill (F)
- a security lock (G)
- door stops (H)
- an anti-lift device (I)
- a ventilator hook (J)

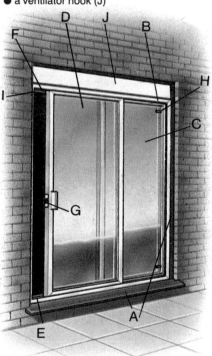

TIP: CUT BACK THE RENDER

You may find that the external render has been carried over the timber frame of your original patio doors at the sides. Where you're fitting new doors of the same size, cut back a little render at top and bottom to reveal the brick edge so you can measure the opening.

CHANGING THE OPENING SIZE

If you're enlarging the width or height of your opening, or you're fitting a new patio door where none existed previously, you'll have to fit a new lintel above to bear the weight of the walling and any load it supports.

original doors are the 'keyhole' style with windows at each side incorporated into the main frame, you'll simply need the overall dimensions of your proposed doors, including the hardwood subframe.

Measure at two points in each direction, and if there's a variation use the smaller one when ordering. You can always fill in any slight gap between the frame and the masonry – indeed, some 'fitting tolerance' is preferable – but if the frame is even fractionally too big you'd have to enlarge the opening.

On rendered walls you'll have to chop out a small area of the cladding at the top and bottom on each side of the existing frames to expose the brickwork so you can measure accurately. When measuring the height, take your reading from the top of the existing frame to the underside of the sill.

The two dimensions you'll end up with – which, in effect, give you the overall size of the opening – are all your supplier will need.

Removing the old frame

If you're simply replacing existing patio doors with new ones of the same size you'll probably be able to carry out the work in one day. But if you have to enlarge – or even decrease – the size of the opening you should tackle the preparation on one day and fit the new doors on the following day.

Before you start work, clear the room of all furniture and carpets, or stack it out of the way at the opposite end to the doors and cover it with dust sheets.

The first job is to dismantle the old doors and windows. If your original doors are wooden, you simple unscrew them from their main frame at the hinges to remove them. Repeat this procedure for any fanlights and side windows.

Often you'll find an old metal door and window unit will be set into a rebated timber frame, and the doors will be hinged to their own metal surround, which is screwed to the woodwork. To remove these you'll have to locate the screws, which will probably be covered by layers of paint.

With all of the screws removed you can take off the doors. They may still be held by bedding putty; if so, use a small wooden block and a hammer from the inside to break the bond so you can lift the doors free of the metal frame.

If there's a fixed light above either the door or opening windows it will probably be connected to the metal frame below by bolts and to the surrounding timber by screws. Use an old screwdriver or a glazier's hacking knife to chop out the putty covering the bolt and screw heads in the fixed light and unscrew them.

With all of the glazed sections removed, you'll be left with just the wooden framework to tackle Cut through each of the vertical rebated sections that may separate the doors

PREPARING THE OPENING

If you're fitting new aluminium patio doors that are the same overall size as your original French windows all you have to do, having removed the old frame, is to tidy up the opening to receive your new frame. But if you're going to extend the size of your opening to take higher, broader doors, you'll have to fit a new lintel above to take the weight of the walling and any load bearing upon it. On solid 225mm (9in) walls you could use a prestressed concrete or hollow steel lintel; on cavity walls you could use a concrete lintel for the inner leaf and a steel support lintel for the outer leaf.

1 *Use a timber straight edge against a spirit level to mark the sides of the opening to be cut on the projecting part of a keyhole-style window and door unit.*

4 *Start to hack off the render from the masonry; remove individual bricks from the top. Force the chisel under a brick to break the mortar bond.*

5 *Cut down onto any bricks that protrude into the opening to give as clean a break as possible, to avoid substantial making-good later.*

from the window about 150mm (6in) above the window sills, and then lever the lower portions away from the walls and from the old sills. Then pull away the top sections from the headpiece of the frame above.

With your club hammer and cold chisel, chop back any rendering that may cover the outer frame so that it's flush with the brickwork (see *Ready Reference*). Next you can cut through the frame jambs about 150mm (6in) above the sills, making your saw cuts at an angle so you can remove the pieces easily (see *Ready Reference*). Use a crowbar to lever out the lower pieces of frame and the sills. Remove the upper sections of the vertical jambs similarly; they'll be held with cut nails driven into the brickwork and you'll need to exert quite a lot of pressure to lever them free.

Remove any nail heads that are left projecting from the wall, then cut the frame head in two and lever it away.

Preparing the opening

If you're going to install a new frame the same size as the original you can simply tidy up the masonry at the perimeter of the opening, ready to accept your new timber subframe (see part 2 on pages 86–90). But if you're enlarging the opening you'll need to fit a new, wider lintel above the first (see *Ready Reference*).

Where you just have to cut back the masonry of a keyhole-style opening (see step-by-step photographs on this page), or when you've fitted your new lintel, you should mark a pencil line down the outside wall using a spirit level and a long timber straight edge to indicate the sides of the new opening. Repeat this procedure on the inside wall, then chop down the lines with your bolster chisel to give a clean cutting edge.

Before you start to chop out the masonry, you'd be wise to fix up a dust sheet or a

2 *Do the same at the other side of the opening, so that you're outlining a square or rectangular opening; mark the inside face of the wall, too.*

3 *Chop down your pencil guidelines with a club hammer and bolster chisel, on both faces of the wall, to give a clean cutting edge at the perimeter.*

6 *When you reach the bottom, cut out the bricks to just below floor level so that you can set your new subframe flush with the floorboards.*

7 *You can make good any damage to the corners of the reveals by fixing metal angle bead onto the masonry, and then spreading on a layer of render.*

READY REFERENCE

CLOSING A CAVITY WALL

If you have a cavity wall with an inner section of bricks or blocks and an outer one of bricks, you'll have to close off the gap between the two leaves and install a vertical dpc before you can fit your new frame. To do this:
● tooth out half- or cut bricks at the perimeter of your opening and replace them with whole bricks laid header-on to form the reveals
● add cut bricks to close the gap
● insert a strip of bituminous felt between the two leaves as a dpc.

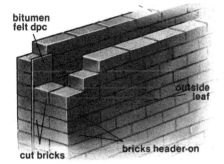

bitumen felt dpc

outside leaf

cut bricks

bricks header-on

BUILDING A PLINTH

If the floor of your room is more than about one brick's depth above the ground outside you should lay a low plinth of bricks across the base of the opening so that you can set your new hardwood timber sill at floor level.

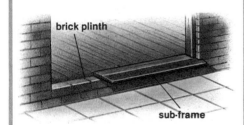

brick plinth

sub-frame

TIP: REMOVING THE OLD FRAME

To remove your old door frame, cut through the jambs about 150mm (6in) above and below the sills and lever out the sections.

make saw cut at angle

---

polythene sheet across the opening, but tacking it to the inside, to contain the considerable amount of dust thrown up during hammering. You should wear goggles as protection against flying fragments.

Using a club hammer and bolster chisel – and starting at the top of the wall – hack off the render on the outside, followed by the plaster on the inside, at each side of the opening to reveal the brickwork.

When all of the render and plaster has been removed, start to chop out the bricks individually. Cut through the half bricks that protrude into the opening at the perimeter line from above.

When you've removed all the masonry to the perimeter of your opening take out the old door sill and give the mortar beneath and to the sides of it a thorough brushing with a stiff-bristled brush, ready to take the wider hardwood sill of your new door. The floor of

your room may be higher than the ground level just outside the opening, in which case you'll have to lay a low plinth of bricks so that the new sill is at floor level.

Cutting out a new opening is relatively straightforward in a solid 225mm (9in) wall: you can simply cut the sides as straight and flat as possible or, for neatness, 'tooth-out' the bricks, removing the cut bricks, and fill in with half bricks placed flat side out. But if you've a cavity wall you'll have to close off the gap (see *Ready Reference*). It's also vital that you incorporate a damp-proof course around the opening to stop any moisture bridging the cavity and causing damp on the inside face of the wall.

This completes the preparation of your opening. See part 2 of this job on pages 86–90 for details of how to fit a timber subframe, followed by your new aluminium patio doors.

INSTALLING PATIO DOORS II — installation

New patio doors with durable aluminium or plastic frames usually come in kit form for easy assembly. Part one of this article described how to prepare the opening; here's how to fit the doors.

Aluminium or plastic-framed patio doors have many benefits over traditional French windows and exterior glazed doors. They're double-glazed, with efficient weather-proofing, operate with a smooth, space-saving sliding action, and admit more light to your room. Also, they're quick and easy to install, and they have an attractive finish which means you never need to decorate them.

Although they're popular as replacements, you can, of course, fit them where there was no opening previously, as long as you install the necessary support for the wall by installing a new lintel.

When you've removed your old frame (see part one of this job on pages 82–85) or you've increased the size of the opening, you can fit your new frame and doors.

Parts of the frame

Your new doors will probably have two, three or four separate panels, depending on the width of your opening, but it's not usual to have all of them sliding – which you have fixed and which opening mainly depends on access to and from your garden and where your furniture is placed indoors.

Although it's possible to have doors made to your own size specifications – and, indeed, containing as many panels as you want – there's a wide range of standard sizes available, which should suit most locations.

When your new patio doors have been delivered you should make sure that all the components have been supplied, by checking them off against the manufacturer's instruction booklet, which should also be supplied with the kit.

Although the individual parts may vary from one maker to another, all of the doors consist of the same basic components (see the *Ready Reference* column on page 83). Basically the installation consists of a hardwood subframe and a metal outer frame into which the doors slot, although plastic-framed doors may not have a subframe.

Your kit should contain the double-glazed door panels themselves, already assembled and with nylon or stainless steel rollers at the bottom; a new hardwood still, generally made from prepared 150x50mm (6x2in) Brazilian mahogany, with two integral jambs that form the sides of the subframe, and a head piece of 100x50mm (4x2in) hardwood, which forms the top of the subframe. These four pieces of timber should be in good, clean condition and they're usually assembled with mortise and tenon joints. The frame may have projecting 'horns' at the sill and head, which protect the corners during storage and transit. You can saw off the head horns when you're ready to fit the frame but you should leave the sill horns in place to make the frame more rigid when fitted. The frame may also have a prepared rebate into which the aluminium frame will fit.

This aluminium frame will probably come in four separate pieces, comprising two jambs, one sill and one frame head. With these there'll also be two short lengths of aluminium, which you use at the door threshold and between the fixed door and locking jamb of the frame head.

Your kit may also include a ventilator unit, which is fixed to the outer metal frame at the top, and ensures a constant flow of air into the room. The security lock should already be fitted to the opening door, and lengths of weatherstrip should be fitted in channels to the frame sections at all meeting faces. All of the screws, brackets and various other miscellaneous items used to assemble the

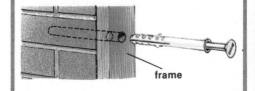

frame will also be provided with the kit.

Other materials you'll need – but which may not be supplied with the doors – are sealants and mastics for weatherproofing. They usually come in tubes for use with special applicator guns. You'll also need some help in fitting the doors – they're very heavy to lift and you'll also need some assistance when setting the doors on their tracks.

Assembling the timber subframe

The first step you'll probably have to make is to assemble the timber subframe, using a little wood glue on each joint. Make sure the tenons are fully seated in their mortises and check that the corners are absolutely at 90° with a try square.

Saw off the head horns, then offer up the assembled frame to your prepared opening to check that it will fit; you'll have to cut out some of the masonry at each side to accommodate the projecting sill horns and remove any brickwork that prevents easy insertion of the frame. Once you're satisfied that the frame will fit snugly, remove it and lay it flat on the ground.

Assembling the aluminium frame

Next, identify each component of the aluminium outer frame to make sure you know how it fits together, then assemble it. It's best if you do this on soft ground – your lawn, for example – or on an old sheet or blanket laid on the ground, so that you don't scratch the surface finish of the aluminium. Take special care to ensure that the side jambs are located properly, and that the locking jamb is on the correct side.

Apply a bead of weatherproofing mastic to the sill and head joins, assemble them and secure with self-tapping screws, through the pre-drilled holes in the frame. Check that the joints are tight, then wipe off any excess mastic. Lift the assembled frame and slot it into the wooden subframe, which is still lying flat, to check it fits. Once you're satisfied that the fit is perfect, remove the aluminium frame and leave it lying flat on soft ground.

Fitting the frames

You can now fit the hardwood subframe into the opening from the outside. If the subsequent components are to fit properly, and the doors to slide without binding, the subframe must be set perfectly square and true – both vertically and horizontally – within the opening. You'll probably have to wedge the frame to get a perfect fit.

Pack out under the sill first with small wooden offcuts to jack up the frame until it touches the top of the opening. Use your spirit level continually on the sill and adjust the wedges until the sill is perfectly horizontal.

Move on to the jambs next, using wedges

FITTING THE TIMBER SUBFRAME

1 *Once you've removed your old frame, assemble the jambs, head and sill of the timber subframe and position it in the prepared opening.*

2 *Place your spirit level on the sill to check it's level. Leave the 'horns' protruding at the sides of the sill and build them into the masonry.*

3 *Use timber offcuts to wedge up the frame at the sill. Check again with your spirit level until you're sure that it's perfectly horizontal.*

4 *Measure both diagonals of the frame by stretching a tape measure from one corner to another. If they're the same, the frame's square; adjust if necessary.*

to adjust and hold the frame in position. Use your spirit level on both the sides and faces of the jambs to check the plumb, then recheck the sill, to make sure that your adjustments to the jambs haven't altered the horizontal level. A long metal straight edge held against the face of each jamb will indicate whether or not the wood is flat and straight: if it's at all bowed you can correct this when you fix the frame finally.

To check that the frame is seated truly square you must measure the diagonals accurately. You'll need someone's help to hold one end of your tape measure at a top corner while you stretch the other end to the bottom diagonal corner. Repeat this procedure for the other diagonal. If there's any variation at all between the two measurements you'll have to re-adjust the sill or the head pieces and possibly re-align the jambs. Only when the diagonals measure

precisely the same and the jambs are exactly vertical should you fix the frame permanently.

To do this, drill clearance holes to take the fixing screws through the jambs and into the solid masonry. Follow a line that will eventually be covered by the aluminium outer frame to conceal the screws. Make a minimum of four fixings on the jamb adjacent to the fixed door, and six on the locking jamb side for additional security in the area of the lock.

Push wallplugs, which have their own built-in screws, through the holes you've drilled in the jambs and into the masonry (see *Ready Reference*); then drive them fully home.

It's possible that by screwing the frame in place you may have secured it in a warped position, so you should check again with a straight edge that the jambs are flat; loosening or tightening the screws or

MAKING GOOD

7 Trowel mortar into the gaps at the perimeter of the opening, taking it onto the frame by about 25mm (1in), then remove the masking tape.

8 Weatherproof the small gap between the metal frame and the timber subframe on the inside face with a silicone rubber sealant.

TIP

9 Make a 'pugging tool' from two offcuts of timber nailed together in a T-shape so that you can more easily push mortar under the sill.

10 When you've made good the sides of the opening inside and out, apply three coats of exterior varnish to the exposed timber subframe.

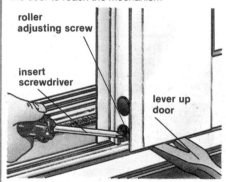
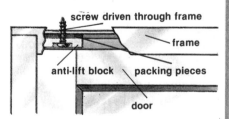
between the wood subframe and the aluminium outer frame on the inside of the installation, then immediately clean off any excess which may have spread onto either frame, with a clean, damp cloth, to prevent smears from spoiling the woodwork.

Do the same on the outside of the installation, but use an exterior frame sealant in a colour that matches either the wood or the aluminium.

Any gap between the external brickwork and the wooden subframe must also be made good. You can fill large gaps with fillets of brick or stone embedded in, and covered by, mortar. Press the mortar well into gaps all round the frame, overlapping the subframe by about 25mm (1in). You can protect the rest of the timber face from smears with masking tape, as mortar will stain the wood quite easily.

In areas where access isn't easy, such as under the sill, make a small 'pugging stick' – simply two pieces of timber nailed together in a T-shape – to help you push the mortar into place.

Making good the frame

The interior plasterwork around your new door must also be made good. Where you've had to cut away sections of plaster at the reveals in order to fit the frame you'll have to replaster complete corners using expanded metal angle bead which you attach to the exposed masonry and plaster over.

Clean the frame thoroughly, then varnish the exposed timber frame, using at least three coats of top-quality exterior varnish. The timber can, of course, be painted, if this is more in keeping with the rest of your house. You can likewise paint the interior woodwork to match the decor of your room.

FITTING A NEW WINDOW I — the opening

As well as admitting light and keeping the elements at bay, windows also perform an important decorative role. If they're in poor condition – or if you don't like their style – why not replace them?

There are numerous reasons why you may decide to remove or replace a window or, indeed, to install a new one. The most common one, however, is likely to be age. Whether your windows are made of wood or metal, they're likely to deteriorate unless you maintain them regularly. It's possible to make minor repairs to the frames by tightening up loose joints, replacing sash cords or even renewing damaged sections of timber with new wood. But if the damage is widespread, the only solution to the problem is to fit a new window.

Equally, your reason for replacing a window may be aesthetic rather than practical. Previous renovations might have included the fitting of new windows that you think are incompatible with the original style and age of the property.

Another possibility is that you feel there aren't sufficient openings to give adequate ventilation, or that the existing ones are in the wrong places. You may also want to make adjustments to the position of your windows within an area of wall to fit in with a new decorative scheme.

If you're replacing your existing window with one of the same size you won't have to worry about providing any support for the opening while you remove the old frame and fit your new one. If you're increasing the width of the frame or making an entirely new window opening, you'll have to install a rigid beam or lintel to support the walling you've removed. Look back at Making a doorway (pages 73–81) for how to cut a hole in a solid brick wall ready to take your frame.

Planning permission

Before you go ahead with your plans to replace your windows you must contact your local Building Inspector with details of what you intend to do. Local planning bye-laws may dictate the type of window you can fit. At all events, you'll have to adhere to the Building Regulations, which ensure that you carry out the work safely and that the structure, when complete, is sound.

Choosing a replacement window

It's important to choose a window that's compatible with the style and age of your house; there are many styles of traditional and modern windows, made in a variety of materials, commonly wood or steel, and nowadays aluminium and sometimes even plastic. Some of these materials, especially if they are badly maintained, will only have a limited life. Anodized aluminium, for example, although it requires little decoration, will oxidise in seaside areas, where there's a salty atmosphere.

Steel windows, although tough and long-lasting, are prone to rust and, like plastic and aluminium, don't always lend themselves to older-style homes, although you can conceal their starkness by painting them. Wood, although it can rot, comes in the widest range of styles and can be painted to match other woodwork in your choice of colour.

Plastic window frames are much more durable than the steel types. They require little maintenance, but have the disadvantage that they don't take paint well, so you're limited to the factory-made colour – usually white. Unless you're making new timber frames to your own specification, you'll be limited in your choice of window size and style by the standard dimensions available. These range from 600 to 2400mm (2 to 8ft) wide and from 450 to 2100mm (18in to 7ft) in height. If you can't find a standard frame size or style that fits your opening – and it's not possible for

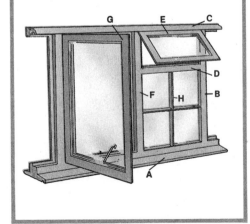
91

MAKING THE OPENING WIDER

1 Brick up on top of the lintel and around the needle, following the original brickwork bond both for a blended look and for strength.

2 Measure the width of your new opening, transfer this dimension to the outer face of the wall and then scribe a line down the wall.

3 Starting at the top, just under the lintel, chop out the bricks individually up to your scribed guideline, saving the whole bricks.

4 Work your way down the window sides, toothing out the brickwork as you go by alternately removing the half or header bricks.

5 If there's a concrete sub-sill in the opening, you can remove it after you've cut back the sides by breaking its bond with the bricks.

6 Clear the opening of debris then begin bricking up the sides with cut bricks to give a square, clean surface for the frame.

7 Build up from the base of the opening, then mortar cut bricks into the toothed recesses so that they are flush with your scribed guidelines. Fit the cut ends first.

8 Check with your spirit level as you work that the sides of your new window opening are truly vertical, or you'll find that your new frame probably won't fit perfectly squarely.

9 Lay bricks to bring the base of the opening to within a brick's depth of the new frame position, copying the brick bond originally used both for strength and a matching look.

paint and their heads may even be counter-sunk and concealed with filler or dowels: scrape away the paint to locate them. You may be able to chisel out the dowels or filler to reach the screw heads but if they're awkward to withdraw – or if nails have been used – simply insert a hacksaw blade between the frame and wall and saw through them.

Use a couple of bolster chisels – or even a crowbar – to lever the old frame from the opening – you can work from the outside or the inside, but you'd be wise to enlist some-one to support the frame while you lever it out and, if it's large, to lift it away.

If you're not intending to save the frame for use elsewhere you can saw through the sill, transom and head near each corner and remove it in pieces.

Clear away any loose mortar, projecting nails and plugs from the opening. If there's a separate concrete or tiled sub-sill you can remove this by breaking the mortar bond with the masonry and levering it free.

Where possible you should try to have the new frame ready to fit as soon as you've removed the old one, but if you're going to alter the size of the opening you won't be able to complete the job in one day. Cover the opening with a large sheet of heavy gauge polythene held in place with timber battens lightly pinned to the wall with masonry nails to keep out draughts and rain.

Altering the opening size

You can fit a deeper window frame in your opening without rigging up any temporary structural support for the walling, but if you're intending to increase its width or height you'll have to prop up the masonry with adjustable metal props and stout timber 'needles' (see pages 76–77) while you reposition the lintel or fit a new, wider one to support the wall and its loading.

When you've positioned the props you can mark out where the lintel is to be fitted, cut a slot for it and then fit the lintel in place. Once it's installed, you can safely chop back the reveals to the new window width.

It's much easier to increase the depth of the opening (see *Ready Reference*): you can simply cut out the brickwork at the bottom to the new depth.

Your new depth of opening may not con-veniently fall at an exact number of bricks, so you'll have to lay a course of split bricks to bring the opening to the correct level.

Making the opening narrower (see *Ready Reference*) is also possible, but you'll need a supply of bricks that match the existing masonry for filling in, or the finished job will look patchy; unless, of course, the exterior walls are going to be rendered. Continue the brick bond in your narrower opening by carefully knocking out all the half bricks down the sides and saving them. Mortar into

FINISHING THE OPENING

1 *If you want to copy a soldier arch used on the original outer wall you'll have to make up a timber former to support the bricks.*

2 *Once the arch is completed you can brick up over it and around the needle, using the bricks you've saved to match the rest of the wall.*

3 *Wait for about a day for the mortar to set before removing the props, but leave the arch former until you're ready to fit the frame.*

4 *Fill in the hole where the needle was inserted and repoint the mortar joints throughout your new brickwork to match the rest of the wall.*

both sides of your 'toothed' wall the required number of whole or cut bricks you'll need to decrease the width of the opening then use the half bricks to fill in between. Any cut bricks at the reveals should be mortared in, cut end first, so you have a neat, square edge within the opening.

When you're increasing the width of your opening you should also 'tooth out' the reveals to fill in with cut bricks.

Closing a cavity wall

A solid 225mm (9in) wall doesn't present many problems when you're replacing a window: all you have to do is increase or decrease the size of the opening, continuing the masonry bond originally used, and then fit your new frame from the inside. But if you have cavity walls you'll have to close off the gap between the two leaves and insert a damp-proof course (dpc) to prevent the

cavity being breached by moisture.

You must also fit a vertical dpc at the sides of the opening. Chop out the half bricks on alternate courses of the inner leaf and lightly tack a strip of bituminous felt to the outer leaf. Mortar nearly whole bricks into the recesses left by the removal of the half bricks; position them header-on, at right angles to the inner leaf so they butt up to the felt strip and close the cavities. Fill in the gaps on alternate courses at the reveals with fillers of brick. Allow the felt strip to project into the reveal so it can butt up to the window frame or locate in a narrow groove in the jamb. You'll also have to fit a strip of dpc along the bottom of the opening separating the two leaves. Your lintel at the top will effectively seal the cavity.

If you are replacing an existing sash window with a purpose-built modern one, don't bother to close the cavity; the space will house the sliding sash weights.

FITTING A NEW WINDOW II – the frame

An old, rotten window frame not only looks unattractive but also admits rain and draughts to your house. Part one of this job dealt with removing the old frame and preparing the opening; part two describes how to fit the new frame.

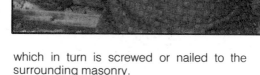

Windows take quite a battering from the elements, so it's hardly surprising that they need regular maintenance to keep them in working order and looking good. But if they've been neglected and deterioration has become too widespread for repairs to be made successfully, you will have to consider replacing them.

Choosing a replacement window
It's not necessary for you to fit exactly the same type of frame as the one removed. There's a vast selection of different ready-made styles to choose from, featuring numerous combinations of fixed and opening panes. If you can't find a suitable off-the-shelf frame, you could even make one to your own specification.

There's no reason why you shouldn't make your new window larger or smaller than the original, but if you're making structural changes such as this you must inform your local Building Inspector both to prevent infringement of local planning bye-laws and to ensure that you carry out the work safely.

To increase the width of an opening you'll have to install a new, longer lintel to support the masonry above, but if you simply want to make a narrower window you can 'tooth-in' matching brickwork at the reveals without disturbing the original lintel. Making the height of the window larger or smaller is best done at sill level to avoid the aggravating job of having to move the lintel.

Any work that involves disturbing the structure of the walls will need the temporary support of adjustable props.

How frames are fixed
Once you've adapted the size – or even the shape – of your opening to accept the frame you should leave the structure for about 24 hours so that any new mortar sets. You can then remove any props or arch formers (see Installing a window 1) and fit the frame into place.

There are a variety of ways you can secure your frame within the opening. A steel or aluminium frame, for instance, can be either bolted to metal lugs inserted in the mortar joints, or first screwed to a timber subframe which in turn is screwed or nailed to the surrounding masonry.

A timber frame can be secured with galvanised metal 'frame ties', which are screwed to the jambs (sides) of the frame and embedded in the mortar joints. Another method of fixing a timber frame is to drive screws or nails through the jambs into wood wedges set in the mortar courses of the brickwork. But the simplest method of all is to screw the frame into plugged holes drilled in the masonry, although this type of fixing isn't as tough and long-lasting as the other methods.

Some new frames have projecting 'horns' at each side of the sill and head piece. Although they're intended to protect the corners while in storage or transit, you can build them into the masonry at top and bottom for a really tough fixing. It's quite common for the head horns to be cut off flush with the jambs and for the sill horns alone to be built into the masonry.

Positioning the frame
Whichever method of fixing you choose, it's imperative that the frame sits perfectly squarely in the opening. If it's crooked or at all warped, for instance, you could find that the opening sashes tend to bind in their frames and a fixed pane of glass, if it's not bedded flat in its rebate, could shatter at even the slightest vibration.

Warping can occur if the lintel and its load bears directly on the frame (this is sometimes caused by settlement of the masonry), so it's usual to leave a slight gap of about 3mm (⅛in) between the lintel and the top of the frame. You can seal this gap with a flexible, non-setting mastic applied by a special 'gun' (see the *Ready Reference* on page 99). It's intended to compensate for any slight movement in the structure; if you were to fill the gap with mortar, the filling could crack and eventually allow moisture to seep inside.

The position of your frame in the opening depends on whether you want to fit a sub-sill or whether the sill built into the frame is going to rest on the masonry at the base of the opening. If you want to make a concrete sub-sill you can cast one in formwork when you've fitted the frame, which you'll have to wedge up to the required height. You can, on the other hand, fit a timber sub-sill. Thirdly, you can simply bed the frame's integral timber sill on a mortar bed.

If you're installing the frame in a cavity wall, you'll have to fit a vertical damp-proof course (dpc) between the two leaves of the closed-off cavity and set them in a groove in the jambs to prevent moisture seeping through; you'll also need to fit a dpc beneath the sill.

You may also want to locate the frame within the opening so that it sits flush with either the inside or outside face of the wall, or recessed from each face to leave 'reveals' on each side (see *Ready Reference*).

When you've decided where and how you're

WINDOW AND SILL CONSTRUCTION

A standard casement window consists of: a head **(1)**; a sill **(2)**; jambs **(3)**; a mullion **(4)** to divide the frame into two panes; a transom **(5)** forming a small top-hinged light **(6)** at the top. There may also be a side-hinged casement **(7)**. On the inside there's a window board **(8)** which may be timber or tiles set in mortar.

The frame is fixed into a cavity or solid brick wall **(9)** with nails driven into wood wedges **(10)** hammered into the mortar joints, or with metal frame ties **(11)** screwed to the frame and set in the joints. Or, horns **(12)** can be built into the masonry. The masonry above the opening must be supported on a beam: either a hollow steel lintel **(13)** with a ledge to take a course of bricks standing upright **(14)**, or a concrete lintel **(15)** with a curving soldier arch **(16)**.

There may be a concrete sub-sill under the frame **(17)**, cast in formwork. A plank **(18)** supported on studs **(19)** makes the base, three battens nailed on top, the front edge and sides **(20)**. A length of sash cord set in the concrete **(21)** makes a drip groove. The reveals **(22)** can be rendered.

READY REFERENCE

POSITIONING THE FRAME

The position of your window frame within the opening depends on whether there's a sub-sill.

If there isn't a sub-sill:
● place the frame near the outside face of the wall with its integral sill overhanging the brickwork by about 25mm (1in), leaving reveals for plastering on the inside of the opening.

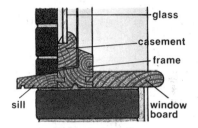

If there is a sub-sill:
● place the frame flush with the inside face of the wall, reducing the amount of plastering necessary or

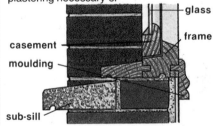

● place it centrally within the opening, leaving reveals on both sides of the window.

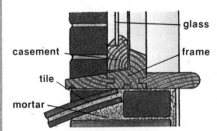

GLASS FOR GLAZING

Glass is sold by thickness and it's important that you buy the correct type for a particular window size. If you choose a thin pane for a large window there's a danger of it flexing and breaking too easily. You should use:
● 3mm glass for panes up to 1sq m (11sq ft) in area
● 4mm glass for larger panes up to 2.1m (7ft) long
● 6mm glass for large panes longer than 2.1m (7ft)

FITTING A TIMBER FRAME

1 Where a timber arch former has been used you will have to remove it before you can fit your new frame within the window opening.

2 Decide into which masonry joints your timber fixing wedges are to be fitted, and hack out a slot using a club hammer and bolster chisel.

3 Cut your wedges to shape using a wood chisel, then hammer them firmly into their slots so that they just protrude into the opening.

4 Lift the frame into the opening and find its approximate position. In this case it should be sitting almost flush with the inside face of the wall.

5 Use timber blocks under the sill to wedge the frame in place beneath the lintel. Leave a 3mm (¹⁄₈in) gap for sealing with flexible mastic.

6 Place a spirit level on the sill to check that the frame is sitting horizontally in the opening; adjust the timber packing if necessary.

7 Check with the spirit level held against the face of the jamb that the frame is square within the opening. Adjust by tapping gently with the handle of a club hammer.

8 Hammer 100mm (4in) cut nails through the jambs into each wedge, punching in their heads. Recheck the level of the frame in case your hammering has dislodged it.

9 Once you're satisfied that the frame is fixed accurately and securely, brick up underneath. Use bricks split along their length if the depth is less than a whole brick.

going to fix your new frame, offer it up to the opening to make sure it will fit.

Fitting a timber frame

Before you finally fit a timber frame you should treat all its surfaces – especially those that will be inaccessible when the frame's fitted – with a coat of wood primer. A new, off-the-shelf frame will probably come ready-primed – it's usually pink in colour – but you'd be wise to give it another treatment in case the factory-applied coat has been damaged in transit.

If you're going to secure the frame by its horns you should chop out slots for them in the masonry at the sides of the opening using a club hammer and bolster chisel. Be very careful, when cutting the holes for the horns, that you don't weaken the bearings, which support the lintel and its load. If you did and the masonry 'dropped', you wouldn't be able to return it to normal without substantial rebuilding.

To screw the frame into wallplugs you must drill the holes in the sides of the opening – three at each side – and insert the plugs. As your frame must be perfectly level and the fixing holes accurately positioned you'd be wise to drill the jambs of the frame first, wedge it temporarily in the opening level and square and mark the wall through the holes with your drill bit.

Remove the frame, drill the holes in the masonry and plug them, then return the frame to the opening, set it level and square again and drive in the fixing screws. Check that the frame is level and square and adjust it if necessary by re-drilling the fixing holes.

To fix the frame to timber wedges you can chop out the mortar joints at two points on each side of the opening and hammer in triangular-shaped timber wedges, cut with a chisel from a length of 50x25mm (2x1in) softwood. Don't cut them too thin or they'll simply split and the fixing nails won't hold securely.

Lift the frame – unglazed – into the opening and temporarily wedge it in place with blocks of wood while you ensure that it is level and square. The jambs should be tight against the triangular wedges; if they're not you'll have to adjust them.

Hold your spirit level against the jambs to make sure that the frame is sitting truly vertical and adjust it if necessary, by tapping gently with the handle of your club hammer. When you're satisfied that it's straight, transfer the spirit level to the top of the sill to check that the frame is truly horizontal. Insert more packing underneath, or remove the existing packing, to set the level. Don't forget to leave a small gap beneath the lintel at this stage. Re-check the vertical once more in case your horizontal adjustments have knocked the frame out of square again, then nail or screw it to the wedges. Check again with your spirit level

that the frame hasn't moved; if it has you may have to release some or all of the fixings and adjust the position of the frame. Once the frame is securely and accurately fixed in the opening you can remove the temporary timber packing.

If you've set the frame above the base of the opening, intending to install a concrete or timber sub-sill in the gap, you'll have to brick up under the frame on the inside face of the wall. You may have to insert bricks split along their length if the gap is less than a course deep.

Mortar in bricks to cover the horns of the frame at the top and bottom, and point in the gap between the jambs and the masonry on the inside of the window frame with mortar, covering the triangular timber wedges. Leave a gap of about 3mm (⅛in) so that you can spread on a layer of finishing plaster flush with the rest of the wall.

Making good the walls

Leave the window for about 24 hours for the mortar to set before making good the wall round the perimeter of the opening with plaster. Where you've left reveals inside the room you can apply a layer of Carlite Browning plaster to the brickwork, followed by a thin layer of Carlite Finish plaster which you can polish to match the rest of the wall.

You can form the corners of the reveals by attaching expanded metal angle beads to the brickwork; they have a 'nosing' at the angle which serves as a guide to spreading on the plaster to the correct thickness. Alternatively you can tack thin timber battens temporarily to the wall at each side of the corner so they project slightly, to serve as thickness guides. Plastering angles and reveals will be dealt with in more detail in a later issue.

The brickwork reveals outside the window can be either left exposed as a feature or rendered with a mortar mix. You can apply the render to the correct thickness by using timber battens as thickness guides in the same way as you plaster internal reveals. Dampen the brickwork with clean water splashed on from a brush to provide a key for the mortar, then trowel it on and smooth it flush with the thickness guide. Leave it to set for about 24 hours before removing the battens and making good the edges of the screed with more mortar.

Fitting a metal frame

Hold the frame against the opening and mark the wall at the sides where the metal fixing lugs are to be recessed. Remove the frame and chisel holes in the masonry with a club hammer and cold chisel to correspond with the lugs. Return the frame to the opening, with the lugs bolted on loosely, and wedge it in

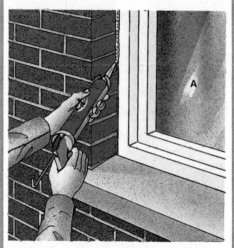
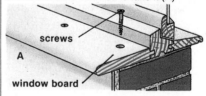
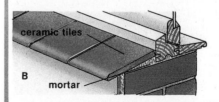

place, square and upright. Push the lugs in their slots and mortar around them using a mortar mix of one part cement to three of sand. Leave the mortar for about 48 hours to set before tightening up the bolts. You can then remove the packing and make good the perimeter of the opening wedges.

An easier, and a much more efficient method, is to screw the frame to a timber subframe, which you fix to the masonry. When you've fitted the frame, seal the joint between it and the subframe with a non-setting mastic.

Making a concrete sub-sill

To set a concrete sub-sill on site, you'll have to erect timber formwork against the wall to make a trough. You'll need a length of board to form the base of the sill, which you can wedge in place on stout timber studs, resting on the ground and attached to the wall with masonry nails. Nail a long batten to the base board to form the front edge of the sill and two shorter ones at right angles to form the ends. You could also use slightly tapered size battens and a thinner nosing button to give the sill a slight shape to the front.

An easy way to make a drip groove under the front edge of the sill, to prevent rainwater from trickling between the bottom of the sill and the wall, is to place a length of sash cord in the base of the trough in the required position, and trowel in the concrete on top. When the concrete has set and the formwork has been removed you'll be able pull the cord free, leaving a half-round groove the length of the sill.

Fill the trough with a concrete mix of four parts sand to one part cement, making sure you don't leave any air pockets, and then smooth the top with a steel float flush with the thickness battens. Leave the formwork in place for about 24 hours for the concrete to harden.

Sealing and glazing the window

Fill the gap between the frame and the brickwork with mortar to within about 10mm (3/8in) of the outside edge of the frame then, when the mortar has set, apply a flexible non-setting mastic over it and between the lintel and the frame (see *Ready Reference*).

You can glaze your new window as soon as possible after it's fitted. But if you have to leave it overnight you can tack a sheet of heavy gauge polythene over the frame on the outside to prevent rain or wind from getting in. What type of glass you use really depends on the type of frame and what the room it's in is used for. But remember to measure accurately the sizes which you require. Leave the newly glazed window for about a fortnight for the putty to dry before applying primer, undercoat and top coats of paint.

If you are installing sealed-unit double glazing with proprietary gaskets, make sure these are correctly positioned.

MAKING GOOD THE WINDOW

1 *Trowel mortar into the gap between jambs and masonry, covering the wedges. If it shrinks on setting you may have to add more mortar.*

2 *If you've made a brick soldier arch over the outside of the opening there may be a curved area of lintel visible, which you can render.*

3 *If you want to render the external reveals, tack battens to them; allow them to protrude into the opening by about 6mm (1/4in). Wet the brick surface.*

4 *Trowel mortar onto the reveals, smoothing it flush with the edge of the timber batten. Remove the batten after leaving for 24 hours.*

5 *Set up timber formwork against the wall to cast a sub-sill. Nail a shelf on studs to form the base with battens nailed on top for the sides. Trowel in mortar and smooth out.*

6 *While the sub-sill is setting, glaze the window. Bed the panes in linseed oil putty, then retain them with glazing sprigs or panel pins and seal with triangular fillets of putty.*

BLOCK PARTITION WALLS

Building a partition is the easiest way to rearrange the rooms of your house – to improve storage or simply to divide a large area into two smaller parts. Lightweight building blocks make a particularly solid structure, and they're easy to work with.

Even with the most ingenious space-saving schemes you may find that one room is simply not enough to cope with all the different activities and storage needs of your household. Often your problems would be solved if you had two rooms where there was one, and a partition is the obvious solution. You could, for example divide an open-plan living and dining room, or make a second WC or a utility room. Or it may simply be that you are dissatisfied with the way your rooms are laid out, and wish to rearrange them. Pages 106–110 describe how you can build a timber-framed partition wall, which you can clad with plasterboard and decorate. But there are advantages to using concrete blocks instead: they give a stronger, more sturdy structure than timber, help to reduce the transmission of sound through the wall and provide a solid fixing for items such as book shelves and picture frames. Blocks also provide a greater degree of heat insulation. Because of their size you can build a fairly substantial floor-to-ceiling room-width wall relatively quickly which has the advantage that you can make it load-bearing

Types of blocks

Building blocks are cast from concrete and come in a range of sizes with various densities (see *Ready Reference*).
Facing blocks have one patterned or decorative face, which is intended to be left bare as a finished surface.
Aerated blocks are the most widely available and the best for an internal partition. They're lightweight, can easily be grooved to take electric conduit or pipes and will take nails and screws. They also provide good heat and sound insulation.
Cellular blocks have cavities which don't go right through the block. They're laid closed end uppermost to give a continuous surface for spreading on the mortar bed for the next course. They have a rough surface which must be plastered.
Dense and **lightweight solid blocks** are rectangular, and can be used for most building work; some can even be used below dpc level. Load-bearing and non-load-bearing types are available; they'll take screws and nails, and can be plastered.
Jointed blocks have tongued-and-grooved ends for slotting together into a strong, load-bearing structure. They have good sound and heat insulation.
Hollow blocks have cavities, which can take pipes and conduits, or they can be filled with concrete or fitted with mild steel strengthening rods.

The best blocks for use inside are the aerated type, which are light in weight and so easier to handle than their heavyweight counterparts, and reduce the total load of the wall as well. The most commonly available size is 440 x 215 x 100mm (17 x 8½ x 4in). They're laid in a similar bonding pattern to bricks for strength, and have mortar joints between.

Planning a partition

You must plan the shape, size and position of your partition wall if you're not to end up with two dull rooms with unattractive proportions, but the most important factor to take into account is whether your floor can support a solid wall of blocks.

If you're building onto a solid concrete floor you can position the wall where you want. Don't worry if the surface isn't perfectly smooth and flat: you can accommodate any

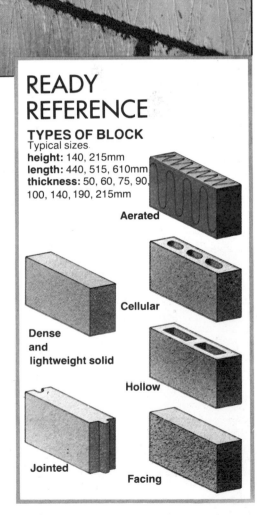

LAYING THE SCREED

1 Spread a 150mm (6in) wide screed of mortar onto the floor where you want the partition and smooth it to about a 9mm (³/8in) thickness with your trowel.

2 Scribe the line on the screed with a trowel against a builder's square to mark the outside of the partition; extend it with a timber straight edge.

3 Measure along the mortar screed to the position where you want the wall to turn a corner and lay a second screed at right angles to the first.

4 Scribe the line around the corner of the screed using your trowel and builder's square and extend it if necessary, with a long timber straight edge.

5 Dry-lay the blocks on the screed against the scribed line, starting at the existing wall, leaving finger-thick joints between each of the blocks.

6 When you've positioned the first course of blocks you can erect the door frame. Check with a spirit level that its position is truly vertical.

unevenness in the thickness of the mortar screed on which you lay the blocks.

A suspended timber floor causes more problems, although you can build onto it if the partition doesn't impose too great a strain on the structure. To ascertain this it's wise to consult your local council's Department of Building Inspectors.

Ground floor joists are usually spaced at 400mm (15in) intervals and supported on timber wall plates, which in turn are mounted on dwarf brick walls 1.3m (4ft 6in) apart over concrete foundations. Here you can build the partition on a stout timber floor plate, which will spread the load of the wall over the floor area. The floor plate should be of 100 x 50mm (4 x 2in) unplaned timber, nailed or screwed to the floor. It's a good idea to fix a 100mm (4in) wide strip of carpet underfelt underneath the plate to help reduce any sound transmission. You can nail strips of expanded metal lath on top of the plate to improve the mortar bond with the blocks.

Upper floors of timber construction aren't sturdy enough to support a blockwork partition and here you should build one with a timber frame. Similarly, upper floors of reinforced concrete construction aren't designed to support the weight of a full-width, room-height block wall, but you can safely build short-length dividers and half-height partitions, the top section of which can be glazed.

Structural requirements

The type of wall you wish to build is entirely up to you. It can be floor-to-ceiling and full-room-width: it can incorporate a window or door (see pages 73–77) or it may be a half-partition. But if you choose a full-width wall there are some important structural rules to keep in mind.

On very long walls you'll have to install a 'vertical movement joint' of flexible mastic every 6 to 9 square metres (20 to 30ft) – usually against a door or window frame – to allow for flexing of the structure. A wall of this size should also be 'toothed' into the existing walls (see *Ready Reference*).

When it comes to finishing off the wall, the choice of surface is again a matter of choice. Concrete blocks can be left bare or simply painted with emulsion, but they're not attractive to look at, and aren't really acceptable anywhere except in a garage or workshop. Other options are to match the partition to adjacent walls, or clad it with plasterboard over wooden battens and decorate it with paint or wallcovering.

Another thing to bear in mind when you're still at the planning stage is the lighting of a newly-partitioned room. Only the smallest of rooms such as a cupboard or WC can cope without natural light, although by incorporating glazing panels in the partition

LAYING THE BLOCKS

1 *Remove the blocks and apply a bed of mortar to the screed, against the scribed line. 'Furrow' the mortar with your trowel so you can bed the block accurately.*

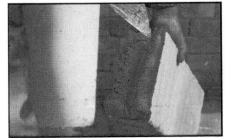

2 *'Butter' one end of the first block with mortar and furrow it with your trowel. The mortared end of the block is butted up to the existing wall.*

3 *Position the block on the mortar bed, parallel with the scribed line on the screed. Tap it gently into place using the handle of your trowel.*

4 *Move to the other end of the partition and lay the two corner blocks on a bed of mortar with finger-thick mortar joints between them.*

5 *Place your builder's level across the tops of the first and corner blocks and tap them level, then fill in the intermediate blocks of the first course.*

6 *As you tap the blocks into place, some mortar will be squeezed out of the joints. Scoop this off with your trowel and re-use it for other joints.*

READY REFERENCE

FITTING A DOORWAY
If your partition is to have a door, use a room-height frame to increase the stability of the wall.

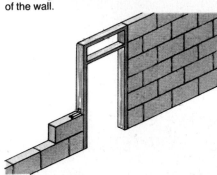

● screw it at the top to the ceiling joists
● secure it at the sides with galvanised metal frame cramps at every second course
● fill the gap between the top of the doorway and the ceiling with wired safety glass, plasterboard or wood panelling.

If you use a normal-size door frame:

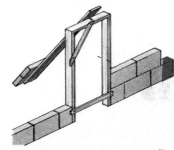

● fit it with temporary timber battens called 'strainers' across one corner and between the uprights at the bottom to prevent the frame from warping under the weight of the blocks
● erect the frame exactly where you want it and prop it in place with a 3m (9ft) long plank with a nail driven into the top.

FORMING A CORNER
You'll have to cut some blocks to size at the corners and the ends to maintain the stretcher bond throughout the rest of the wall.

● form the corner at ground level with full blocks then cut three-quarter-size blocks (A) for the second and then for the alternate courses
● use bricks or cut 100mm (4in) pieces of blocks (B) to use at each course on alternate sides of the corner.

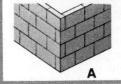

A　　　　　　　**B**

you can make use of light from windows in adjoining rooms. It's illegal, though, to position a partition wall so that it divides a window, and it's not, in any case, an attractive solution.

Another important factor in positioning your partition is whether you'll block access to underfloor cables and pipes. You must also consider whether electricity, gas and water supplies, and even the central heating system, can be extended into your new room. Also allow for adequate ventilation such as an extractor fan or a window with an opening fanlight.

The easiest way to provide access to the new room is to build a doorway into the partition, otherwise you'll have the extra job of cutting one in an existing wall. Whichever method you choose you'll have to fit a lintel over the door as support for the blockwork or brickwork above (see pages 73–81 for details). Alternatively you can make a room-height frame (see *Ready Reference*), in effect dividing the partition into two parts and providing the structure with greater strength. The upper part of the frame can be glazed with wired safety glass or panelled with plasterboard.

Before you decide upon a final plan for your partition it's wise to check with your

BUILDING THE PARTITION

1 *Build up the corner and end of the partition to the fourth course, 'stepping back' at each course. Check the angle with a spirit level.*

2 *Fix a stringline as a guide to laying the intermediate blocks. Push the pin into the vertical joint, with the string wound over the pin.*

3 *At the other end, take the string over the last block, around the corner and push in the pin diagonally opposite. Use a brick to hold the string in place.*

4 *Infill with blocks to the stringline. Butter one end of each block and lay it on a bed of mortar applied to the laid blocks to make fitting easier.*

5 *Secure the partition to the wall and door frame with metal frame cramps at every second course. Mark the screw holes on the wall with a pencil.*

6 *Drill holes at these marks to take the fixing screws for the frame cramp and insert plastic or wooden wallplugs into the holes.*

7 *Screw the frame cramp to the wall. There's no need to cut a recess in any of the blocks; the cramp is buried neatly in the mortar joint.*

8 *A mortar joint is all you'll need at ceiling level. Apply mortar to the top edge of the block and to the blocks already laid to make fitting easier.*

9 *Point the ceiling joint with a small pointing trowel. Use a small hawk to carry the mortar. Allow the structure to set before finishing.*

local council's Building Control Department that you aren't infringing any Building Regulations. If you don't, and are found out, you could be required to demolish the wall.

Marking out the partition

Before you start to build the wall on a solid floor you must remove any loose floorcovering such as linoleum, sheet vinyl, carpet or tiles, so that you have a firm, flat base for the blockwork. You can lay the blocks directly onto thermoplastic, vinyl or ceramic tiles as long as they're firmly stuck down. You should also remove any wallcovering from the existing wall where the partition is to be fixed.

Mark on the floor in pencil or chalk parallel lines that indicate the exact position of the partition, and carry them up the adjacent wall or walls to ceiling height. Use a spirit level and a long timber straight edge to ensure these guidelines are evenly spaced and straight. Next, chisel out a section of the skirting board and ceiling moulding, if any, between the guidelines so that the blocks can be laid flush with the wall; this makes for a sturdier structure and means that you don't have to cut any blocks to shape. When the partition's built you can fit new skirting and moulding to match that on the adjacent wall. You also need to chop out 'bonding pockets' in adjacent walls so that the new structure is properly tied in (see *Ready Reference*).

To support the blockwork during construction you'll need a temporary timber batten called a 'wall profile', which you should nail lightly to the existing wall against the guideline marking the outside face of the partition. You can make use of a chimney breast or other feature that extends into the room as a wall profile (see photographs).

Space out the blocks dry for the first two courses, without using any mortar, so that you can plan the best bonding pattern with as few cut blocks as possible. You'll probably find that stretcherbond, as used in brickwork, is the best and simplest arrangement. When placing the blocks, leave finger-width joints between them (see photograph 5, page 102). You'll have to cut some blocks to size for corners and ends to maintain the bond throughout the

CUTTING A SOLID BLOCK

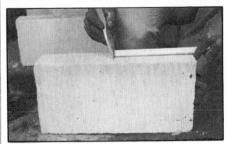

1 *To cut a block into two pieces, measure across one end the distance required and scribe a line at this point using a bolster chisel.*

2 *Tap the bolster chisel along the scribed line with a club hammer to make it deeper but don't hit it too hard or you may shatter the block.*

3 *Turn the block onto one face and scribe a line across, then around and onto the other face. Tap lightly along the line with the bolster chisel.*

4 *Place the bolster chisel on the centre of the face side of the block and hit it sharply with the club hammer to break it cleanly along the lines.*

rest of the wall. Alternatively, you could use bricks to fill in some spaces. When you've dry-laid the first two courses of blocks you can fix the door frame, if any, in place. Hold it erect with a temporary timber strut (see *Ready Reference*).

Laying the blocks

Once you're satisfied with the position and bond of the dry-laid blocks you can remove them and start to relay them, this time bedding each in mortar.

To do this, spread a 150mm (6in) wide screed of mortar about 9mm (⅜in) thick onto the floor over your guidelines and trowel it smooth. Then scribe a guideline marking the outside face of the wall onto the screed using your trowel and a timber straight edge. Bed the first course of blocks in mortar up to the line, starting at the wall profile. Make a mortar joint with the existing wall.

The most accurate way of working is to build up the corners or ends of the wall first, to about four courses, so that a string line can be stretched between them at each course as a guide to laying the intermediate blocks. Check constantly with a long spirit level as you work that the partition is level and upright.

Unlike brickwork, laying blocks that are going to be plastered or boarded doesn't call for perfectly regular size joints between the blocks. So long as there's sufficient mortar between each one, and they're laid so that the face is vertical, minor irregularities in thickness don't affect the strength of the structure. If you're building a large, room-width wall it's wise to carry out the work over two days to give the mortar in each part time to set. To tie the partition to the existing wall of the house you can either recess alternate courses of blocks into bonding pockets cut into the wall or insert galvanised metal frame cramps at these positions (see photographs 5-7, page 104).

Finishing the partition

If your partition is to be in a garage or utility room you might not feel a perfectly smooth, plastered finish is necessary, in which case you can simply form 'struck' or bevelled mortar joints with a bricklayer's trowel as you work and then give the wall a coat of emulsion paint when the mortar has set.

On the other hand, if the partition is to be in a habitable room within the house you won't want to see the outlines of the individual blocks. Here you should spread on two coats of plaster (see Working with plaster). You can then either paint or wallpaper the partition to match adjacent walls.

Alternatively, you can screw or nail horizontal timber battens directly to the blockwork and clad the surface.

EXPANSION JOINT

If you're building a very long wall it's advisable to include a vertical 'movement' joint every 6 to 9m (20 to 30ft). Using a flexible mastic compound (available from builders' merchants) instead of mortar, the joint allows for a little movement in the solid structure and prevents cracks appearing in the mortar joints. If you're including a door or window, alongside the frame is an ideal place for the joint.

movement joints

BONDING POCKETS

To form a strong bond with an existing brick or block wall and to prevent sideways movement of the partition, 'tie-in' the blocks at alternate courses.

● cut bonding pockets 50mm (2in) deep x 130mm (5in) wide x 245mm (9½in) high (to allow for mortar joints) in the existing wall with a club hammer and cold chisel
● slot the last whole block of alternate courses into the bonding pockets, bedding them in mortar.

LINTEL OVER DOOR

You'll need to install a lintel over the doorway to support the blocks above. Because of the lintel's size you'll have to fill the gap above with bricks or cut blocks.

For more information about using lintels see BUILDING TECHNIQUES 13.

BUILDING A STUD PARTITION WALL

Building a partition wall gives you two rooms where you only had one before. Surprisingly, you don't have to be a skilled craftsman. Here's how to build a simple framework.

Sometimes, even after the most careful planning and the cleverest space-saving schemes, one room just won't do all the jobs you want it to do. Perhaps you've got a combined kitchen and dining room, but you could really do with one of each. Maybe the house needs a second toilet. Or, try as you may, you can't squeeze everyone into the available bedrooms.

In any of these situations the answer could be to build a timber-framed partition wall. That may sound daunting, but it's not. An ordinary partition — even one that stretches from floor to ceiling and right across the room — needs only simple carpentry and easily obtainable materials. You can even incorporate a door, overhead glazing, or a serving hatch without much extra trouble.

Putting together a partition is simplicity itself. One long piece of wood (the 'head' or 'top plate') is fixed to the ceiling. A second piece (the 'sole plate') is fixed to the floor. Uprights run between them; these are the 'studs', which is why the structure is usually called a 'stud partition'. Between the studs run short horizontal spacers called 'noggins'. That's the framework, and all you do after building it is to nail sheets of cladding, which are usually plasterboard, to it.

The planning stage

A partition wall will make quite a difference to your house, and it needs to be made properly. Here, as so often, thoughtful planning is the key to success.

Be careful, for example, that you do not accidentally create two narrow, gloomy cupboards. Think about lighting in particular. Only in very small rooms such as toilets can you rely solely on artificial light. Elsewhere, you may be able to 'borrow' light through windows in the partition itself. Existing outside windows may take care of the situation — but you should avoid, at all costs, the temptation to site the partition so that one window sheds half its light on each side. It will look terrible, and it's against the law.

Ventilation needs similar attention. A habitable room must either have a mechanical ventilator, or one or more ventilation openings so constructed that 'their total area is not less than one twentieth of the floor area of the room and some part of the area is not less than 1.75m above the floor'. In other words, a room 3 × 4.5m (10 × 15ft) needs a window about 840mm (33in) square; and the top of the window must always be above head height.

Another point to consider is access. You'll do well to plan the partition so that you don't have to put a new doorway in an existing structural wall. It's far less work and just as effective to include one in the partition.

You must also consider how the ceiling joists run. This is important because you'll have to fix your partition to them, not just into the ceiling plaster. They're probably spaced regularly, but you'll have to find their exact positions by tapping and making small holes, or by removing the floorboards above. If they lie at right angles (or nearly) to the intended line of your partition, there's no problem. If you want the partition to run in the same direction as the joists, think carefully. You'll have to position it directly underneath a joist, fit a new joist and fix it to that, or fit 50 × 50mm (2 × 2in) bridging pieces between existing joists at regular intervals and fix the top plate to them. Moreover, an especially long and/or tall partition may be too heavy for the floorboards alone to support — so you'll have to make similar decisions about the floor joists.

Have a look at the electricity, gas and water supplies, and see that any necessary modifications to these won't be too difficult to make.

READY REFERENCE

USING JOINTS

Although skew-nailing will make quite a strong framework, there is a slightly more complex and craftsmanlike alternative. This is to use a wide housing joint instead. Mark out the housings across both plates at the same time with a try-square.

The four corners of the frame will have rebate joints; so will the bottom corners of the door opening.

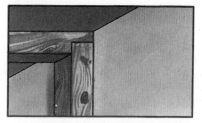

And lastly ring the local council. Unless you are converting a house into flats, you don't need planning permission. But you can't be too careful where the Building Regulations are concerned, because they deal with things like fire hazards and proper ventilation. The council should be able to tell you whether your plans conform.

When you've thought about all this and worked out a likely scheme, it's a good idea to sketch it out on paper. If there's a hidden snag, you'll find it staring at you in black and white, and you can deal with it before it causes any trouble.

Constructional details

Something you'll need to decide is how far apart the studs should be. Studs set at '600mm (2ft) centres' (i.e., with their centres that distance apart) give what is really the maximum spacing, and 450mm (18in) will make an even more rigid structure.

You should also measure and take into account the sizes of whatever cladding material you'll be fixing to the wooden framework. Plasterboard, for example, is standarised at 2440 × 1220mm (8 × 4ft) and 3050 × 1220mm (10 × 4ft). You might therefore want to arrange the studs so that there's one every 1220mm (4ft). Putting them at either 600mm (2ft) or 400mm (16in) centres would ensure this.

The door opening, of course, needs to be wider. Take its size from that of the door you plan to use, plus 3mm (⅛in) clearance either side and thickness of extra 'lining' pieces of, say, 100 × 25mm (4 × 1in) wood, fixed round its inside at top and sides. These should be wide enough to cover the edges of the cladding on both sides of the partition. A window opening should be lined in the same way (see *Ready Reference*, page 110).

It's unlikely, of course, that you'll be able to fit an exact number of whole sheets of cladding from wall to wall or floor to ceiling. So you'll need to cut some to fit. Besides, the walls and ceiling may not be dead straight or true, so you'll need to mark and cut the edges of the sheets which adjoin them, to make them fit snugly. Luckily, plasterboard is extremely easy to cut.

Noggins need only be placed 1220mm (4ft) above the floor, and again at 2400mm (8ft) if the ceiling is higher — assuming you'll be using 2400 × 1200mm (8 × 4ft) sheets.

Starting work

First, of course, you'll need to buy your timber. This is made easy by the fact that all the pieces (except for door and window linings, which are added later anyway) are the same cross-sectional size. This can be as massive as 100 × 50mm (4 × 2in), but 75 × 50mm (3 × 2in) is quite big enough for most purposes, and 75 × 38mm (3 × 1½in) will

FIXING TOP AND SOLE PLATES

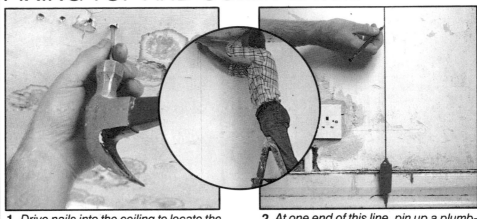

1 *Drive nails into the ceiling to locate the exact centre of the joist (or joists) to which the top plate will be fixed. Mark the new wall's position on the ceiling.*

2 *At one end of this line, pin up a plumbline to mark the exact centre of the top plate (inset). Mark a true vertical line down the side wall to floor level.*

3 *Cut the sole plate to length. Suspend the plumbline further along the ceiling line and position the sole plate using plumbline and wall marks as guides.*

4 *Nail the sole plate in place (inset – use screws and plugs on solid floors). Then cut the top plate to length and drill screw clearance holes through it.*

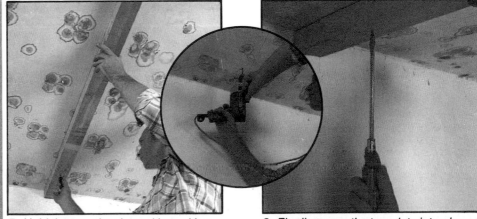

5 *Hold the top plate in position, with a helper or a stud to support it, and mark the screw positions. Drill pilot holes into the joist or joists (inset).*

6 *Finally screw the top plate into place using 90mm (3½in) screws. Check that it is precisely aligned with the sole plate by suspending the plumbline at each end.*

BRICKS

**You may think bricks are all the same.
They're not. There are thousands of different bricks
available, and it really does pay to choose
the bricks that are right for the job you're doing.**

Bricks are one of the most versatile of all building materials. To make the most of their qualities though, you must choose the right one for the job. Basically, two things affect your choice: how the brick is to be used and whether the final appearance is important.

For most do-it-yourself jobs, strength can be ignored. Even 'weak' bricks are more than adequate for, say, a garden wall, or a small outhouse. Similarly it's not important if bricks have slots, holes, or 'frogs' in them — unless the top face is visible. These are there to make the brick lighter and key with mortar better.

What you must not ignore if you're laying bricks outside is their weather resistance. Bricks are divided into various 'qualities' according to their ability to resist extremes of temperature.

Internal quality bricks have no weather resistance at all. As their name implies, they can only be used indoors — outside they would quickly disintegrate.

Ordinary quality bricks are suitable for exterior use, but will not stand severe exposure to the elements. This means they can be used to form the bulk of a free-standing wall, but not its coping. Ordinary quality bricks are also unsuitable for retaining walls and for brickwork underground. Here, the almost complete weather resistance of *special quality* bricks is required. These are very dense and very durable.

In terms of looks, if the brickwork is to be covered with rendering, plaster, or some form of cladding, it doesn't matter what they look like. Where appearance is important, you'll find a host of 'facing' or 'faced' bricks for use indoors or out.

Engineering bricks
Technically, engineering bricks are all special quality, but they are really more than that. They are extra special: very hard, very strong, regular in size and colour,

and almost completely impervious to water. Their major drawback is that they are expensive, so reserve them for situations where their virtues are really needed (eg, lining manholes, building an indestructible damp proof course into a wall, and so on). They come in two classes — A and B — which describe their exact strength and water resistance, but there are few DIY jobs where the choice is critical. You may also find bricks described as semi-engineering, but since there is no recognised definition of this type, you need to ask to find out what they are recommended for.

Commons
Bricks described as commons aren't meant to be beautiful. They are rough looking and vary considerably in colour, but they are relatively cheap and are normally either internal or ordinary quality. Some are sufficiently attractive to be left exposed (in which case they need protection by a coping). But in most cases they're used in situations where they will be covered up with some form of cladding which shields the bricks.

Faced and facing bricks
Both faced and facing bricks are designed to be put on display. The difference between them is that while faced bricks have only one or two sides that are presentable, facing bricks are attractive no matter which way you look at them.

Facing bricks made from clay are available in a variety of colours — reds, yellows, greys, blues, blue/greens, etc — and a combination of colours (called multi-coloured bricks). They also come in several textured finishes; some with commonsense descriptive names ('sand faced', 'rustic' and so on); some with names that indicate the methods of making ('hand mades', 'wire cut' etc). They offer the widest range and the best way to decide which you want is to go and look

at the bricks themselves — they are available in ordinary and special qualities.

Standard 'specials'
A wide range of these bricks is made to coordinate with standard bricks. They're designed to give either protection (eg, copings) or a finishing touch to the top of a wall or an end (eg, single, double or left and right hand bullnose). Radial headers and stretchers allow you to create a curve without cutting bricks or making the mortar joints thicker. These plus plinth headers and stretchers are the ones most useful in DIY work, and if not stocked can be ordered at builders' merchants. Most are available in ordinary or special quality; copings should always be special quality.

Calcium silicate bricks
These are made from either a mixture of sand and lime, or flint and lime. They're the same size and used in exactly the same way as clay bricks. Because of the way they're made, they are much more uniform in colour and size than clay bricks. There are a total of 6 classes available, but, as with classes of engineering bricks, most of them are to do with the bricks' strength. Basically, they fall into two categories: those designed to be on show (facing bricks), and those that aren't. Sandlime and flintlime bricks contain no soluble salts and efflorescence can only occur if salts come from the ground or materials stacked against them. For severely exposed places, specify class 3 or 4.

Concrete bricks
These are similar to calcium silicate bricks but are made from either portland cement or sulphate resisting cement. Concrete bricks are as uniform as calcium silicate bricks and are classified in exactly the same way. Good quality concrete bricks closely resemble the clay bricks they are designed to imitate.

Faced bricks

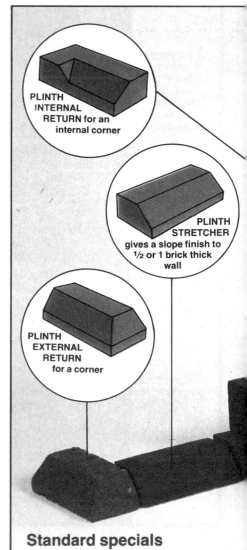

PLINTH INTERNAL RETURN for an internal corner

PLINTH STRETCHER gives a slope finish to ½ or 1 brick thick wall

PLINTH EXTERNAL RETURN for a corner

Standard specials

Standard bricks

Various brick types and colours are manufactured in different areas. If you select those from a local range they'll be more likely to blend with the colour and character of buildings in the area, and your delivery cost will also be lower.

Commons   **Facing bricks**   **Engineering bricks**   **Calcium silicate bricks**   **Concrete bricks**

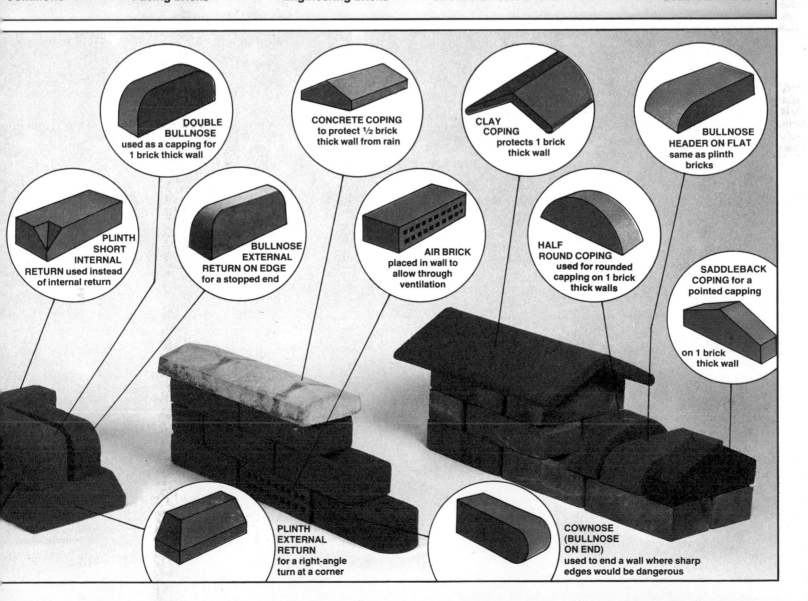

DOUBLE BULLNOSE used as a capping for 1 brick thick wall

CONCRETE COPING to protect ½ brick thick wall from rain

CLAY COPING protects 1 brick thick wall

BULLNOSE HEADER ON FLAT same as plinth bricks

PLINTH SHORT INTERNAL RETURN used instead of internal return

BULLNOSE EXTERNAL RETURN ON EDGE for a stopped end

AIR BRICK placed in wall to allow through ventilation

HALF ROUND COPING used for rounded capping on 1 brick thick walls

SADDLEBACK COPING for a pointed capping

on 1 brick thick wall

PLINTH EXTERNAL RETURN for a right-angle turn at a corner

COWNOSE (BULLNOSE ON END) used to end a wall where sharp edges would be dangerous

CEMENT, SAND AND AGGREGATE

Mortars and concrete are precise mixtures of cement, sand, aggregates and other additives. It's important to use the right ingredients for the best results.

You can't do much in the way of building work without having to mix up some mortar or lay some concrete, and if you're going to get good results you have to know the difference between the various types of cement, sand, aggregates and other additives you'll need. First, cement.

Cement

Cements are used to bind the sands and aggregates of a mortar or concrete mix together to give it strength. They set by the action of water, and for this reason they must be kept dry until they are used. Cement that has been stored in damp conditions and has partially hardened into lumps will not set properly and should not be used. Cements are usually sold in 50kg (1cwt) bags, but smaller sizes are available.

Portland cement is not a brand but a type of cement, and is made by several manufacturers. There are two commonly-used types.

Ordinary Portland cement (commonly abbreviated OPC) is the least expensive and most widely-used cement and is suitable for all normal purposes.

Masonry cements are used for making bricklaying mortars, for bedding tiles and for backing renders for decorative wall finishes, including roughcast and pebbledash. They are not suitable for making concrete.

A masonry cement is not all cement; there are other materials added to improve the mix. It needs only the addition of sand to give a good mortar, and therefore it is simple to use. You can also add colouring pigments to change the mortar colour, but nothing else. Masonry cement is sold in 50kg (1cwt) bags.

Lime

Mortars and rendering mixes made with Portland cement and sand only are not ideal because they are too strong for general use and can be difficult to work with. Lime can be added to reduce the strength and to greatly improve the workability of the mix. It retains water well, which assists the proper hardening of the cement. The addition of lime to a mix also gives a degree of flexibility to the hardened material, making it less likely to shrink and crack.

ordinary Portland cement

lime

White Portland cement is made from white raw materials. It is used for making white mortars for pointing brick or stone walling, and for making white concrete for special decorative work. It is comparatively expensive.

white Portland cement

Various mixes are recommended for different jobs, but in all cases the lime is similar. Builder's merchants sell 'white lime' for work where a light colour is required, or the cheaper 'grey lime' for all other work. Lime is sold in 25kg (½cwt) bags.

Plasticisers

Instead of adding lime to a mortar mix to make it workable, another additive, called a plasticiser, can be mixed in to produce minute air bubbles which act as a 'frictionless aggregate' in the mix.

Good-quality plasticisers are based on a resin that limits the

amount of air bubbles to a certain proportion. This improves the resistance of the hardened mix to frost damage.

Plasticisers are sold in liquid or powder form under various brand names. Liquids are easier to measure out and mix in than powders. They are available in 1 litre cans — enough to mix with four 50kg bags of cement.

Sands

Sand is the bulk material of mortars, renderings and floor screeds. It should be clean and well-graded. Sand is cleaned either by washing with water or by dry screening. Dry-screened sands are often better than washed ones, as they retain their finest particles and these can help to produce a more workable mix.

A well-graded sand is one that has particles of various sizes. The smaller particles fill the gaps between the larger ones, and so less cement is needed to bind them all together to make a strong material. Poorly-graded sands include a lot more air space and extra cement would have to be used.

Sharp sands are coarse and are generally washed. They are best suited for floor screeds and fine

sharp sand

concrete mixes. They can produce strong, durable mortars but they are slightly more difficult to work with. *Soft sands* (often called builders' or bricklayers' sands) contain large proportions of fine particles, including clay, which makes them unsuitable for good mortars. They are used for binding or filling hard-core sub-bases to floor slabs, drives and paths.

soft sand

Silver sand is a naturally-occurring and extremely pure white sand. It is used in work where appearance is important – for example, with white Portland cement to make white or light-toned pointing mortars and white concrete. Silver sands are fine and not well graded. Additional cement is needed to make a mortar with good strength and durability.

silver sand

Bulking is a factor that must be allowed for when using sand. The proportion of sand in a mix is given by volume, and this figure always refers to dry sand. In practice, all the sand you buy will be damp to some extent. Damp sand increases in volume – sometimes by up to 40 per cent – so you should measure out extra sand to allow for this.

Coarse aggregates

Coarse aggregates are mixtures of strong stones, not chippings, and are the main material forming concrete. They are usually graded by sieving to diameters of 5 to 20mm (about ¼ to ¾in). Grading of the particle sizes throughout the material is needed for strong concrete, but the range of sizes varies for different jobs. For this reason, always tell your supplier what you require the aggregate for.

All-in aggregates (commonly called ballast) combine sand and fine coarse aggregates, and are usually used where the precise strength of the concrete is unimportant.

Bulk-buying sand and aggregates

Large quantities of sands and aggregates are traditionally sold loose by volume, measured in cubic metres or parts of cubic metres. In some areas, builders' merchants now sell sand and aggregate by weight in 25kg (½cwt) bags, which you could collect yourself, and also in ½ tonne (approx 10cwt) and 1 tonne quantities which are delivered to the customer either

all-in aggregate

loose or in canvas bags off-loaded by a crane on the special delivery vehicle.

Buying small quantities

DIY shops now offer small bagged quantities of most of the commonly used sands and aggregates as well as ordinary Portland cement and lime. Sizes vary from 6kg (approx. 13lb) to 50kg (1cwt).

fine concrete mix

The range often also includes various general-purpose mixes for popular uses, including:
sand & cement mix – for floor screeds, laying crazy paving and repair work in damp locations;
bricklaying mortar mix – for general bricklaying and internal rendering;
coloured mortar mix – for bricklaying with coloured mortars;
fine concrete mix – for paths, steps, kerb surrounds, etc, where a fine

finish is needed;
coarse concrete mix – for foundations, setting fence posts and clothes line posts etc.

Most of the blended products do not state the exact composition of the mix. Read the application list printed on the bag carefully to make sure you have chosen the correct one for your job.

sand & cement mix

The range of mixes and pack sizes has been carefully worked out to provide a choice to suit commonly-occurring jobs around the home and garden. They save wastage and eliminate the trouble of buying and mixing together the separate ingredients. However, for some jobs it may be preferable to mix your own materials to the particular specification you require for the work.

coarse concrete mix

Special-purpose additives

The basic properties of standard mixes for mortars, renders and concretes can be modified by the inclusion of special-purpose additives. Here is a selection of the most common.

Colouring pigments are used to add colour to mortars and concrete. The pigments are stirred into the wet mix, and must be inert and colour-fast. Adding too much can weaken a mortar and reduce its

durability, so follow the instructions provided with the pigment.

Pigments are sold in powder form in 1kg and 5kg (2.2 and 11lb) tins. The maximum amount usually recommended is 5kg per 50kg bag of cement. The stockist will have colour charts indicating the effect of various proportions of the pigment. When using pigments, keep a record of the amount added to the mix and work with accuracy to keep the colour constant.

Waterproofing additives are used to make mortars and concretes waterproof. They come as powders or liquids, and can be used with Portland cement mixes, but some are not suitable for use with masonry cements. Check the manufacturer's instructions carefully when using these additives.

Well-compacted concrete is essential for waterproof work. Do not expect the additive to do the job at the expense of good workmanship.

Frost-proofers are additives used when working in cold weather. The frost resistance of a hardened

mortar, render or concrete is dependent on the strength of the basic mix; select a suitable specification and make sure that it is properly made up and used, and the work will be frost-resistant once is has set.

Frost-proofing additives are intended to give protection to work only during construction. Avoid working with mortars, renders and concrete when there is a risk of frost. Never start work in freezing weather, but if there is a risk of frost on new work or incomplete work, protect it with insulating covers such as hessian sacks, old blankets, or straw and the like, covered with polythene sheet or tarpaulins.

There is no effective frost-proofer to allow mortars and renders to be laid in near freezing conditions. However, concrete can be protected in low temperatures by the addition of an accelerator/hardener to the mix. This causes heat to be generated in the new-laid concrete, which should be covered as soon as practical in order to keep in the heat.

CONCRETE PAVING SLABS

Gone are the days when the local garden centre could offer you only paving slabs in dull grey or off-white. Today, a wide range is available in many colours and textures.

With slabs now made in an ever-increasing range of colours, textures and patterns, there's no longer an excuse for creating a concrete jungle in your garden. Your patio or path can have the mellow finish of old stone, the warm appearance of brick or cobbles, or the look of exposed aggregates.

What are concrete slabs?

Essentially concrete slabs, whatever appearance they might assume, are all made of the same material – cement. This reacts with water to form a hard, solid material. Crushed stone or gravel (coarse aggregate) and sand (fine aggregate) are added to form the body of the mix and provide strength and bulk. The cement-and-water paste coats the particles of aggregate and binds them all together into the dense mass known as concrete.

The cheapest slabs are simply cast in a mould of the required shape. A finish is then applied to the top face.

Pressed concrete slabs are stronger than cast slabs – although more expensive. They're hydraulically pressed during manufacture using many tonnes of pressure to compact and consolidate the fresh concrete. The result is a strong, double product.

Cast concrete slabs for garden use are generally 50mm (2in) thick, whereas pressed slabs are about 40mm (1½in) thick and a bit easier to lift and lay.

You might see concrete slabs described as made from 'reconstituted stone', the implication being that they are different from (and better than) concrete paving. All concrete is, in a sense, reconstituted stone. Manufacturers of this product, however, set out to simulate in concrete the appearance of a particular natural stone. Authentic stone is used for the aggregates, pigments are added and the product is made in moulds; themselves cast from an actual piece of stone in order to capture the correct texture.

Shapes and sizes

Most slabs are square or oblong, and come in a wide range of sizes, based on a 225mm (9in) or 300mm (12in) module. The most common sizes are:
225 x 225mm (9 x 9in)
300 x 300mm (12 x 12in)
450 x 225mm (18 x 9in)
450 x 300mm (18 x 12in)
450 x 450mm (18 x 18in)
600 x 300mm (24 x 12in)
600 x 450mm (24 x 18in)
600 x 600mm (24 x 24in)
675 x 450mm (27 x 18in).

Not all manufacturers make all of these sizes. The ones based on a 225mm (9in) module are the most useful, as they're appropriate in scale for most gardens. None of these sizes is too arduous to work with but

normal precautions against back injury should always be taken. Bend the knees rather than the spine when lifting them, and watch your fingers and toes when stacking them: a 450 x 450mm (18 x 18in) slab weighs about 16.6kg (37lbs).

In addition to rectangular slabs you'll also find a wide range of other shapes – such as hexagons, and circles – although some are available only from specialist suppliers.

Hexagons, for instance, are particularly useful for making winding paths since you can change direction at 60° as well as at right angles. The commonest size measures 400mm (16in) in width between parallel sides. To obtain straight sides for a patio or path of hexagonal slabs half-hexagons are available.

Circular slabs come in various diameters and you can make a path of attractive stepping stones set in a lawn.

Estimating numbers

Estimating how many slabs you'll need to pave a given area is a matter of simple arithmetic with square and rectangular types. As a general rule, plan the size of your paved areas so that whole slabs are used when possible.

The easiest and most accurate way to work out how many slabs you'll need is to draw out the area you want to pave on squared paper, using one square to represent one slab.

Estimating the numbers of hexagonal slabs can be more difficult, although most manufacturers provide guides in their leaflets. When you're ordering your slabs it's wise to allow a few extra for breakages.

Colours and textures

Colour and texture must really be considered together. Relatively smooth, flat slabs can generally be found in the widest range of colours – from off-white, buff, yellow, brown and red to green, grey and dark slate.

With slabs designed to look like natural stone manufacturers naturally use stone colours. These include York stone in both buff and grey, Cotswold and a neutral stone grey. The most authentic looking slabs, however, are composed of two shades – a mixture of grey over buff to give a York – stone look and red with overtones of greys to simulate red sandstone.

Left: You can buy paving slabs with special cut-outs for paving around trees and all sorts of textured patterns that you can lay in swirling, interwoven designs.

Not all slabs are made to simulate natural stone; there's a wide range of other surface textures and patterns available. These range from a cobbled effect to more uniformly-patterned designs.

Slabs with relief patterns such as these are made in conventional sizes and shapes but you can also buy radius slabs to make a circular pattern contained within a square. Alternatively, some can be laid in such a way that they form interwoven swirling patterns or an overall herringbone effect.

A different approach to colour and texture is adopted with 'exposed aggregate' slabs.

Right: Surface finishes for square and rectangular slabs vary from smooth and riven to exposed aggregate.

Below: With pressed slabs you get patterns resembling brick, stone or mosaic in various shapes and sizes. With hexagonal slabs, two different edging slabs are available.

hints

Stacking slabs correctly

To prevent accidentally chipping the corners and edges of your slabs, and marking their faces, stack them on edge in pairs, face to face, against a wall, with their bottom edges on timber battens.

Handling slabs

Slabs are heavy and cumbersome to carry. The best precautions you can take are to wear heavy-duty shoes to protect your feet in case you should drop a slab on them, and gloves to protect your hands, especially if the slab has a rough surface. Grip the edges of the slab firmly and lift them with your knees bent and your back straight. Alternatively, you can hold the top corners of the slab and 'walk' it on its bottom corners.

Laying slabs in patterns

You've a lot of freedom in the way you lay your slabs. You can lay only one shape, size and colour or you can mix them to give various patterns.

GARDEN WALLING BLOCKS

If you're building walls in your garden, you don't have to stick to brickwork. There is a wide range of walling stone, natural or man-made, to choose from.

M any projects in the garden involve building free-standing walls, either for their decorative effect or to give shelter and privacy or to act as earth-retaining walls on sloping or banked sites.

In some areas, natural stone is still readily available at a price that makes it a worthwhile consideration for wall construction, but otherwise there is a good selection of reconstituted stone and high-quality precast concrete masonry blocks which come in a range of sizes and which offer an attractive alternative. In most areas the larger garden and DIY centres and builders' merchants keep good stocks. Stone merchants too, should not be overlooked as many offer quite an extensive range of reconstituted stone and precast concrete garden walling products as well as quantities of natural stone.

Reconstituted stone

Reconstituted stone blocks are made from concrete in which the aggregate is crushed natural stone and the sand and cement content is carefully selected so that the finished product closely resembles natural stone. They can be smooth, but most blocks have a texture intended to simulate traditional split stone walling.

These blocks are made in a co-ordinated range of sizes that can be laid in traditional stonework bonding patterns – either coursed or random. Precise sizes vary between makers and different brands are not generally interchangeable if regular bonding is to be maintained. But any size can be used on its own or together with others from the same co-ordinated range to produce the desired bonding pattern. The block sizes allow for joints 10mm (⅜in) thick. There is a choice of about half a dozen natural stone colours; yellows, reds, greys and greens predominate. They can be used in mixtures to produce a multi-coloured walling.

Not all faces of the blocks are textured; often only one long face and one end is intended to be exposed, while the others are flat and smooth for neat bonding. Check this point when you are planning your wall and estimating quantities. If you want the wall to look good on both sides you may have to use two blocks back-to-back if the blocks themselves have only one textured face. Some ranges also include special blocks for corners and the ends, and also coping stones for finishing off the top of the wall.

Reconstituted stone can be used outside for the walls of buildings, extensions, garages and greenhouse bases, for boundary walls, retaining walls and barbecues; it is also ideal for use inside the house for fireplaces and decorative feature walls.

Simulated dry-stone walling

An interesting variation among reconstituted stone walling blocks is one which is moulded to give the appearance of eight or nine individual 'stones'. The false joints are deeply recessed, and for the best effect the 'real' joints should also be deeply recessed, and should be made with a mortar to match the colours of the block.

These blocks are faced on one long side and on both ends. They can be used to turn corners, but if

SCREEN WALLING BLOCKS

you want both sides of the wall to appear the same, then a double thickness wall will be required. The standard block size is 527 x 145 x 102mm (20¾ x 5¾ x 4in) which, allowing for a 6mm (¼in) thick joint, gives a work size of 533 x 152 x 102mm (21 x 6 x 4in). Half blocks are available for the half lap at the ends of the wall so that a soundly bonded wall can be built without cutting blocks. It is worth planning the work to suit the sizes of the block, as cutting will spoil the continuity of the pattern of false jointing. Special coping stones are made to suit single and double-leaf walls and square piers constructed from standard blocks.

These blocks are particularly suitable in the garden for retaining walls, boundary walls, piers for pergolas or pierced screen wall blocks, raised planting beds, seats and barbecues. As both ends are properly faced, a pierced screen or 'honeycomb' wall can be built with them as a design variation.

Concrete facing blocks

The lightweight concrete blocks used in houses for partitions and the inner leaf of cavity walls are not suitable for use in the garden, as they are not weather-resistant. Special concrete facing blocks should always be chosen for any outdoor work. They are walling blocks with a high-quality face intended to be left exposed. A wide variety of colours and textures are available, including sculptured, exposed-aggregate and split stone finishes. Usually they are made with dense concrete, but some types of lightweight blocks are made with dense weather-proof facing finishes. They are made in the standard work sizes of 450 x 225mm (18 x 9in) and 400 x 200mm (16 x 8in). Both sizes allow for 10mm (⅜in) thick mortar joints and they are made in several other thicknesses. Very thick ones are generally hollow to save weight. Other sizes are made to co-ordinate with these standard blocks for use at the ends or corners of walls. There are also other block sizes for special effects, including random course walling.

Facing blocks must be laid bonded – with vertical joints staggered – to give the wall strength. They can be cut with a bolster and club hammer, but it is best to set out the work to use whole block sizes as far as possible.

Decorative bricks

As an alternative to walling blocks of reconstituted stone, you could consider using specially coloured bricks – not the ordinary stocks or facing bricks used for house-building, although these would often be suitable, but special types

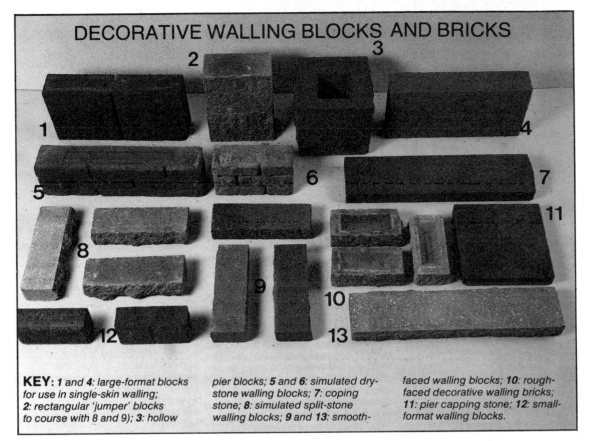

DECORATIVE WALLING BLOCKS AND BRICKS

KEY: *1 and 4: large-format blocks for use in single-skin walling; 2: rectangular 'jumper' blocks to course with 8 and 9); 3: hollow pier blocks; 5 and 6: simulated dry-stone walling blocks; 7: coping stone; 8: simulated split-stone walling blocks; 9 and 13: smooth-faced walling blocks; 10: rough-faced decorative walling bricks; 11: pier capping stone; 12: small-format walling blocks.*

resembling dressed stone on their exposed faces and available in yellows, reds, greens and greys. The advantage these have over walling blocks is the presence of a frog (or indent) that helps to increase the bond strength – a useful bonus on exposed walls or earth-retaining structures. They are the same size as an ordinary brick.

Pierced screen wall blocks

Open screen walls made from pierced blocks can provide an attractive feature to give partial shelter or as a background for plants. They can be used to screen a patio, to build a carport wall or a porch screen, or to hide an unsightly area such as a compost heap or the dustbin.

The blocks are made from dense concrete, often white or near white, although some makers offer them in grey or other colours. Designs are generally based on geometric patterns. Some are laid in groups of four to give a larger interlocking design. Many manufacturers also make co-ordinated blocks which are not pierced; these can be incorporated in the pattern for special effects or they can be used where full screening is required in the general run of the decorative pierced walling.

Designs vary between manufacturers and different brands may not be interchangeable. Precise sizes may vary too, but they are generally a nominal

300mm (12in) square (including an allowance of 10mm (⅜in) for joints) and build a wall approximately 90mm (3½in) thick.

Pay attention to choosing the correct mortar mix for use with these blocks. White blocks should be laid either with a mortar made with white cement and silver sand to match, or else with a darker and deliberately contrasting mortar. The light grey colour of plain mortar made with ordinary Portland cement does not offer sufficient contrast and tends merely to look dirty. Take care to keep the mortar off the face of the blocks when laying them, so as to avoid the risk of staining. Align and level the blocks carefully and finish the joints neatly, as the square grid pattern will accentuate any irregularities.

Screen wall blocks are not laid with a lapped bond, but are 'stack-bonded', one on top of the other with the mortared joints aligning throughout. Stack-bonding is not as strong as lapped bonding, so a wall that is more than a couple of blocks high needs supporting piers. These piers should usually be every 3m (10ft), but follow the manufacturer's instructions for high walls or exposed locations. For extra strength, reinforcing mesh can be bedded in the horizontal mortar joints.

Piers can be built of bricks, or reconstituted stone or concrete walling blocks, but perhaps the simplest method is to use tailor-made screen wall pilaster blocks:

these are made to suit end, intermediate, corner and intersecting positions and have holes through the centre so that a steel rod can be threaded through, extending into the concrete foundation, to provide extra reinforcement for high walls; the hole is then filled with a weak concrete mix.

The tops of the pilasters are finished off with special caps, and copings are made to lay along the tops of the screen blocks. These strengthen the top of the wall, as the cappings each cover two or three blocks; they also help to shed rainwater, so minimising staining of the wall surface.

It is essential that this walling be laid on a flat base, so if you have a sloping site you will have to level it up in steps by building a dwarf wall in solid blocks or bricks. Even on a flat site this is often preferable, as two or three courses of bricks or stone walling is more practical next to soil than pierced blocks.

Mortars for garden walls

Never use mortars consisting of straight Portland cement and sand for building garden walls, since cracking is likely to result. The textbook mix is 1:1:6 cement:lime:sand, but other suitable mixes for this work include 1:4 masonry cement:sand and a 1:5 cement:sand mix with added proprietary plasticiser. In all cases the mix should be workable but not sloppy.

PLATFORM TOWERS

Whether you are decorating the outside of your house or carrying out vital repairs, you need to be able to reach the heights comfortably and safely. A platform tower does the job perfectly.

The main use of a platform tower is for gaining safe access to the upper storey of a house – for example when painting the upstairs walls and woodwork, or when you need to be able to get at gutters, chimney stacks or the roof. Most can also be used indoors, either as a platform for painting ceilings or, more usefully, for creating a working platform for decorating the stairwell.

The most common type of platform tower is made from steel sections that are simply slotted together. A typical height for such a tower would be 4.8m (16ft) from the ground to the platform, allowing heights of up to 6.5m (22ft) to be reached.

The tower components
For this type of tower, the main components are the *frame sections*. These are made from tubular steel, welded together to form an H-shape with two cross pieces, and slot together in parallel pairs to form the tower. The steel is either painted or galvanized to protect it from corrosion.

Most towers are about 1.25m (4ft) square, but some manufacturers also make half-width frame sections for a rectangular tower – useful for access in confined spaces.

As well as steel towers, there are also aluminium alloy towers. These have main frames about 2m (6ft 6in) high, linked by fixed platforms and fitted with an internal staircase that acts as a structural brace (see photograph, page 840).

There are three kinds of *feet* that you can fit to a platform tower. The cheapest is a simple fixed baseplate. Its disadvantage is that all four feet have to be at the same level, a problem overcome by using adjustable feet instead. Mobility can be achieved by fitting the tower with lockable castors.

All kinds of tower have diagonal *braces* or tie bars, which keep the tower rigid and, incidentally, also provide a handy grab rail when you are climbing the inside of the tower.

The *platform* itself usually consists of a number of stout boards. Some systems offer prefabricated platform sections instead of planks. Most towers also have toe boards which slot in on edge round the platform to stop paint tins and tools cascading to the ground or on to someone's head.

To top off the tower, a *guard rail* is fitted all round. It is absolutely vital to fit guard rails properly and to use them at all times.

When building towers above a certain height against a building, *outriggers* can be fitted to the two outside corners of the tower to increase its stability. These avoid the need to tie the tower to the building.

Optional extras
Many tower manufacturers offer other accessories and extras, usually intended to widen the usefulness of the tower. These include ladder sections, hinged platforms, staircase frames, trestle feet and workbench attachments.

Buy or hire?
Because of the cost, most people will hire a tower rather than buying one. Always order well in advance, and check on delivery that all the components are present.

SAFETY RULES

When building a tower:
● ensure that the feet are resting on firm ground
● on soft ground, set the feet on stout planks
● check that the tower is standing level, and adjust the feet if necessary
● check that the height recommendations are not exceeded; fit outriggers or tie the tower to the building if they are
● beware overhead power lines
● fit guard rails and toe boards round the platform.

When using a tower:
● lock castors, if fitted, before starting to climb
● climb the inside, NOT the outside, of the tower
● don't lean ladders against towers
● don't attempt to move a tower if anyone is on the platform.

When dismantling the tower:
● don't throw components to the ground; pass them to a helper
● don't force components apart; tap them with a hammer and a block of wood if they are stiff.

hints

Interlocking toe boards are a vital safety feature, stopping you from slipping beneath the guard rails or knocking tools to the ground.

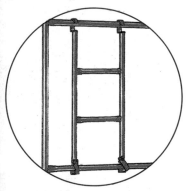

You can fit a hinged platform section alongside a fixed landing panel for easy access.

Small clip-on ladder sections bridge successive H-frames to make climbing the tower easy.

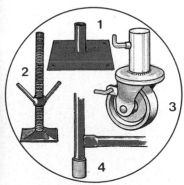

You can fit fixed base plates (1), adjustable ones (2), lockable castors (3) or rubber feet (4 – for indoor use only).

● it's often difficult to reach upstairs walls with a ladder when a single-storey flat roof gets in the way. Build a cantilevered arrangement like this, resting the feet of the cantilevered part on boards to protect the roof surface.

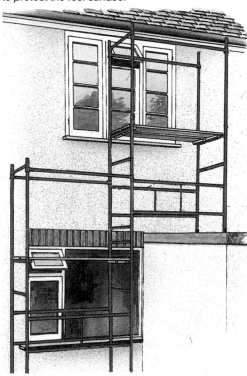

● where the cantilever aims to bridge a pitched roof, protect the tiles with sandbags and again use boards to help spread the load. Use narrow H-frames to reach over a shallow roof.

● if you want access to the area above a door that is in constant use, build a tower at each side of the door and link them together with two frames.

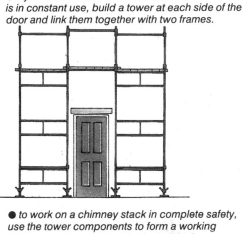

● to work on a chimney stack in complete safety, use the tower components to form a working platform as shown. Rest the feet of the frames on boards laid on sandbags, and use a roof ladder for access.

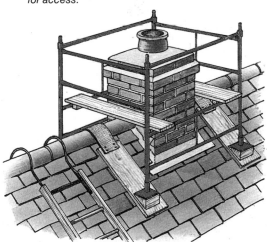

● you can use tower components indoors as well – to make a low mobile work platform for painting ceilings (left), or a stepped platform for decorating in stairwells (right). A special staircase frame is usually used for this arrangement.

SAFETY GEAR

Lots of jobs around the home can be dangerous, dirty, or just plain unpleasant. There's a wide range of protective clothing and accessories designed to help you get on with the job while keeping clean and reducing the risk of accidents.

There are times when you simply cannot avoid working in hazardous situations or with potentially dangerous materials and machines. And accidents will happen. The trick is to minimise the risk by following the safety rules appropriate to the job and by wearing the right gear.

This need not be anything elaborate. It all depends on what you are doing. If you are working with machinery, the 'right gear' may mean nothing more than buttoning your shirt sleeves and taking off your tie so they will not get tangled in the moving parts. If you are standing on a ladder for long periods, it may simply mean wearing comfortable 'sensible' shoes to reduce 'foot fatigue'. The right gear can even mean clothes which protect you from the weather, including warm gloves and sweaters, waterproofs or a sun hat. If you are too cold or too hot, your concentration will go, leaving you prone to errors. If you are extremely cold, you may actually injure yourself without knowing it.

But of course there are also times when only specialist equipment will give you the protection you need. The range available is detailed below.

Safety glasses/goggles
These will protect your eyes from dust, harmful liquids, and also from the flying debris produced by such jobs as chiselling masonry.

The cheapest are like ordinary spectacles, with impact-resistant plastic lenses. To stop things getting past them, more expensive types also have protective side screens, or curved main lenses. They are light and comfortable to wear, even for extended periods, but, like ordinary spectacles, have a tendency to slip if you are doing anything really active.

For greater protection, particularly against dust and liquids, safety goggles are better. To ease the problem of perspiration, the body of the goggles contains ventilation holes. Many can be worn over ordinary spectacles.

Protective masks/respirators
To stop you inhaling harmful dust, sprayed paint and so on you will need one of these.

The cheapest and most widely available consist of a simple replaceable cotton gauze pad mounted in an aluminium frame contoured to fit over the nose and mouth. For more demanding work, there are also moulded rubber and plastic masks (normally referred to as 'respirators') which accept more efficient replaceable cartridge filters. These filters are generally designed to filter specific substances, and it's important that you choose the right type. For example, some work against dust; others against the vapours produced by spray painting.

Heavy-duty gloves
If you want to avoid blisters, gardening gloves will probably do the trick. For some jobs though, you need far greater protection against abrasion on rough surfaces, cuts from sharp edges, and/or corrosive chemicals, and should wear purpose-made heavy duty gloves.

There are three common types. One is a chrome leather version, either with double thickness palm, or armoured with metal staples, to give good protection against cuts and abrasions.

Natural rubber gloves are the usual choice against corrosive chemicals. Unlike their domestic washing-up counterparts, these are not only proof against chemicals, but also have good resistance to tears, snags and abrasion. There are ordinary medium weight versions and also heavy gauntlets with extended cuffs to protect the forearms.

Then there are PVC gloves. Most are equivalent to medium weight gloves; some perform like chrome leather but give a degree of chemical resistance as a bonus.

Overalls
When tackling a dusty, dirty or potentially messy job, these simply stop your ordinary clothes getting in too much of a state.

They don't offer much more than splash protection though, particularly against oil, grease, paint and so on. If it's cold you will still have to wear old clothes underneath (if its warm, for many jobs you can just wear the overalls).

Work boots
If you have ever dropped a brick on your foot, or can imagine how it feels, the advantages of wearing a good strong pair of boots with steel-reinforced toe caps when carrying out general maintenance and building work are immediately obvious. They are not expensive, and since most have hard-wearing leather uppers and oil and alkali resistant rubber soles, they do represent very good value for money. Protective shoes made to the same standards are also available. The only thing they are not much good at is coping with mud and deep water, so, if you are digging trenches, wear your wellingtons.

Safety helmets
More commonly known as 'hard hats', these are really worth considering only if you are engaged in substantial demolition work, or intend to go clambering up professional type scaffolding. They can be hired. They are normally made from glass fibre or high density polythene and should have a fully adjustable harness allowing you to make them fit well enough not to fall off. The gap between harness and helmet also cushions any impact, so never wear a helmet without a properly adjusted harness. As an added safety precaution, make sure the helmet conforms to British Standards (BS5240 to be precise).

Ear protectors
These are designed to protect your ears from the damage that can result from prolonged exposure to high levels of noise.

Most are foam plastic filled plastic muffs mounted on a plastic covered sprung-steel headband. For the sake of general safety, when you are wearing the protectors you should still be able to hear moderately loud noises in your vicinity (so you can hear warning shouts for example) which is why they are preferable to ordinary ear plugs.

Knee pads
You will really appreciate these when tackling a job which means spending hours crawling about the floor. Some are simple cushioned rubber mats, others are strapped onto your knees. If you can't buy them, improvise with pads of cloth, or some old cushions.

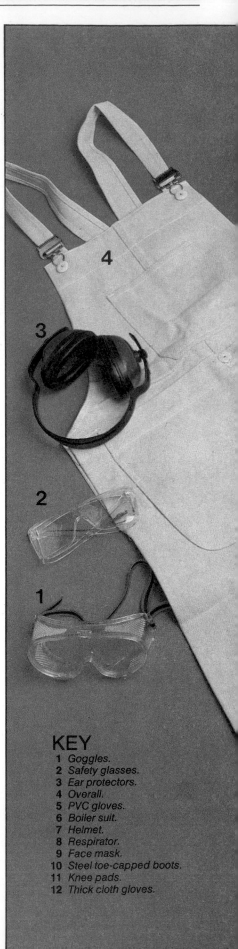

KEY
1 Goggles.
2 Safety glasses.
3 Ear protectors.
4 Overall.
5 PVC gloves.
6 Boiler suit.
7 Helmet.
8 Respirator.
9 Face mask.
10 Steel toe-capped boots.
11 Knee pads.
12 Thick cloth gloves.

MASONRY TOOLS

The term 'masonry' can mean anything from a brick or piece of stone to a complete wall, so it is important to be specific when choosing the right tool for a cutting or shaping job.

The hardness of the material to be worked is, perhaps, the most important consideration when choosing masonry tools. Some stone-cutting tools are designed for use only on relatively soft stones such as sandstone, and to use them on a hard stone like granite could cause damage to the tool or workpiece. Most 'brick' tools are intended for use on ordinary, relatively soft bricks and tend not to cope with hard engineering bricks, which have to be treated more like hard stone. Some are tempered just to cut brick and nothing else, whereas others may cut a variety of materials; it is important to check. When dealing with mixtures of materials, the general rule is to pick a tool that will handle the hardest element in the mixture.

Cutting and shaping tools

The commonest tools for cutting and shaping masonry of all types are cold chisels. There are several general-purpose and specific versions.

The **flat-cut cold chisel** is frequently used on masonry for splitting, chopping out, cutting chases and, occasionally, rough shaping. Like the rest of the cold chisel family, it is a hexagonal steel bar with a cutting tip formed at one end – in this case a straightforward wedge-shaped tip a little wider than the bar. The other end has chamfered edges to prevent chipping when struck with a heavy hammer.

The **cross-cut cold chisel** also known as the Cape chisel, has a cutting edge very much narrower than the bar from which it is made, allowing it to cut slots and grooves with great accuracy.

The **half-round cold chisel** is a variation of the cross-cut chisel and may also be known as the round-nosed chisel. It has a single cutting bevel ground into the tip to produce a semi-circular cutting edge. Used mainly for cutting grooves, it can produce rounded internal corners as well.

The **diamond-point cold chisel** is yet another variation of the cross-cut chisel and is sometimes known as the diamond-cut chisel. It has a diagonally-ground single cutting bevel. Use it for making V-shaped grooves and neatly angled internal corners.

The **plugging chisel** is otherwise known as the seaming chisel or seam drill. It has a curious slanting head, and is used for removing the mortar pointing in brickwork. Two types are available: one with a plain head and the other with a flute cut into the side to help clear waste material.

The **concrete point** is a fairly rare cold chisel that tapers to a point rather than a normal cutting edge and is used for shattering concrete or brickwork in areas previously outlined with a flat chisel.

The **dooking iron** is intended for cutting holes through brickwork and stone. This extra-long, flat-cut cold chisel has a narrow 'waist' let into the bar just behind the head to help prevent waste from jamming it in the masonry.

The **brick bolster** has a extra-wide, spade-shaped head and is designed to cut bricks cleanly in two. Most have a 100mm (4in) wide cutting edge, but other widths can be found, and care should be taken not to confuse these with other types of bolster chisel such as the mason's bolster (see below) or even the floorboard chisel. They are not tempered in the same way and may be damaged if used incorrectly.

The **mason's chisel** comes in two varieties. Narrow versions look like ordinary cold chisels, but the wider versions are more like brick bolsters. They are intended for general shaping and smoothing of stonework. The very narrow types (sometimes called edging-in chisels) are used to make a starting groove for a bolster when splitting large blocks and slabs.

The **mason's bolster** is a much tougher tool than the brick bolster, being designed for use on stone or concrete. Use it to split blocks and slabs, or to smooth off broad, flat surfaces.

Breaking tools

When it comes to breaking up solid masonry, heavier-duty tools are needed. The **pickaxe**, usually known simply as a pick, is the tool most people think of for breaking up masonry. It has a pointed tip for hacking into hard material and a chisel or spade tip for use on softer material such as ashphalt. In practice, though, you may find it easier merely to crack the masonry with a sledge hammer (see below) and then use the spade tip of the pickaxe to grub out the debris. Neither tool is worth buying, hire them instead.

The **club hammer** is a double-faced hammer used for breaking up masonry and for driving chisels and bolsters. It is also known as the lump hammer.

The **brick hammer** is designed specifically for driving cold chisels or bolsters when cutting bricks. It has a head that incorporates a chisel end for trimming the brick after it has been cut.

The **sledge hammer** is used for directing heavy blows at masonry in order to break it up. For light work, it should be allowed to fall under its own weight, but for more solid material, it can be swung like an axe.

Electric hammers and hydraulic breakers

If you have a lot of demolition work to do or have to break through thick concrete, it is possible to hire an electric hammer to do the job. This will come with a variety of points and chisels.

If no electricity supply is available, then you can hire a hydraulic breaker which is powered by a small petrol driven compressor.

Saws for masonry

For cutting blocks and slabs, or even masonry walls, a hand or power tool can help to achieve a neat finish.

Although the **masonry saw** resembles a normal woodworking saw, its extra-hard tungsten carbide teeth and friction-reducing PTFE coating are capable of slicing through brick, building blocks and most types of stone.

A large two-man version, which has a detachable handle at one end so that an assistant can help pull the saw through, will even cut through walls. Unfortunately, with the exception of small **chasing saws** used to cut electric cable channels in walls, using masonry saws is very hard work.

The **cut-off saw** is just another name for a heavy-duty circular saw which may be electrically or petrol driven. The key to cutting masonry, though, is not so much the power of the saw as the special cutting wheel – a rigid disc of tough abrasive that grinds its way through the stone. Various grades are available to match the material being cut.

Such saws are professional tools that can be hired if there is sufficient work to warrant it, or if a particularly deep cut is required. However, if you already own a circular saw, you should be able to buy a masonry cutting disc for it. Take care, though, to get the right grade for the job.

The **angle grinder** is usually used to cut and grind all types of metal – pipes, rods and sheets. However, fitted with the appropriate stone-cutting disc it can also be used to make cuts and shallow channels in brick, stone and concrete. It is extremely useful for cutting earthenware drainpipe sections.

Tools for drilling holes

When drilling holes in masonry of any type, it's vital to use a drill bit or other tool that is specially hardened to cope with the task. Never attempt to use ordinary twist drills.

Masonry drill bits allow you to drill into brick, stone, mortar and plaster with an ordinary hand or electric drill. Each has two small 'ears' at the end to help break up the waste, and is tipped with tungsten carbide.

Special long versions and extension sleeves are available for drilling right through walls.

Core drill bits are used for boring large-diameter holes – up to 50mm (2in). The bit is a hollow tube that cuts out a 'plug' of material much like a woodworking hole saw. A reduced shank allows it to be fitted into a normal drill chuck.

One thing that masonry drill bits cannot cope with is hard aggregate, such as that found in concrete. One solution is to break up the aggregate particles with a **jumping bit** as they are met. This is a hole boring tool that is driven in with a hammer and twisted by hand at the same time. Sometimes the bit is mounted in a special holder and is interchangeable with bits of different sizes. The **star drill** is a heavier-duty one-piece relation of the jumping bit, and has four tapered flutes to clear debris as the drill is hammered into the masonry.

Electric percussion drills look like normal electric drills and are used in the same way, but there is an important difference. While the drill bit rotates it is hammered in and out, offering the benefits of the twist drill and jumping bit in one.

If you intend buying such a tool, make sure the hammer action can be switched on and off as required and that it has a strong steadying handle. Also, check that it is powerful enough for your needs. This may be indicated by the wattage of the motor or by the chuck size; generally, the larger the chuck capacity, the more powerful the drill.

Make sure that any bits you use with the hammer action are designed for such use, since otherwise they may shatter.

Finally, remember that safety goggles or glasses are essential when using masonry tools.

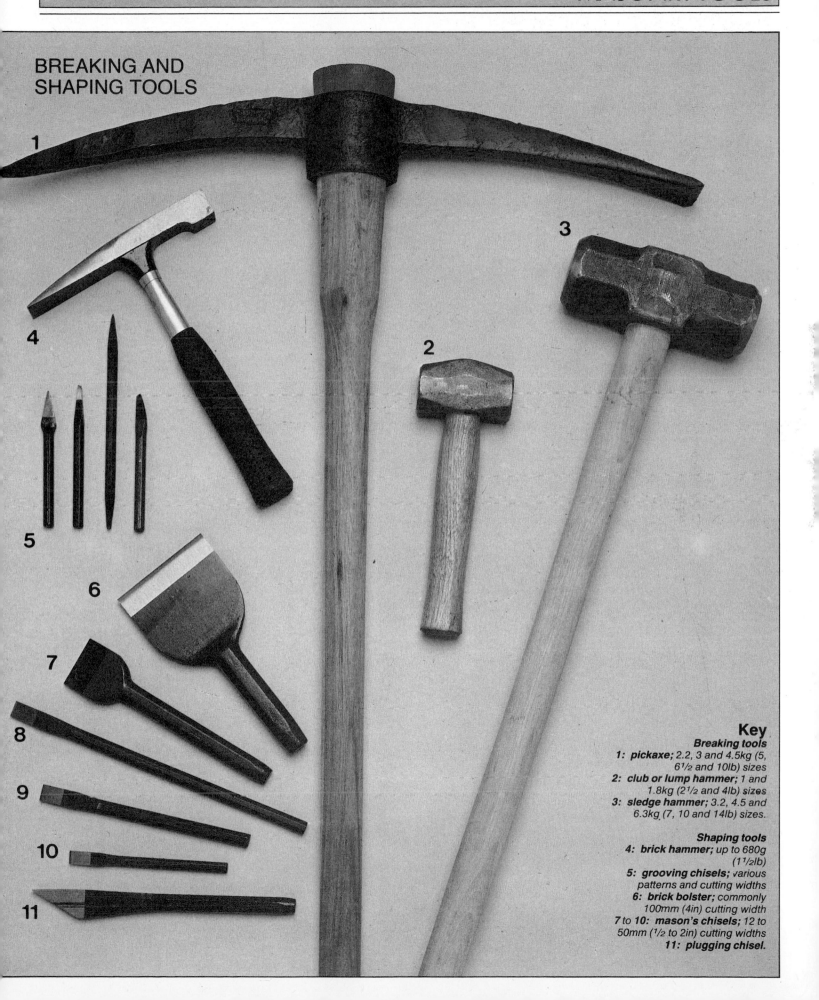

BREAKING AND
SHAPING TOOLS

1

4

3

2

5

6

7

8

9

10

11

Key
Breaking tools
1: pickaxe; 2.2, 3 and 4.5kg (5,
6½ and 10lb) sizes
2: club or lump hammer; 1 and
1.8kg (2½ and 4lb) sizes
3: sledge hammer; 3.2, 4.5 and
6.3kg (7, 10 and 14lb) sizes.

Shaping tools
4: brick hammer; up to 680g
(1½lb)
5: grooving chisels; various
patterns and cutting widths
6: brick bolster; commonly
100mm (4in) cutting width
7 to 10: mason's chisels; 12 to
50mm (½ to 2in) cutting widths
11: plugging chisel.

CUTTING AND DRILLING TOOLS

1: **masonry saw** with tungsten carbide-tipped teeth
2: **angle grinder** with masonry cutting discs
3: **interchangeable cutters** for jumping bit (4); diameters match screw gauges

4: **star drill;** diameters match masonry bolt sizes
5: **jumping bit** holder and cutter
6: **hammer-action drill** with depth stop, plus masonry drill bits
7: **circular saw** with masonry cutting disc.

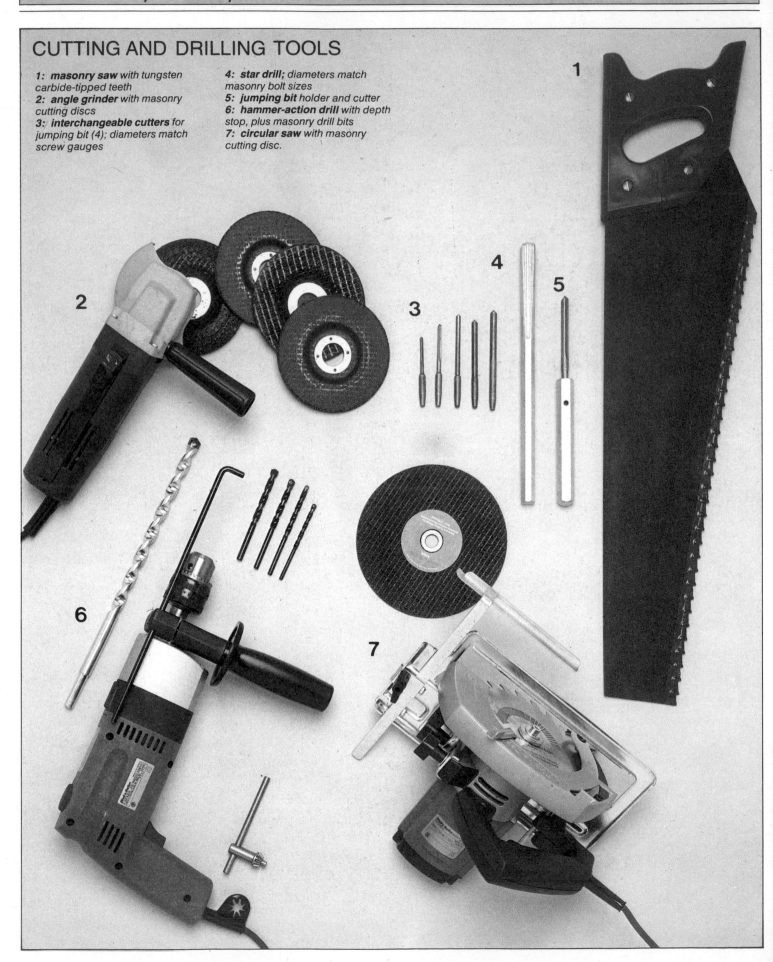

BUILDING RULES AND REGULATIONS

If you propose to carry out any work to improve, enlarge or modify a building, you must obey certain rules and regulations. These can be rather confusing, but here's an idea of what's involved.

In Britain there are two main sets of rules governing building work. These are the Town and Country Planning Acts and the Building Regulations. These rules are quite separate and cover different sorts of things. In Inner London the London Building Acts replace the Building Regulations, and Scotland and Northern Ireland have their own rules too.

The Planning Acts govern the way in which land is developed, stipulating what kind of building can be built on that particular spot. The Building Regulations, broadly speaking, lay down methods of construction and materials, and cover certain other internal works.

You may, therefore, need Building Regulations approval for certain work – knocking down an internal wall for instance – but not planning permission. Other work, such as putting up a garden fence, may need planning permission but not Building Regulations approval. In general, though, most building work will require approval under the Building Regulations.

Where to get help

The whole system of rules and regulations is very complicated and because of this there is often a temptation not to bother about getting permission. But you ignore the need for it at your own peril. For the local authority can issue an order compelling you to undo the work – and put the building back in its original state. If you refuse, it can impose a hefty fine for every day of your non-compliance. It even has the right to do the work itself and charge you for it, although it would only do that in extreme cases. But if a year has passed since you did the work, the authority has to get an injunction before acting.

So if any job you want to tackle does require planning consent or Building Regulations approval, you will, in many cases, require the help of an expert, for example an architect or surveyor. With many Building Regulations applications you'll need engineering calculations to show that the construction will be strong enough. Even architects get the help of an engineer for these calculations.

Moreover, some of the rules are rather vague. Often they are saying little more than that a construction or component must be fit for its purpose. That leaves a lot of leeway for local authorities to put their own interpretation on the Regulations.

To find out if the project you have in mind does require official approval, the simplest thing to do is to approach your local authority. The department that supervises the Building Regulations is called the Building Control Department in England and Wales, and the Building Authority in Scotland; in Inner London you should get in touch with the District Surveyor. To ask about planning you should get in touch with the Planning Department.

When contacting them, just say you have a query about the Regulations or the planning rules and you will be directed to the right office. Tell the officials what you would like to do and ask if permission is needed and if it is likely to be granted. Architects often take this way out and there's no reason why you shouldn't do the same. Most officials are only too anxious to be of assistance. Their main concern is to see that the rules – which after all were devised for your health, safety and comfort – are followed. And they will often give you valuable advice.

However, to save you – and them – unnecessary bother, it's worth knowing a little about what the rules and Regulations do cover, and what work is exempted.

Planning permission

The planning laws cover the way in which land is developed. In particular they cover: building work such as home extensions; change of use such as converting a garage to a living room or dividing a house into flats; and other visible exterior work such as altering the access to your property or erecting a garden wall. However, a certain amount of work is classified as 'permitted development' and can be carried out without planning permission provided it conforms to certain restrictions of size and location. But you will still need Building Regulations approval of course.

For example, you can build an extension without having to get planning permission as long as its volume is less than 70 cu m (2472 cu ft), or, alternatively, as long as it is less than 15 per cent of the volume of the original house (up to a maximum of 115 cu m/ 4060 cu ft), whichever is the greater. For terraced houses, the figures are 50 cu m (1766 cu ft) or 10 per cent. For this rule, the term 'original house' means the house as it was first built or as it stood on 1 July 1948. The volume is calculated from the external dimensions and includes the volume of the roof. However, you would need planning permission if the extension projects beyond the 'building line' (usually the front wall of the house) or above the roof line, if it obstructs the view of drivers on bends and corners, or if it needs new access from a class A or B road.

Despite these restrictions there is still enormous scope for building a garage or extension, or both, without bothering about planning permission. Moreover, with one of the most popular forms of home extension, the loft conversion, you are not adding significantly to the volume of the house, but simply making use of space that would otherwise be lying idle. Dormer windows do of course count as extra space, but their volume is unlikely to be very large.

One point to note is that the volume of permitted development is the total volume allowed. If your home already has an extension this must be taken into account. The volume of porches, sheds, greenhouses, dog kennels and other outbuildings, do not count towards your extension limit and you don't need planning permission to erect them as long as they conform to certain restrictions of size and location. See the drawing on this page for more details.

Other works which are exempt from planning permission are general repairs and maintenance which do not affect the external appearance of the building – repointing brickwork for example. Nor is permission needed for internal work, though you would need it if this involved 'change of use' of the property such as converting a house into flats, or a non-habitable room such as a garage into a habitable room or starting to run a business from your house. Converting flats back into a house, however, does not need permission.

How to apply

If the work you intend to do is not part of the permitted development then you'll need to apply for planning permission. It's worth going along to your local planning department to discuss the work with them, as they will be able to help you fill out the application forms and give you advice on the drawings and documents you'll need to provide. In most cases you will have to fill in four copies of the application form, and make detailed scale drawings. If you are getting a builder to do the work or you're employing an architect, then they can make the application on your behalf.

You can, instead, apply for 'outline planning permission'. This is useful where you are considering buying a house but want to know in advance whether you are likely to get permission for what you want to do. Only simple drawings are needed for this so you should be able to make them yourself. Of course, you would still need full permission before you started work.

The planning department will send you a decision notice after about five to eight weeks to let you know if the work has their approval or not. You may be given full permission or only be allowed to do the work subject to certain conditions such as using materials to match the rest of the house. If the application is rejected the authority should give you their reasons and you may then be able to alter your plans to make them more acceptable. If you consider their refusal to be unreasonable you can appeal to the Department of the Environment within six months of receiving the decision notice.

DO YOU NEED PLANNING PERMISSION?

There are three cases where you will always need planning permission regardless of any of the other rules. These are:
● *if the work will cause danger by obstructing the view of people using a public highway*
● *if the work requires new or wider access to a classified road, and*
● *if the work is restricted or prohibited by the original planning permission for your house.*

A garage (1) *built in a conservation area or, in other areas, built within 5m (16ft) of your house, is treated as a house extension. If it is more than 5m away it is treated as an outbuilding. See the relevant section for each case.*

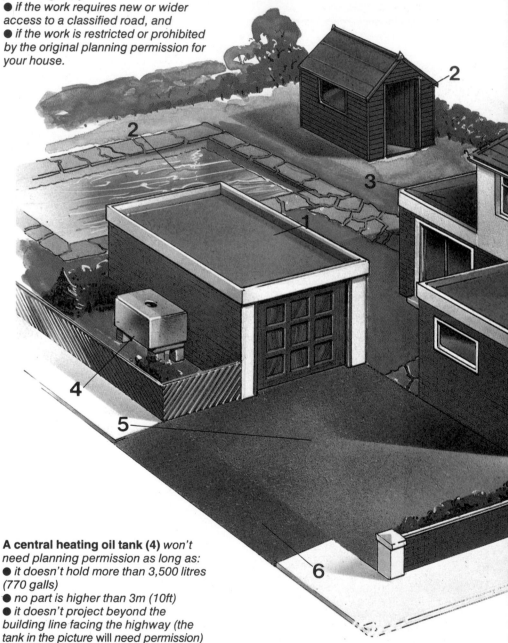

A central heating oil tank (4) *won't need planning permission as long as:*
● *it doesn't hold more than 3,500 litres (770 galls)*
● *no part is higher than 3m (10ft)*
● *it doesn't project beyond the building line facing the highway (the tank in the picture will need permission)*
Headstanding for a car (5) *does not need permission as long as it is constructed within your garden and the car is used mainly as a private vehicle.*

A new access (6) *will usually need permission unless it's to an unclassified road and is required for a development such as a garage, which does not itself need permission.*

An outbuilding or other structure (2)
– shed, rabbit hutch, swimming pool, etc – does not need permission if:
● *it won't be used for business*
● *no part projects beyond the building line of the house facing a highway*
● *it is not more than 4m (13ft) high if it has a ridged roof, or 3m (10ft) otherwise*
● *not more than half the original garden will be covered by building structures.*

An extension or loft conversion (3)
won't need permission as long as:
● *the extra volume is within the permitted allowance (see page 185)*
● *it doesn't project above the highest part of the house*
● *it doesn't project beyond the building line which faces a highway*
● *no part that comes within 2m (6ft 6in) of the boundary is more than 4m (13ft) above the ground*
● *the extension doesn't result in more than half the original garden being covered with buildings (these last two points don't apply to loft conversions)*
● *it is not a separate dwelling.*

Building Regulations
With the planning laws just described, the do-it-yourselfer is most interested in the exceptions to the rules, but this is not the case with the Building Regulations. They affect almost every aspect of house construction and cover both the materials and the methods used. In particular the Regulations are concerned with:
● materials used and site preparation
● structural stability
● fire resistance
● damp resistance
● thermal and sound insulation
● ventilation of rooms
● open space beyond windows
● room heights
● construction of stairways
● drainage and sewage disposal
● WCs and water sources
● chimneys, flues and fireplaces
● electrical installation (Scotland).

Repairs and replacements
General repairs and decorations are about the only things that are not covered by the Regulations. You can, therefore, decorate your house as you wish and lay down any floorcovering. You can also make minor repairs such as patching plaster, repointing brickwork, replacing a rotten floorboard, etc. Even where the regulations do make stipulations – about, say, gutters and downpipes – no one is likely to bother if you take down rusty old cast iron ones and replace them with new plastic ones of the same size.

But large-scale repairs may be classed as replacements and you would need approval for the work. For instance, if there were a few tiles missing from the roof you could replace them without anyone worrying about the size of battens to which the tiles are fixed or the fire resistance of the roofing felt below. But, if you're replacing the whole roof, the council will certainly insist that it is built to conform to the Regulations. The same is true of floors. However, in both these cases, it may well be that your council would skip the formality of a proper application, but you should still inform them of the work you intend to do.

Replacement windows are not normally a problem, except that in conservation areas and on listed buildings, they should not alter the external appearance of the house.

You do need permission *if you intend to change the use of the property. This includes starting to run a business, building an independent annex, converting a house into flats, etc.*

You don't need permission *for general repairs and internal alterations, nor to erect a TV aerial (though you would for a flagpole or radio mast), nor to demolish part of the house or any outbuilding. But remember your property may be covered by other conservation or listed building regulations. And you may need Building Regulations approval for some of these jobs.*

Porches (7) *don't need permission if*
● *the floor area is 2sq m (22sq ft) or less*
● *no part is higher than 3m (10ft)*
● *no part is less than 2m (6ft 6in) from a boundary.*

Fences (8) *need permission if they are more than 1m (3ft 3in) high along a boundary with a highway, or 2m (6ft 6in) elsewhere. Hedges are exempt.*

New look
You must get approval for any structural alterations or any work involving interference with the drains. One of the most obvious examples of this would be the taking down of a load-bearing wall. Here, the local authority must ensure that the work meets the requirements as the consequences could be disastrous. The same applies to the removal of chimney breasts. In fact in London, you need a

BUILDING REGULATIONS REQUIREMENTS

You must get Building Regulations approval for almost all building work you tackle, except for general repairs and re decoration. It is impossible to give all the requirements in detail, but here are some examples of the more common ones.

A loft room *must comply with all the fire and structural regulations. This will usually mean strengthening the floor and fitting fire doors.*

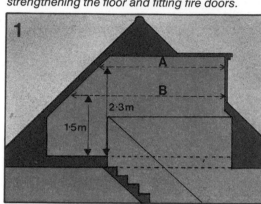

A habitable room (1 and 5) *must be at least 2.3m (7ft 6in) high, but in a loft this rule is relaxed slightly. It must be 2.3m high only over part of the floor area, not over the whole floor. That is, the floor area below A must be at least half the area below B.*

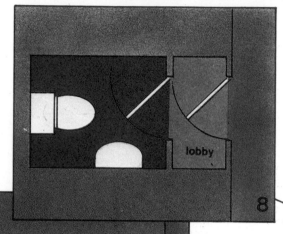

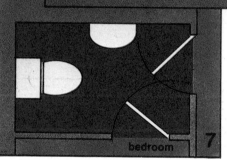

A room with a WC *must have two doors between it and a habitable room (this includes a kitchen), but the lobby could contain a basin or bath (8). A WC can lead off a bedroom (7), but if it is the only one in the house, it must have a second entrance which doesn't pass through the bedroom.*

Extensions (6) *that are habitable rooms must be at least 2.3m high – a kitchen or scullery can be less. The area of openable window must be at least ¹⁄₂₀ the floor area. The materials and the methods of construction used must obey all the rules, and these will be specially concerned with foundations, dpms and drainage.*

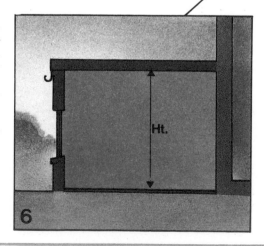

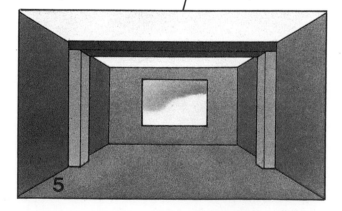

Knocking two rooms together (5) *will mean consulting a specialist to calculate the correct size of beam to comply with the rules.*

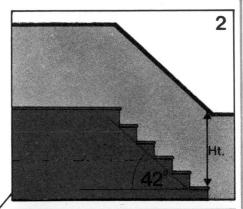

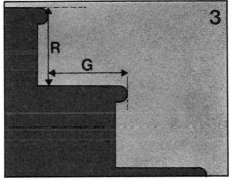

A new staircase (2) *must have at least 2m (6ft 7in) headroom, and a handrail at a height of 840 to 1000mm (33 to 40in). The maximum pitch allowed is 42°. Each 'going' (G) must be equal and so must each 'rise' (R). There are regulations governing their dimensions, but an off-the-shelf stairway will conform to these.*

With flue pipes (4), *the rules determine how near windows they can be and how high above the roof they should discharge. Balanced flue outlets must have a guard if they are below 2m (6ft 6in) from the ground.*

'chimney breast certificate' before you remove a chimney breast from a party wall, in case undue strain is put on the remaining chimney breast on the other side.

Fireplaces of course must be installed to conform with the Building Regulations, otherwise they could be dangerous. And if you move a WC or put in an extra one then you must also get approval as it involves alterations to the drains.

Extensions

When it comes to large-scale new work such as building an extension – whether it takes the form of extra living accommodation, a garage, a porch or a conservatory – then it must be constructed in line with the Regulations. (You may need planning permission, too.) Nowadays, of course, many porches and extensions are bought as prefabricated buildings. Provided they have been manufactured by a reputable company they will be all right but you must still get approval before you start. You must get special approval if the extension will cover a drain or sewer.

Loft conversions, too, must satisfy all the Regulations and this will mean providing the correct type of staircase, proper structural support for the floor, and the correct fire insulation. You will certainly need the help of an architect for this.

Getting approval

The first thing to do, as always, is to discuss your plans with the Building Control Officer. Take along a rough scale drawing if possible. He may suggest how the work should be constructed and what materials you should use. He will also explain how to make the application. The number of drawings and other details you have to provide depends on the type of job you're doing. You will usually have to submit an estimate of the cost of the work, and pay the relevant fee. The fee you have to pay depends on the cost of the work covered by the Building Regulations, and for small jobs there's no fee.

The local authority must approve or reject your plans within five weeks unless the time is extended by written agreement. Once you have approval, you must give 24 hours' notice before starting work and before commencing various stages of the work such as covering up foundations, damp courses, drains, etc. You may be given a set of postcards that you can send to the Building Control Officer to give the notification. If you don't give the notice, the local authority can require you to pull down or cut into the work so that it can be inspected.

In Inner London the situation is slightly different. You don't have to get approval but you must give the District Surveyor at least 48 hours' written notice before you start work.

You may also have to provide scale drawings of the work, and you'll have to pay a fee. The District Surveyor will then inspect the work at various stages to make sure the work complies with the Regulations.

Other rules and regulations

Apart from the Planning Acts and the Building Regulations there are certain other rules affecting the development of your property and the work you can do.

If you live in a conservation area then the permitted development is restricted and you can do nothing to alter the exterior appearance of your house without special planning permission. And if you live in a listed building you will need listed building consent for *any* alterations.

The original planning permission for the house may have included some restrictions on the type of work you can do. The original deeds to the property may contain a restrictive covenant preventing you doing certain work even though you may have planning permission; this is particularly common on large estates. If you have a mortgage you should consult the lender as well.

There are certain other regulations concerning the work you can do. For instance, water authorities have their own rules. There is no obligation in law for you to get permission from them for the work you have in mind, but anything you do must be in accordance with their rules and they can, if they wish, inspect the work and demand alterations. You can replace a tap or install a shower without any worries, but if you propose ambitious new plumbing schemes you should discuss your plans with the authority – their address will be on your water rate demand. They will have firm views on the size of tanks and cisterns, and will want to ensure there is no risk of contamination of the water supply.

In Scotland, electrical installation work is governed by the Building Authority and the regulations must be followed. But in England and Wales there is no law requiring you to get permission from anyone. However, for your own safety, you should ensure that all wiring jobs are carried out according to the standards laid down by the Institute of Electrical Engineers (IEE). In fact, you may only get approval for an extension, say, on condition that all wiring is done in accordance with these rules. And, of course, the electricity board can refuse to supply houses where they feel the wiring has not been done properly.

Finally, there are tree preservation orders that must be obeyed, and restrictions on advertising material that can be displayed. It's hardly likely, though, that anyone will bother you if you want to stick a notice advertising the local jumble sale in your window.

PART 2

HOME DECORATING

PAPERHANGING

Modern wallcoverings and adhesives have made paperhanging a far less difficult job than it used to be, but every home has its awkward corners and you need to know how to approach these if you're going to get good results.
The techniques are the same whatever type of wallpaper you're hanging – even if you're tackling a ceiling.

PAPERING WALLS
the basics

No other wall covering can quite so dramatically alter the look and feeling of a room as wallpaper. Correctly hung paper makes the walls sharp and fresh, and to achieve this finish there are important things to know. What do you do if the walls are out of true? Where's the best place to start? How do you prevent bubbles and creases? The answers are here.

Wallpapering isn't so much an art, it's more a matter of attention to detail. And perhaps the first mistake that's made by many people is expecting too much of their walls. Rarely are walls perfectly flat, perfectly vertical and at right angles to each other. So the first and most crucial part of hanging wallpaper is to prepare the walls properly. Obviously you can't change their basic character — if they're not entirely flat or vertical, you're stuck with them — but you can make sure that the surface is suitably prepared so that the new paper will stick.

This means that any old wallpaper really should come off before you do anything else. Papering on top of old wall coverings won't *always* lead to disaster, but it will quite often simply because the new adhesive will tend to loosen the old. The result will be bubbles at best and peeling at worst.

Adhesives

Always use the correct adhesive for the wallcovering and follow the manufacturers instructions for mixing. Using the wrong paste can result in the paper not sticking, mould growth or discoloration of the paper.

A cellulose-based adhesive is used for all standard wallcoverings. There are two types, ordinary and heavy-duty which relates to the weight of the paper being hung. Heavy-duty pastes are for heavyweight wallcoverings. Certain brands of paste are suitable for all types of wallcoverings — less water being used for mixing when hanging heavy papers.

Since vinyls and washable wallcoverings are impervious, mould could attack the paste unless it contains a fungicide. Fungicidal paste is also needed if the wall has previously been treated against mould or if there is any sign of damp.

Some wallcoverings (like polyethylene foam, some hessians and foils) require a specially thick adhesive which is pasted onto the wall. Follow manufacturers' instructions.

Ready-pasted papers are exactly that and require no extra adhesive — although it's useful to have a tube of latex glue handy for finishing off corners and joints which mightn't

have stuck. (The same applies to all washable wallpapers).

Glue *size* (a watered down adhesive) is brushed over the walls before papering to seal them and prevent the paste from soaking in to the wall. It also ensures all-over adhesion and makes sliding the paper into place easier.

Although size can be bought, most wallpaper pastes will make size when mixed with the amount of water stated in the instructions.

If you buy a proprietary size and the wallcovering you are using needs an adhesive containing fungicide, make sure that the size you buy also contains a

fungicide. Use an old brush to apply and a damp cloth to clean off any that runs on to paintwork. It can be difficult to remove after it has dried. Sizing can be done several days or an hour before.

Where to begin

The traditional rule is to start next to the window and work away from it, but that is really a hangover from the days when paper was overlapped and shadows showed up joins. Today, papers butt up, so light isn't the problem. But as inaccuracies can occur with slight loss of pattern, you have to be able to make this as inconspicuous as possible. In an average room, the corner nearest the door is the best starting point. Any loss of pattern will then end up behind you as you enter the room. In a room with a chimney breast, hang the first drop in the centre and work outwards from both sides of the drop

Problem areas in a house (recesses, arches, stairwells) are dealt with later in this chapter.

Measuring and cutting

Measure the height of the wall you want to paper using a steel tape measure and cut a piece of paper from the roll to this length, allowing an extra 50mm (2in) top and bottom for trimming. This allowance is needed for pattern matching, and to ensure a neat finish at skirting board and ceiling.

Lay the first drop — that's the name given to each length of paper — pattern side up on the table and unroll the paper from which the

second drop is to be cut next to it. Move this along until the patterns match, then cut the second drop using the other end of the first as a guide. Subsequent lengths of paper are cut in exactly the same way, with each matching the drop that preceded it.

Remember some wallpapers have patterns that are a straight match across the width, while others have what is called a drop pattern that rises as it extends across the width. With drop match papers the second length will begin half a pattern repeat further along the roll. Length 3 will match length 1, length 4 will match length 2 and so on.

For things to run smoothly, you should establish a work routine when paper hanging. Cut all the wall drops first (so you only have to measure once) and cut bits for papering above windows and doors as you come to them. If you paste say 3 drops, the first will have had its required soaking time

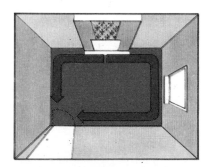
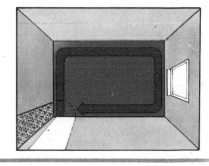
HOW TO CUT AND PASTE

1 Mark the pasting table with lines at 150mm (6in) and 300mm (1ft) intervals. Measure wall drop and use guidelines to cut your first length.

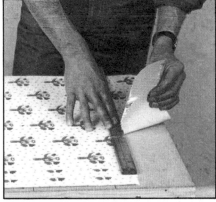

2 Use the first length as a guide for the other drops, matching the pattern carefully. Tear off the waste against a wooden rule.

3 Lay all the drops pattern down, overhanging the far edge of the table. Pull the first drop to the near edge and paste it from centre to edges.

4 Fold pasted end, paste the rest and fold in. Now fold up the whole drop and leave it to soak. The top of the longer fold always goes to the top of the wall.

PAPER HANGING TECHNIQUES

1 Place chosen pattern on ceiling line with waste above. Align side edge with vertical and turn waste onto adjacent wall. Brush up to ceiling first, then corners and edges, and then down. Open out short fold last.

2 Mark cutting line for waste at ceiling and skirting board with a pencil — ends of scissors won't fit creases neatly and can give a thick line which causes you to cut the paper inaccurately and will give an uneven look at ceiling and skirting.

3 To cut waste, pull short length of paper away from wall so pencil line catches the light. Cut using full length of blades — hurried, short cuts can make the edges jagged. Brush paper back on wall so that it is perfectly flat.

4 Reduce waste on adjacent wall to 6mm (¼in) to lessen bulk when paper overlaps from other direction.

5 Continue along wall matching the pattern horizontally. Press drop onto wall so long edges butt.

6 As each drop is hung, brush up first, then to edges and finally down to remove any trapped air.

7 To turn a corner, measure between hung paper and corner at the top, middle and bottom of wall. Add 6mm (¼in) to widest width, then use this measurement to cut the pasted and folded drop into two. Set aside offcut for new wall.

8 Hang drop to complete wall, brushing the waste round the corner. Find the new vertical and mark the line the width of offcut from the corner. Check this measurement at the top, middle and bottom of wall. If the same, hang offcut.

9 If corner is out of true, offcut and wall measurements will differ. To disguise pattern loss, hang the offcut so waste laps onto completed wall. Brush into corner, run pencil down crease line and cut waste.

(with medium weight paper) by the time the third is pasted and folded and is ready to be hung. With heavy papers paste, fold and soak 6 drops at a time as extra soaking time is needed.

Avoiding bubbles

The purpose behind soaking time (apart from making paper supple enough to handle) is to give it time to expand to its natural limit. On the width this can be 6mm-12mm (¼in-½in) and the average wall-size drop will gain 24mm (1in) on the length – this explains why you have more to cut as waste than you started with.

If you haven't given paper the time it needs, it will expand on the walls – but its spread will be contained by adjoining drops and so you get bubbles in the central part.

Soak medium weight papers for 3-4 minutes, heavy weights for about 10. Ready-pasted papers don't need too long a soaking, but to ensure they get wet all over, roll drops loosely and press into water till they are completely covered.

Pasting and soaking

Position the paper with its top edge at the right-hand end of the table (or at the other end if you're left handed). Paste it carefully to ensure that all parts, the edges especially, are well covered. Work from the centre outwards in herring-bone style using the width of the brush to cover the drop in sweeps, first to the nearest edge, then the other – excess paste here will go onto second drop, not the table. Cover two-thirds of the drop, then fold the top edge in so paste is to paste. Move the drop along the table and paste the remainder, folding bottom edge in paste to paste. Because the first folded part is longer than the other, this will remind you which is the

top. Fold the drop up and put aside to soak while you paste the others.

This technique will give you a manageable parcel of paper to hang no matter what length the drop – but always remember to make the first fold longer – this is the one offered to the ceiling line. If in doubt mark the top edge lightly with a pencil cross.

Hanging pasted paper

Wallpaper must be hung absolutely vertical if it is to look right, so always work to a vertical line (see *Ready Reference*).

Position your step ladder as close as possible to where you want to work, and climb it with the first length of paper under or over your arm. Open out the long fold and offer the top edge up, placing the pattern as you want it at the ceiling with waste above. Align the side edge of the drop with your vertical guide line, allowing the other side edge to turn onto the adjacent wall if starting at a corner. Smooth the paper onto the wall with the paperhanging brush, using the bristle ends to form a crease between wall and ceiling, and at corners. When brushing paper into place, always work up first then to the join, then to the side edge, then down. This will remove trapped air.

As soon as the paper is holding in place, work down the wall, brushing the rest of the drop in position, opening out the bottom fold when you reach it. Again use the bristle ends to form a good crease where paper meets the skirting board.

The next step is to trim off the waste paper at the top and bottom. Run a lead pencil along the crease between the ceiling or skirting and the wall — the blades or points of scissors wil make a line that's too thick for accurate cutting. Gently peel paper away from the wall and cut carefully along the line with your scissors. Finally brush the paper back in place.

Hanging the second drop is done as the

Ready Reference

HANGING TO A VERTICAL

For perfect results wallcoverings must be hung absolutely vertical. You can't trust the corners of rooms to be perfectly true so you must
● mark a vertical line on the wall against which the first length can be aligned
● mark a similar line on the next wall every time you turn a corner

Mark line on first wall 25mm (1in) less than a roll's width from the corner, using a plumb bob and line
● hold the line at the top of the wall and allow the bob to come to rest just above skirting board level
● mark the string's position at three points on the wall with a pencil
● join up the marks using a long straight timber batten as a ruler

PAPERHANGING TOOLS

Plumb bob and line: for establishing a true vertical. Any small weight attached to a string will do.
Pasting brush: it's thicker than a paint brush and about 150mm (6in) wide. A paint brush will do as a substitute.
Paperhanger's scissors: for trimming on or off the wall. Long-bladed household scissors can be used instead.
Paperhanging brush: for smoothing paper onto walls and into angles. Use a sponge on washable and vinyl papers.
Seam roller: for ensuring good adhesion along seams (not used with embossed papers). A cloth-wrapped finger does almost as well.
Pasting table: for pasting lengths prior to hanging, it's slightly wider than a standard roll width. Any table over about 1.8 metres (6ft) long can be used.

Estimator

Most wallpaper is sold in rolls 10.05m (11yds) long and 530mm (21in) wide. Calculate rolls needed by measuring perimeter of the room and height from skirting board to ceiling.

WALLS	Distance around the room (doors and windows included)										
Height from skirting	10m 33'	11m 36'	12m 39'	13m 43'	14m 46'	15m 49'	16m 52'	17m 56'	18m 59'	19m 62'	20m 66'
2.15–2.30m (7'–7'6")	5	5	5	6	6	7	7	8	8	9	9
2.30–2.45m (7'6"–8')	5	5	6	6	7	7	8	8	9	9	10
2.45–2.60m (8'–8'6")	5	6	6	7	7	8	9	9	10	10	11

The number of rolls needed can be greatly affected by the frequency of pattern repeat. With a large pattern repeat, buy an extra roll.

first except that you have to butt it up against the edge of the first length, matching the pattern across the two. The secret here is not to try and do it all in one go. Get the paper onto the wall at the right place at the ceiling join but just a little way away from the first length. Now press against the paper with the palms of your hands and slide it into place. Using well-soaked paper on a wall that's been sized makes this easy, but if you're using a thin wallpaper press gently as it could tear. Butt the paper up after pattern matching and brush into place.

When trimming waste from drops other than the first, cut from where the lengths butt to ensure even ceiling and skirting lines.

Hanging ready-pasted wallpaper
With these you won't need pasting table, bucket and pasting brush but you will need a special light plastic trough made for the purpose. Put it below where the first drop is to be hung and fill with water – covering the floor with layers of newspaper will soak up accidental spillages. Don't try to lift the trough; slide it along the floor as the work progresses.

Cut each drop so patterns are matching, then roll the first one loosely from the bottom up with the pattern inside. Place it in the trough and press it down so water can reach all the parts covered with paste. Leave for the required soaking time (check manufacturers' instructions but, it's usually between 30 seconds and 2 minutes), then pick the drop up by the two top corners and take it to the ceiling line. Press onto the wall using an absorbent sponge to mop up and push out air bubbles. Press firmly on the edges with the sponge or a seam roller, then trim waste.

COPING WITH WALL FITTINGS ... AND CREASES

Few walls present a perfectly clear surface for paperhanging. Almost all will contain such small obstacles as light switches and power points, while some may carry wall-mounted fittings such as curtain tracks and adjustable shelving. Small obstacles can be papered round with some careful trimming, but larger obstacles are best taken down from the wall and replaced when you have finished decorating. That way you will get a really professional finish.

Creases can also spoil the look of your work. If they occur, take steps to remove them before the paste dries. Here's how.

1 To cut round light switches, mark centre of plate, insert scissor tips and cut out towards plate corners.

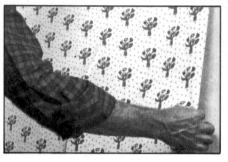

1 Creases are a common fault where the wall is out of true or if you haven't brushed the paper out properly.

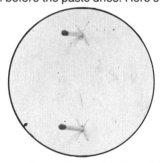

1 Use matchsticks, pushed head out into wall plugs, to show where wall fittings have been taken down.

2 Crease tongues of paper against edges of plate, lift away from wall, trim along line and brush back into place.

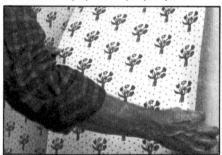

2 To remove the crease, peel the paper from the wall to a point above the crease – to the ceiling if necessary.

2 Brush paper firmly over match heads so they pierce it. With hanging complete remove matches and replace fittings.

3 With washable and vinyl papers push a strip of rigid plastic against plate edges and trim with a sharp knife.

3 Brush the paper back into position – across towards the butt join, then to the other edge and down to the bottom.

PAPERING A STAIRWELL

Even if the walls are flat, papering a stairwell presents problems. The awkward angles, height of the walls and long lengths of wallcovering make for special difficulties of access and handling, but you'll find that these can be overcome.

Hanging wallpaper in an ordinary room is not too difficult. But with stairwells there are awkward corners and long lengths to cope with.

Gaining access

The chief problem in wallpapering a stairwell is that of gaining access to the walls you are papering. This is because of the height of the walls and the awkward angles involved.

It is essential to have a safe working platform and to set this up in the right way to suit the layout of the stairwell and the way the stairs rise. You can hire special platforms for decorating the stair/hall area, or use the components of a tower platform. Alternatively, you can use ladders and steps linked with scaffold boards (see page 143).

A particularly useful item of equipment is a hop-up, a small platform which you can make yourself (see *Ready Reference*).

Preparation

Before you start decorating, remove the handrail and any other wall-mounted obstacles so you can get at the wall. Then prepare the walls properly so the new wallcovering will stick. Always remove any old wallcovering; some will peel off, although with most types you will have to soak and scrape them off.

Once the walls are stripped, you can work out where to begin hanging. You should position the longest drop of wallcovering first, and to establish where this will be, measure the height of each wall in the stairwell. (You will need a long tape and someone to help you when you are measuring the wall in a stairwell.) Then, starting as close as possible to this point but about 50mm away from any obstacles – such as a door or window opening – take a roll of the wallcovering you are going to use and move it along the wall to estimate where succeeding widths will fall. If, according to your calculations, there will be a join between lengths within 50mm of an external corner (at another window opening, for example), change your starting point slightly and measure again so you avoid this. Then mark off where this first drop will be hung.

When you have established where you will hang the first drop, use a plumbline to work out a true vertical at this point. Coat the line with chalk, pin it to the top of the wall and allow it to hang. Then, at the skirting, hold the plumb bob with one hand, pluck the string with the other and let it snap back against the wall to leave a vertical chalk line on the wall. Alternatively, instead of coating the plumb line with chalk, fix it in place, allowing it to hang down, and then place a long straight timber batten so the edge is exactly against the line, and use the batten as your guide to draw a true vertical line down the wall. Remember to plumb a new line every time you turn a corner.

Hanging the wallcovering

The decorating sequence is the same as for any other area – see the techniques already covered. If the wall is bare plaster, start by applying size to the wall to prevent the paste soaking in. Then measure and cut the wallcovering to length, remembering to allow for the angle of the skirting board if applicable, paste it and allow it to soak. If you are using a ready-pasted wallcovering, place your water trough in the hall or on the landing, not on the stairs where you are likely to knock it over. Wallcoverings hung by the

PREPARATION

1 To prepare the wall surface you will have to remove the existing wallcovering. In this case it is vinyl which is easy to remove; it is simply peeled off.

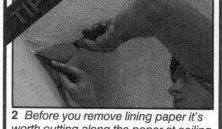

2 Before you remove lining paper it's worth cutting along the paper at ceiling level or you may find you tear off the ceiling paper with the lining paper.

3 When working at a high level make sure that the ladders and scaffold boards you are working from are firmly secured and well supported to ensure safety.

4 To remove paper from the wall when preparing to hang a new wallcovering, soak it thoroughly with a damp sponge. Leave for a while, then soak again.

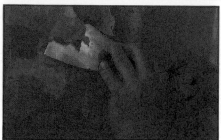

5 Use a scraper to take the paper off the wall and scrape off old flaking paint at the same time. Wash the wall down to remove any remaining bits.

6 When you have established where you will hang the first length, use a plumbline to make sure you get a true vertical and mark a pencil line on the wall.

HANGING THE WALLCOVERING

1 Place the first drop up against the wall, using the line you have drawn as a guideline to get it straight. Get someone to help you hold the long drop.

2 Use a soft-bristled wallpaper-hanging brush to smooth the covering into place. Leave an overlap at the top and bottom for trimming when the drop is fixed.

3 Hang subsequent lengths of wallcovering so they butt join and so the pattern matches. Trim each piece; a scraper will help as a guide.

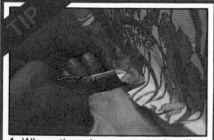

4 Where there is a curve cut into the overlap so the paper will fit round the curve easily without puckering.

5 You can then trim off the overlap in the same way as at a door surround, using a scraper to help guide the knife as you trim along the bottom edge.

6 For convenient paper hanging you will have to remove a wall handrail. This can be replaced when the wallcovering is fixed and the adhesive completely dry.

SAFE WORKING PLATFORMS

1 stairs with quarter landing

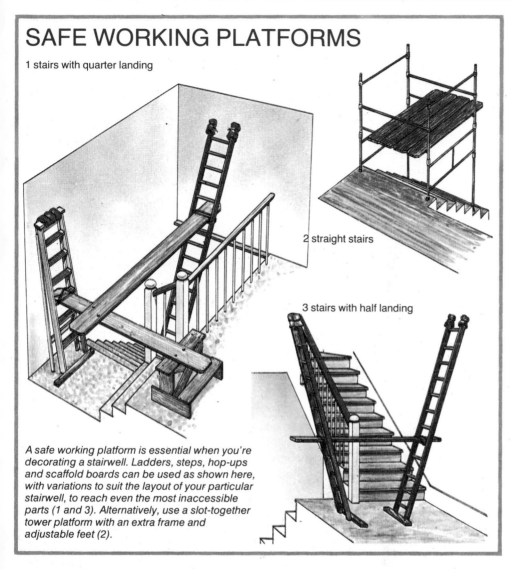

2 straight stairs

3 stairs with half landing

A safe working platform is essential when you're decorating a stairwell. Ladders, steps, hop-ups and scaffold boards can be used as shown here, with variations to suit the layout of your particular stairwell, to reach even the most inaccessible parts (1 and 3). Alternatively, use a slot-together tower platform with an extra frame and adjustable feet (2).

Ready Reference

CARRYING LONG LENGTHS

To make it easier to carry a long length of wallcovering, fold it in concertinas and then drape it over your arm.

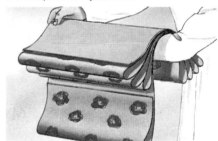

BEWARE ANGLED SKIRTING

When measuring up remember that lengths meeting the stairs skirting must be measured along their longer edge, not their shorter one.

EQUAL SOAKING TIME

To minimise the risk of stretching
● allow the same amount of soaking time between pasting and hanging on each length
● if you do find the paper has stretched, match the pattern as best you can at eye level, where bad matching would be most noticeable.

YOU'LL NEED HELP

It's best not to try hanging long lengths of paper by yourself; the weight of the paper may cause it to stretch or tear. Get someone to take the weight and unfold the paper as you work down the wall.

TIP: TRIM NARROW PIECES DRY

Where long narrow strips are needed, measure up and trim the drop approximately to size before pasting. This is easier to handle than having large waste pieces covered in paste flapping around.

OVERLAPS WITH VINYL

Vinyl will not stick to vinyl where you are using ordinary paste. If an overlap is unavoidable use a special vinyl overlap adhesive.

---

paste-the-wall technique are particularly easy to hang in stairwells, because you are handling lengths of dry wallcovering.

Because the lengths of paper for the wall at the side of the stairs will all be of a different size – caused by the rise of the stairs – it is better to cut and paste one length at a time, unlike straightforward rooms where you can cut and paste several lengths at a time.

Hang the first and longest length of wallpaper, using the vertical line you have marked on the wall as a guideline to get it straight. Then work round the stairwell from this length, making sure the pattern matches as you go along.

If your staircase is curved at the bottom the wallcovering is likely to pucker as it fits around the curve. To prevent this, you can snip into the overlap at the foot of the wall at intervals so the paper is more flexible in its fit.

Coping with long drops

A problem unique to stairwells is the length of paper you are handling – often as much as

4.5m (15ft) long. Apply paste liberally so it is less likely to dry out before you have fixed the bottom of the length. (It's worth keeping a small amount of adhesive ready to apply where the adhesive has dried out before the wallcovering is fixed.) Fold the pasted paper in concertinas (see *Ready Reference*) and then gather up the folds and drape the folded-up length over your arm to carry it.

Because the weight of the paper may cause it to stretch or tear as you are hanging it, try to get someone to help you take the weight. Where there is no one available to help, you will have to sit on your scaffold board, or other form of support, and allow the bottom of the drop to unfold gently to skirting board level. Then you can take the top up to the ceiling and start brushing it into the correct place.

Remember too, that when you are trimming along the bottom of a length of wallcovering that meets the staircase skirting, you will be trimming at an angle rather than horizontally as at the foot of a wall in a room.

PAPERING AWKWARD AREAS

The techniques for papering round tricky areas like corners and reveals are quite basic. But care and patience is required if you are going to get really professional results from your paperhanging.

Although the major part of wallpapering, hanging straight lengths is fairly quick and straightforward. The tricky areas – corners, doorways and so on – which call for careful measuring, cutting and pattern matching are the bits that slow the job down. There's no worse eye-sore than a lop-sided pattern at a corner; but if you use the right techniques you can avoid this problem.

You have to accept in advance that the continuity of a pattern will be lost in corners and similar places; even a professional decorator can't avoid this. However, he has the ability to match the pattern as closely as possible so that the discontinuity is not noticeable, and this is what you have to emulate.

Things would, of course, be a lot simpler if all corners were perfectly square, but this is rarely the case. When you wallpaper a room for the first time you are likely to discover that all those angles that appeared to be true are anything but.

You can, however, help to overcome the problem of careful pattern matching at corners by choosing a paper with the right design (see *Ready Reference*). The most difficult of the lot to hang are those with a regular small and simple repeat motif. The loss of pattern continuity will be easy to spot if even slight errors are made. The same is often true of large, repeat designs. With either of these types, a lot more time will be involved and it could well take a couple of hours to hang a few strips around a single window reveal.

Sloping ceiling lines are another problem area and certain patterns will show it up clearly. You can understand the nuisance of a sloping ceiling by imagining a pattern with, say, regular rows of horizontal roses. Although the first length on the wall may be hung correctly to leave a neat row of roses along the ceiling line the trouble is that as subsequent lengths are hung and the pattern is matched, you will see less and less of that top row of roses as the ceiling slopes down. And, conversely, if the ceiling line slopes upwards, you will start to see a new row of roses appearing above. So, despite the fact that each length has been hung

vertically, the sloping ceiling will make the job look thoroughly unsightly.

Internal and external corners

Before you begin papering round a corner, you must hang the last full length before the corner. Your corner measurement will be done from one edge of this length. You can use a steel tape or boxwood rule to measure the gap to the corner (see *Ready Reference*) and then cut the piece required to fill it, plus a margin which is carried round onto the new wall. Since it's likely that the walls will be out of square and that the margin taken round the corner will not be exactly equal all the way down, it's obvious you would have a terrible job hanging the matching offcut strip to give a neat butt join.

For this reason you must hang the matching offcut which goes on the 'new' wall to a true vertical and then brush it over the margin you've turned onto this wall. You should aim to match the pattern at the corner as closely as possible. Since the paper overlaps, the match will not be perfect, but this is unavoidable and will not, in any case be noticeable as the overlap is tucked into or round the corner out of sight (see *Ready Reference*).

Papering round window reveals

Unless you intend to paper just one or two walls in a room you will eventually have to cope with papering round a window. Pattern matching is the problem here, but you should find cutting the paper to fit above and

below a window is not too difficult provided you work in a logical order (see box opposite). But you may have to be prepared for lots of scissor work when you cut out strips of paper for the two sides and top of the reveal to ensure the pattern matches the paper on the facing wall. (It's worth getting into the habit of marking some sort of code on the back of each piece of paper before it's cut up so you will be able to find matching pieces quickly.)

Make sure that you don't end up with a seam on the edge of the reveal, where it will be exposed to knocks and liable to lift. Before you begin work on the window wall, take a roll of wallcovering and estimate how many widths will fit between the window and the nearest corner. If it looks as though you will be left with a join within about 25mm (1in) of the window opening you should alter your starting point slightly so that, when you come to the window, the seam will have moved away from the edge of the reveal.

Where the lengths of paper are positioned on the window wall obviously depends on the position of the window, its size and the width of the wallpaper. But the ideal situation occurs when the last full length before you reach the window leaves a width of wall, plus window reveal, that measures just less than the width of the wallpaper. You can then hang the next length so its upper part goes on the wall above the window, the lower part on the wall below it and (after making two scissor cuts) turn the middle part to cover the side of the window reveal. The edge of

PAPERING ROUND A WINDOW

Top: Fill the narrow gap left on the underside of the reveal with a small offcut.
Above: The papering sequence; piece 7 fills the gap left on the reveal by piece 6.

Ready Reference

TIP: CHOOSE PATTERNS CAREFULLY
In rooms full of awkward corners and recesses, pick a paper with a random, busy design which the eye doesn't try to follow. This will help disguise the fact that a corner is out of square, or a ceiling is sloping.

MEASURING AT CORNERS
When you are measuring for the width of paper required to fill a corner gap:
● measure from the last full fixed length to the corner at the top, middle and bottom of the gap
● take the largest measurement; for an internal corner add 12mm (½in) and for an external corner 25mm (1in) to give you the width to cut from the next length
● the offcut left is used on the 'new wall' and overlaps the 12mm (½in) or 25mm (1in) strip turned round the corner.

TIP: TURN NARROW STRIPS
Never try to take a lot of paper round a corner. If you do, you will end up with it badly creased into the angle of the corner, and the part that is taken onto the 'new wall' will be completely askew.

AVOID OBVIOUS JOINS
On an external corner the overlap of the edges of the two strips of paper which cover the corner should be positioned where they will be least obvious (eg, on a chimney breast it is better to make the overlap on the side wall rather than have it on the wall facing into the room).

PAPERING ROUND A DOORWAY
Ideally, you'll use the minimum of paper if you centre a full-width strip of paper over the door opening. Where the door is close to a corner, fit a narrow strip above the doorway. Pattern discontinuity will be least noticed in between two full strips.

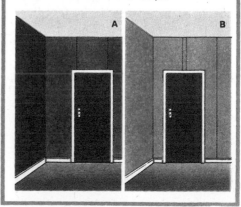

the middle part can then be creased and trimmed so it fits neatly up against the window frame.

Go on to hang short lengths of wallpaper above the window, cutting them so their lower parts can be taken on to the underside of the top window reveal, and again trim them so they fit neatly up against the window frame. When you reach a point where the reveal on the opposite side of the window is less than the width of the wallpaper away from the last edge hung, you should stop and repeat the papering process below the window between the sill and skirting board, trimming as you go.

You can then hang the next full length in the same way as the one you hung on the first side of the window. You should, first, however, hang a plumbline over the pieces in place above the top and bottom of the window then hang the full length to the plumb-line, trimming any slight overlap on the new length if necessary. (By doing this, you will ensure that the lengths to be hung on the rest of the wall will be truly vertical.)

Often, however, the position of the last full length at the window will fall so that the paper does not cover the reveal at the side of the window, and in this case you will have to cut matching strips to fill the gap. Similarly, you

will have to cut strips to fill the gaps on the underside of the reveal at the top of the window.

Dormer windows
In attics and loft rooms there will be sloping ceilings and dormer windows with which you will have to contend. If you decide to paper rather than paint the sloping ceiling, then you treat it in the same way as you would a vertical wall; there are no unusual problems involved, other than the peculiar working angle. Remember, too, that if you choose the wrong type of paper the irregular pattern-matching could give unfortunate results.

Paper the wall alongside the window and then round the window itself, moving on to the wall below the other side of the sloping ceiling (see step-by-step photographs). Finally, you can paper the dormer cheeks.

Chimney breasts and fireplace surrounds
Special rules apply to chimney breasts. For a start, since they are a focal point in the room, any pattern must be centralised. The design of the paper will affect where you begin to hang the wallpaper. Where one length of paper contains a complete motif, you can simply measure and mark off the central point of the chimney breast and use a

PAPERING AN INTERNAL CORNER

1 *Hang the last full length before the corner. Then measure the gap (see Ready Reference) to determine the width to be cut from the next length.*

2 *Cut from the next length a piece which will overlap 12mm (¹/₂in) round the corner. Then paste and fix it in position so it fills the corner gap.*

3 *Measure the width of the matching offcut strip of paper and use a plumbline to mark a guideline on the wall this distance from the corner.*

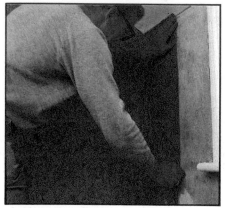

4 *Hang the offcut so its cut edge overlaps the matching edge of the first corner piece and its 'good' edge aligns with the vertical guideline.*

FLUSH WINDOWS

1 *Fix the last full length of paper before the window and pull the excess across. Cut round the sill and fix the paper beneath it.*

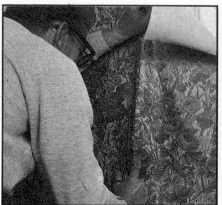

2 *You can then trim off the excess paper which runs alongside the window. Now press and brush the pasted paper into position.*

3 *Work along the wall underneath the window, fixing, creasing and trimming as you go. Afterwards you can fix the paper on the other side of the window.*

plumbline at this point to help you draw a vertical line down the centre. You can then begin hanging the wallpaper by aligning the first length with this line.

On the other hand, if it is the type of paper where two lengths, when aligned, form a motif, you will first have to estimate the number of widths which will fit across the chimney breast and then draw a line as a guide for hanging the first length of paper so the combined motif will, in fact, be centralised.

Your order of work should be from the centre (or near centre) outwards and you will then have to turn the paper round the corners at the sides so you form an overlap join with the paper which will be applied to the sides of the chimney breast. Follow the usual techniques for measuring and papering round external corners, remembering in particular not too take too much paper round the corner.

When it comes to fireplace surrounds, there are so many varying kinds of mantelshelfs and surrounds that only general guidance can be given. Usually the technique is to brush the paper down on to the top part of the wall and then cut it to fit along the back edge of the mantelshelf. You can then cut the lower half to fit the contours of the surround. If it's a complicated outline then you'll have to gradually work downwards, using a small pair of sharp scissors, pressing the paper into each shape, withdrawing it to snip along the crease line, then brushing it back into place.

If there is only a small distance between the edge of the mantelshelf and the corner, it's a lot easier if you hang the paper down to the shelf and then make a neat, horizontal cut line in the paper You can then hang the lower half separately and join the two halves to disguise the cut line.

PAPERING ROUND A DORMER

1 Where the dormer cheek meets the junction of the wall and ceiling, draw a line at right angles to the wall on the ceiling by the dormer cheek.

2 Draw a vertical line at right angles to the first line on the dormer cheek. You can then fix the first length of paper in place on the dormer cheek.

3 Work along towards the window, trimming as you go. Gently tear along the overlap to feather its edge so you won't get a bulky join later.

4 At the window, crease along the side of the frame by running the edge of the scissors along it. You can then carefully trim along the creased line.

5 Return to the small gap which needs to be filled at the narrow end of the dormer cheek; fix this piece in position, crease and trim.

6 Mark a straight line on the sloping ceiling to serve as a guideline for fixing the first length of paper on the underside of the dormer cheek.

7 Cut a piece of paper so it reaches from the point you have marked up to the window and brush it into position ensuring that it covers the feathered edges of the overlap.

8 At the junction of the wall and ceiling you will have to cut round awkward angles. You can then go ahead and brush the paper into its final position.

9 Finally, you can brush the strip of paper which fills the gap between the wall and the underside of the dormer cheek into position to finish off the dormer area neatly.

PAPERING CEILINGS

One way to cover up a ceiling with cracks or other imperfections is to use lining paper or a textured wallcovering and then paint over it. But a good alternative is to make a special feature of the ceiling by using decorative paper.

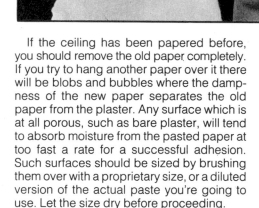

Papering ceilings can be a rather daunting prospect, even to the experienced home decorator. In fact, once you have mastered the basic technique of paperhanging, ceilings are quite straightforward and you are likely to be presented with far fewer problems than on walls. There will be no windows, few (if any) corners and not so many obstacles with which you have to deal.

If you intend to paint the ceiling it's usually best to hang a lining paper or a textured paper like woodchip first to hide the inevitable blemishes of a plaster ceiling. Or you might decide to choose a fine decorative paper and make a feature of the ceiling with it. Most of the papers that are suitable for walls can also be used for ceilings.

But before you opt for papering, it makes sense to consider the alternative: if the sole objective is to get a textured surface which will cover up cracks and bumps, you can do it just as well with a textured paint. Using a woodchip paper would only make sense if you were skilled at papering and wanted to save money; in any case, you'll still have to paint it. However, if you want a smooth ceiling or a decorative surface of distinction then papering is for you.

The equipment you'll need
You will need the same equipment as for papering walls, with the addition of a safe working platform that spans the width of the room (see *Ready Reference*). You should check with your supplier that the paper of your choice is suitable for ceilings (some heavier types may not be) and ask him to provide a suitably strong adhesive, including fungicide if it is a washable vinyl paper. Such papers are extremely suitable for high humidity environments like bathrooms and kitchens.

Preparing the surface
The surface to which you fix the paper must be clean and sound. This means washing down existing paintwork with detergent or sugar soap and then sanding it with a fine abrasive paper or pad to provide a key for the adhesive. Distempered ceilings, often found in old houses, must be scrubbed to remove the distemper, or the paper will not stick.

If the ceiling has been papered before, you should remove the old paper completely. If you try to hang another paper over it there will be blobs and bubbles where the dampness of the new paper separates the old paper from the plaster. Any surface which is at all porous, such as bare plaster, will tend to absorb moisture from the pasted paper at too fast a rate for a successful adhesion. Such surfaces should be sized by brushing them over with a proprietary size, or a diluted version of the actual paste you're going to use. Let the size dry before proceeding.

New plasterboard, often used in modern construction, needs painting with a primer/sealer before decoration. It is also wise to fix a layer of lining paper before your main decorative paper if you are hanging heavyweight or fabric wallcoverings.

Decorating perfectionists always recommend using lining paper anyway, whatever the surface. There is no doubt it does improve the final appearance, particularly on older surfaces or with thinner papers. Lining paper comes in different thicknesses or 'weights' and you should consult your supplier about a suitable grade.

One last preparation tip: don't leave cracks and dents in ceilings for the paper to cover. Fill them and sand them smooth, particularly at joins between plasterboards, and at the wall/ceiling angle. Think of your paper as a surface that needs a good smooth base, and not as a cover-up for a hideous old mess.

Planning the job
Consult the estimator panel (see *Ready Reference*) to gauge the approximate number of rolls you will need; also think about the pattern of your intended paper. Can you cope with a complex drop pattern on a ceiling, or would you be better off with a straight match? A bold paper that looks fine on walls might be a bit overpowering above your head. Is your ceiling good enough for a plainish paper, or do you need texture to draw the eye away from the ravages of time that appear in all old lath-and-plaster ceilings?

Modern papers are designed for the strips to be butted against each other, not overlapped. This means the traditional pattern of working away from, but parallel to, the main source of natural light is not essential. You will generally find it easier working across the narrowest dimension of the room. Well-applied paper will tend not to show the joins too much anyway, particularly if the pattern draws the eye.

All ceiling papering starts from a line which is strung or marked across the ceiling 10mm (³⁄₈in) less than the width of the paper away from the wall. The 10mm (³⁄₈in) on the length of paper which runs next to the wall allows for the walls being out of square and its overlap is trimmed off at the wall and ceiling junction. You can chalk a line and snap it against the ceiling between two tacks to make a mark, or just pin it temporarily in place and butt the first strip of paper against it.

MARKING UP AND PASTING

1 *Measure in from the width of the paper minus 10mm (³⁄₈in), to allow for an overlap at the wall, and mark this distance on the ceiling.*

2 *Make another mark at the opposite end, the same distance from the wall. Use a chalked line to link the marks, then snap the line onto the ceiling.*

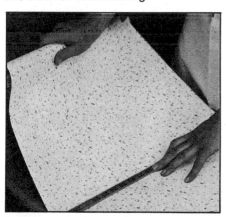

3 *Cut or tear the lengths of paper. You should allow 100mm (4in) excess on each piece to give an overlap of 50mm (2in) for trimming at each end.*

4 *Apply paste to the back of the paper and fold it into concertina folds as you go. Paste enough lengths to allow adequate soaking time.*

5 *Take the last fold in the length to meet the first, short, fold so the edges meet without paste getting on the front of the paper.*

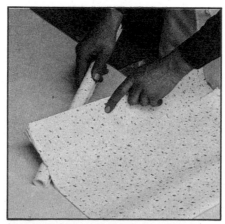

6 *Slip a spare roll of paper under the folded-up length; this will serve as a support for the paper so you can carry and hold it easily.*

Ready Reference

ESTIMATOR

Distance around room	Number of rolls 10.05m x 530mm (33ft x 21in)
10-12m (33-39ft)	2
12-14m (39-46ft)	3
14-18m (46-59ft)	4
18-20m (59-66ft)	5
20-22m (66-72ft)	6

TIP: WHISK YOUR PASTE

To speed up the process of mixing paste, use a kitchen whisk to beat up the mix.

A SAFE WORKING PLATFORM

Set up two stepladders and a solid plank, at a height where you can comfortably touch the ceiling with the palm of your hand.

TIP: HAVE TOOLS TO HAND

Have the necessary tools with you (in the pocket of an apron or overall) when you're on the working platform to save you scrambling up and down more than you need.

PREVENT WASTAGE

If you are pattern matching, paper in the direction which will save long bits of waste paper left over after cutting the lengths.

LINING PAPER

If you are hanging lining paper, remember that it should be hung at right angles to the paper which goes over it.

PAPERING TECHNIQUE

With the concertina-folded paper supported by the spare roll held in your left hand (if you are right-handed; vice versa if you are left-handed) pull one fold out taut and then brush it into place, working outwards from the centre to avoid trapped air bubbles. Repeat with the other folds.

TIP: TRIM ROSES NEATLY

Don't be tempted to remove the cover of a ceiling rose to trim the paper round it; inaccurate cutting may mean there are gaps when the cover is replaced. Instead:
● trim round the fitting with the cover in place leaving a slight overlap (see step-by-step photographs)
● remove the cover and press the overlap into place.

FINAL TRIMMING

When the last piece of paper has been hung you may need to spend some time on final trimming if the walls and ceiling do not meet squarely and evenly.

HANGING STRAIGHT LENGTHS

1 *Hang the first length on the 'room' side of the chalk line, not next to the wall. Brush the paper into place gently but firmly.*

2 *Brush the ends carefully into the angles where walls and ceiling meet, and trim. Then hang the next length alongside the wall.*

3 *The lengths should be butt-jointed. Use a seam roller to ensure well-stuck edges by running it gently over the length of the seam.*

4 *Trim off the overlap at the ends and side (if necessary) of each length of paper. Use a scraper as a guide for the knife for accurate cutting.*

5 *Wipe off any excess adhesive where the overlap has been before it dries, or it will leave ugly marks on the wall surface.*

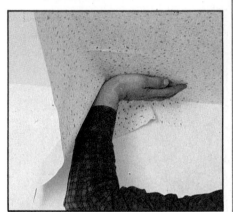

6 *You can now go ahead and hang the next length on the other side of the first piece hung. Continue until you have covered the entire ceiling.*

It makes sense to get all the lengths measured and cut out in advance, and pasted up in batches of twos or threes (depending on your speed of working) to give adequate soaking time for the type of paper you are hanging; check the manufacturer's instructions on this point. Cut all the strips, including those which will be trimmed for chimney breasts, to full room dimensions plus 100mm (4in) excess for trimming.

The concertina fold
The secret of successful ceiling papering is the correct folding technique, as you paste, so that the paper can be transferred to and laid out against the ceiling surface in a smooth manner. Each fold of the concertina should be 300mm (1ft) wide approximately, apart from the first, which can be shorter (see step-by-step photographs). It's worth practising folding with dry paper first.

Hanging the paper
Assemble the working platform securely at the correct height across the whole length of the room, beneath the area where the first strip is to be pasted. Before you get up there with a fold of wet, pasted paper, make sure you have the tools you will need to hand.

The last-to-be-pasted section of each length is first to go on the ceiling; tease off this first section and brush it into place. Continue to unfold the concertina in sections, brushing it down as you go and checking it is straight against the guideline.

Trimming and seam rolling
When you trim, you should make sure the paper butts exactly up to covings, but allow a 5-10mm (¼-⅜in) overlap down to the surface of the walls you intend to paper later. Except with embossed papers, you should roll the butt joints between strips with a seam roller.

Light fittings or shades should always be removed, leaving just the flex hanging down. Turn the power off, to ensure safety.

If a chimney breast falls parallel to the run of the paper, you will need your scissors handy to take out an approximate piece as you work along the platform. It's worth anticipating this before you get up there; mark a rough line on the paper at the approximate position of the chimney breast. Cut out the chimney breast piece, leaving an excess of about 15mm (⅝in) for detailed trimming when the whole strip is in place.

If the strip ends at a chimney breast there are less problems. Remove any vast unwanted sections as you work and trim to fit later. External corners are dealt with by making a V-cut so that one flap of the paper can be folded down the inside alcove edge of the chimney breast (or trimmed there if you are working to a coving).

PAPERING ROUND OBSTACLES

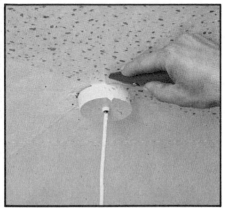

1 If there is a ceiling rose, use a knife or scissors to make a little slit in the paper so it fits round the rose; don't cut too deep.

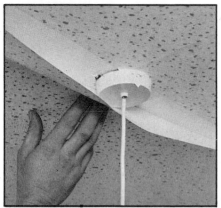

2 Hang the next length so it butts up against the previous one; at the rose take the paper over the top of the obstacle.

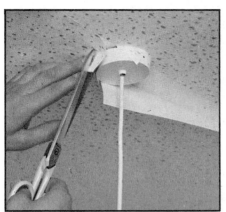

3 Again, make slits in the paper so it fits round the rose; this will allow you to brush the rest of the length of paper in place.

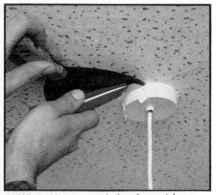

4 When the paper is in place, trim round the rose. Place the edge of a scraper between the knife and ceiling so there's a slight overlap.

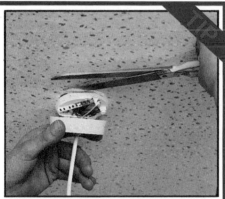

5 Turn off the power, remove the rose cover and press the overlap into place. When the cover is replaced it will conceal the cut edges completely.

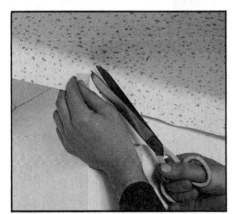

6 Where the paper meets an alcove, make a slit in the paper in line with one corner of the alcove and then in line with the other.

7 You can then brush the paper into place in the normal fashion so it fits neatly into the gap between the two corners. Trim the overlap along the wall leading to the alcove.

8 Fix the next length so it butts up against the previous one. Adhesive may ooze out when seams are rolled; so long as the paper is colourfast you can remove it with a damp sponge.

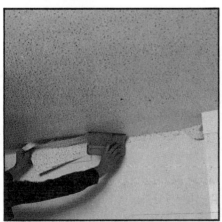

9 Measure up and cut the last narrow piece, allowing for an overlap of about 25mm (1in) at the wall and ceiling junction. Paste and brush it into place; trim to complete the job.

HANGING RELIEF WALLPAPER

If you want a change from the flat surface which ordinary wallpaper gives, you can hang a relief wallcovering with a raised, embossed pattern for a different look on walls or ceilings.

Wallcovering: Crown Anaglypta Arabesque RD132

O ne way of covering up a poor wall or ceiling surface is to use a relief or embossed wallcovering. It must be stressed at the outset that the wall or ceiling should be in sound structural condition, but these types of wallcoverings will provide an ideal disguise for minor defects such as hairline cracks, a rough finish or slight unevenness in the surface. Even where the surface is perfect, you may simply decide that you like the look which a raised pattern can give.

Frequently, embossed or relief wallcoverings are referred to as 'whites' because they come only with a white finish. Most of them require overpainting (you can, of course, paint them white, if you wish) so the paper is protected against dirt, moisture and reasonable wear and tear. Painting over a wallcovering normally means that it won't be an easy job to remove it later, so it's usually best to hang a relief wallcovering only if you intend leaving it in place for some time. (Although a steam stripper will make removal easier.)

There is a wide range of relief wallcoverings available which vary in design, thickness, depth of embossing, quality, strength, method of manufacture and price.

Woodchip wallpapers

One of the most commonly used of the 'whites' apart from lining paper is woodchip wallpaper. This relatively thick paper is made from soft wood-pulp with small, medium or large chips of wood added during the manufacturing process. These chips create the textured surface.

Woodchips are hung in normal fashion; you paste the back with a paste suitable for medium weight papers and butt-join lengths of paper before trimming off the overlaps. The cut lengths must be allowed to soak and become supple before hanging, but be careful that you don't oversoak them (follow the manufacturer's instructions as to the length of soaking time) or it is more likely you will tear the paper when trimming.

Low-relief embossed papers

This range of wallpapers, which includes Anaglypta, is also made from pulped wood

fibre. During manufacture two sheets of paper are bonded together with a water-resistant adhesive. Before the adhesive dries, the paper is run through shaped steel rollers, one with a raised pattern and the other with corresponding indentations, to stretch the soft paper and create the embossed effect.

The back surface of the paper has hollows and you need to take extra care when hanging these types of wallcoverings to ensure that the hollows are not squashed flat against the wall. You should use a heavy-duty adhesive and allow the paper to soak (usually for 10 minutes) and become supple before hanging. Take care that the edges are well pasted.

High-relief embossed papers

The majority of good quality high-relief 'whites' are made in a similar manner but often using cotton linters (short cotton fibres), china clay and resins rather than pulped wood fibre to produce the 'paper'. These ingredients give a more durable wallcovering and enable it to be given a greater

depth of embossing. Supaglypta is the best known example of this type of paper.

Depending on the design, high-relief embossed papers can often require some depth of drop matching to maintain pattern repeats. Soaking times (use a heavy-duty adhesive) should therefore be kept as constant as possible so that each length stretches, before and during hanging, to the same degree.

Blown vinyls

Classed as 'whites' and intended to be over-painted, blown vinyls are made from a type of vinyl bonded to a paper backing. During manufacture the vinyl is heated to make it expand, then before it cools it is passed through a machine which embosses a pattern into the surface. The result is a wallcovering with a slightly soft, spongy feel. But despite this softness, blown vinyls are strong, easy to handle and create few hanging problems.

You should hang a blown vinyl wallcovering with a heavy-duty or ready-mixed paste containing a fungicide; these types of wallcovering do not require soaking. You can

PREPARING ANAGLYPTA

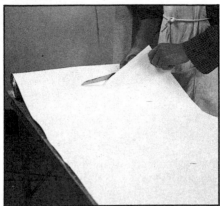

1 *Measure and cut the paper so there will be a 50mm (2in) overlap at the top and bottom. Mark the top so you'll hang the lengths the same way.*

2 *To ensure accurate pattern matching place the length to be cut alongside a cut length and make a slight tear to indicate where to cut.*

3 *Brush on the adhesive, filling all the hollows. If it is the correct consistency the brush will lift the paper from the table for a few seconds.*

4 *Fold the paper, taking care not to crease the folds, and leave the length to soak for 10 to 15 minutes (follow the instructions on the roll.)*

LINING WALLS

It's advisable to line walls and ceilings with lining paper before you hang a relief wallcovering. Remember to:
● hang it the opposite way to which the wallcovering will run
● never overlap the edges of the lining paper; they should be butt joined or you can leave a slight gap between lengths.

TIP: DON'T ROLL SEAMS

Never use a seam roller to flatten the butt joins between lengths of a relief wallcovering or you risk flattening the embossed pattern. Use a paperhanger's brush to press the seams lightly into place.

TIP: OVERLAP JOINT

Where it is necessary to overlap lengths of a relief wallcovering at a corner, tear the edge of the first length which reaches round the corner and then run a seam roller over the feathered edge to flatten it down before fixing the adjoining length over it.

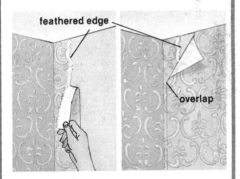

feathered edge

overlap

PAINTING RELIEF WALLCOVERINGS

Relief wallcoverings can be painted using a brush or roller. The first coat should always be an emulsion paint but you can, if you wish, follow this up with a coat of solvent-based paint. The exception is Lincrusta which should always be painted with a solvent-based paint or, if a wood effect is wanted, it can be treated with scumble, a thin oil-based covering which gives a 'grainy' effect.

TIP: FLATTEN AIR BUBBLES

The painting process will show up any air bubbles trapped behind the paper. As the paint dries the air bubble will probably flatten again but if this does not happen:
● use a razor blade to make two careful cuts diagonally across the bubble
● push more adhesive under each flap and press the paper back
● wipe off excess paste from the paper surface, allow to dry and then repaint.

then paint them like any other relief wallcovering, and they can be scrubbed clean. When you want to remove the wallcovering you peel off the vinyl layer leaving the paper lining on the wall. This can be left in place to serve as a lining paper for the next covering, or else it can be soaked and stripped off completely.

Pre-finished vinyl reliefs

Another type of relief wallcovering comes with a textured or plain vinyl surface. It is pre-finished so it does not require over-painting (though you can paint it if you wish), and it is bonded to a paper backing. These can be regularly wiped clean and are easily removed by peeling them off.

There are also vinyl relief wallcoverings with a printed decorative embossed surface designed to give the appearance of wall tiles, wood panelling or other effects.

Lincrusta types

Lincrusta is a heavy, solid, embossed wallcovering made from a combination of oxidised linseed oil and fillers bonded to a paper backing. During manufacture the putty-like surface is embossed while still soft, and is then left for 14 days to mature and dry out. It is available in two versions – one intended to be overpainted and the other already finished.

As this type of wallcovering is heavy and will easily pull away old, poorly-adhering emulsion or other paints, you should take special care in preparing the wall surfaces. They must be thoroughly clean, made good and should also be given a coat of size.

To hang Lincrusta, first cut it into drop-matched lengths, allowing an extra 50mm (2in) for later trimming at the base. The top edges of each length should be cut to fit precisely. Then trim the edges of the lengths

HANGING ANAGLYPTA

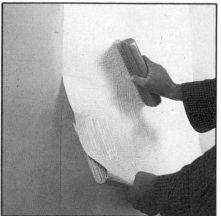

1 Mark where the first length will fall (here the edge just reaches the central point of the chimney breast) and then gently brush it in place.

2 To give you a clear guideline for trimming the relief paper, mark off the cutting line by running a pencil along the wallcovering.

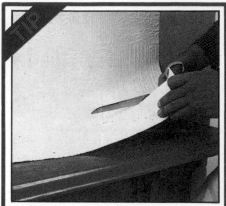

3 Use scissors to trim the paper. Don't use a knife as you are more likely to tear the paper because of its softness (from soaking).

4 Fix the next length of wallcovering, butting it up against the previous length. Don't overlap; any slight gap will be filled by overpainting.

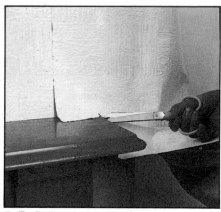

5 To fit the paper round a mantelpiece cut into the overlap at several places. Make sure that you don't cut too deep.

6 Similarly, where the paper will have to fit round an external corner, make a cut into the overlap at the top and bottom.

7 At a fire surround mark off the cutting line with a pencil, use scissors to trim the overlap, then brush the trimmed edge into place.

8 There should be at least 25mm (1in) of paper lapping round an external corner (here there's much more) which you brush into place.

9 At an internal corner brush one length into the corner. Ideally, tear the overlap (see Ready Reference), and cover it with the next length.

using a straight edge and a sharp knife (Lincrusta is one of the few wallcoverings which require edge trimming). Offer each length up to its intended position and make any cutouts required for light switches or other obstacles.

You should then dampen the paper backing with warm water applied with a sponge to allow the material to expand fully and make hanging easier. Leave it to soak for up to 30 minutes on a flat surface with two lengths laid back to back, then wipe off any excess water.

Brush special Lincrusta glue onto the damp backing paper; work fairly quickly and aim for even coverage. Position each length immediately after it is pasted, and use a soft cloth to press the wallcovering gently but firmly into position, working from the top downwards. Trim the bottom length with a sharp knife and you can then go ahead and hang the other lengths, butting each tightly up against the next. Because of its thickness and the nature of its surface, Lincrusta does not easily bend round corners so you will have to cut and butt join it at corners as neatly as possible. As with other types of wallcoverings, you're unlikely to get perfect pattern matching at corners because the walls will probably be slightly out of true.

It is very difficult to remove Lincrusta and you are quite likely to damage the wall behind in the process if you try to remove it, so it's worth thinking carefully before you decide to hang this type of wallcovering. It is, however, extremely durable, so can be used where ordinary relief wallcoverings might be prone to damage – in stairwells, for example.

Novamura

Although not really a relief wallcovering and certainly not a 'white', there is another slightly textured wallcovering worth describing which is made from an unusual material and hung in an unusual manner.

This is Novamura, which is a foamed poly-ethylene wallcovering. It is extremely lightweight and supplied in standard-size rolls in a wide variety of designs. It is soft and warm to touch and possibly the easiest wall-covering to hang.

Instead of pasting lengths cut from the roll, the paste is applied directly to the wall; the roll is unfurled down the wall onto the pasted area and then trimmed. This method eliminates the need for paste tables, mixing buckets and other paperhanging paraphernalia and takes comparatively little time.

Novamura must nevertheless be treated with some care and should not be overstretched. Although it can be wiped clean it should not be scrubbed.

To remove it you simply peel it away from the wall, with no soaking or pre-treatment required.

PAINTING ANAGLYPTA

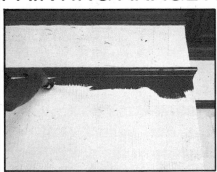

1 *Use a brush to cut in at the edges; applying a silk-finish emulsion paint will emphasise the embossed effect more than a matt one.*

2 *The job will go more quickly if you use a roller to paint the rest of the wallcovering; paint it in bands, working down the wall.*

HANGING NOVAMURA

1 *Apply adhesive containing a fungicide to the wall, covering an area slightly wider than the width of the wallcovering.*

2 *Apply the wallcovering directly from the dry roll without cutting individual lengths. Smooth it into place with a damp sponge.*

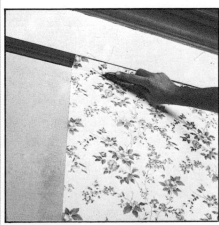

3 *Crease the wallcoverings at the joins between wall and ceiling (or picture rail) and skirting, then trim with scissors or a sharp knife.*

4 *Hang the next piece in the same way, butting it up against the preceding piece and making sure the pattern matches as you hang it.*

USING CERAMIC TILES

Tiled walls present one of the most attractive and hardwearing
finishes available, and there is now a huge range of colours,
patterns and sizes to choose from.
Ready-mixed adhesives make the fixing easy; all you have
to do is plan out each area carefully before you start.

CERAMIC TILES
for small areas

Ceramic tiles are easy-clean, hygienic and hard wearing. By starting with a small area in your home where these qualities are needed – like splashbacks or worktops – you'll not only grasp the basics but also gain confidence to tackle bigger things.

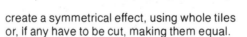

Modern ceramic tiles are thin slabs of clay, decorated on one side with coloured glazes. These are baked on to give the tile a hard, glassy surface resistant to water, heat and almost all household chemicals. The clay from which tiles are made, which is known as the biscuit, varies and you need to know the differences before you choose the tile to use. The thinnest ones with a pale coloured biscuit are good on all vertical surfaces (including doors where extra weight puts stress on the hinges).

If the biscuit is reddish/brown it has been high baked (vitrified). The thicker and darker coloured it is the more strength the tile has — floor tiles, for example, are usually big in size as well as thick in biscuit.

Work surfaces need tiles that are strong to withstand weights of heavy pots, while splashbacks and bathroom surfaces can take lighter, thinner ones.

Types of tiles

Within each range of tiles there are usually three types. *Spacer* tiles have small projections on each edge called lugs which butt up to the neighbouring tile and provide the correct space for grouting (with these it is very hard to vary the width of the grouting). *Border* tiles are squared off on all sides but are glazed on two adjacent edges — these give a neat finish to outer corners and top or side edges. *Universal or continental* tiles have no lugs and are square on all edges. All three can be used successfully in small areas, but do remember that if tiles do not have lugs you have to include grouting space in your calculations — the thinnest tiles need to be spaced by nothing more than torn-up pieces of cardboard, 6mm (¼in) tiles are best with a matchstick width in between.

Tiles are sold by the sq metre, sq yd, boxed in 25s or 50s, or can be bought individually. Boxed tiles usually advise on adhesive and grout needed for specific areas. When buying, if there's no written information available always check that the tile is suitable.

How to plan the layout

When tiling small areas you don't have much space to manoeuvre. The idea in all tiling is to create a symmetrical effect, using whole tiles or, if any have to be cut, making them equal.

Knowing about the different sizes of tiles helps in the planning. For example, if you know the width and height or depth of the surface you intend to tile, you can divide this by the known size of tiles until you find the one that gives the right number of whole tiles. Remember that the width of grouting has to be added to the measurement with non-lugged tiles – and except with the very thinnest tiles this can be slightly widened if it saves cutting a tile.

If you're prepared to incorporate cut tiles into the planning remember:
● on the width of the tiled area, place equal cut tiles at each end
● on the height, place cut tiles at the top edge
● on the depth (eg, window-recesses) put cut tiles at back edge
● frame a fitting by placing cut tiles at each side and the top

A mix of patterned or textured with plain tiles is best done first on metricated graph paper. This will help you see where you want the pattern to fall.

Fixings should be made in the grouting lines where possible. Some tile ranges have soap dishes, towel rails etc attached to tiles so they can be incorporated in a scheme, but if these don't suit your purposes, you can drill the tiles to screw in your own fitting (see page 160).

A working plan

All tiles should be fixed level and square so it's important to establish the horizontal and vertical with a spirit level. Draw in the lines with pencil. If you plan to tile where there is no support (eg, on either side of a basin or sink) lightly pin a length of 50 x 25mm (2 x 1in) timber below the tiling line – the batten will prevent the tiles slipping.

On doors you may have to consider adding a timber surround to keep the tiles secure as they will be subjected to movement (also see section on *Adhesives* below).

Adhesives and grouting

The choice of both of these depends on where the tiles are to be fixed. In a watery situation (eg, a shower cubicle or a steamy kitchen) it is important to use a waterproof variety of both, even though you might have

Ready Reference

TILE SHAPES AND SIZES

Ceramic tiles for walls are usually square or oblong in shape. The commonest sizes are shown below. The smaller sizes are usually 4mm (⅝₂in) thick, while larger tiles may be 6mm (¼in) or more in thickness.

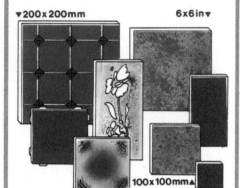

▼200 x 200mm 6x6in▼

100x100mm▲
50x50mm▲
▲4¼ x 4¼in

HOW MANY TILES?

Square or oblong areas
● measure lengths and width of the area
● divide each measurement by the size of tile you're using, rounding up to the next whole number if you get a fraction
● multiply the two figures to give the number of tiles needed

Awkwardly-shaped areas
● divide area into convenient squares or oblongs
● work out each one as above adding up the area totals to give the final figures

Patterns using two or more different tiles
● sketch out design on graph paper, one square for each tile (two for oblong tiles); use colours to mark where different tiles fall
● count up totals needed of each pattern, counting part tiles as whole ones

Add 10% to your final tile counts to allow for breakages

ADHESIVE/GROUT

For each square metre of tiling allow:
● 1.5kg (about 1 litre) of adhesive
● 150g of grout

TIP: AVOID NARROW STRIPS

Less than about 25mm/1in wide is very difficult to cut. When planning, if you see narrow strips are going to occur you can:
● replan the rows to use one less whole tile with two wider cut pieces at either end
● or increase the grouting space slightly between every tile in the row

HOW TO HANG TILES

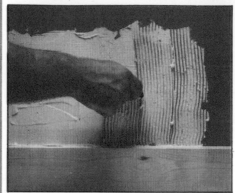

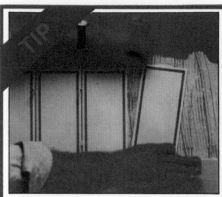

1 Spread ceramic tile adhesive to cover 1 sq metre, then 'comb' with notched spreader. To support tiles where no other support exists, pin a horizontal timber batten to the wall.

2 When positioning tiles it is important to twist them slightly to bed them. Don't slide them as this forces adhesive between joints.

3 Form even grouting spaces between tiles without lugs with pieces of matchstick. Or you can use torn-up cardboard from the tile packaging or similar if you want only a narrow grouting space.

4 Remove matchsticks or card after all tiles are hung, and grout 12-24 hours later. Press grout into the spaces using a small sponge or squeegee, making sure no voids are left in either vertical or horizontal spaces.

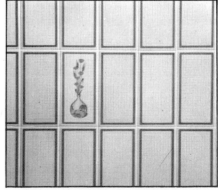

5 After 10 minutes, wipe off excess grouting with soft cloth. Use fine dowelling (sand the end to round it) to even up and smooth the lines. Fill any voids that appear with fresh grout to prevent water penetration.

6 When grouting is dry, polish the tiles with a soft cloth so the area is smooth. All the surface needs now is an occasional wipe-down although non-waterproof grout may tend to discolour as time goes by.

to wait for 4-5 days before exposing the tile surface to use.

All ceramic tile adhesives are like thin putty and can be bought ready mixed in tubs or in powder form to be made up with water. They are what is known as thin-bed adhesives in that they are designed to be applied in a thin layer on a flat even surface. The spread is controlled by a notched comb (usually provided by the manufacturer but cheap to buy where you bought the tiles) to make furrows of a specified depth. When the tiles are pressed on with a slight twist, the adhesive evenly grips the back of the biscuit.

Special latex-based adhesives (usually, two-part products which have to be mixed before using) have much more flexibility and are good for tiles where there is any movement (eg, on doors).

Spread the adhesive on an area no more than 1 sq metre (1 sq yd) at a time, or it will lose its gripping power before you have time to place the tiles. If you remove a tile, before refixing comb the adhesive again.

Grout gives the final finish to the tiled area, filling the spaces between the tiles and preventing moisture getting behind them and affecting the adhesive. Grouting can be done 12-24 hours after the last tile has been pressed into place. Grout can be standard or waterproof (with added acrylic), and both are like a cellulose filler when made up.

If you only make up one lot of grouting, you can colour it with special grouting tints – but remember that it's hard to make other batches match the colour. Waterproof grouting cannot always take these tints.

Press grout between the tiles with a sponge or squeegee and wipe off excess with a damp sponge. Even up the grouting by drawing a pencil-like piece of wood (eg dowelling) along each row first vertically, then horizontally. Do this within 10 minutes of grouting so it is not completely dry.

Leave the tiles for 24 hours before polishing with a clean dry cloth. Wash clean only if a slight bloom remains.

Tiles should never be fixed with tight joints for any movement of the wall or fittings will cause the tiles to crack. Similarly where tiles meet baths, basins, sinks etc, flexibility is needed – and grout that dries rigid cannot provide it. These gaps must be filled with a silicone rubber sealant

Techniques with tiles

To cut tiles, lightly score the glaze with a tile cutter to break the surface. Place the tile glazed side up with the scored line over matchsticks and firmly but gently press the tile down on each side. If using a pencil press on one side, hold the other. Smooth the cut edge with a file. Very small adjustments are best done by filing the edge of the whole tile.

CUTTING TILES

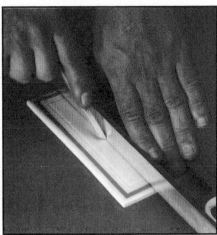

1 Before a tile will break, the glaze must be scored — on the edges as well as surface. Use a carbide-tipped cutter against a straight-edge.

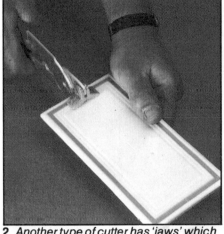

2 Another type of cutter has 'jaws' which clasp the tile during breaking. (It also has a small 'wheel' for scoring through the glaze on the tile).

3 No special tools are needed with other tile-breaking methods. For medium thick tiles use a pencil, for thin tiles use matchsticks.

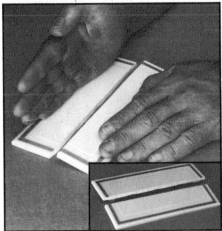

4 Place pencil centrally under tile and score line, hold one side and press firmly on other. With thin tiles, press lightly both sides.

To remove a narrow strip of tile, score the line heavily by drawing the tile cutter across the tile more firmly several times in the same place. Then use pincers to 'nibble' the waste away in small pieces and smooth the edge. Glaze on broken tiles is as sharp as glass, so be careful not to cut yourself.

Templates for awkwardly shaped tiles are not difficult to make. Cut the shape in card, place on a tile and score a line freehand with the tile cutter. Any straight score marks can be deepened afterwards, using a straight edge for support. Then nibble away the waste with pincers. If there's a large amount to be cut away, score the waste part to divide it into sections, then nibble away. A good tip is to do this on a soft or padded surface so the tile doesn't break in the wrong place.

Suitable surfaces

The ideal surface for tiling is one that's perfectly flat, dry and firm. Small irregularities will be covered up, but any major hollows, bumps or flaking, need to be made good.

Plastered walls and asbestos cement sheets: perfect for tiling, but wait a month after any new plastering to allow the wall to dry out completely. Unless surface has been previously painted, apply a coat of plaster primer to prevent the liquid in the tile adhesive from being absorbed too quickly.

Plasterboard: again, ideal for tiling as long as it's firmly fixed and adjacent boards cannot shift. (If they did the joins would probably crack). To prepare the surface, remove all dust, wipe down with white spirit

Ready Reference

TOOLS FOR TILING

Tile cutter: essential for scoring glaze of tiles before breaking them. Score only once (the second time you may waver from the line and cause an uneven break).
Pincers: these are used for nibbling away small portions of tile, after scoring a line with the cutter. Ordinary pincers are fine for most jobs, but special tile nibblers are available.
Special cutter: combines a cutting edge (usually a small cutting wheel) with jaws which snap the tile along the scored line.
Tile file: an abrasive mesh, used as a file to 'shave' off small amounts.

TIP: TO DRILL A TILE

● make a cross of masking tape and mark the point where you want the hole
● drill after adhesive and grouting have set using lowest speed or a hand drill with masonry bit — too much speed at the start will craze the tile
● once through the glaze, drill in the normal way

● cut tile into two along line corresponding with centre point of pipe; offer up each half to the pipe
● mark freehand semi-circles on tile to match edge of pipe; score line with tile cutter and nibble away waste with pincers

SHAPING TILES

5 *Edges of broken tiles need to be smoothed off — use a special tile file mounted on wood, a wood file or rub against rough concrete.*

6 *To cut an awkward shape, make a card template. Place it on the tile and score glaze on the surface and edges with the tile cutter.*

7 *On a soft surface, use pincers to take tiny nibbles out of the tile. If you're over enthusiastic you'll break off more than you intended.*

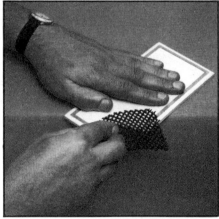

8 *Once the waste has been slowly but surely nibbled away, smooth up the edge. Files are also useful when a whole tile needs a slight trimming.*

to remove grease, then treat with primer.
Paint: old emulsion-paint needs to be cleaned thoroughly with sugar soap or detergent to remove all traces of dust and grease. Gloss paint needs to be cleaned thoroughly; remove any flaking paint then roughen up whole surface with a coarse abrasive to provide a good key for the adhesive.
Wallpaper: DO NOT tile directly onto wallpaper, as this can be pulled away from the wall by the adhesive. Strip it off completely.
Wood and Chipboard: perfect for tiling as long as it is flat and adjacent boards cannot shift. Treat with an ordinary wood primer.
Laminates: joins and small, minor blemishes in the surface can be covered up so long as the entire sheet is soundly fixed and absolutely flat. Its smooth face must be roughened with course abrasive to provide a key for the tile adhesive.
Old ceramic tiles: the thin biscuit ceramic tiles are excellent for tiling over as they add little to the wall's thickness and won't protrude beyond existing fittings. Loose and cracked tiles will have to be removed. Scrape out the grouting surrounding the tile using an old, thin screwdriver or something similar, then, beginning in the centre and working outwards, remove the tile using a club hammer and cold chisel.

Small sections or mis-shapen pieces (as around a new fixture) can be built up level with neighbouring tiles with cellulose filler.

The area should then be sealed with plaster primer or emulsion paint to finish the surface.

CERAMIC TILING WALL TO WALL

Ceramic tiles are an ideal decorating material for they make a room look good for years and require virtually no maintenance. But covering several walls with tiles is a large-scale job which needs a methodical and careful approach if you are to achieve the best results.

Jem Grischotti   Tiles: Rustica Roberta pattern   Flooring: GAF terra cotta cushion vinyl Coburg

The all-in-one look that wall-to-wall tiling can give has to be planned carefully to avoid expensive and time consuming mistakes. How to do this may depend on whether you want to include special patterns in the design, but following certain rules will give a desirable symmetry to the look.

One of the hardest tasks will probably be choosing the tiles for there's a vast array of shapes, sizes and colours available. Having picked out the ones you want though, don't buy until you've done the planning – for the plans of each wall should tell you whether the pattern will work in the room or would be lost in the cutting or amid the fittings.

Plans on paper also give you an instant method of working out how many tiles to buy (counting each cut one as a whole, and adding 2-5% for unintended breakage) including the number which will need to be border (two glazed edges) or mitred (on square or rectangular universal tiles) for the top row of half-tiled walls or external corners. Buy all the tiles at once, but do check each carton to make sure there's no variation in the colour (this can occur during the firing of different batches).

Planning on paper

The best possible way to start planning for a large expanse of tiling is not on the wall, but on paper. Graph paper is ideal, particularly if you intend including a mix of plain and patterned tiles, or a large motif that needs building up. Of course, advance planning is also essential if you're tiling round major features like windows, doors, mirrors, shower cubicles and so on.

You need separate pieces of graph paper for each wall you intend tiling. Allow the large (1cm) squares on the paper to represent your tiles — one for a square tile of any size, two for a rectangular tile; this will give you a scale to work to. Now mark up sheets of greaseproof paper with your actual wall sizes using the scale dictated by the tile size on the graph paper. Measure and outline on the see-through paper the exact position and in-scale dimensions of all fixtures and fittings (see the planning pictures on page 162).

At this stage, the objective is to decide how to achieve the best symmetrical layout for your tiles — the 'ideal' is to have either whole or equal-size cut tiles on each side of a fixture.

First you have to mark in the central guide lines. For instance, on *walls with a window* draw a line from the sill centre to the floor, and from the centre of the top of the window to the ceiling. If there are *two windows* also draw in the central line from floor to ceiling between them. Mark the centre point above a *door* to the ceiling and also indicate the horizontal line at the top of the door. In the same way draw in a central line from the top of a *basin or vanity unit* to the ceiling.

For all these lines use a coloured pen for you have to be aware of them when deciding where whole tiles should be positioned. But they're only the starting point — other potential problems have to be looked at too.

Place the see-through paper over the tile sizes on the graph paper so you can see how the tiles will fall in relation to the guide lines. Now take into account the following important points:
● The first row above the lowest level — either the floor, the skirting board or a wall-to-wall fitting — should be whole tiles. If necessary, change this to prevent a thin strip being cut at the ceiling.
● Check where tiles come in relation to fittings. If very thin strips (less than 38mm/1½in) or narrow 'L' shapes would need to be cut, move the top sheet slightly up, down, left or right till the tiles are of a cuttable size — areas to watch are around windows, doors and where one wall meets another.

Placing patterns

When you are satisfied that you have a symmetrical and workable arrangement you can tape the top sheet in the right position on the graph paper, then start to plan where you're going to position your patterned tiles. Use pencil this time in case you change your mind and want to make adjustments. These are the points to watch:
● Don't place single motif patterns at internal corners where they would have to be cut — you won't find it easy to match up the remaining piece on the adjacent wall.

Ready Reference

TILING SEQUENCES

You can use the 'step' method (see page 55), or build 'pyramids'. Here are the sequences for different bonds.

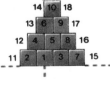

Running bond staggers the tiles. Place the first one centrally on your vertical line.

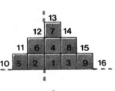

Jack-on-Jack has the joints lined up. Work either side of your vertical line.

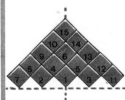

Diamond bond puts plain or outlined tiles at an angle. Place the first centrally on the vertical, fill in 'triangles' last.

161

● If the pattern builds up vertically and horizontally over four or more tiles, 'centre' the pattern on the wall so that cuts are equal at both ends. If pattern loss can't be avoided with designs of this type at least it can be kept to internal corners.

● Whole tiles should be used on both faces of external corners.

Now butt each of the wall plans up to the other to make sure that the patterns relate both vertically and horizontally.

Planning on the wall
When there are no complicated tiling patterns involved and walls are free of interruptions such as windows, it's often easier to do the planning directly on the wall itself. Here, the simple objective is to place the tiles symmetrically between the corners. And to do this, all you need is a tiling gauge which you can make.

A tiling gauge is like a long ruler, except that it's marked off in tile widths. Use a long, straight piece of timber ideally about 25mm square (1in square) and remember to include the grouting gap between tiles as you rule off the gauge. If you're using rectangular tiles, mark the widths on one side, the lengths on the other.

Holding the gauge against the walls —

first vertically, then horizontally — tells you instantly where the whole tiles will fit in and where cut tiles will be needed. But first you must find the centre of each wall. Measure the width — doing this at three places will also tell you if the corners are vertical (hang a plumb line or use a spirit level to make absolutely sure) — and halve it to find the centre point. Use the tiling gauge to mark this vertical centre line with a pencil, then hold the gauge against it. Move it up or down until you have at least a whole tile's width above the floor or skirting board — this can be adjusted slightly if it avoids a thin piece of tile at ceiling height — then mark off the tile widths on the vertical line itself.

Now hold the tiling gauge horizontally, and move it to left or right of the vertical line if thin pieces of tile would have to be cut near windows or fittings, or to make cut tiles at both ends of the wall equal. Following this adjustment, mark the wall and draw in a new vertical line if necessary. The wall can now be marked horizontally with tile widths. Keeping to the same horizontal, mark up adjacent walls in the same way.

At corners, whether internal or external, don't assume they're either square, vertical or even. An internal corner is the worst place to start your tiling for this very reason, but it

doesn't matter if you position cut tiles there. On external corners use the tiling gauge to work inwards in whole tile widths.

You can also use the tiling gauge to check that your graph plan is accurate, and make any necessary adjustments.

Putting up battens
Once you have determined that your plan is correct, fix a length of perfectly straight 50mm x 25mm (2in x 1in) battening across the full width of the wall — use a spirit level to ensure that the batten is horizontal. Use masonry nails to fix it in place but do not drive them fully home as they will have to be removed later. If using screws the wall should be plugged. The batten provides the base for your tiling and it's important that its position is correct.

If more than one wall is being tiled, continue to fix battens around the room at the same height, using the spirit level to check the horizontal. The last one you fix should tie up perfectly with the first. If there are gaps, at the door for example, check that the level either side is the same, by using a straight-edge and spirit level to bridge the gap.

Once the horizontal battens are fixed, fix a vertical batten to give yourself the starting point for the first tile. Use a spirit level or plumb line to make sure it's positioned accurately.

Fixing tiles
Begin tiling from the horizontal base upwards, checking as you work that the tiles are going up accurately both vertically and horizontally. Work on an area of approximately 1 sq metre (1 sq yd) at a time, spreading the adhesive and fixing all the whole tiles using card or matchsticks as spacers as necessary. Make sure no excess adhesive is left on the surface of the tiles.

Next, deal with any tiles that need to be cut. You may find the gap into which they fit is too narrow to operate the adhesive spreader properly. In this case spread the adhesive onto the back of the tiles.

When all the tiling above the base batten has been completed wait for 8-12 hours, before removing the battens, and completing the tiling. Take care when removing the base batten that the tiles above are not disturbed — the adhesive is unlikely to be fully set.

Dealing with corners
Your original planning should have indicated how many border or mitred tiles you will need for tiling external corners or for the top line of tiles on a half-tiled wall. You will find external corners, those which project into the room, in virtually all tiling situations — around boxed-in pipework, or around a window or door reveal, or in an L-shaped room.

Where you are using universal tiles at an

PLANNING TILE LAYOUT ON PAPER

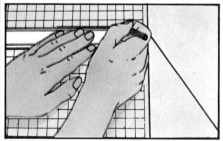

1 *On graph paper with large (eg, 1cm) squares, let each square represent one whole square tile. Strengthen the grid lines with coloured pen if necessary.*

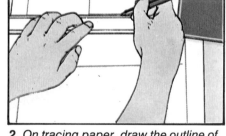

2 *On tracing paper, draw the outline of each wall to be tiled, and mark in doors and windows. Use the scale 1cm = the actual tile size (eg, 150mm).*

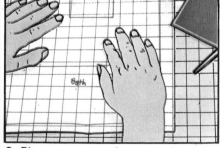

3 *Place greaseproof over graph paper and move it around till you get the most manageable size cut tiles, especially near fixtures, ceiling and floor.*

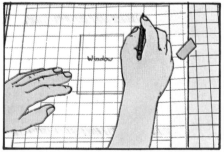

4 *Tape the top sheet in place, then mark the pattern in with pencil. Do each wall the same so that the alignment of the horizontal is correct.*

Jem Grischotti

external corner, start at the corner with a whole tile — it should project by the depth of the mitre so that the mitre on the other face neatly butts up against it with a fine space for grouting in between.

With window reveals the correct method is to tile up the wall to sill level, cutting tiles if necessary. Fit whole tiles either side of the reveal, then again cut tiles to fill the space between those whole ones and the window frame. Attach whole border or mitred tiles to the sill so they butt up against the wall tiles. If using square-edged tiles the ones on the sill should cover the edges of those on the wall so the grouting line is not on the sill surface. If the sill is narrower than a whole tile, cut the excess from the back — not the front. If the sill is deeper than a whole tile, put cut tiles near the window with the cut edge against the frame. Continually check the accurate lining up of tiles with a spirit level.

Some vertical external corners are not as precisely straight and vertical as they should be and this can lead to problems of tile alignment. The use of a thick-bed adhesive will help to straighten out some irregularities where a corner goes inwards (a thin-bed helps where the wall leans outwards). Buying a 'flexible' adhesive will give you both qualities. As a general rule it is

PLANNING ON THE WALL

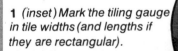

1 *(inset) Mark the tiling gauge in tile widths (and lengths if they are rectangular).*

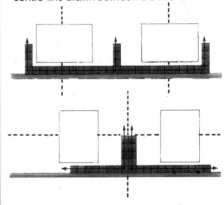

2 *Use a plumb line to check that the wall is vertical.*

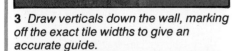

3 *Draw verticals down the wall, marking off the exact tile widths to give an accurate guide.*

4 *Check each horizontal with a spirit level, then mark tile positions from floor to ceiling.*

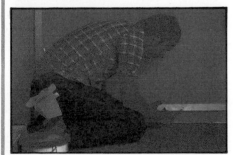

5 *Place horizontal batten at least a tile's width above floor or a fitting using masonry nails or screws.*

6 *Fix vertical batten and begin to tile where the battens meet. Spread adhesive to cover 1 sq metre (1 sq yd).*

Jem Grischotti

TACKLING TILING PROBLEMS
Whenever a fitting, a door or window interrupts the clean run of a wall, it becomes the focal point of the wall. So you have to plan for symmetry *round* the features. Here are some guidelines:

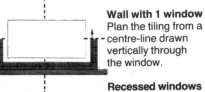

Wall with 1 window
Plan the tiling from a centre-line drawn vertically through the window.

Recessed windows
Again work from a centre-line drawn vertically through window. But make sure that whole tiles are placed at the front of the sill and the sides of the reveals. Place cut tiles closest to the window frame.

Wall with two windows
Unless the space between the two windows is exactly equal to a number of whole tiles, plan your tiling to start from a centre-line drawn between the two.

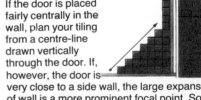

Wall with door
If the door is placed fairly centrally in the wall, plan your tiling from a centre-line drawn vertically through the door. If, however, the door is very close to a side wall, the large expanse of wall is a more prominent focal point. So plan the tiling to start one tile's width from the frame. If the frame is not exactly vertical, you'll be able to cut tiles to fit in the remaining space.

MAKE YOUR OWN TILE BREAKER

1 *Use a timber offcut wider than the tile as the base. Use 3mm (¹/₈in) ply for the top and sides.*

2 *Stack ply strips on both sides till the same height as the tile, then pin. Nail on the top piece.*

3 *The breaking part needs to be as wide and deep as the tile, with the opening on the top a half tile long.*

4 *Score the glaze on the top and edges with a carbide-tipped cutter. Put the tile into the main part.*

5 *Slip on the breaking part so the score line is between the two. Hold one side while you press the other.*

6 *The tile breaks cleanly. This aid costs nothing and will save you time when tiling a large expanse.*

TILING CORNERS

1 *At an internal corner, mark amount to be cut at top and bottom. Break the tile, then fit in position.*

2 *File the remainder until it fits the adjacent area with enough space left for a fine line of grout.*

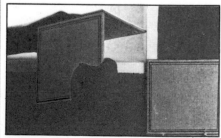

3 *On a window sill, use a whole tile at the front and make sure that it overlaps the one on the wall-face underneath.*

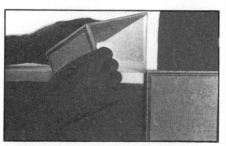

4 *Mitred edges of universal tiles and glazed edges of border tiles give a better finish to external corners.*

better to concentrate on lining up your border or mitred tiles perfectly vertically with only minute 'steps' between tiles, then bedding spacer or ordinary tiles behind to correspond with the line. Don't forget that if you do have to create a very slight stepped effect, you can reduce the uneven effect between the corner tiles and others by pressing in extra grouting later.

Internal corners seldom cause serious problems as cut tiles can be shaped to suit fluctuations from the truly vertical. Don't assume when cutting tiles for a corner that all will be the same size — the chances are that they will vary considerably and should be measured and cut individually. Another point: don't butt tiles up against each other so they touch — leave space for the grouting which will give the necessary flexibility should there be any wall movement.

Tiling around electrical fittings

When tiling around electrical fittings it is better to disconnect the electricity and remove the wall plate completely so that you can tile right up to the edge of the wall box. This is much neater and easier than trying to cut tiles to fit around the perimeter of the plate. Cut tiles as described in the illustration on pages 51 and 52 and fit them in the normal way with the plate being replaced on top, completely covering the cut edges of the tiles. This same principle applies to anything easily removable. The fewer objects you have to tile around the better, so before starting any tiling get to work with a screwdriver.

You have the greatest control over the end result if at the planning stage you work out where you want to place fittings such as towel rails and soap dishes, shelves and the like. Some tile ranges offer them attached so it's only a matter of fitting them in as you put the tiles up.

Tiling non-rigid surfaces
On surfaces which are not totally rigid or which are subject to movement, vibration or the odd shock, tiles should not be attached using adhesive which dries hard as most standard and waterproof types do. Instead use adhesives which retain some flexibility. These may be cement-based types with a latex rubber content, or acrylic adhesives. You may have to surround a non-rigid surface with wooden lipping to protect the tiles.

TILING AROUND FIXTURES

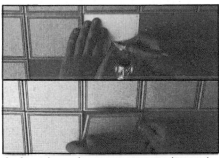

1 *At awkward corners use card to make a tile-size template. Place it on the tile and score the shape, then gently nibble out the waste with pincers — the smaller the bits the better.*

2 *Where basins, baths, kitchen sinks or laundry tubs meet tiles, seal the join with silicone caulking to keep out water. Caulking comes in various colours to match fixtures.*

3 *After the adhesive has had time to set, the tiles are grouted both to protect them and to enhance their shape and colour.*
Accessories can be bought already attached to tiles, can be screw mounted after drilling the tile, or if lightweight can be stuck on to tiles with adhesive pads.

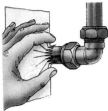

MOSAIC TILING

You don't have to be a skilled craftsman to decorate a surface with modern ceramic mosaic tiles. They come in a variety of designs and their small size makes it easy to tile round curves and obstacles.

Decorating a surface with mosaics – small pieces of material such as stone, glass, tile or shell – is an art form with a long history. The main drawback with the traditional method was that you needed an artist to design the mosaic and, usually, a highly skilled installer to fit them – all of which was expensive. Today, however, there are mosaics available as ceramic tiles that you can lay yourself.

Modern ceramic mosaic tiles come in a wide variety of shapes, sizes and patterns and can be used both indoors and out. In the kitchen they are ideal as wall surfaces or as a practical and attractive worktop which will be easy to clean and extremely hardwearing. An alternative to a completely tiled worktop is to have an inset area of mosaic tiles close to the hob on which you can put hot pans (see *Ready Reference*). In the bathroom, mosaics can be used as a splashback to the basin and bath, to tile the floor and walls or as an attractive finish to the inside of a shower cubicle.

Elsewhere in the house, mosaic tiles can be used for interesting effects. You don't have to stick to wall or floor surfaces either; mosaics will also make an unusual coffee table top, or could be set into a wooden frame to create a pot stand or even a cheeseboard. The small size of the tiles makes them easy to apply to curved surfaces: the smallest ones can even be used to cover unsightly columns or large pipes.

Types of mosaics
Most mosaic tiles are supplied on backing sheets. This means that the sheet itself can be cut to fit the tiles round doors, windows, light switches and fittings. In effect, it keeps the cutting of tiles themselves to a minimum.

The tiles are available glazed or unglazed, and come in various shapes, from 22mm (¾in) square, to round, hexagonal or Provencale (see *Ready Reference*). The number of tiles on a sheet varies from 12 to about 80 depending on the size and shape of each tile. Some sheets come with a paper facing over the front of the tiles, and this has to be removed after the adhesive has set so

that the grouting can be completed. The disadvantage in using such sheets is that you cannot see the overall effect of the tiles right away. To overcome this problem, most mosaic tiles are now produced with either a nylon or perforated paper backing. The added advantage with this type is that you can, if you wish, make minor adjustments to the placing of each tile during laying, by cutting through the backing mesh with a sharp knife and sliding the tile to its ideal position.

Buying mosaics
Ceramic mosaic tiles may be available from local do-it-yourself shops, but specialist ceramic tile shops will usually have a far greater selection. The staff in a specialist shop may also be able to advise you on the right mosaic tiles for the job you have in mind – they're not all suitable for kitchen work surfaces, for example, because of the lead content of the glaze.

Adhesives and grout
Adhesives and grout for mosaic tiles are the same as are used to fix other ceramic tiles. You can either buy separate products, or go for a combined adhesive and grout that will do both jobs. If the mosaic tiles are to be fixed in an area likely to get wet, as in a

shower, bathroom or kitchen, use a waterproof type. For outdoor use (eg, tiling a porch floor) pick a frostproof adhesive. Remember you can add colour pigments to grout to obtain a coloured, rather than the usual, white, finish. This technique can be most effective, especially if it's used on a work surface where a darker coloured mosaic is used.

MARKING UP THE

1 *Measure across the wall to find the central point to help you determine where to fix the first whole sheet of tiles at the corner of the room.*

FIXING TILES ON A WALL

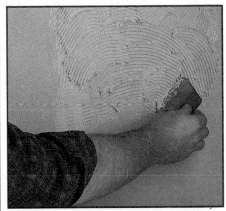

1 *Spread adhesive on the wall to take the first sheet of tiles. Don't use too much adhesive at a time or it will set too soon and be wasted.*

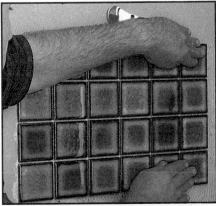

2 *Press the first whole sheet of tiles firmly into place, checking it is in the right position. Continue fixing whole sheets of tiles and then off-cut strips.*

3 *When the whole sheets and off-cut strips are in place, you can mark off tiles which need cutting to fill the gaps at the end of the wall.*

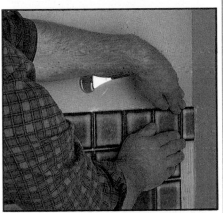

4 *Fix the cut tiles in place, leaving a grouting gap between them and the whole tiles. Clean off excess adhesive with a damp sponge as you work.*

TILE POSITION

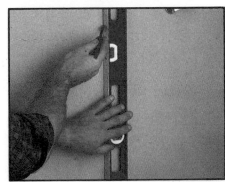

2 *Measure up from the floor where you want to fix tiles. Aim to have a whole sheet of tiles fixed immediately above the lowest point of the floor line.*

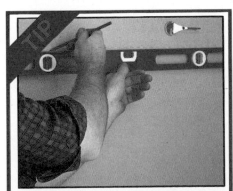

3 *Draw a line across the wall to show where the top line of the tiles will come to. You can use this as a guide for getting the tile sheets straight.*

Ready Reference

SHEET SIZES FOR MOSAICS
● Small, square mosaics usually come in sheets measuring about 300mm (12in) square, though larger sheets measuring 600 x 300mm (24 x 12in) are available.
● Shaped tiles are available on sheets measuring 470 x 300mm (18½ x 12in) or 547 x 350mm (21 x 14in).

TILE SHAPES
Most mosaics are square or rectangular, but other shapes are also available – round, hexagonal and Provencale are the commonest.

CHOOSE THE RIGHT TYPE
Check that the tiles you intend using are suitable:
● for exterior use (eg, on a patio) mosaics must be frostproof or vitrified
● for floors, select flooring quality mosaics
● for kitchen work surfaces, check that the glaze on the tiles does not contain lead.

THE TILING GAUGE
Use a 2m (approx 6ft) length of 50 x 25mm (2 x 1in) softwood and mark the width of a number of mosaic sheet sizes along it, allowing the same gap between sheets as between individual tiles. In small rooms use a shorter batten.

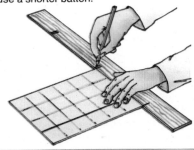

167

CUTTING TILES

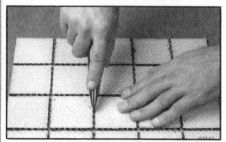

1 To cut off strips of tiles from a sheet, simply trim through the mesh or perforated paper backing with a sharp knife to get the right number of rows.

2 To cut a single tile, score a cutting line with a tungsten-carbide-tipped tile cutter. Break the tile along the line using a tile cutter with angled jaws.

3 To cut shaped tiles mark off a cutting line using a template as a guide, then score along the cutting line using a tungsten-carbide-tipped cutting tool.

4 Nibble away at the waste area with a pair of tile nips taking out only small pieces at a time. Smooth any rough edges with a carborundum stone.

TILING ROUND A WC

1 Lay a whole sheet of tiles so the outer row fits round the corner of the WC base. Tear off individual tiles which will need to be replaced by cut tiles.

2 With the remainder of the tiles in the sheet fixed in place, mark off a cardboard template for cutting tiles. Once cut to shape, fix the tiles in place.

3 Lay tiles over the rest of the floor area. Make sure you work in small areas at a time so the adhesive doesn't harden before you're ready.

4 Fix strips of tiles to the floor in the same way as fixing a whole sheet; allow for a grouting gap. Mark off the tiles for cutting at the edges.

Preparing the surface

The surface on which you are tiling should be clean, flat, dry and firm. You should allow a newly plastered surface to dry out for at least a month before tiling it; make sure old plaster is sound by removing all loose particles with a brush. Dusty or porous plaster can be treated with a stabilising primer to prevent the liquid from the adhesive being absorbed too quickly.

Mosaics can be applied on top of paint as long as the paint film is sound. If the paint is flaking, you should scrape it off as thoroughly as possible. Don't use a chemical stripper, and avoid using a solvent-based adhesive for fixing the tiles (most are water based, but check first).

Old ceramic tiles provide a suitable surface if they are perfectly flat. Any chipped or broken tiles should be removed and the gap filled with mortar or adhesive, and any loose tiles should be firmly restuck. You should also remove dirt and grease from the surface of the tiles.

Don't attempt to lay mosaic tiles on concrete unless it is absolutely sound and dry. (If it's not perfectly flat, the small size of the mosaic tiles will be able to accommodate any unevenness, but it'll still show.) If you want to tile over wooden floorboards, cover the floor first with sheets of plywood or chipboard (special water-resistant, resin-bonded sheets are available for very 'wet' areas like bathrooms). This will prevent any slight movement of the floorboards causing the tiles or the grouting to crack.

Where to start on floors

The best way of planning your tiling and deciding where to start is to treat a sheet of tiles as one tile. In effect this means you can use a tiling gauge to find the correct starting point in the same way as for laying ordinary ceramic floor tiles (see pages 204–209). Where a whole sheet

GROUTING TILES

1 Use a sponge to spread the grout over the tiles, taking care to press it down firmly into the gaps so they will be properly sealed off.

won't fit, you simply cut whole tiles off the sheet — and leave the cutting of individual tiles until last. Check with a square that you have a right-angled starting point, and adjust your starting point if the cut pieces are too thin for convenience.

In a small room where there is a prominent feature such as a WC, it may be more sensible to begin tiling outwards from the feature and work towards the walls. In cases like this you should measure up and find the central starting point. Adjust its position if it means you will have to cut very thin pieces of tile by including one less mosaic tile in each complete row.

Mosaics on wall surfaces

On a wall you can use a tiling gauge to mark off where complete sheets of tiles will fall, and so establish your starting point in the same way as for fixing larger ceramic wall tiles (see Ceramics tiling, pages 161–165). Use a plumbline and a spirit level to establish a true vertical and horizontal. Aim to position the tiles so there will be a whole mosaic sheet width (with a grouting gap at the bottom) immediately above the floor line or skirting board.

Find the centre point of the wall or the centre of a window, and measuring from this point work out where the last whole sheet of tiles in each row will be; then mark off your starting point by finding where one of these will fall at a suitable level — usually just above the skirting board. Again, adjust your starting point if you will have to cut pieces of tile which are too thin. On a reasonable size wall you can fix a horizontal and vertical batten which meet at the starting point to serve as guides for fixing the sheets. On a small area this is not essential.

Fixing mosaics

It's easier to work in small areas when fixing the tiles, one sheet at a time, otherwise there's a risk of the adhesive going off before you've finished making the final adjustments. Spread the adhesive over an area no greater than 1 sq m (about 11 sq ft) and fix the first sheet of tiles in place. You can then lay the other whole sheets, remembering to leave the same gap between each sheet as there is between the individual mosaics. On a floor you can gently tamp the sheets of mosaic down with a wooden batten to make sure they are level and securely fixed. When all the whole sheets are in place, the next step is to cut the strips of mosaic to fill the gaps at the perimeter of the wall or floor. Then, if necessary, mark off any individual pieces of mosaic to be cut, and fix these in place.

Mosaics are ideal for tiling round curved fixtures, such as a WC. You simply butt a sheet of mosaics against the base of the WC and push it up so some of the tiles will fit round the corner. You can then tear off individual tiles to fit round the front part of the WC base. Usually you will still have to fill some gaps with cut, shaped tiles. For this you will need to make a cardboard template of the required shape and mark this off on the individual tiles to be cut. With very small gaps, a bit of extra grouting won't look out of place or upset the clean lines of the tiles.

Grouting mosaics

You should allow the adhesive to set before applying the grout and follow the manufacturer's instructions carefully. As when you are applying adhesive, work over only about 1 sq m (11 sq ft) at a time. Allow the grout to dry for about 24 hours before walking on the floor. However, if the mosaics have a paper facing, you can apply the grout to the back of the sheet making sure all the gaps between the tiles are well filled. The tiles should then be laid quickly on the adhesive and when dry the paper facing has to be removed (see *Ready Reference*). Then the grouting can be finished neatly as shown below.

2 Use a smooth rounded stick, such as a length of dowel, to smooth off the joins in the grouting so there won't be any ugly bumps or gaps.

3 Remove excess adhesive with a damp cloth or sponge before the grout dries. When the grout has set, you can complete final polishing with a dry cloth.

FLOORCOVERINGS

Changing your floorcoverings can be an expensive job, and
certainly means considerable upheaval while the old flooring
is lifted and the new one laid.
Using the right techniques ensures a perfect fit and long life,
whether you're laying materials off the roll or in tile form.

STRIPPING TIMBER FLOORS

Sanding wooden floorboards is dusty, time-consuming work, but it's not difficult. You'll find the effort well worthwhile when the boards are transformed into an attractive floor surface.

Using floorcoverings can be expensive, particularly if you have to deal with passages, stairs or landings as well as main rooms. As an alternative you could decide to leave a wooden floor uncovered after treatment to make it an attractive surface in its own right. Since timber is one of the most versatile flooring materials there is, it will fit in with most styles of decor, whether modern or traditional. It's extremely hardwearing and easy to look after. And, just as important, it has a warmth you don't get with most modern floorings of comparable durability.

You can, if you wish, lay a new timber floor, if the old one is rotten or in a bad state of repair, finishing it with stains or varnish to bring out the natural beauty of the wood. But the chances are you won't need to go to this expense. You may well have a wooden floor already which you've covered up. The old floorboards may not look much when you first expose them but if you sand them smooth to take off the uneven top layers engrained with dirt you'll be surprised how beautiful they can become, especially after they've been coated with varnish to make the grain pattern clear.

Checking out the floor

Of course, ordinary floorboards are not intended to be displayed, so you cannot guarantee good results. A particularly unattractive, inferior grade of timber may have been used. Or the boards may have been badly laid or badly looked after. The only way to find out is to lift any floorcovering and see for yourself. You can make a preliminary survey simply by lifting a corner of the floorcovering; but to be absolutely sure the whole floor should be exposed.

When you lift the existing floorcovering, take care to remove any fixing nails and the remains of flooring adhesive. Many flooring adhesives are soluble in white spirit (turps) or petrol. But obviously, if you're using petrol you must ensure the room is adequately ventilated. Don't smoke while you're doing the work.

The look of the timber grain is important, but here much depends on personal taste. Some people like wooden floors to have even, restrained grain patterns; others feel that, unless the pattern is striking and irregular, the floor doesn't look like real wood. It's up to you, but do allow for the fact that any grain pattern will become slightly more pronounced once the boards have been sanded and sealed.

You should also see if the floorboards have been stained, and if so, whether or not the staining covers the entire floor: it was once popular to stain the edges and cover the central unstained portion with a carpet or linoleum square. If the staining has been carried out over the whole of the floor area there shouldn't be any problem with sanding and sealing later. Thoroughly sand a trial area by hand to get an idea of the finished result. If you don't like the way the floor looks, you can try restaining it experimentally; alternatively try to lighten or remove the existing wood stain with a proprietary wood bleach. Border staining can be more of a problem because of the need to match the border with the unstained part of the floor. Again, experimenting with stains and bleaches is the only answer; make sure you sand the test area first. If, when later you come to tackle the job in earnest, you give the floor its main sanding after staining, there is a risk that the old and new stains will respond in rather different ways.

Preparing the surface

When you've got a good idea of what the final result will look like, you can turn your attention to the physical state of the floor. Are there lots of large gaps, wider than 2 or 3mm (up to 1/8in) between boards? If there are, the finished floor may well turn out to be excessively draughty so you will have to fill the gaps before sanding. To maintain the floor's 'natural' look involves tailoring a fillet of timber for each gap and you may well decide, as a result, that a wooden floor simply isn't worth the effort. Watch out, too, for signs of excessive localised wear resulting in dips and ridges that no amount of sanding will remove. And, finally, check for signs of woodworm. This must be treated, but, remember, woodworm treatment will not restore the appearance of the affected wood.

If, at this stage, things don't look too promising, there are three remedies to consider which may provide you with the solution you require.

The first is a cure for gaps. All you do is lift every single board and re-lay them closer together: not difficult but very hard work. Next there is the remedy for boards disfigured by wear or woodworm, and you can also use it to overcome the problems associated with stained boards. Again, all you do is lift and re-lay the boards, but this time, you re-lay them with what used to be the underside uppermost. This is also very hard work, and there is a possibility that the underside of the boards may look no better; a good builder should have laid the boards with the worse side face down when the house was built.

Because of the amount of work involved with both of these solutions it's best to consider them as a last resort. You could instead adopt the third remedy: give up the idea of sanding the existing boards and cover them with new ones. Such 'non-structural' boards are available in a variety of hardwoods and softwoods, so the results can be very rewarding indeed in that you will end up with a very attractively coloured and grained floor surface. However, this type of floor is likely to prove very expensive and rather tricky to lay. The actual techniques involved will be covered in a later article.

If, on the other hand, you check the boards and discover that they are suitable for sanding, you should fill any gaps and make sure there are no protruding nails or screws. These should be driven well below the surface otherwise there could be dire consequences when you are sanding (see *Ready Reference*). Giving screws an extra half a turn should do the trick; otherwise unscrew them, drill out a deeper countersink and replace them. For nails which cause you a problem you will need a nail punch (if you don't have one you can use an old blunt nail instead) to drive the offending nails home so they can't cause any further nuisance.

Sanding the floor

Sanding floorboards is in essence, no different to sanding any piece of natural timber. You must work your way through coarse, medium and then fine grades of abrasive until you achieve the desired finish. It's simply that you are working on a larger scale than usual.

However, this question of scale does create a few complications. First, there will be a great deal of dust flying about, and a lot of noise, so you must protect yourself with the appropriate safety equipment (see *Ready Reference*). You must also take steps to stop the dust being trodden all round your home. Second, the job will be far too large for sanding by hand and, in any case, the average DIY power sander wouldn't be up to the task. What you need are two special floor sanders, and these you will have to hire. (See below for tips on hiring.)

The first sander looks a bit like a lawn mower, but is in fact a giant belt sander and its role is to tackle the bulk of the floor. It has a revolving rubber-covered drum set on a wheeled frame which can be tilted backwards to lift the drum from the floor. You wrap a sheet of abrasive round the drum to provide the sanding surface. There is a bag attached to the sander into which a fan blows the wood dust and particles produced by the sanding process. The second sander is a sort of heavy duty orbital sander, and it is used to tackle the parts the main sander cannot reach. It works on the same principle as the large sander (you attach an abrasive sheet to a rubber pad) but, being small and lighter, it's easier to manoeuvre.

You won't be able to rely entirely on these labour-saving devices, though. After machine sanding there will be small unsanded patches left, usually at the edges of the floor and these will have to be sanded by hand or scraped with a shave hook or some other form of scraper.

The need to hire equipment raises a further complication: careful planning is needed to keep the cost to a minimum. As always, the best way to start is by shopping around the hire shops in your area to find the best price. In particular, look for firms that give discounts for extended periods of hire (for example, one where the weekly rate is cheaper than say, four or five days at the day rate) and find out how much flexibility there is in allowing you to switch rates should you decide to keep the sanders for a day or two longer than originally anticipated. This is important because, although it's only sensible to keep the period of hire to a minimum by doing all the preparation (punching nail heads below the surface and so on) before you pick up the equipment, and returning it as soon as you've finished, floor sanding is physically very demanding, and may well take longer than you think.

Check up, too, on the cost of the abrasives. If there is a marked difference in price between two shops, it may be due to the fact that, while one offers ordinary glasspaper, the other offers a more modern synthetic paper which will last longer and clog less readily, and so works out cheaper than it appears. You will also encounter differences in the way abrasives are provided. For example, some shops will give a refund for any abrasive you don't use. A point to remember here is that as it's difficult to estimate exactly how much abrasive you will need it's wise to take an amount which appears surplus to requirements. If you take this precaution you will avoid the annoying situation where you have to down tools and buy extra abrasive.

PREPARING THE FLOOR

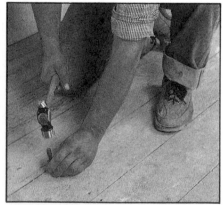

1 *Go over the entire floor, punching all nail heads well below the surface. If screws have been used, check they're adequately countersunk.*

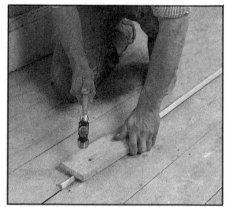

2 *Cut thin fillets of wood to fill gaps between the boards; hammer them in, protecting the edges of the fillets with a block of softwood.*

3 *Plane the fillets flush with the surrounding surface, taking off a little at a time to prevent chipping and splintering.*

ORDER OF WORK

After you have checked that the floor is in a suitable condition for sanding, with gaps filled and no protruding nails or screws, you should adopt the procedure indicated below when using the large and small sanding machines. The arrows indicate in which direction the sander should be moved.

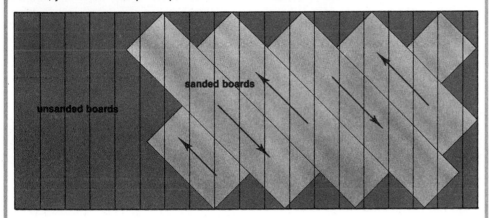

1 Use the large sander in a diagonal direction across the boards in order to flatten them out and remove thoroughly the top dirt-engrained layer.

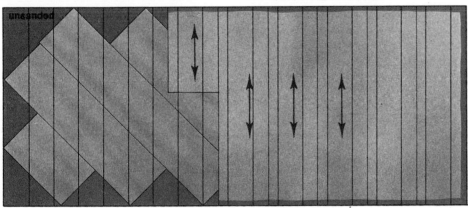

2 Work in strips along the boards. Work down a strip, then with the machine on, move back along the strip. Switch off when you reach your starting point.

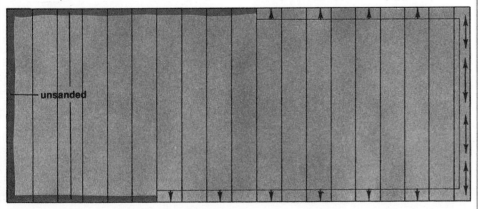

3 When the floor has been sanded as in (2), with first coarse, then medium and fine abrasives, you can use the small sander on the perimeter of the floor.

Ready Reference

PUNCH NAILS DOWN
Make sure there are no protruding nails or screws in the floor surface before you begin sanding, because:
● if screws or nails are less than 2-3mm (1/12-1/8in) below the surface of the boards there's a good chance they will tear the abrasive sheets
● a protruding nail will cause an explosion of flying bits of abrasive which can be dangerous; it may also damage the sander.

KEEP DOORS AND WINDOWS CLOSED
To prevent dust from permeating other areas of the house, keep doors closed. Close the windows, too, to allow the dust to settle so it can be vacuumed up.

SAFETY EQUIPMENT
Sanding is extremely dusty, very noisy work, so you should wear the appropriate equipment to protect yourself. A mask, to prevent you from breathing in dust, is a must; you should also consider ear muffs to protect your ears from the din, and goggles so dust and flying bits of grit don't get in your eyes.

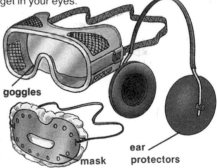

goggles

mask

ear protectors

ELECTRICAL SAFETY
To prevent nasty accidents, you should make sure the electrical cord is out of the path of the sander. One way to do this is to drape the cord over your shoulders as you are working.

FLATTEN WARPED BOARDS
Use the weight of the sander to flatten the edges of any warped boards in the first **stage** of sanding by running the sander diagonally across the boards.

SAND WITH THE GRAIN
When you are sanding in strips down the length of the room in the second stage of sanding, work in the same direction as the grain of the timber or you will cut deep, difficult-to-remove scratches in the surface.

SANDING AND SEALING THE BOARDS

1 Fit a large floor sander with a coarse grade of abrasive; the paper is locked into a slot in the revolving drum of the machine.

2 You can now start sanding the floor by running the sander diagonally across the floorboards to remove the rough and dirty surface layer.

3 Continue sanding the floor in this way until the bulk of the floor area has been treated; the sander will flatten out any warped boards.

4 Sand a strip down the length of the room. Work in the same direction as the boards and allow the sander to pull you along.

5 Sand this strip again, dragging the sander backwards. Repeat for the rest of the floor. Afterwards, sand using medium then fine grades of paper.

6 Use a small sander to sand round the perimeter using progressively finer grades of paper. Work in the direction of the grain.

7 You can use a shave hook to scrape stubborn areas at the edges. Other areas that the machines have missed will have to be sanded by hand.

8 Allow the dust to settle, then vacuum the floor clean, paying particular attention to the gaps between the floor and skirting.

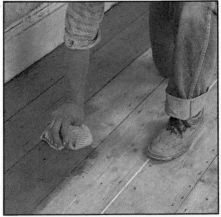

9 To reduce the amount of sealant needed, apply polyurethane varnish, diluted with white spirit on a clean cloth to prime the boards.

Finally, you should make sure that the shop from which you hire the equipment will give you adequate tuition on how to use and clean the sanders. If you damage them through misuse, or return them dirty, you will have to pay more.

Finishing the floor

Having dealt with the sanding, the final thing you have to consider is how to finish the floor: that is, add to its decorative quality and protect the boards from scratches and other types of wear.

If you feel that the boards are too dark to leave as they are after sanding you can apply bleach to lighten them. Use a proprietary wood bleach and follow the manufacturer's instructions for applying it. The fumes from the bleach can be at the least unpleasant and at worst dangerous, so make sure you keep the windows open and wear a protective face mask.

You may want to change the colour of the boards, as well as lighten them. You could use coloured polyurethane varnish for this, but as the surface of the floor becomes subject to wear, so the colour may become thin in some places, highlighting the wear more strongly than you would wish. So it's better to use wood stains which colour the timber itself and then seal with clear polyurethane varnish. Again apply the stain according to the manufacturer's instructions as to the number of coats needed. Work in the direction of the grain when you are applying the stain. (Stains, which come in a variety of colours, allow you to go in for different attractive decorative effects.)

Polyurethane varnish is by far the best choice for sealing the floor, simply because it is so hardwearing and easy to look after. You should choose a brand that is available in large cans rather than in the small tins you are probably familiar with. You'll need a lot to give the floor the two or three coats it requires, and buying such a large amount in small cans can work out very expensive. It's up to you whether you choose a polyurethane giving a high gloss, a satin look or a matt finish; it all depends on the style of the room as a whole. However, it's worth bearing in mind that a very high gloss will show marks more readily and may make the floor rather slippery.

Care and maintenance

To look its best, a wooden floor should be kept free of dust; regular vacuuming will attend to this. If you like a shiny look you can polish it with a proprietary floor polish. Dirty marks can be removed with a damp cloth or mop; more stubborn marks may require treatment with a proprietary cleaner. Where the finish or floorboard has been slightly damaged, such as by a cigarette burn, you will have to sand down the affected area until the signs of damage are removed and then apply polyurethane to reseal it. If there is more extensive damage you will have to remove the affected floorboards, replace them (or use them with the undamaged side face up), sand to provide a smooth surface and reseal.

Take care when you are moving bits of furniture about that they don't scratch the surface (see *Ready Reference*). There's not much point in spending the time and energy it takes to get an attractive varnished wooden floor surface only to spoil it in a few careless minutes.

10 *Follow the priming with at least two, preferably three, coats of polyurethane varnish applied with a brush, working with the grain.*

11 *Allow each coat to dry, then rub lightly down with medium glasspaper to provide a key for the next. Use a damp cloth to remove dust.*

LAYING FOAM-BACKED CARPET

Having wall-to-wall carpet is most people's idea of floorcovering luxury. You can even lay it yourself if you choose the right type of carpet.

Carpet is warm and luxurious underfoot, a good insulator, which is particularly important in flats and upstairs rooms, and still something of a status symbol when fitted in every room – particularly in the bathroom. Modern methods of weaving carpets, and the development of new synthetic fibres, have made some forms of carpeting relatively inexpensive, but it is silly to buy carpet just because it is the conventional thing to have; or for its luxurious image and status.

Consider whether it is a practical proposition for your home. Carpets in bathrooms where there are young children splashing about, (or where the lavatory is situated in the same room) may not be a wise choice. Carpets in kitchens (even the special 'utility' area type) are not always practical at the cooking/washing up end of the room, (although the eating end can be carpeted to co-ordinate with a more easycare surface at the 'business' end of the room). In family rooms, childrens' bedrooms and playrooms, halls and dining rooms, a washable surface may be the answer, softened with large cotton rugs (these can be cleaned in a washing machine), a carpet square or rush matting. But for the sitting room, master bedroom, stairs and corridors, there is really no substitute for carpet.

Choosing carpets

So how do you decide exactly which type of carpet to buy? Of course, you will start by looking for a colour or pattern you like, but a trip to a local carpet specialist or department store can often result in complete confusion once you have seen the range. As a general guide, you should choose the best quality (and consequently the most expensive) you can afford for heavy 'traffic' areas such as hallways, stairs, landings and main living rooms. You can then select the lighter weights and cheaper grades for the rooms which get less wear, like bedrooms, bathrooms and so on.

The carpet industry has produced a labelling system which divides the carpets into categories. In each case the label gives details of how the carpet is made, what fibres have been used and how durable it is likely to be.

This is quite a useful guide, but you should also ask for advice from the salesman. Here are some of the terms it helps to know.

Carpet weaves

The traditional types of carpet are known as Axminster and Wilton, terms which refer to the way they are woven.

An **Axminster** carpet is usually patterned and has an extensive choice of colours within the design. The backing is jute or hessian, sometimes strengthened by polypropylene. Different fibres and blends of fibres are used, but an Axminster is frequently woven in an 80 per cent wool and 20 per cent nylon mixture, and also from acrylic fibres, which resemble wool in appearance and feel.

Axminsters come in many different widths, up to 5m (16½ft) wide. They also come with bound and finished edges, known as carpet 'squares', although they are not necessarily square in shape. This type of carpet can be turned round within a room to even out the wear.

A **Wilton** carpet is usually plain or two-tone, although there are some patterned Wiltons made with a restricted number of colours. The carpet is generally close-textures with a velvet, looped, twist-and-loop, or a mixed cut-and-loop pile (called sculptured or carved). Any yarn not used on the face of the carpet is woven into the backing, to add to the thickness, and the backing is usually jute

or hessian.

Different fibres and blends of fibres can be used in the construction, but Wiltons are usually made with 100 per cent wool pile, the 80/20 blend (as Axminster) or from an acrylic fibre.

Wilton carpet is woven in widths from 700mm (27in) to 2m (6ft 6in), which are then seamed together when the carpet is to be fully fitted; 3.75m (12ft) widths are also available in some ranges and can be bound to form a carpet 'square'.

Tufted carpets are a more modern type which has been developed during the last 25 years. Tufted carpets come in many different fibre mixtures including wool and wool blends. Widths vary from 1m (3ft) to 5m (16½ft). The tufts are 'needled' into a ready-woven backing and anchored by adhesive; when the main backing is hessian, this can be given a coat of latex to secure the tufts. Foam backing can then be stuck to the main backing; a high-quality foam-backed tufted carpet does not need an underlay.

Bonded carpets are made face-to-face, with the carpet pile held between two specially-treated woven backings. The carpet is then 'sliced' down the middle at the finishing stage, and becomes two carpets. The pile can be cut to different lengths to give a carpet with a texture ranging from a shaggy pile to a velvety velour. Fibres can be wool, wool blends or several different synthetics, and the carpet is usually plain. Widths are as for Axminster carpets.

Needlefelt or needleloom carpet is not really woven. A fibrous material is needled into a strong backing to create a looped ribbed pile or one which looks like dense felt. The fibres used are normally synthetic and the carpet has a rather harsh texture. The backing can be resin-coated hessian or foam, and the surface can be printed or plain. Various widths are available.

Broadloom or body?

These are terms used to describe the width of carpet. **Broadloom** carpets are 1.8m (6ft) or more wide, and are the practical choice for fitted carpets in all but the smallest rooms. **Body** carpets are usually 700 to 900mm (27 to 35in) wide, and are intended for use on stairs and in corridors, although they can be seamed together to cover larger areas.

Carpet fibres

All the carpets previously mentioned can be made in several different types of fibre or different blends, which creates still more confusion.

Acrylic fibres are the synthetic fibres most similar to wool. They have long-lasting qualities, and good resistance to flattening, but are not quite so springy as wool. They tend to soil more easily than a natural fibre, but they can be treated to resist staining and to be anti-static. Acrylic fibres come under many brand names, such as Courtelle and Acrilan.

Nylon is a hardwearing fibre, which has a characteristic shiny look. It soils easily, and can look flat and sad if it is the only fibre used in the carpet construction, but when added to other fibres it increases the durability con-

siderably. Nylon is frequently used in an 80/20 mix with wool.

Polyester is a soft fibre, used to create fluffy light-duty carpets. It is not very hard-wearing and does become flattened easily, but it can be blended with other fibres.

Polypropylene is a fairly tough fibre, which is often used to create 'cord' effect carpet. It does not absorb liquid, so it is often used for carpet tiles and carpets for kitchen and utility rooms.

Viscose rayon is not used very much these days, and has poor wearing and soiling qualities, but it can be used as part of a blend of fibres quite successfully.

Wool is the traditional carpet fibre, and no real substitute for it has yet been found. Wool is warm, hard-wearing, resilient and does not soil easily; from the safety point of view it also resists the spread of flame. It is used alone, or blended with other fibres. The most widely-used blend, 80 per cent wool and 20 per cent nylon, gives the best performance.

Other carpet types

Apart from the diferent methods of carpet making, and the various blends of fibres, you will find there are many other words in the carpet salesman's vocabulary, which loosely cover what might be called carpet styles, or types.

Cord carpets, for example, come in several styles. Originally the only type was a haircord, which was made from natural animal fibres, and was very hardwearing. This is now very expensive and is not frequently used, but there are some blends of animal hair with synthetic fibres available, and some much cheaper cords which are not particularly hard-

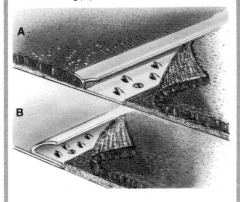
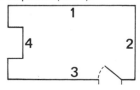
PREPARING THE FLOOR

1 *Lift old floorcoverings completely, and remove all traces of underlay. Nail down any loose boards securely with 38mm (1½in) nails.*

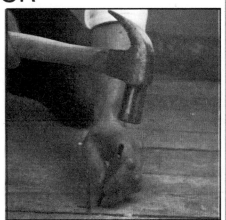

2 *Use a nail punch and hammer to ensure that all the nail heads are flush with, or driven below, the surface of the boards.*

wearing. Other types of cord carpet include the Berbers; which have a looped pile and look homespun. Originally these were made from un-dyed, coarsely-woven wool, by Berber tribesmen. Now they are made in many different fibres, including blends of wool and synthetic fibres. These are often called Berber-style.

Hardtwist is a curly, crush-resistant pile, which is sometimes called twist pile. This is frequently found in high-quality Wiltons, in wool or wool blends, but may also be found in all-synthetic carpets.

Shag pile carpets have a long pile, which can be plain or kinked and with a richly textured shaggy surface. The pile needs raking if it is very long, to maintain its appearance, and it is not a practical carpet to choose for areas which get a lot of wear, on stairs, or in halls for example.

Shadow pile is another fairly new development in carpet style. The pile is dyed so it has contrasting colour or tone, usually darker at the base, lightening towards the tip. The pile is usually shiny (synthetic fibres) and when the carpet is walked on the dark tones show as 'shadows'.

Sculptured pile is usually made by combining a looped and cut pile to form a self-coloured pattern, although sometimes different colours can be used. Fibres can be natural, synthetic or a mixture of both.

Printed carpets are another fairly recent development. The carpet is woven and then a design is printed on the surface via computer-controlled dye injection systems. They often resemble Axminsters in colour and design, but on closer examination you can see the pattern does not go right through to the backing. The fibres used in this range are usually synthetic, and the pile is frequently very close and sometimes looped or corded.

Planning and estimating

As with any other floorcovering, start your planning by taking accurate measurements of the room at ground level with a steel tape or yardstick. If possible, work out a scale plan on squared paper, marking in the recesses, corners, angles, projections and so on. Take this with you when you shop for carpet, so the salesman can work out exactly how much you need. It is usual to multiply the room measurements to get square yards or square metres, and you will find most carpeting is sold by the square yard or metre, although some types are still sold by the linear yard or metre.

With the more expensive types of carpet with hessian backing, it is wise to call in an expert to lay the carpet for you, unless you have had a great deal of experience laying other types of carpet and floorcovering. Otherwise you risk marring an expensive carpet if you make a cut in the wrong place; what's

LAYING THE LINING

1 Unroll the lining down the length of the room. Smooth out the strip and staple down both sides 50mm (2in) in from the edge.

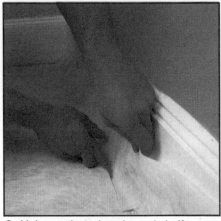

2 Using a sharp handyman's knife, cut off a strip of the lining 38mm (1½in) wide between the line of staples and the skirting board.

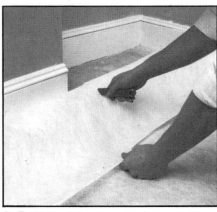

3 To fit the lining into an alcove, lay the strip up against the face of the chimney breast and make a cut with your knife in line with its corner.

4 Staple down the cut end of the length as before, after ensuring that it is perfectly flat. Then cut off the border strip next to the skirting board.

5 Continue covering the rest of the floor with the lining, overlapping each succeeding strip with the previous one by about 25mm (1in).

6 Stick double-sided self-adhesive tape down all round the edge of the room where you have cut off the strip of lining. Do not remove the release paper.

POSITIONING THE CARPET

1 Unroll the carpet parallel with the longest wall, and position it so that there is an overlap at the skirting board all round the room.

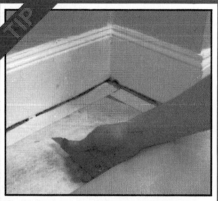

3 At fireplaces gauge the depth of the alcoves using your cutting knife as a guide. Add 75mm (3in) to allow for the final trimming.

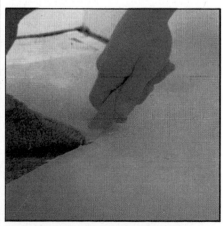

5 Cut across the end of the tongue of carpet that fits into the alcove, taking care not to cut into the pile underneath the tongue.

2 Roughly trim off the excess carpet with a sharp handyman's knife to leave a 75mm (3in) overlap all round; cut through the foam backing behind.

4 Cut into the alcove as you did with the lining. Make the first cut parallel with the side of the chimney breast and allow the tongue to fall into place.

6 At the corner of the chimney breast, make a diagonal cut on the underside of the carpet, and trim across the face of the chimney breast.

Ready Reference

CUTTING IN AT DOORWAYS

At doorways carpet should extend to a point under the centre of the door. To get an accurate fit round architraves and door stops, start making release cuts in the overlap at one side of the door opening, until the tongue falls neatly into the door opening. Then trim it to fit neatly under the threshold strip (see *Ready Reference*, page 177).

COPING WITH BAY WINDOWS

It's often easier to cope with odd-shaped bay windows by trimming the two flanking walls first. Then
● pull the carpet down the room until its edge is across the 'mouth' of the bay

● measure the depth of the bay, and cut a strip of wood to match this measurement
● use it to trace off the profile on the carpet, marking the line with chalk

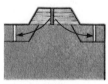

● trim along the marked line and slide the carpet back into place against the wall containing the bay.

FITTING ROUND PIPEWORK

Where pipes to radiators come up through the floor, you will have to cut the carpet to fit neatly round them. To do this
● make an incision in the edge of the carpet, parallel with one edge of the pipe
● measure the distance between wall and pipe, and cut out a small circle in the carpet at this distance from the edge
● fit the carpet round the pipe.

FITTING ANGLES

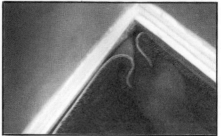

1 *To fit the carpet tightly into an angle, press your thumb firmly down into the corner as shown.*

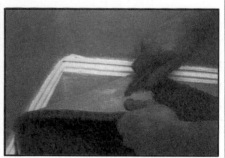

2 *Pull up the corner, keeping your thumb in place, and make an incision just beyond the end of your thumb.*

3 *Cut cleanly across the corner in line with the incision, and press the carpet back in position.*

TAPING SEAMS

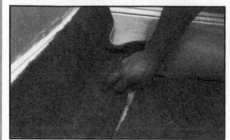

1 *Carefully trim the edges of the two pieces to be joined, and check that they butt neatly together.*

2 *Cut a piece of carpet tape to the length of the join, peel off the release paper and bed one carpet edge on it.*

3 *Position the other piece of carpet over the tape, and press it down firmly right along the join.*

FINAL TRIMMING

1 *Press the carpet tightly into the base of the skirting board with the back of an old knife or a pair of scissors.*

2 *Turn back the carpet and cut off the excess, using the score mark made by the knife back as a guide.*

3 *Peel off the release paper from the border tape and press the carpet firmly into place.*

more, it will wear out prematurely unless it is tensioned correctly during installation. This involves fitting special toothed gripper strips all round the perimeter of the room, and hooking the carpet on to the teeth once it has been pulled taut across the room.

The foam-backed types are, however, easier to lay yourself, because tensioning is not necessary.

If you are having the carpet professionally laid, ask for a written estimate and check carefully to see whether the price includes underlay or not, and if not, how much extra this will be. With an expensive carpet it may be wise to get several quotes from different firms. Some firms quote a price for carpet 'laid', but again check to see whether underlay is included in the price.

There are several different types of underlay – at different prices. The cheapest is the conventional brown felt, but there are also rubber and synthetic foams, including one on a coarse hessian backing. Foam-backed carpets definitely do not need underlay.

Laying carpet
It is usual to plan and lay carpet so the seams (if any) come in the least obvious place and where the 'traffic' is lightest. When the carpet has to be seamed, both pieces must be laid so the pile is going in the same direction, otherwise the colour would appear slightly different on each side of the seam. The floor should be clean, level and free from dust and debris. Punch down any nail heads that are proud of the floor surface, and nail down any loose boards. If the boards are very uneven, cover them with sheets of hardboard pinned down at 230mm (9in) intervals to disguise the ridges. Otherwise simply lay stout brown paper or nylon lining to prevent dust from blowing up between floorboards.

Never lay a new carpet down on top of an existing one; the worn areas will quickly transfer themselves to the new carpet. It is not wise to use old underfelt either.

Do not lay a carpet with a latex backing, or a latex underlay, in rooms which have underfloor central heating, as you could find it gives off an unpleasant smell.

LAYING HESSIAN-BACKED CARPET

There's no denying that laying hessian-backed carpet requires a fair degree of skill. But with care and some practice you can learn how to use a knee kicker to stretch this type of carpet into place and so provide a longlasting floorcovering.

Most really heavy quality carpets will not have a foam backing and therefore need to be laid with a separate underlay. A traditional method of securing such carpet is to 'turn and tack' it; the carpet is folded under at the perimeter of the room and non-rustling tacks are then driven through the fold to hold it to the floor. The underlay is cut to size so it meets the folded-under edge of the carpet. The problem with this method is that the tacks will be visible and will leave indentations in the carpet; also, you are likely to end up with scalloped edges and the carpet will be difficult to remove.

Consequently, most carpets which do not have a foam backing are laid using a system without tacks: the carpet is stretched over wooden or metal strips containing two staggered rows of angled pins which hook into the back of the carpet. This method provides an invisible fixing and it's quite simple to lift the carpet off the pins if you want to take it up later. But it's a much more complex method of fitting and fixing carpet than sticking down a foam-backed carpet (see pages 176–180).

Your chief problem is likely to be the stretching process: if you stretch the carpet too much it will tear; if you stretch it too little there will be lumps, which apart from being unsightly, will wear through quickly because of their exposed position.

A good professional fitter will be able to get the tension right according to the feel of the carpet. So at the outset it's worth considering the benefits of calling in an expert. Your chief guideline here will probably be cost and value for money. Fitting charges are, in fact, similar whether you are laying an inexpensive or a costly floorcovering. So, obviously, the costs of professional fitting relative to an expensive carpet make more sense than with a cheap one.

Bearing all this in mind you may decide you want to go ahead and fit your own carpet. There are many examples of successful DIY carpet fitting and yours may well be one of them. To ensure a good result it is worth practising fitting techniques on an old carpet you're going to discard before you begin on your new one. And it's certainly worth tackling a simple rectangular room, with no awkward alcoves or bays, first of all, so the job will not be too complicated.

Tools and equipment
After you have measured up you can order the amount of carpet and underlay you'll need. Take a scale plan of the room along to your supplier so he can work out how much you need and check with him on the type of underlay which will suit the carpet you have chosen. A good quality underlay improves the feel of the carpet underfoot and, by serving as a buffer between the carpet and floor, helps to ensure even wear. It will also compensate for small defects if the floor is level but not perfectly smooth. For extra protection against dirt and dust rising up through the floorboards on a wooden floor you can lay paper or nylon lining underneath, so you will need to buy this as well.

You will also have to buy adequate carpet gripper. Gripper strips (commonly called smooth edge) can be nailed or glued to the floor. Strips intended for nailing come complete with pins for fixing to timber floors or masonry nails for fixing to solid floors. You will, obviously, have to buy adhesive of a suitable type (check with your supplier) if you are going to glue the strips in place.

In addition, you will require hessian tape and adhesive for joining lengths of carpet and, if you are going to fix the underlay, staples (and a staple gun), tacks, adhesive or self-adhesive tape.

You will probably already have most of the tools required for this type of work: knife, shears, tin snips for cutting the gripper, hammer, bolster chisel and steel tape or wooden measure. You will also need a knee kicker to hook the carpet onto the gripper. This is relatively expensive, so it makes sense to hire one if, as is likely, you don't intend to go in for regular carpet fitting.

Preparing the floor surface
The floor surface must be level, smooth and dry. Wood floors can be sanded or covered with hardboard or an underlay; if the only problem is protruding nails you should punch the nails down or countersink the screws. Damp may also be a problem which needs tackling at a more basic level. If the floor is concrete, or has a composite surface, unevenness can be treated with a self-levelling screed (see pages 208–209 for more details of how to do this).

The first stages
If you have decided to fix a paper lining, you will have to spot-glue, staple or tack it to the floor. You can then fix the gripper in place;

FIXING GRIPPER STRIPS

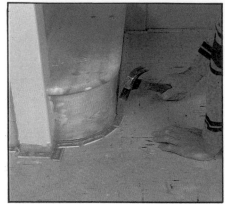

1 *Cut the strips to length and nail them down so there's a gap of just less than the carpet thickness between them and the wall.*

2 *Cut short lengths and lay them with small gaps between them to follow a curve. Use a minimum of two nails to fix each piece in position.*

LAYING THE UNDERLAY

1 *Roll out the underlay and then position it so one end just comes up to the edge of the gripper strips fixed along one wall.*

2 *Cut the underlay so the end of the first length reaches the edge of the gripper strips along the opposite wall. Cut and lay other lengths.*

4 *Neatly trim what's left of the overlap so it fits exactly up to the edges of the gripper strips in the same way as for straight lengths.*

3 *At a curve or an angle, leave an overlap, and cut it at intervals so it fits around the obstacle. Then roughly trim off the excess.*

Ready Reference

TIP: AVOID BURIED PIPES

Solid floors often have pipes running close to the floor surface, so if there is a radiator in the room it's better to stick down the gripper along the length of the wall to which the radiator is attached rather than risk nailing it.

GULLY WIDTH

The space between the edge of the gripper and the wall is known as the gully. Its width should be slightly less than the uncompressed thickness of the carpet.

FIXING THE FIRST EDGE

To hold the carpet firmly down during stretching you will have to use what's known as the 'starting edge technique'. This is used to hook the carpet along the first two walls to be fitted; the carpet is hooked along the other two walls by stretching. Select a starting corner (one where you will have a reasonably uninterrupted run of walls is best) and follow this procedure:
● ease the edge of the carpet up the wall about 10mm (3/8in)
● rub your fingertips along the carpet over the gripper with a steady downward pressure so the back row of pins start penetrating the warp (A)
● use a hammer to press the carpet down between the gripper and the wall (B)
● don't try to turn the compressed carpet into the gully at this stage or you will release the pressure on the pins.

A

B

LAYING THE CARPET

1 Place the carpet roughly over the underlay, then adjust its position more exactly. Arrange it so the edges 'climb up' the walls all round.

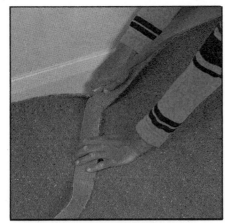

2 Trim off most of the surplus so there's an overlap of about 50mm (2in) at the wall and floor join; this makes the carpet easier to handle.

3 Adjust the teeth of the knee kicker so they grip the carpet backing, hold the head down firmly, then 'kick' the pad with your knee.

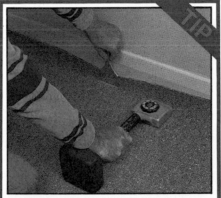

4 When making the next 'kick' use a bolster to hold down the carpet where you made the previous one so it doesn't spring back off the pins.

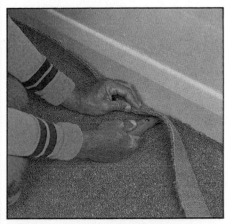

5 When all the carpet has been stretched and fixed in place, trim off the excess so there's about 10mm (³/₈in) lapping up against the walls.

6 Use a bolster or thin piece of wood to press the overlap neatly into the gully between the gripper strips and the walls ensuring a snug fit.

lengths of gripper can be placed end-to-end on straight walls. Recesses, bays and projections can be tackled by cutting the gripper into small pieces which you position to follow the contour of the wall. You can tack or stick the gripper down as you go along or when it is all in position. Tacking will also anchor the paper-felt lining. Where it is being stuck and a lining has been used, be careful to stick the gripper to the floor and not just to the lining, which should in fact be cut away within about 50mm (2in) of the wall all round the room.

With all the gripper satisfactorily in place, you can put down the underlay. It does not have to be fixed to the floor; lengths can simply be placed so they butt join without being secured. If you handle the carpet carefully, it should not disturb the underlay when you pull it over. If you feel happier securing the underlay, you can spot-stick it to the subfloor or anchor it to board floors with tacks or a stapling gun and tape successive lengths together where they abut.

If you have stuck the gripper down and it has been in place for the time recommended in the manufacturer's instructions, it's worth going round and trying to pull it off to make sure the adhesive has set really hard.

Laying the carpet

Unroll the carpet and place it roughly in position with the excess 'climbing up' the walls. Make sure the pattern (if any) is square and that the pile is leaning away from the light to prevent uneven shading in daylight. Position it so any seams will not be in areas of hard wear, such as doorways. You can roughly trim the overlap so the carpet is less cumbersome to handle when you are fitting it. Make sure you have left nothing under the carpet which shouldn't be there. You can then walk all over it and leave it to settle so that it flattens out.

As with foam-backed carpet, when you are trimming the carpet, and specially when you are cutting down into the overlap so it will fit round a corner or curve, make sure you do not cut too deeply or you will ruin the final effect. This and getting the tension right are likely to be your two major problems. Go round the room hooking and stretching in the required direction (see *Ready Reference*). Once you have hooked the carpet, stand back and take a look at it. It may not look straight and you might feel that it would be worth taking it off and starting again. Remember that one of the benefits of the tackless gripper method is that it's easy to hook and unhook a carpet so that you can get the adjustment right.

Where the carpet meets another type of floorcovering in a doorway, you can secure it with a threshold strip. You simply nail this down and then press the carpet onto the pins in the strip.

TRIMMING EDGES

1 *Where the corner forms a curve, cut down into the overlap so the carpet will fit round the curve; take care not to cut too deep.*

2 *At an external angled corner turn the carpet back and cut diagonally at the corner for a short distance and then straight towards you.*

3 *Trim off the bulk of the overlap, let the carpet flap back against the walls and then trim the overlap again for a perfect final fit.*

JOINING LENGTHS

1 *Lay the lengths of carpet so they butt against each other, then cut a length of hessian tape and place it so it fits beneath the two edges.*

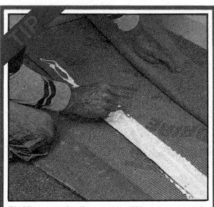

2 *Use a small carpet offcut to spread adhesive along the tape. Take care that you don't get adhesive on the front of the carpet.*

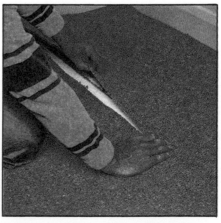

3 *You can then flap the edges back into position so they are held in place by the adhesive, and press the carpet down firmly along the seam.*

Ready Reference

STRETCHING CORRECTLY

To fit the carpet properly you should carry out the stretching and hooking in the following order:

● start at corner A and hook the carpet about 300mm (12in) along walls AB and AC. Stretch from A to B and hook on about 300mm (12in) of carpet along wall BD

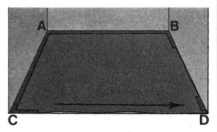

● hook the carpet along the full length of wall AB, then repeat in direction A to C. Stretch the carpet from C to D and hook it on. Stretch across the width of the carpet from wall AB as you hook onto wall CD

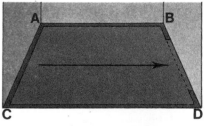

● stretch across the full length of the carpet from wall AC as you hook on the wall BD.

ADJUSTING THE KNEE KICKER

There are two sets of pins of different widths in the head of the knee kicker. The thinner pins are adjustable, so the amount they project from the head can be increased or decreased. You adjust them to suit the type of carpet, so:
● if you are laying a shag pile carpet, the thinner pins should project enough to grip the carpet backing; if they are too short they will snare the pile; if too long, they will become embedded in the underlay and will pull it out of place
● for smooth pile carpets you will need to use the thicker pins only.

LAYING CARPET ON STAIRS

Carpet provides an attractive covering for stairs, and will cut down considerably on noise levels in the home. Fitting a stair carpet is relatively straightforward providing you use the right techniques.

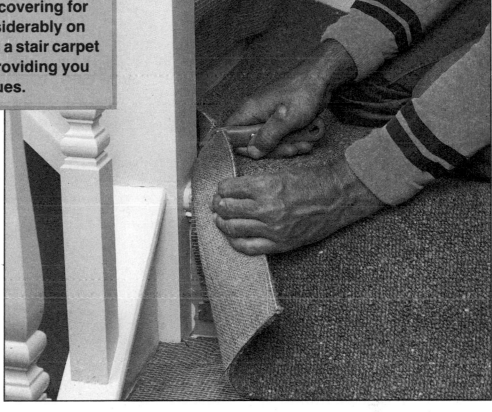

If you intend to fit a stair carpet you will first have to make sure that the carpet you have in mind is a suitable type. Since stairways are subjected to a lot of use, the carpet must be durable and hardwearing. The label on the carpet may help you make your choice; for example, carpets suitable for light wear only may be labelled as 'not recommended for stairs'. On the other hand, some ranges will be labelled as being specifically suited for use on stairs and others as being suitable for the whole house, including stairs. If the staircase is very heavily used and you require the carpet to last a long time, you will have to go for one of the toughest quality.

Foam-backed carpets are generally unsuitable for stairs; the cheaper light-weight ones tend not to be sufficiently durable and the heavier ones can be too inflexible to fit properly. You should also avoid carpets with a long pile which could impede movement and make the edges of the treads more difficult to locate. Again, some carpet patterns may obscure the outline of the treads or make people feel dizzy. Carpets with these kinds of patterns can be a safety risk, especially where elderly people will be using the stairs.

After you have chosen the carpet you must decide either to call in a professional to lay it or to go ahead and lay it yourself. The complexity of the job is a factor to take into account here; for example, if you want to cover a spiral staircase with a carpet fitted 'edge to edge', that is across the complete width of the stairs, it would normally be advisable to have a professional installation. A straight flight is likely to cause less problems, particularly if you intend to have a carpet runner which simply runs down the centre of the stairs and doesn't cover the complete width.

Measuring up

You will then have to work out how much carpet you'll need. The amount will be affected by the way you intend fitting the carpet: that is, edge-to-edge or as a carpet runner. If you have decided on an edge-to-edge fitting and the staircase is a regular width all the way up, you may find that this measurement

coincides with one of the regular widths in which carpet is supplied. If the staircase is narrower than a regular width, you can buy the regular width, trim the carpet to size and seal the cut edge. Where the staircase is a width which is going to waste a great deal of carpet in trimming you might decide to buy broadloom carpet and cut it into strips to match the stair width.

To calculate the length of stair carpet required you should add the height of all the risers to the depth of all the treads and then add on an additional 38mm (1½in) for each step to allow for the space taken by the underlay. Where there are curved nosings at the edges of the treads you will also have to allow for these – add 50mm (2in) for each nosing. Where you are using a carpet runner you can add on an extra 500mm (20in) to the length so you can reposition the carpet later to even out wear (see *Ready Reference*).

On a curved staircase measuring up is more complicated. You will have to calculate the bends separately, taking the largest dimensions of the winder treads which go round the corners.

As well as the quantity of carpet, you will also have to work out how much underlay to order. The underlay is cut in strips, with a

separate piece used for each step. Order an amount of underlay which will ensure that each strip is big enough to cover the treads and lap round the nosing so it can be secured to the riser beneath. Check with your supplier about a suitable type of underlay to use with the carpet you have chosen (remember that the better the quality the more wear and sound insulation it will give).

The preparation

As when you are fitting carpet on a floor, the stair surface must be in a suitable state; both treads and risers should be flat, smooth and dry. Check that they are in sound condition; this may involve nailing down loose treads or removing and replacing faulty treads or risers with new timber.

Unless you happen to have bought one of the few types of foam-backed carpet which are suitable for stairways you will have to fit an underlay before you go ahead and lay the carpet. And before you do this, if you are using the tackless gripper system, you will have to nail the gripper strips to the treads and risers. Fix the grippers to the back of each tread and the bottom of each riser so the pins face into the angle. The gap between the grippers on tread and riser should be

FIXING THE GRIPPER AND UNDERLAY

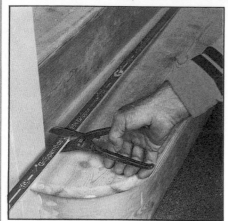

1 Use tinsnips to cut the gripper to size; its width should match that of the tread, measured where the tread meets the riser.

2 Fix the gripper strips to the treads by driving in the nails with a hammer; check that the gripper's teeth are not flattened as you do this.

3 Fix the gripper to the risers; there should be a gap of 15 to 18mm (⁵/₈ to ³/₄in) between the gripper strips on the tread and riser.

4 On a landing, nail the gripper strips in place so the gully between the strip and wall is just less than the carpet thickness.

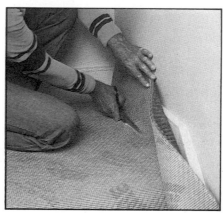

5 Place a strip of underlay in position on the landing and then trim it so it reaches the edges of the gripper strips.

6 Trim the underlay on the landing so it just reaches down to the edge of the gripper strip fixed to the first riser beneath the landing.

7 Use a staple gun to fix the underlay securely in place on the landing and then to fix it above the gripper strip on the riser beneath.

8 Work down the stairs, continuing to cut strips of underlay to size and fixing them in place between the gripper strips.

9 Where there is a bullnose tread at the bottom of the stairs you will have to cut the underlay so it fits the shape of the curved tread.

equal to about twice the thickness of the carpet, to allow the carpet to be tucked down between the grippers. If you are using special right-angled stair grippers, you don't have to worry about a gap. Where you are fixing a carpet runner you should cut the gripper strips 38mm (1½in) shorter than the width of the carpet so the method of fixing won't be obvious when the carpet is finally fixed in place.

You will have to cut the underlay into strips so there is a separate piece for each step. If you are fitting a carpet runner the width of the underlay should be about 38mm (1½in) less than the width of the carpet so it won't be visible under the carpet edges. Where you are using gripper strips, each piece of underlay should just reach the edges of the gripper strips on the tread above it and the riser below it. If you are using tacks to fix the carpet, each piece of underlay can be slightly longer, but you must allow enough room (ie, stair uncovered by underlay) to drive in the tacks which secure the carpet. The underlay can be tacked down, or, to make the job go more quickly, you can use a staple gun to staple it in place. If you are using a carpet runner, you should make sure the underlay is centrally placed (measure and mark off its position before you attempt to secure it). At the same time as you mark off the position of the underlay you can mark the position of the carpet runner so it too will eventually be centrally placed. Care taken at this stage will save you spoiling the look of the stairs later.

Where you are fitting edge-to-edge carpet, treat a landing as you would a floor; that is, cover it with underlay, except that the underlay should lap down over the edge of the landing onto the first riser beneath it. Where you will be fixing the carpet with gripper strips this overlap should reach to just above the gripper strip which you have fixed in place on the top riser.

Laying the carpet

Of the various methods you can use to secure the carpet in place, stair rods provide the simplest one and the tackless gripper system the most difficult (but it also gives the most 'professional' look). Don't forget that if you are using a foam-backed carpet, you can use stair rods instead of special right-angled grippers to hold it in place. You may already have stair rods holding an old stair carpet which you want to replace: these can be removed and used again. Or you may choose to buy new ones; they come in a range of types, including simple streamlined ones and more ornate versions, so you should be able to choose a variety which gives you the look you want for your staircase. Remember that it is simple to move a carpet if you have used stair rods to secure it and that they are the easiest of the various fixing methods to

take up and re-fix. So do bear this in mind.

With the next method, tacking, you should start at the top tread. First, centre the carpet if it is a runner and allow an extra 13mm (½in) for turning under where the carpet meets the top riser. This riser will be covered by the carpet which laps down from the landing. Turn the allowance under and tack the carpet down in one corner, then stretch it so it fits smoothly across the tread and tack it down at intervals of about 100mm (4in) across the riser. Then continue down the stairs, tacking it at the edges in the angles formed by the treads and risers. Make sure it's firmly stretched over the nosings as you go. To complete the job, drive in more tacks at 100mm (4in) intervals across the risers at the angles between treads and risers and, where you have made an allowance for moving the carpet at the bottom, tack up the sides of the folded-under carpet on the bottom step.

For an invisible fixing you will have to use the tackless gripper system. You can use a bolster to stretch and fit the carpet over the gripper strips (see step-by-step photographs) and in this case you should again begin work from the top downwards. But, if you prefer, you can instead use a knee-kicker to get the tension you want, in which case you will be working from the bottom step upwards. With the roll of carpet resting further up, push the carpet into the gully on the first (bottom) step so it is tightly held. Then roll the carpet further up the stairs and, using the knee-kicker on the second tread to pull the carpet tight, push the carpet into the gully between this tread and the second riser. Continue in this way, pulling the carpet tight (but not too tight) as you go, until you reach the top of the stairs.

Left-over carpet at the top and bottom can be tucked into the top and bottom risers and tacked firmly down. Sometimes it is tucked under another carpet at the top and bottom of the stairs; sometimes it continues to meet another carpet, and at other times it is finished with a binder bar. It all depends on the existing arrangements at the top and bottom of the staircase.

On stairs with winders where you are fitting edge-to-edge carpet, you will have to cut separate pieces for each step (see Ready Reference). To help you get the shape right it's worth making a paper template of each winder and using this as a guide when you are cutting the carpet.

Where you have cut the carpet to width from a wider measure you will have to seal it at the edges before you lay it. Otherwise the backing will fray, tufts will work loose from the edges and the appearance of the carpet will be spoiled. To seal the edges, run strips of latex adhesive along the underside and allow it to dry before you go ahead and fit the carpet.

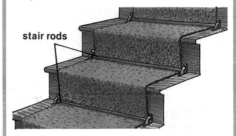

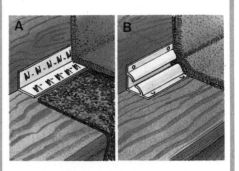

LAYING VINYL FLOOR TILES

Vinyl tiles are supple, easy to handle and don't take much time to lay. They come in many colours and designs so you should have no trouble finding tiles of the type you want.

Vinyl tiles are ideal for use on kitchen and bathroom floors because they are waterproof and resistant to oil, grease and most domestic chemicals. They have the advantage over vinyl sheet flooring in that they are easier to handle, and also, if you make any mistakes when cutting, they will be confined to individual tiles. So if you have a room where you will have to carry out quite a lot of intricate cutting to make the floorcovering fit round obstacles or awkwardly shaped areas, it would be well worth considering laying tiles rather than sheet material.

The tiles come in a wide variety of patterns and colours, with a smooth gloss finish or a range of sculptured and embossed designs. They can be bought with or without a cushioned backing. Cushioned tiles are softer and warmer underfoot, but more expensive than uncushioned tiles. However, even among tiles without a cushioned backing there is a wide variation in price. The cost of a tile is usually a fair indication of its quality, so, in general, the dearer the tile the longer it will last. However you don't need to be greatly concerned about this: even the cheapest tiles can have a life of twenty years in average domestic use, and long before then you will probably wish to remove or cover up the tiles. (On average floorcoverings are changed every seven years.) So your choice of tiles will probably be based simply on the fact that you like the colour or pattern and feel it will fit in well with the rest of the decorative scheme in the room.

Preparing the surface

The floor surface on which you intend to lay vinyl tiles should be free of dust and dirt, so you should go over it first of all with a vacuum cleaner. Then check that the subfloor is in sound condition.

If it is a timber floor you will have to repair any damaged boards, and if the floor has been treated in whole or in part with stains and polishes these will stop the tile adhesive from adhering properly, and will have to be removed with a proprietary floor cleaner. There may be gaps between the boards and they could possibly be warped and curling at the edges. You can cure these faults by

lining the floor with hardboard without adding much to the cost of the job or the time it takes to do it. First inspect the floor; punch home any protruding nails and countersink any screws. Replace missing nails. Where a board squeaks because it is loose, screws will hold it in place more securely than nails.

Hardboard sheets 1220mm (4ft) square will be a manageable size for this type of work. To condition them, brush water at the rate of ½ litre (2/3 pint) per 1220mm (4ft) square sheet onto the reverse side of the sheets. Then leave them for 48 hours stacked flat back to back in the room where they will be laid so they will become accustomed to its conditions. When fixed they will dry out further and tighten up to present a perfectly flat subfloor.

You can begin fixing the hardboard in one corner of the room. It's not necessary to scribe it to fit irregularities at the walls; small gaps here and there at the edges of the boards will not affect the final look of the floor.

Fix the sheets in place with hardboard pins at 150mm (6in) intervals round the edges and 225mm (9in) apart across the middle of the sheets. Begin nailing in the centre of a convenient edge and work sideways and forwards so the sheet is smoothed down in place. On a floor where there are water pipes below, use pins of a length which will not come out on the underside of the floorboards.

The sheets should normally be fixed with their smooth side down so the adhesive will grip more securely; also the pin heads will be concealed in the mesh.

Nail down the first sheet and work along the wall. When you come to the end of a row of sheets, you will have to cut a sheet to fit. Don't throw the waste away; use it to start the next row so the joins between sheets will not coincide. When you come to the far side of the room you will have to cut the sheets to width. Again, don't worry about scribing them to fit the exact contours of the wall.

On a solid floor, check to see if there are any holes or cracks and whether it is truly level and smooth. Fill in holes and small cracks with a sand/cement mortar. Large cracks could indicate a structural fault and, if in doubt, you should call in an expert. To level an uneven floor, use a self-levelling compound, applying it according to the manufacturer's instructions.

When dealing with a direct-to-earth floor you will have to establish whether it is dry or not. There's no point in attempting to lay the tiles on a damp floor: you will get problems with adhesion and in time the tiles themselves will curl and lift.

One difficulty is that dampness in a floor is not always immediately apparent, especially if there is no floorcovering. (If the floor has a sheet covering you should lift up a corner of the covering and inspect beneath for any signs of damp.) A slight amount of damp can rise up through floors of quarry tiles or concrete and evaporate in a room without being noticed.

To test for damp you can heat up a plate of metal over a gas ring or blowlamp, or heat a brick in the oven for about an hour, then

LAYING SELF-ADHESIVE TILES

1 *Sponge primer over the floor and leave it to dry for 24 hours. It will help the tiles to form a secure bond when they are fixed in place.*

2 *Snap two chalk lines which bisect at the floor's centre. Dry-lay a row of tiles along one line to find out the width of the cut border tiles.*

3 *Adjust the first (centre) tile if the cut tiles will be too narrow. Fix the tiles in place by peeling off the backing and pressing them down.*

4 *With the first row in place, continue fixing the tiles, working in sections, until all the whole tiles are laid. You can then lay the cut border tiles.*

5 *Place a tile over the last whole tile in a row and another one over it butted against the wall to use as a guide to mark the cutting line.*

6 *Leave the backing paper on when cutting the tile with a sharp knife. Remove the paper and press the cut border tile in place.*

Ready Reference

TILE SIZES
Vinyl tiles are sold in packs sufficient to cover 1 square metre (1 square yard). The most common size tile is 300mm (12in) square.

FIXING TILES
Some tiles are self-adhesive; you simply pull off a backing paper, then press the tile down in place. Others require adhesive; this should be special vinyl flooring adhesive.

TIP: MAKE A TRAMMEL
A simple device called a trammel can help you find the centre of a room. Take a batten about 900mm (3ft) long and drive a pin through the batten near each end.

FINDING THE CENTRE OF THE ROOM
In an irregularly-shaped room you can find the room's centre in this way:
● strike a chalk line to form a base line, parallel to and 75mm (3in) away from the wall with the door
● place the centre of your trammel on the centre of the base line (A) and use the trammel to mark points B and C on the chalk line
● with one pin of the trammel placed in turn on points B and C, scribe two arcs, meeting at D
● strike a chalk line through points A and D to the wall opposite (this line will be truly at right angles to the base)
● find the centre of the line through A and D to give the centre point of the room (E), then draw a line across and at right angles to it using the same technique.

TILING AN L-SHAPE

1 *At an external corner, place the tile to be cut over the last whole tile in one of the rows of tiles which adjoin at the corner.*

2 *Place another tile over the tile to be cut, but butted up against the skirting and use it as a guide to mark the cutting line.*

3 *Place the tile to be cut over the last whole tile in the other row leading to the corner. Use another tile as a guide for marking off.*

4 *Cut the tile along the marked lines with the backing paper on. Test if the cut tile fits, then peel off the paper and fix it in place.*

TILING ROUND AN ARCHITRAVE

1 *Make a template of the area round the architrave. Always test a template out: put it in place before using it on the tile to be cut.*

2 *When the template fits, use it to mark out the required shape on the tile. Cut the tile, remove the backing paper and press it in place.*

place it on the floor. If a damp patch appears on the floor or moisture gathers underneath the metal or brick this indicates that damp is present. Another test is to place a sheet of glass on the floor, seal its edges with putty, then leave it for a couple of days. If moisture appears underneath it is again a sign of damp. These methods are, however, rather hit-and-miss and you may feel it's worth calling in an expert to give a true diagnosis.

Curing a damp floor is a major undertaking which may involve digging up the existing floor and laying a new one with proper precautions taken against damp. You should seek professional advice here.

Existing sheet floorcoverings should be removed before you start laying vinyl tiles. You can, however, lay them over existing vinyl tiles provided these are in sound condition and are securely fixed. If they are not, you will have to remove them before you fix the new tiles. To lever them up, use a paint scraper, or even a garden spade (the long handle will give you plenty of leverage).

Marking up
You should start laying tiles from the middle of the floor. To find the centre of a room which is a reasonably regular shape you should take one wall and, ignoring any bays, alcoves or projections, measure and mark its centre. Go to the wall opposite and do the same. Between these two centre points you should snap a chalked line. Snap a second chalk line from the middle of the other two walls: the point where the lines meet is the centre of the floor.

If you are going to tile an irregularly-shaped room you should strike a chalk line, to form a base line, parallel to and 75mm (3in) away from a wall which has a doorway in it. You can then strike a line at right angles to the base line and stretching to the wall on the other side. The centre of this line will be the centre point of the room; draw a line through this centre point parallel to the base line. (Instead of using a large square to help you draw the lines at true right angles, you can use what's known as a trammel; see *Ready Reference*.)

Laying the tiles
When you come to lay the tiles, the first one is all-important. There are four possible positions for it. It can go centrally on the centre point; neatly inside one of the angles where the centre lines cross; centrally on one line and butting up to the second, or centrally on the second line and butting up to the first.

You should choose the position that gives you the widest border of cut tiles round the room. Very narrow cut strips at the edges will tend to give an unbalanced look, especially if you are laying the tiles in a dual colour or chequerboard pattern. So set out the tiles dry

TILING ROUND A WC

1 *Butt a paper template, which is the same size as a tile, against the base of the WC and mark off the shape of the WC on the template.*

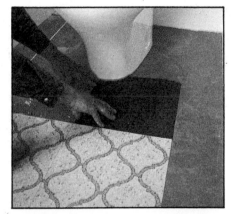

2 *Cut the template to shape, then test to see if it fits exactly round the WC base and between the base and the whole laid tiles.*

3 *Place the template over a whole loose tile (check the tile is the right way round for pattern matching) and mark off the cutting line.*

4 *Use a sharp knife to cut the tile to shape following the marked line. You can then remove the backing paper and fix the tile.*

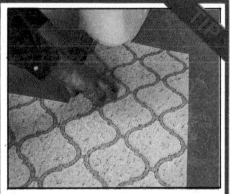

5 *Aim to get the tile position right first time. Tiles can be taken up and restuck, but will lose some of their adhesive in the process.*

6 *Continue to make templates and fix shaped tiles round the curved WC base. You can then fix the cut border tiles next to the walls.*

(that is, not stuck down) to find out which position for the first tile gives you borders with the largest cut tiles. In a regularly-shaped room this will be quite straightforward; a couple of dry runs should make things clear. In an awkwardly shaped room, especially if it has a lot of alcoves or projections, you will have to make several of these practice runs. When you've decided on your final starting position, draw round the outline of the first tile to be placed.

When you've stuck down your first tile you can begin laying the rest. If you are laying tiles which require adhesive, you should apply this to as large an area as you can cope with in one go; possibly a square metre (square yard). Butt all the tiles accurately up against each other, and check that they are precisely aligned. Then apply firm hand (or foot) pressure to bed them firmly in place.

It's normal practice to stick down all the full tiles, known as the 'field', leaving a border of cut tiles to be fitted round the edges.

If you are laying self-adhesive tiles, you simply peel off the backing paper and press each tile into place. Where you have to cut tiles, don't peel off the backing until the cutting-to-size is completed. Should a tile be misplaced, lift it quickly and relay it correctly; the adhesive 'grabs' quickly and later attempts to lift the tile will probably tear it.

Cutting tiles

Vinyl tiles can be quite easily cut using a sharp knife and a straightedge. For an intricate shape make a template first.

Border tiles can be marked up for cutting in the usual way; that is, you take the tile to be cut, place it on the last complete tile in the row, place another tile over the first one but jammed hard against the wall and use this tile as a guide for marking off the cutting line

on the first tile (see step-by-step photographs). The main thing wrong with this method is that it can leave a narrow border in which it is difficult to apply adhesive, with the consequent risk that the border tiles will not adhere properly.

Another method, which avoids this problem, is to lay the field except for the last full tile in each row. Then take a tile and place it against the last full tile in the field. Place another tile on top of the first one and jammed against the wall. Use this second tile as a guide to cut through the first (and it will itself become the last full tile fixed in the relevant row).

The two tiles can temporarily be placed on top of the field, adjacent to the position they will occupy, while you cut the rest of the border. When you come to stick the border tiles down you will have plenty of room in which to wield your adhesive spreader and ensure adequate coverage.

LAYING CORK TILES

Cork tiles will provide you with a floor surface which is warm, wears well and is quiet to walk on. In addition, they are the easiest of tiles to lay.

You can use cork floor tiles in bathrooms, kitchens, dining rooms and children's rooms; anywhere, in fact, where any other resilient floorcovering (eg, vinyl sheet or tiles, or thermoplastic tiles) could be used. They are warmer and quieter than most other floorcoverings and tend not to 'draw the feet', unlike, for example, ceramic tiles, which are very tiring if you have to stand round on them for long periods. They will look particularly elegant if they are softened with rugs or rush matting and blend equally well with modern or traditional style furniture and décor

Ordinary cork tiles are made from granulated cork, compressed and baked into blocks; the natural resins in the grain bond the particles together, though sometimes synthetic resins are added to improve wearing and other qualities. The tiles are cut from these blocks so they are 5mm (¼in) or more thick. 'Patterned' cork tiles (see below) are made by alternating wafer-thin cork veneers with thicker layers of insulating cork and sealing with a protective PVC surface.

Types of tiles
Cork tiles have an attractive natural look; usually they are a rich honey-gold, although there are some darker browns and smoky tones. Dyed cork tiles are available in many different colours ranging from subtle shades to strident primary colours. There are also 'patterned' tiles which have an interesting textured, rather than a heavily patterned look; these come in natural colours as well as red, soft green and rich dark smoky brown: the colour tends to 'glow' through the top surface of cork. One design gives a subtle miniature checkerboard effect. Other tiles come with designs (such as geometric patterns) imprinted on them.

For floors that are likely to get the occasional flood or where spills and 'accidents' are inevitable, such as in kitchens, bathrooms and children's rooms, it is wiser to use pre-sealed types of tiles (see *Ready Reference*). The cheaper seal-it-yourself types are, however, perfectly adequate for living rooms, bedsitting rooms and halls.

Preparing the surface
As with other types of tiles and resilient floor-coverings the subfloor surface on which you lay cork tiles must be smooth, clean and free from lumps, bumps, protruding nails, tacks or screws. Where floorboards are uneven, it's best to cover them up with flooring-grade chipboard, plywood or flooring quality hardboard, either nailed or screwed down securely. Remember to stagger the sheets of chipboard or other material to avoid continuous joins. Then, if there is any floor movement it will not disturb the tiles fixed on top and cause them to lift or be moved out of alignment.

There must also be adequate ventilation underneath a wooden subfloor. Poor ventilation can cause condensation which could lead to the rotting of the floorboards and the floorcovering above them. If the floor is laid at ground level, or directly to joists or battens on ground level concrete, you should protect the cork from moisture penetration by covering the timber with bituminous felt paper before laying hardboard or plywood. The paper should be fixed with bituminous adhesive; and you should allow a 50mm (2in) overlap at joins and edges.

Solid subfloors, such as concrete or cement and sand screeds, should be thoroughly dry. Make sure the floor incorporates an effective damp-proof membrane before laying the tiles: this can

ESTABLISHING THE STARTING POINT

1 *Find the centre points of two opposite walls. Stretch a string line between them, chalk it and snap a line across the floor.*

2 *Repeat the procedure, but this time between the other two walls. Where the two lines intersect is the exact centre of the floor.*

3 *Dry-lay a row of tiles along the longest line from the centre point to one wall. Adjust the other line if necessary (see* Ready Reference*).*

4 *Lay a row of tiles along the other line from the centre point and again adjust to avoid wastage or very narrow strips at the edges.*

is irregularly shaped, divide it into rectangles and measure each one separately. If you take these measurements to your supplier, he should be able to help you calculate the quantity of tiles you will require. Or, as many tiles are sold ready-boxed with a guide to quantities printed on the box, you can study the guide to work out the number of tiles you'll need.

If you plan to buy tiles of contrasting colours, and to form a border pattern, or to lay them so you get a checkerboard effect, you should plan out the design on squared paper first. Divide up the floor area so each square represents a tile, and colour the squares in different colours to represent the different colours of the tiles so you can judge the effect. You can then calculate the quantity needed by reference to your plan.

Laying tiles

Whichever type of tile you are laying, it is best to work at room temperature, so don't switch off the central heating. Leave the tiles in the room overnight to condition them.

Make sure you have enough tiles and adhesive on the spot; you don't want to have to stop work halfway through the job and go out and buy extra. Collect together the necessary tools: measure, chalk and string, pencils and ruler or straight edge, notched trowel or spreader, sharp knife, cloth and white spirit. If you are using the seal-later type of tile you will need a sander and brush or roller plus sealer.

As with other types of tiles, cork tiles look best if they are centred on the middle of the room and any narrow or awkwardly shaped tiles come at the edges. So you'll have to establish your starting point (see *Ready Reference*) at the centre of the room. You can then begin laying whole tiles, working from the centre outwards. It's best to work on a quarter of the floor at a time; when all four quarters of whole tiles are laid, you can cut and fix the border tiles. If you are using adhesive, you may have to spread only about one square metre (1 square yard) at a time before it is ready to take the tiles. In other cases it will be best to cover a larger area with adhesive, so you don't have to wait too long to bed the tiles, increasing the length of time it will take to complete the job. Since the length of time needed before the adhesive is ready to take the tiles does vary depending on the type of adhesive, you should follow the manufacturer's instructions.

If tiles have to be cut to fit round obstacles such as door architraves, WC bases, or wash stands you can use a scribing block to mark the outline you require. Make up a paper template or use a special tracing tool (which has little needles which retract to fit the shape) if the shape is particularly complicated.

be in polythene sheet form, a cold-poured bitumen solution, or a hot pitch or bitumen solution. If the subfloor is porous or flaky and tends to be very dusty, you can use a latex floor-levelling compound to cover it. This is also practical for very uneven floors. The solution is poured on, left to find its own level and then allowed to dry out before the final floorcovering is laid.

Other floors, such as quarry or ceramic tiles, can have cork laid on top, but they have to be degreased, dewaxed and keyed by rubbing them with wire wool; once again, a floor-levelling compound may be necessary. With flagstones laid directly on the ground there could be damp or condensation problems; it may be best to take up the existing floor and re-lay it, probably a job for a professional to do. Alternatively, the floor could be covered with a layer of rock asphalt at least 16mm (⅝in) thick but you will need to call in

professional help for this. (Always seek expert advice if you are worried about the state of the subfloor; the expense incurred will be worth it to get successful results when you are laying the final floorcovering.)

If there is already a linoleum, vinyl sheet, tile or other resilient floorcovering on the floor, you are advised to take this up, then resurface or rescreed it if necessary; alternatively, use a floor-levelling damp-resistant latex powder mix, or an epoxy surface membrane. If it is not possible to remove the old floorcovering, you should use a proprietary floor cleaner to degrease and dewax it and then key the surface by rubbing over it with wire wool.

Planning

Measure the room, at floor level, using a steel tape or wooden measure; don't use a cloth tape as these stretch in use. If the room

Ready Reference

MARKING OUT

For a balanced look, aim to cut your edge tiles to equal size on both sides of the room. To do this, establish the centre point of the floor, using chalked string lines (see Ready Reference, page 191):
● if, when you've dry-laid a row of tiles from the centre point out to the wall, a gap remains of more than half a tile-width at the wall end (A), adjust your chalked line half a tile-width off-centre (B); this will save undue wastage later when you are cutting the perimeter tiles.

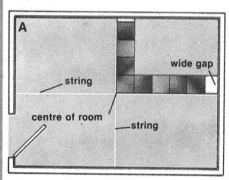

● if, however, by moving the chalked line you are left with very narrow perimeter strips (less than 75mm/3in wide) leave the centre of the floor as your starting point; there will be wastage but narrow cut perimeter tiles won't look very good and should be avoided if possible
● when marking out, avoid narrow strips at door thresholds where they will be subjected to a lot of wear
● adjust your starting point so you don't end up with narrow strips round a feature of the room, such as a chimney breast.

CHECK UNSEALED TILES

Be sure to lay unsealed tiles the right way up. They have a smooth top surface and a bottom surface which is rougher to provide a key for the adhesive. You can judge which surface is which by running your fingers over the tile.

LAYING WHOLE TILES

1 *Use a notched spreader to apply adhesive to a quarter of the floor area, using the marked lines as a guide to the area to be covered.*

2 *Place the first whole tile in the centre right angle which has been coated with adhesive. Check that it aligns with the guidelines.*

3 *Lay a row of tiles following the guidelines, treading each tile down gently but firmly to make sure it is securely bedded.*

4 *Work across the floor until that quarter is covered with whole tiles. Then lay tiles on the other quarters of the floor area.*

For some awkard shapes (eg, fitting tiles round an L-shape or in an alcove) you can mark out the pieces to be cut by placing a whole tile or tile offcut up against the skirting and the tiles which are already in place and draw the required shape on it. Cork tiles are very simple to cut: all you need is a sharp knife and a straight edge to guide it; there is no risk of breakages as there may be with other tiles which are more difficult to cut, such as ceramic types.

Sealing tiles

If your tiles are the seal-after-laying type, you will have to sand the floor carefully, using a powered sander, to ensure the surface and joins are smooth. Dust carefully; you can wipe the tiles with a slightly damp cloth to remove excess dust but take care not to saturate the tiles. Leave them to dry and then seal them, using a brush or roller to apply the sealer.

If you attach your applicator to a long handle, you can avoid bending or crawling on all fours; work from the furthermost corner, backwards to the door. Leave each coat to dry thoroughly, before applying the next one. There will always be more than one coat of sealer but the exact number will depend on the type of wear to which the floor will be subjected (see *Ready Reference*).

Ideally, you should leave the sealer to dry for a few days before you walk on the floor, but if you have to use the room, seal half the room at a time. Cover the unsealed part with brown paper so it can be walked on without damaging or marking the cork. When the sealed part is completely dry, you can seal the other half.

Don't wash a new cork floor for at least 48 hours after laying and sealing; ideally it should be left for at least five days. It's worth

LAYING BORDER TILES

1 *To cut border tiles accurately to size, place the whole tile to be cut exactly on top of the last whole tile in a particular row.*

2 *Place a second tile over it, this time butting it up against the skirting. Use its edge as a guide to scribe a line on the first tile.*

3 *Remove the tile to be cut and make a deeper mark. The tile should then break through cleanly when gentle pressure is applied.*

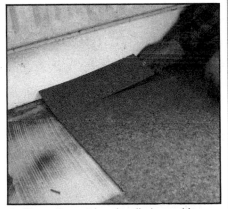

4 *Place the cut border tile in position against the skirting. You may need to apply extra adhesive to its back to ensure secure fixing.*

TILING AN L-SHAPE

1 *As when cutting other border tiles, use a tile as a guide to scribe the outline of one side of the L onto the tile to be cut.*

2 *Move the tile to be cut and the guide tile to the other side of the L and use the same method to scribe its outline for cutting.*

3 *Remove the loose tiles, cut through the back of the tile along the scribed lines and then fix the tile in position so it aligns with the whole tiles.*

putting up with grubby marks for a few days rather than running the risk of moisture penetrating the flooring and reducing its useful life.

Care and maintenance

Once pre-sealed tiles are laid, or the unsealed type has been properly sealed, it will probably be unnecessary to do more than wipe over the floor with a damp mop or cloth to keep it clean. To remove grease or dirt, add a few drops of liquid detergent to the washing water; wipe over again with a cloth rinsed in clean water to remove any traces of detergent. If there are some particularly stubborn marks, made, for instance, by rubber-soled shoes, or paint or varnish spots, you should be able to remove them by rubbing gently with a little white spirit on a damp cloth.

An important point to remember when you are cleaning your cork floor is that you must take care not to overdampen the floor or the tiles may lift. Also, never use strong abrasive cleaners as these can damage the PVC wear layer.

If you like a fairly glossy surface or are worried about scratches on the floor, you can use an emulsion wax polish on top of the sealed tiles. However, never use a wax floor polish as the surface could become too slippery.

Sometimes a tile can become damaged. If the area which needs repair is small (a cigarette burn hole, for instance) you can fill it with shavings from a cork out of a bottle and reseal the tile. For more extensive damage, you should remove the tile carefully and replace it with a spare one; reseal if this tile is an unsealed type with the number of coats of sealer required to give it adequate protection.

Ready Reference

TIP: STORE TILES FLAT

If you take tiles out of their box, weight them down to keep them flat when you are storing them.

FIXING TILES

Fixing methods and adhesives vary. Some adhesives should be applied to both the back of the tiles and floor, others to the floor only; follow the manufacturer's instructions. Remember:
● pre-sealed tiles are always fixed with adhesive
● unsealed tiles are often fixed by driving in 5 headless pins, one at each corner and one in the centre, a technique which may be combined with adhesive (the pin holes can be filled, if necessary, and will then be covered up by the sealer).

REMOVE EXCESS ADHESIVE

As you lay the tiles, wipe off any adhesive from the front of the tiles with a soft cloth which has been dipped in white spirit.

CUTTING ROUND PIPES

To cut a tile so it fits round a pipe, make a cardboard template of the shape required and trace the shape onto the tile. Then cut a slit from the hole made for the pipe to the skirting board; this line will be almost invisible when the tile is fixed in place.

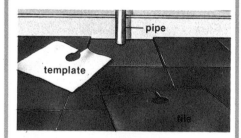

SEAL TILES PROPERLY

Cork is porous and fairly absorbent, so proper sealing is essential; if the tiles get wet, they swell and lift and have to be trimmed and re-stuck. For unsealed tiles, several coats of sealer will be necessary for real protection:
● in areas of ordinary wear, apply two or three coats of sealer
● in heavy wear areas you will need to apply 4 or 5 coats.

TRIM DOORS

To allow doors to open freely after the cork floor has been laid you may have to trim along the bottom of the door to give adequate clearance.

LAYING TILES IN AN ALCOVE

1 Place a tile over the fixed tiles with its corner butting up against the skirting and make a mark on the 'wrong' side at the correct distance.

2 Repeat this procedure, this time to make a mark on the adjacent edge. Transfer the marks to the front of the tile and draw a line between them.

3 Cut along the drawn line to give the required shape and then place the cut tile in position so it aligns properly with the whole tiles.

4 Use the same techniques to cut the next tile. If there is a pipe against the wall, butt the tile up to it and mark where it's to be cut.

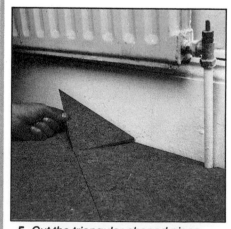

5 Cut the triangular-shaped piece required to fill the gap between the two larger shaped pieces and fix this in position so that it butts right up against the skirting.

6 To complete the job, cut the corner piece to shape and fix it in place. For economy, you can cut these smaller shaped pieces from any tiled offcuts which you may have available.

LAYING SHEET VINYL

Vinyl provides a tough, easy-to-clean floor surface which is ideal in kitchens, bathrooms and other areas of the house where floors are likely to be subjected to heavy wear or spillages. It's also straightforward to lay.

Vinyl flooring was developed in the 1960s and revolutionised the smooth (and resilient) flooring market. At first it was a thin and rather unyielding material. But it was something which could be laid fairly easily by the DIY enthusiast; and this was a breakthrough because its predecessor, linoleum, had had to be professionally laid. Since then, vinyl flooring has been greatly improved and there are now several different types available.

Types of vinyl
The cheapest type of vinyl is known as a 'flexible print' and has a clear wear layer on top, with the printed pattern sandwiched between this and the backing. Then there are the cushioned vinyls, which are more bouncy underfoot and have a soft inner bubbly layer between the wear layer and the backing. They are often embossed to give them a texture, which is particularly successful when the embossing enhances the design, as with simulated cork or ceramic tile patterns. Finally, the most expensive type is solid flexible vinyl, made by suspending coloured vinyl chips in transparent vinyl to create colour and design which goes right through the material and consequently wears longer.

All three types come in a wide variety of colours and designs ranging from geometric and floral patterns to simulated cork, wood block, parquet, ceramic tiles, slate and brick. Some ranges include special glossy no-polish surfaces. Also, there is a special 'lay-flat' type which does not have to be stuck down, except on very heavy wear areas or at doorways. Some vinyls can be folded without cracking, but as with carpets, a good guide to durability is price: the more expensive the flooring, the longer-lasting it is likely to be.

Buying vinyl
To work out the amount of vinyl you'll need, measure up the floor using a metal tape; note down the measurements and then double-check them. Draw a scale plan of the room on squared paper, marking in all the obstacles, door openings and so on.

Take the measurements and plan to your supplier, who will help you to work out quantities. Remember to allow for walls which are not quite true and for trimming the overlap (see *Ready Reference*).

Whatever the type, vinyl is available in standard sheet widths (see *Ready Reference* again). Choose one in a wide width for use on a floor where you do not want to have a seam. (A wide sheet can be difficult to lay so make sure you have someone to help you – If you are going to lay sheets of a narrower width which will have to be joined, remember to allow for pattern matching when buying.

Check the manufacturer's instructions for fixing and order the correct adhesive and other sundries. Make sure you get the right amount; there is nothing worse than running out of adhesive halfway through the job.

A roll of vinyl is usually 30 to 40m (100 to 130ft) long and the retailer will cut off the length you want, re-rolling it for you. Take the roll of vinyl home and leave it, loosely rolled, in the room where it is to be laid for about 48 hours. This will allow it to become acclimatised and it should then be easier to lay. Do not stand it on edge as this can crack the material and take care not to damage the ends when you are transporting or storing the roll.

Preparing the sub-floor
Vinyl must be laid on a sound, reasonably smooth and even sub-floor if the best results

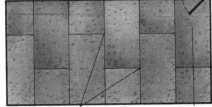

LAYING VINYL IN A RECESS

1 *With the vinyl fixed in place at the straightest edges of the room, deal with awkward areas like a recess. First trim at the corners.*

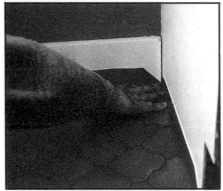

2 *Turn back the vinyl and spread a band of adhesive round the edges of the recess. You can then push the floorcovering firmly into position.*

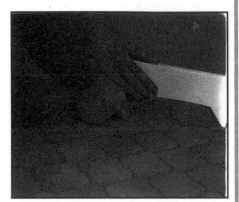

3 *To complete the job, use a sharp knife to trim off the overlap. Again, make sure there are no bubbles by smoothing the vinyl down.*

along the wall so its profile is marked on the vinyl. To cut along this line you can use a knife and straight edge (with the straight edge on the vinyl which will be used), or if the line is very wobbly, use scissors.

With the first length fitted, you can then place the next length of vinyl parallel to the first, matching the pattern exactly, and cut off the required length, again allowing for extra overlap at the ends and sides. Some people cut all the required lengths first before fitting, but if the room is not perfectly square and several widths are being used, there could be a mismatch.

If the two sheets overlap, the excess will have to be trimmed away. Place one on top of the other, aligning the design carefully, and cut through the two sheets together at the overlap, using a knife and straight edge. Remove the trimmings and then adjust the second sheet to fit doors, skirtings and so on, trimming where necessary.

Where there are more than two sheets, repeat the fitting procedure, making sure the pattern matches.

If you are renewing the skirting, to get a perfect fit you can fit the material first and put the skirting on after the vinyl is laid. Remember, though, that this may make it difficult to take up the floorcovering when you need (or want) to change it.

Fitting extra-wide flooring

The technique is largely the same as for fitting strips of vinyl except there will not be any seams to stick, or pattern matching to do. You should start by laying the flooring out fully – you will probably need help for this – and try to find a long straight wall against which the first edge can be laid. Then make diagonal cuts at each corner to allow the flooring to be positioned roughly, with the

excess material 'climbing up' the skirting board or wall. Trim away the excess, leaving a 50 to 75mm (2 to 3in) overlap all round. Scribe the first wall, if necessary, then trim and ease the flooring back into its exact position. Deal with corners, projections, and obstacles as you work your way round the room, leaving the same overlap; finally trim to a perfect fit.

Fixing vinyl

How you fix vinyl will depend on the type; always follow the manufacturer's instructions. As vinyl can shrink it's wise to stick it down immediately before or after trimming it. To stick the edges you should first turn them back and apply a 75mm (3in) wide band of adhesive to the sub-floor, using a serrated scraper in a criss-cross motion, and then press the vinyl into position immediately. This will usually be at doorways, round the edges of the room, or round obstacles. Where heavy equipment will be pulled across the floor regularly (a washing machine for example) it is worth sticking down the entire area.

At the seams, you should make the width of the spread adhesive generous – 150 to 200mm (6 to 8in). Again, turn back the edges, apply the band of adhesive to the sub-floor and press the vinyl back into position immediately. Wipe away any adhesive which seeps through the seam or round the edges of the vinyl immediately, as this can discolour the flooring if it hardens.

At the entrance to rooms, particularly in heavy traffic areas, or if you have used the 'lay-flat' type of vinyl, you can fasten down the vinyl with a ready-made threshold strip These come in metal, wood or plastic and are also used to cover joins between two different materials, such as vinyl and carpet.

Cleaning and maintenance

Once you have laid your floor you will need to look after it. Always wipe up any spills immediately, particularly hot fat and grease. It is also wise to protect the surface from indentation by putting heavy pieces of furniture on a piece of hardboard, or standing legs and castors in castor cups.

Some of the more expensive vinyls have a built-in gloss, so they do not need polishing. This type can be mopped with a damp cloth.

Never use a harsh abrasive cleaner on any type of vinyl floor as this could damage the surface layer. The glossy surface should not wear away, but if it does become dull in heavy traffic areas, it can be recoated with a special paint-on liquid provided by the manufacturer.

The less glossy vinyls will need regular sweeping or vacuuming and mopping. It also makes sense to use a clear acrylic polish, applied very sparingly according to the manufacturer's instructions and then buffed gently. Wash occasionally with warm water and a mild liquid detergent, and don't apply lots of coats of polish, or you will get a thick discoloured build-up, which spoils the look of the floor; 2-4 coats over a 12-month period is plenty. Always let the floor dry thoroughly before walking on it, after it has been washed or polished.

Once several coats of polish have built up, you will have to strip off the polish and start again. To do this, add a cupful of household ammonia to a bucket of cold water, to which a little washing-up liquid has been added. Scrub the floor with this, taking care not to saturate it too much. When the old surface begins to break down, wipe it with an old soft cloth, rinse thoroughly with warm, clean water and dry before applying a new protective coating.

CUTTING ROUND OBSTACLES

The best way to get a neat floor when fitting vinyl round obstacles such as bathroom fittings is to make a template of paper or cardboard which is slightly larger (by about 25mm/1in) than the obstacle. Place one sheet of paper up against the basin pedestal, WC base or whatever, and tear it round so you have half the obstacle's shape on it. Then repeat the procedure with another sheet of paper for the other half.

Fit the template round the obstacle and use a scribing block and pencil to give the exact profile. Then lay the pattern over the flooring and use the block and pencil to reverse the procedure and transfer the exact outline onto the vinyl by running it round the inside of the line. You can then cut and fit; you will have to make a slit in the edge of the vinyl in some cases to get a snug fit at the skirting. Carefully trim away any excess material round the obstacle once the flooring is placed in position. Fix the vinyl according to the manufacturers' instructions.

Making a template

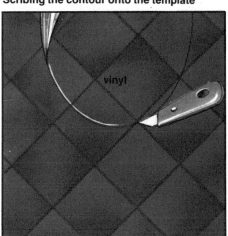

Scribing the contour onto the template

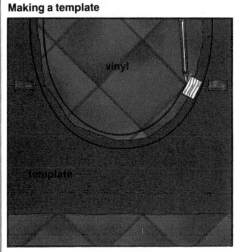

Scribing the contour onto the vinyl

Cutting the vinyl

Ready Reference

FITTING CORNERS

To fit vinyl:
● at internal corners, gently push the vinyl into the corner and cut away the excess, diagonally across the corner, until it fits. Cut a little at a time and pare the edge carefully
● at external corners, press the vinyl into the corner, pull up the excess and cut to allow the vinyl to fall into place round the corner; then trim the excess.

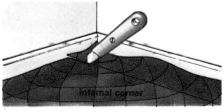

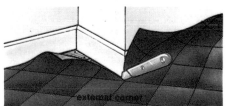

FIXING METHODS

Sheet vinyl can be fixed either by sticking it down all over or only at the edges and seams. Check the manufacturer's instructions.

'Lay-flat' vinyls do not have to be stuck down but they must be firmly fixed at doorways by glueing, or another method. Double-sided tape may be used to secure seams.

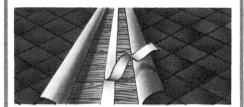

TIP: SMOOTH OUT BUMPS

If there are any bumps in the vinyl after you have laid it fill a pillowcase with sand and drag this round the floor to iron them out.

TIP: HIDING GAPS

If you have an unsightly gap between the skirting and the floor, because the walls are very uneven or your vinyl has shrunk, you can pin painted quadrant beading to the skirting round the room to hide the gap.

If you wipe up spills at once you should not get any stains on vinyl flooring, but sometimes they become marked from tar or grit trodden into the house; some types of shoe can leave black scuff marks, and cigarette burns are not unknown.

If normal cleaning doesn't remove marks rub them very gently with a very fine grade wire wool, used dry. Take care not to rub too much of the surface layer away. Wipe with a damp cloth, and reseal/polish the area if necessary. Some grease marks can be removed with white vinegar, others with petrol or lighter fuel. Always, however, wipe the area immediately with clean water.

Any badly discoloured or damaged area may have to be patched, so save any offcuts of sufficient size for this purpose.

GROUTING TILES

1 When the adhesive has set, you can grout the joints. Use a sponge or a rubber squeegee to force the grout into all the gaps.

2 Wipe off the excess grout as you work with a damp sponge; if you allow it to set hard it will be very difficult to remove later.

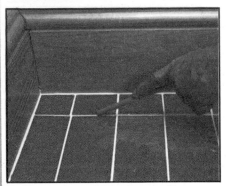

3 Use a piece of thin dowel with a rounded end to smooth off the joints. Don't be tempted to use a finger as grout could irritate your skin.

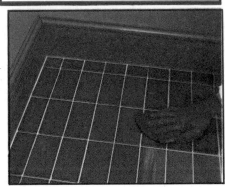

4 Leave the grout to set for the recommended time, and then polish the surface all over with a clean, dry cloth to remove the last traces of grout.

PREPARING FLOOR

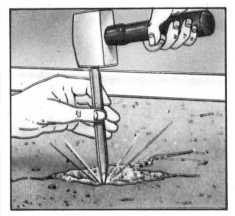

Clean out the small depressions and cracks to be filled with a club hammer and chisel. Beware of flying chippings.

Use a trowel to fill in the depressions with mortar and to level off to provide a suitable surface for the tiles.

hollows under the tiles will become weak points later on.

You can proceed with the tiling in 1 sq m sections until all the tiles are in place, then leave them for at least 24 hours. The tiles must not be walked on during this time so that any risk of them being knocked out of place or bedded too deeply is avoided. If you have to walk on the tiles, lay a sheet of plywood or chipboard over them first to spread the load. When 24 hours – or longer; check the manufacturer's instructions – are up, you can remove the spacers. Check with the adhesive manufacturer's instructions to see whether you need to allow extra time after this before you begin grouting.

Cutting tiles

You will have to cut each tile individually since you will almost certainly find variations around the room. Place the tile which is going to be cut against the wall and on top of the adjacent whole tile. Mark it off for cutting.

Using a straight edge as a guide, score the tile surface and edges with a scribing tool. You *can* use a hand tile cutter to cut and break the tile along the scoreline; but its probably worthwhile hiring a special floor tile cutter to make the job easier.

To cut a tile to give an L-shape you will need to use tile nips to nibble away at the waste area. You can use a tile file, carborundum stone or coarse glasspaper to smooth off the rough edge. For curved shapes (eg, to fit round a WC pedestal), you will need to make a template and again use tile nips to nibble away at the tile.

Grouting the tiles

Mix the grout according to the manufacturer's instructions; make up only a small amount at a time and, as with adhesive, work in areas of 1 sq metre (11 sq ft). Apply it with the straight edge of a rubber float, or a sponge or squeegee, making sure the joints are properly filled. Pack the grout firmly into the joints and smooth off using a small rounded stick – don't try using a finger as the grout is likely to irritate your skin.

It's best to remove excess grout (and adhesive) as soon as possible. If it sets it will be difficult to remove.

Filling cracks and hollows

If you have a concrete floor which is flat, dry and level you can go ahead and lay tiles without further preparation. Often, however, the floor is not level or there are cracks and small hollows on the surface. Indentations should be filled with mortar (a 3:1 sand:cement mix is suitable) mixed to a creamy but not too runny consistency. For mortar with a good bond add some PVA bonding solution to the mix. Cut back the holes to a clean shape and brush out any loose material so it doesn't mix in with the mortar making it difficult to get a smooth surface. You can also coat the holes with a PVA bonding solution to help the mortar adhere.

SURFACES FOR TILING

Levelling a concrete floor

A concrete floor which is out of true can be levelled using a self-levelling flooring compound so it is suitable for tiling. For the compound to form a smooth, even surface it should only be applied to a floor which is clean and free from dust, oil, grit or grease so you should first sweep the floor and then scrub it thoroughly (1). You may find you have to use a proprietary cleaner to remove stubborn greasy patches. The compound comes in powder form and you will have to mix it up according to the manufacturer's instructions so it forms a runny paste (2).

If you try covering the entire floor in one operation, it's likely the compound will set into large pools which are difficult to join up. It's better to work in small areas; you can delineate your working area by forming a bay using timber battens. Pour the compound onto the floor (3) and then spread it out as evenly as possible using a steel float (4), any marks from the float will disappear quickly. The compound will set within a couple of hours. If you want extra thickness you can apply a second coat once the first is hard.

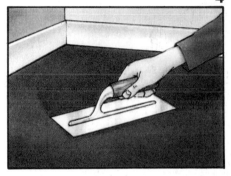

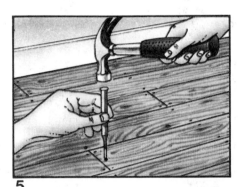

Laying plywood over a timber floor

A floor which is subject to movement will disrupt tiles laid over it so if you intend tiling over a suspended wooden floor you will first have to make the surface as firm as possible by covering it with a layer of man-made boards. Water-resistant resin-bonded plywood is a suitable material as it will resist penetration by the damp adhesive you will be spreading over it and you will avoid the problem of rotting boards. The boards should be at least 12mm (½in) thick. To prepare the floor to take the plywood you should punch any protruding nails below the surface (5) at the same time checking that the floorboards are firmly secured. You can then go ahead and fix the sheets of plywood to the floor (6) using nails spaced at 225mm (9in) intervals across the middle of the sheets and at 150mm (6in) intervals round their perimeter. You will have to cut the boards to shape round any recess or alcove (7), and where there is a pipe run, fix narrow strips of ply-wood over the pipes to make access to them easier. Make sure you stagger the joints; this will prevent any floor movement causing the tiles to break up in a run across the floor.

LAYING QUARRY TILES

Quarry tiles will provide a highly attractive natural-looking floor surface in kitchens, bathrooms, hallways and other areas which receive hard wear. They can also be used outdoors – as a patio surface, for example.

G lazed ceramic floor tiles are ideal as a floorcovering in kitchens, bathrooms, utility areas and WCs, but, whether plain or patterned, they are also expensive. This is where unglazed ceramic tiles, commonly known as quarry tiles, compare well. Like glazed tiles, quarry tiles are hardwearing and easy to clean but they are cheaper and, if you want really good value for money, they're well worth considering. They come in subtle shades of brown, red or yellow and will fit in with almost any décor, whether modern or traditional.

Buying quarry tiles

You'll first have to decide on the type of tiles you want (see *Ready Reference*) and their size. Where thickness is concerned, it's worth asking your supplier for advice. Obviously, the thicker the tile, the more hardwearing it is likely to be, but, in practice, few domestic situations warrant anything more than the thinnest of the range. There's also the question of shape: in addition to ordinary square-edged tiles, you'll find RE and REX tiles – with one and two rounded edges respectively – for use on steps (none of these, by the way, has spacer lugs). And, to complete the job, most manufacturers offer a range of skirting tiles, including those for straight runs, internal and external corners, plus stop ends. You can use these in place of timber skirtings and they are ideal in situations where water is likely to be splashed around, providing protection against moisture penetration.

Measuring up

For a rough estimate of how many tiles you need, measure the length and width of the area to be tiled using the size of a whole tile plus the width of a joint as your unit of measurement. Round each dimension up to the next whole number then multiply the two together to find the number of tiles required to cover the whole floor area.

If the area you're going to tile is an awkward shape, perhaps because of sanitary fittings, built-in units and so on, it's better to work out the number of tiles you need accurately with the aid of a floor plan drawn to scale on graph paper, so long as it's not too large. The floor

will look best if the tiles are arranged symmetrically, so remember this when you are drawing in the position of each tile. Add up the number of tiles, counting each cut tile as a whole tile.

Preparing the surface

Your aim should be to provide a surface which is sound, stable and free from anything likely to stop the tiles sticking, such as dirt, grease, dust, polish and moisture.

With bare concrete you will usually only need to give it a thorough clean, though if the surface is at all powdery you will also have to treat it with a stabilising solution. You may need to give highly polished concrete additional attention, depending on the type of adhesive you intend using. With some adhesives you have to roughen the surface to provide a key. This is not an easy task and you may decide that it's worth looking for an alternative fixing product.

Suspended timber floors require rather more preparation. You should begin by checking that the floor shows no sign of movement when walked on, as any problem of this kind will be increased by the weight of the tiled surface. Loose boards should be refixed with screws and, while you're about it, you should punch all nail heads well below the surface. Overall 'springing' of the floorboards caused by sagging joists presents rather more of a problem for the simple reason that the cure involves virtually rebuilding the floor. In this case it may be better to give up the idea of tiling the floor.

Assuming the floor is sound, the next step is to ensure that the underfloor space is adequately ventilated: in other words that there are sufficient airbricks. You can then level off the surface of the floor with a covering of exterior-grade plywood sheets (see *Ready Reference*). If you intend using adhesive to fix the tiles, check with the manufacturer's instructions to see whether the plywood has to be treated with a special primer before you apply the adhesive.

If you can do so without too much trouble, you should lift existing vinyl sheet or tile floorcoverings and treat the floor surface beneath as already described. You can generally afford to leave existing floor tiles in place. Remove any damaged sections, together with those which have come loose, then fill in any deep depressions that result with mortar. The tiling adhesive should be able to accommodate minor lumps and bumps in the floor. Finish by thoroughly cleaning the floor, making sure you remove all trace of dirt, grease and polish. (Certain tiling adhesives are unsuitable for use over plastic floorcoverings so remember to check for this with the adhesive manufacturer's instructions.)

Depending on the thickness of the floorcovering formed by the tiles plus adhesive or mortar, you may have to remove and refix the skirting boards. If you do remove them, you will have to make good the wall where they were fixed in place, whether you intend to replace them with skirting tiles or to replace the original skirtings when the tiling is finished.

LAYING THE TILES

1 Establish a starting point for the first whole tile and temporarily nail the guide battens in place. Check they are square using a set-square.

2 Use a tiling gauge to work out the position of a third batten, four tiles in from one fixed batten, and temporarily nail it in position.

3 With a spirit level check that the battens are level. If they are not you will have to pack them up (see Ready Reference).

4 Use a trowel to spread a layer of mortar in the bay formed by the battens; aim to get the mortar coverage as even as possible.

5 Draw a notched dragging board over the battens so the mortar is smoothed down to the correct distance below the battens.

6 Using your tiling gauge as a guide, bed the tiles by hand, making sure you leave the correct grouting gap between them.

7 When you've bedded 16 tiles by hand you can go over them again with a block of wood, tamping them down into the mortar bed. Check they're evenly laid with a spirit level.

8 With the first 16 tiles in place, remove the third batten and fix it in place so it forms another bay for fixing the next area of tiles. Fix all the whole tiles in this way.

9 When a section of tiles is laid securely, you can cut tiles for the border areas and fix these in place. Make sure you don't disturb the whole tiles when you are doing this.

CUTTING TILES

1 *Score deeply along the cutting line with a tile cutter. If the tile has ribs on the underside, score in the same direction as the ribs.*

2 *To help the tile break cleanly, hold it carefully and use a pin hammer to tap the tile sharply on its underside just beneath the scored line.*

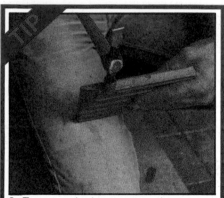

3 *To cut an L-shape, score the shape onto the tile and then tap away at the back of the waste with a hammer so it's thinner and easier to remove.*

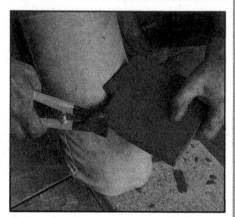

4 *Use tile nips or pincers to nibble away at the waste, taking out small pieces at a time so you don't risk breaking the tile.*

Laying the tiles

Whether you are going to lay the tiles on a mortar bed or adhesive you will first need to mark up a tiling gauge. You can make up a gauge rod from a 50x25mm (2x1in) timber batten. Lay a row of tiles on the floor, spacing them the correct distance apart, and then transfer the tile positions on to each batten with a pen or pencil.

It's best to begin tiling next to a long, straight wall, preferably the wall furthest from the door. As when laying glazed floor tiles you will have to establish a right-angled starting point for the first whole tile (see Laying ceramic floor tiles). Temporarily nail timber battens in place to indicate the starting point and to serve as a guide for the rest of the tiling. Where you are laying the tiles on mortar and the mortar is simply used as an adhesive, the battens' thickness should equal twice the thickness of the tiles; where

the mortar is to double as a screed their thickness should equal the thickness of the screed (usually 50mm/2in) plus the thickness of a tile.

Then, if you are tiling on mortar, use the gauge rod to work out the position of another batten four tiles in from one of the battens already in place, and temporarily nail this batten in position. You now have a 'bay' formed by the three battens and it is within such bays that you work across the floor, spreading the mortar and bedding the tiles area by area.

If you are using adhesive, once you have fixed battens to indicate your starting point and to serve as guidelines for the rest of the tiling, you can begin to apply the adhesive, spreading on enough to cover about 1sq m (1sq yd) of floor area at a time. If you are laying the tiles on a 3mm (⅛in) thick bed of adhesive you simply pour some adhesive onto the floor, spread it out as evenly as possible to the required thickness with a trowel or steel float

TILING A SKIRTING

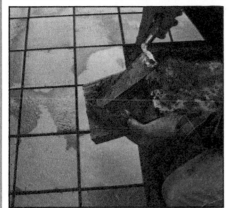

1 *When the skirting board has been removed you can proceed to butter the back of the skirting tiles with mortar; aim for an even coverage.*

2 *Press the skirting tiles carefully into place, leaving a grouting gap between them and making sure they align with the tiles on the floor.*

3 *Where necessary, you will have to fill in the gap between the skirting tiles and the rest of the tiles with narrow pieces of cut tile.*

TILING A STEP

1 *Start by covering the riser. Cut the tiles so they will reach 13mm (1/2in) above the top of the step, then butter their backs and press them into place.*

2 *Then spread a layer of mortar onto the step tread so it just reaches the top of the riser tiles. Smooth the mortar so it's even and level.*

3 *You can then go ahead and fix the lipping tiles on the tread to form a neat nosing at the front of the step. Fill in with cut tiles at the back.*

and then lightly rub the surface with a serrated scraper.

If you are applying a 6mm (1/4in) bed of adhesive you could apply it in areas delineated by timber bays as when using mortar. However, it is easier to lay a 3mm (1/8in) thick bed as described and then to butter the necessary additional adhesive onto the back of each tile just as you are about to lay it. Alternatively, apply the entire 6mm (1/4in) of adhesive to the tile.

Once the adhesive is down you can press the first square metre of tiles firmly into place. Take care that the whole of each tile is firmly in contact with the adhesive and that there are no gaps or pockets of trapped air. Once two or three tiles are down, use a spirit level to check that they finish flush with each other, then repeat this test as each subsequent tile is pressed in place. When you have covered one square metre, clean off any adhesive that has strayed on to the surface of the tiles before moving on to put down more adhesive and tiles. It's important to do this before the adhesive sets.

When you are fixing tiles in mortar it's best to work in sections when you are laying the cut tiles. Otherwise you risk disturbing the whole tiles which are already laid.

If you wish, instead of bedding the tiles in a dry, crumbly mortar (see *Ready Reference*) you can use a mix like this as the base and then spread a runnier mix over the top in which to bed the tiles.

Cutting tiles

Quarry tiles are cut in much the same way as any other type of ceramic tile. You score the surface with a tile cutter, or where you are cutting an L-shaped piece you nibble away at the waste with pincers or tile nips. Having said that, it's worth remembering that these floor tiles are thick and it's best to take care to score deeply into the tile. If you tap the underside of the tile sharply with a hammer just beneath the cut line it will break more easily. Nibbling away at waste with pincers may still prove troublesome and in some cases it could be worth resorting to the use of a cold chisel and hammer to chip off the tile to the shape you want. You will have to work with care, resting the tile on a firm bed of newspaper for

GROUTING TILES

1 *Leave the tiles for at least 12 hours without disturbing them and then spread grout over the surface with a sponge or plastic spreader.*

2 *To remove the excess grout, first rub a cloth diagonally across the joins, taking away as much of the excess as possible.*

3 *Then, with most of the hard rubbing done, work along the joins with the cloth to neaten the finish. This saves you removing too much grout from within the joins.*

support, to stop the tile from cracking. Alternatively, you can thin the waste part of the tile to make it easier to nibble it away.

Tiled skirting

According to the traditional method of tiling, tiled skirtings are always laid before the floor is tiled. However, you may find it easier to get a neat result, matching the skirting's joins with those between the floor tiles, if you fix them after tiling the floor; this is perfectly acceptable. In this case, make sure you leave the correct gap between the floor tiles and walls to take the skirting tiles.

If you are working with tiling adhesive, use this to fix the skirting tiles to the wall in exactly the same way as when you are fixing tiles to the floor. If you are using mortar, apply this to the wall using a steel float, aiming for a continuous bed roughly 6mm (¼in) thick. Alternatively, you can butter the back of each tile with mortar, taking care that the whole of the back surface is covered.

Finishing off

Where the tiles have been laid on adhesive, leave them at least 12 hours before you grout them. Where you have laid them on a mortar bed this 'waiting time' should be increased to 24 hours.

In both cases it's worth reducing the risk of disturbing the tiles if you have to walk on them by spreading your weight on 'crawl boards' roughly 900x600mm (3x2ft) made from chipboard or some equally rigid sheet material.

The grouting is done in much the same way as when you are grouting other ceramic floor or wall tiles, in that you rub the grout over the tiles so it fills the joints and then clean off the excess. Do make sure that you are using a grout which is designed for floors and that you don't remove too much grout when cleaning off (see step-by-step photographs). Most grouts which are suitable for use with floor tiles are cement-based and are likely to irritate the skin, so avoid unnecessary contact with the grout by wearing gloves. Remember you can buy coloured grout or add colour to a standard type of grout if you want to match the colour of the tiles or set them off in coloured grout which provides a striking contrast.

After grouting you should leave the floor for a day or two to harden and then wash it thoroughly using water and detergent. You can finish off by applying a proprietary tile sealer or, if you like, floor polish, but tiles which have been laid outdoors must never be polished.

A word of warning: do be careful when you are carrying out this first floor wash. Take care that you don't use too much water. The floor, in particular the grout and adhesive, will not be up to a heavy soaking for at least a fortnight.

METHODS OF FIXING

There are two ways of fixing the tiles:
● they can be fixed in a mortar bed; useful where you are tiling over a new concrete floor as the mortar bed also provides the floor's finishing screed
● alternatively, they can be fixed with tile adhesive; the adhesive bed should be 3mm (⅛in) thick for regular, smoother tiles and 6mm (¼in) thick for rougher type tiles. Use a thick bed for tiles with studs on the underside or where the floor is slightly uneven.

THE RIGHT MORTAR MIX

A fairly dry crumbly mix of 1 part cement to 3 parts sharp sand is suitable.

TYPES OF ADHESIVE

Quarry tiles can be laid with ordinary floor tile adhesives.

TIP: LEAVE A GROUTING GAP

When you are laying the tiles leave a gap 3mm (⅛in) wide between each tile and at the skirting board for the grout.

LEVELLING BATTENS

Where you are fixing the tiles in a mortar bed, you may have to pack up the battens forming the 'bay' surrounding the mortar with pieces of card to level them.

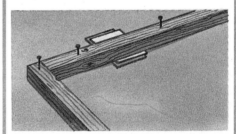

MAKING A DRAGGING BOARD

Take a piece of timber long enough to span the two formwork battens. Cut notches in the bottom edge so that the edge can rest within the battens about 12mm (½in) above the floor surface, ie, at the eventual depth of the mortar layer.

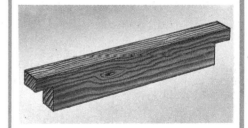

LAYING HARDWOOD FLOORS

Hardwood flooring comes in a variety of types and timbers. It can provide you with a particularly elegant floor without your having to spend a great deal of money.

If you want a wooden floor and have decided that sanding and sealing existing floorboards would be inappropriate, you can simply lay hardwood flooring over the floorboards or, for that matter, over a solid concrete floor. Wood flooring is available in several varieties of hardwoods: oak, teak, iroko, beech, sapele, mahogany, maple and walnut, for example. It can be particularly decorative in terms of grain, figure or colour and with a few rugs scattered over it, a hardwood floor can add real elegance to a room. In addition to its decorative qualities the flooring will be hardwearing, durable and easy to clean and maintain.

Another factor in its favour is cost: you can get an attractive hardwood floor for less than the price of a good quality carpet with underlay. And, besides lasting longer, the timber will stand up better to spills and dirt.

Choosing the flooring

The type of hardwood flooring which is most widely available is mosaic flooring, which comes in panel form (see *Ready Reference*). Normally, mosaics are the most flexible of the various types of flooring and therefore the easiest to lay, though those joined by wire and glued together at the edges are more rigid. If you decide to use mosaic panels, you might choose to have types made from different timber on the same floor, building them up into a pattern.

Traditional solid timber parquet blocks are still available, though most manufacturers and importers restrict themselves to supplying the professional floor layer. One or two varieties are, however, available on the DIY market. The problem with blocks is their rigidity, so that it's all too easy to end up with some that have edges sticking up over which people, especially young children or elderly people, might trip. Furthermore, there's the problem of setting out the patterns. Traditional herringbone can be tricky and the trouble with brick bond is that any expansion of the blocks due to moisture absorption from the atmosphere will be in the same direction. Also, since the blocks must go on a flat, rigid floor you must be painstaking with your preparation.

The advantages of block flooring are that the blocks are usually a high quality material which will last a lifetime and you can choose your own pattern (mosaics, on the other hand, always come in basket-weave form).

Wood strip floorings can be laid on top of existing timber or concrete floors; some varieties can also be fixed direct to joists and so can take the place of floorboards. The latter types are therefore particularly worth considering if you are faced with renewing a timber floor or having a house custom-built for you. Laminated strips are always pre-finished, so if you want to avoid having to sand the floor and finish it you might choose this type of flooring. Mosaic panels and solid strips are sometimes pre-finished, sometimes not. Unfinished types are less expensive to buy than their pre-finished counterparts, but you will have to sand and finish them.

When buying the flooring remember to allow about five per cent extra for wastage when you are cutting to fit or to remove any defect. Also, if you have underfloor heating you should check with your supplier that the type of flooring you have in mind is one which will not be affected by the heating.

Preparation

The floor must be in sound condition and as level as possible before you lay hardwood flooring over it. One point to remember here is that the more level the sub-floor is before you lay the new flooring, the less sanding you will have to do when finishing.

On a timber floor you will have to punch home protruding nails or countersink screws; knots should be planed down. You may also have to remove any accumulated polish or stains; this is particularly important if you are using adhesive to fix the flooring or it will not stick properly. Instead of going to this trouble, however, you could cover the floor with sheets of hardboard or plywood to ensure a clean level surface. Condition hardboard first, before you lay it, by brushing water into its mesh side and then stack it flat, with the sheets back to back, and leave it in the room where you're going to use it for 48 hours.

It's worth using relatively small sheets of hardboard, say 1220mm x 1220mm (4ft x 4ft) because these are easier to handle than large sheets. Start laying the hardboard in one corner of the room. You don't have to take too much trouble and aim for an absolutely perfect fit; there's no need, for example, to scribe the hardboard so it exactly follows the outline of the skirting. If you are going to use adhesive to fix the hardwood flooring, lay the hardboard mesh side up to help the adhesive to grip properly. Fix the sheets by nailing them at 100mm (4in) centres round the edges and 150mm (6in) centres in the middle. Begin in the middle of one and work forwards and sideways so that the sheet will lie truly flat. When you come to the end of a row, use the

LAYING AND CUTTING PANELS

1 Snap a chalked line alongside a straight wall. It should be the width of a panel, plus 12mm (¹/₂in) to allow a gap for expansion, away from the wall.

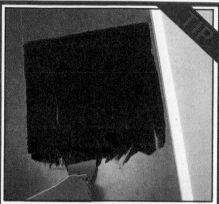

2 Using the chalked line as a guide, spread on the adhesive with a notched spreader. When working, protect your hands and clothing from the adhesive.

3 Lay the first row of panels along the wall, 12mm (¹/₂in) away from it. Butt the panels against each other, making sure they are aligned.

4 Continue spreading adhesive and laying the panels; check they're in straight rows. When the whole ones are laid you can lay the cut border panels.

5 To mark off a panel to be cut, place it over the last full panel in a row. Place another one over it 12mm (¹/₂in) away from the wall to use as a guide.

6 When you have marked the cutting line you can go ahead and cut the panel. Use a tenon saw and work with the panel face side up.

offcut from the sheet you've cut to size to start the next row so the joins in the sheets won't coincide; this helps to prevent any movement of the floor occurring in a continuous line down the joins and disturbing the flooring above.

With solid floors there could be a damp problem. If, after you've tested for damp (for example, by heating a metal plate, placing it on the floor and seeing if moisture forms underneath), you are in any doubt at all about the condition of the floor, you should take precautions against damp by laying a damp-proof membrane. The exception to this rule is where you are going to use bituminous adhesive to stick the flooring down, since the adhesive itself will prevent moisture from penetrating the flooring. If you are going to fix the flooring to battens set into or placed on the floor, make sure you use battens which have been preservative-treated.

The other question to consider with a solid floor is how level it is. If it is uneven you should level it using a self-levelling screeding compound (see Laying ceramic floor tiles, pages 208–209, for more details).

Apart from the state of the floor you will also have to examine the door. Your new floor might stop the door from opening properly; test for this by placing a piece of flooring under the door. If necessary, you will have to take the door down, trim the required amount off the bottom and then re-hang it.

You should also condition the flooring. Buy it at least a week before you intend laying it, then unpack it and leave it in the room where it will be laid so it can adjust to the atmosphere; stack it so the air can circulate freely around it.

Setting out

You can start laying mosaic panels, strips and wood blocks alongside the longest uninterrupted wall in a room. You should check first that the position in which you intend to lay your first row won't mean you have to cut very narrow pieces to fit on the other side of the room by dry-laying a row of panels across the room. In the case of strips and blocks it would be easier to work this out on a scale drawing of the floor. Also, check by dry-laying a row of panels alongside the wall that there won't be very narrow cut pieces at the ends of the rows. If necessary, adjust your starting point, then snap a chalked line down the room to serve as a guide when you are fixing the first row. A tip here: if you want, instead of snapping a chalked line you can make a mark at each end of the room in the relevant position, drive in a nail at each mark and then tie a length of string so it's tightly stretched between them. Unlike a chalked line this can't be prematurely rubbed out.

If you are laying wood blocks in an intricate pattern, you would be better off starting from

LAYING PANELS IN AN ALCOVE

1 At the corner leading into the alcove, place the panel to be cut to fit round it on the last full panel in one of the rows which meet at the corner.

2 Place another panel over the panel to be cut, 12mm (1/2in) away from the wall and use this as a guide to mark off one side of the required L-shape.

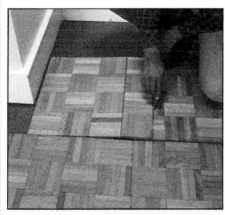

3 Repeat this procedure at the end of the other row of panels leading to the corner, to mark off the other side of the L-shape on the panel to be cut.

4 Cut the panel, spread on adhesive and lay the L-shaped panel. Take care to wipe off any adhesive from the front of the panels before it dries.

5 You can now fit the cut border panels at the back of the alcove. Mark them up for cutting in the usual manner before spreading the adhesive.

6 Lay the cut panels so they align with the full-size panels, and make sure there is an expansion gap of 12mm (1/2in) between them and the wall.

Ready Reference

TYPES OF WOOD FLOORING

There are different types of hardwood flooring available. They include:
● mosaic flooring which consists of thin fingers of wood (generally only 8mm/5⁄16in thick) fixed together in a series of squares on a panel to form a basket-weave pattern and stuck to a backing pad of bituminous felt. (Some are, however, wired together and glued at the edges; some are also tongued-and-grooved.) Usually there are 5 fingers per square and 16 squares per panel
● traditional parquet wood blocks which can be laid in different patterns. They must be laid on a flat, rigid base and are usually laid on a solid floor though they can be fixed to suspended timber floors. They are stuck down and are sometimes interlocked by tongues and grooves
● strip flooring, ie, a series of strips rather like very narrow short floorboards. They may be solid and thin (9.5mm/3⁄8in) or quite thick (19 to 23mm/3⁄4 to 7⁄8in). Other types are laminated, either coming in pieces designed to look like a solid strip of wood or having a veneer which is split up into strips. They are longer than wood blocks and are usually laid side by side in straight runs. They can be 'secret nailed' to wood floors, joists or battens or glued together along the tongued-and-grooved joints and laid 'floating' on solid floors.

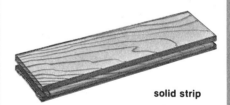

solid strip

FLOORING PATTERNS

Apart from the figure and colour of the wood, the patterns in which wood block flooring is arranged are also a source of interest. Arrangements include various types of basket-weave patterns, brick bond and herringbone patterns.

double herringbone

brick bond

FIXING MOULDING

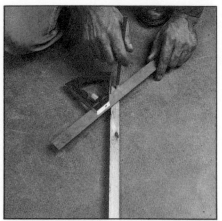

1 *Use a combination square to mark off 45° angles on lengths of moulding which will meet at a corner. When cut they should form a neat mitre join.*

2 *Use the moulding to cover the gap left for expansion round the perimeter of the room. Fix it by driving panel pins through it into the skirting.*

3 *At a corner, nail two lengths of moulding so they form a mitre join. You can seal the moulding later at the same time as you are sealing the floor.*

DOORWAYS

1 *Where a panel will have to be cut to shape to fit round an architrave, trace the outline of the architrave from a template onto the block.*

2 *Cut the panel to the required shape; a jigsaw is ideal for this sort of work. You don't need to allow for an expansion gap in the doorway.*

3 *To finish off the job, fix a length of moulding so it fits just over the edge of the shaped panel and covers the expansion gap along the wall.*

the middle of the room, as the effect will be much neater this way.

For a herringbone pattern you should first mark a line or stretch string tightly between the mid-points of two opposite walls. Then, starting at the centre of that line, dry-lay the blocks at an angle of 45° to the line. Once the rows on each side of it are in place the rest are positioned automatically. With other patterns, begin from the middle, setting out your blocks dry first to make sure you get the edge cuts equal and not too small. To prevent them from moving during the setting out, you can pin the odd one here and there on a timber floor.

Laying and cutting flooring

Having worked out your starting point and set up guidelines to help you get it straight, you can go ahead and lay the flooring. If you are using a bitumen-based adhesive, spread it on the floor so it covers an area only slightly larger than the piece of flooring you are laying, then very carefully place the flooring in position. This type of adhesive is very messy to work with and you should aim to avoid getting any on the face of the flooring as it can be difficult to remove; if any does adhere to the flooring surface, scrape it off immediately before it has a chance to set. Also, it's worth wearing gloves when you're applying it and clothes that you don't mind getting possibly permanently marked.

To get tongued-and-grooved boards to slot together fully, you can knock them in using an offcut to protect the exposed tongue. Secret nailing (see *Ready Reference*) will provide a professional-looking fixing. If you're laying strip flooring over joists you should make sure than no two joints between strips are within 150mm (6in) of each other, in any direction to ensure a sound and stable floor surface. (Before you begin laying the flooring check also that the joists are in reasonable condition; you might need to add a splint to an uneven joist to provide adequate support for the flooring.)

In some cases, it is recommended that besides allowing a gap for expansion round the perimeter of the flooring that you leave small gaps (of about 1mm) between the individual units of flooring. Check with the manufacturer's instructions.

The normal procedure is to lay all the whole pieces of flooring first, however you happen to be fixing them, and then to fill in with the cut pieces at the borders. Cutting should be done with a fine-toothed saw; check that it's sharp before you start cutting. Where you have to cut out an intricate shape, for example to fit round an architrave or a WC, a jig saw will make the job much easier and will reduce the risk of splintering the wood so it has to be recut, thus lessening the likelihood of wastage. Make a template of the area where

SEALING

1 *Sand the floor to provide a clean, even surface, removing any high spots between the panels. To make the job go more quickly, use an orbital sander.*

2 *Remove dust arising from the sanding, and then brush on a thin coat of special wood flooring sealer over the panels (and the moulding).*

3 *For a good finish, wait until the sealer dries, then buff it gently with worn, fine sandpaper or steel wool to provide a key for the second coat.*

intricate cutting will be required, and test the template by placing it on the floor in the relevant position before you trace its outline onto the flooring. It makes more sense to remake an inaccurate template than to waste flooring by cutting it to the wrong shape.

If you are using cork strips (see *Ready Reference*) to fill in the gaps you've left for expansion at the perimeter of the room, you may find that some of the intricate cutting which would otherwise be required will not be needed. Round a fluted architrave in a doorway, for example, you can simply cut the flooring as if it were a square corner and then fill in with the flexible cork strip.

Finishing the floor

If you have laid flooring which is not pre-finished, you will have to give it a sanding first to smooth it over. In fact, one of the advantages of using an unfinished type of flooring is that sanding may in any event be necessary to remove the odd high spot here and there.

You can tackle the floor in a small room by hand or with a portable powered orbital sander, but on larger rooms you'll need a heavy-duty floor sander (which you can hire) and an edging sander for the borders. Since these sanders are powerful you should take care when using them; many of the wooden flooring materials have thin surface veneers and you run the risk of going right through them. It's best to use only a fine abrasive belt for this reason.

Seal off the room in which you're using the sanders, and wear a dust mask because they generate an enormous amount of dust. Remember too to wear ear protectors as they're also very noisy to work with. Sharp edges or nail heads can rip the abrasive belt, causing bits to fly around; this can be dangerous so make sure you've punched home nails and removed splinters from the flooring before you start.

Aim to be very careful not to scratch the floor surface. To avoid this you should always sand along the grain, never across it. Even when you're using the edge sander, move it along the grain only. In patterns where the grain is going in all directions (such as basket-weave) the trick is to approach such patterns at a 45° angle.

Finally, you'll have to seal the floor. Floor sealers come in matt and gloss versions and you will need two or three coats, according to how fine a finish you want. For a good-looking result, it's worth sanding each coat (except the final one) lightly with very fine glasspaper to provide a key for the following coat. If you do this, wipe the floor surface with a cloth moistened with white spirit to pick up any dust. If you wish, you can apply a little polish to the flooring once the sealer is properly dry.

Ready Reference

FIXING FLOORING

Some brands of hardwood flooring are self-adhesive. Others are stuck in place with a bitumen-based adhesive. Sometimes they are nailed down (on timber floors only). A few just lock together. In some cases both nailing and adhesive are recommended. Follow the manufacturer's instructions, whatever type of flooring you are fixing.

TIP: ALLOW FOR EXPANSION

When laying the flooring, allow a gap at the perimeter next to the wall to take account of expansion when the timber absorbs moisture. The gap should be about 12mm/½in wide (check with the manufacturer's instructions) and can be covered later by lengths of quandrant moulding nailed to the skirting, or else fitted with special cork strips (see below).

TIP: SECRET NAILING

Tongued-and-grooved floorings can be fixed by secret nailing: the nail is driven through the top of the tongue at an angle and punched home through the main body of the block or strip so it becomes invisible in the finished result. (If you use a punch with a hollowed end you're less likely to damage the flooring.)

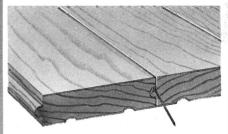

CORK EDGING STRIPS

Instead of using strips of quadrant moulding to cover the gaps left for expansion at the perimeter of the flooring (see step-by-step photographs) you can fill the gaps with special cork edging strips (about 7mm/¼in thick and 12mm/½in wide). These strips are ideal for filling in round curves or awkward areas such as a fluted architrave in a doorway.

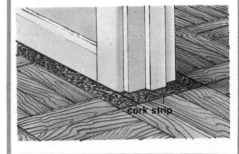

cork strip

LAYING WOODSTRIP FLOORING

Hardwood strip flooring can be laid over an existing floor or, provided it's a suitable type, directly over the joists. In either case, it should prove extremely durable.

The various types of hardwood flooring can be divided into three main types: mosaic panels, wood block and hardwood strip. Of the three, wood blocks require the most skill to lay and with these, unless you're feeling really confident, you may decide to leave the job to a professional. Mosaics were specifically developed for the DIY market; the techniques required for laying them have been explained in Laying hardwood floors. Laying strip flooring can be more or less complicated depending on the type of flooring selected and where it is going to be laid. The general skills you will require for this are described here, and how to lay one particular type of strip flooring is shown in detail in the step-by-step photographs.

Preparation

First of all you must get the existing floor ready to receive the flooring. Preparation is particularly important with floors, since safety, as well as appearance, is involved. An uneven floor could cause someone to trip, and this could be serious, especially in the case of an elderly person.

Floorboards will often be unsuitable as a base for applying hardwood flooring, as shrinkage will probably have caused gaps to appear between them. Some, or all, may have curled up at the edges because of warping. You can, however, use a relatively simple and inexpensive method of correcting this: by lining the floor with hardboard.

A chipboard or plywood floor in good condition presents the perfect base for a hardwood floor. Suspended concrete floors, such as one finds in very modern houses and high-rise buildings, also make a good base. However such a floor may have 'ripples' caused during the 'tamping-off' of the top screed and may be slightly uneven here and there. In that case, it should be treated with a self-levelling compound (see pages 208–209 for more details).

Modern direct-to-earth floors are usually in concrete and these make superb sub-floors, although they, too, may need to be treated with a self-levelling compound. Older solid floors, in quarry tiles and flag-

stones, are not suitable, and even an older concrete floor may be subject to damp. In this case a new damp-proof membrane will have to be laid.

Once you've got the sub-floor into a suitable condition you may still have to carry out some preparatory work before you can begin laying the flooring. For example, some manufacturers recommend that you put down a layer of polythene sheeting or polystyrene first, others supply a special underlay. On floorboards one manufacturer recommends that you put down layers of newspaper. The question of an underlay will arise when you plan to install a so-called 'floating floor' – that is, one which gets its stability by the strips being fixed to each other, but not to the sub-floor itself.

Methods of laying

If you wish, you can remove the skirting before you lay the flooring; when it's replaced (slightly higher up than its original position) it will conceal the gap you've allowed for expansion at the perimeter of the floor area. Otherwise you will have to fill the gap with special cork strips designed for this purpose, or else nail quadrant moulding or similar to the skirting in order to hide the gap.

It's usually recommended that you begin laying strip flooring along the longest wall you will be laying parallel to, starting in one

corner. Remember that with a timber sub-floor you should lay the strips so that they run at right angles to the floorboards. You should lay complete rows, starting with the tongue outwards in the case of tongued-and-grooved flooring. Make sure you get the first run straight; don't rely on your walls being perfectly square and an accurate guide. Instead stretch a taut string line, or snap a chalked line which you have ensured is true by the standard methods (see photograph 1 on page 216), alongside the wall. Use this to help you get a straight run of strips. In order to protect the tongues and the edges of the strips of wood, use a wooden block when you are knocking the strips together. An offcut of the flooring will be suitable.

The manufacturer may recommend 'secret nailing' – that is, where the nail is driven through the top of the tongue at an angle and punched home through the main body of the strip so that it is invisible in the finished flooring. If, instead, you nail straight through the face of the strips you will have to fill all the nail holes with matching stopper. With the clip-type system no nails are necessary; the longitudinal joints of the strips are secured by the clips. You will, with this system, need to use a woodworking adhesive to fix the ends of the strips together. By glueing the header joints you'll stop them dislodging.

PREPARATION

1 *It's usual to remove the skirting before you lay the flooring. You'll also have to cut away the bottom of any architrave to match the thickness of the new flooring.*

2 *Remove any debris and chippings from the floor surface and make sure it's level. Then lay down polythene sheeting over the entire floor area.*

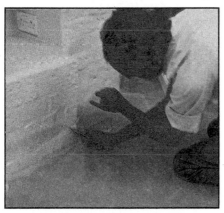

3 *The polythene will help protect the new flooring against moisture. Cut it so there's an overlap of about 100mm (4in) at the floor's perimeter.*

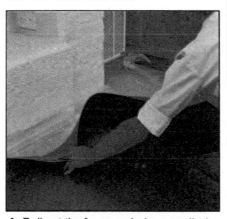

4 *Roll out the foam underlay supplied with the flooring and cut it to length. It should reach to within about 25mm (1in) of the walls all round the room.*

If you are using adhesive, you should follow the manufacturer's instructions as to which type to use and where to apply it. For example, one manufacturer specifically states that the adhesive should be spread on the top side of the groove and not just squirted in so it lies on the groove bottom.

With the strip system which has interlocking 'ears', the individual strips can either be secret-nailed or glued together.

Where you are laying tongued-and-grooved flooring over the joists rather than over an existing floor, (obviously you should use a thick type of strip flooring for this), then so long as the ends of the strips are tongued-and grooved it's not necessary to make the joints fall over the joists. However, the joints should not be closer than 150mm (6in) to each other in any direction.

You will have to cut flooring to fit the ends of the room and go round obstructions.

Finishing the surface
Obviously, if you have chosen a pre-finished flooring you will save yourself the time and trouble of finishing the surface. If you have bought an unfinished type of strip it may be necessary to sand the surface after you've laid the flooring, and you can hire a floor sander for this. You should normally require only fine grades of belt, but a coarse grade may be necessary in some instances. Sand the floor with the coarsest grade first and then sand using progressively finer grades. Take care as you work; you don't want to gouge out the surface so that all the effort you have spent laying the flooring is wasted. (For fuller information on sanding floors see Stripping floors, page 85.) When all the dust from the sanding has been removed you can apply the recommended number of coats of varnish or seal according to the manufacturer's instructions.

LAYING THE FLOORING

1 Laying begins alongside the longest straight wall, or failing that, the one with the least obstructions. Mark where the first straight run of timber will go.

2 In this case, you will also have to cut the flooring which runs next to the wall to shape. Scribe onto the timber the profile to be cut.

3 Cut the timber as required. Before you cut flooring to length, make sure the strips which make up the flooring will end up with the joints staggered.

6 You will need to leave an expansion gap of about 10mm (³/₈in) round the room, so cut timber wedges of this size and insert them at the perimeter.

7 Drive fixing clips into the adjacent lengths of flooring. They should be arranged so they will be no closer than 75mm (3in) to any other clips.

8 To interlock the tongues and grooves of adjacent lengths, drive them together using a hammer and an offcut of the flooring to protect the edges.

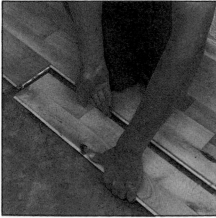

11 With the end groove glued, position the next length so it will align with the neighbouring lengths of flooring at its end and side.

12 You can then drive the length of flooring into place at the header and side joints, again protecting the tongue with an offcut of the flooring.

13 Continue in this way until all the floor is covered. You work back and forth down the length of the room, clipping and glueing as required.

4 Turn the first length of flooring so its back is facing you, then drive in the toothed end of a clip into the groove channelled in the timber.

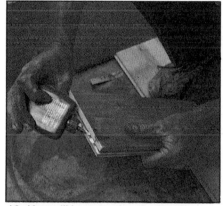

5 Fix other clips in the same way; they should be spaced about 750mm (30in) apart along the length of the flooring. You can then lay the first lengths.

A MAT WELL

1 It's unlikely that the walls will be perfectly square, so use a sliding bevel to measure the angle. Transfer this measurement to the flooring.

9 As these offcuts show, you fix a clip in one length and the pressure of the floor drives the untoothed end into the groove on the neighbouring length.

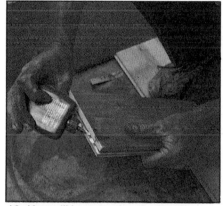

10 You will have to glue the header joints. Apply woodworking adhesive along the bottom inside of the groove on the piece to be joined.

2 You can use the mat itself to mark off on the flooring the rest of the shape which will need to be cut. Use an ordinary saw or jig saw to cut the timber.

14 Where you won't be fixing a skirting at the outer edge you will need to insert special flexible cork strips to keep the flooring in place.

15 For a neat effect trim the polythene overlap. Replace the skirting, insert cork strips or fix beading to cover the gap you've left.

3 Cut the other strips which will fit round the mat to size and shape, and fix them in place, clipping and driving the lengths together in the normal manner.

LAYING CARPET TILES

Like fitted carpet, carpet tiles can provide warmth and softness underfoot, but they don't require anything like the same sort of skill to lay them.

Carpet tiles are small squares of carpet which you can lay side by side to create a fitted carpet look. You could of course choose to lay ordinary fitted carpet but carpet tiles have advantages that make them well worth considering. For example, since the majority are loose-laid (carpet tiles which require sticking down are available, but only in heavy 'contract' ranges for industrial and commercial use), laying carpet tiles is extremely simple. You certainly won't need to call in a professional carpet fitter for the job. You don't even need an underlay. What's more, they are just as easy to take up again (though some may stick to the floor beneath in heavy traffic areas) which means that, normally, you can remove badly-stained examples for cleaning or else simply move the tiles around to even out wear.

You can also remove the tiles completely if you are redecorating the room, though it's worth pointing out here that you may have a little trouble in achieving the same neat fit as you had before as the tiles may have spread with use. And finally there is the financial aspect. Although not exactly cheap, allowing for the savings you will make on fitting them, carpet tiles tend to be a good deal less expensive than fitted carpet.

What's available

In spite of their advantages, carpet tiles are not very widely available so you should expect to do a fair amount of shopping around before you find exactly what you want.

Basically, the choice is between carpet tiles designed specifically for heavy-duty areas where looks and feel aren't terribly important, and those designed as a straightforward carpet substitute. In the former category, you'll find versions that look rather like needlecord, as well as quite a few very rugged examples made by embedding synthetic fibres, which are often quite coarse in texture, in a fibrous reinforced base. In the second category, you can expect the tiles to have a proper pile, though quality varies considerably with price. At the lower end of the price scale the 'pile' may amount to nothing more than synthetic fibres embedded vertically in a rubber backing. If you pay a

little more you will begin to be offered tiles that approach the quality of normal carpet, with a more luxurious feel.

Calculating quantities

If you simply want to create a plain fitted carpet look, measure the length and breadth of the room using the length of a tile as your unit of measurement. Round each dimension up to the nearest whole number and multiply them together to get the total number of tiles.

If you intend to create a pattern, you will have to work out the quantities of each colour more carefully. It's best to draw up a scale floor plan of the room; then, on this draw a grid to represent the positions of the individual tiles. Colour in the grid to produce the design you want and count up the number of tiles required. Count cut tiles as whole tiles.

Preparation

As with most floorings, the surface on which the tiles are laid must be clean, level and free from damp. So take special care over preparation, levelling concrete floors with a self-levelling compound and floorboards with sheets of plywood or hardboard pinned down all over (see pages 208–209 for more details).

Setting out

Although with carpet tiles which have a thick pile the joins between tiles should in theory be invisible, they nearly always show to some extent in practice, so it's worth going to the trouble of laying the tiles symmetrically.

This is done in exactly the same way as for vinyl and cork floor tiles (see pages 190–193 and 194–198 respectively). You stretch a chalked string line between the mid-points of opposite walls and snap it down onto the floor to leave a cross at the centre of the room. Then lay two rows of tiles in an L-shape, starting at the cross and lining up the edges of the tiles with the chalk lines, working out towards the walls until cut tiles are needed to fill the gaps. If your first layout means that you would have cut tiles which are too narrow (see *Ready Reference*) restrike the guide-lines in a slightly different position, up to half the length of a tile away from the first set of lines, and try again. Keep trying until you have achieved the required layout.

Laying and cutting tiles

Once you've found a suitable arrangement you can begin laying the whole tiles, starting with one which goes in the angle of the guide-lines where they meet at the centre of the room (see step-by-step photographs).

You will eventually have to cut tiles to fill the gaps at the edges. Most tiles can be cut with ordinary scissors; scissors with contoured plastic handles are best, allowing you to apply the pressure needed to cut thick tiles without too much discomfort. Alternatively, you can use a sharp knife. The only thing you have to watch, apart from the obvious need to cut a straight, true line is that when cutting tiles which have a pile, you don't shave off the pile at the edge of the piece you want to use. Although the cut edge will be up against the wall, the bald line sometimes spreads and can look quite unsightly after a short time.

To work out where you make the cut you can, with tiles which have no pile, use the same trick as you would with cork, vinyl or ceramic tiles. That is, you lay the tile to be cut over the whole tile which will be its neighbour, then lay another whole tile on top with its edge butted against the wall to serve as a guide to mark the cutting line on the tile to be cut. The snag with this method is that because there is a certain amount of 'give' in the tiles, it tends not to be very accurate.

A more sensible approach, therefore, is simply to measure the width of the cut tile required. To allow for the fact that the walls may not be exactly straight or out of square, take three readings, one at each end and one in the middle of the gap to be filled and transfer these measurements to the back of the tile you are going to cut using a very soft pencil. Don't use a felt-tipped pen; on rubber-backed tiles in particular, the ink may not dry, with the result that it transfers itself to the pile of the tile you are cutting via the scissor blades, or it may stain tiles you have already laid when you throw aside the offcut. If you feel fairly confident you can, in fact, cut down on the measuring and marking part of the process when it comes to cutting tiles. You can take the tile to be cut, and with its back side facing you, place it so it butts against the wall and exactly over the gap to be filled, then make nicks on the back with a sharp knife to indicate where it should be cut and, finally, cut it to size (see step-by-step photographs).

Finishing off

With all the tiles in place, it's worth leaving them for a few days to settle down under normal use. If they spread it may be necessary to re-trim the edges around the walls.

You can then carefully lift the tiles round the edge of the room and re-lay them, sticking them down with a single strip of heavy duty double-sided sticky tape, positioned close to the edge of the tiles which faces into the room. If you have been unable to avoid narrow cut tiles you should use 'tramlines' of adhesive tape, with an extra line of tape running close to the wall. Sticking down tiles on the perimeter is not essential but it helps to stabilise the tile arrangement and prevents further movement. On very large floors in heavy traffic areas it may even be desirable to fix perhaps one in three rows of whole tiles right across the floor.

You should fit ordinary carpet threshold strip to protect the edges of the tiles at doorways and eliminate the risk of them lifting and forming a ridge which you could trip over. Do remember to vacuum the floor thoroughly to remove any surplus lint.

LAYING THE FLOORING

1 Snap chalk lines which cross at the room's midpoint. Adjust this point if it means you'll have narrow cut tiles. Use the lines to get the tiles straight.

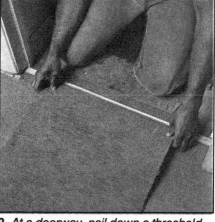

2 At a doorway, nail down a threshold strip. This will give you something to work against when the tile edge is pressed into it.

3 Lay the whole tiles. When you reach the outer edge, take the tile which will fill the edge gap and nick it slightly at either end to mark where to cut it.

4 Still working on the back of the tile, join up the nicks with a sharp knife using a straightedge to guide you. Then slice right through the tile.

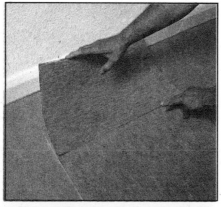

5 The cut tile is now ready to be fitted in place. If it's the right size it should stay in place in much the same way that a complete tile does.

6 It's best if you work in a quarter of the floor area at a time. Check that the tiles are straight as you work and cut them to fit at the perimeter.

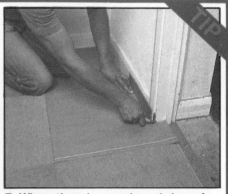

7 *Where there is an awkward shape for the tiles to be fitted round, such as the base of a WC or an architrave, make a cardboard template of the shaped area.*

8 *Place the template on the back of the tile to be cut and trace round it with a pencil. You can then cut out the shape with a sharp knife.*

9 *Fit the shaped tile in the same way as you would any other, butting it against adjacent tiles and, in this case, press it under the threshold strip.*

10 *When cutting a tile to fit round the angle formed by an alcove, nick on the back on two adjacent sides to indicate where it should be cut.*

11 *Cut the tile to the required shape and then lay it in place. Here, another tile will have to be cut to fill the gap near the alcove back wall.*

12 *Vacuum the flooring to remove surplus lint. The tiles shown here have been laid with the pile directions at right angles for a chequerboard look.*

Ready Reference

TILE SIZES
Carpet tiles are commonly available in the following sizes: 300, 400 or 500mm (12, 16 and 20in) square.

CREATE YOUR OWN PATTERN
Patterned tiles are not commonly available (though many heavy-duty tiles have a flecked effect). You could, however, create your own pattern by:
● using tiles of different colours and arranging them in either a simple chequerboard pattern or some sort of geometric design, or

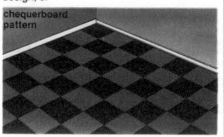

chequerboard pattern

● for a more subtle effect, choosing tiles with a distinct pile direction (normally indicated by an arrow on the backing) and laying alternate tiles with the pile directions at right angles.

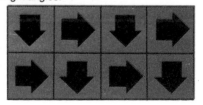

TIP: ALLOW A FEW TILES EXTRA
When you are buying the tiles, buy two or three more than the number required to cover the floor area to allow for mistakes (this is particularly worthwhile if the shape of the room damands awkward cutting). You may in fact be compelled to buy extras where the tiles are sold in packs rather than singly. But don't buy too many extras as it's too expensive.

TIP: AVOID NARROW CUT TILES
If possible you should avoid having cut tiles which are less than 100-150mm (4-6in) wide. Apart from the difficulty of cutting narrow strips of carpet tile, such small areas tend not to lay flat.

CHECK PILE DIRECTION
For a normal carpet effect the arrows on the back of the tiles should all point in the same direction.

UNUSUAL WALLCOVERINGS

Once you've mastered the basic paperhanging techniques,
you can tackle some of the more exotic wallcoverings now on the
market, and add the final touches to any room by putting
up friezes, decorative borders and cornices to match
its architectural style.

HANGING FABRICS ON WALLS

Hessian and other fabric wallcoverings are ideal as a cover-up for less-than-perfect walls. They can give a softer, richer look to a room and provide an ideal backing for prints, pictures or other items on display.

There are many fabric wallcoverings available. Some are nubbly and tweedy; others have a delicate silky or moiré (watered silk) surface; some are like damask: woven figured material. There are wallcoverings with wool and linen strands stretched across a backing to give an overall effect of striped, half-woven cloth; fragile grasscloths (strands of natural grasses bound lightly into a mat on a paper backing); and other coverings with an Oriental effect such as raw silk and split bamboo. There are thick sound-deadening felts; wallcoverings with a leather look, including crushed and brushed velvety suedes; ones with cork slivers on a coloured, or foil, background (which glints through the cork 'skin') and last, but by no means least, ever-popular hessian which comes in a natural oatmeal colour, various dyed colours and also in a special 'sized' version intended for over-painting.

Most of these wallcoverings are paper-backed, which makes hanging easy and straightforward. Some, however, are not. Ordinary upholsterers' hessian, for example, which is only about one-third of the price of the paper-backed version, can be hung on walls; but a different hanging technique is required (see *Ready Reference*). A point to bear in mind, if you are considering hanging one of the more expensive speciality wallcoverings like silk, grasscloth or cork, is that while they come with a paper backing, which prevents stretching and wrinkling, you cannot afford to make any mistakes in measuring and cutting; also these types of wallcovering stain very easily if any paste gets onto the surface.

Real fabric of almost any type can also be hung to cover walls, so long as it is firmly woven, but usually it is not stuck into place; instead, one of two other fixing methods are used. With one method, a staple gun is used to staple the fabric to battens which are in turn stapled to the wall. With the other, special plastic fabric-fixing track is fixed to the wall and the fabric tucked into this. Either way, the fabric can be removed fairly easily for cleaning, or when you are ready to change it again.

Choosing and buying wallcoverings

While taste is obviously an individual matter and you will choose the type of wallcovering according to the look you want (and the amount you are prepared to pay), the different textures of the various fabric wall-coverings do tend to make them appropriate for use in particular settings. The silks, moirés and grasscloths tend to look better in a more traditional setting whereas corks, suedes, wool weaves and tweedy effects complement a modern décor and blend particularly well with exposed brickwork, timber cladding, slate and stone. Hessian usually looks right in both modern and traditional settings, is a perfect foil for pictures, prints or other exhibits and is frequently used on one specific wall area to back a prized collection.

Quite a few fabric wallcoverings have a 'random' match, which means you don't have to allow for pattern-matching when buying. However, where there is a very heavy texture or a definite striped effect running horizontally across the material, some pattern matching may be necessary if the results are not to be disappointing. Some speciality wallcoverings, like grasscloth, can have a rather untidy look when hung, but this is characteristic of the material and it is supposed to have a random-match effect. If you think this is likely to worry you, buy something a little less defined in texture.

When buying, try to see as large a sample as possible before making up your mind. If you can, see two rolls unwrapped and placed side by side and also try to see them arranged vertically as they'll be seen when hung. The more expensive wallcoverings must usually be ordered in advance from specialist decoration shops, and you may only be able to select from smallish samples. In which case, try to have an arrangement with the supplier so you can return the material for a credit if it does not match the sample to your satisfaction.

Check the width and length of roll before ordering; many fabric wallcoverings are imported and may not conform to standard sizes. So if you don't check you risk ordering too much or little.

Also remember to check carefully for colour variations between rolls. Colour differences will be only too apparent when the wallcovering is in place.

HANGING LINING PAPER

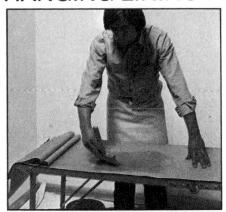

1 *Measure and cut the paper, allowing for an overlap at both ends of the room. Paste the back, folding the paper into concertina folds.*

2 *Hang the first length horizontally across the wall. Then hang the second length so it butts against it, pulling the concertina folds out.*

3 *Use a wallpaper brush to smooth the paper into place and ensure an unwrinkled surface; if right-handed, you should work from right to left.*

4 *At the corners of the room, you will have to trim off the overlap. As a guide for the knife you can use the edge of a scraper to get a clean cut.*

Preparing the surface

As with any wallcovering, the wall must be properly prepared first. This means old wallpaper should be stripped off and the wall washed clean of any old paste and size. Cracks, holes and indentations should be filled, any crumbling, or otherwise faulty plaster should be cut and filled, and the whole area should be smoothed down and then sized with a weak coat of size.

Newly-plastered surfaces must have dried out throughly; cracks should be filled, 'nibs' of plaster smoothed down and any efflorescence rubbed off with a cloth or brush. It is wise to apply a diluted coat of alkali-resisting primer, brushed well into the plaster.

Previously-painted surfaces should be washed down to remove grease and dirt and then rubbed down with glasspaper to provide a good 'key'; this is particularly important with a gloss-painted surface. Again, fill any cracks and holes and sand them down after filling.

Lining the wall

Before fixing a fabric wallcovering you should first line the wall with lining paper. The need for this is obvious with unbacked fabrics but it is equally important with other types of fabric wallcoverings since it will greatly improve the appearance of the finished result.

The lining paper should be hung horizontally (starting from the top of the wall) so there is no risk of the joins coinciding with those in the wallcovering. The edges of the paper should be butt-joined and surplus paper trimmed neatly into the corners of the room at each end. For the final length on a wall, you should trim the length roughly to size before pasting it and carry out final

Ready Reference

WALLCOVERING SIZES

Fabric wallcoverings are sometimes sold by the roll and sometimes by the metre. Sizes vary but typical widths are:
paper-backed hessian: 889mm (35in), 914mm (36in)
silk: 762mm (31in)
grasscloth: 914mm (36in)
tweed: 685mm (27in)
fine wool: 690mm (27in)
open-weave wool: 750mm (30in)
bouclé: 690mm (27in)
suede: 700mm (28in)
cork: 762mm (31in), 530mm (21in).

AVOID HEAVY-WEAR AREAS

Care and cleaning can be a problem with many fabric wallcoverings so they're best confined to areas where they won't get too much wear or be subject to grubby fingers or heating stains.

CROSS-LINE WALLS

Always cross-line the walls with lining paper first.
● if the wallcovering is very heavy, use a fairly thick lining paper
● for open-weave fabric, paint the paper first in the same colour as the fabric.

HANGING METHODS

The method of hanging depends on the type of wallcovering (check the manufacturer's instructions):
● paper-backed hessians and some other paper-backed fabrics can be hung like ordinary wallpaper. You paste the backing and, when hanging, work down from the top of the wall
● unbacked hessian and other speciality wallcoverings are hung by the paste-the-wall technique and, when hanging, you may in some cases have to work from the bottom of the wall up.
● to avoid shading, some wallcoverings should be 'reverse hung'. Each alternate length is reversed, as it is cut from the roll, and hung in the opposite direction from the previous length.

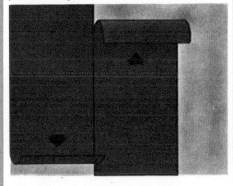

HANGING UNBACKED HESSIAN

1 Measure and cut the hessian to the required length, allowing about 100mm (4in) top and bottom. Cut enough for most of the room.

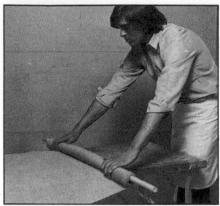

2 Roll the first length round a stout tube or a strong stick (a piece of old broom handle is suitable) with the right side of the hessian facing in.

3 Using a plumbline as a guide, mark the wall vertically into strips which will be the width of the overlap narrower than the hessian width.

4 Spread the adhesive on the wall with a brush, using feathered strokes, but don't apply it too thickly. Stop short of the drawn line on each side.

5 While the paste is still wet, start unrolling the hessian onto the wall from the roll you've made, using the lines on the wall as a guide.

6 To smooth the hessian into place and ensure it is securely fixed, run a clean paint roller over it when it is in place between the guidelines.

7 Hang the next length in the same way as you hung the first; make sure that you leave an overlap of at least 25mm (1in) between the lengths to allow enough material for trimming.

8 Hang hessian round the room. Before you carry out any trimming, leave the adhesive to dry to allow for shrinkage. Then trim to size at the top, bottom, and at joins.

9 At an internal corner, you will have to trim one length neatly into the corner, then fix the adjoining piece and trim the overlap to ensure you form a neat butt join.

MAKING A NEAT BUTT JOIN

.1 *Place a straight edge over the middle of the overlap between two lengths of hessian and then run a sharp knife through both lengths.*

2 *You can then peel off the surplus hessian; with the top waste piece removed you will be able to see and remove the piece underneath.*

3 *Paste the wall underneath the hessian on both sides of the join. Use a small brush and work carefully to ensure no adhesive gets on the front.*

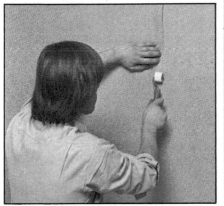

4 *With a seam roller, gently run over the two edges to make a neat butt join. Make sure you don't press too hard or you risk a shiny surface.*

trimming above the skirting board when it has been brushed into place.

If you are hanging an open-weave fabric, such as furnishing hessian, it's worth painting the lining paper in the same colours as the hessian so it won't be conspicuous if it shows through the fabric.

Hanging wallcoverings
Depending on the type of wallcovering, you may be cutting and pasting several lengths or one length at a time. Or you may use the paste-the-wall technique.

If the material is to be reverse hung (see *Ready Reference*), mark the back of each length with an arrow to indicate which way each piece is to go.

If you are using paper-backed hessian, you can trim off the overlap at the top and bottom as you go along, but for an unbacked type you should leave the adhesive to dry to

allow for shrinkage before you start to trim.

Turn hessian well round external angles as you do not want a raw edge on an exposed wall area. On inside angles, cut the corner length material into two strips and butt-join them in the angle (use the overlap technique – see step-by-step photographs – if appropriate).

Looking after fabric wallcoverings
For fabric wallcoverings to look their best, they will have to be dusted every few months. Gently run the upholstery attachment of a vacuum cleaner over the wallcovering (alternatively, you can brush it down with a soft brush). If there are any stains on the fabric, use dry-cleaning fluid to remove them (after testing the fluid on an inconspicuous area like behind a picture – to make sure it doesn't cause discolouration). Loose seams should be pasted down again.

DECORATING WALLS WITH CORK

Cork in tile, panel or sheet form provides an easy-to-fix wallcovering which is highly decorative and warm to the touch. It will also add to your peace and quiet by insulating against noise.

You may decide to decorate one or more walls of a room in your house with cork simply because you like the look of it. But there are practical advantages in doing this as well. You will also be providing extra insulation as, apart from its decorative qualities, cork deadens sound, is warm to the touch and keeps heat in and cold out. Also, it doesn't cause condensation and will absorb a certain amount of moisture. It can be quite hardwearing, taking its share of knocks and bumps without bruising, and many of the ranges of cork tiles, panels, sheets and rolls available are treated to be fully washable and steam-proof.

Where to use cork

Because of its highly decorative quality and natural texture, cork usually looks best as a feature wall, or forming a focal point on a chimney breast, or in an alcove, or behind some display shelves. But because of its insulating quality it is ideal on the inside of walls which face away from the sun, particularly if a bedhead or seating is placed next to them. Cork tiles on a ceiling can help reduce noise and also add warmth; in children's rooms, teenage bedsitting rooms, family living rooms, hobby areas, even the kitchen, a panel of cork can also provide a place to pin pictures, posters and memos. Pre-sealed cork is practical for kitchens and bathrooms so long as it does not come in direct contact with the bath, sink or basin edge (you can isolate it with a row of ceramic tiles). It can also be used to face doors, cover window seats and ottomans, or cover screens and bath panels – so long as you select the right product.

Types of cork

Cork for walls comes in several different types. Some is made by pressing the cork into layers, or mixing cork chippings with a binder, and then cutting it into sheets, tiles or panels of various sizes, thicknesses and textures. Sometimes, to get a rougher home-spun look, the actual bark of the cork tree is peeled, mounted on a backing and sold for decorative purposes. The backing may be coloured, and if the cork is slivered thinly

enough, this backing will show through, giving a hint of colour to the cork. This type may be sold as panels or sheets.

Another attractive cork wallcovering is made by shaving the cork so thinly that it is almost transparent and because of the natural uneven texture, the effect is like hand-crocheted lace. This is then mounted onto a foil backing which glints through the layer of cork. This type is usually sold in sheets or by the roll, as wallpaper.

A new development is a wallcork which is laminated to crêpe paper so it is extremely flexible and can be bent round curved surfaces. This type comes in a natural finish, which can be painted, and also in several colours. It is sold by the linear metre, off the roll.

Most wallcorks are presealed, either waxed or treated with a sealant, which makes them washable; some come unsealed including some of the heavily textured types and the very open granular tiles.

Buying and planning

Cork tiles, panels and sheet come in various sizes. When you have decided on the type you want to use you will have to work out how much you will need to order from your supplier. Remember the cardinal rule that you should always order more than will be exactly required to cover the wall, to allow for any mistakes, accidents or errors when you are putting the cork up.

You may decide to fix tiles or panels in a particular pattern, for example, so they create a diamond or herringbone design. If so, it's best to work out the design on paper

first; then, after you've prepared the surface, you can square up the wall and mark the position of each tile or panel on it. (Remember you can also create interesting effects by using light and dark tiles to form a chequerboard pattern or to form a border or 'framed' effect; but you shouldn't need to mark up the wall for this.)

Preparing the surface

As with any other form of decoration, cork must be hung on a properly prepared surface. If you are going to cover a wall with cork which has already been decorated you should strip off old wallpaper, scrape off any flaking paint and fill any deep holes; cut and re-plaster any crumbling 'live' areas. If the plaster is porous, prime with PVA primer diluted 1:5 with water.

Gloss or emulsion-painted walls can be keyed by rubbing over them with glasspaper to roughen the surface, but as the paint can sometimes cause the adhesive to break down, most cork suppliers recommend lining a painted wall with heavy lining paper before fixing the cork in position. Follow the instructions supplied with the particular product you intend using. If you are going to use lining paper, remember to cross-line the walls, that is, hang the paper horizontally just as you would before hanging a good quality wallpaper or fabric wallcovering to avoid the risk of joins coinciding.

If you are hanging sheet cork wallcovering and using a heavy-duty wallpaper paste to fix it, it may be necessary to prime the wall surface first with a coat of size or diluted wallpaper paste.

FIXING THE FIRST TILE

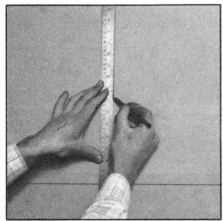

1 *Work out how the tile pattern will fall on the wall by drawing central horizontal and vertical lines. Adjust these to avoid awkward cuts.*

2 *Starting at the centre, spread adhesive in one of the angles formed by the lines. (With contact adhesive apply it to the back of the tile as well.)*

3 *Cover an area slightly larger than a tile, then align the first tile using the horizontal and vertical lines as a guide to the exact position.*

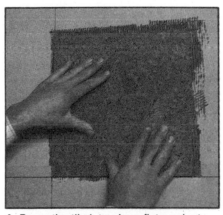

4 *Press the tile into place flat against the wall, taking care not to let it slip out of line as you do this. It's crucial you get the tile correctly positioned.*

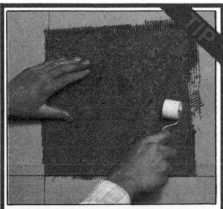

5 *Roll the tile with a wallpaper seam roller to get a better bond particularly at the edges. Be careful not to get adhesive on the roller.*

6 *If any adhesive gets onto the face of the tile wipe it off with a damp cloth before it sets. With some adhesives you may need to use white spirit (turps).*

Ready Reference

CHOOSING THE RIGHT CORK
Cork swells when it gets wet and could become distorted and start peeling off the wall. It therefore makes sense to
● use a pre-sealed type for kitchens, bathrooms and areas where you are going to have to wipe off sticky finger marks, or
● use a type of cork which can be sealed after hanging in these areas.

TIP: CONCEAL CUT TILES
When you are planning the layout of the tiles you are going to use on a wall, aim to place cut tiles where they won't draw attention. For example:
● it's best to have cut tiles at the skirting rather than at the ceiling
● on a chimney breast, butt cut tiles up to the junction between the chimney breast and wall rather than to the outer corner of the chimney breast.

TIP: MAKE DEMOUNTABLE PANELS
Because of the adhesive used to fix them, cork tiles can be difficult to remove once they are up; if you try to scrape them off you may either have large lumps of cork left stuck to the wall or large holes left in the plaster. To help you make it easier to have a change of decor later:
● fix the cork to panels of plasterboard, hardboard, partition board, chipboard, plywood or other dry lining
● fix the panels to battens which are screwed to the wall; these can be unscrewed and removed when you choose.

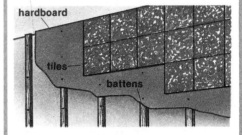

TILES IN HOT SPOTS
If you are fixing cork tiles to a chimney breast where a fire will be used, behind a radiator or other 'hot spot', it is best to put adhesive down the edges of the tiles as well as on the back to make extra sure of a secure bond.

PREVENT FIRE RISK
Many adhesives suitable for use with cork are highly inflammable. Therefore, when using them, make sure all pilot lights are switched off and turn off any electric or gas fires. Don't smoke or work near a naked light, and provide adequate ventilation.

FIXING OTHER TILES

1 *Apply more adhesive then butt the second tile into place using hand pressure and a roller. Then continue to fix all the whole tiles.*

2 *Where the tile has to be cut, for example, to fit at the edge of a chimney breast, you should first place it over the last whole tile in the row.*

3 *Butt another tile up against the corner so that it overlaps the tile to be cut; use this as a guide to mark off a cutting line with chalk or pencil.*

4 *To cut the tile, place it on a firm surface then use a sharp kife to cut along the marked line. Use a straightedge as a guide.*

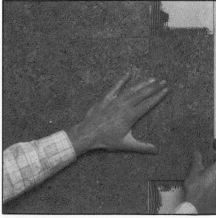

5 *Coat the exposed wall with adhesive and fix the cut tile in the same way you've fixed the whole tiles. Continue marking up, cutting and fixing the tiles.*

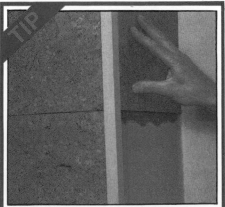

6 *When you've completed the front of a chimney breast you can tile the sides. Work so the cut edges go into the junction with the wall.*

Tools and equipment

You are already likely to have most of the tools and equipment required for covering walls with cork, particularly if you have hung some other type of wallcovering before. You will need a sharp knife to trim the cork, a straightedge, a notched adhesive spreader (sometimes supplied with the adhesive) or a pasting brush, a plumbline and chalk or pencil, a T-square or set square, a wallpaper seam roller and (for sheet cork) a wallpaper hanger's roller (which is wider than a seam roller). You will also require a tape measure and, to cut bark-type cork, a fine-toothed tenon saw. A pasting table (or some other suitable surface) may be needed; put this in a good light so you can see that the back surface of the tile or sheet (where these are pasted on the back rather than pasting the wall for fixing) is completely covered. As you'll be working at a height for part of the fixing process you'll need a stepladder. Make sure this is in sound condition so it will provide you with safe, secure access.

Fixing the cork

When you are fixing cork tiles or panels, as with all tiling, the setting-out is vitally important. The tiles should always be centred on a focal point or wall, so you end up with cut tiles or panels of equal width in the corners or at the edge of a chimney breast. Once you have established your central point and squared up the wall for the first line of tiles, tiling should be quite straightforward; the tiles are fixed with contact adhesive applied to the back of the tile and the wall or with an adhesive which is applied to the wall only.

Sheet cork is hung in different ways (see *Ready Reference*). The crucial thing here is to hang the lengths of cork to a true vertical and to plan the layout so cork which has to be cut to fit in width will come at the corners where any unevenness (due to the walls being out of square) will be least likely to be noticed.

Finishing touches and maintenance

If you put up cork tiles, panels, or sheet cork which are not sealed you can seal them with a transparent polyurethane varnish (a matt finish looks best). Dust the surface thoroughly and apply two or three coats of varnish; you may find a spray-on type is easier to apply than one which you brush on but this is only economical if you don't have too large an area to cover.

Most wall corks (whether sealed or unsealed) can be cleaned by dusting them down (use a cloth or the soft brush attachment on your vacuum cleaner). Most of the sealed corks and the crêpe-backed cork can be wiped with a damp cloth. The paper and foil-backed corks may not be wipable, so check before you buy, and don't hang them in a place where they will get dirty quickly.

HANGING SHEET CORK

1 Use a plumb line to mark off a guide line for fixing the first length. It should be less than the width of the cork sheet away from the corner.

2 Mark off more lines the width of the cork sheet apart along the wall. You can then apply the adhesive; in this case with a notched spreader.

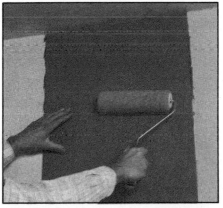

3 Trim the first length to size at the ends and then fix it in place; work down the wall and use a wide roller to help you smooth the cork in place.

4 Fix the next length by applying adhesive and then butting the cork up against the first length. Continue to fix cork lengths along the wall.

5 At a corner, measure the width at several places down the wall. Transfer these measurements to the cork and cut it to fit exactly.

6 Fix the corner length in place. It should have been cut to fit an out of square wall. The other adjacent (cut) corner length butts up to it.

Ready Reference

FINISHING RAW EDGES

If you will get a 'raw' edge down the side where you are fixing tiles to the face of a chimney breast only or where thick, soft types of tiles will meet at an exposed corner, protect the tile edges with a wooden lipping or moulding. For this you:
● attach the lipping (of the same thickness as the tiles) with pins or adhesive down each vertical angle before you start tiling
● tile up to the liping as if it were an internal angle
● stain the lipping the same colour as the tiles so it will be barely noticeable or coat it with clear varnish to make it more of a feature in the decorative scheme.

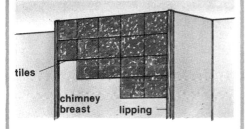

tiles

chimney breast   lipping

TIP: REMOVE EXCESS ADHESIVE

If you Inadvertently get adhesive on the front of the cork you may be able to remove it by rubbing with your finger when the adhesive is partly set. If it dries before you notice it, rub it gently with a cloth moistened with white spirit (turps). You may need to reseal or touch up the surface with wax polish when the cork is dry in order to hide the marks.

FIXING CORK SHEET

Cork in sheet form can be fixed in various ways. When you are fixing it, remember that
● with some types you use a special cork adhesive, applied to the wall
● with others you apply a heavy-duty wallpaper adhesive to the back of the cork or to the wall (check with the manufacturer's instructions)
● unlike wallpaper, which you trim after fixing, each length of cork should be cut exactly to fit before you hang it
● the joins between the lengths of cork shouldn't be rolled with a seam roller, as this will simply make the joins more obvious and spoil the overall look.

BARK-TEXTURED CORK

It's a pity to seal a really heavily textured bark cork, as part of its appeal lies in the matt, almost crumbly surface. Another point is that this type of cork should not be hung where it gets constantly knocked or touched, nor used as a noticeboard or pinboard or it will show signs of wear.

PUTTING UP FRIEZES & BORDERS

Patterned friezes and borders can help give a room a touch of style, and they can be used to hide cracks or make a tall room seem smaller – while adding very little to your decorating costs.

Friezes and borders, narrow strips of paper patterned to match the wallpaper in a room, are a traditional form of decoration. They were often either stuck below the picture rail or at the top of the wallpaper to hide the trimmed edges. Sometimes they were used below or above a dado rail, or to 'trim' an attic ceiling by hiding the join between sloping and flat areas.

Their popularity faded for some time but they are now making a comeback. Many of the co-ordinated ranges of wallcoverings, fabrics and beddings now available include border designs, and a definite 'bordered' look is commonly seen in upholstery and curtains. As well as being used with painted walls, borders can be teamed with a papered area, with either a simple texture or a co-ordinating design. There are also some heavily embossed friezes, which can be painted to contrast or tone with the scheme before they are hung, and a border or frieze effect can be created with painted bands of colour or with stencilled designs (see pages 164-167 for details).

Using friezes and borders

Of course, a border can still be used to bridge the gap between ceiling and wall or to hide any unevenness, or for that matter to cover decorating mistakes such as paint drips from the ceiling, the smudges and splodges of an inexperienced decorator, or to hide badly trimmed paper at the top or bottom of the wall. But they are intended to be an integral part of the decorative scheme and should not be thought of simply as a cover-up device. They can be used for various decorative purposes and it's worth taking some time to study the wide range available to see which would suit your requirements.

You can use a bright border to enhance a dull colour scheme, to introduce an 'accent' colour to a monochromatic scheme, or to tie several colours in a room together (the border could link carpet, curtain and wall colours, for example). Alternatively, you could use a quiet frieze to tone down a vivid scheme. Friezes and borders can be used to carry colour through from one room to another, creating a sense of continuity. For instance,

in a 'through' room with an arch or doorway between, one half might be decorated with patterned walls and the other half plain-painted but trimmed with the companion border design. In the hall you could have a dado rail with paint below, paper above and the rail emphasised with a border and the same pattern echoed at cornice or picture rail. You could then hang a companion design wallpaper with a co-ordinating pattern in an adjoining bedroom or sitting room.

You can use borders to play eye-deceiving tricks to improve the proportions of a room. In a hall which is too tall, you could use a deep border below the cornice or coving at ceiling level, and hang a matching or companion border at dado height or to emphasise the dado rail, then decorate below and above to contrast. In a sitting or dining room which looks too tall and where you wish to lower its apparent height, you could hang a very deep frieze (or two rows of a narrower one) just below the coving; or if there is none, leave a strip about twice the width of the border between the ceiling and the top edge, painted to match the ceiling. A very long room can be made to seem shorter if you use borders to form panels on the longest wall, or to outline the two shorter end walls. In an uninteresting box-like room, you can add interest by creating a focal point with a border design or, in a clinical bathroom, add a border design above the tiles to give warmth and character. Borders can also link with a fabric braid used to trim curtains or bedcovers and upholstery.

Trimming your own border

If you want a particularly bold border and have difficulty in finding just the right design, you can trim your own from wallpaper or a vinyl wallcovering which has a positive stripe in the pattern or a definite shape which will give an emphatic silhouette.

You may want to create a dado effect for a hall or breakfast area behind bench seating, to protect the lower part of the wall, or to give a splashback effect behind a dressing table, basin or kitchen worktop. Tile-type designs or definite geometric patterns are particularly suitable; you cut the top, following the pattern to form a castellated, scalloped, or serrated effect. In a bathroom or kitchen, and in children's rooms, you can even use offcuts of sheet vinyl flooring to form a border or splashback.

Suitable surfaces

Borders are applied right at the end of decorating; in fact, sometimes they may be added some time later. They need to be applied to a smooth, clean, dry wall area and if the walls are covered with heavily embossed paper which has been painted over it may not be possible to apply a border because it won't adhere securely to the surface. If a border is not well stuck it is likely to peel at the edges, which looks unsightly. If you want to apply a border to a textured wallcovering, it's well worth doing a trial run on a small area of wall first, to make sure it will stick, rather than risking wasting time and money on doing the whole room.

FIXING A PASTED FRIEZE

1 *Measure down the wall and mark off where the base line of the frieze will come; the top should be a few millimetres below the picture rail.*

2 *Lightly pin a batten to the wall to serve as a guide for marking off the base line. Check that it's truly horizontal with a spirit level.*

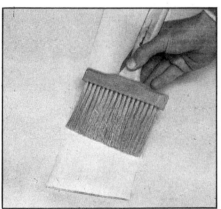

3 *After you've adjusted the base line where necessary you can go ahead and paste the back of the frieze, applying an even coat of adhesive.*

4 *Hold the pasted frieze up to the wall and then smooth it into place. If it's a long length you may need to fold it into concertina folds first.*

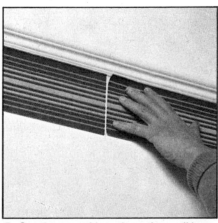

5 *Continue working along the wall in this way. Where you need to join lengths of frieze, butt the cut ends, taking care that the pattern matches.*

6 *Remove any excess adhesive and then, unless the frieze is an embossed type, run over it with a seam roller to make sure it is well stuck down.*

Ready Reference

BORDER SIZES

Friezes and borders come in a variety of widths from 18mm (¾in) up to about 450mm (18in), and also in different lengths (though many are available in 9m/29¼ft lengths). They are available from wallpaper stockists; some may have to be ordered from a pattern book where small samples are shown.

CHOOSING THE RIGHT DEPTH

When deciding on the depth of your border you'll get best results if you:
● choose a narrower width (and smaller design) border for small areas
● choose big, bold ones for larger rooms
● when in doubt, cut a template from paper and try the effect first before ordering; (if you are going to make a panel or outline, make a template the same size as the panel and fix it to the wall with sticky tape, to see how you like it.

FIXING METHODS

With many friezes and borders you can buy (or those you've trimmed yourself), you fix them by applying adhesive to the back and then applying them to wall. (Or you can paste the wall instead). Some types are ready-pasted and you use water to activate the paste before fixing them as with ready-pasted wallpaper.

TYPES OF ADHESIVE

The type of adhesive you should use depends on the material from which the border is made:
● for paper friezes, use ordinary wallpaper adhesive
● if the frieze is vinyl or you are sticking a frieze or border to a vinyl wallcovering, use a heavy-duty or ready-mix tub paste
● if you are using sheet vinyl flooring to form a border or splashback, use the recommended flooring adhesive.

TIP: THE SIZE OF BRUSH

To apply adhesive you'll need a brush of a suitable width; use a small one for a narrow border and a wide one for a deeper frieze. A clean paintbrush or an artist's brush is often most suitable.

TIP: MARK UP CAREFULLY

For a professional-looking result it's essential that the frieze or border is fixed (or appears to be fixed) in a straight, horizontal line. You will have to mark up a true horizontal and then adjust slightly where necessary so the picture rail, dado or cornice does not appear to be askew. Use chalk or pencil to make the guideline so rubbing it out is simple.

237

Tools and equipment

It's important that you don't end up with your frieze or border askew, so you'll need the appropriate items of equipment to ensure this: a plumbline, try-square, spirit-level and a length of batten to serve as a straightedge. You'll need a brush of suitable size (see *Ready Reference*) to apply the paste – unless you're using a ready-pasted decoration – and scissors for cutting the frieze or border to the correct length and for mitring the corners. Unless the decoration is an embossed type, you'll also require a seam roller to smooth down the top and flatten the seams for a neat result.

Hanging borders

The important thing to remember when you are hanging borders is that you need to establish a true horizontal line. However, if you are following a cornice, picture rail or dado rail you may find that the original is not actually horizontal. In that case, try to follow the line with the edge of the border just a few millimetres below or above the edge of the rail or cornice and rely on your eye, adjusting the width between the edge of the border and line you are following, so the border appears to be straight but the rail does not look too obviously at an angle.

To get a horizontal line to follow, use your plumb line, and try-square or spirit level and the batten to help you draw a straight line in chalk or soft pencil (see step-by-step photographs). If you have someone to help you, you won't need to pin the batten to the wall, since one person can position and check for accuracy while the second person draws the line.

If you are hanging a ready-pasted trimming you treat it in the same way as you would if you were hanging ready-pasted wallpaper. If it has to be cut to size, immersed in water until the paste is activated and then stuck in place; you smooth it out with a sponge or clean cloth.

Where you will be pasting the back of the trimming, you cut it to length and apply the paste, taking care not to get paste on the front of the paper. Hang it, following the line you've drawn on the wall, and smooth it out carefully with a sponge or clean brush (a conventional paperhanger's brush may be too wide).

A final tip: if you find paperhanging difficult and messy you could cheat and cut a border or frieze from self-adhesive material. Materials of this type are not very wide, but to get a sufficiently long length you could cut down the length instead of across the width. If you do use this type of material, you will need another person to help you; otherwise work in short lengths so you get it in exactly the right position first time, as the adhesive will stick firmly once it touches the wall surface.

FIXING BY PASTING THE WALL

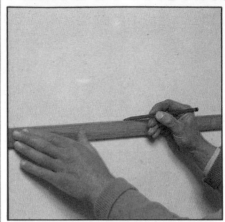

1 *Measure the width of the frieze, then draw two horizontal lines this width apart across the wall to mark where you want the frieze to be fixed.*

2 *Load a brush or roller with adhesive and then spread a fairly generous even coat on the wall between and up to the lines you have marked.*

3 *Holding the rolled-up frieze in one hand, apply the loose end at the end of the wall, gently pressing it onto the pasted surface.*

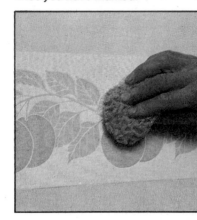

4 *Unroll the frieze and work your way across the wall, smoothing the frieze into place by pressing it all over with a clean, damp sponge.*

5 *When you reach the end of the wall you can cut off the frieze with a sharp knife or scissors to form a neatly finished edge. Press this in place.*

6 *Clean off excess adhesive from the face of the frieze and surrounding wall using a clean damp sponge. Then run a seam roller over the frieze.*

FORMING A PANEL

1 To use a border to make a panel on the wall, first draw in the outline in pencil, using your spirit level and plumbline to get the lines true.

2 Smooth a pasted length of border vertically on the wall so it overlaps the horizontal line by at least the depth of the border you are using.

3 Cut another length of border and smooth it into place, following the horizontal line so it overlaps the vertical length you've fixed.

4 Take a straightedge and place it diagonally between the inner and outer edges of the corner; then cut along it using a sharp knife.

5 Peel off the trimmed overlap on top, then lift back the horizontal length and peel off the trimmed overlap which is underneath it.

6 You will now have a neatly mitred corner which you can smooth back into place. Repeat the process to form the other edges and corners of the panel.

Ready Reference

READY-PASTED TRIMMINGS

Where you intend hanging a narrow trimming which is a ready-pasted type, it may be more practical to activate the adhesive by laying the trimming face down on the pasting table and brushing the back with tepid water (use a clean brush) rather than immersing the narrow strip in a bowl or trough of water.

PANELS AND OUTLINES

If you plan to hang a border paper to form a panel or to outline a wall area, you will have to mitre the corners. You will find some designs, with a definite directional pattern, may not be suitable for this type of treatment, so check before you buy.

MAKING YOUR OWN BORDER

To make your own border from wallpaper or a vinyl wallcovering, you cut the top out to shape and leave the bottom flush.

TIP: LONG FRIEZES

If the area where you are going to apply the frieze is a very long one it may be impossible to hang the frieze in one go without difficulty. In this case:
● if you decide to cut it, do so where the join will not be obvious, and follow either a line or shape in the design (cutting round the edge of a flower shape, for example)
● you can also use this technique if you have to join the material because you are starting another roll.

TIP: REMOVE SURPLUS ADHESIVE

Wipe off immediately any surplus paste which oozes out from the edge of the border. The same applies to any water/paste which may trickle down the wall when you are applying a ready-pasted trimming. Otherwise you risk ruining the trimming and the rest of the wall decoration.

USING A SEAM ROLLER

When you have applied the border you can run a seam roller over it to make sure that it adheres securely. But never use a seam roller if the border is of an embossed type or you will spoil the raised pattern.

PUTTING UP COVING

You can enhance the decorative effect of a room – and hide defects – by adding coving and a complementary centre to the ceiling. Installation is quite straightforward and it should be no trouble to find a variety which suits your room.

When you are planning your decoration scheme, don't forget the ceiling. Often this simply ends up being painted white and without ornament. Sometimes this may be the right solution but at others a more imaginative treatment can enhance the overall appearance of a room.

You can use colour on the ceiling to make a very tall room appear lower; or change the proportions of a box-like room to make the shape seem more interesting; or even increase the apparent size of a small room. Alternatively, you can add some form of ornament to the ceiling surface. In bathrooms and bedrooms where you will be aware of the ceiling much more often than in other rooms – when you are lying in the bath or in bed – it's particularly worth making the view more interesting.

Ornamental ceilings can be created either by using cornices – mouldings fixed in the angle between the wall and the ceiling – or more simple coving which links the two surfaces. (There is a clear distinction architecturally, but here both will be referred to as coving.) Ceiling centres – ornamental mouldings fixed in the middle of the ceiling – will provide an attractive focal point.

In practical terms, a nice, neat coving between wall and ceiling, apart from looking more elegant and 'finished', will hide the joints between ceiling and wall decorations or hide cracks, wires or pipes; sometimes it may be continued to form a pelmet for curtains or blinds, or to conceal strip lighting. Ceiling centres, used to complement coving, will also disguise a poorly plastered ceiling, hide joins, bumps and electrics and are a perfect foil to attractive light fittings like chandeliers.

Types of ceiling ornaments

It is still possible to find a craftsman who will 'sculpt' a decorative coving or ceiling centre for you but this is likely to be prohibitively expensive. It is cheaper to use some form of prepared, preformed coving or ceiling centre.

These come in various materials which break down into four categories: fibrous plaster, plasterboard or gypsum, plastic and wood. Fibrous plaster covings and ceiling centres are available in different styles, mostly traditional. Plasterboard or gypsum covings are streamlined and simple to install. Of the various plastic types there are covings and ceiling centres made from glass fibre and also ones made from cellular plastics such as polyurethane and expanded polystyrene: these are all light and easy to handle. There are also covings and ceiling centres made from a new plastic resin product that looks like genuine plasterwork and can be sawn, drilled and sanded like wood; and, unlike the other plastics, it is fire-resistant.

Wood covings – a final variant – are particularly effective in a room with walls completely or partly covered in wood cladding where they will provide a feature in keeping with the rest of the room.

Types of adhesives

Manufacturers usually recommend a suitable adhesive – always check with their instructions when buying the coving or ceiling centre. Adhesives come ready-mixed or, for fixing plasterboard or gypsum coving, in powder form – you mix the adhesive with water.

As a guideline, fibrous plaster ornaments should be stuck with a wall panel adhesive or a contact adhesive – it will be easier to manage if an application gun is used. Plasterboard or gypsum coving is fixed with plaster – you can use this to fill any gaps as well. Glass fibre is fixed with the same types of adhesive as fibrous plaster. For polyurethane you will need a ready-mixed paste adhesive which again can be used to fill gaps. Polystyrene should be stuck with a special expanded polystyrene adhesive of

PREPARING THE SURFACE

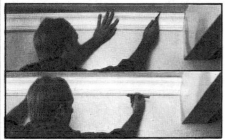

1 *Using a length of coving as a guide, mark guidelines on the ceiling and on the wall. Continue the lines so they go right round the room.*

2 *Score along the guidelines with a handyman's knife or other sharp instrument as a first step to removing the wallpaper from the ceiling and wall.*

3 *Scrape off wallpaper and flaky paint in the area between the guidelines. Soak paper if necessary, taking care to protect wallpaper lower down the wall.*

4 *Provide a key so the adhesive grips properly by slightly roughening the surface, gently scoring the area where the coving will be fixed.*

the type used to fix ceiling tiles. Plastic resin ornaments are fixed in a similar way to wood. Choose a wood adhesive such as PVA, synthetic resin adhesive, a multi-purpose type, or even a wall panel adhesive in an easy-to-apply gun. For wooden covings you will need a wood adhesive – this is often used in conjunction with nails or screws.

Any adhesive is only really effective if it is applied to a clean, dust-free surface. New plaster should be allowed to dry out before

multi-purpose, wood, or expanded poly-styrene adhesives are used, although the plaster/gypsum filler type can be used on damp plaster.

Always follow the manufacturer's instructions carefully when using any type of adhesive. If you are using an adhesive which is likely to 'go off', or harden quickly, work on manageable lengths of coving at a time. With powder adhesives, don't guess how much water to add, follow the instructions.

CUTTING A MITRE

1 *When using a mitre box, place the coving so the 'ceiling' edge is at the bottom of the box and use the slots in the box to provide a saw guide.*

2 *Where a paper template is provided, mark the cutting line using the template as a guide and then carefully saw along the marked line.*

Ready Reference

CUTTING MITRES

● Check coving orientation in box before cutting – the 'ceiling' edge should be on the base of the box.
● Lengths with one internal and one external mitre (A) have parallel cuts done in the same box groove; lengths with two external mitres (B) or two internal mitres (C) are cut using both box grooves (one for each end).

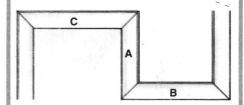

MAKING A MITRE BOX

● Make the box from timber about 450mm (18in) long and 19mm (¾in) to 25m (1in) thick, with internal dimensions chosen so the coving is held exactly at 90° within the box.
● Mark out the 45° angles using a combination square or basic geometry.

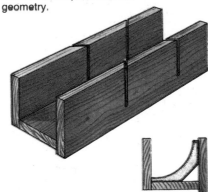

FIRE HAZARDS

Never paint foamed plastic coving or ceiling centres with gloss or other solvent-based paints as you will create a fire hazard – the painted plastic could rapidly spread flames in a fire.

EASY ELECTRICS

So you don't have to remove – and risk damaging – a ceiling centre to get at wiring, remove the existing ceiling rose and rewire to a junction box installed in the ceiling void – access can then be gained from above.

Planning

As with all decorating operations, time and care spent on planning will pay off later, helping you make sure of a successful result. To judge the optimum coving depth before buying, cut a paper template to a likely depth and a length of 1.5 to 1.8m (5 to 6ft) and pin it in the angle between the wall and ceiling where the coving will go. This should be long enough for you to gain an idea of the finished effect. If it seems wrong, (ie, too shallow or too deep), repeat the operation with a template of a different depth until you have the right size.

Having decided on the depth of the coving, the next step is to measure up the ceiling accurately. If it is going to be a difficult shape to deal with – for example, if there is a chimney breast or corners which are out of square – make a scale plan of the ceiling on squared paper. This way you will be able to work out exactly where the joins will come in the lengths of coving and where you will need to cut or mitre the coving for the corners. Use your plan or measurements as a guide for ordering the correct amount of coving.

A ceiling centre is going to be a focal point of interest, and it is essential therefore to choose one which is the right size for the room. They range in size from 150mm (6in) to 685mm (2ft 3in) in diameter; smaller ones suit smaller rooms and larger ones large rooms. To help you decide on the size of the ceiling centre, you can again make a paper template to gain an impression of the finished effect.

Marking up and preparation

You will need to mark guidelines for fixing the coving. You can use a piece of coving to indicate where lines should be drawn at the correct level on wall and ceiling.

The surface must be properly prepared. You will need to make sure all old wallpaper, flaking paint or distemper is removed from between the guidelines. It is also advisable to fill any cracks. Leave the filler to harden and then, if necessary, sand smooth. Bumpily filled cracks could throw the coving out of alignment, making it look distorted. With some types of adhesive you will also have to provide a key, so the adhesive grips properly, by slightly roughening the surface of the wall and ceiling where the coving will be fixed.

For a ceiling centre you can cut a paper or cardboard template round which to draw a guideline before preparing the surface in the same way as preparing for fixing coving. Make the template slightly smaller – by about 6mm (¼in) – than the actual ceiling centre so areas where paper or paint have been removed will not show when the ceiling centre is in place.

Cutting coving

Measure the coving for length. Remember that corners will have to be mitred and that there is a different technique for internal and external angles (see *Ready Reference*). Some preformed coving comes with a special template provided in the pack to make cutting and mitring easier – you place the template on the coving and trace the required mitre shape with a pencil. If you are using coving which does not have such a template provided, you will need to make up a mitre box which you can use to hold the coving while you cut it at the correct angle (see *Ready Reference*). For cutting you will need a fine tooth saw and you should cut from the face of the coving to ensure you get a clean edge.

Fixing coving

A plaster/gypsum adhesive will have to be mixed according to the manufacturer's instructions. If the job is likely to take a while, mix up only part of the adhesive at a time so you don't waste any if it dries out too soon. With some types of adhesive you will need to dampen the surface to be coved with water. If the surface is very porous you will have to seal it with a coat of diluted emulsion or PVA adhesive first.

You can then spread out the adhesive onto the back edges of the coving. Push each length firmly into position and hold it in place until it sticks. If you are using a contact adhesive, spread it on the back of the coving. Press the coving in position, then pull it away immediately and leave for about 10-20 minutes – the honeycomb structure of the adhesive will be on coving, wall and ceiling surfaces. Then fix the coving back in position and adjust its positioning at once as the adhesive will harden quickly and will be firmly bonded within an hour.

Heavier covings may have to be nailed or screwed, as well as stuck, into position. You should use galvanized nails or rustproof screws spaced 500mm (20in) apart, and, so they won't be visible on the finished surface, punch the nails below the surface with a nail punch, or countersink screws and fill the holes you have created with surplus adhesive or with cellulose filler.

Scrape off surplus adhesive which squeezes out from under the coving. (Sometimes this can be used to fill nail holes and gaps. Otherwise, you will have to use a cellulose filler).

Fixing ceiling centres

Ceiling centres are fixed in the same way as coving. Heavier types may need extra support from nails or screws: make sure the heads are countersunk or punched home and fill the gaps with adhesive or other filler.

If the ceiling surface is bad and you want

FIXING COVING

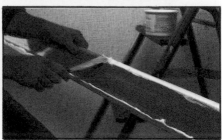

1 *Butter the adhesive on the back edges of the coving with a filling knife – try to avoid getting adhesive on the front of the coving.*

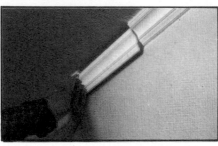

5 *Where coving is to fill a gap between lengths already fixed, hold a piece up so it rests against one fixed length and mark a cutting line on the other end.*

to use a textured paper to help disguise this, it is easier to paper the ceiling first and then cut out the area to be covered with the ornament rather than fixing the ceiling centre and then papering round it.

Where a ceiling centre is to be used to enhance a central light fitting, you will also have to cope with the electrics. As a first step, you will have to remove the existing bulb and lampholder. Where the ceiling centre has a hollow in the middle, it may be possible to leave the existing ceiling rose in place and fit the new ceiling centre over it. Simply pull down the flex through the hole in the middle of the new centrepiece (some already have holes bored; with others you may have to make the hole).

With other types of ceiling centres, which are flatter in the middle, you may have to remove the existing rose and replace it with a terminal connector strip which will fit in the space available before fixing the new ornament into position to conceal it. Both these solutions have the disadvantage that if at a later date you wish to gain access to the wiring, you will have to remove the ceiling centre. As an alternative, you can rewire the light so access can be gained from above (see *Ready Reference*).

If you have a very heavy chandelier, it may be necessary to have a hook to support it –

2 *Offer up the coving to the fixing area and, when you are sure it is in the right position, press it firmly into place. The adhesive will squeeze out of the edges:*

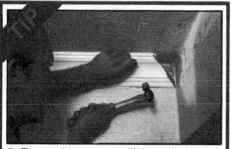

3 *To provide support till the adhesive sets, drive nails into the edges of the coving. These can be punched home or removed and the holes filled later.*

4 *At a corner, place coving so mitred edges meet and fix it in position. You can then use a filling knife to smooth adhesive down for a neat joint.*

6 *After you have cut the filler piece and applied adhesive, offer it up and install it so it butts against the lengths of coving already fixed*

7 *Remove excess adhesive by running a filling knife along the edges of the coving. This can be used to fill in any gaps, joins or nail holes.*

8 *For final cleaning up, use a sponge which has been soaked in clean water to remove any adhesive from the coving face, the wall and ceiling.*

coming through the hole in the middle of the decorative centre – and this will have to be fixed to a beam or joist to take the weight. This may also determine the position of the fitting, since there may not be a conveniently placed central support.

Decoration

If you intend painting the ceiling, emulsion paint, which can be applied without silting up any of the more decorative mouldings, is particularly suitable. A matt or eggshell lustre-finish oil-based paint can also be used, but this is not very suitable for delicate mouldings. Lastly, you can use multi-purpose paint (ie one which can be used on walls, ceilings and woodwork). Gloss and other solvent-based paints should never be used on plastic.

Colour is a matter of personal choice but usually the 'bed' – the flat part of the ceiling – looks best in a colour which can be dark, rich or strong if the room is fairly tall and paler if it is low. The relief decorations can be picked out in white or any other contrasting neutral shade, or in a pale, toning or contrasting colour. Give the ceiling decorations their first coat, then paint the ceiling itself with two coats, taking particular care at the edges and where it meets the ornaments. Apply a final coat to the decorations.

FIXING A CEILING CENTRE

1 *Draw round a paper template which is slightly smaller than the ceiling centre. You can then prepare the surface within the marked area.*

2 *Spread adhesive on the outer rim at the back of the ceiling centre, feed the flex down through the hole in the middle and fix the centre in place.*

3 *Run a filling knife round the edge of the ceiling centre to remove excess adhesive between the centre and ceiling.*

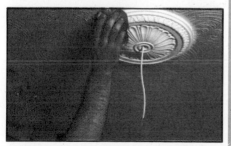

4 *Use a damp sponge to wipe off traces of adhesive left on the surface of the centre and ceiling.*

UNUSUAL EFFECTS WITH PAINT

Walls and ceilings can be painted in a variety of attractive ways using techniques like stippling and rag-rolling. The finished effect is unique, and you need only a few simple tools to achieve it. If you prefer a bolder effect, stencils and murals offer a striking alternative.

CREATING COLOURED WALL FINISHES

If you fancy a change from the usual expanse of emulsion painted walls, you could try one of these broken colour finishes. They're quick and easy to do.

Painted walls will always be popular because they're quick and easy to decorate and paint manufacturers offer hundreds of colours to choose from. Walls, however, are usually the largest surface in a room and if you're not careful they can look very bare and uninteresting. Professional decorators have always known this and they use many different methods, some of them centuries old, to give a painted surface more texture. These methods – including stippling, sponging, rag-rolling and dragging – all involve 'breaking up' or 'distressing' the paint in some way so that two or more colours mingle together to give a wonderful depth to the wall.

For all these finishes a base coat is first painted on the wall in the usual way; then other coats are applied using one of the special techniques. The effects can be varied depending on the colours chosen for the two coats. You can use two slightly different shades of the same colour for a subtle, gentle effect, or use dark or contrasting colours – deep reds on white for instance – for a bold, rich finish. You can also afford to experiment with bolder colours than you would normally dare to choose because the 'distressing' techniques will always tone down the colour depth.

Preparation
With all these techniques you will get the best effect if you prepare the surface well before you start.

Old wallpaper must be stripped off and any remaining paste should be washed off thoroughly. Painted surfaces will just need a good wash down with a cleaning solution. Start at the bottom of a wall and work your way upwards; then, with clean water and a soft cloth, go over the wall again, this time starting at the top. Walls painted in gloss must be rubbed down with medium-grade glasspaper to provide a good key for the base coat.

Cracks should be filled with an interior-grade filler. Undercut the edges of the crack a little and damp the area slightly. Leave the filler a little proud of the surface, and then sand it down level when it's dry.

Walls that are just plain shabby would benefit from being lined with a good-quality lining paper. Hang the lengths vertically, not horizontally as you would if you were going to hang wallpaper on top, and butt-join the edges for a near-invisible seam. That said, though, a few of these techniques, such as sponging and ragging-on, will actually disguise slightly shabby plasterwork as they will distract your eye from any unevenness. But, ideally, you should always aim to provide a perfectly flat, even wall surface – and for dragging, this is essential.

What you do next depends on the paint finish you intend to use. If the finish needs a base coat of an oil-based eggshell, then first apply an oil-based primer/sealer or undercoat. An emulsion base needs no primer or undercoat, but you may need two coats for good coverage, especially on new plaster.

Tinting paint
The most economical way of buying paint is to buy a large tin of the correct type – matt, silk, undercoat or eggshell – and then to mix your own shades by adding small amounts of universal stainers or even artists' paints (see *Ready Reference*). This way you can get exactly the shade you want – to match curtains or carpets for instance. But, if you don't feel up to this, several of the paint manufacturers offer a large range of colours that they'll mix up for you. This will save you the uncertainty of mixing your own but they are rather more expensive

Use the right paint
Traditionally, professional decorators have always used a special paint called a transparent oil glaze or 'scumble' glaze for these special finishes. The glaze is colourless or white and has to be tinted to the right colour and thinned at the rate of two parts glaze to one, two or even three parts of solvent. A glaze has the advantage of being very slow drying, so the distressing techniques can be carried out without panic. Oil paints tend to dry out more quickly.

However, many professional decorators are now using a paint 'glaze' which is simply thinned oil paint. The best type of oil paint to use is trade flat white which gives a nice matt finish. But this is rather difficult to find and you can work quite well with ordinary comm-

SPONGE STIPPLING

1 *Pour a little paint into a shallow dish or onto a board and spread it around with the back of a spoon or a palette knife to give a thin even layer.*

2 *It's essential to use a real marine sponge for this technique. Dip it into water until it expands to its full size and then squeeze it out well.*

3 *Grip the sponge firmly and dab it lightly into the paint. A quick dab is all you need as you don't want it to soak up a lot of paint.*

4 *Keep a sheet of scrap paper handy – lining paper is ideal – and test the print, dabbing until you get the right density of paint.*

5 *Now work lightly over the whole wall, refilling the sponge as necessary. Aim for an even coverage and a regular speckled effect.*

6 *Leave the wall to dry and then repeat the process with the second colour. The base will always dominate, but will be changed by the sponged colours.*

ercial eggshell paint. If you do want a matt finish with an oil-based paint you can always use an oil-based undercoat. Buy one as near to the right colour as possible and then tint it to the right shade. Don't use gloss, as this would be far too shiny for walls.

Of course, you don't have to use oil-based paints for all these techniques. Many of them work equally well with emulsion paint – whether silk or matt – and, in fact, this would be the first choice for techniques such as sponge stippling, ragging-on, colour washing and, possibly, bag-graining.

The techniques

Most of the paint finishes described here can be divided into two basic categories. The first covers all the techniques where a top coat of paint is dabbed or sponged onto a base coat that has dried. This includes sponge stippling and ragging-on. Both these methods work well with a base and top coat of ordinary matt emulsion. But you can use an eggshell base and a thinned eggshell or glaze for the top coat if you wish.

The second method includes bag-graining, rag-rolling, dragging and stippling. With all these techniques the top coat is painted on and then treated in some way while it is still wet to break up the colour. These methods generally work best with oil-based paints – eggshell for the base and thinned eggshell or glaze for the top coat. You *can* use a thinned emulsion paint for the top coat but you would have less time to work on it before it dried.

The technique for this last category is to paint a narrow strip of wall – 600mm (2ft) wide is best – then go over it with the rag, bag or whatever and paint the next strip of wall before the first has dried. It is essential to keep a wet edge to the paint or you'll end up with a patchy result. If you can get someone else to paint on the top coat while you follow closely behind with your chosen technique, so much the better. The work will go much more smoothly this way.

Finally, for a long-lasting finish, coat the walls with a clear, matt, polyurethane varnish.

Sponge stippling

This gives a very pretty informal finish, and is quick and easy to do. Emulsion paint is picked up on a sponge and dabbed onto the wall in an irregular pattern. It's left to dry and the wall is gone over again with another colour. Sponge stippling works best with a soft pastel shade for the base coat and slightly darker shades of the same colour family for the top coats. You can also use contrasting colours, but in this case it's best to keep them all fairly pale. You can vary the effect by sponging on dark colours for a stronger speckled effect, or use lighter or diluted paint for a soft, marbled look.

RAGGING ON

1 *Spread a thin layer of paint round a shallow dish, bunch up the rag and dip it lightly in the paint. Test the print on some scrap paper.*

2 *Dab the rag on the wall with a light touch, refilling the rag as necessary. Keep refolding the rag, leaving even spaces between each print.*

RAG-ROLLING

1 *Use an oil-based eggshell paint or scumble glaze for the top coat; dilute it with equal parts of white spirit (turps) and mix well.*

2 *Soak a fine cotton rag in white spirit (turps) first, then squeeze it out well. This will prevent it clogging with paint too quickly.*

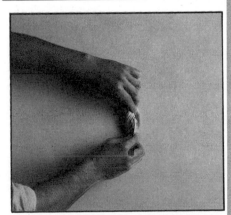

3 *Brush on the paint next, but don't cover too large an area or the paint will dry before you get to it. A strip 600mm (24in) wide is about right*

4 *Bunch up the rag into a sausage shape and roll it over the wet paint glaze. Keep changing direction but take care not to skid over the surface.*

Ready Reference

QUANTITIES OF PAINT

Most techniques use thinned paint so you'll need less paint than usual.
● sponge stippling: one litre of each colour is sufficient for an average room
● ragging-on: one third the quantity required for one coat of base colour
● bag-graining: half the quantity needed for one coat of base colour
● rag-rolling: half quantity needed for one coat of base colour
● dragging: half quantity needed for one coat of base colour
● colour washing: one litre is sufficient for an average room.
For more information on how much paint you need for walls see pages 12-15.

TIP: MIX ENOUGH PAINT

If the technique you're using needs diluted paint, try and mix up enough for the whole room. If you do seem to be running out of paint, finish the wall you're on and mix up another batch adding any paint you've got left. That way, any slight change of colour from one wall to the next won't be noticeable.

MAKE A TEST FIRST

Before starting on the wall it's advisable to practise the technique first. Do this on an out-of-the-way patch of wall or, better still, prop up a board and pin a length of prepainted lining paper to it.

For **sponge stippling** test:
● spacing of the prints
● pressure on the sponge
● thick and diluted paint

For **ragging-on** test:
● different types of material
● different folds and spacing of prints
● thick and diluted paint

For **bag-graining** test:
● thickness of the top coat – if you apply too much paint it will run so brush it out more. It will also run if you've diluted it too much so add more paint and try again

For **rag-rolling** test:
● different folds and method of rolling
● thickness of the paint (see bag-graining)

For **dragging** test:
● different brushes
● thickness of the paint (see bag-graining)

For **colour washing** test:
● brushing technique
● different dilutions of the colour wash.

BAG-GRAINING

1 *You'll need an ordinary polythene bag and some rags. Half-fill the bag with the rags, push them well in and tie or secure the neck of the bag.*

2 *If you're using emulsion paint for the graining coat, dilute it with an equal amount of water. Eggshell paint should be diluted with white spirit (turps).*

3 *Using a wide brush, paint a section of wall about 600mm (24in) wide. Apply a thin coat of paint which covers the ground colour evenly.*

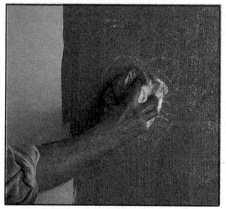

4 *Press the bag lightly over the wet paint and overlap the prints slightly for an even, crinkled finish. Continue painting and graining the wall, a section at a time.*

It is essential to use a real marine sponge for this technique. A man-made one just won't work as the pattern it produces will be too hard-edged and regular.

Ragging-on
This is very similar to sponge stippling, except that a small piece of bunched up rag is used to apply the paint. You can experiment with different materials to get the effect you want – try net, muslin, cotton sheet and sacking. The finished effect also depends on the size and fold of the rag. If you want a regular, repeating pattern, keep the same rag with the same folds for the whole wall. This however, is difficult to do and it's best to keep refolding or changing the rag and aim for an irregular pattern. The most convenient size for the rag is about 300mm (12in) square, but again, experiment to find the size that suits you best.

Like sponging, ragging-on works well with a slightly darker colour ragged over a lighter one, but it looks equally good with the colours reversed. For a softer print you can dilute the top coat with up to 50 per cent of the solvent.

Rag-rolling
In contrast to ragging-on, this method uses a bunched up rag which is rolled over still wet, diluted eggshell paint or glaze.

Soft, fine cotton rags cut into 300mm (12in) squares are best, and you'll need a good supply of these as they soon get soaked with paint. It's best to keep refolding the rag from time to time and altering the directions of the rolling movements, since otherwise the pattern may become annoying and insistent. You should aim for an even and uniform coverage. The pattern produced is similar to soft crumpled silk and is well suited to formal rooms such as some dining rooms.

Bag-graining
Here the texture is produced by going over the wet paint with a graining bag – that is, a polythene bag filled with rags. It gives a much finer texture than rag-rolling, looking rather like crushed velvet. It's easy to do; you just press the bag over the wall and, from time to time, wipe off the excess paint that builds up on the bag. It works best on a white background – either eggshell or silk. Any colour can be used for the top coat, with the darker colours giving a bold effect.

Dragging
Dragging is one of the more difficult techniques to master, since the object is to drag a dry brush over the wet paint to produce regular vertical lines down the wall. Here's where proper glaze works best; if you use oil paint the stripes will tend to merge together a little – though you may prefer this. The trick is to drag the brush in a relaxed way with the bristles only lightly touching the surface. If you're tense, your arm is sure to shake and the stripes will wobble. You can buy special dragging brushes which have extra-long bristles but these are difficult to find and very expensive. As an alternative, a wide paper-hanging brush will do quite well.

Stippling
Stippling is easy to do and produces a beautiful finely textured finish. All you do is paint on diluted eggshell or glaze over an eggshell base and then go over the wet paint with a special stippling brush. You must hit the wall square on to stop the brush skidding over the surface.

Stippling is often used to obliterate any brush marks on the top coat before doing other techniques like dragging and rag-rolling.

Real stippling brushes are rectangular, about 100 x 75mm (4 x 3in) and are made of fine bristle. Their only drawback is that they are difficult to find and very expensive. But you can experiment with an old clothes brush or a soft-bristled hairbrush.

Colour washing
This is a splashy technique best suited to country rooms, kitchens and playrooms. The top coat – of emulsion – is thinned much more than usual – as much as 8 parts water to 1 part of paint. This is then slapped onto the wall in haphazard strokes using a wide brush, leaving lots of the base colour showing through. When this is dry the process is repeated using the same colour, but this time brushing over the bare patches to give a dappled variation of colour. It's a messy business and you'll need plenty of protection for the floor as the paint is liable to run off at first. Don't worry though; enough paint will stick on eventually and the second coat of paint will cover up any unevenness.

DRAGGING

1 *Here, a scumble glaze is being used. Thin the glaze with an equal amount of white spirit (turps) and then pour it into a paint kettle.*

2 *To tint the glaze, take a small amount of artists' oil paint (or universal stainer) and mix it with some glaze. Then add this to the glaze and mix well.*

3 *Paint on the glaze in a smooth, even layer. Finish off with vertical strokes of the brush to prevent a criss-cross finish when you start dragging.*

4 *Use a dragging brush or, as here, a paperhanging brush and drag it smoothly down the wall. Overlap each strip for a regular striped effect.*

STIPPLING

1 *A proper stippling brush is very expensive so it's worth experimenting – with an old clothes brush, for example. It must have a level surface like this.*

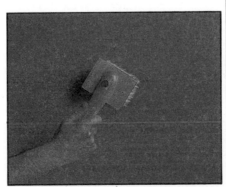

2 *Simply hit the wall square on with the brush – hard at first to even out the paint and then more softly for a fine stippled finish.*

Ready Reference

TIP: STOP AT A CORNER

If for any reason you can't do the whole room in one session, stop at a corner and do the next wall when the first is dry.

COVERING UP MISTAKES

Apart from dragging, all the other techniques produce a broken finish and any slight irregularities in the pattern or thickness of paint won't be too noticeable. But mistakes can happen so here's what to do:
● if you sponge or rag on a thick blob of paint, let it dry; then go over it again, this time with the sponge or rag dipped in the *base* colour
● if you're rag-rolling or bag-graining and the paint is too thick, simply go over it again with a clean rag or bag
● keep a clean cloth handy soaked in water or white spirit (turps) as appropriate to wipe off any paint from skirtings or ceiling
● if you're rag-rolling and the paint starts to dry out before you get to it, go over the paint surface with a new rag soaked in white spirit (turps).

MIX YOUR OWN COLOURS

If you're using a scumble glaze you'll have to mix your own colours, but you can do so with paint as well. Universal stainers are available for oil and emulsion paints. You can also use artists' oil colours for oil-based paints, and artists' gouache, acrylic or poster paints for emulsion paints.

For oil paints take a small amount of colour in a dish or on a palette and add paint gradually, mixing until the colour is dispersed. You can then add this mixture to the main body of the paint. Repeat with more colour until you get the right shade. For emulsion paints, dissolve the colour in water first.

USING SCUMBLE GLAZE

Transparent oil glaze or 'scumble' glaze has the advantage of being very slow drying and will stay put rather than run out into a smooth layer. It is therefore ideal for many of these techniques as you'll have more time to work on the finish – up to two hours – before it starts to go off. The glaze will need thinning and colouring before use. It is available from specialists decorating suppliers.

TAKE CARE WITH SOLVENTS

When you've finished rag-rolling you'll be left with a pile of rags soaked in paint and solvent. Let these dry out before throwing them away. They are highly inflammable and could even catch fire spontaneously if left bunched up in a confined space.

STENCILLING WALLS AND FURNITURE

If you want to give walls, furniture or even floors a unique decorative finish, stencilling offers plenty of opportunities. This method of applying a painted pattern is easily mastered.

The art of stencilling can be learned quickly and is an effective way of giving a personal touch to all manner of fixtures and fittings in the home. Anything from a simple frieze design around a wall to an intricate pattern on a piece of furniture can be achieved with stencils, and they are an inexpensive way of brightening up what would otherwise be plain surfaces.

Stencilled designs should be simple, but two or more basic patterns can be combined to create a more intricate effect. Some traditional stencil designs incorporate many different shapes and colours, but usually two or three of each, on a natural or plain coloured background, make the most satisfactory combination.

Make or buy?

Ready-made stencils are available from craft, art or graphic design shops and other specialist suppliers; some are pre-cut in acetate and others are made from the traditional material, oiled card. Acetate is the most expensive, but the surface is easily wiped clean, and such stencils may be used again and again. Oiled card is also easy to clean and does not absorb paint, preventing smudges unless you move the stencil carelessly. However, it eventually deteriorates. These ready-cut designs come in a wide range of sizes, shapes and motifs.

There is nothing to stop you cutting your own stencils, as both acetate and oiled card should be available from the same source as the pre-cut stencils. It is possible to buy books of patterns which may be traced on to the stencil material; some patterns are printed on stiff paper and could be used for stencilling themselves, if only a short life is required. If you have some artistic skills you might even draw up your own design, or adapt a wallpaper, fabric or tile pattern.

Deciding size and colour

You may have to adjust the size of the pattern, particularly if you intend using the same design on several different surfaces for a co-ordinated effect. A delicate floral pattern might look delightful on a small chest of drawers, but would be quite lost on a large area of wall. It is not too difficult to scale any design up or down, using squared paper (see *Ready Reference*).

Once you have worked out the size and shape of the basic stencil design, and the area you plan to cover, think about the colours you want. Colours that contrast with the background are best, dark colours over pale backgrounds looking good if simple bold motifs are chosen. Lighter colours over dark backgrounds are better suited to more delicate designs.

If you plan to use two or more colours to make up a single pattern, test the effect first to see how they look together. The best way to judge the finished job is to cut out a few of the motifs from thick paper, colouring them with the paints you intend using. Hold these coloured shapes against the surface you want to stencil and move them around until you achieve a satisfactory balance. Then, stick them in place with adhesive tape until you are ready to mark out the guide lines for the stencil itself.

As an alternative, you could paint a length of lining paper with the intended background and stencil the design on to it in the chosen colours. Pin or tape this into position and leave it there for a few days to make sure you are completely happy with the result. Different types of light can change the appearance of colours quite dramatically, so look at your patterns carefully under both natural daylight and the artificial lighting you will use in the room to be decorated.

Materials and tools you will need

Apart from the actual stencils you are using, or the sheets for cutting your own, you will need a selection of basic materials and hand tools.

The type of paint you choose will depend on the surface you are treating. Ideally, it should be quick-drying. Apply a gloss or coloured wood stain to floors and furniture, and emulsion paint to walls. The latter is particularly good because it is easily removed if you make a mistake. You will need a solvent suitable for whatever type of paint you use, and some masking tape.

A black felt-tip pen is adequate for marking out the pattern on the stencil material, unless you are using acetate, in which case a special drawing pen will be needed. The latter will mark the acetate permanently, whereas other types of ink will simply rub off.

For cutting stencils, use a sharp craft knife, or possibly an artist's scalpel if the pattern is intricate. A piece of chipboard, blockboard, or even a sheet of thick glass with its edges taped, will serve as a cutting board.

Stencil brushes are specially made for the purpose and have short, stiff bristles which give a characteristic stippled look to the finished pattern. They come in various sizes and you should select them to match the size of the job. If you prefer, you can use paint pads, which are particularly useful when covering large areas. Even normal paint brushes will suffice, providing care is taken not to force paint under the stencil around the edges of the cut-outs.

MAKING A STENCIL

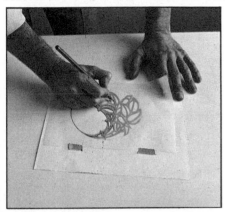

1 *You can draw out your own designs or copy something else, such as a tile. Tape a piece of tracing paper over the design and trace it out with a pencil.*

2 *The traced design is transferred to the stencil card by placing a sheet of carbon paper over the card and then drawing over the traced outline again.*

3 *Place the stencil card onto a suitable cutting board and carefully cut out the various shapes. Using a scalpel with a round handle will aid accurate cutting.*

4 *After cutting the stencil, compare it with the original design, and check that you have made all the cut-outs. Trim any rough edges so that you get a fluid line.*

One or two sponges will be useful for wiping off any smudges but these, too, can be used for applying paint if the design lends itself to this treatment.

You should never apply paint direct from the can as you may overload the brush, so equip yourself with some old saucers or a palette made from a piece of board.

Careful marking out of the surface to be painted is essential if the pattern is to look right. Therefore, you will also need a plumb-line, some chalk, a T-square or set square, a spirit level and a straightedge.

Cutting your own stencils

To cut your own stencils, first transfer the design on to the acetate or oiled card. If using the former, simply lay it over the chosen design and trace over this with the drawing pen. In the latter case, you can use carbon paper to transfer the design. Place the carbon over the card and then put the design on top, making sure that all three layers are aligned. Trace over the outline of the design with a pointed instrument like a ballpoint pen or a knitting needle. Mark out a separate stencil for each colour you intend using.

Hold the acetate or card firmly on the cutting board with drawing pins or masking tape, and carefully cut out the shape. Make the cut line as fluid as possible, and if you do find a slightly ragged edge, smooth it gently with flour-grade glasspaper after removing the stencil from the board.

Keep the original design, storing it flat, so that you can make further tracings if necessary. In fact, if you plan to stencil a large area where the same shape will be repeated frequently, it is a wise move to cut more than one stencil in the first place. Lay them on top of each other to make sure the design is exactly the same on each. Also do this if

Ready Reference

SCALING PATTERNS

If you intend using the same pattern on a number of different surfaces, you may want to increase or reduce its size to suit its position. To do this:
● draw or trace the original design on to squared graph paper
● then, if you want to increase the size, draw up another grid on a clean sheet of paper, making the squares larger. If, for example, you wanted to double the size you would make the squares twice as large, and so on
● copy the design on to the second grid, square for square, and you will achieve the necessary enlargement automatically
● to reduce the size of the pattern, draw it on a grid of smaller squares.

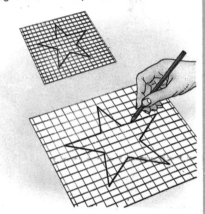

TIP: TRY OUT THE DESIGN

Before you start stencilling, make a series of 'proofs' from tissue paper. Trace through the stencilled motif, using coloured crayons or pencils to fill in the shapes with solid colour. Fix these roughs to the area to be stencilled and move them around until you achieve the effect you want. Tissue paper is particularly useful if you have to superimpose several designs or colours on top of each other. It will allow the background colour to show through, as well so you can more accurately judge the effect than you could if using an opaque material.

BRUSHES FOR STENCILLING

Stencil brushes are unlike normal paint brushes in that they have short, stiff bristles. Various sizes are available.

MARKING OUT

1 Mark the wall carefully to provide a guide for placing the stencil. Use a chalked line to mark a horizontal guide, checking with a spirit level if necessary.

2 Vertical guide lines can be made with the aid of a set square placed with its base edge against the horizontal line. Use white chalk as this won't stain the paint.

3 Finally, offer up the stencil to ensure that you have achieved the right spacing of the marks. Pencil guide lines and notches in the stencil will help you to align the pattern.

STENCILLING A FRIEZE

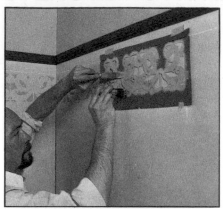

1 When more than one colour is used, apply one at a time. Use the brush with a stippling action, building up several layers of paint.

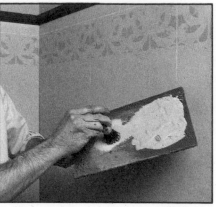

2 Use a palette, pouring a small amount of paint on to it at a time. Dip the brush in and tap it out on the palette until almost dry. Excess paint causes runs.

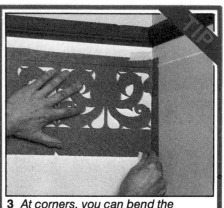

TIP

3 At corners, you can bend the stencil so the design is continuous. Score the stencil lightly with a knife and bend it round a straight edge.

4 Apply the second colour when the first has dried, taking extra care to align the stencil so that the colours register. Hold the stencil flat with a bladed tool.

several different stencils form part of the same pattern. When all are aligned correctly, punch holes or cut notches through them so that perfect alignment is possible each time they are used.

Preparing the surface
As with all forms of decorating, the secret of a successful stencilling job lies in sound preparation of the surface. Make sure it is clean, dry and dust-free. Repair damaged plasterwork, sanding, painting or sealing walls and woodwork. If treating a floor, sand it smooth and punch any nail heads below the surface. New furniture will need sealing with clear polyurethane varnish if it is un-painted, and old furniture may need stripping before resealing or painting.

A stencilled pattern can even be applied to a textured surface, so uneven walls can be lined with a textured paper first. However,

if the surface undulates too much, the pattern will make this more obvious.

To ensure correct placing of the stencil each time, mark out the surface with horizontal base line marks and vertical divisions to match the stencil edges. Use the plumbline, chalk, square and spirit level as necessary to achieve this.

Applying the pattern
Place the first stencil in position, fixing it with masking tape; other types of self-adhesive tape may damage the painted surface. Pour some paint on to your palette and dip the tip of the brush into it. Don't overload the brush with paint; check for this by trying it on a piece of scrap paper or board first. Then dab the colour firmly on to the background through the cut-out in the stencil. Take care not to dislodge the edges of the cut-out or you will smudge the pattern. Work from the

STENCILLING FURNITURE

The techniques you use for stencilling a design on a piece of furniture are much the same as you would use for stencilling a wall. You must, for example, make sure you have the stencil correctly positioned (one thing to watch out for on furniture is mouldings; it's best to arrange things so you won't be trying to paint a stencil over them). Also, you should take care not to smudge the edges of the pattern, so don't overload the brush or use a paint which is too watery. Proper preparation is a must: with old furniture you might have to strip off the existing finish and reseal with new paint or varnish; new furniture may also require sealing with paint or varnish before you apply the new decoration.

1 *To position a design in the centre of the top, mark the diagonals in chalk and put similar pencil marks through the stencil design.*

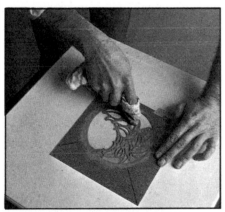

2 *After applying the colour to this central design, most of the paint was wiped off with white spirit to leave an unusual 'faded' finish.*

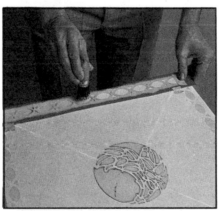

3 *Finally, a decorative border was applied to the top. Taping the stencil in place with masking tape prevents it moving and smudging the pattern.*

edges to the middle, and when all the cut-outs have been filled with colour leave the paint to harden off for a few moments. Then, peel off the stencil, replace it in the next position and repeat the stippling process. Work right across the surface to be stencilled, using one colour at a time. If you would have to place the stencil on top of wet paint to tackle the next area, do alternate areas instead – pattern repeats 1, 3, 5 and so on – and return to do 2, 4, 6 etc when the paint has dried and you can quite safely place the stencil over it.

If the stencil cut-outs become clogged, or there is paint on the surface, wipe it clean each time you reposition it.

It is a good idea to try out the stencil and your stencilling technique on a piece of paper before trying the job in earnest. This is particularly important if you intend stencilling furniture, where mistakes are difficult to rectify.

Finishing off

Proper care will mean you can use the same equipment again. There is little point in saving money by decorating with a stencil, only to waste the money you have spent on equipment by failing to take the few simple measures required for its maintenance. So, when the job is finished, remove any chalk marks from the surface, thoroughly clean all tools and the stencils, storing everything away carefully. Keep the stencils flat in a dry place, separating one from another by a layer of tissue or greaseproof paper.

On furniture and floors, apply a coat of clear polyurethane varnish to protect the pattern. A matt finish will suit most surfaces. However, heavy-wear areas, like floors, may need several coats, and you might prefer to use a semi-gloss or gloss finish for these. Make sure the stencilled pattern is absolutely dry before applying any protective finish.

Ready Reference

STENCILLING TECHNIQUE
The stencil brush should be used with a dabbing motion at right angles to the surface being painted. This is to prevent the paint from creeping beneath the edges of the stencil and spoiling the outline of the pattern. Take care not to overload the brush, as this may also cause paint creep.

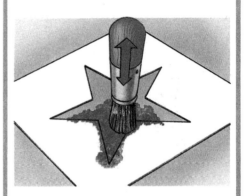

AEROSOL ALTERNATIVES
Although it is normal to carry out stencilling with a brush, you could do the job with aerosol paints such as those sold for touching up car paintwork. These come in a wide range of colours and would provide the opportunity for trying metallic finishes. However, the paint is very thin and several coats would be necessary. Take care not to put too much on at once, as it may run.

Aerosols are rather expensive and should not be used over oil-based paints. Make sure you pick a solvent and protective finish that are compatible.

PROVIDING SAFE ACCESS
If you are working at a high level, applying a decorative frieze to a wall for example, you can avoid having to work at arm's length by making a platform from two stepladders with a scaffold board at a comfortable height in between.

PAINTING MURALS

While the idea of painting a picture on a wall may seem daunting you'll find that a mural is surprisingly easy to execute. You don't need special artistic abilities to achieve a successful result.

Paint is not just for plain walls; it can be used to produce any pattern in any colour. And painting a wall with a mural or wall-pattern will give you a personalised form of decoration which is also inexpensive. You can use this technique to change the visual impression which a room gives; a mural will add an extra dimension to a blank wall or a really tiny room, can reduce the apparent size and give a more homely, cosy look to a vast wall area, or transform a dull, dark corridor, providing colour and interest where there was none before. In a tiny hall, with little light source, you might try painting an imaginary window on the blank stair well wall, complete with curtains, window box and view. In a narrow corridor you could use the trompe l'oeil (literally 'deceive the eye') technique, with, for example, pillars and a vista all down one side, or paint an imaginary doorway (it could be a French door with a view beyond) with trees in tubs to each side. In a bathroom or WC, a simple design of colours, waves, rolling hills or a permanent herbaceous border can be used to good effect.

Remember too that if you find a doorway or awkwardly placed pipe, projection or alcove gets in the way of your design you can turn them into an integral part of the mural. You can even include a piece of old furniture in the overall design by 'painting' it into the background; in fact this is a good way of hiding ugly architectural features, or making a junk shop buy blend in with its surroundings.

Proper preparation

Acting on impulse may result in a fine free-style mural, but it could be a waste of artistic effort if the wall surface is in poor condition, or you are painting over wall (or lining) paper which has started to peel, or old, porous, greasy emulsion paint.

So you should start out by providing yourself with a smooth, clean, non-absorbent surface. You will, where necessary, have to smooth down old plaster, fill any cracks and rub the filled areas down with glasspaper afterwards. If the plaster is in good condition, you can paint the wall in a suitable background colour; a standard mid-sheen or matt oil-based finish makes a perfect background for mural painting. Poor plaster can be lined; for this, you should choose as smooth a type of paper as possible and one which is of fairly heavy quality. If the walls are already covered in smooth wallpaper which is in good condition, you can give them a couple of coats of oil-based or emulsion paint, but don't choose a shiny finish (you can, of course, paint over lining paper in the same way). One point here: woodchips and other embossed or relief wallcoverings are not really suitable for mural-painting as it's difficult to get a straight or clearly defined line on the bumpy surface they provide; so if you've set your heart on painting a wall pattern you should remove wallcoverings of these types (and smooth and clean the surface) before you begin.

Materials you'll need

You can use emulsion or resin-based paints (painting murals is an attractive way of using up paint leftovers; you can intermix different colours of the same type of paint together to produce a wider colour range if you wish). You can also tint your own paints using artists' gouache or acrylic colours; these are expensive and can be used neat or thinned with a suitable medium, but though they are fine for small details their cost makes them impractical for large areas. Coloured stains can also be used neat (some of the woodstains now available come in a wide range of colours to give you a fairly reasonable amount of choice) or to tint, and you can even add fine details to your mural with felt pens or crayons.

You will also need an assortment of brushes: artists' brushes with fine points for details (a 'lining fitch' is a suitable type) and outlining the area to be painted, and ordinary decorators' 12 or 25mm (½ or 1in) brushes (or you could use artists' wedge-shaped oil brushes instead) for filling in the outlined areas. Larger brushes or rollers may also be necessary, depending on the design. Paint pads are also useful if you want to create texture interest, or a sponge can be used to create a stippled effect.

A mahl stick, on which you can rest your arm when painting, will help keep your hand steady and reduce the risk of smudging.

Suitable thinner (white spirit/turps or whatever) will depend on the type of paint you are using, as will the paint brush cleanser. You'll also require chalk or charcoal to transfer the design to the wall, and a plumb-line and spirit level to make sure you get the design square onto the surface. You may well need masking tape to get clean lines and perfectly straight edges, or you could use low-tack

THE FIRST STAGES

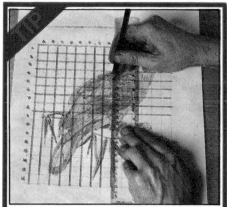

1 *Divide your original drawing up into squares and label the grid. Later the labels are transferred to the wall to make referring to the drawing easier.*

3 *Then use chalk to mark off the first horizontal at right angles to the vertical lines. Check with a spirit level to make sure it's absolutely true.*

5 *Referring back to your original drawing with its numbered or lettered grid, begin to fill in each square on the wall with the design (in chalk).*

2 *Measure the wall area to be covered by the mural to find out where the grid lines will come. Then use a plumbline to mark off a true vertical with chalk.*

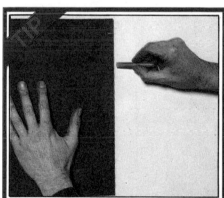

4 *Draw the outer grid lines. Then use a marked piece of paper as a guide to mark the rest, which you can draw or snap onto the wall with chalked string.*

6 *Continue filling in the squares until the whole design has been transferred to the wall. Then check to see if you've made any mistakes.*

Ready Reference

CHOOSING THE GRID SIZE

When you are dividing your original design into a grid to help you transfer it accurately to the wall, the size of the squares will depend on the complexity of the design:
● if the design is intricate, divide it into small 12mm (½in) squares
● if it is simple you can get away with larger squares of say, 50mm (2in).

TIP: PAINT THE WALL

Before you sketch the outline of the mural on the wall, first paint the area to be covered by the mural white. This provides a good base and may save you using two coats of colour.

TIP: OUTLINE AREAS FIRST

Even where you are attempting a free-hand design it's best to first draw its outline in chalk (preferably light-coloured so it won't show through the paint).

USE MASKING TAPE

When a straight line is required, rule the line in pencil first and then apply masking tape. Don't press it into place too hard or it may pull off the freshly applied paint when you remove it.

AIDS FOR DESIGN

There are a number of aids you can use to help you draw designs on the wall:
● diamonds, hexagons, or shaped bands of colour can be transferred to the wall by means of a template, cut from stout card
● triangular shapes can be made by drawing round a set square
● for circles you can use a compass, or draw round household objects like a bowl or glass; if you plan a large circle you can use a drawing pin, length of string and a pencil; pull the string taut and move the pencil round to draw the circle.

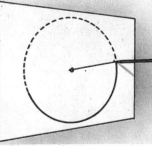

● for small intricate details you can buy a plastic or cardboard stencil (from artists' supply shops) and draw the outline with a pencil through the hole pierced in the stencil.

PAINTING THE MURAL

1 Mix up the paints where necessary and then pour them into containers which will be easy to hold. Assemble a range of brushes of different sizes.

2 Work from the top down. A mahl stick, which you can buy or make from a length of dowel with cloth tied to the end, will make painting easier.

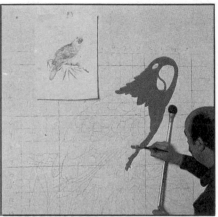

3 Continue to fill in the first area of colour. Try to work outwards from a wet edge, so you don't get a band of dried paint that could cause ugly ridges.

4 Begin painting the next colour. Where it will adjoin the previous colour, check that the first one is thoroughly dry or you will risk smudging it.

5 Continue painting with the other colours. When the larger areas have been completed you can go back and fill in the finer details.

6 Let the paint dry. You may then find, particularly with paler colours, that you need to apply a second coat to cover up the lines of the grid.

7 Again wait until the paint is thoroughly dry. Then clean the chalked grid off the wall by rubbing over it carefully with a damp cloth or sponge.

8 If you wish you can make the outline sharper and its details more obvious by drawing a black line exactly over it using a felt-tipped pen.

9 When the ink has dried, seal and protect the mural by applying polyurethane varnish; if you worked with emulsion paint, use emulsion glaze.

draughtsman's tape (available from good stationers) instead.

Where you will be working at a height you will need a stepladder, or some other form of working platform; make sure, whatever you use, that it is securely positioned. Painting can be a messy job and you should protect your clothing and also the furniture and floor (a dustsheet or old newspaper will suffice) and don't forget to have a plentiful supply of rags available for wiping off brushes and your hands.

Finally you'll need varnish (a clear, matt polyurethane type is best) to protect your finished masterpiece, so it can be wiped down occasionally and won't fade away.

Deciding on the design

The choice of design, is of course entirely up to you; this is the chief reason why painting a mural can be one of the most satisfying forms of decoration to carry out, in that it gives you the freedom to express individual ideas. Having said that, if you are artistic then the sky can be the limit but if you are not, a word of warning: choose a relatively simple design – one you feel confident of handling – for your first attempt.

For inspiration you could look at classical murals, browse through a few books on cave paintings, the art of Pompeii, old tapestries or ethnic or folk art. You can look at landscapes and views, you might even have a photograph of an outdoor scene which you have taken yourself which would transfer to a mural. If the picture is in slide form, and you have a projector, it is sometimes possible to project the design directly onto the blank wall and to sketch in the outline.

Putting the idea on the wall

Once you have decided on the design you should sketch it out on paper and colour it in (with a photograph or picture you've cut out this may not be necessary). Your next step is to transfer this design to the wall, and so that you can get as accurate a representation as possible, the best way to do this (unless you are particularly skilled at freehand drawing) is to use the grid technique. With this you divide the original design up into a grid and then draw a larger grid on the same scale on the wall to provide guidelines for drawing the outline of the mural and for painting it later (see step-by-step photographs). So that your final picture will not end up askew it's essential that you get the grid squarely drawn onto the wall, so make plentiful use of your plumbline, spirit level and try square when you are marking it out.

You can then carefully work your way down the wall filling in one square of the grid at a time with the outline of the design; use your original drawing as a guide.

If you are using the projection technique

mentioned earlier you will not need a grid, but it would be wise to establish a true horizontal and vertical and make sure the projected design is correctly positioned before drawing round it.

Another situation where you can dispense with the grid technique is if you decide to use geometric patterns; here there are all sorts of aids available for making sure you get the shape you want clearly and accurately outlined on the wall (see Ready Reference). You could, in some circumstances, find that a combination of the grid technique and drawing aids will give you the result you want.

Applying the paint

With the design transferred to the wall you should stand back and look at it carefully and critically, for this is the moment in which you should make any alterations and adjustments necessary. It's a simple matter to rub out any offending chalk or charcoal lines with a cloth, and then redraw them correctly.

When you've got your design exactly how you want it you can begin the painting. Make sure the paint is thoroughly mixed, with the appropriate amount of thinners added, where necessary, and that your brushes are clean, dry and ready for use.

It's best, if possible, to work from the top of the wall downwards as you paint, and to start on the large flat areas of colour.

Use your fine brush to draw in the outline and for filling in on a fairly intricate design; on an uncomplicated job fill in with a larger one to complete the job faster.

When the main, flat painting is completed, you can add shading, modelling, special details or highlights. Sometimes a textured effect can improve a design; you can, for example, stipple the side of a treetrunk by dabbing the paint with a sponge for a more natural effect. Or you might decide to highlight fruit or flower petals with off-white or pale-coloured glaze. Another technique to use when you have completed the mural is to improve the definition of the shapes it contains by outlining them with a thin black line. You could use paint and an artist's brush for this where the design is very simple, but on a more complicated wall-pattern it's much easier and quicker to use a spirit-type felt-tip pen (and you're probably less likely to make mistakes as well).

Finally, however satisfying you've found the process of creating your own wall picture or design, it will have taken you some time to produce. You will want it to last and so you will need to provide it with a protective coating. When the mural is thoroughly dry, you should brush on polyurethane varnish or other suitable sealant so the surface will stand up to wear and tear and so you will be able to clean off any grubby marks without fear or impairing your carefully-wrought design.

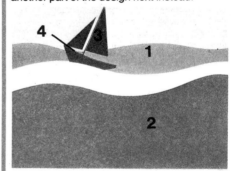

PART 3

HOME CARPENTRY

BASIC TECHNIQUES

Whether the woodworking job you are planning to carry out is a simple or a complicated one, you will not get far without first mastering the basic carpentry skills.

T-JOINTS FOR FRAMING

There's a mortise-and-tenon joint for almost every purpose. Pegs and wedges (29 to 31) add strength and can be very attractive, especially in a contrasting wood. You can even wedge pegs. When using double wedges (30), drive them in with alternate strokes so that they enter the cuts evenly.

31 can be a knock-down joint if unglued.

As a general rule, make mortises one-third the thickness of the piece (24 to 31, 33, 34 – and see also 3, 4, 5). This avoids both weakening the tenon and splitting the mortise piece.

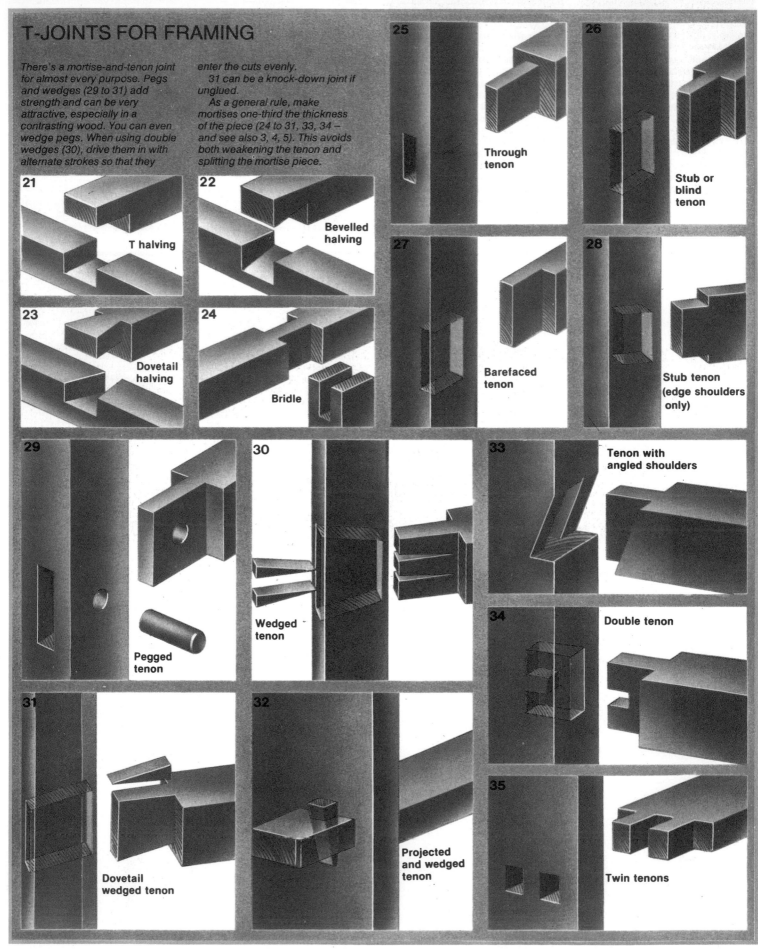

21 T halving

22 Bevelled halving

23 Dovetail halving

24 Bridle

25 Through tenon

26 Stub or blind tenon

27 Barefaced tenon

28 Stub tenon (edge shoulders only)

29 Pegged tenon

30 Wedged tenon

31 Dovetail wedged tenon

32 Projected and wedged tenon

33 Tenon with angled shoulders

34 Double tenon

35 Twin tenons

SIMPLE JOINTS

It's often thought that only elaborate joints give good results in woodwork. It isn't true. There are simple ways to join timber, and one of the simplest is the butt joint. It's easy to make, can be used on natural timber or man-made boards, and it's neat. What's more, given the right adhesive and the right reinforcement, a butt joint can also be strong enough for most purposes.

The great thing about butt joints is their simplicity. You can use them on any kind of timber or man-made board, provided it isn't too thin – not under 6mm (¼in). The only problem you will run into is where you are joining chipboard. A special technique is needed here to get the screws to grip, as is explained later.

Although it is possible simply to glue two pieces of wood together, unless you add some kind of reinforcement the result won't be very strong. So in most cases, the joint should be strengthened with either screws or nails. The question is which? As a rule of thumb, screws will give you a stronger joint than nails. The exception is where you are screwing into the endgrain of natural timber. Here, the screw thread chews up the timber to such an extent that it has almost no fixing value at all. Nails in this case are a much better bet.

Choosing the right adhesive

Even if you are screwing or nailing the joint together, it ought to be glued as well. A PVA woodworking adhesive will do the trick in most jobs, providing a strong and easily achieved fixing. This type of adhesive will not, however, stand up well to either extreme heat or to moisture; the sort of conditions you'll meet outdoors, or in a kitchen, for example. A urea formaldehyde is the glue to use in this sort of situation. It isn't as convenient – it comes as a powder that you have to mix with water – but your joints will hold.

Choosing the right joint

There are no hard and fast rules about choosing the best joint for a particular job. It's really just a case of finding a joint that is neat enough for what you're making, and strong enough not to fall apart the first time it is used. And as far as strength is concerned, the various kinds of butt joint work equally well.

Marking timber

Butt joints are the simplest of all joints – there's no complicated chiselling or marking out to worry about – but if the joint is to be both strong and neat you do need to be able to saw wood to length leaving the end perfectly square.

The first important thing here is the accuracy of your marking out. Examine the piece of wood you want to cut and choose a side and an edge that are particularly flat and smooth. They're called the face edge and face side.

Next, measure up and press the point of a sharp knife into the face side where you intend to make the cut. Slide a try-square up to the knife, making sure that its stock – the handle – is pressed firmly against the face edge. Then use the knife to score a line across the surface of the timber. Carry this line round all four sides of the wood, always making sure that the try-square's stock is held against either the face edge or the face side. If you wish, you can run over the knife line with a pencil to make it easier to see – it's best to sharpen the lead into a chisel shape.

Why not use a pencil for marking out in the first place? There are two reasons. The first is that a knife gives a thinner and therefore more accurate line than even the sharpest pencil. The second is that the knife will cut through the surface layer of the wood, helping the saw to leave a clean, sharp edge

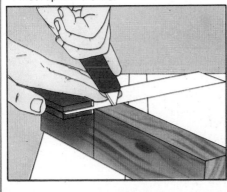

Sawing square

One of the most useful – and easiest to make – aids to sawing is a bench hook. It'll help you to grip the wood you want to cut, and to protect the surface on which you are working. You can make one up quite easily, by gluing and screwing together pieces of scrap timber (see *Ready Reference*).

You also need the ability to control the saw, and there are three tips that will help you here. Always point your index finger along the saw blade to stop it flapping from side to side as you work. And always stand in such a way that you are comfortable, well balanced, and can get your head directly above the saw so you can see what you are cutting. You should also turn slightly sideways on. This stops your elbow brushing against your body as you draw the saw back – a fault that is often the reason for sawing wavy lines.

Starting the cut

Position the piece of wood to be cut on the bench hook and hold it firmly against the block furthest from you. Start the cut by drawing the saw backwards two or three times over the far edge to create a notch, steadying the blade by 'cocking' the thumb of your left hand. Make sure that you position the saw so that the whole of this notch is on the waste side of the line. You can now begin to saw properly using your arm with sort of piston action, but keep your left (or right as the case may be) hand away from the saw.

As the cut deepens gradually reduce the angle of the saw until it is horizontal. At this point you can continue sawing through until you start cutting into the bench hook. Alternatively, you may find it easier to angle the saw towards you and make a sloping cut down the edge nearest to you. With that done, you can saw through the remaining waste holding the saw horizontally, using the two angled cuts to keep the saw on course.

Whichever method you choose, don't try to force the saw through the wood – if that seems necessary, then the saw is probably blunt. Save your muscle power for the forward stroke – but concentrate mainly on sawing accurately to your marked line.

Cleaning up cut ends

Once you have cut the wood to length, clean up the end with glasspaper. A good tip is to lay the abrasive flat on a table and work the end of the wood over it with a series of circular strokes, making sure that you keep the wood vertical so you don't sand the end out of square. If the piece of wood is too unmanageable, wrap the glasspaper round a square piece of scrap wood instead and sand the end of the wood by moving the block to and fro – it'll help in keeping the end square.

DOVETAIL NAILING

This is a simple way of strengthening any butt joint. All you do is grip the upright piece in a vice or the jaws of a portable work-bench, and glue the horizontal piece on top if it – supporting it with scrap wood to hold the joint square – and then drive in the nails dovetail fashion. If you were to drive the nails in square, there would be more risk that the joint would pull apart. Putting them in at an angle really does add strength.

The only difficulty is that the wood may split. To prevent this, use oval brads rather than round nails, making sure that their thickest part points along the grain. If that doesn't do the trick, try blunting the point of each nail by driving it into the side of an old hammer. This creates a burr of metal on the point which will cut through the wood fibres rather than parting them.

Once the nails are driven home, punch their heads below the surface using a nail punch, or a large blunt nail. Fill the resulting dents with wood stopping (better on wood than ordinary cellulose filler) and sand smooth.

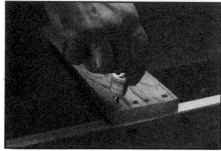

1 *Drive nails at angle: first leans to left; next to right, and so on.*

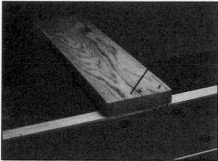

3 *Fill resulting dents with stopping compound to cover up nail heads.*

THE OVERLAP

This is the simplest of all and is one you can use on relatively thin timber. The example shown is for a T-joint, but the method is the same if you want to make an X-joint.

Bring the two pieces of wood together as they will be when joined, and use a pencil to mark the position of the topmost piece on the one underneath. To reinforce the joint, countersunk screws are best, so mark their positions on the top piece of wood, and drill clearance holes the same diameter as the screw's shank – the unthreaded part – right the way through. The screws should be arranged like the spots on a dice (two screws are shown here, but on a larger joint where more strength is needed five would be better) to help stop the joint twisting out of square. Enlarge the mouths of these holes with a countersink bit to accommodate the screw heads, and clean up any splinters where the drill breaks through the underside of the wood.

Bring the two pieces of wood together again using a piece of scrap wood to keep the top piece level. Then make pilot holes in the lower piece using either a bradawl or a small drill, boring through the clearance holes to make sure they are correctly positioned. Make sure the pilot holes are drilled absolutely vertically, or the screws could pull the joint out of shape. Finally, apply a thin coating of adhesive to both the surfaces to be joined (follow the adhesive manufacturer's instructions), position the pieces of wood accurately and, without moving them again, drive home the screws.

3 *Reassemble joint and bore pilot holes in bottom piece with bradawl.*

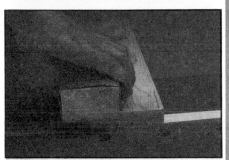

2 With nail punch or large blunt nail, hammer nail heads below surface.

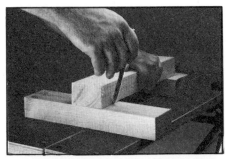

4 When stopping is dry, sand flush with surface of surrounding timber.

CORRUGATED TIMBER CONNECTORS

Another simple way of holding a butt joint together is to use ordinary corrugated timber connectors. Simply glue the two pieces of wood together, and hammer the connectors in across the joint. Note that they are driven in dovetail fashion – the fixing is stronger that way.

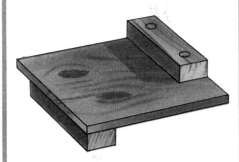

For strength, hammer in connectors diagonally rather than straight.

Ready Reference

MAKING YOUR OWN BENCH HOOK

This a very useful sawing aid to help grip the wood when cutting. Hook one end over the edge of the workbench and hold the wood against the other end. Make it up from off-cuts and replace when it becomes worn.

You need:
● a piece of 12mm (½in) plywood measuring about 250 x 225mm (10 x 9in)
● two pieces of 50 x 25mm (2 x 1in) planed softwood, each about 175mm (7in) long. Glue and screw them together as shown in the sketch. Use the bench hook the other way up if you're left-handed.

TIP: SAWING STRAIGHT

● hold wood firmly against bench hook and start cut on waste side of cutting line with two or three backward cuts
● decrease angle of the saw blade as cut progresses
● complete cut with saw horizontal, cutting into your bench hook slightly

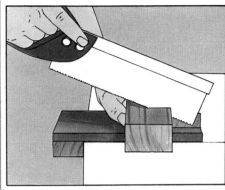

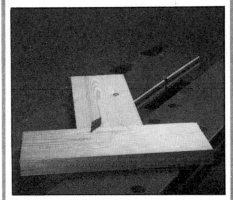

1 Bring pieces squarely together. Mark position of each on the other.

2 Drill and countersink (inset) clearance holes for screws in uppermost piece.

4 Apply woodworking adhesive to both pieces and press them together

5 Carefully drive in screws. If they're tight, remove and lubricate with soap.

TIP: TO SMOOTH CUT END

● rub with a circular motion on glasspaper held flat on the workbench, so you don't round off the corners
● on large pieces of wood, wrap glasspaper round a block of wood and rub this across the cut end

FIXING INTO CHIPBOARD

Because neither nails nor screws hold well in chipboard, how do you hold a butt joint together? The answer is that you do use screws, but to help them grip, you drive them into a chipboard plug. Chipboard plugs are a bit like ordinary wall plugs. In fact, you can use ordinary plugs, but you have to be careful to position the plug so that any expanding jaws open across the board's width and not across the thickness where they could cause the board to break up.

The initial stages of the job are exactly the same as for the overlap joint – marking out, drilling the clearance holes, and so on. The difference is that instead of boring pilot holes in the second piece of wood, you drill holes large enough to take the chipboard plugs. Pop the plugs into the holes, glue the joint together and drive home the screws.

Incidentally, if you can't use any sort of plug at all – for example, when screwing into the face of the chipboard – the only way to get the screw to hold properly is to dip it in a little woodworking adhesive before you drive it home.

1 *Bring pieces together and mark position of overlap with a pencil.*

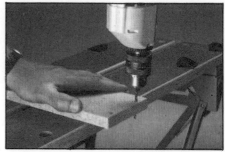

2 *Drill and countersink clearance holes in overlapping piece.*

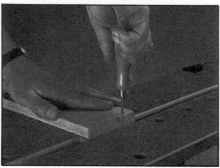

3 *Mark screw positions through holes onto end of second piece.*

4 *Drill chipboard to take plugs, then glue and screw joint together.*

REINFORCING BLOCKS

The joints described so far are fairly robust, but if a lot of strength is needed it's worth reinforcing the joint with some sort of block. The simplest is a square piece of timber.

First drill and countersink clearance holes through the block and glue and screw it to one of the pieces you want to join so that it's flush with the end. To complete the joint, glue the second piece in position, and drive screws through into that. You can arrange for the block to end up inside the angle or outside it. Choose whichever looks best and is easiest to achieve.

With the block inside the angle, you'll have a neat joint and the screw heads won't be openly on display. However, in most cases it means screwing through a thick piece of wood (the block) into a thin piece (one of the bits you want to join), so it's not as strong as it might be. If greater strength is needed work the other way round, driving the screws through the pieces to be joined, into the block. You can neaten the result to a certain extent by using a triangular rather than a square block.

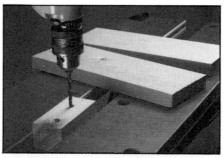

1 *Drill and countersink clearance holes through reinforcing block.*

2 *Glue and screw block in place level with end of one piece of wood.*

3 *Glue second piece in place and drive screws into it through block.*

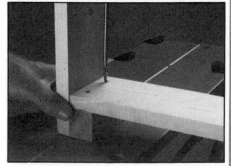

4 *In some cases this joint looks better with block outside angle.*

JOINTING BLOCKS

Made from plastic, these are just sophisticated versions of the wooden blocks you can make yourself, and they're used in similar situations. Their only real advantage is that they tend to give a neater result when you're working with veneered or melamine covered chipboard, but only because they come in the right colours. There are basically two kinds to choose from.

The simplest is just a hollow triangular 'block' that comes with a snap-on cover to hide the screws. More complicated versions come in two parts. You screw one half of the block to each piece of wood, and then screw the two halves together using the machine screw provided. It's essential here that both halves of the block are positioned accurately, and since the blocks vary from brand to brand in the details of their design, you should follow the manufacturer's instructions on this point.

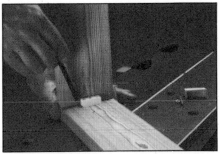

1 *Screw half of block to one piece of wood and mark position on other.*

2 *Next, screw second half of block in place on second piece of timber.*

3 *Finally, connect both halves of block using built-in machine screw.*

4 *Treat blocks that come in one piece as wooden reinforcing blocks.*

ANGLE IRONS

If still greater strength is needed, use either an angle iron or a corner repair bracket to reinforce the joint. These are really just pieces of metal pre-drilled to take screws and shaped to do the same job as a reinforcing block (the angle irons) or to be screwed to the face of the two pieces of timber across the joint (the flat T-shaped and L-shaped corner repair brackets).

In either case, bring together the pieces of wood to be joined, position the bracket, and mark the screw holes. Drill clearance and pilot holes for all the screws, then screw the bracket to one of the pieces before glueing the joint together and screwing the bracket to the second piece. They don't look very attractive, so use where appearance isn't important, ie, at the back of a joint, or where the joint is going to be concealed in some other way.

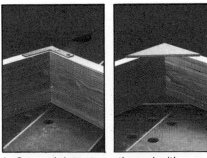

1 *Corner joints strengthened with plywood and an angle repair iron.*

2 *T-joints can be simply made with angle irons or repair brackets.*

SKEW NAILING

There'll be some situations where you cannot get at the end of the wood to use dovetail nailing. Here you must use skew nailing instead. This means glueing the two pieces securely together and then driving a nail into the upright piece of wood at an angle so it also penetrates the horizontal piece. Put a couple of nails into each side of the upright so that they cross. To stop the upright moving, clamp a block of wood behind it or wedge it against something solid.

Stop movement while driving nails with scrap wood block and G-cramp.

HALVING JOINTS & simple mitres

Getting joints to fit snugly is one of the major objectives in carpentry, and nothing introduces the techniques so well as the halving joint. As for the perfect finish, that's the role of the mitre.

There are many situations in woodwork when you need a joint that's fast and simple, but also neat and strong. And this is where halving joints come into their own. Despite their simplicity, they're very effective joints because the two pieces of wood are cut so they interlock together, either face to face or edge to edge, making the joint as strong as — if not stronger than — the timber itself. They are used almost exclusively for building frameworks, joining the rails (side pieces) either at a corner or in a cross absolutely flush. You end up with a frame that's neat enough to be on show and sturdy enough to need no reinforcement.

Mitre joints, though not strictly speaking considered halving joints as there's no interlocking, are halved to make up a perfect 90° angle. In this section, only the simple mitre is dealt with — the more complicated forms (eg, mitred secret dovetails) are covered in another section.

Strength of joints

There are three things that affect the strength of a halving joint — the size of the timber, the quality of the timber, and any reinforcement you add.

The size of timber is important because it governs the amount of adhesive in the joint; the greater the areas glued together, the stronger the joint will be. Usually problems only arise when you are trying to join thin pieces of timber together — it's almost impossible to get the joint to stay rigid. Regarding timber quality, hardwoods rarely present a problem, but with softwoods, splitting can occur which will seriously weaken the joint. You should, therefore, reject timber containing knots, cracks and other potential weak spots.

In many cases, the correct adhesive is all the reinforcement you need — use a good quality PVA woodworking adhesive, or, if the joint will be subjected to heat or moisture, a urea formaldehyde woodworking adhesive. If still greater strength is required — this is more likely on corner halving joints than on cross halvings — you should drive screws through the overlaps, or, for a more natural look, drill a hole right through and glue in a length of dowel. Both the dowels and screws are set like the spots on a dice to stop the joint twisting.

Simple butt joints (see pages 27-31) must be reinforced in some way to have strength, but with mitred butt joints this would defeat the decorative aim. Because of this, they are normally reserved for situations where strength is not required — picture frames and decorative edgings, such as door architraves for example.

Marking corner halving joints

Having sawn the ends of the two pieces of wood to be joined perfectly square (see pages 263–267) place one piece on top of the other, and mark the width of the top piece on the one below. Carry this mark right round the timber using a knife and a try-square, then repeat the process, this time with the bottom piece of wood on top.

Next divide the thickness of the timber in two. You need a single-tooth marking gauge for this: it consists of a wooden shaft with a sharp metal pin called a spur near one end, and a block of wood (the stock) which can be moved along the shaft and be fixed at any point with the aid of a thumbscrew.

Position the stock so that the distance between it and the spur is roughly half the timber's thickness, and place it against one edge of the wood. Use the spur to dent the surface of the timber, then repeat with the stock against the other edge. If the dents co-incide, the gauge is set correctly. If they don't, reset the gauge. Don't try to make small adjustments by undoing the thumbscrew and moving the stock — you'll go on for ever trying to make it accurate. Instead, with the screw reasonably tight, tap one end of the shaft sharply on a hard surface. Depending which end you tap and how hard you tap it, the setting will increase or decrease by the merest fraction.

With the setting right, wedge one end of the timber into the angle of a bench hook, place the stock of the gauge firmly against the timber's edge and holding it there, score the wood from the width line to the end. You'll find this easier if, rather than digging the spur right into the wood, you merely drag it across the surface. Score identical lines on the other side and the end.

Use a pencil to shade the areas on each piece of wood that will form the waste (the top of one, the bottom of the other), then grip the first piece upright in a vice. The lower down you can get it the better. If you can't get it low, back it with a piece of scrap wood to reduce vibration. Using a tenon saw, carefully saw down until you reach the width line — the first one you marked. The golden rule of sawing any kind of joint is to saw on the waste side of the marked line (it's *always* better to saw or chisel off too little rather than too much since you can always take off a little more but you can never put it back). And remember that the closer the fit, the

MAKING A CORNER HALVING JOINT

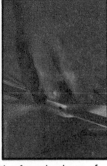

1 *First mark the width of each piece of wood on the other. Then, using a knife and square, continue these width lines round all four sides of each piece.*

2 *To mark the thickness line, set a marking gauge to half the thickness of the wood and, holding the stock firmly against one edge, scribe the line.*

3 *It's easier to start sawing at an angle, then gradually bring the saw to the horizontal. Keep the wood gripped firmly in the vice until you're finished.*

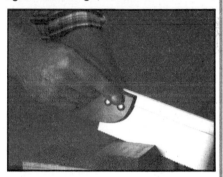

4 *Transfer the wood to a bench hook and cut down along the width line to remove the waste wood. Be sure to cut on the waste side of the guide line.*

5 *Smooth both parts to be joined with glasspaper and apply adhesive. Clamp together with a G-cramp until dry, protecting the wood with scrap timber.*

6 *When the adhesive has set, drill holes for reinforcing wood screws or dowels. If using screws, countersink the hole to take the screw head.*

WHERE TO USE HALVING JOINTS

Halving joints are usually used for making frameworks. Here you can see which joint to use where, and how each one is assembled.

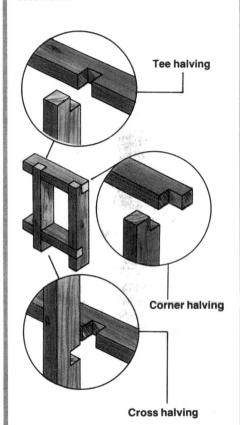

Tee halving

Corner halving

Cross halving

TOOLS FOR HALVING JOINTS

For measuring and marking: use a *handyman's knife* rather than a pencil for marking; use a *marking gauge* on each face of the joint — it'll be more accurate than using a tape measure; a *try-square* ensures accurate squaring off.
For cutting: use a *tenon saw* and a broad-blade *chisel* (25mm/1in) for cutting out cross halvings.

TIP: LABELLING JOINT PARTS

Avoid mixing up the pairs of joints by labelling the two parts with a letter and a number as soon as you cut them.

stronger the joint will end up. Basically, it should fit like a hand in a glove.

Remove the wood from the vice, put it on a bench hook and cut down along the width line to release the waste wood. Again make sure you cut on the waste side of the line and be prepared to make final adjustments with a chisel. Treat the second piece of wood in exactly the same way, then bring the two together and check the fit.

You can use either a chisel or a piece of glasspaper to take off any unevenness in the timber, although it'll be quicker to use a chisel to clear out the edges so that the corners are absolutely square. When the pieces finally fit neatly, spread adhesive on both faces of the joint and hold them in place with a G-cramp (protecting the wood's surface with scrap timber) until the glue has set. Remove the cramp, and add any re-

MAKING A CROSS HALVING JOINT

1 *First mark out the waste area to be removed, then cut down the width lines with a tenon saw.*

2 *Hold the timber in a vice or against a bench hook and remove the waste by chiselling at a slight upward angle.*

3 *Do the same on the other side until there's a 'pyramid' of waste in the middle. Gradually flatten this.*

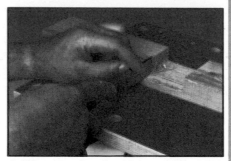

4 *When nearing the thickness line, hold the cutting edge at an angle to the wood grain. Trim fibres in the corners.*

The next step is to turn the wood round and slope the other edge to leave a sort of pyramid of waste. With that done, pushing the chisel through the wood rather than hitting it, gradually flatten off the pyramid until you have brought it level with the half-way lines. You'll get a neater finish here if, in the final stages, you work with the chisel's blade flat but at an angle to the grain of the wood. Finally, again pushing the chisel, remove any ragged fibres lodged in the angles of the housing.

Once you've sawn and chiselled out the housing in the second piece of wood, the next step is to try fitting the two together. Don't try forcing them if they don't quite fit — you're in danger of splitting the wood. Instead, carefully chisel off a fraction more wood, bit by bit, until you can fit the pieces together without undue force. If, on the other hand, you've cut the housing too wide so the fit is very loose, you'll have to add some reinforcement like screws or dowels, and fill in the gaps with a wood filler, stopping or a mixture of fine sawdust and PVA adhesive. It's not worth trying to add a wedge unless the gap is very wide (over 6mm/¼in) because the result can be very messy.

Making a mitre joint

With wood that's square or rectangular in section, the first job is to make sure that both pieces are absolutely squarely cut. Use the try-square to check this — if they're not, it's better to cut another piece of wood than attempt to make adjustments. Next, place one piece on top of the other to form a right angle. Mark an internal and external corner on both, then take them apart and carry the marks across the edge with a knife and try square. Join up the marks on each piece of wood — this will give sawing lines at 45° Mark the waste side of each with a pencil.

Wood that is raised on one side (eg, mouldings for picture frames) cannot be marked in the same way as the pieces won't sit flat on each other. The easiest way is to mark the

inforcing screws or dowels that may be needed, drilling pilot holes first.

Making cross halving joints

The difference between cross halving joints and corner halving joints is that you cannot remove the waste using only a saw. You have to make a 'housing' and for this you need a chisel (see pages 276–279 for more details of halving joints).

Saw down the width lines to the halfway mark and make additional saw cuts in between to break up the waste — these can

be the same width as the chisel blade to make chipping out easier. Grip the work in a vice, or on a bench hook, and now use the chisel to remove the waste. This is done in four stages. Guiding the chisel blade bevel uppermost with one hand and striking the handle with the palm of your other hand — for this job your hand is better than a mallet — reduce the edge of the timber nearest to you to a shallow slope ending a fraction above the halfway line. Don't try to remove all the wood in one go or it will split. Remove just sliver at a time.

MAKING MITRES

1 *With square or rectangular wood, cut ends absolutely square and stack to form a right angle. Then mark the inner and outer corners on both pieces.*

2 *Carry lines down each edge with knife and try square, and score a line between corner marks to create an angle of 45°. Shade waste in pencil.*

3 *Press the wood against the bench hook and keep the saw at a shallow angle. Cut the diagonal, using the line on the edge to keep the saw vertical.*

THE SIMPLE MITRE

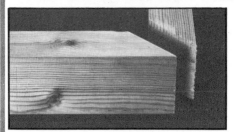

1 *The ends of two battens are cut to 45° and, when fixed together, make a 90° angle in this simplest of mitre joints, ideal for picture framing.*

2 *With thick timber frames, use corrugated steel fasteners driven into the back of mitre joints, where they will not be seen from the front.*

3 *Another method of strengthening a fairly thick mitre joint from behind is to pin triangles of plywood across the corner, out of sight.*

4 *Ready-made angle brackets with pre-drilled, countersunk screw holes make a quick, rigid and hidden fixing for two mitred battens in a frame.*

point of the mitre (the corner point) and then to use a simple *mitre block* to cut the angle. A mitre block not only helps you support the piece of wood (like a bench hook) but also has saw cuts at 45° in the back face to guide the saw. Then you only have to line up the mitre point on the wood with the saw now set at the correct angle. You can make a mitre block yourself — see *Ready Reference.*

Mitre aids

There are other devices available to help you cut mitres accurately. A proprietary *jointing jig*, for example, guides the saw either at right angles or at 45°; a *mitre box* is like a mitre block but has an extra side so that the whole length of the saw is kept in line.

Without these devices, getting the angles right isn't easy — but if necessary you can use a bench hook, driving in two nails so the wood is held against the block and the line of cutting is free of the bench hook. This is not as easy as using one of the other methods. Mark the wood so you know the sawing line, then place it in the mitre block, box or jig, to line up with the appropriate groove to guide the saw. If the wood you are cutting is very thin, put some blocks of scrap wood under the device to bring it up to a reasonable height. Insert a tenon saw into the guide slot and, holding it level, saw away.

There are only two things that can go

wrong. If the block is old, the 'guide' cut may have widened, resulting in an inaccurate cut. A larger tenon saw may help, but really the only answer is to hold the saw as steady as possible. The other common error when cutting mouldings and the like is to cut two mitres the same — that is two right-handed or left-handed angles, instead of one of each. This can be avoided by always marking the waste on the wood, and checking that the saw is in the correct guide slot before you begin.

Clean up the cut ends with glasspaper, taking care not to alter the angle, and glue and cramp the joint together. For frames, special mitre cramps are available, but you again make up your own. From scrap wood, cut four L-shaped blocks, and drill a hole at an angle through the point of each L. Feed a single piece of string through the holes of all four blocks, position the blocks at the corners of the frame and tie the string into a continuous loop. To tighten up, twist the string around a stick, and keep twisting the stick to draw the blocks together. You can then wedge the stick against the frame to stop it untwisting until the adhesive has set.

There are three ways to strengthen mitres — with timber connectors, plywood triangles or metal angle repair irons. For frames they should be fitted from behind, either by glueing, or glueing and pinning (see the photographs above).

Ready Reference

MAKING A MITRE BLOCK

Mitre blocks and boxes already have 45° angle cuts made as a saw guide. Rather than buying one, you can make one that's used in the same way as a bench hook. You'll need:
● a piece of 19mm (¾in) plywood measuring about 250 x 150mm (10 x 6in)
● a 250mm (10in) length of 50 x 50mm (2 x 2in) softwood – or hardwood such as beech if available
● a 250mm (10in) length of 50 x 25mm (2 x 1in) softwood.

Glue and screw together as shown in the diagrams, then
● use a combination square, or make a template by folding a square piece of paper in half diagonally, as a guide for the 45° angle saw cuts
● square the lines down both faces of the block, and cut the slots with a tenon saw.

MAKING A MITRE CRAMP

You can make a simple cramp for small mitred frames from 4 L-shaped softwood blocks. Drill holes through one leg of each block, thread string through holes and tie tightly to hold blocks against frame corners.

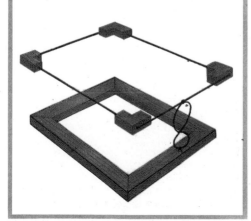

MAKING JOINTS WITH DOWELS

Called wood pins or pegs, dowels are lengths of hardwood with an important role to play in simple carpentry. They can be a decorative part of joints made with them, or be there for strength alone. Few tools are needed but the secret of success lies in using them accurately.

There are two basic ways in which you can use dowels in woodworking joints. You can drive a dowel through such joints as a half lap instead of using a nail or screw, or you can use them to make joints in their own right by drilling holes in one piece of wood, glueing in dowels, and then slotting these into corresponding holes in the second piece.

The dowel joint proper is used mostly in furniture making where it provides a neat joint of great strength without intricate cutting and without the need for unsightly reinforcement. Dowels can also be used to repair furniture.

In any joint, the size of the dowel is very important. Use a small one in a big joint and it won't have sufficient strength; use one that's too large and the holes you drill to accommodate it will weaken the wood. Ideally you should choose dowels which are no more than one third the thickness of the timber into which they will be fixed.

The thickness of the wood must be considered, too, for the dowels must have sufficient space between them and at each side otherwise when they're hit home or pushed into their corresponding holes the wood will split. So follow the carpenter's 'one third rule' and mark the width as well as the thickness into three (ie, a 9mm/⅜in dowel will need at least the same amount on both sides of it). And don't forget that planed wood can be up to 5mm less all round than the dimensions you ordered, and three into this size might not give you enough room for a successful joint.

Types of joints

There are different types of dowel joint. The simplest and easiest to make is the *through* dowel joint in which the dowel peg passes right through one piece of timber and into the other, sometimes passing through this as well if it's thin enough. Because in either case the ends of the dowels show, they are often used as a decorative feature of the article you're making.

If you don't want the ends of the dowels to be seen, you must make a *stopped* joint. In

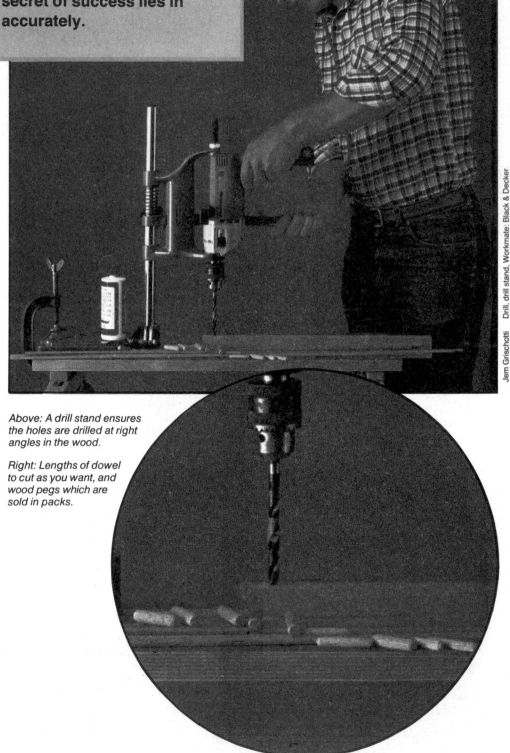

Above: A drill stand ensures the holes are drilled at right angles in the wood.

Right: Lengths of dowel to cut as you want, and wood pegs which are sold in packs.

Jem Grischotti   Drill, drill stand, Workmate: Black & Decker

JOINTS MADE WITH DOWELS

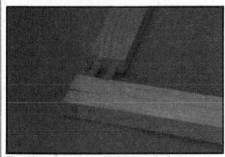

The through dowel joint ready for assembly. The dowels are firmly embedded in one piece and will pass right through the other.

When assembled the through joint shows up the dowels. Cut them a little longer so after cramping they can be planed flush with the wood.

The stopped joint has dowels in one piece which will go into the other far enough to ensure rigidity but won't be seen on the other side.

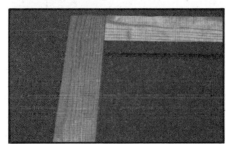

A close fit for the finished stopped joint. When drilling the holes they should be slightly deeper than the dowel to hold any excess adhesive.

Mitred dowel joints can be tricky to make as you can't use the 'pin' method (see next page) for marking up because of the 45° angle.

The hidden strength in this joint is the two different lengths of dowel. Very effective for frames where you don't want reinforcement to be seen.

A halving or half lap joint made at a corner can either be glued and screwed or, if it will be on show, made secure with dowels which fit into holes placed like spots on a dice.

The completed dowelled halving joint gives one overall look of wood. The same effect can be achieved by topping countersunk screws with dowel pellets cut from an offcut of the wood.

Jem Grischotti

Ready Reference

BUYING DOWELS

Dowel lengths from timber merchants are sold in these diameters:
● 6mm (¼in)
● 9mm (⅜in)
● 12mm (½in)
Larger diameters – 16mm (⅝in) and 19mm (¾in) – can be softwood rather than hardwood.

TIPS TO SAVE TIME

● Buying grooved dowel saves you having to groove it yourself.
● **Pre-packed dowels** are bought in packs containing short lengths of diameters such as 4mm, 8mm and 10mm. They are fluted (finely grooved) and the ends are chamfered.
● **Dowel pellets** finish woodwork where screws have been countersunk. They should fit the hole exactly but be fractionally deeper so they can be planed back when the adhesive has set. Buy pre-packed, or cut your own from offcuts using a special plug attachment for an electric drill.

TOOLS

● **try-square and marking gauge** are essential for accurate marking up
● **electric drill** held in a drill stand for perfectly plumb holes
● **mallet** for tapping in the dowels
● **block or ordinary plane** for finishing a through joint
● **cramp** to hold the joint until the adhesive has set

CHAMFER DOWEL ENDS

If cutting your own dowels rub the cut ends with medium-grade glasspaper to give a gentle chamfer (it makes the dowel go in more easily).

Apply woodworking adhesive to the meeting faces of the wood as well as brushing or squirting it into the holes.

MARKING UP

1 With wood that's rectangular or square in section, use a marking gauge to make the central line on the edge where the dowels will go.

2 Divide this central line into three, then draw two lines at right angles.

3 Lightly tap small panel pins into the wood at the two centre points. Snip off their heads leaving about 3mm (¹⁄₈in) protruding.

4 Holding the second piece of timber firmly against a bench hook or edge of the try-square, press the pins in to mark the drill positions (inset).

Jem Grischotti

this the peg doesn't go right through either piece of timber. This is perhaps the most common dowel joint.

Joint shapes
Dowels can be used to make joints of various types, including L-joints, T-joints and X-joints between rails or boards, and three-way joints between rails and posts, as in furniture-making. They can also be used to reinforce edge-to-edge joints between boards, for example when making a drawer.

Cutting dowels
Cut dowels to length with a fine-toothed tenon saw, holding the dowels in a bench hook or a vice. For through joints, cut one dowel slightly longer than the combined thicknesses of the timbers, so that the ends can be trimmed flush after the joint is assembled. For stopped joints, cut the dowels slightly shorter than the combined depths of the holes into which they fit, and lightly chamfer the ends using glasspaper, a chisel or a proprietary dowel sharpener (which works just like a pencil sharpener).

Dowels need a shallow groove cut in their sides to allow excess adhesive to squeeze out as the joints are assembled. With much

practice you can do this with a chisel or tenon saw (having cramped it lengthways in a workbench), but it is probably easier to buy grooved dowel in the first place – in lengths you cut to size yourself, or for small jobs as pre-packed pegs. If buying pegs make sure you choose ones that correspond with the bit size for your drill.

Marking hole positions
First, use a try-square to check that the meeting faces or ends of the timber to be joined are cut perfectly square and are of the same thickness. You can then mark the positions for the dowel holes. Set a marking gauge to half the width of the timber, and mark a line down the middle of the end of one length of timber. Determine exactly where on this line the centre of the holes will be – the ideal is that they should be from 25mm (1in) to 50mm (2in) apart and never nearer than 19mm (³⁄₄in) from the edges. Using a try-square, draw lines across the gauge line to mark the exact centres of the holes.

To mark matching holes in corresponding positions on the second piece of timber use the following method to ensure accuracy. Drive small panel pins into the first piece at the positions you've marked for the holes.

Leave the pins slightly proud of the surface and snip off their heads with pliers. Bring the two pieces of wood together in the correct joint position, and the heads of the pins will mark where the holes are to be bored in the second piece of timber. Remove the pins with pincers before drilling.

Where you are joining two horizontal rails to an upright at a corner, you should stagger the holes, otherwise the dowels will clash inside the upright.

Cutting holes
Holes for the dowels can be made either with a hand drill or an electric drill. In each case, obviously, the bit used must match the diameter of the dowel. The main difficulty is that you must ensure the bit is truly at right angles to the timber you are drilling, or a dowel that protrudes from one hole will not fit snugly into the hole in the matching timber.

You can use an electric drill held in a drill stand to guarantee that the bit is truly at right angles to the timber. Or where the timber is too large for this you can use a dowelling jig to ensure accuracy. Where you are cutting a through dowel joint, you can avoid this problem by cramping both pieces of wood together in a vice and boring through both.

For stopped joints, the hole you bore should be slightly deeper than the depth to which the dowel penetrates, to leave a small reservoir for any excess glue that is not squeezed out along the groove. A depth gauge ensures this. Various types for both hand and electric drills are available but you can improvise by making your own. Either stick a bit of tape on the bit's shank, carefully positioned so that the distance between its lower edge and the end of the drill exactly equals the depth of the hole required. Or you can take a length of timber – 25mm (1in) or 38mm (1½in) square according to the diameter of the dowel – and bore a hole right through its length. Cut this timber to length so that when it is slipped onto the bit's shank, the part of the bit left protruding will cut a hole of the right depth. In both cases you should take your measurement to the cutting end of the drill only – not to any threaded or shaped lead-in point.

For a stopped dowel joint, drill holes so the dowels will penetrate each piece of timber by between one-half and two-thirds of the timber's thickness.

Fixing and finishing dowels
Always check first that the joint is a good fit and is accurately square before applying PVA adhesive. You can then squirt adhesive into the holes, but since you risk applying too much this way, it is better to brush the

DRILLING HOLES

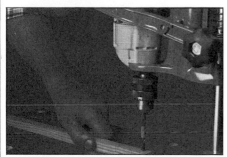

1 To ensure that holes will be in exactly opposite positions on a through joint, drill both pieces of wood at the same time.

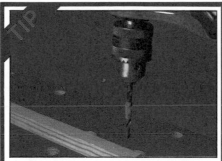

2 The depths you have to go to for a dowel joint can be marked on the bit with a piece of tape, allowing a little extra at both ends for glue.

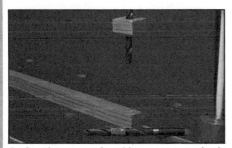

3 Another way of making sure you don't go too deep is by making a depth gauge from a scrap of timber. Or you can buy a proprietary gauge.

4 A dowelling jig has holes for different sized bits. When you cramp it over the wood use spare timber to prevent the screw marking the wood.

adhesive onto the dowel before tapping it into place with a mallet — you can use a hammer but you should protect the dowel with a block of wood. You should also apply adhesive to the meeting faces of the timber.

The glued joints should be cramped until the adhesive has set.

With through joints and halving joints, you now saw off the bulk of the protruding dowel

and use a block plane to trim the end flush. You can use an ordinary plane for this, but it must be set for a very fine cut. Smooth off any remaining roughness with glasspaper.

If using dowel pellets, hit them into place over the countersunk screws (with the ones you've cut yourself make sure the grain follows that of the wood). Plane off excess after the adhesive has dried.

MAKING THE JOINT

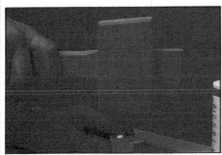

1 First check that the dowel fits snugly, but not too tightly. Then apply adhesive and gently tap it into place with a mallet.

2 After cramping to allow the adhesive to set, finish off a through joint by planing away the excess along the side of the wood.

Ready Reference

RULES FOR DRILLING HOLES
● make them the same diameter as the dowels
● they should be a little deeper than the dowel's length
● slightly countersink these where the pieces of wood meet

TIP: DOWELLING JIG
With a drill use a dowelling jig so the holes will be straight and square.

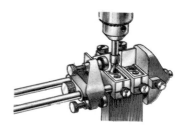

WHAT CAN GO WRONG?
The most common problems are:
● the dowels being too tight. Forcing the joint together causes the wood to split – so always check the fit first
● the joint being forced out of alignment because the holes were drilled out of line with one another – always check the alignment before finally applying the adhesive

MITRED DOWEL JOINTS
● use a mitre box for accuracy
● place mitred pieces together in a cramp and mark them at the same time
● the dowel at the outer corner should be shorter than the one at the inner corner

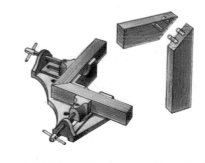

Dowelling jig: Buck & Ryan   Jem Grischotti

Block plane: Stanley Tools   Jem Grischotti

STOPPED HOUSING WITH SHOULDER

1 *After marking out the housing on the upright (except on the front edge), mark where it stops, about 19-25mm (3/4-1in) inside the front edge.*

2 *With the marking gauge still at the same setting, mark the shoulder depth across the shelf end and a little way down each of its faces.*

3 *Set the gauge to 1/3 the thickness of the upright, and mark the housing depth on its back edge only. Bring the side marks down to meet it.*

4 *Use the same setting to mark the shoulder width on the front edge and both faces of the shelf, meeting the marks you've made for the depth.*

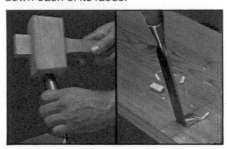

5 *Roughly chisel out the first 25mm (1in) or so of the stopped end of the housing – across the grain and up to the sides, then back towards the end.*

6 *Cut the sides of the housing with a tenon saw. You'll need to use short careful strokes so as not to bang against its inner end.*

7 *Clear out the housing with a mallet and chisel, inching forwards at an angle if the chisel won't reach all the way in when held flat.*

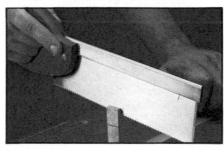

8 *Saw down into the front edge of the shelf until you reach the marked depth of the shoulder, being careful not to overshoot.*

9 *Chisel into the endgrain to remove the waste and complete the shoulder; or you can use a saw – but again, don't cut too deep.*

blade is narrower than the housing you're cutting out, you'll need to make several parallel, overlapping cuts.

Putting it together
When you assemble the joint before glueing, to see if it fits, you may think that it's too tight and you need to pare away wood from the housing or the shelf.

But be sure not to overdo this – and be careful where you remove it from. A shaving off the wrong place can allow the end of the shelf to rise or fall so that it's no longer level.

If, on the other hand, the joint turns out to be very loose, you'll need thin slivers of wood or veneer to pack it out.

For maximum tightness, strength and squareness, a housing joint should really be glued, then cramped together while the adhesive sets. Where a shelf or shelves fit between a pair of uprights, as usually happens, your best plan is to glue and cramp the whole structure up at once, so as to get it all square in one go. Use sash cramps (long bars of steel with two adjustable jaws) and simply place the structure between them, with the shelf running along their length, and blocks of scrap wood positioned on the outside of the uprights to protect them from the pressure of the jaws. You'll probably have to borrow or hire the sash-cramps. When using them, you need to

check the structure constantly for squareness, as cramping, unless done correctly, can cause distortion.

You can always reinforce a housing joint by nailing through the outside of the upright and into the endgrain of the shelf, concealing the heads by punching them in and plugging the holes with wood filler.

On the whole, screws are best avoided, since they grip badly in endgrain; but for a chipboard shelf you can use special chipboard screws – or ordinary wood screws each driven into a special plastic plug, or 'bush', which is pressed into a pre-drilled hole in the end of the shelf. You can disguise screwheads with plastic covers.

BAREFACED HOUSING JOINT

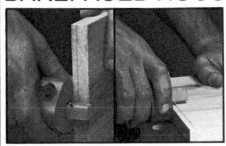

1 At ⅓ the shelf thickness, mark the rebate depth along its end and across its edges; likewise mark across the upright's edges and inner face.

3 Saw out the rebate depth across the shelf with a tenon saw, using careful strokes to keep it the right side of the line.

5 Measure the full shelf thickness and set your marking gauge to that measurement by holding it against the rule.

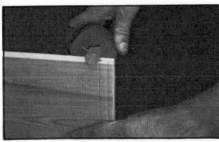

7 Mark the depth of the housing on the back edge of the upright, only ⅓ of the way across: any further and you'll weaken the joint.

2 At ⅓ the upright thickness (very likely the same as the shelf thickness), mark your rebate width across the top face and both edges of the shelf.

4 Chisel out the rebate width along the endgrain. You'll get a more accurate result if you do it in several goes rather than all at once.

6 Pressing the gauge against the end of the upright, mark across its face and edges where the bottom of the shelf will be positioned.

8 Cut the housing just like the basic one, taking care not to break off the end. After glueing, nail through into the tongue for extra rigidity.

Ready Reference

TIPS FOR BETTER HOUSINGS
● a cramped-on batten is useful as a saw guide
● a third saw-cut down the centre of a wide housing will help the removal of waste

● for short housings in narrow wood, set the piece on edge and chisel vertically for greater accuracy

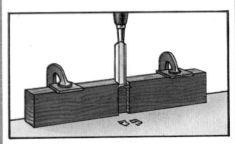

● use a rule or try-square to check that the housing has a level bottom

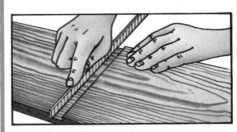

● for pairs of uprights, use the housings in the first to mark out those in the second; this will ensure a level shelf

● a chipboard shelf can be secured with chipboard screws driven into special plastic plugs.

Jem Grischotti

HANGING A DOOR

1 To check the height, wedge the door against the hinge side of the frame using an offcut that gives the correct clearance at the bottom.

2 Mark the area that has to be removed using a try-square for accuracy, then saw off. On a panel door, take equal amounts from top and bottom.

3 To check the width, offer the door to the frame against the hinge side and wedge with offcuts that give the correct clearance top and bottom.

4 Hold the door steady when planing: saw and chisel a housing in scrap wood and press in a wedge.

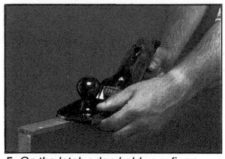

5 On the latch edge hold your finger under the side of the plane to prevent it rocking. On top and bottom, plane inwards so end grain doesn't splinter.

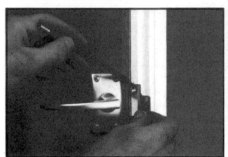

6 When the door hangs properly, put in the handle. Rub the tongue with chalk, then open and shut it till the frame is marked with keep plate's position.

Jem Grischotti

Plane: Stanley Tools

Altering dimensions

Enlarging a door, by adding a strip of wood, carries the risk both that it will be too obvious and that it will eventually fall off. But the job can be tackled fairly easily if you first plane the edge of the door straight – keeping your finger at the side of the plane will prevent it falling off the narrow surface. Next, cut your strip to length and plane it to the exact extra size you require – making sure it's a little proud of the door thickness on both sides. Glue and nail it on, and lastly plane it flush with the door face so that when painted it makes an inconspicuous join.

More commonly, however, you'll have to make your door smaller. To take off large amounts you'll need a ripsaw or a powered circular saw; guide it along a batten firmly cramped to the door. After sawing, plane the edge smooth.

Alterations like this are relatively easy on panel doors – but remember to saw similar amounts off both opposite edges to avoid lopsidedness, and be careful not to destroy the joints. A flush door, unless the core is solid, is a very different proposition. A cellular core (made of wood strips laminated together or a honeycomb of kraft paper), a narrow timber frame, and the hardboard or plywood faces are all there to

make the door lightweight. And you risk mutilating any or all of them if you try to alter the width (the height's all right, for you can make a new piece to glue and nail in at the top or bottom if you need to).

So, if you need to take off more than a little, buy a panel door. If you must have a flush door and you can't get one that fits or is about 10mm (⅜in) larger, buy one slightly undersize and add lippings all round to make up the extra height and width.

A fitting finish

Once the door fits the frame you can add the hinges. If you're re-using the existing hinge recesses in the frame, support the door in the opening parallel to the upright and mark on it where their tops and bottoms are. If you're cutting new ones, mark their positions on both door and frame.

Remove the door and, using a try-square and marking-gauge, mark out all new recesses – a hinge should fit flush with both the door edge and the edge of the frame. Carefully chisel out the recess and screw one side of the hinges to the door, checking that they lie neatly in place.

The standard steel or brass butt hinges you need can be bought anywhere. Another option is self-closing 'rising butts' which will

carry the door clear of the floorcovering as it opens, and enable it to be lifted off if necessary without unscrewing them – good if you're redecorating. If the door's not going to have a lot of weight put on it (eg, on a cupboard) light and shorter hinges are best. Choose those that can be surface-mounted and you won't have to chisel out recesses.

Support the door in position again, and fix the hinges to the frame with one screw each. See whether the door swings and closes properly; if not, you can take it off again and make various adjustments to the way the hinges sit in the frame.

The final step is to fill any defects, to sand the door down, and to paint or varnish it. On an external door in particular, make sure you include the top and bottom edges in your treatment (the bottom will have to be dealt with before the door is hung) so that damp cannot penetrate and swell or rot the door.

Hinges should not be painted as this can interfere with the pivot action – and the constant friction of the door will cause the paint to chip anyway. If made of ferrous metal, they can rust, so they should either be primed with a metal or rust-inhibitor primer or coated with a clear lacquer. A non-ferrous metal like brass won't rust but it can tarnish, so clear lacquer is a good idea in this case.

PUTTING ON THE HINGES

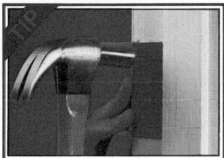

1 *If old hinge positions are unusable fill in with 3mm (¹/₈in) hardboard or ply. Nail in place, fill with wood filler.*

2 *Mark up the new hinge positions on the frame using a combination square to get the width measurement right.*

3 *Make the first shallow cut with the chisel bevel down. Turn it bevel up to smooth the recess.*

4 *Wedge the cut-to-fit door in the frame with correct clearance at side, top and bottom. Mark hinge positions.*

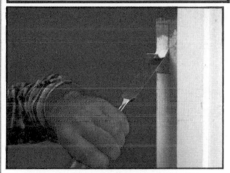

5 *With the door held in the block cramp, use a marking gauge, then a try-square to mark recesses.*

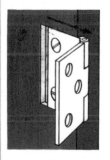
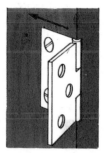

6 *Use a 25mm (1in) chisel to make the recess (the hinge must lie flush). Drill holes, screw hinges to door.*

7 *Wedge door so the hinges fit the recesses in the frame. Mark, then drill the central holes only.*

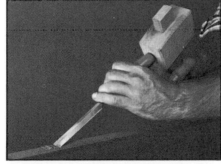

8 *Put screws in central holes, then check that the door closes properly. Adjust if necessary, add other screws.*

Ready Reference

TIPS: REMOVING OLD SCREWS
● use a screwdriver that fits the slot exactly (scrape out any paint first)
● if the slot is damaged make a new one with a hacksaw at right-angles to the old
● if the screw won't budge put the screwdriver in the slot and tap it with a hammer or mallet; or heat the screw with a blow-torch, then leave to cool and contract before trying to remove
● the last resort is to drill out the screw using a power drill.

PROBLEM CHECKLIST
If the door swings open or closed by itself the hinges are not taking the weight equally. To do this they must be vertically above each other, so you'll have to move one of them either backwards or forwards across the frame.

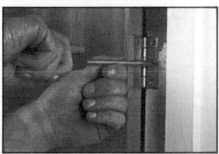

If the door sticks at the lock edge you can either deepen the hinge recesses in the frame or shave a little off the lock edge.

If the door springs open when you shut it the hinge recesses are too deep. Pack the back of the hinge with a piece of cardboard cut to the shape of the recess.

If the bottom of the door isn't parallel with the floor glue and pin on a wedge-shaped lipping. When planed flush and painted it should not be seen.

Remember to make all the adjustments while each hinge is held only by its central screw. Only when the door fits well should you drive in the rest.

Jem Grischotti

FITTING FRONT DOOR FURNITURE

A door looks naked without the right fittings. These make it attractive, and help it do its job. Installing them requires few special skills – just some careful planning and accurate workmanship.

When you buy a door, it comes without 'furniture' – as tradesmen call handles, letter plates, street numbers, knockers and the rest. You'll have to obtain and fit these yourself; there is an immense variety of styles available.

But the most important items, though they don't strictly come under the same heading, are of course locks and latches. First of all, let's run over the most important difference between the two. A latch has a bolt which is kept closed – ie, protruding – by a spring. It's opened by turning a handle, but closes again the instant this is released. A lock, on the other hand, has no spring, and is both opened and closed by a key or handle, or both.

A mortise lock (or latch) is so called because it fits into a deep mortise which you cut in the edge of the door. This far-from-impossible task is the most demanding you're likely to face when fitting out a door: if you can tackle it successfully, you should certainly be equal to the others.

It involves carefully marking the position of the mortise, drilling out the bulk of the waste to the right depth, cleaning up the hole with chisels, and chiselling a larger shallow recess to take the 'forend' of the lock or latch (plus the faceplate which is screwed over it).

You'll also need to cut a hole for the handle spindle, or for the key – drilling in either case, and elongating the keyhole with a padsaw. In the case of a 'sashlock', which combines a lock with a latch, you'll need both these holes.

Moreover, some types of mortise lock have a cylinder mechanism (round, oval or 'dual-profile' – pear-shaped) which passes through the door, so you need a hole for that instead of a keyhole. An ordinary round cylinder needs a sizeable hole, which – like a mortise – will require a bit and brace, or a spade bit in a power drill. Pear-shaped and oval holes can also be made with twist bits; enlarge them with a padsaw or chisel.

The body of a rim lock (or latch), on the other hand, is screwed to the inside of the door. It doesn't require a separate hole for a key or handle. But all except the cheapest rim locks have a cylinder mechanism, which again needs a hole through the door face.

Choosing and fitting locks and latches

For internal doors, a mortise latch – or even just a catch – is usually enough, and it's unobtrusive. An external door needs a latch, too, so you can open it from inside without a key. But, of course, it also needs at least one lock.

In many homes, it carries a cylinder lock called a 'nightlatch', which is halfway to being a latch. A rim nightlatch (the usual type) opens from inside with an integral handle as well as from outside with a key.

Though sprung, it can be retained in the open or closed position with a locking knob on the inside called a snib. However, a nightlatch isn't secure unless it's a 'deadlatch': that is, unless the bolt can be 'deadlocked' immovably in the closed position from outside. This is either done with a key – a procedure usually known as double-locking – or else happens automatically as you close the door. Often the handle can be deadlocked too.

A nightlatch, therefore, should be accompanied by a good mortise lock – preferably a five-lever model.

All locks and latches also have a part which goes on the door jamb – see *Ready Reference*. In the case of mortise fittings, it's a 'striking plate' (usually flat, with a rectangular hole in the centre) which is screwed into a recess cut to fit. More secure types have a sort of box on the plate, which is mortised into the timber of the door frame. Rim fittings have a 'staple' or 'keep', which again incorporates a box for the tongue, and is usually partly recessed. In both cases, you fit these components after the main lock – closing the door and using the lock itself to mark the right position on the jamb with the aid of a square.

Apart from security and convenience, there's one thing to bear in mind when choosing locks and latches: the construction of the door they are fitted to. A panel door should present no problem unless its stiles (uprights) are exceptionally narrow, in which case you need a special narrow-stile lock or latch. It's wise, too, not to cut mortises in or near timber joints.

A flush door, unless it's solid throughout, will have at least one solid 'lock block' in its largely hollow core – the position or positions of which should be indicated on the door itself. For a secure fixing, it's important that the lock or latch should be sited there and nowhere else.

Fitting a letterplate

Apart from locks and latches, the only item of door furniture whose installation could remotely be described as complicated is a letterplate.

This consists of a metal surround with a hinged and sometimes sprung flap to cover the hole, plus maybe a knocker and/or a handle. Its siting demands some thought.

On a flush door, it too will have to be placed over a special block. A panel door usually affords more choice – but, if there's no rail (cross-member) at a height which is suitable from the point of view of looks and the postman's comfort, you may have to position it vertically.

If the rear of the plate lies flat against the door and the flap opens outwards, your best plan is to position the plate accurately, lift the flap and draw round the inside to give the outline of your intended hole. Otherwise, you'll have to rely on careful measurement to determine the hole's size and position.

If you have a jigsaw with a blade long enough to pass through the door, cutting the hole is straightforward. If not, you'll probably have to resort to a wide, robust chisel and mallet, perhaps after drilling a series of holes closely spaced round the edge. A padsaw is an alternative, but cutting the hole with it will be a long, hard job.

Finish the inside of the hole (and any mortises) in the same way as the rest of the door to stop moisture from penetrating.

The actual fixing of the plate will be via bolts or machine screws which pass through holes drilled right through the door. If these are overlong, shorten them with a junior hacksaw.

A useful accessory for the inside of the door is a letterbox to catch your post – thus protecting it from children, pets and feet, and saving you from stooping.

Other items

Handles are fitted (and usually sold) separately from the mortise latches which they operate, and almost always in pairs. They're simply screwed to the door face in the same way as the escutcheon plates which cover keyholes. A square-sectioned steel spindle, cut to length if necessary with a hacksaw, passes through the door between handles.

For a sashlock, you can use the type of handle which incorporates a keyhole as well.

A common adjunct, especially for internal doors, is a finger-plate – often decorative – which prevents dirty finger-marks on the door itself. It too is screwed on. Knockers and house numbers are bolted, screwed, nailed, self-adhesive or secured by spikes protruding from the back.

A door viewer – the wide-angle lens which enables you to eye callers without their seeing you – comes in two halves, which are simply screwed together through a single pre-drilled hole.

For doors by which you don't leave the house, such as most back doors, bolts are an extra security measure. The mortise bolt, a simple type of mortise lock usually operated by a serrated key, is better than the traditional 'barrel' or 'tower' bolt, which can be more easily forced open.

FITTING A CYLINDER RIM LOCK

1 Drill a hole for the cylinder after marking its position from the lock's mounting plate, or with a template if one is supplied by the manufacturer.

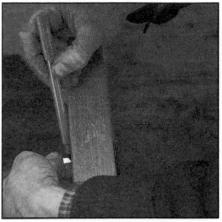

2 Fit the cylinder and 'rose' through the hole, and mark where to cut off the connecting bar (including any extra length required). Cut with a hacksaw.

3 Screw on the mounting plate, after marking the screw positions (from the fitting or template) and making pilot holes with a drill or bradawl.

4 Insert the cylinder and rose through the hole again, and make sure the connecting bar engages in the slotted pivot in the mounting plate.

5 Insert the connecting screws through the mounting plate and into the threaded lugs in the back of the cylinder, and tighten them to hold it in place.

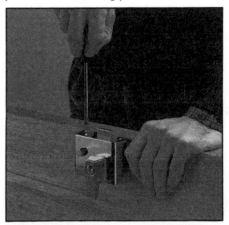

6 Screw the main body of the lock to the mounting plate via the screws in the case. Fit the keep to the door jamb.

FITTING A LEVER MORTISE LOCK

1 *Decide the height at which you want the lock to go, place it on its side on the door edge, get it square, and mark the height of the casing.*

2 *Set a mortise gauge to the thickness of the casing, centre it on the door edge, and score along. Alternatively, use an ordinary marking gauge.*

3 *Choose a spade or auger bit that matches the thickness of the casing, and use tape to mark on it the lock's depth from the front of the faceplate.*

5 *Using chisels, turn the row of holes into a clean, oblong mortise. Insert the lock to test the fit, and shave the mortise further if necessary.*

6 *Insert the lock casing fully into the mortise (being careful that it doesn't jam) and mark all round the fore-end with a sharp pencil.*

7 *To chisel the recess for the fore-end and faceplate, first make a series of cuts across the grain. Work very carefully while doing this.*

9 *Position the faceplate and fore-end back to front, to check whether your recess is the right depth. Chisel it a little deeper if necessary.*

10 *Position the lock accurately against the face of the door, and mark through the keyhole (plus the spindle hole, if there is one) with a bradawl.*

11 *Drill the hole (or holes) right through the door, and enlarge the keyhole with a padsaw. Fit an escutcheon plate (keyhole plate) over it.*

4 *Drill a row of holes to depth, being sure to stay exactly between your height and thickness marks. At all costs, you must keep the drill vertical.*

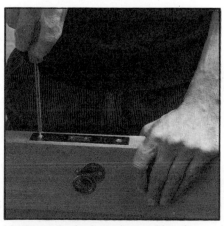

8 *Chisel vertically along the sides of the recess (gently, so as not to split the timber) and then remove the waste with the chisel bevel-upwards.*

12 *Insert the lock again, position the faceplate and drive in the screws. Sometimes the lock and faceplate each have a separate pair of screws.*

LETTERPLATES

1 *Measure the size of the cutout you'll need to make in the door. It may have to be off-centre – for example, if it must include room for the flap mechanism.*

2 *Mark your measured rectangle on the door, drill a hole inside the line, and cut it out – using a jigsaw for speed if you have a long enough blade.*

3 *Finish the hole neatly, and cut out recesses for the threaded lugs if necessary. Then drill holes for the bolts, fit the plate and tighten the nuts.*

Ready Reference

DOOR JAMB FIXINGS

For a **mortise** fitting: extend the bolt (if any), push the door to, and mark where each tongue comes on the frame (A). Then square the marks across to the doorstop, position the striking plate, mark round it, and chisel a shallow recess plus one or two mortises (B). Screw the plate on.

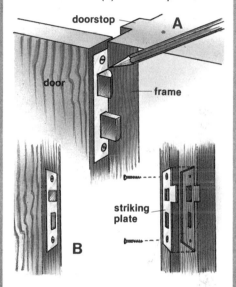

For a **rim** fitting: mark the frame opposite the edges of the case (C). Position the keep, mark round it, chisel a recess and screw it on (D).

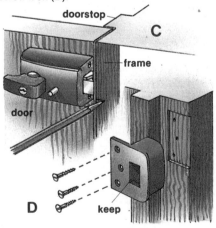

TIP: BEWARE 'HANDING'

Latches (and some handles) only fit one way round. Before buying, know which 'hand' you want. A door that's hinged on your **left** and opens towards you ('anti-clockwise closing') takes a **left-hand** latch with a **left-hand** handle on your side, and a right-hand latch and handle on the other.

SHELVING: THE BASICS

There are lots of ways of putting up shelves. Some systems are fixed, others adjustable – the choice is yours. Here's how both types work, and how to get the best from each.

Deciding how much shelving you'll need is always tricky – because, the more shelves you have, the more you'll find to go on them! So it's always wise to add an extra 10 per cent to the specification when you start planning.

Think carefully about what you want to store and display, and try to categorise it by size and weight. The size part is fairly easy. Concentrate first on the depth (from front to back) and length; a collection of paperback books, for instance, might need 3.5m (10ft) of 150mm (6in) deep shelves. Having the shelves a bit deeper than you really need is always worthwhile, and if you add 10 per cent the length should look after itself.

Next, the heights in each grouping will tell you roughly how far apart the shelves must be. Most paperbacks are 175mm (7in) high – allow an extra 25mm (1in) for easy access and removal.

Finally, weight. The trouble here is that, even if you weigh what you'll be storing, you can't translate the result into shelf, bracket and fixing materials or sizes. Instead, think in terms of light, moderately heavy and very heavy. Items such as the TV and stereo, while not especially weighty, are best treated as very heavy, because it would be nothing short of disastrous if a shelf did give way under them!

Shelf design

Where you put the shelves affects the amount of storage you can gain, how you build them, and the overall look of the room itself. This last may not be important in a workshop, for instance, but in a living room, where the shelves may well be the focal point, a bad decision can be serious.

The obvious spot for shelving is against a continuous wall. This offers most scope to arrange the shelves in an interesting and attractive way. An alcove is another possibility. Shelving here is neat, and easily erected; it is a very good way of using an otherwise awkward bit of space. A corner has similar advantages if you make triangular shelves to fit – though they're really only suitable for displaying plants or favourite ornaments.

Planning it out

If appearance matters and you're putting up a lot of shelves, a good way to plan is by making a scale drawing of the whole scheme to see how it looks. Then check for detail. If your TV has an indoor aerial, make sure you have room to adjust it. With stereo systems, ensure the shelf is deep enough to take all the wiring spaghetti at the back. And do think about the heights of the shelves from the floor (see *Ready Reference*).

Finally, make sure you provide adequate support for the shelves and the weight they'll be carrying. There is no very precise method of gauging this, but you won't go wrong if you remember that for most household storage a shelf needs support at least every 750mm (30in) along its length. This will usually be enough even with chipboard, which is the weakest of shelving materials. But bowing may still be a problem, so for items in the 'very heavy' category it's advisable to increase the number of supports by reducing the space between them.

Which material?

Chipboard is usually the most economical material, and if properly supported is strong enough for most shelving It can be fairly attractive, too, since you can choose a type with a decorative wood veneer or plastic finish. These come in a variety of widths – most of them designed with shelving in mind.

Natural timber, though more costly and sometimes prone to warping, is an obvious alternative. You may have difficulty obtaining some timber in boards over 225mm (9in) wide, but narrower widths are readily available. For wider shelves, another way is to make up the shelf width from narrower pieces. An easy method is to leave gaps between the lengths and brace them with others which run from front to back on the underside, forming a slatted shelf.

Blockboard and plywood are also worth considering when it comes to building shelving. They are both a lot stronger than chipboard and have a more attractive surface which can be painted or varnished without trouble. However, in the thickness you need at least 12mm (½in) – plywood is relatively expensive; blockboard is cheaper, and chipboard cheaper still. All these man-made boards need to have their edges disguised to give a clean finish. An easy yet effective way to do this is just to glue and pin on strips of timber moulding or 'beading'. Also remember that the cheapest way to buy any of these boards is in large sheets (approximately 2.4m x 1.2m/8ft x 4ft), so it's most economical to plan your shelves in lengths and widths than can be cut from a standard size sheet.

Shelves needn't be solid, though. If you want them extra-thick, for appearance or strength, you can make them up from a timber frame covered with a thin sheet material. Hardboard is cheap, but thin plywood gives a more attractive edge; alternatively use a timber edging strip.

BRACKET SHELVING

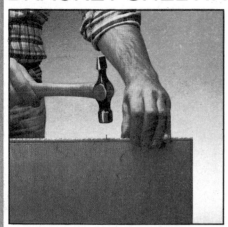

1 *If your shelves are of man-made board, a good way to give them neat edges is to pin on decorative 'beading', mitred at the corners.*

2 *Begin by screwing the shorter arm of the bracket to the shelf. Position it squarely and in such a way that the shelf will lie snugly against the wall.*

3 *Using a spirit level as a guide, mark a pencil line along the wall at the height where you want the top of the shelf to be positioned.*

4 *Hold the shelf, complete with brackets, against this line, and mark with a pencil through the screw holes in the brackets, so you know where to drill.*

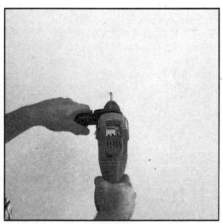

5 *Drill holes in the wall with a power drill, using a masonry bit if necessary, and being sure to keep the drill straight. Then insert plastic plugs.*

6 *Hold the shelf in position, insert one screw in each bracket and tighten it halfway; then insert the others and tighten the whole lot up.*

Ready Reference

PLANNING SHELVES

When you design storage, plan ahead and think about *how* you're going to use it.

Height. Keep everyday items well within reach. That means between 750 and 1500mm (30 and 60in) off the ground.
Depth. Shelves that are deepest (from front to back) should be lower, so you can see and reach to the back.
Spacing. An inch or two over the actual height of the objects means you can get your hand in more easily.

HOW TO SPACE BRACKETS

Space brackets according to the shelf thickness. Heavy loads (left) need closer brackets than light loads (right).

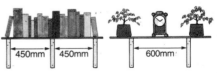

450mm   450mm   600mm

12mm (½in) chipboard

600mm   750mm

12mm (½in) plywood
19mm (¾in) chipboard

750mm   900mm

19mm (¾in) plywood

ADJUSTABLE SHELVING

1 Metal uprights come in a range of sizes, but occasionally they may need shortening. If so, you can easily cut them down with a hacksaw.

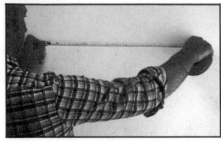

2 After using your level to mark the height for the tops of the uprights, measure along it and mark out the spacings between them.

3 Hold each of the uprights with its top at the right height, and mark through it onto the wall for the position of the uppermost screw hole only.

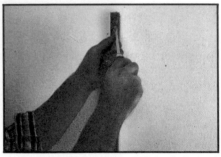

4 Remove the upright, drill the hole and plug it if necessary. Then replace the upright, and fit the screw – but don't tighten it completely.

5 With the upright loose, hold a level against it and adjust it till it's vertical. Then mark through it for the other screw positions.

6 Hold the upright aside and drill the other holes. Plug them, insert the screws and tighten them all up – not forgetting the topmost one.

7 Now you can screw the bracket to the shelf, aligning it correctly and taking particular care over how it lines up at the back edge.

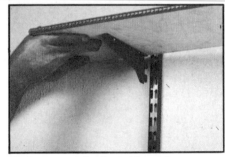

8 One type of adjustable system uses brackets with lugs at the back. It's easiest to let these lugs project behind the shelf when screwing on brackets.

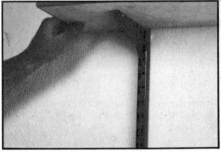

9 The lugs simply hook into the slots in the uprights. Changing the shelf height is just a matter of unhooking them and moving them up or down.

10 If you want the back edge of the shelf right against the wall, notch it with a tenon saw and chisel to fit round the upright. Inset the bracket on the shelf.

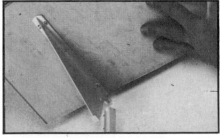

11 The channel system is different. First of all, you engage the bracket's upper lug in the channel and slide it down, keeping the lower one clear.

12 When you reach the position you want, level the shelf and the bracket, so as to slide its lower lug into one of the pairs of slots down the upright.

Fixing shelves

The simplest method of fixing shelves is directly to the wall, using brackets. L-shaped metal brackets of various sizes and designs are available everywhere – some plain and functional, some with attractive lacquered or enamelled finishes. It's just a question of choosing ones about 25mm (1in) less than the shelf depth, spacing them the right distance apart and screwing them to both shelf and wall.

If you're filling up your shelves with books, the support brackets won't be seen. But if you're using the shelves for ornaments, the brackets will be visible, so choose a style that blends. Alternatively, you can make up your own brackets from two pieces of timber butt-jointed into an L shape and braced with a diagonal strut or triangular block.

The fixing technique is the same either way. First you draw a line on the wall where the shelf is to go, using a spirit level. Next, fix the brackets to the shelf and put the whole assembly up against the line. Mark on to the wall through the pre-drilled screw holes in the brackets; then take the shelf away and drill holes in the wall, filling each with a plastic plug. Lastly, drive in one screw through each bracket; then insert the rest and tighten them all up.

Because the accuracy of this method relies largely on your ability to hold the shelf level against your line, you may find it easier to work the other way round. By fixing the brackets to the wall along the guide line, you can then drop the shelf into place and screw up into it through the brackets. This works, but you must position the brackets with great care, and avoid squeezing them out of position as you screw them into the wall. That isn't always easy. For one thing, many brackets don't have arms which meet at a neat right angle. They curve slightly, which makes it hard to align the top of the shelf-bearing arm with the line on the wall.

Making a firm fixing

Remember that the strength of all brackets depends partly on the length of their arms (particularly the one fixed to the wall) and partly on the strength of your fixing into the wall. The longer the wall arm in proportion to the shelf arm, the better; but it's also important to use adequate screws – 38mm (1½in) No 8s or 10s should do – and to plug the wall properly. In a hollow partition wall you really must make sure you secure the brackets to the wall's wooden framework and not just to the cladding. Even if you use plasterboard plugs or similar devices, a lot of weight on the shelf will cause the brackets to come away from the cladding and possibly damage the wall.

Of course, there is a limit to how much weight the brackets themselves will take.

Under very wide shelves they may bend. With shelves that have heavy items regularly taken off and dumped back on, and shelves used as desk-tops, worktops and the like, the movement can eventually work the fixings loose. In such cases it's best to opt for what's called a cantilevered shelf bracket. Part of this is set into the masonry to give a very strong fixing indeed. Details of its installation vary from brand to brand, but you should get instructions when you buy.

Alcove shelving

All proprietary brackets are expensive. However, for alcove shelving there's a much cheaper alternative, and that is to use battens screwed to the wall. All you do is fix a 50 x 25mm (2 x 1in) piece of softwood along the back of the alcove, using screws driven into plastic plugs at roughly 450mm (18in) centres. Then screw similar ones to the side walls, making sure that they line up with the first. In both cases, getting the battens absolutely level is vital. In fact, it's best to start by drawing guidelines using a spirit level as a straight edge.

A front 'rail' is advisable where the shelf spans a wide alcove and has to carry a lot of weight. But there's a limit to what you can do. With a 50 x 25mm (2 x 1in) front rail and battens, all on edge, 1.5m (5ft) is the safe maximum width.

A front rail has another advantage because, as well as giving man-made boards a respectably thick and natural look, it also hides the ends of the side battens. So does stopping them short of the shelf's front edge and cutting the ends at an angle.

The shelf can be screwed or even just nailed to the battens to complete the job.

Movable shelves

Unfortunately, both brackets and battens have one big drawback: once they're fixed, they're permanent. So you might consider an adjustable shelving system which gives you the chance to move shelves up and down. Such systems consist of uprights, screwed to the wall, and brackets which slot into them at almost any point down the length.

There are two main types. In one, brackets locate in vertical slots in the uprights. The other has a continuous channel down each upright. You can slide brackets along it and lock them at any point along the way, where they stay put largely because of the weight of the shelf. With both types, brackets come in standard sizes suitable for shelf widths, and there's a choice of upright lengths to fulfil most needs.

Many proprietary shelving systems of this sort include a number of accessories to make them more versatile. These include book ends, shelf clips and even light fittings.

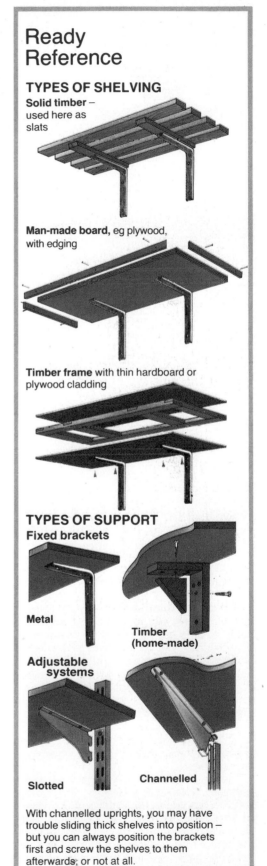

Ready Reference

TYPES OF SHELVING

Solid timber – used here as slats

Man-made board, eg plywood, with edging

Timber frame with thin hardboard or plywood cladding

TYPES OF SUPPORT

Fixed brackets

Metal

Timber (home-made)

Adjustable systems

Slotted

Channelled

With channelled uprights, you may have trouble sliding thick shelves into position – but you can always position the brackets first and screw the shelves to them afterwards; or not at all.

PANELLING WALLS WITH TIMBER

Natural timber panelling can transform your walls like no other material, bringing warmth and atmosphere to even the least promising room. Yet the technique of installing it is easily mastered.

Cladding interior walls with natural timber is an age-old decorative technique. Nowadays, it's most popular in the form of narrow boards.

They look extremely attractive and have other advantages too. Panelling is a perfect cover-up for plaster in poor condition, and for lumpy walls often found in older houses. Moreover, it has excellent insulation properties.

If you plan to panel one or more of your walls, go and see what the timber merchant has to offer. Cedar, ramin, mahogany and meranti are all possible woods for the purpose. But by far the most popular is 'knotty pine' — softwood of various species with knots that would be unacceptable in ordinary joinery work. It's available from almost all suppliers. The commonest size is 100 × 12mm (4 × ½in), in lengths up to 3m (about 10ft). Width and thickness, as usual, are nominal: since the timber is planed smooth, these dimensions will actually be smaller.

Most boards used for panelling have a protruding tongue along one edge, and a groove in the other, so that each piece fits into the next. Quite often both outer edges are chamfered, forming attractive V-shaped grooves when the boards are interlocked; hence the name 'TGV' — tongued, grooved and V-jointed.

Boards with concave faces are also obtainable as in 'shiplap', which has one edge rebated to overlap the thin edge of the next board. It's almost always used horizontally. Horizontal cladding creates the optical illusion that the wall is wider than it really is: vertical cladding makes it seem taller.

Battening the wall

All cladding is normally fitted onto 50 × 25mm (2 × 1in) rough sawn softwood battens, which are themselves nailed or screwed to the existing solid wall.

They're unnecessary if the wall is a hollow partition construction which is framed with vertical studs and horizontal noggins to which the cladding can be nailed. But be quite sure you're nailing through into the timber frame and not just into its covering, which is usually plasterboard and thus won't hold the nails well.

If cladding the inside of an external wall, you can keep out damp with a vapour barrier such as polythene sheeting. You simply place it under the battens before you fix them to the wall. Even if you don't include a vapour barrier, it's wise to treat the battens and the back of the cladding with wood preservative, in case condensation leads to rot. And the job also offers a unique opportunity to fight heat loss, for you can easily place insulating material between the wall and the cladding.

Buying the timber

If the shop prefers to supply panelling in assorted lengths, it will be cheaper to buy it that way, rather than in the exact dimensions you want; but many suppliers now sell TGV in pre-cut bundles, containing timber in lengths of 1800mm (just under 6ft), 2400mm (8ft) or 3000mm (10ft).

To work out how many lengths of vertical cladding you need, divide the wall width by the board width — remembering that the board's face will be only about 90mm (3½in) wide if it's nominally 100mm (4in).

For horizontal cladding, divide the wall height by the board width. For board length, just measure the wall — though on wide walls you may have to fit boards end-to-end.

Before buying boards always check them — especially knotty pine — for splits, loose knots, discolouration and twisting. Don't be afraid to reject bad ones.

Battens should run at right angles to cladding; in the case of diagonal panelling, either vertically or horizontally. They should be spaced about 600mm (24in) apart, except that the first and last in a row of vertical battens should be at either end of the wall. And you'll always need battens next to doors, windows and other fitments, and under any butt joints between the ends of boards.

Buy your cladding at least two weeks before use, and keep it inside the house. This is because your home will be warmer than the place the timber has been stored. The heat will reduce the amount of moisture in the wood, which will make it shrink. You should therefore give this time to happen *before* you fix the cladding in place; otherwise it will shrink afterwards. That may result in tongues coming out of grooves, which will leave unsightly gaps.

As soon as you get the cladding home, lay it flat on the floor (provided the floor is dry) in small piles, with boards face to face. Leave it for a fortnight, shuffling the boards around every few days. Don't attempt to dry them out artificially, as this will be sure to warp them.

FIXING THE BATTENS

For a professional finish, the wall battens to which the cladding boards are fixed should not follow any undulations in the surface. You can test whether your wall surface is uneven by holding a timber straight edge against it horizontally and vertically; you will then be able to see at a glance where lumps or hollows fall. The examples here are for vertical cladding; the hollows are exaggerated.

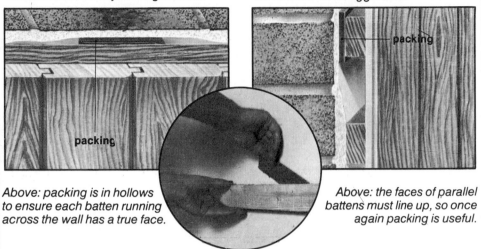

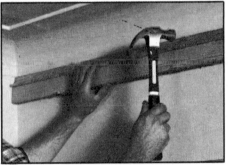

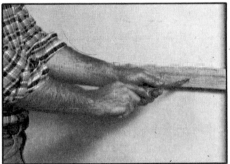

Above: packing is in hollows to ensure each batten running across the wall has a true face.

Above: the faces of parallel battens must line up, so once again packing is useful.

Inset: hardboard is an ideal packing material

1 *Fix battens with No 8 screws, 600mm (2ft) apart and 63mm (2½in) long – long enough to go through the plaster. Masonry nails are an alternative.*

2 *To form a neat link between the bottom of an existing cornice and the top edge of the cladding, use scotia moulding. Butt the cladding up to it.*

Fixing the cladding

If the wall is solid, use masonry nails, or screws in plastic plugs, to fix the battens. Take care not to drive them into cables or pipes; be especially careful round electrical fittings. The important thing is to get the battens at a constant level, both vertically and horizontally. Insert pieces of hardboard, plywood or scrap timber behind them where necessary. On a slightly concave wall, for example, you'll have to pack behind the centres of the battens to get them truly vertical, whereas on a convex wall you'll have to pack behind the top and bottom of each batten.

Then position a piece of cladding as the first in the row – usually against a side wall (against the ceiling for horizontal cladding). If the side wall isn't vertical, or is uneven, you'll have to scribe the board – see page 370 — and cut to the resulting pencil line.

Place the first board so the tongue is ready to fit into the next piece, and nail the board to the battens. Another method, which avoids your having to conceal the nail heads, is to fix this first board in position over the battens using a contact adhesive. This will hold it firmly in place straight away without nailing or cramping. (Note: no other adhesive will achieve this.)

You can nail the next board through its tongue, angling the nails inwards. The heads will be covered by the groove in the following board. Use this 'secret' nailing for all the other boards too, except the last. With cladding other than tongue-and-groove, such as shiplap, there is no tongue; so secret nailing means

see page 370

Ready Reference

FINISHING TOUCHES

Whatever area of cladding you have been fixing, you will need to finish off the edges where the cladding meets other walls, ceilings, skirting boards and openings.

INTERNAL CORNERS

Finish off with quadrant, triangular or scotia moulding, pinned into the angle.

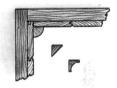

CEILINGS

Where there is an existing coving, stop the cladding just below it and fill the gap with scotia moulding (A). Otherwise take the cladding up to ceiling level and finish with quadrant or other beading (B).

EXTERNAL CORNERS

Where the cladding covers both walls, plane off the tongue for a neat overlap, and cover it if you wish with a decorative moulding (C). If only one wall is covered, finish off with a vertical strip of wood pinned to the ends of the horizontal battens (D).

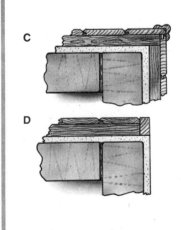

FIXING THE CLADDING

1 Hold the first board vertically against the side wall – or its skirting, if the cladding goes that far down. Lightly pin the board to the battens.

2 Scribe the board with a pencil pressed against a block of wood 50mm (2in) wide and run down the side wall. The mark follows the wall profile.

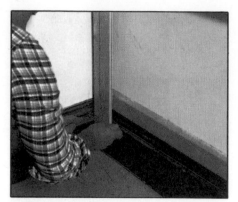

3 For a neat result, scribe around the shape of the skirting too. A second pencil can take the place of scrap timber as a guide for this.

6 Then fix the first board to the battens permanently by driving 25mm (1in) panel pins through its face. (On stud partitions you'll need 38mm/1½in pins.)

7 Before nailing each subsequent board, ensure a snug fit by tapping an offcut held against it. Check with a spirit level, and adjust it if necessary.

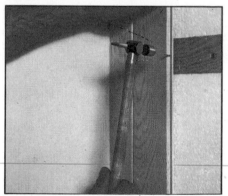

8 Nail at an angle through the board's tongue – but not too near the end, or you'll split the wood. The groove in the next board will cover the pin heads.

placing the nails where the rebated edge of the next board will cover their heads.

Repeat the fitting and nailing process right across the wall, checking that each board is still vertical (or horizontal). When you get to the end, it's unlikely that the last board will fit exactly, so you'll probably have to scribe it.

Even once you've cut it to shape, you may have trouble squeezing it in if you've already nailed all the other boards in position. There are two ways of dealing with this. One is to fit the last three or four boards at the same time, inserting the tongues in the grooves and then springing them into place, before nailing through their faces. The other is to plane or chisel off the back of the groove in the last board, and simply lay the board onto the battens – fixing it either with impact adhesive, or nails.

An external corner (eg, the end of a chimney breast) means planing off the tongue, at least from the last board. If the cladding continues round the corner, give the angle a neat finish by butting the grooved edge of the next board

at right angles against the tip of the last one, perhaps pinning a length of right angle or 'birdsmouth' (L-shaped) moulding neatly over the join. If the cladding ends there, your best bet is to nail a small rectangular-sectioned piece of planed timber (say 32 × 13mm/1¼ × ½in) to the ends of the battens so that it covers the edge of the last board as well. This method will also work at a door frame.

At an internal corner, just butt the boards together, or butt the last one against the next wall if the cladding ends there.

A quadrant, triangle or scotia moulding will give added neatness; you can use this along the junction with the ceiling too, or below a ceiling moulding.

Skirtings and other features
If the wall you're panelling has an existing skirting board, it's best left on and used as a batten, nailing the cladding to it. If it's thinner than the other battens, you'll need to pack it out first. So nail on a strip of timber, hardboard or thin ply-

wood, to bring it to the right thickness.

You can also use it as a recessed plinth. This will prevent the bottom of the cladding from being scuffed or damaged. Stop the cladding short of the floor, so that it ends some way up the skirting. Or fix the bottom of the cladding to a batten nailed immediately above the skirting, leaving the whole of the skirting exposed.

Alternatively, you can put new skirting over the cladding. With horizontal cladding, back the skirting with short lengths of board, nailed one to each batten, rather than wasting a whole board behind the skirting. Another form of skirting is a quadrant moulding (nailed to the cladding, not the floorboards, in case of timber movement).

If the old skirting is thicker than the battens you'll have to take it off carefully, or it will prevent you from nailing the cladding flat. If it's an obsolete pattern, removing it has the advantage that you can still match the room's other skirtings, because you can put it back on top of the cladding.

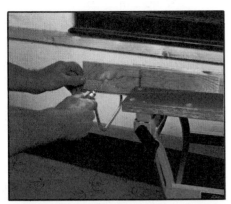

4 Take down the board and cut out the skirting profile with a coping saw or power jigsaw. Then cut along the rest of the board with a rip saw.

9 At a window, door or end wall, pin the last board to the second last and use an offcut of cladding to scribe it. Then remove it, cut it to shape and fit it.

5 To prevent heat loss through the wall, place polystyrene insulation board, of the same thickness as the battens, between them.

10 You'll need to cut short boards for some places, such as under a window. The bottom edge of the cladding can often be nailed to existing skirting.

Ready Reference

MORE FINISHING TOUCHES

Finishing off cladding neatly at a doorway, skirting boards and round electrical accessories can be tricky. Here are some solutions.

DOOR FRAMES

Fit cladding up to the door frame, then pin a vertical strip to the ends of the battens and add new door architrave moulding.

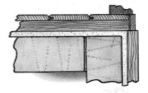

SKIRTING BOARD

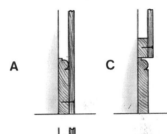

Pin the cladding directly to the skirting at floor level (A) or higher (B), or fix battens just above the skirting board (C).

ELECTRICAL FITTINGS

Pin battens round surface-mounted fittings (D) and cut the cladding to fit flush with the edges of the mounting box (D). The face plate may not be exactly flush with the cladding surface.

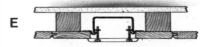

Remove flush fittings, and refix to the cladding with a new box and proprietary fixing lugs (E).

Like skirting, the architrave round doors and windows can either be removed or left. If you remove it, finish the cladding with strips of wood, in the same way as for any external corner where panelling ends; for decoration fit architrave (new, or old if it's in good condition) on top of the boards. If you leave the old architrave, fit battens up against it where necessary, nail the cladding to those, and cover its edge with a right-angle, birdsmouth or rebated moulding, planed to fit.

Electrical sockets also need battens next to them. A surface-mounted box generally needs no further treatment, since its face will end up more or less level with the surface of the cladding.

The simplest way of dealing with a flush-mounted box is to re-fix it to the wall surface, put battening and cladding next to it, and screw the face plate back on to overlap the cladding. If a flush-mounted box is too deep or shallow for this, use it as if the cladding were plaster-board. That is, attach special metal lugs to the

sides of the box, so that screwing on the face plate clamps the box to the cladding.

Wall-mounted light fittings can usually be dealt with by re-fixing them onto the cladding, having drilled a hole through it for the wires.

The cladding, of course, will need to be cut round all projecting features.

Surface finishes

As you fix the cladding, punch any visible nail heads below the timber surface. Then, when you've finished, you can fill the holes with a matching-coloured wood filler. Next, sand the entire timber surface with fine grade abrasive paper. An orbital sander will take much of the hard work out of this job.

When you've prepared the surface in this way, you can apply a stain, if you want to give the wood a deeper, richer or brighter colour. Follow this with a clear varnish in a matt, satin or gloss finish according to your taste.

BUILDING BASIC BOX FURNITURE

Almost all storage furniture today is built on the box principle, which is also the quickest and easiest method when you're doing it yourself. Here are the joints and techniques you need to make hard-wearing, good-looking pieces.

Apart from tables and chairs, just about all furniture is used to contain things. You can make a very good container in the obvious way: by taking five boards – a top, a bottom, two sides and a back – and joining them together at the corners. That's the essence of what is called box construction.

According to its size and how you fit it out with shelves, partitions, drawers, hinged or sliding doors, and so on, you can turn your box into almost anything: for example, a wardrobe, a sideboard, a chest, a cupboard, a bedside or bathroom cabinet, a kitchen unit, a set of bookshelves or a hi-fi unit.

Using chipboard

The box method is ideal for modern man-made boards. Natural timber, especially hardwood, has the draw-back that it's very difficult to get in widths over 225mm (9in), so you can only use it to build shallow cabinets. With chipboard, plywood and blockboard there's no such restriction.

Because it combines cheapness with good looks, veneered or plastic-faced chipboard is the most popular material for box furniture construction. Useful thicknesses are 12, 15 and 18mm (½, ⅝ and ¾in). Boards are normally 2440 or 1830mm (8 or 6ft) long, and come in widths from 150mm (6in) to 1220mm (4ft). Naturally, it's most economical to make items in sizes which utilise standard-size boards with the minimum waste.

Chipboard edges are unsightly, so boards are veneered or plastic-covered on the two long edges as well as on both faces. But you'll still have to conceal the bare short edges, plus any which you expose when cutting up the board. You can often do this by choosing the right joints. Otherwise, you can buy iron-on self-adhesive edging strip at the same time as the board. Or, for greater durability, use a timber lipping (ie, a suitable strip of plain wood or a decorative timber moulding glued, pinned on and stained to match if necessary).

Plastic-faced chipboard (which can be covered in either relatively soft PVC or more durable plastic laminate) needs no finishing treatment, but it's usual to varnish or oil wood-veneer boards. You can paint the latter if you prefer. Both materials give even the simplest box furniture a really professional look. In fact, they're so easy to work with that you need a very good reason to choose anything else.

You can of course buy chipboard without veneer or plastic facing, but after the necessary finishing processes for furniture its cost would end up about the same anyway.

A disadvantage of chipboard is that it's the weakest of man-made boards. Across a horizontal span of about 900mm (3ft) it will even sag under its own weight. So you need to support it at a maximum of 750mm (30in) intervals – even less, if it's to carry heavy objects. Remember that books, records, hi-fi and video equipment, and the TV set, are very heavy indeed.

Other materials

The strongest alternative is blockboard, which comes in standard sheets of 2440 x 1220mm (8 x 4ft) and is usually 19mm (¾in) thick. It's also the most expensive of the boards, but because of its great strength you can use it unsupported over spans twice as great as chipboard. Its main disadvantage is that the ends of the core, which is made of battens, present an unattractive appearance and need to be disguised like the edges of chipboard.

A good substitute for blockboard is 12mm (½in) thick plywood, which is almost as strong yet somewhat cheaper. In addition, its edges are neater than those of blockboard. For a smaller piece of furniture – say, a tiny bathroom cabinet – you might get away with plywood 9mm (⅜in) or even 6mm (¼in) thick. Plywood comes in standard sheets the same size as blockboard, but is also often available in smaller pieces.

Both plywood and blockboard usually require some finishing treatment. You can always add your own plastic laminate (using a contact adhesive). This is rather expensive, but will give you an extremely attractive and hard-wearing result. Veneered or plastic-faced plywood, and blockboard, is also obtainable.

Joints for boxes

Having chosen your material, you need to decide what type of joint to use at the corners of the box. If you have little or no

FROM BOXES TO FURNITURE

The box idea is enormously useful, because you can develop it in so many ways. Just by adding to it, and mixing the different features, you can turn a box into almost any item of furniture you want.

Think of a box

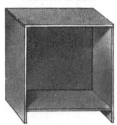

You can add a shelf   **a divider**   **a door**   **a drawer**   **You can extend the top**

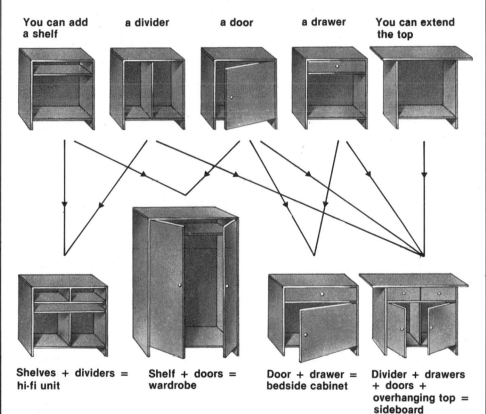

Shelves + dividers = hi-fi unit   **Shelf + doors = wardrobe**   **Door + drawer = bedside cabinet**   **Divider + drawers + doors + overhanging top = sideboard**

Ready Reference

POWER TOOL JOINTS

With a router, or even a circular saw, you can cut several strong corner joints in man-made boards, reinforcing them with strips of wood if necessary. Cut edges need veneering.

rebate   **double rebate**

mitre   **mitre with loose tongue of 4mm (3/16in) plywood**

FITTING A BACK

You can nail a back to the edges of the box – or to strips of wood which are screwed inside it.

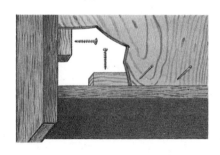

MAKING A PLINTH

You can easily make the 'toe recess' type of plinth with a strip of 100 x 25mm (4 x 1in).

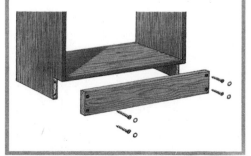

expertise with power tools, the glued butt joint – where the edge of one board meets the face of another – forms the basis every time (see pages 263–267).

You can use it by itself, but usually it's reinforced. There are several ways of doing this. Firstly, you can use nails, by punching their heads below the surface and filling the holes with wood stopping. Secondly, you can use screws – either double-threaded or chipboard screws, or ordinary screws driven into plastic bushes which have been previously inserted into holes drilled in the thickness of the board. Conceal the screw heads with plastic tops.

Thirdly, and for a stronger fixing still, you can use dowels (see pages 272–275 for details), glueing them in after lining the pieces up carefully and drilling appropriate holes. Here again there are two options. You can drill right through the outer piece in the same way as for screws, leaving the heads of the dowels to be sanded smooth as a decorative feature. Alternatively, use stopped dowels: in other words, drill only part of the way through the outer piece, so the heads are concealed.

A dowelled or plain glued butt joint will

BASIC BUTT JOINTS

1 First cut all the pieces to size, after carefully marking them out with a try-square and straight edge. A power saw with a fine blade cuts fast and cleanly.

2 To avoid mix-ups during assembly, mark each piece with its name, and mark both halves of each joint with appropriate matching letters or numbers.

3 The simplest board joint is the plain glued butt joint. The cut edge must be straight and square, and the joint needs careful cramping to keep it aligned.

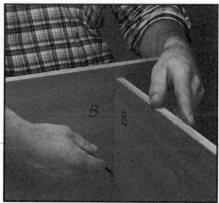

5 Chipboard screws are even stronger. First of all, place the edge half of the joint carefully against the face half, marking its position if necessary.

6 Mark screw positions as well. If the joint isn't at a corner, you may have to measure their distances in from the edge for a really accurate result.

7 Drill holes, a little smaller than the screw diameter, through both pieces before inserting the screws. Use No 8 screws on 18mm (¾in) thick board.

need to be cramped while the glue is drying if it's set square and tight. You can use sash cramps, or improvise your own cramping arrangements.

But there are other and even simpler ways of improving a butt joint; they involve placing reinforcements inside the angle. The easiest of all is to use plastic jointing blocks (see pages 263–267 again), which you screw to both pieces. They make a very rigid fixing even without glue. Stronger still is a square- or triangular-sectioned strip of wood, glued on and nailed or screwed to both pieces. Either of these reinforcements can be used in addition to screws, nails, dowels or glue alone.

Design features

Cut your pieces so that any existing edging

strip will be where you want it on the finished box, and so that the grain of the face veneers will run in the same direction up the sides and across the top. The latter will give the box a more unified look.

Bear in mind that even the cleanest cut may damage the face veneer on the underside of a board, so you'll want that side to be the less visible of the two.

Usually the top of the box sits on the sides, which thus support the top corner joints. It can even overhang them, giving a larger and more useful surface. However, either type of construction does mean you'll have to conceal the edges at each end of the top. The problem doesn't arise with the bottom or with intermediate shelves, for their ends will be concealed by the box's sides.

If you are adding a door or drawer to your box, think carefully at the design stage to make sure you get the details right.

For a really neat job, shelves and dividers can be fitted in housings (see pages 40-43 for details). However, you can't cut housings in plastic-faced boards, and in any case you may find plastic jointing blocks, or other proprietary fittings such as shelf supports, easy to use and just as effective.

Even the best-jointed and most substantial box is quite easily distorted into a lozenge shape. That is, until you fit the back. This need only be made from hardboard of 4mm (³/₁₆in) plywood, and can be glued and pinned onto the back edges of the boards. It's best to make it about 3mm (⅛in) too small all round, so that it's less easily seen from the top or sides. Alternatively, you can inset it – either in stopped rebates in all four edges, or against narrow strips of wood which are themselves screwed a little way inside the box.

A plinth is another feature on many pieces.

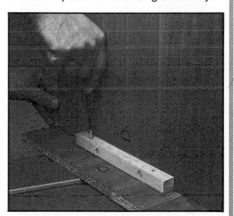

4 *Nails are one way of reinforcing a glued butt joint. Always have a wet rag handy to wipe off any excess adhesive which is squeezed out during assembly.*

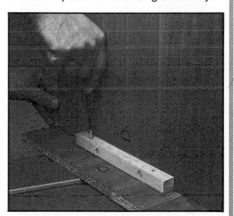

8 *A square-sectioned strip of wood is another good reinforcement. Position, mark, drill and glue it; then drive chipboard screws both ways.*

The word covers two different things. One is the traditional cabinet base, built separately out of four lengths of 100 x 25mm (4 x 1in) planed softwood used on edge, which fits over the bottom of the box. The corners are mitred or butt-jointed and reinforced with triangular wooden blocks, glued or screwed in place, which also serve as supports for the box when it's located inside the plinth. This type of plinth is mainly for decoration.

The other type is really a toe recess. It's formed by raising the bottom of the box and fitting a piece of timber below it, along the front. The timber is fixed at each end into notches cut in the bottom corner of each side. The fixing can be done by any of the jointing methods already described. This type of plinth helps to prevent stubbed toes and damage to the cabinet, and is particularly common on kitchen base units and living-room wall units.

STOPPED DOWEL JOINTS

1 *Draw a line down the face of one board in exactly the position where you want the centre line of the other board's edge to meet it.*

3 *Drill dowel holes in both pieces, positioning them accurately on the marks. Adhesive tape round the drill bit warns you when it's gone far enough.*

2 *Mark the dowel positions along this line, on both pieces, making sure each pair of marks matches exactly. Dowels should be 150-225mm (6-9in) apart.*

4 *Put the pieces together, having first inserted glue and dowels into the set of holes you've drilled, and having spread adhesive along the joint.*

FINISHING TOUCHES

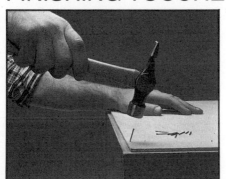

1 *4mm (3/16in) plywood makes a good back for a box. Drive panel pins through it at an angle, so that they don't come through the board faces by accident.*

2 *Glue and pin beading onto the edges, for decoration and to hide those which you've cut. The shelf and bottom are inset to conceal the beading's ends.*

HANDYMAN PROJECTS

Making things from wood is one of the most satisfying hobbies, and there is literally no limit to what you can create with the skills you have acquired from earlier chapters.

BUILDING CUPBOARDS IN ALCOVES

Built-in cupboards save you money because you use your walls instead of side, back and top panels. Fitting them neatly and snugly is just a matter of knowing the right methods.

M aking freestanding storage furniture that's rigid and stable – even fairly simple box-type pieces – calls for accuracy, plus a certain amount of basic woodworking ability and design sense. It's certainly worth taking the trouble to acquire these. But you may be unsure of your skills, especially when it comes to large items – or perhaps you just don't want to take chances.

The answer is built-in units. These are almost sure to be structurally sound, because they're anchored to the walls – and often to the floor and ceiling too. They don't usually require any joints more complex than halvings (see pages 268–271 for details). And, of course, fitting storage facilities into alcoves and odd corners is an excellent way to make the most of available space.

But any built-in cupboard does face a disadvantage. The walls of your room will probably not be flat or true. Although (at least in modern homes) the masonry itself will be vertical, and walls will be square with one another, it's impossible to apply plaster to a uniform thickness over an entire wall, so there will be variations. This means you'll have to take some trouble to make your cupboard fit.

Working in an alcove

Let's suppose you're building a cupboard in an alcove – the most obvious place, and a very sensible one. What you need to know first is the alcove's width at its narrowest.

This is very hard to find accurately with a tape measure, because it's flexible and the casing gets in the way. Instead you can use 'pinch rods'. Improvise these from a couple of pieces of square-sectioned timber – say 25x25mm (1x1in) or 38x38mm (1½x1½in). Each should be longer than half the width of the alcove. Hold them together horizontally inside the alcove, and slide them until the end of each one meets a side wall.

Now move them up and down the alcove until you've found its narrowest part, and tilt them till you're sure they're level – that is, when they show the shortest width yet still have both ends touching the walls.

Then, grasping them tightly, draw a pencil line across both, so that you can re-assemble them in the correct position. Take them down from the wall and measure their combined length.

Making a frame

Your next job is to make a simple rectangular frame, to the overall width you've just measured. This consists of two cross pieces, plus two uprights which can be any height you choose – possibly dictated by the height of ready-made doors (such as louvre doors) if you plan to fit them.

You can use square or rectangular timber for the frame, making the corners with halving joints, glued together and then screwed from the inside. Keep checking the frame for squareness as you assemble it. To ensure it stays square during the rest of the job, tack battens of thin timber diagonally across two opposite corners.

Place the frame in the alcove where you want it, and fix it by drilling and screwing through the frame sides into wall plugs. Alternatively, if the frame is made of rectangular timber such as 50x25mm (2x1in), you can screw vertical battens to the wall at either side and fix the frame to them, with timber strips or plastic jointing blocks. Use a spirit level to make quite sure it's upright. If it leans forward, the doors will always tend to fall open; if it slopes backwards, they'll be

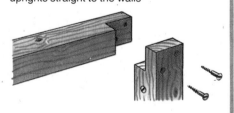

inclined to stay shut. And of course, the frame needs to be set truly horizontal too.

The frame probably won't fit exactly. If it's too wide, you can plane it down; take an equal amount off both sides. On the other hand, there may be gaps. Don't attempt to make the timber follow the contours of the wall if this is so.

If the gaps are narrower than about 5mm (³⁄₁₆in), you can stop them up with filler, which will be disguised with paint. A length of foam plastic draught strip, inset about 3mm (¹⁄₈in) back from the front, and inserted before you screw the frame to the wall, makes an excellent backing for the filler.

If you don't want a painted finish, glue and pin moulding (eg, quadrant) to the front of the frame so it hides the gaps. Hold it in position, mark it as best you can and shape it with a file; then re-position, re-mark and re-shape it till it hugs the wall tightly.

Wider gaps call for the insertion of packing strips of thin timber, plywood or hardboard before adding the moulding.

Supporting the top

If the cupboard doesn't reach to the ceiling, it will need a top. This can be of blockboard or plywood – painted, veneered or covered with plastic laminate if you wish. But, as always, proprietary veneered or laminated chipboard is a cheap and attractive alternative. If you decide on this, bear in mind that it comes in standard widths, with each long edge ready-finished. So, unless you're lipping the front edge yourself in any way, you need to fix the frame at a distance from the back wall that allows you to make use of one of these widths.

Think about the details beforehand: do you want the top to overhang the cupboard doors, or to project even further? The treatment of the front edge is one of the small points which make all the difference to the final appearance of the unit, so it's worth making sure you've got it right from the start. A few of the possibilities are shown in *Ready Reference*. Small strips of decorative mouldings such as astragal, ogee, scotia and even glass bead may come in handy as ways of giving the edge a slightly softer and more interesting look, and getting away from the functional effect of straight lines everywhere.

In any case, allow enough extra width for trimming the top panel to fit the contours of the back wall.

Supported on the frame at the front, the top rests at the back on a corresponding horizontal batten screwed to the wall. This must be at exactly the same height as the top of the frame. You can use a spirit level to achieve this. If your level is too small, place it on top of a straight length of wood.

For a cupboard that rises above eye level,

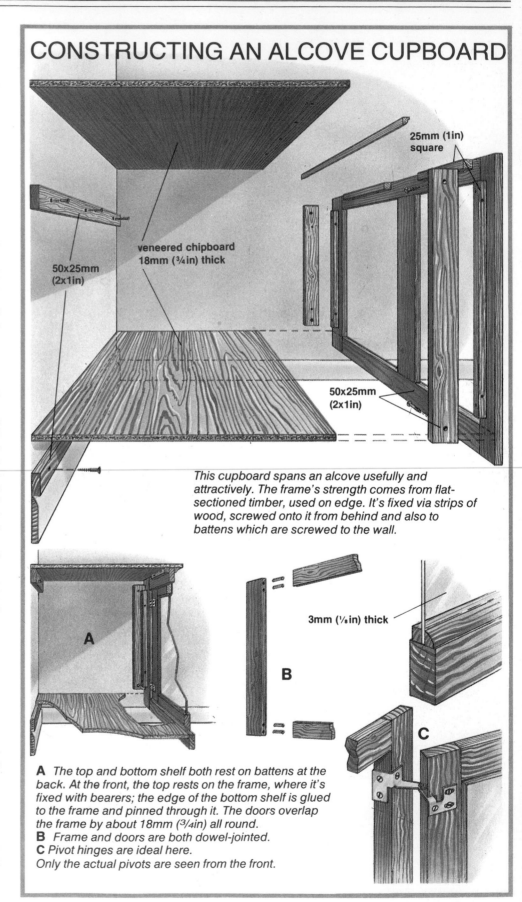

CONSTRUCTING AN ALCOVE CUPBOARD

25mm (1in) square

veneered chipboard 18mm (¾in) thick

50x25mm (2x1in)

50x25mm (2x1in)

This cupboard spans an alcove usefully and attractively. The frame's strength comes from flat-sectioned timber, used on edge. It's fixed via strips of wood, screwed onto it from behind and also to battens which are screwed to the wall.

A

3mm (¹⁄₈in) thick

B

C

A *The top and bottom shelf both rest on battens at the back. At the front, the top rests on the frame, where it's fixed with bearers; the edge of the bottom shelf is glued to the frame and pinned through it. The doors overlap the frame by about 18mm (³⁄₄in) all round.*
B *Frame and doors are both dowel-jointed.*
C *Pivot hinges are ideal here.*
Only the actual pivots are seen from the front.

MAKING THE FRAME

1 Cut 'pinch rods' to find the alcove width. Slide them apart till each meets a wall, mark across both, and measure their combined length.

2 Make up a front frame for the cupboard to this width. Use dowels or halving joints; glue them and if possible cramp the frame together.

3 If the side uprights overlap the cross members, not the other way round, they'll be easier to plane down later if necessary.

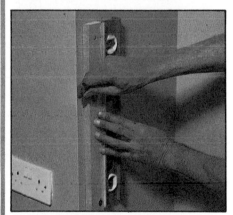

4 Cut two battens, and hold one vertically where you want it on the wall, allowing for frame and door thickness. Mark its position.

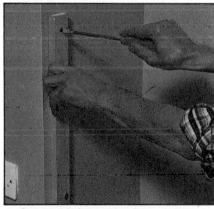

5 Screw this batten in place, using wall plugs, after making sure that it's not long enough to get in the way of the bottom shelf.

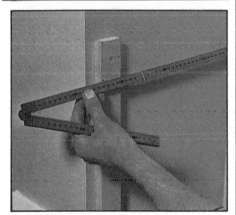

6 Measure its distance from the back wall, so you can position and fix another batten the same distance from the wall at the other side.

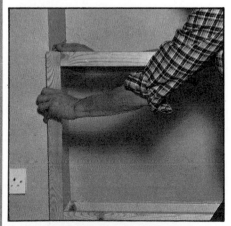

7 Place the frame in position, and mark it if it's too wide. Alternatively, it may need packing out with timber or thin board.

8 If the frame is too wide, plane a bit from both ends. Bevelling each edge inwards across the thickness will give an even easier fit.

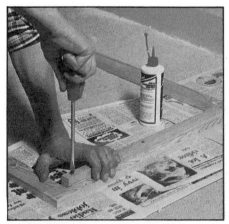

9 Glue and screw a fixing block down each side of the frame, insetting it by the thickness of the battens you've fastened to the wall.

COMPLETING THE UNIT

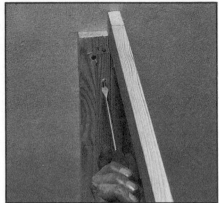

1 *Re-position the frame, and glue and screw in the other direction through each fixing block, attaching it to the batten.*

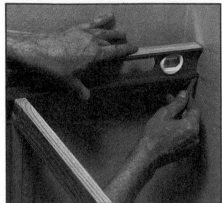

2 *Use a level to mark on the back wall, in at least two places, the position of the bearer which will support the cupboard's top.*

3 *After making similar marks for the bottom shelf, add a second mark below each one, to indicate the shelf thickness accurately.*

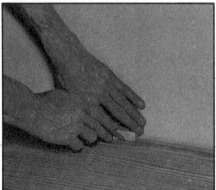

5 *After checking the side walls and cutting each shelf to fit at either end, scribe the contours of the wall along its back edge.*

6 *Fit the top shelf into position. Fasten it to the cross-bearers with plastic jointing blocks, or more strips of wood glued and screwed.*

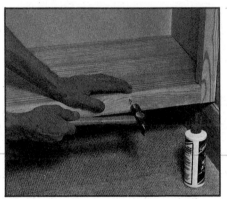

7 *After positioning the bottom shelf, glue and pin into its front edge through the front cross-bearer, to give it extra rigidity.*

you needn't even use chipboard for the top. Thin plywood or hardboard will do. However, hardboard should never span a greater distance than 450mm (18in) without support. This is bound to mean fitting an extra bearer or two from front to back, halved across the front cross piece and rear batten.

Fitting the top

Next, you need to make the top. First, use pinch rods to see if the alcove is the same width at front and back. If the angles are more or less square and the walls straight, go ahead and cut the top to size. Whatever you do, don't make it any smaller than the space; rather leave it a bit too big, then trim the back edge and one end with a plane, filing or Surforming where necessary to ensure that you have a perfect fit.

If, on the other hand, the end walls are well out of true, you'll have to make angled cuts at either end. Cut pieces of cardboard to fit by trial and error, then use them as templates to mark out the top panel before you saw it.

Lastly, note where the top needs trimming at the back. If the back wall is very bumpy, it's best to scribe the top to fit. That means holding it a bit less than 25mm (1in) from the wall, and placing a small block of 25mm (1in) thick timber there, with one face against the wall. Hold a pencil against it, and move both block and pencil along the top. This will give you a line on the board which follows the contours of the wall, so you can cut along it for a perfect fit.

The top can be held in place by screws driven up through the battens and frame if the timber is square in section, or otherwise through small strips of timber screwed to the inside faces of the frame and battens.

Fitting a bottom panel

A cupboard that stops short of the floor will need a bottom shelf panel, which should be measured and prepared in just the same way as the top. It rests on a batten screwed to the wall at the back, also like the top.

You can position this level with the top of the bottom cross piece in the frame, notching the panel at the front corners so it fits round the uprights and rests on the bottom cross piece. In that case it can act as a doorstop if you cut it short of the front. Or, cutting it even shorter, you can let it rest on a small additional bearer (say 25mm/1in square). This can be screwed to the inside of the cross piece, and positioned so that the panel is flush with the top of the cross piece. For the same result, you can simply glue and pin the front edge of the panel through the cross piece. Either way, you'll need to adjust the height of the rear batten accordingly.

Further possibilities

If you want shelves inside the cupboard, they too can rest on bearers screwed to the

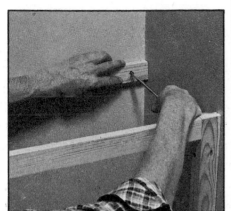

4 Screw the top bearer to the wall, keeping its upper edge against the pencil marks. Screw the bottom bearer against the lower set of marks there.

8 A small moulding (eg, a glass bead), glued and pinned below the top overhang, improves its looks. Now add doors to the unit.

walls at the back and sides. Alternatively, you can make them adjustable, in case your storage requirements change. Just use one of the proprietary systems described on pages 288–291.

If your cupboard reaches to the floor, you'll have to take account of the skirting board. One option is to take it off (for replacement or re-use), complete your cupboard, saw the skirting to length, and re-fix it to any stretches of wall that are visible outside the cupboard – and inside it, too, if you wish. The other possibility, where the skirting isn't too thick, is to scribe and cut away the frame of the cupboard to fit.

Full-height cupboards

An alcove cupboard that reaches to the ceiling as well as the floor presents its own problems. In theory you could build a frame to the correct size, slide it into position, and fix it in the way already described. But, since

it would be the same height as the room itself, it would be difficult to manoeuvre into position. You'd do far better to assemble it all in place.

It pays, however, to be wary. Filling or packing gaps isn't really satisfactory for such a large structure. Place a spirit level vertically against each wall. If either of them is out of true by more than, say, 20mm (¾in) along its length, or if any curves in it are deeper than that, cut the upright member of the frame to a length equal to the height of the alcove at its lowest and scribe it to fit the wall – using a pencil and block of wood while holding the timber precisely vertical. Then cut halving joints in each end.

A bottom frame cross piece is also needed to act as a doorstop, if nothing else. Cut it to length (ie, as long as the alcove's narrowest width), and screw it to the floor, making sure it's truly level. (Incidentally, before driving screws or nails into a floor, you should always try to make sure there are no water or gas pipes underneath. If in doubt, choose screws too short to pass through floorboards.)

Then glue the joints, and screw both uprights to the wall. Cut the top cross piece to the same length as the one on the floor. Joint it to the tops of the uprights, screwing it to a ceiling joist if possible. If you've worked accurately, it will be horizontal, and square to the rest – but do check!

Lastly, fit any intermediate cross pieces. You may need one to help support a shelf, and perhaps act as a doorstop, if you plan to create a small cupboard at the top.

Bottom and top panels aren't necessary in floor-to-ceiling units, but it doesn't cost much – and it makes a neat-looking touch – to fit a cupboard floor of plywood or hardboard.

Adding doors

Doors, or course, are what complete the cupboard. They can be sliding or hinged, and in construction they can be flush – perhaps consisting of single pieces of board – or else panelled. They can even be glazed; louvres are also a popular feature.

All these types can easily be installed in the front frame of the cupboard. For sliding doors, you fit tracks or channels; others can be hinged to the timber uprights, either overlapping them or inset between them. On a wide cupboard, you can always add extra uprights.

Whatever plan you decide on, it's always sensible to sort out the details before you buy any materials or begin work on the project. In both construction and design you'll find it pays dividends to think of the doors as an integral part of the unit.

You'll find more information given on pages 306–309.

Ready Reference

FITTED CUPBOARD POSSIBILITIES
At the top
Details 1 to 4 use 'lay-on' doors (ie, doors which overlap the front frame).

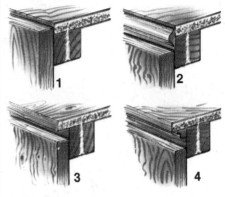

1 Door overlaps top
2 Using decorative edging
3 Top overhangs door
4 Overhanging top and moulding
5 Inset door with timber strip as doorstop, glued and pinned to the underside of the top frame member.

At the bottom
The bottom panel rests on a timber strip, and a lay-on door is fitted.

An inset door uses the bottom panel as a doorstop.

ADDING DOORS TO BASIC BOXES

Doors for furniture should be much more than an afterthought. In usefulness and appearance, they make all the difference – so it's vital that they look good and work smoothly.

When you're building cabinet furniture or fitted units, it's worth considering from the outset how you're going to make and fit the doors.

The first decision you have to take is whether they'll be hinged or sliding.

Sliding doors

Sliding doors don't create any obstruction in the room when open – you're never likely to bang yourself on them. What's more, if they're small and light they can be extremely easy to fit. But they have the big disadvantage that only half the cupboard is accessible at one time (a third, if you fit three doors). This can be a real irritant.

Folding doors, of course, are a variant which avoids that particular problem. However, for all folding doors, and for large and heavy sliding doors such as those on a wardrobe, you'll need special mechanical fittings, which come with their own detailed instructions. To make sure you buy the right pattern, get the overall construction of the cupboard clear in your mind first – but don't buy any materials or begin construction, because some types of sliding and folding gear require a minimum door thickness, and all affect the doors' other dimensions. So you'll have to finalise these details after buying the fittings, rather than before.

For smaller items (eg, wall-hung bathroom cabinets), it's quite enough to have doors of thin plywood or hardboard which slide in simple channels glued and/or screwed to the inside of the cabinet at top and bottom. These channels can be wooden or plastic; in either case, top channelling is slightly deeper than bottom channelling. This enables you to push each door up into the top channel first, before positioning it over the bottom channel and dropping it into place without its falling out at the top.

Sliding doors should, of course, be of such a width that they overlap each other when they're all closed. Lightweight ones will slide more easily in their channels if their width is greater than their height. Rubbing the doors' bottom edges with soap or candle wax will make for an even easier ride – and plastic channelling is smoother than wood.

Hinged doors

Hinged doors can be fitted in either of two ways: inset or lay-on. An inset door fits inside the cabinet. A lay-on door overlaps its front, either wholly or partly. Each type gives quite a different look, so think carefully about the effect you want before deciding which to choose.

Inset doors are a bit harder to fit, because you have to achieve a more or less accurate and consistent clearance all round – variations will be noticeable, and the door may stick if it sags even slightly on its hinges after fitting.

If you've decided on a natural varnished timber finish for an inset door, try to make it an exact push fit in the opening. Subsequent cleaning-up and sanding, before you apply the finish, will make it just the right size. If you're going to paint it, aim to leave 3mm (⅛in) all round, after sanding, so that the various coats of paint do not cause it to bind.

Another thing an inset door needs is some kind of doorstop to close against. This could be a strip or strips of timber, fixed inside the cabinet, or the bottom and top panels of the cabinet itself – or, perhaps most commonly, a catch (see below). Remember that you can place the doorstop so the door closes flush with the front of the cabinet, or slightly inside it. Again, your choice is dictated by looks.

Fitting hinges

Your choice of hinges for hanging the doors on the cabinet must of course be made at the same time. Some hinges are suitable for inset doors, some for lay-on doors, and some for both.

The traditional butt hinge, for example, can be used for either arrangement. With an inset door, it's screwed to the edge of the door and the inner face of the cabinet side. With a lay-on door you just reverse the process, screwing the hinge to the inner face of the door and the front edge of the cabinet, so that its knuckle projects at the side.

Either way, you have to mark out the hinge positions with a pencil, try-square and marking gauge, then cut recesses for them in the door or cabinet or (more usually) both.

A modern alternative is the concealed hinge. This is a much more complex mechanism which actually lifts the door out from the frame rather than simply letting it swing. While its primary purpose is to allow lay-on doors to open to 90° within the overall width of the cabinet (which a butt hinge cannot achieve), some kinds of concealed hinge can also be used for inset doors.

Cranked hinges do a similar job – though only on lay-on doors – and their shape makes them especially easy to locate in position. However, they're only partly concealed.

FITTING SLIDING DOORS

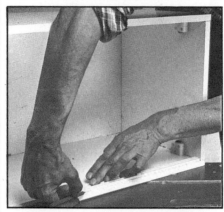

1 *Cut the top and bottom channelling to length; align it where you want it in the cabinet, and mark out its position in pencil.*

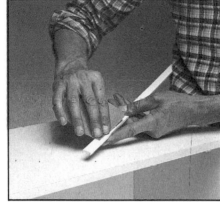

2 *Roughen the bottom of the plastic channelling to provide a 'key', then fix it back on with contact adhesive (the type you spread on both surfaces).*

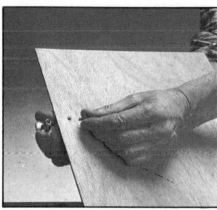

3 *After measuring for the doors and cutting them to size from thin plywood or hardboard, drill for and fit handles in matching positions.*

4 *Fit each door by pushing it up into the top channel, then swinging it into position and letting it drop into the bottom channel.*

Pivot hinges are a third possibility.

What's more, you can get 'lift-off' and 'loose-pin' types of butt, cranked and pivot hinges which enable you to fix one leaf to the door and one to the cabinet separately before putting the two together – eliminating the need to hold or prop an unwieldy door in position as you screw the hinges to the cabinet.

If you're not using one of these types, the rule is to fix the hinges to the door first, then to the cabinet.

Plain doors

You can make doors for furniture in two main ways. The simpler type is made from a single slab of man-made board. You can, of course, use veneered or plastic-faced chipboard, two parallel edges of which will be ready-finished. To take advantage of that, you'll want to design your cupboard so that its doors can simply be cut to length (ie, height) from a standard width of board. This is easier with lay-on doors, since their dimensions – unlike those of an inset door – aren't dictated by the exact size of the opening. On the latter you may find yourself having to shave the ready-finished edges with a plane to make the door fit properly, which would be a pity.

Blockboard and plywood don't present these problems, since they don't come ready-edged, and their bare edges are in any case more acceptable. When using them, you can simply saw the door to size (making it slightly too big rather than too small), offer it up and plane off bits where necessary.

You can give a plain one-piece door a professional look by using hockey stick moulding round the edge, taking the moulding's thickness into account all round as you prepare the door to fit the opening. You can also use other mouldings to decorate its face if you wish.

WAYS OF FITTING DOORS

An inset door (A) closes inside the cabinet. A lay-on door (B) closes against its front edges.

inset door   lay-on door

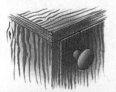

CHOOSING A CATCH

Magnetic catches are useful because the plate doesn't have to be lined up perfectly. (A), a light model, fits in a drilled hole. (B) and (C) screw onto the surface; the double version (C) deals with two doors at once.

Ball catches are neat. The cylinder fits into a drilled hole; its faceplate (if any) into a chiselled recess. The striking plate's lip guides the ball into a small countersunk socket, preventing damage to the cabinet edge. The double type (C) has a screw for strength adjustment.

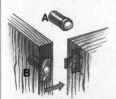

Roller catches work by sprung rollers. Both parts (like many furniture fittings) have elongated holes, for adjustment after inserting the screws.

Automatic latches are unique in opening, as well as closing, simply by pressure – you don't pull the door.

USING BUTT HINGES

An inset one piece door
with plain butt hinges

1 Mark on the door edge the distance of each hinge from the top and bottom, and square these marks across with a knife and try-square.

2 Place a hinge against each mark, and score another mark at its other end. This will give you the length of the hinge recess.

3 Chisel out a recess, the width and depth of one hinge leaf. If this recess is as wide as the door edge, you can make saw cuts for it first.

4 After screwing each hinge to the door so the knuckle just protrudes in front, align the door and mark each hinge length in the cabinet.

5 Mark the width of each hinge position in the cabinet. A marking gauge, set to the width of a single hinge leaf, is ideal here.

6 Screw the hinge to the cabinet. In veneered chipboard, don't cut a recess; instead, make the recess in the door twice the usual depth.

7 If you're using a magnetic catch, screw it in place after ensuring the door fits. Inset it by the thickness of the door and plate combined. Then position the plate on the catch.

8 Close the door firmly, in such a way that the little bumps on the back of the plate make dents on the inside face of the door. If necessary, loosen the screws and adjust the catch.

9 Remove the plate from the catch, use the dents to position the plate on the door, make a hole with a bradawl in the appropriate position and screw it in place.

MAKING A FRAMED DOOR
A lay-on framed door with cranked lift-off hinges

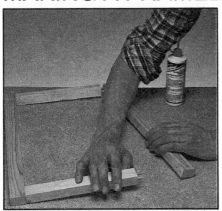

1 *The frame is easily assembled with glued dowel joints. Cramp it to a flat surface to stop it twisting while the adhesive sets.*

2 *Cut the hinge recesses for a lay-on door in its inner face, instead of in the edge. Mark them out carefully with a marking gauge first.*

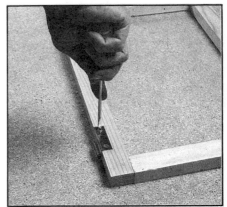

3 *Screw one half of a lift-off hinge to the cabinet, the other separately to the door. The cranked type locates over the door edge.*

4 *The spindle half of the hinge goes on the cabinet, spindle upwards. Place the door on these spindles to check its alignment.*

5 *Mitre a small quadrant moulding or glass bead neatly and tightly, then glue and pin it round the inside of the frame at the front.*

6 *Lay the glass in place, then pin strips of wood all round at the back. Don't glue them in case you ever need to remove the glass.*

Framed doors

The other type of door consists of a frame with some kind of panel fitted inside it. This has a rather more traditional look, and an attractiveness all of its own. You can easily make the frame from four pieces of plain rectangular-sectioned timber – a typical size would be 50x25mm (2x1in); use dowels for the corners, or mortise-and-tenon joints. (Plain mitre joints aren't strong enough.)

Make sure that you cramp all the components during assembly. Twisting is a common problem when assembling a frame, so it's wise to cramp the whole thing to a flat surface while the adhesive sets.

Then glue and pin a quadrant moulding or glass bead round the inside of the frame and just inside its front edge. Lay in a sheet of thin plywood or 3mm thick glass, marked and cut to fit, and hold that in place with a thin strip of timber, say 6mm (1/4in) square,

pinned round at the back.

You can buy ready-made frame-and-panel doors, in which the frame is specially shaped – a tricky job for the inexperienced woodworker. Louvred doors are another attractive variation on this theme which it would be most unwise to tackle yourself – and unnecessary, since they're so widely available.

Choosing a catch

A catch is a vital piece of hardware for most cupboards with hinged doors – though some concealed hinges have a spring that holds the door closed without one.

The best catch for the do-it-yourselfer is undoubtedly the magnetic type, since it will still work even if its magnet doesn't exactly face the striking plate. So it remains unaffected even if the door drops out of alignment over a period of time.

Other types of catch include friction, roller, double roller, ball, double ball and peglock. None of them share the advantage of magnetic catches, though the single ball catch has the virtue of being unobtrusive.

However, one very clever and useful device is the automatic latch, which – though hidden from outside the cabinet – springs open, as well as closed, simply by hand pressure.

If you're fitting only a single catch, it's wise to place it behind the spot where the door handle will be, to avoid uneven tension on the door, catch mountings and handle.

Choosing a handle

Handles, perhaps more than anything else, make or mar furniture. Here, as so often, the best plan is to go to a good hardware store. Most types of handle either screw into or bolt through the surface of the door.

BUILDING BUNKS: THE BASICS

Bunk beds save space. What's more, children love them, so it's easier to persuade them that bedtime has arrived! Bunks must be strong – but that doesn't mean they aren't straightforward to make.

Here's a way to build a set of very simple freestanding bunks. Like any furniture design, it's only one of many possible variations, and you can regard it as a basis for adding your own ideas. In particular, you can vary the dimensions to suit your needs.

However, a word of warning is necessary before going into the details of the construction. When you build bunks, you're making something which rises well above the floor, and which will be used by active, boisterous children. Your paramount consideration must be that of safety. Be quite sure that everything is firmly fixed, that the whole thing is rigid and stable, and that there's no danger to either the child in the top bunk or the one below.

As when constructing any other type of bed, you should begin with the mattresses: everything must fit round them. If making or buying new ones, go for the smallest single bed size. Children don't need that much sleeping space – and the larger the mattresses, the more cumbersome the structure you'll have to build.

Of course, if you're using mattresses you already own, they must both be exactly the same length and width. The thickness isn't so important.

Using box construction

Solid pine is the ideal material throughout for the construction – none of the flat sections are wide enough for veneered boards to be useful.

Each bunk is a box frame, with bearers inside it for the mattress base. A sensible size for the four sides of the frame, not too wide and not too weak, is 100x25mm (4x1in). For easy bedmaking, build the frame's slightly larger than the mattresses – say 25mm (1in) extra all round. Screw bearers of 50x25mm (2x1in) timber to the

sides and 25mm (1in) square timber to the ends, about 25mm (1in) below the top edge. Leave a gap in each end bearer and screw on an extra bearer below it (see photograph 10 on page 117).

Then join the corners of the frame together. Bear in mind that you shouldn't screw or nail into end grain. And the frame sides won't be wide enough to include a strip of wood or plastic jointing blocks as an internal reinforcement. This leaves three possibilities: see *Ready Reference*. One is dowels, and the second is a barefaced housing joint (see pages 276–279 for details). If you arrange things so that the shorter pieces (the head and foot) overlap the sides, you'll end up with an especially neat finish: the end grain, which is less attractive, will be hidden by the bedposts. The third possibility is a halving joint in the width. This is probably the strongest of the three.

You will in any case need to glue the joint well with PVA adhesive. Rough usage by children means you'll have to forget the idea of making each bunk capable of being dismantled. Instead, for real strength, it pays to glue every joint, even when it's screwed or nailed as well. (But you can make bunks that turn into separate beds – see below.)

Adding the bedposts

The four bedposts – one at each corner – are 75x50mm (3x2in). When deciding on their length, take into account the distance from the bottom of the lower bunk to the floor (say 300mm/1ft); the height of the lower bunk and its mattress; the clearance between that and

Ready Reference

BUNK CORNER JOINTS
There are three suitable ways of joining frame corners without screwing or nailing into end grain, and where there's no room for a timber reinforcement or plastic jointing blocks in the internal angle.

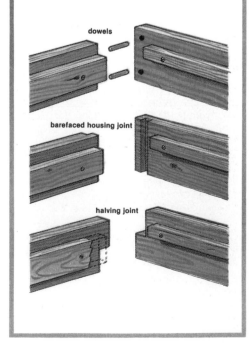

dowels

barefaced housing joint

halving joint

BUILDING THE STRUCTURE

1 One cut in each direction with a tenon saw is enough to make the halvings for the four corners of each bed frame.

3 Glue and screw two more bearers to each end at the same height, plus a third lower down to support the central longitudinal bearer.

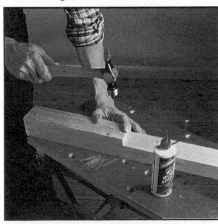

5 Cut the bedposts to length, then glue and nail 300mm (1ft) of 75 x 25mm (3 x 1in) timber flat against the bottom of each, planing it flush.

2 After notching the side bearers to take the cross-bearers, glue and screw them inside the frame sides, 20mm (3/4in) from the top edge.

4. After glueing each frame corner joint, drive in one nail each way to cramp it – checking constantly that all the joints are square.

6 Laying the posts on the floor, glue and screw the lower frame flush with their outer edges, resting it against the top of the 75 x 25mm (3 x 1in) timber.

Ready Reference

BUNK BED SIZES
These dimensions should be right for children's bunks – depending on the age and size of the occupants.

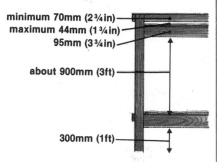

minimum 70mm (2¾in)
maximum 44mm (1¾in)
95mm (3¾in)
about 900mm (3ft)
300mm (1ft)

FIXED LADDERS
75 x 25mm (3 x 1in) slats, screwed at each end to the outer sides of the bedposts, and with their top edges rounded.

maximum gap 44mm (1¾in) to top of mattress

One upright is 50mm (2in) square, screwed to the sides of the bunks; the other is the bedpost. The rungs can be pieces of broomstick – or more pieces of 50 x 50mm, housed at both ends, their top edges rounded. This type of ladder is unsuitable for bunks which separate.

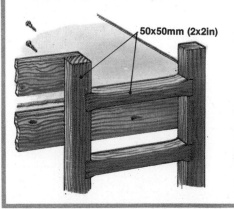

50x50mm (2x2in)

311

COMPLETING THE BED

1 Cut two longer pieces of 75 x 25mm, and glue and nail one along each post, so their bottom ends butt against the lower bed frame.

2 After adding the top frame and the other two posts, glue and screw a reinforcement across each end, flush with the top of the lower frame.

3 Glue and screw a guard rail above the end of the top bunk where necessary. Otherwise put another reinforcement across it.

4 Glue and screw a side guard rail, where needed, to the insides of the posts – flush with their tops, and butting against the end guard rail.

5 Insert the central bearer, after cutting notches in its top edge to take the cross-bearers, plus another notch in the bottom of each end.

6 Lastly, after inserting the two cross-bearers in the notches in the side and central bearers, fit a piece of pegboard into each bunk.

the bottom of the top bunk (say 900mm/3ft); and the height of the top bunk (including mattress and a guard rail). This will make something over 1500mm (5ft).

The two frames must be fixed to the posts very securely indeed – you don't want the disaster of the top bunk crashing down onto the occupant of the bottom one in the middle of the night. You can use glue and screws, driving the screws through the frame sides and into the bedposts. Countersink them well, so that they won't cut your hands or tear the fabric when you tuck the bedclothes in. Glue and dowels would be even better. Either way, use two per post per bunk.

You'd do well to give this fixing some support. This can take the form of lengths of 75x25mm (3x1in) planed timber glued and nailed to the inside of each post, below the bottom bunk and in between the two bunks, so the edges of the sides butt against them.

Using planed timber
Here you may well come up against a minor problem which often arises when, as is usually the case with non-structural carpentry, you buy your wood ready-planed from the timber merchant. The sizes are inconsistent, and can vary by as much as 6mm (1/4in).

You'll have asked for 75x50mm (3x2in), 75x25mm (3x1in), and so on. You'll have received timber which is narrower and thinner than the size in question – the 'nominal' size – because some of it has been planed off at the mill. This, of course, is universal practice, and – provided you expect it – it should cause you no problems.

The snag is, however, that the amount that's planed off isn't always the same. It can vary by 3 or 4mm (1/8 or (3/16in). You can often get over that by designing your work to allow for the variation. But you'll still have difficulties when it comes to matching two

pieces. Here, the 50mm (2in) side of the 75x50mm (3x2in) probably won't match the 50mm side of the 75x25mm (3x1in) although it's known by the same measurement.

The way out, of course, is to wait till the glue has set, then use your plane and trim the wider piece till it matches the narrower one exactly. That's why you need at least one bench plane in your tool kit. It saves your having to rely on what the timber merchant provides.

Bearers and guard rails
At this point you can fit the cross-bearers and the central longitudinal bearer in each bunk, plus the sheet of pegboard which forms the mattress base. Instead of pegboard you can use slats of timber, say 75 x 19mm (3 x 3/4in), spaced their own width apart and screwed down onto the side bearers. If so, it's best to support the central

bearer in a different way – see page 453. Slats are especially suitable for sprung mattresses.

You also need at least one guard rail for the top bunk, to stop a child from falling out of bed while asleep. Fix a rail wherever the bunk isn't next to a wall. For each long side of the bunk, you can just extend the posts upwards and screw a further length of 75 x 25mm (3x1in) timber to their insides – horizontally, so it runs between them. But this isn't such a good method at the ends, because the rail will be too far in. Instead, screw it to the outsides of the posts, using brass screws in cups for decorative effect.

It's extremely important to leave only a small gap between the bottom edge of the guard rail and the top of the mattress, to avoid the very real danger of heads or limbs getting stuck there. The maximum gap is 44mm (1¾in).

Reinforcing the structure
The only snag with this design is that it doesn't have much strength if it's subjected to pulling or racking from side to side. It demands too much from the frame corner joints: within a few weeks or months of use energetic children may well succeed in pulling them apart!

One simple answer is to include reinforcing pieces. These too can be of 75x25mm (3x1in) timber, and each one should be glued and screwed in place across the end, exactly like an end guard rail. If you position its upper edge flush with the top of the frame, you'll neatly cover the end grain in the halving joints. And this is another case where brass screws will make an attractive feature out of a necessity, especially if used in brass cups.

Such reinforcements are needed on both ends of the bottom bunk, and on the top bunk at whichever end doesn't possess a guard rail. Of course, if you're screwing slats between the posts anyway – see below – they'll give all the strength you require.

Separating the bunks
You may find it useful to be able to make your double bunk into two separate beds.

You can arrange this without much alteration in the design – but, when you're designing and making a 'knock-down' assembly of this kind, you need to take special care that the fixing in question is solid. One method is to make each post in two parts, of which the upper rests on the lower. Do the same with the 75 x 25mm (3 x 1in) timber which is fixed to the inside of the post – but 75mm (3in) further up, so that you're left with a staggered joint. Then you should bolt the end of the thicker piece, which protrudes downwards, to the end of the thinner piece, which protrudes upwards.

You should use two bolts for each post, plus washers, and do the nuts up very tightly with a spanner. For safety's sake, it might be sensible to use two nuts on each bolt.

Alternatively, you can follow the same procedure without staggering the joint, and drill corresponding holes in the end grain of the 75x25mm – one in the top end of the bottom piece, and one in the bottom end of the top piece. Glue a piece of broomstick into the first hole, and use that as a locator.

The posts should extend 300mm (1ft) below the bottom of each bunk, to form legs, and 600mm (2ft) above the top of the bottom bunk's mattress. This will provide your 900mm (3ft) clearance between the two.

If you want to make the beds identical, extend the posts 600mm (2ft) above the top bunk as well. This will leave you with tall 'goalposts' when the beds are separated. But you can make these look good (and stabilise the structure) by screwing slats of 75 x 25mm (3 x 1in) timber to their outer faces at each end.

Installing a ladder
You'll need a ladder for access to the top bunk. Slats are one possibility here, too: run them up just far enough for the top one to serve as a guard rail. Space them about 250mm (10in) apart, and round over their top edges with a file so they'll be easier on the feet.

Alternatively, you can make a detachable ladder. Simply take two pieces of 75 x 38mm (3 x 1½in) timber to form the uprights, drill through them both at once, and glue in lengths of broomstick (which is cheaper then dowel) for the rungs. Then reinforce the fixing by nailing into the rungs through the edges of the uprights.

If you don't want the ends of the rungs to be visible, you'll have to drill stopped holes separately in each upright, which is a trickier job. Mark out the holes' positions together as far as possible, so that they match.

A reasonable overall width for the ladder is 300mm (1ft). Hang it from both bunks at once with two pairs of proprietary ladder brackets. These are just hooks which you screw into the edges of the ladder uprights.

Finishing touches
You can paint or varnish the bunks, as you wish. But, whatever finish you choose, do give the whole thing a really thorough sanding, in order to round off all the corners. There must be no sharp edges on which children can hurt themselves, and no splinters to penetrate their skin as they clamber over the bunks in their bare feet.

A bright-coloured stain followed by a clear polyurethane varnish might give a cheerful and durable, yet natural, look.

FITTING DRAWERS TO CABINETS

Drawers are the classic way to get easy access to your storage space. Making and fitting them needn't be complicated: it's just a matter of knowing the best methods; and there's plenty of choice.

The word 'handy' could have been invented for drawers. They're indispensable in sideboards, in kitchen units, in desks, in bedside and dressing tables (and of course in chests of drawers!). You can install them in shelf units and even under beds.

If you're thinking of making and fitting drawers to your furniture, the important thing is to be familiar with the options available. There's a method for every purpose, and most are well within the beginner's capacity.

Drawer construction

A drawer, of course, is simply a box without a top. But, because it's constantly pulled out, its front corners are subject to particular stress. That's why traditional dovetail joints are best for the job – you can't pull them apart. However, it would be foolish to pretend they're easy to cut unless you've had a bit of experience. And other methods will do quite well for all practical purposes.

The easiest option of all is to buy a drawer kit. These consist of specially shaped plastic moulding to form the four sides of the drawer (three, if you're using your own front panel – see below) plus corner pieces which form a permanent connection.

The only piece you may need to provide yourself is the bottom panel, which fits into grooves already made in the sides. For a smaller drawer this can be hardboard; but thin plywood is much stiffer, and should be used for larger drawers and any which will be heavily loaded.

The only secret with drawer kits is to follow the instructions closely. So why bother with any other method? Mainly because the sides come only in standard heights, and these may be too shallow. Making your own drawers gets over this problem. The best material for the four sides is undoubtedly solid timber, though multi-ply is an alternative. The minimum thickness you need is about 10mm (⅜in), so you could use 12mm (½in) thick timber which has been planed. Choose the width that makes the best use of the space inside the cabinet. But don't make drawers deeper than their likely contents, or you'll waste space.

For the crucial corner joints, you have several choices – even without using power

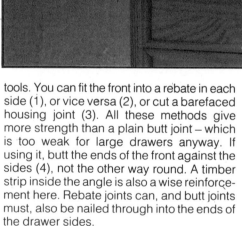

tools. You can fit the front into a rebate in each side (1), or vice versa (2), or cut a barefaced housing joint (3). All these methods give more strength than a plain butt joint – which is too weak for large drawers anyway. If using it, butt the ends of the front against the sides (4), not the other way round. A timber strip inside the angle is also a wise reinforcement here. Rebate joints can, and butt joints must, also be nailed through into the ends of the drawer sides.

The other possibility is dowels (5). They too are stronger if placed sideways.

Rear corners come under less strain, so making them is even simpler. The drawer sides often run past the back, to support the drawer when fully extended. You can either house the back into them (6) – stopping the housing near the top for neatness if you prefer (7) – or butt-joint it (8).

Just glueing and pinning the bottom panel to the bottoms of the sides isn't strong enough for most purposes. It can be grooved in all round instead; but the most convenient way of fitting it is in a grooved *drawer slip* moulding (9), which you can buy ready-machined from timber merchants. Mitre this and glue and

pin it inside the drawer front and sides round the base. If you make the back narrower than the sides, you can slide in the bottom panel underneath it from behind as the last step in assembling the drawer, and just pin it up at the back.

Alternatively, you can make the back the same height as the sides, and simply glue and pin a mitred timber strip, square in section, all round the inside of the box. Lay the bottom panel on that. If you want it to be removable for cleaning, just leave it loose. If not, either glue and pin it in place, or (for a more professional result) mitre a quadrant beading and fix it above the panel in the same way (10).

Whatever you do, cut the bottom panel accurately to size and shape, so it will help to keep the whole structure rigid.

One more type of drawer is ready-made from plastic in its entirety. It's strong and easily cleaned. But, although there's a range of sizes, you naturally cannot arrange or alter any of its dimensions to suit your own requirements. You need to design your furniture to accept it – and you'll need to take special care to make the cabinet accurately to size so the drawer fits into it properly.

WAYS OF MAKING AND HANGING DRAWERS

Choose from these methods when you're putting drawers together from timber or plywood – and when you're fitting them.

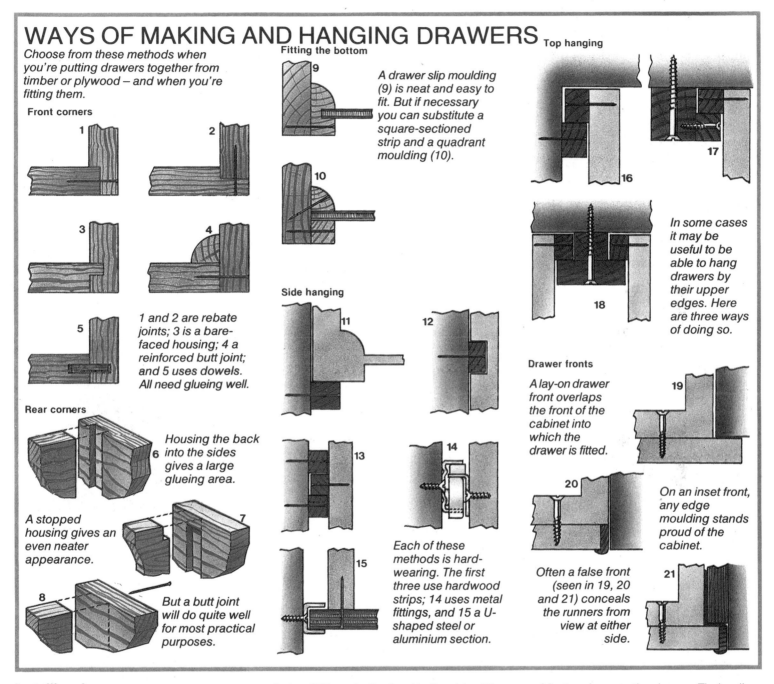

Front corners

Fitting the bottom

A drawer slip moulding (9) is neat and easy to fit. But if necessary you can substitute a square-sectioned strip and a quadrant moulding (10).

Top hanging

In some cases it may be useful to be able to hang drawers by their upper edges. Here are three ways of doing so.

1 and 2 are rebate joints; 3 is a bare-faced housing; 4 a reinforced butt joint; and 5 uses dowels. All need glueing well.

Rear corners

Housing the back into the sides gives a large glueing area.

A stopped housing gives an even neater appearance.

But a butt joint will do quite well for most practical purposes.

Side hanging

Each of these methods is hard-wearing. The first three use hardwood strips; 14 uses metal fittings, and 15 a U-shaped steel or aluminium section.

Drawer fronts

A lay-on drawer front overlaps the front of the cabinet into which the drawer is fitted.

On an inset front, any edge moulding stands proud of the cabinet.

Often a false front (seen in 19, 20 and 21) conceals the runners from view at either side.

Installing drawers

Fitting drawers, too, embraces a number of possibilities. In the traditional method the drawer is the full width of the cabinet interior, and its sides simply rest on the cabinet bottom, or more usually on *runners* fixed to the cabinet sides (11). This system is not only simple but hardwearing. It also demands something above the drawer to stop it tipping forward as you pull it out. In modern box construction, this is usually the top of the cabinet itself, or the runners of the drawer above.

Nowadays, however, drawers are often *side hung:* in other words, the runners are halfway up the drawer sides. Often a strip of timber (12) or plastic, fixed to the side of the cabinet, fits into a groove along the side of the drawer. This takes up no extra space, so that the drawer still fills the whole width of the cabinet.

The sides in plastic drawer kits have grooves already made to mate with such strips. In timber or plywood, however, you'll have to cut them yourself. A simpler way to get a similar result is to glue and pin two parallel strips of timber to the cabinet side – leaving space for a third strip, glued and pinned to the drawer side, to slide between them (13).

Alternatively you can use metal runners (14). These come in two parts, one screwed to the cabinet and one to the drawer. Their rollers ensure a really smooth action – especially useful if you expect heavy loads.

You can even hang drawers with a timber strip fixed near the top of each side, instead of halfway up. This rests on a timber runner fixed to the cabinet (16). The arrangement can be adapted so that the drawer is hung from the underside of the top (17) – useful if you can't use one or both of the drawer or cabinet sides.

There's yet another option. This is to hang the drawer by means of its bottom panel – running it out past the sides, so that its edges can slide in metal or plastic U-sections (15),

ASSEMBLING THE CARCASE

1 *After cutting all the shelves to the same length, mark and cut housings for the divider halfway along the shelves above and below it.*

2 *Use one of the housings as a guide to mark the position of the halving to be cut in the shelf which the divider crosses.*

3 *Measure halfway across the shelf for the depth of the halving. Then cut the divider to length, and measure and mark it out likewise.*

4 *Cut the matching halvings in the divider and the shelf it crosses; use a tenon saw across the grain and then a chisel to chop out the waste.*

5 *Align both uprights exactly and mark on them the height of each shelf (at a point which is halfway across the shelf's thickness).*

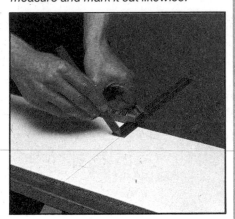

6 *Use a combination square at the same setting to mark the exact dowel positions on both the uprights and on all the shelf ends.*

7 *Drill all the dowel holes, glue the dowels into the shelf ends, and fit all but the top and bottom shelves to the uprights when the adhesive sets.*

8 *Screw the top and bottom shelves into position with plastic jointing blocks, or any other appropriate jointing technique.*

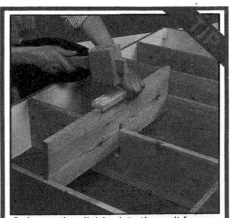

9 *Insert the divider into the unit from the back, using scrap wood to prevent damage to its rear edge as you tap it into position.*

ADDING REINFORCEMENT

1 *Fix a stiffening rail across the top, screwing it to the uprights and the underside of the top shelf with jointing blocks.*

2 *Glue and pin the plinth rail to the front edge of the bottom shelf (which is cut narrower than the other shelves to allow for this).*

3 *Use steel angle repair brackets to hold the plinth firmly to the uprights and thus help to keep the whole unit rigid as well.*

4 *Glue and pin lengths of timber, as long as the uprights are wide, to the ends of the top shelf in order to conceal them.*

5 *Glue and pin further lippings to both long edges of each upright to enhance the unit's appearance and give it extra rigidity.*

6 *Lastly, fill all nail holes with wood stopping of the appropriate shade, and varnish the timber parts to improve their looks and durability.*

will accept a number of different types of stud.

Lastly, there's a very neat way to make the shelves in a freestanding unit fully adjustable. This is to use 'bookshelf strip' – metal strips with continuous rows of slots, into which you clip small metal lugs; the shelves rest on these. The strips (of which you'll need two each side) can be simply screwed to the insides of the uprights, or fitted into vertical grooves if you've got the power tools to cut them.

A home-made version of this system uses removable dowels in regular vertical rows of drilled holes.

Installing dividers

For the distances you can safely span with various thicknesses of various materials, see page 289. Really wide shelves may need extra support in the middle. Vertical dividers will provide this, and can also add to looks and usefulness. They're usually housed or dowelled in at top and bottom, and halved over intermediate shelves.

Alternatively, a square- or rectangular-sectioned timber upright, fixed to the front edges of the shelves, will help matters. It can be glued and pinned to the shelves, dowelled in or notched over them.

Frame shelving

If you only think in terms of box construction, you limit the scope of your projects. A shelf unit's sides can just as well be open frames as single slabs. This gives a lighter look, and also avoids the problems of using man-made boards. But you do need to pay even more attention to making the structure rigid. You'll certainly need extra strengthening pieces running from side to side.

Shelves can be supported in most of the ways already mentioned – with the additional possibility of placing them on the cross pieces in the frames themselves. These cross pieces can even be pieces of broomstick – in other words, each upright is in effect a ladder, with the shelves resting on the rungs.

Box modules

In fact, as far as freestanding shelves are concerned, the possibilities are limitless. One more example may help to demonstrate this. There's no reason why you shouldn't make your 'shelving' up as a stack of completely separate open-fronted boxes. They needn't even be the same depth from front to back. Such a system lets you rearrange its shape completely at will. Its main disadvantage is that most of the panels are duplicated, so the cost of materials goes up. But moving house is easy: each box doesn't even need packing!

As long as you make the structure rigid, the choice of design is yours.

MAKING KITCHEN BASE UNITS

Kitchen units are really nothing more than simple boxes with a few frills added. Here's how to design and build them – and how to arrange them for maximum convenience.

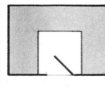
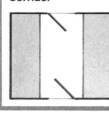

Nowadays even fancy-looking kitchen fitments don't mean complicated joinery and laborious cabinet-making. When you get beneath their patterned worktops and behind their solid timber doors and drawer-fronts, they simply consist of a series of boxes.

These are almost always made from plastic-laminated chipboard, and you can soon build similar ones yourself by the straightforward box-construction methods described in detail on pages 296–299. What's more, you can easily add the refinements which give a really distinctive result.

However, there's no point in just knocking up kitchen units without giving the job a good deal of thought first. That goes for all types of furniture, of course; but the average kitchen is such a busy place that any faults in design will make themselves felt especially sharply.

Kitchen planning
You have to remember that four distinct activities take place in your kitchen: the storage of food, its preparation, the actual cooking, and the serving.

Food storage space includes the larder, the refrigerator and the vegetable racks. Food preparation centres around the sink, and neighbouring worktops. For ease of plumbing, the washing machine usually has to go near the sink. Cutlery needs to be stored in this area too.

When it comes to cooking, the cooker is obviously the most important element; but pans and other utensils should also be stored nearby.

Serving is done from a worktop. If the kitchen is big enough for a breakfast bar, that should be in this area too.

A kitchen's efficiency depends on how easily it allows you to move within and between these activities. For a smooth work-flow, a kitchen should really be circular. That's impossible unless you live in a light-house, so this ideal pattern has to be modified according to the shape of your kitchen and the position of its door. Despite the enormous range of room plans and sizes, there are only three basic kitchen layouts: the L-shaped, the U-shaped and the corridor – and you can't choose which you want.

So how are all the activities to be fitted in? the best item to start with is the sink. In most homes this has to go on an outside wall, in order to get access to the drains, and many people like to site it in front of the window so that they can look outside as they work.

Next, take the cooker. This is often used in conjunction with the sink. Furthermore, it's a good idea to have a worktop on each side of the hob, and between the hob and sink, because things often need to be laid down there. In a corridor kitchen, sink and cooker should be against the same wall, so that you don't have to carry containers of boiling water across the room.

With these two main elements in position, you can surround them with your units. Always keep the workflow in mind. Tall cupboards should be in a corner or at the end of a run, so as not to interrupt the worktop surface. This even applies when you have split-level cooking, with separate hob and oven, and the oven is housed in a tall unit because the oven doesn't need such constant attention as the hob.

ADDING A DRAWER AND DOOR

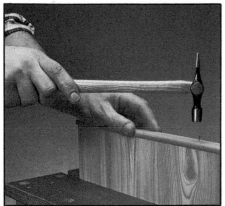

1 Cut out the drawer-front, and if necessary glue and pin on a strip of moulding (eg, hockey stick), to conceal its top edge.

2 Cut and assemble the drawer, following the makers' instructions if using a kit; then attach the drawer-front, with its handle.

3 Insert the drawer into the unit, and mark the position of the bottom edge of the drawer-front. This will give the exact height for the door.

4 Cut the door to size, mark the hinge positions, and fix the hinges to the door and the completed box. Put the drawer back on its runners.

Similarly, it doesn't matter if, in a corridor kitchen, the oven is against the opposite wall to the sink, because you don't carry boiling water to and from the oven.

But if for some reason you have to include units of different heights in your scheme, try to make sure you don't change height next to the hob; it's important to be able to slide pans easily on and off it.

What dimensions?
Another vital consideration is how high your units should be. A height of 900mm (3ft) is usual for the sink, hob, worktops and any other surface on which you work while standing up. Of course, this isn't perfect for everyone, but on the whole it's a good compromise. Why not conduct a few tests to discover the height which is exactly (rather than just approximately) right for you?

The standard depth (from front to back) for all kitchen units is 600mm (2ft). This matches the depth of most kitchen appliances; it provides ample space on the worktop and in the cupboards underneath; and it means you can still install a 300mm (1ft) deep unit on the wall above without banging your head on it.

Lastly, you'll probably want to make worktops as long as you can. Unless you have a really enormous kitchen, it's most unlikely you'll find yourself with too much working space!

In the corner, of course, you'll have cupboard space which is inaccessible. The two commonest solutions to this are to include extra frontage at an angle, and to install a special proprietary revolving corner unit which means you don't have to reach inside.

As for materials, timber-veneered chip-

board is an alternative to the plastic-laminated variety, but you'll have to varnish (if not paint) it to keep out moisture.

What width?
It's usually impractical to make a single box which runs right along the wall. Instead, make a series of smaller ones. You can choose any width you like for these units, and the sensible plan is to follow that of the cupboard doors you're going to put on. Among the widths available in veneered and plastic-faced chipboard are 300, 375, 450, 525 and 600mm (12, 15, 18, 21 and 24in) – so just select one of these. The long edges are already covered with matching edging strip, so it would be silly to lose them by cutting the board lengthwise to a non-standard width.

You can also buy very stylish ready-made louvred and panelled doors, which will give a sophisticated look with no extra trouble.

In all probability, you'll find that the total length of your units doesn't divide exactly by any standard width of board. But that doesn't matter, because you have a certain amount of leeway. For a start, there are two different ways of hanging the doors. Instead of insetting each door between the sides, top and bottom of the box, you can have lay-on doors, which overlap the front edges – and that means you can vary the amount of overlap. (Special hinges are needed for this – see *Ready Reference*).

Alternatively you can leave the odd amount as a gap between units (eg, for storing trays). The minimum width for this is about 100mm (4in), and 150mm (6in) is ideal.

Building the box
The only major difference between a kitchen unit and any other piece of box furniture is that its top doesn't form part of the basic structure. Instead, you fit two cross-bearers between the sides – one at the front, one at the back – with plastic jointing blocks.

The front cross-bearer can be of 50x25mm (2x1in) planed timber, but if you make the back one 50x50mm (2x2in) it's thick enough for you to screw through it later, when you come to fix the unit to the wall for stability. At that stage you may need to remove at least part of the skirting board for a close fit.

Add a back to the unit by pinning a piece of hardboard or thin plywood to the edges of the box (see pages 296–299 for details). This will help to keep it rigid. Fix units together side-by-side with screws, or preferably with special plastic fittings called cabinet connecting screws (see *Ready Reference*). And lastly, add a worktop which extends along the whole run of units – fastening it by screwing up through the cross-bearers.

You can buy worktops ready-made to a

standard width of 600mm (2ft), and covered with an extra-tough plastic laminate which is curved ('postformed') round the front edge so it can't chip. If using a laminate, be sure you get a worktop grade, and not a 'vertical' grade (used on vertical surfaces only), which is thinner and less durable.

Even with the right grade, there are limits to its heat-resistance (you can't put pans onto it straight from the hob), and you can't chop on it. A still tougher material is ceramic tiles, which you could lay on a chipboard base; but these are more expensive, and noisy in use.

Whatever its surface, the worktop should overhang the front of the units – including any protruding doors and drawer fronts – by about 25mm (1in). This makes it more convenient to work on. A recessed plinth at the bottom (see pages 296–299) will keep your feet well clear of the base of the unit while you work.

It's important to make sure no water seeps down behind the worktop, otherwise it will get into the edge of the chipboard and damage it. You can get special plastic mouldings to fit in this gap. Otherwise, silicon sealant along the junction with the wall may do the trick; but a strip of timber – say 50x25mm (2x1in) planed, glued, and nailed or screwed, into the back edge of the worktop to form an upstand – will provide extra protection. It will also help to bring the worktop forward a bit, which is necessary if it's to overhang a unit of the same depth.

You may well find that an uneven floor makes it hard to line units up properly. The answer is to pack them up where necessary, eg, with wedges. Serious discrepancies call for either levelling the floor or adjusting the height of the units' sides.

Doors and drawers

When you come to fit the doors, there are quite a number of varieties of hinge. Your best bet is to go to a good hardware store, see what's in stock and ask for advice. The basic choice is between traditional butt hinges, and modern types which enable you to use a lay-on arrangement without obstructing the doors of neighbouring units when open.

If you're using an inset door, you'll need something for it to close against: either a strip of wood, or perhaps a metal or plastic catch.

You may want a shelf inside the unit. The way to fit this is either on top of wooden battens screwed to the sides, or with proprietary shelf fittings – of which, again, there's quite a range.

You can either run the doors all the way up to the top, or fit drawers as well. Drawers can be made yourself out of solid timber and plywood, or bought in the form of plastic kits whose components you snap together. They can run either on strips of hardwood or plastic, or on metal fittings with built-in rollers. Both types of runner have to be screwed to the sides of the box. So if you want two or more drawers side-by-side (eg, on a double unit) you'll usually need to install dividers between them, to which you can screw the runners.

The trick when fitting a drawer is to make its front overlap the edges of the box sides – like a lay-on door. That way you cover up any discrepancies in the alignment. And you can add the drawer-front as an ornamental extra, perhaps of solid timber, screwing it to the existing front panel of a drawer that's already made up. When measuring and marking up the front, be careful to get it square – and the right height, so that it extends up to the bottom of the worktop and down to the top of the door.

But don't rely on an overlapping front to prevent the drawer sliding too far in. This will place too much strain on its fixings. Instead, screw a block of wood or something else (eg, a piece of what you're using for the runners) to each side of the unit in the appropriate position near the back. Alternatively, make use of the rear cross-bearer, or its plastic jointing blocks, for the same purpose.

Wire trays are another form of sliding storage that many people find convenient. They can be fitted instead of shelves, or indeed, in addition to them.

You'll find a lot more information about how to fit drawers and doors on pages 306–309 and 314–317.

Doubling up

The basic unit can also be doubled in width and fitted with a pair of doors. If you do this, it's best to add a divider in the middle to give the worktop extra support; notch the divider at the top corners to fit the cross-bearers.

A double unit will take a sink, let into a hole specially cut in the worktop. In this case you'll probably want to put a shelf below the sink so as to make some self-contained cupboards, and then run the divider up to the shelf.

Other fittings

If you go to a good stockist, you can enhance your kitchen units with a tremendous range of proprietary accessories. These include extending tabletops; pull-out ironing boards; telescopic towel rails; plastic and ceramic scoops for liquids and dried foods such as rice and sugar; foot-operated door openers, useful if your hands are full; built-in waste bins which pull out or fit on the inside of cupboard doors; fitted chopping boards; fitted bread boxes; and so on.

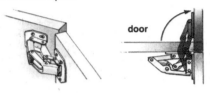
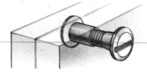
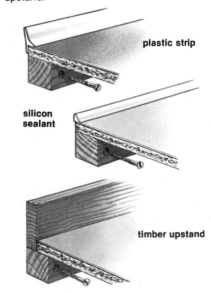

FITTING A KITCHEN : 1

Ready-made cabinets are the classic way of providing kitchen storage. Some come factory-assembled, others in kit form. Installing them is straightforward when you know the tricks of the trade.

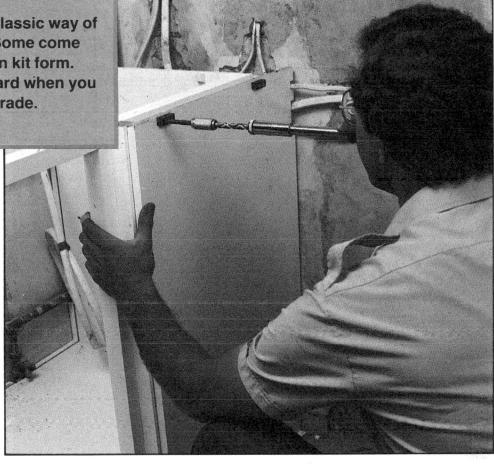

Nowadays, fitting out a kitchen almost always means installing a series of floor-standing and wall-hung cabinets – usually called 'units'.

These are highly standardised. Floor-standing or 'base' units consist of two side panels, a base panel, a thin back panel, and a recessed plinth at the front. There's usually a stiffening rail at the back as well, and there are often shelves inside.

There's no top panel, because the idea is to fill all the available space in the room simply by installing units side-by-side (using ones whose widths most nearly achieve this), and then to cover the whole lot with single lengths of worktop.

To allow this, widths vary considerably; 300, 500 or 600mm (12, 20 or 24in) makes a 'single' unit, 1000 or 1200mm (39 or 47in) a double, and 1500mm (59in) a triple. As for other dimensions, base units are almost always about 870mm (34in) high and 600mm (2ft) deep from front to back. Wall units come in several heights, but most are only 300mm (1ft) deep.

Variants include corner units, tall larder and oven-housing units, tray spaces, open shelf units, and a number of others.

Melamine-faced chipboard is pretty well the universal material for side and base panels, plinths, shelves and even stiffening rails. The back panel is usually melamine-faced hardboard. Most worktops are of chipboard too, but faced with a thicker and tougher laminate. The standard worktop thickness is 30mm (1³⁄₁₆in); the width is usually 600mm (2ft), and many lengths are available. Special double-edged worktops (and special units) are available for 'islands' in the centre of large kitchens.

The real variety comes in doors and drawer-fronts, which are made in any number of materials and finishes, and provide most visual impact in the average fitted kitchen.

Why units?

It's still possible, of course, to fit out a kitchen without units. You can fix softwood battens to the walls, floor and/or ceiling, and use them for mounting shelves, dividers, end panels, extra front rails and uprights, doors, and so on (see pages 105-109 and 155-159 for further information about this method).

However, any professional woodworker will tell you that chipboard is cheaper than time. It always makes more sense for him to install square, uniform cabinets – built in his workshop or factory with the aid of time-saving machines – than to spend long hours on site cutting everything to fit individually.

The do-it-yourselfer's time is free, so the equation is rather different. But there's no doubt that units do simplify things, and the extra cost of duplicated side panels in a row of cabinets is probably balanced by that of all the softwood you need to do it the other way. Besides, battens need lots of wall-fixings, whereas base units require only a couple of screws each. Under the added weight of the worktop, they won't shift.

Working with units

While planning for your basic kitchen requirements you can also be choosing the units you want. Its up to you to sort out your personal priorities from the vast selection on the market. The main differences lie in price, in finish, and in the number of variants and accessories available.

Once you've managed to settle on a short list of likely purchases, you can take the design a stage further by working out which combination of sizes will best fill the space at your disposal. Expensive ranges make this job easier because they generally come in a greater number of different widths.

Provided your measurements are accurate, most small irregularities such as uneven floors and walls can be overcome during installation. One thing that's worth a specific check, however, is whether the walls are square to one another. If any meet at much more or less than 90°, you may have to cope with the discrepancy by setting one or more rows of units away from the wall – and this may mean a slightly wider worktop to cover the resulting gap.

There are three types of unit: ready-assembled, flat pack, and home-made (see pages 322–326).

The carcases, doors and drawers of flat-pack units (plus the worktops) all come in separate cartons. Your first task is to check that everything you've ordered is actually present. But don't put the cabinets together until you need them, or they'll take up an enormous amount of living space.

HANGING THE DOOR

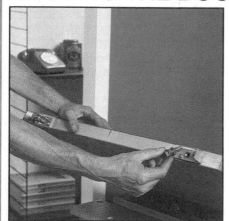

1 Screw the hanger bolts into the plates on the top edge of the door, so their ends protrude down into the holes you've drilled.

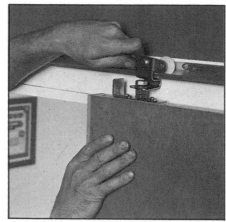

2 Slide the wheel units onto the track, and slip the hanger bolts into them – first loosening the nuts to let you do this easily.

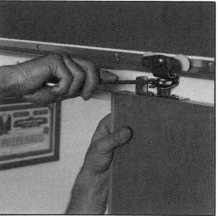

3 Turn each bolt, so the door rides up or down on the thread, to get the door level and give a slight clearance above the floor.

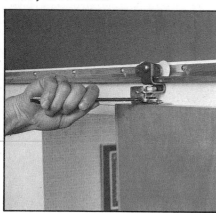

5 Tighten the bottom nut against the plate itself, so as to keep the door at the right level and to prevent vibration loosening the nuts.

6 Fit a piece of timber in position, if necessary, to narrow the opening and so eliminate gaps when the door is closed.

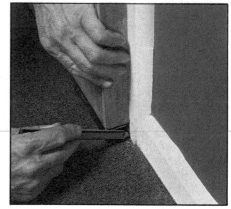

7 With the door hanging truly vertical and fully closed, mark exactly where the bottom corner of its opening edge comes.

9 Slide the door across so that the guide fixed to the floor engages in the channel fitted to the door's bottom edge.

10 Move the door so the guide is just hidden, and screw a plastic doorstop (if supplied) to the batten as a buffer for the top plate.

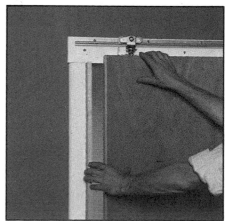

11 Close the door, and adjust the position of the filler piece down the jamb so the door edge meets it in the way you want.

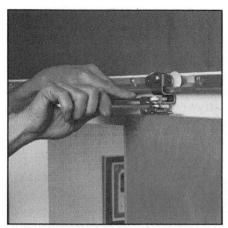

4 *Lock the bolt onto the wheel unit by holding its head with one spanner and using another to adjust the nut immediately below it.*

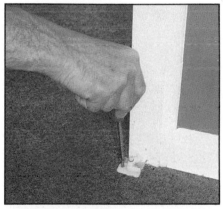

8 *Open the door fully, and screw the guide cam, block or wheel to the floor in accordance with the mark you've just made.*

12 *Finally, nail the filler piece in position, and complete the job by fitting a pelmet (if desired) to conceal the track and the batten.*

shaped timber strips which are attached to the back edge of the door (ie, the trailing edge as you close it). One other system, however, is worth a special mention. It uses a bottom guide channel with a kink in it, which causes the door to close hard against the door frame, thus eliminating gaps. When you open the door, the kink throws it clear again so that it can slide freely.

Special sliding doors

Although the average doorway needs only a single sliding door, wide ones usually need two or even three. This especially applies to openings, such as those in fitted wardrobes, which take up the full width of a room or alcove – because there's no wall for a single door to slide against when it's opened. For this purpose there are double tracks which enable the doors to slide past each other. These are generally suitable only for ceiling (rather than wall) mounting, but they make it easier to achieve the same net result than by using two single tracks.

There are also 'sympathetic' gears, with which one door automatically opens (or closes) when you open (or close) the other. These, however, differ in requiring sliding (ie, wall) space on both sides of the doorway.

Lastly, you can mount doors so that they slide inside a cavity. You actually build a false wall around the doorway, using plasterboard and timber studs, so that the door disappears neatly into the gap between the real and false walls as you open it. This is certainly neater than the standard arrangement which leaves the open door in plain view; and, if you line the opening in the new wall with architraves and skirting boards which match those around, it could solve the problem of making sliding doors blend with older and distinctly styled houses.

Carrying out the installation

Since the various makes of sliding door gear do differ, you'll naturally have to stick to the manufacturer's instructions to make sure you get the fixing details right. However, the basic principles of installation are common to all.

The first step is to gain a clear idea of how you want the door to fit against the frame when closed, and how the door and frame will look from all angles. There are many ways of modifying the frame to achieve various results, both functionally and in terms of appearance, several are illustrated on page 332. A lot will depend on the style of the rooms and the furniture in them, as well as the neighbouring doorways on either side, and on the width of the new door.

On the door side of the doorway, you'll always need to cut away at least the overhead section of the existing architrave – flush with the top of the opening – in order to accommo-

date the batten for the track on which the door slides.

In some cases you can leave the rest of the architrave, and simply add an extra piece or pieces of timber to the inside face of the door lining to act as a doorstop. But it's often neater to remove the architrave down the jamb against which the door closes, and substitute a thicker piece of wood as a doorstop, fixed to the face of the wall rather than inside the lining. You may even want to replace the lining of that jamb altogether with a wider piece.

When you've fitted the door, you may also need to widen or thicken the lining of the opposite jamb – by replacing it or adding a piece – to fill any gap left when the door is closed.

Once you've sorted out these major points, the remainder of the job should be straightforward, if not exactly routine. First you need to get the track-bearing batten level on the wall overhead, packing it out if the wall is crooked. Then cut the metal track itself to length (ie, slightly more than twice the door width), get that level too, and screw it to the batten.

You'll need to fit the guide channel to the bottom edge of the door before hanging it, which you do by means of plates, hanger bolts and rollers. You can make fine vertical and lateral adjustments with the appropriate nuts – both before and after screwing the guide block, wheel or cam to the floor and aligning the door with it.

Finishing off

A few other touches finish the job off. It's quite a good idea to add one or two small plastic or rubber doorstops (usually supplied as part of the kit) to prevent the door from opening too far, and make a pelmet (see *Ready Reference*). There's also the fitting of handles, plus a latch or lock if you want one, to be considered.

Your pelmet will need to be fixed to the wall invisibly for appearance's sake. Two possible answers are timber battens and metal angle brackets. In both cases, you'll probably need to screw the ends of the pelmet to the wall via these fixings first, before adding the front and top panels (otherwise you won't be able to get at the wall-fixing screws).

With imagination, a pelmet can be turned into a really impressive feature. You can look in the shops for a suitable moulding, and mitre it neatly round the upper edge of the pelmet to form a cornice. Or you can use panel mouldings of various types to make rectangular patterns right across the front.

Fitting a sliding door isn't a job you can do in a few moments – but you may well find it easier than hanging a door on hinges, and you're almost bound to end up with a smoothly gliding result.

FITTING A KITCHEN :2

Provided you've accurately positioned and levelled your base units, it should be no problem to install the worktops, wall units, doors, drawers, shelves and accessories which will complete your fitted kitchen. Here's how to ensure a trouble-free job.

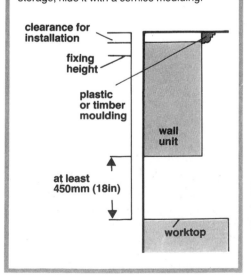

Kitchen fitting is a classic example of a job you can tackle the right way or the wrong way.

The right way is very definitely to start as shown and described on pages 327–330. That is, by levelling and fixing the assembled base-unit carcases at a height determined by the highest floor point around the walls, ensuring the fronts are flush as well.

At the same time, you'll probably find yourself adding an extra panel to blank off the interior of each straight corner unit – that is, the half which has no door because it disappears under the adjacent worktop. Another little detail requiring attention may be the fixing of small sections of board to blank off the plinth recess where two straight units join at a corner. Look at the step-by-step photographs on page 329 for a clear view of these operations.

Any tall units, such as oven housings and larders, need to be assembled and fixed in position at this stage too (though they can't, of course, be made level with the other base units): see page 330. In addition, you can fit their 'top boxes' now.

Adding worktops

Your other preliminary task is to provide adequate support and fixings for the worktops.

As a rule the support simply comes from the base units themselves, plastic joint blocks being screwed to their side panels to hold the top in place. However, overhanging ends will need different arrangements – usually just a batten or a strip of board fixed to the wall, or to the side of a tall unit if the worktop butts against that.

In the particular kitchen shown here, the worktop runs through a floor-to-ceiling opening, making a serving counter with a hatch above. The space below it, which would otherwise offer from outside an unsightly view of the fridge, is closed by a transverse panel fixed to the walls.

Worktops must be cut to length, marked, and then shaped to fit round obstacles and hug the contours of the walls – though tiles or an upstand (of wood or plastic) will conceal smallish gaps. A jigsaw and Surform are useful tools here. With the former, remember that positioning the panel upside-down will prevent chipping the laminate as you cut.

Once each section of top fits to your satisfaction, you'll be able to mark cut-outs for the hob and sink. Don't make them over-large.

When all is ready, lower and fix each section of worktop in place. Butt joins are usually covered with strips of purpose-made aluminium profile – cut to length by you and often screwed to the end of the appropriate piece before it's positioned.

Installing wall units

Now you're ready to put up the wall units. Start by deciding on a suitable gap between their undersides and the worktop – at least 450mm (18in), so you can easily see to the back of the worktop and store appliances there.

Add to that gap the height of the wall units, but subtract the distance by which their fixings are set down from their tops. Subtract, too, any clearance needed above them to drop them into place.

Mark the resulting fixing height along the wall or walls, using a spirit level, and screw the fixings on there. If the walls are out of square, packing behind the fixings may be needed first, so the cabinet fronts will be at right-angles in each corner.

Wall-unit fixings vary a lot, from simple timber battens to clever two-part brackets. The latter let you adjust the units' heights after you've hung them.

Ready Reference

DECIDING HEIGHTS

When choosing and installing wall units, bear in mind that you'll need certain minimum clearances:
- between worktop and units
- between units and ceiling.

If the latter gap is too small to allow storage, hide it with a cornice moulding.

clearance for installation

fixing height

plastic or timber moulding

wall unit

at least 450mm (18in)

worktop

INSTALLING WORKTOPS

Most worktops nowadays have a rounded ('postformed') front edge, though some have timber lipping.

All are expensive, so take special care when marking and cutting them. It's easy to ruin one with even a small mistake. In particular, don't forget to reverse everything as appropriate when working with the board face-down.

See Ready Reference for more details of how to go about shaping tops to fit, and to accommodate inset fitments.

Very often, worktops rest entirely on base units, simply bridging the gaps which house appliances. But sometimes – as in this kitchen – there are overhanging ends which also need support. Battens are used here, but many ranges offer special legs for the purpose; sometimes, too, you can use panels.

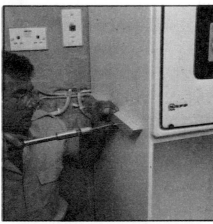

1 Where the end of a worktop meets a vertical surface, such as the side of an oven housing, a screwed-on batten is often the best way to support it.

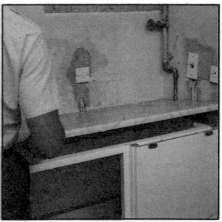

2 Scribe and cut the first section of worktop (in this case the left-hand one) to fit round obstacles such as pipes, and lower it into position.

3 If the hob goes over a unit, mark the unit's internal size on the underside of the worktop before setting out on it the complete cutout you'll need.

4 Cut out the hob opening and replace the section of worktop. Tiles or an 'upstand' will conceal any small gaps caused by uneven walls.

5 Where the worktop passes through the opening to form a hatch, a piece of board (or a timber batten) is screwed to the wall for support.

6 Below the worktop in the hatch, a panel fixed with plastic joint blocks closes the opening and conceals the fridge which will go inside.

7 Cut out the sink hole with a jigsaw, just like the opening for the hob. Subsequent worktop sections are fitted like the first one.

8 Worktop joins are often finished with a metal strip. Screw it on before the worktop goes in, or push it in later for easy removal when cleaning.

INSTALLING WALL UNITS

1 *Measuring up from the worktop, rule a level line across the wall at the exact height where you'll be screwing on the wall-unit fixings.*

2 *Drill and plug the wall, and screw the fixings on. To avoid problems, make sure they're firm and correctly aligned. The screws should be at least No 10s.*

3 *Start with a corner unit, lifting it up onto its fixings. You may have to cut carcase panels round obstacles first, just as with base units.*

4 *As you fit subsequent units, check them for level at top or bottom. Proprietary fixings generally allow adjustment with a screwdriver.*

5 *A corner wall unit, like a corner base unit, usually needs a front panel to close off half its interior. You may need to take it down first.*

6 *Start the next row in a corner too. Out-of-square walls may mean considerable packing if the cabinets are to meet each other at right-angles.*

With all these systems, there's no need to hold the cabinet in position while fixing into the wall. However, it's still a very good idea to cut battens which will support each cabinet on the worktops as you offer it up, eg when marking for cutouts round obstacles.

Wall units are never tight up against the ceiling. This is not only because they must usually be lowered slightly onto their fixings, but also because they tend to sag very slightly afterwards – and, more importantly, because a sagging ceiling might otherwise prevent their doors from opening properly.

The resulting gap can easily be filled with a suitable timber or plastic moulding to avoid a dirt trap on the cupboard tops.

The units are assembled in a very similar way to base units. Here too, installation always starts in a corner, where a blanking-off panel may again be needed.

Check that they're level and that the fronts are flush. Then cramp each pair carefully together in order to fix them to each other. You can do this either with special plastic 'cabinet connector screws' or else with ordinary metal screws – best driven in where they'll be hidden, for example by the hinges. You can fasten the base units together in the same way at the same time.

Now is also the time to add any narrow panels or short shelves to fill odd gaps beside units. If they're to butt against walls, scribe them to fit over any irregularities.

Moreover, some types of plinth, screwed on from the front, are added at this stage – as are specialised accessories like built-in waste bins, pull-out fittings, carousels, wire racks and so on.

Finishing off

Provided all the units are square (check by measuring the diagonals of each to see if they're equal), the doors can now go on.

All mass-produced kitchen units these days have concealed hinges – complex-looking devices which in fact make life a lot easier on this particular job. They press-fit into ready-drilled circular recesses in the unit doors, where two screws secure them.

Then you just offer up each door to the cabinet and screw the other end of each hinge to it, using the pilot holes already there. Backward, forward, upward and downward adjustments are made by means of integral screws, so you should have few difficulties in ensuring rows of perfectly aligned doors.

Drawers, if any, come in kit form and are simply slid into the units. Shelves will most likely rest on plastic supports which you push into pre-drilled holes.

And that's about it. Unless you've installed home-made units with separate timber or wood-veneered doors, the cabinets won't even need any finishing treatment . . . so your fitted kitchen is complete.

BUILT-IN WARDROBES

Fitted cupboards are not only cheaper than ready-made furniture; they're neater, too. And you can choose from any number of different details to suit your own needs and tastes.

The traditional wardrobe is, of course, a completely freestanding unit with a bottom, a top and four sides. Many people possess one as a hand-me-down, and there are plenty of handsome, well-crafted examples.

However, if you're thinking about providing storage facilities from scratch, movable furniture has at least four important disadvantages when you compare it with built-in pieces.

The first is its cost. Except perhaps for the very cheapest (and shoddiest) off-the-shelf wardrobes, you'll find it cheaper to buy the materials and fit your own units – simply because the walls, floor and ceiling of the room replace (instead of duplicating) some of the panels of the cupboard. This saves space, too; and it means you don't have to devote much thought to the often tricky question of making the cabinet rigid.

The second point is that factory-made furniture won't necessarily fit neatly into the room. A freestanding wardrobe that's too big for an alcove can be a real nuisance, obstructing free movement and even light. This problem, of course, doesn't arise at all when you design your own scheme to fit the room.

And when it comes to style, you needn't simply accept a manufacturer's idea of what constitutes elegance. There's a vast range of alternatives.

Lastly, all ready-made wardrobes create a natural dust-trap above and below. A fitted unit scores here, too, provided you run it right up to the ceiling.

Thoughtful design
So think positively. Aim to build a wardrobe – or a whole set of cupboards – which meets all your requirements.

The first consideration, naturally, is what you're going to store, and how much space it will take up. Look at pages 288–291 and 322–326 for details where crockery, cutlery and other objects are concerned. When it comes to clothing, your best guide is a close look – tape measure in hand – at all the items likely to be involved. Coats, trousers, and so on must hang clear of the floor; and you need to be sure you provide enough depth from front to back if you're planning to hang your garments sideways.

At the same time, consider the room itself, including existing furnishings (beds, for example), in relation to where you're going to site the cupboard. One obvious place, of course, is in an alcove (see pages 105-109 for more details), where it will be completely unobtrusive, and construction will be easiest of all. But it can just as well run right across one end of the room. Alternatively, it can start or stop (or both) part of the way along a wall, with the addition of side panels at one or both ends.

Visual effect, as well as convenience, plays a big part here. Even before you think about the details of materials, trim and finish, you know that full-width and full-height fitments will have cleaner (or, if you prefer the word, starker) lines than smaller ones.

They may provide other bonuses, too. Suppose, for example, that you have an unused and unsightly fireplace. There's no reason why you shouldn't build cupboards which run in a continuous line not only across the alcoves on either side, but also in front of the chimney breast, thereby concealing the whole thing. You could fit a fixed panel over the fireplace, but install shallow shelves behind doors in the cupboard area above the mantelpiece. Other items – pipework, perhaps, or even a washbasin or shower cubicle – can be hidden in the same way.

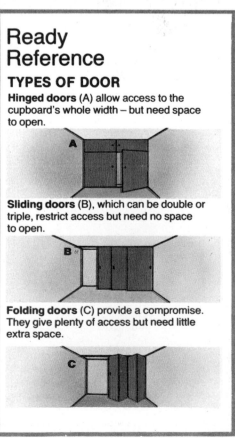

Ready Reference

TYPES OF DOOR

Hinged doors (A) allow access to the cupboard's whole width – but need space to open.

Sliding doors (B), which can be double or triple, restrict access but need no space to open.

Folding doors (C) provide a compromise. They give plenty of access but need little extra space.

339

DESIGNING CUPBOARDS

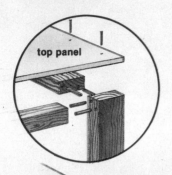

Above: One very natural location is in an alcove. A cupboard here makes use of what can be an awkward corner, while taking up no actual living space.

Above: You can also run cupboards right across the room. If appropriate, you can use both alcoves and hide the chimney breast too.

You can choose from many ways to construct fitted cupboards.

Above: Not only can you build the whole frame out from the wall behind, you can also add a panel overhead (top). This is often handy for long-term storage of objects too bulky to fit inside, such as suitcases.

Frame members which aren't fixed to the floor, wall or ceiling will require at least simple jointing.

plastic jointing blocks

side panel screwed from inside

counterbored screws

Above: Cupboards needn't run all the way from wall to wall. Stop them short if necessary. Side panels can be fixed from outside (far left) – being either cut from thick board, as shown, or cut from thin plywood and pinned on. More neatly, they can be attached from inside (left), for example with counterbored screws.

PREPARING FOR WARDROBE DOORS

1 Your first job is to locate the joists and decide where to make your fixings. Then check whether the ceiling is level along that line.

2 If the ceiling isn't flat, you'll need a batten to take up the unevenness. Hold it in position and scribe the ceiling's contours onto it.

3 Plane the upper face of the batten down to the scribed line, so that it will fit snugly into place across the ceiling without any gaps.

Basic construction

One way to approach fitted-cupboard design is to think of a frame, screwed to the walls, floor and ceiling, on which doors are hung.

If you're using timber for this frame, it needs to be wide enough for wall fixing, and also thick enough to take hinges if any. Timber measuring 50x50mm (2x2in) or 75x38mm (3x1½in) is likely to be suitable; for various possible fixing details, see pages 301–305 for additional information. Remember that you'll almost certainly have to scribe the uprights to match the exact shape of the wall for a true fit.

If the cupboard runs from wall to wall and from floor to ceiling, you can get away without cutting corner joints, because all the pieces are fixed in position. If it stops short in either direction, at least one upright or crosspiece will need jointing in carefully. Mortise and tenon, bridle, halving and dowel joints are all possibilities. Top panels can be nailed to the frame from above; they can be of any board thick and strong enough to bear what's likely to be stored on them. Side panels – of blockboard, chipboard (plain, veneered or plastic-faced) or plywood – are best screwed from inside for strength and neatness, though you could economise by using 6mm (¼in) plywood, pinned from outside.

Fitting doors

Doors can be hinged, sliding or folding. Hinged doors can of course be lay-on or inset – see pages 306–309 for details. Lay-on doors are less trouble to fit, because they're unaffected by frames that are out of square; in fact, the doors will cover up any misalignment of the frame. Moreover, the frame makes separate doorstops unnecessary. See

You have a wide choice of possible hinge types, but make sure you take both the cupboard and hinge design fully into account before deciding which hinges to use.

Sliding and folding doors are very popular alternatives. You buy the track and sliding gear as a kit; it will come complete with fixing instructions. On a floor-to-ceiling cupboard, you need a secure ceiling fixing in order to mount the track safely. Cavity fixings into plasterboard (often secure enough in other situations) won't do. If you can't fix through into ceiling joists – and can't take up the floorboards upstairs in order to fit noggins between the joists and fix into those – go for hinged doors instead.

Sliding or folding doors which are fitted on a full-height cupboard can enable you to do without a frame altogether. You simply fasten their track directly onto the ceiling, and allow the doors to slide right from wall to wall. This is probably the easiest system of all to install. If a wall is uneven, fix a strip of timber down it to cover the gaps down the edge of the closed door. If, on the other hand, you're incorporating a side panel, fix that to wall, floor and ceiling via battens or even plastic jointing blocks. (You could hinge a door to it instead.)

Even sliding doors' obvious drawback – that they allow access to only part of the cupboard at any one time – can sometimes be overcome. If you run the unit across a chimney breast as suggested above, the doors from each alcove can slide into the middle and thus out of the way.

Look at pages 331–335 for further details on choosing and fitting various types of sliding doors. The principles are just the same whether you're installing them in a doorway or in a cupboard.

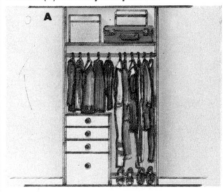
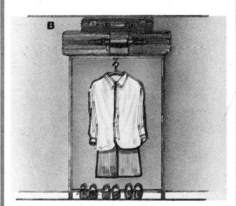
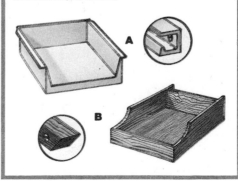

4 Re-position the batten, and use the spirit level again to check whether its lower face is now true. If not, plane it down a bit further.

5 When you've got the alignment right, drill and countersink the batten, drill the ceiling, and finally, screw the batten into position.

COMPLETING THE CUPBOARD FRONT

1 For sliding doors, screw the track onto the batten. Remember to allow for the depth of any beading to be fitted down the sides – see 9.

2 Cut each side upright to length (to fit under the ceiling batten) and mark on it the height of the skirting-board. Square the mark across the piece.

3 A good way to gauge the skirting-board's thickness is with a combination square; loosen the screw and adjust the square accordingly.

5 Fit the upright against the wall and check it for plumb in both directions. Then, if necessary, scribe and cut it, or else pack out any gaps.

6 Screw both uprights into position. With hinged doors, and often with sliding doors, you'll want to fix a similar batten to the floor as well.

7 Cut the doors to size, allowing for clearance and any overlap. For sliding doors, add wheels or sliders as instructed by the manufacturers.

9 Make adjustments so the doors hang properly. For sliding doors, fit floor guides, and pin beading down each side to hide gaps and exclude dust.

10 Often a pelmet strip (say 12mm/½in thick), nailed in position, is useful to hide the track and any ceiling batten when sliding doors have been hung.

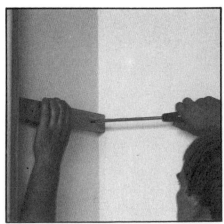

11 If you want an interior shelf, just screw battens to all three walls, ensuring they're level, and place a board on top of them.

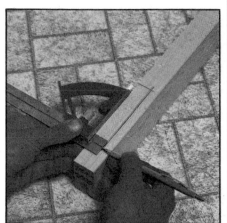

4 *Then you can hold a pencil against the square, run both down the side of the upright, and cut away the waste area you've marked out.*

8 *Hang the doors. Wheels or sliders just hook onto the track; hinges usually require screws. Either way, you'll probably need a helper.*

12 *Lastly, add door handles, plus whatever finishing treatment you think is appropriate, in order to make your fitted wardrobe complete.*

Making doors

The doors' appearance, of course, makes or mars the whole thing. But there's no limit to your choices here. For a start, they can be either full-height, or split at a certain level (available sizes may well decide this particular question for you).

As for materials and finishes, you can use plywood or blockboard, suitably edged, varnished or painted (chipboard is less than ideal because of its weight). You can decorate it with slim timber mouldings. You can paper it, or paste some fabric onto it, to match the rest of your decorations. You can use decorative wallboards, ready-made louvred doors, or even mirrored glass. And, in addition to sliding and folding tracks and gear, some firms supply aluminium edging which forms part of the hanging system, and turns sheets of board into handsome doors.

You can even buy complete 'cupboard fronts' – sets of hinged doors already hung in over-large frames, which can be cut down to the height you want. Scribed panels will hide any gaps at floor and ceiling level.

Internal details

Inside the unit, the first necessity is a rail for hanging clothes. Chrome- and brass-plated tubing is readily available; you can fix it either with the special brackets made for the purpose, or in notches cut in the upper edges of wall battens at either end.

At least one shelf, often at high level, is very useful. Use whichever fixing is most appropriate – see pages 288–295, and in particular *Ready Reference*, page 319. Choose the material and thickness according to what it will have to carry.

The occasional drawer, too, is invaluable for storing underclothes, socks and so on. Consult pages 314–322 for constructional details and fitting methods. Since the drawer will be behind doors anyway, dustproofing isn't vital, and the front is often cut lower than the sides for easy access. You could also consider sliding wire or plastic trays – more commonly found in kitchen units, but also available in versions suitable for wardrobes.

Whatever details you choose, a properly designed fitted unit may well enable you to do away with other storage furniture altogether in a particular room. And of course, there's nothing to prevent you from combining it with open shelving to make a complete 'wall system'. This can provide space for books, ornaments, plants and whatever else you like – as long as the structure is strong enough to support it.

However you design the system, the crucial point is convenience. Try to ensure that each run of shelving gives the space you require at a height that's appropriate for the items concerned.

Ready Reference

FITTING SLIDING DOORS

The commonest type of sliding door gear (A) features wheel units which you fix to the tops of the doors, plus a track which you fix to the ceiling – directly or via a batten. Then you simply hook the wheels onto the track.

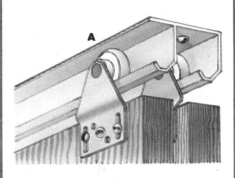

Also available, for lighter duty, are plastic sliders (B) instead of wheels. These too engage in a metal track.

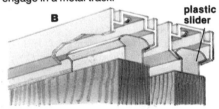

plastic slider

Although heavy-duty gear may have a bottom track too, the usual way of keeping the doors on course is plastic guides screwed to the floor or frame.

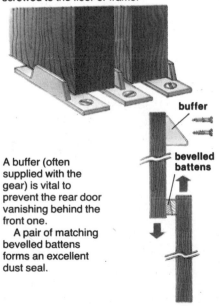

buffer

bevelled battens

A buffer (often supplied with the gear) is vital to prevent the rear door vanishing behind the front one.

A pair of matching bevelled battens forms an excellent dust seal.

PART 4

HOME ELECTRICS

TOOLS & ACCESSORIES

Before you can contemplate carrying out any electrical work in your home, you must make sure you are familiar with all the components that go to make up the system.

Understanding ELECTRICS

In theory, you could do electrical jobs knowing nothing about electricity, given accurate step-by-step instructions. But you can't deal with any part of an electrical installation in isolation — everything is linked. And unless you understand how each part of the system works you have no way of knowing if you are making a mistake. With electricity, ignorance is dangerous.

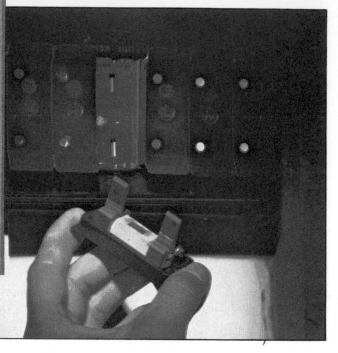

We're all familiar with lights and power sockets, but how does the electricity reach them so we can use it? In fact, electricity enters your home along one thick cable (the service cable), passes through a large 'service fuse' and into a meter which records the amount you use. Everything up to and including that meter belongs to the electricity board, and is their responsibility. Everything beyond is the householder's property, which is perhaps why installations vary so much.

In a modern installation — one wired in the last 30 years — there are two wires carrying electric current that lead from the meter to what is called the consumer unit. These wires are known as the meter tails — one is termed live, the other neutral.

On the inlet side of the consumer unit there's a switch with which you can turn off the power altogether, but the unit's principal job is to divide up the power and send it round your home through a network of cables.

These cables are organized into circuits. There are circuits for lights, power sockets and so on, each with its own fuse in the consumer unit. The cables themselves run under the floor, above the ceiling and may even be visible on wall surfaces, although more often they are buried within them.

In older installations, instead of a consumer unit there may be individual fuse boxes protecting separate circuits. And each of these fuse boxes will have an isolating switch to cut off power to the circuit it controls. These fuse boxes are connected direct to the meter by

> **WARNING:** *Electricity is dangerous. Before touching any part of the fixed wiring in your home, turn off the power at the main switch so you can be sure no current is flowing anywhere in the system.*

live and neutral meter tails. Alternatively the fuse boxes may be supplied from a distribution board which in turn is connected to the meter.

Sometimes, even with a consumer unit you may find separate fuse boxes. This is normally the result of the system having been extended.

What are circuits?

If you take a battery, and connect a wire to the positive (+) terminal, and another to the negative (−), then bring the free ends of the wires together, electricity will flow from positive to negative along them. That's a circuit. You can build a torch bulb and holder into it to prove it works. Break the circuit by cutting one wire, and the light goes out (the flow of current has stopped), and it will stay out until the cut ends are rejoined. That's a simple switch.

Of course, the circuits in your home are a good deal more complex than that, and their design varies according to whether they supply lights, power sockets or whatever. Even the electricity is different. Instead of flowing in one direction, it goes back and forth 50 times a second — hence its name *alternating current*, or AC for short.

But the principle is the same., Think of 'live' as positive, 'neutral' as negative, and you will see that for any appliance such as an electric fire to work it must have wires connecting it to the live and neutral terminals in the consumer unit. Those wires may be contained in a single cable, but the link must always be there, with switches *en route* to make or break it, and for safety reasons, switches are on the live wire.

What are fuses?

The main service cable has its fuse; the various circuits have theirs in the consumer

unit or fuse box and if you remove the back of a flat-pin plug you'll find a fuse in there.

Think of an electric light bulb. It gives out light because electricity passing through the filament (the fine wire just visible inside the bulb) makes it very hot. If you pass enough electricity through any wire, it will also heat up. If that wire happens to be a circuit cable, an appliance flex, or the service cable to the meter, then the consequences would. be serious. So, to protect them, a weak link called a fuse is built into the circuit.

Most fuses are just thin pieces of wire. They can be fitted to rewirable fuse carriers, in which case you can replace them, or they may be in ceramic cartridges, in which case you throw them away and fit another. In any event, the fuse's thickness is described in terms of how much electricity — expressed in amps — is theoretically needed to melt it.

The word 'theoretically' is important because, in fact, fuses aren't particularly accurate or reliable. For this reason, a more sensitive device called a miniature circuit breaker (MCB) may be used instead. It's just a switch that turns off automatically when danger threatens. Once the fault responsible for the overload is put right, you switch-on again.

Why cables?

It would be far too complicated to wire a house like a battery and bulb circuit using individual wires. Instead, the copper wires carrying the electricity are encased in PVC insulation to stop them touching and making their circuit in the wrong place — what's called a short circuit — and then bound together in PVC sheathing to form a cable. In this way, the live, neutral and earth wires can be run as one, even though each one is still connected up separately.

Different kinds of cable are used for different jobs.

Earthing

The purpose of the earth wire within the cable is to make up the earth continuity conductor (ECC). This is an essential safety feature of any electrical installation. Its role is to act as a 'safety valve' in the event of a fault, causing a fuse to blow or an MCB to trip to isolate a faulty circuit or faulty appliance from the mains supply. In doing so it could prevent the risk of fire or someone being electrocuted.

Earth wires are connected to the metal parts of switches, socket outlets, fittings and appliances (and even plumbing) in a really up-to-date system. Electricity will flow along the line of least resistance, so that if by some mishap any of these parts became live (by coming into contact with a live conductor) the earth wire would offer a line of 'less' resistance. In effect the faulty current would travel along the earth wire rather than through a person touching the live metal part. And the extra current passing through one circuit would

be sufficient to blow the fuse or activate the MCB.

Unfortunately this doesn't always happen – so, for added safety, a special device called a residual current circuit breaker (RCCB) can be fitted to detect the slightest leakage of current to earth. It shuts off the power within milliseconds – quickly enough to save a life – at the first sign of a fault.

RCCBs can be added to an existing system, or included within the consumer unit in a new installation. They usually protect all the circuits in the house and also act as a mains on/off switch.

Ring circuits

For getting electricity to the power points, the most common system of wiring is what's called a 'ring' circuit. Wired in 2.5mm² two-core and earth cable, most homes have one such circuit for each floor of the house.

The two-cores and the earth wire are connected to their terminals in the consumer unit (or fuse box) and then pass through each power socket in turn before returning to their respective terminals in the consumer unit (fuse box). The circuit is protected by a 30A

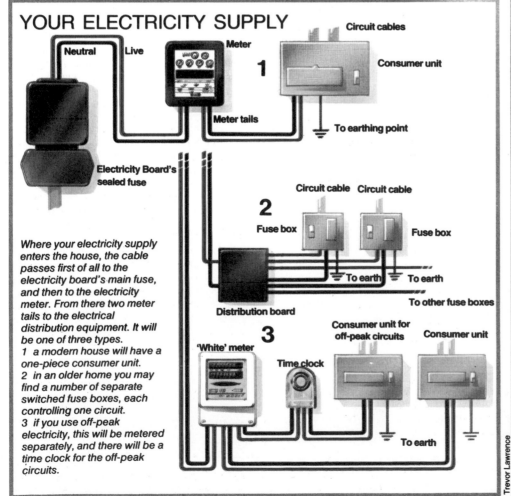

YOUR ELECTRICITY SUPPLY

Neutral | Live | Meter | Circuit cables

1

Consumer unit

Meter tails

To earthing point

Electricity Board's sealed fuse

Where your electricity supply enters the house, the cable passes first of all to the electricity board's main fuse, and then to the electricity meter. From there two meter tails to the electrical distribution equipment. It will be one of three types.
1 a modern house will have a one-piece consumer unit.
2 in an older home you may find a number of separate switched fuse boxes, each controlling one circuit.
3 if you use off-peak electricity, this will be metered separately, and there will be a time clock for the off-peak circuits.

Circuit cable | Circuit cable

2

Fuse box | Fuse box

To earth | To earth

To other fuse boxes

Distribution board

3

'White' meter | Time clock | Consumer unit for off-peak circuits | Consumer unit

To earth

fuse. The advantage of this system is it allows the cable to cope with more sockets than if it made a one-way trip (see Radial circuits – right). In fact, you are allowed as many sockets as you like on the ring, so long as the floor area served by the circuit doesn't exceed 100 sq metres (1,080 sq ft). What's more, you can increase the number of sockets by adding 'branch lines' off the ring. These are called 'spurs' and break into the ring via a junction box, a spur connection unit, or an existing socket. You are allowed as many spurs as

there are sockets on the ring, and each spur can supply one single, double or triple socket, or one fixed appliance via a fused connection unit. Until a recent change in the IEE Wiring Regulations, a spur could feed two single sockets, and you may find such spurs on your existing circuits.

Of course, with all those sockets, there is a risk of overloading the circuit, but in the average family home it's unlikely that you'll have enough sockets in use at any one time. The circuit may carry up to 30 amps of current

which is equivalent to having appliances and portable lamps using 7,200 watts of power all switched on together. It's doubtful that you would want all this on at the same time, but it's wise not to go above this level of power use. If the circuit does overload, the fuse will blow. or the MCB will switch off.

Radial circuits

Unlike ring circuits, radial circuits consist of a single cable that leaves the fuse box and runs to one or more sockets. In older homes in the UK, before ring circuits were introduced, all power circuits were wired as radials. Since homes had (and needed) only a few sockets, individual circuits were usually run to each one from the fuse box. The sockets themselves were rated at 2A, 5A or 15A, and had round holes to accept round-pin plugs. Such circuits will probably have been wired in rubber- or lead-sheathed cables, which deteriorate with age (see pages 14 and 15), and are not able to satisfy the far greater electrical demands of a modern household. It's wise to have such circuits examined by a qualified electrician, and best of all to have them replaced.

Radial circuits are, however, also used in modern wiring systems where a ring circuit could be inappropriate for some reason. There are two types, with different current-carrying capacity.

A 20A radial circuit uses 2.5mm² cable and

A ring circuit originates from a 30A fuseway in the consumer unit. Protection may be by an MCB rather than a rewirable or cartridge fuse.

Spurs are sometimes added when the ring circuit is installed to save on the wiring runs. They are usually connected at a three-terminal junction box.

Socket outlets on a ring circuit take the fused 13A flat-pin plug. They can have one, two or three outlets on the faceplate; the best have switches.

Jem Grischotti

THE RING CIRCUIT

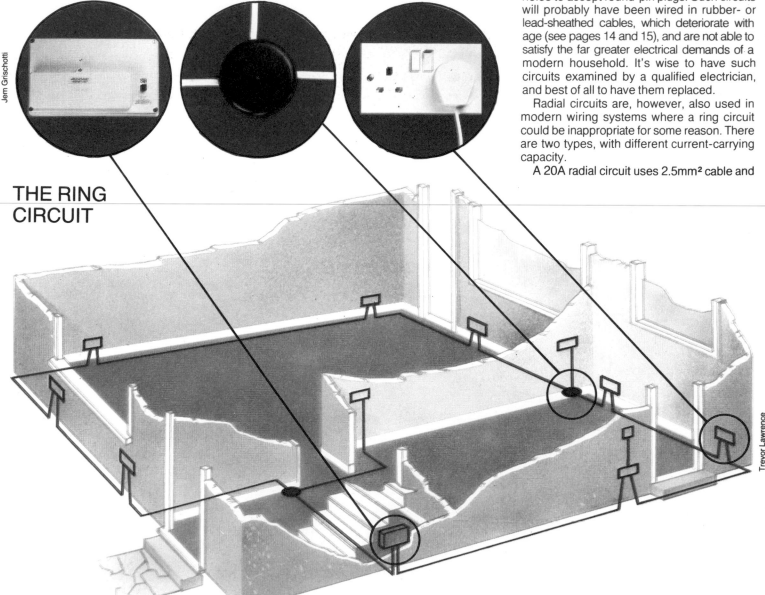

Trevor Lawrence

is protected by a 20A fuse (rewirable or cartridge) or an MCB in the consumer unit (or fuse box). It can supply an unlimited number of 13A socket outlets and fixed appliances using 3kW of power or less, providing they are within a floor area not exceeding 20 sq metres (about 215 sq ft).

The other type of circuit is the 30A radial which is wired in 4mm² cable and can feed a floor area of up to 50 sq m (540 sq ft). It can be protected by a 30A cartridge fuse or MCB, but not by a rewirable fuse.

These restrictions on floor area mean that several radial circuits would have to be installed to cover the same area as a ring circuit. This is one of the reasons why the 'ring' is now the most common method of wiring in the UK, but radial circuits can supplement an overworked ring circuit.

Special purpose circuits

In addition to rings and radials, your home may have special circuits which supply only one outlet or appliance. Cookers, immersion heaters, instantaneous showers and the like are wired in this way and each has its own individual fuse. In effect, these circuits are just radials that have had both the cable and fuse sizes 'beefed up' to cope with the often heavy demands of the appliances they supply — for example, a large family-size cooker might need a 45A fuse, and 6mm² or even 10mm² cable.

Because electric night storage heaters all come on together they could overload a ring circuit; consequently each one is supplied by

The various radial power circuits originate from fuseways in a consumer unit or from individual fuse boxes. They are protected by fuses or MCBs.

Modern radial circuits have sockets that take 13A flat-pin plugs. Older radials with lead or rubber-sheathed cable take round pin plugs.

Even if you have ring circuit wiring, radial circuits are used for special purposes, such as supplying a cooker. It may also contain a 13A socket outlet.

A fused connection unit sometimes supplies a fixed appliance on a radial circuit. This could be a wall mounted heater or an immersion heater.

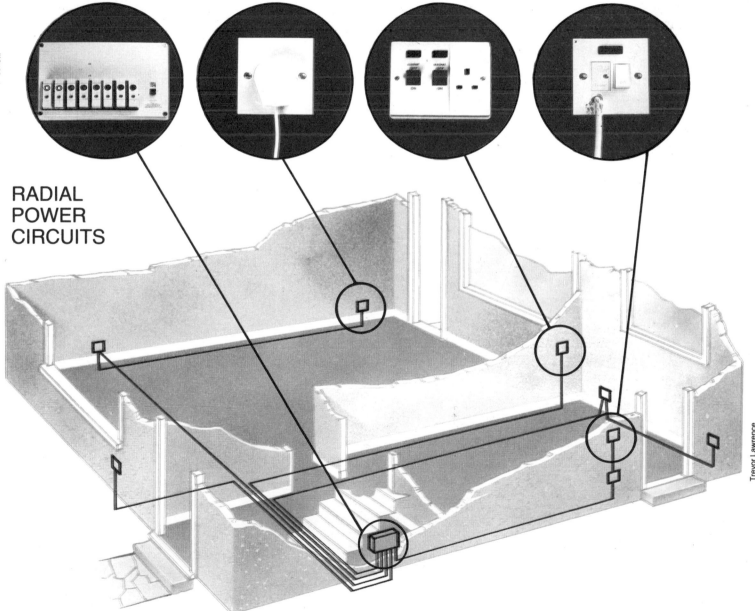

RADIAL POWER CIRCUITS

Jem Grischotti

Trevor Lawrence

LIGHTING CIRCUITS

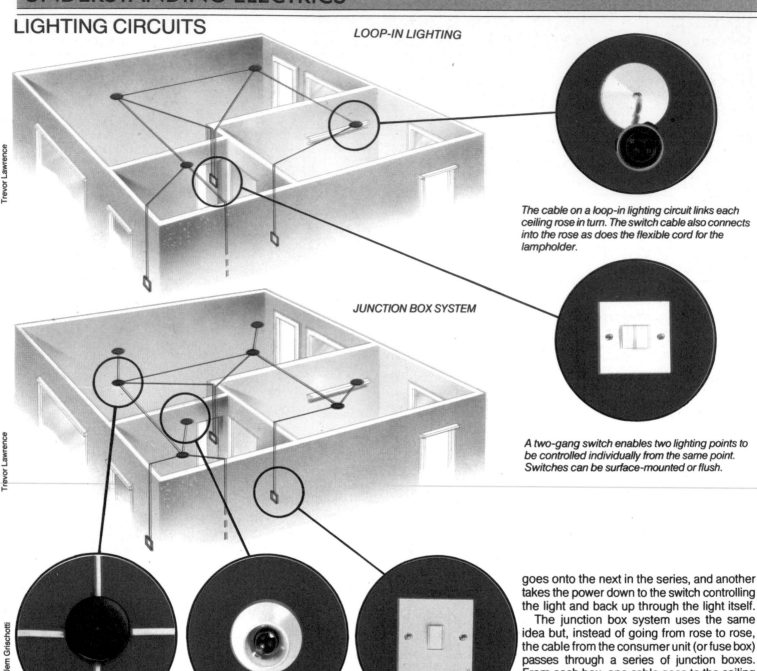

LOOP-IN LIGHTING

Trevor Lawrence

The cable on a loop-in lighting circuit links each ceiling rose in turn. The switch cable also connects into the rose as does the flexible cord for the lampholder.

JUNCTION BOX SYSTEM

Trevor Lawrence

A two-gang switch enables two lighting points to be controlled individually from the same point. Switches can be surface-mounted or flush.

Jem Grischotti

With junction box wiring the main cable runs between four–terminal junction boxes. The other cables go to the lighting point and the switch.

Batten holders are used to fit a light close to the ceiling. In bathrooms, they must have a 'skirt' to prevent contact with metal on the fitting or bulb.

The simplest switch is a one-gang type mounted on a faceplate. They can be either surface mounted or recessed to be flush with the wall.

a separate radial circuit protected by a 20A fuse. The fuses are housed in a separate consumer unit which is linked to a sealed time clock and uses off-peak electricity.

Lighting circuits

Two systems of wiring lighting circuits are in common use, and it is not unusual for an installation to contain a little bit of each. One is called the loop-in system; the other the junction (or joint) box system.

With the loop-in system, a cable (normally 1.0mm² but sometimes 1.5mm²) leaves a 5A fuse in the consumer unit (or fuse box) and is connected to the first in a series of special loop-in ceiling roses. From this rose, one cable

goes onto the next in the series, and another takes the power down to the switch controlling the light and back up through the light itself.

The junction box system uses the same idea but, instead of going from rose to rose, the cable from the consumer unit (or fuse box) passes through a series of junction boxes. From each box, one cable goes to the ceiling rose or light, and another to the switch that controls it. This system is particularly useful, for example, when fitting wall lights as there is little space at the back of a wall light fitting for looping-in.

Lighting circuits are rated at 5 amps, which means they can take a load of up to 1,200 watts. In effect, they could supply 12 lamp-holders containing bulbs of 100W each or smaller. But as you may want to fit bulbs with higher wattages, it is usual for a lighting circuit to supply up to eight outlet points, so separate circuits are required for each floor.

Strictly speaking it's better to arrange the circuits so that there is more than one on each floor — this means that you won't be in total darkness if a fuse in the consumer unit blows.

TOOLS FOR ELECTRICAL JOBS

Electrical work, like so many other jobs about the home, can be carried out more successfully and more quickly if you have the right tools to hand. Here is a selection of what you will need for installation work, and also to enable you to cope with emergencies.

To carry out electrical work properly without causing damage to cables and other household fittings, you'll need to have the right tools for the job. Most DIY enthusiasts will already have many of the tools needed for such heavy work as raising and replacing floorboards and chopping out chases in walls to bury cables. Very often the car tool kit will produce spanners for dismantling appliances when renewing flexible cords or heating elements.

Nevertheless, if you are contemplating carrying out your own electrical installation work, you should assemble a tool kit to cope with all the jobs you are likely to encounter. That way not only will you find the work much easier, but you'll also be able to ensure that the final result reaches a professional standard that will give you great satisfaction.

Screwdrivers
A minimum of three straight-tipped screwdrivers is required: a small, thin-bladed electrician's screwdriver for reaching shrouded grub screws in electrical fittings; and medium and large size normal screwdrivers. A selection of crosshead screwdrivers may also be helpful in dealing with Pozidriv and similar screws.

There are two other screwdriver types which you may find useful: a ratchet screwdriver with a chuck to accept a range of different driver bits, and an offset screwdriver. The latter is a simple steel bar, the ends of which are bent at right angles and terminate in a straight tip at one end and a crosshead tip at the other. It is ideal for reaching awkward screws, particularly when servicing electrical appliances.

Bradawls
A bradawl is needed for piercing holes in timber and plaster to mark the position of fixing screws for appliances and their mounting boxes or brackets.

Pliers
Pliers are among the essential tools for electrical work. They are used to grip and bend wire, and to hold small items such as nuts and washers in confined spaces.

Electrician's pliers are similar to engineer's pliers but have insulated handles suitable for working with voltages of 240 volts or above. However, remember you should never carry out any work on an installation unless the power has been turned off, so the presence of insulated handles is only an extra safeguard.

Complementing the standard electrician's pliers should be a pair of long-nosed pliers, which may also be obtained with insulated handles.

Cutters and strippers
Small side cutters are used for cutting the ends of fuse wires when rewiring circuit fuses, and for trimming cable and flex cores when making connections. The jaws are shaped to get close in to the work and still allow knuckle room to grip the handles.

A pair of wire strippers of the adjustable type to fit the various sizes of insulated conductor will permit the insulation to be removed efficiently without damaging the conductor itself. Also available is a cable stripper which will remove the outer sheathing of a cable without cutting into the insulation of the conductors inside. This is much safer than using a knife.

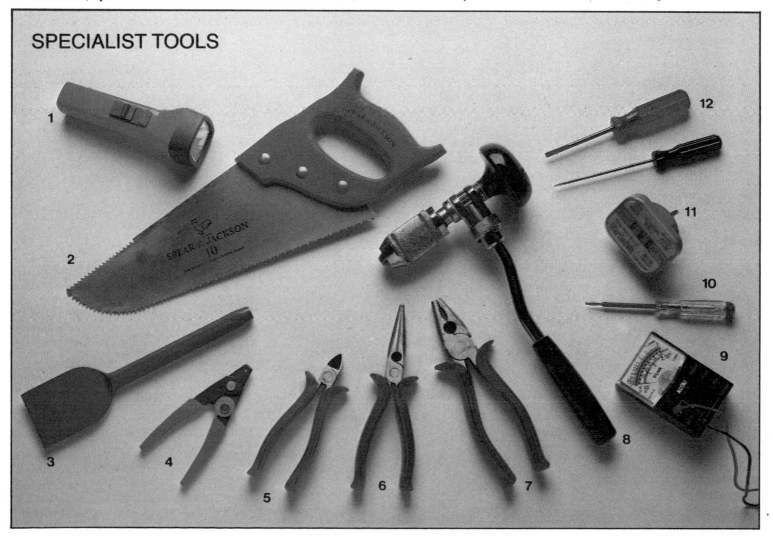

SPECIALIST TOOLS

GENERAL-PURPOSE TOOLS

Handyman's knife
If you can't get hold of the type of cable stripper mentioned previously, a handyman's knife will do for trimming the insulation and cable sheathing, providing it is used carefully. Also, it it useful for trimming floor coverings when lifting and replacing floorboards.

Grips and wrenches
Where metal conduit, armoured and mineral-insulated cables are used, an adjustable spanner will be

SPECIALIST TOOLS
There are a number of specialist tools (below) which are essential for any electrical installation work. These will enable you to get perfect results with the minimum of effort.

KEY
1 *Torch*
2 *Flooring saw*
3 *Floorboard chisel*
4 *Adjustable wire stripper*
5 *Side cutters*
6 *Long-nosed pliers*
7 *Snub-nosed pliers*
8 *Joist brace*
9 *Continuity tester*
10 *Neon screwdriver*
11 *Ring-main tester*
12 *Screwdrivers*

needed. A companion tool is the locking wrench which also has adjustable jaws, but they can be locked on to the workpiece to apply great pressure, leaving the hands free.

Hammers
Ideally, your tool kit should include three types of hammer, and you may already have some of them. A claw hammer is used for general work, a pin hammer for fixing cable clips and a club hammer for driving cold chisels.

Chisels
A selection of cold chisels will make installing cable runs and mounting boxes easier. A short, sharp, small-diameter chisel should be used for chopping out cable chases and recesses in plaster. Deeper recesses in brickwork and masonry can be cut with a thicker 150 to 200mm (6 to 8in) long chisel. A longer (at least 300mm/12in) thin chisel is ideal for cutting holes through brick walls.

The electrician's bolster chisel is useful for lifting floorboards; you drive it between the boards to split off the tongues and then lever them upwards. The wide blade spreads the load.

Since a certain amount of wood cutting is involved in laying cables

beneath floors, a set of general-purpose wood chisels will also prove to be invaluable.

Saws
Various types of saw are needed in electrical work since metal, wood and plastic need to be cut.

For cutting plastic trunking, floorboards and other timber, you'll need a tenon saw.

Cutting down into floorboards and removing the tongues when lifting boarding can be done with a special floorboard saw. This has a curved blade, allowing the waste material to be cleared quickly from the groove the saw cuts, and so reducing the likelihood of damaging adjacent woodwork when cutting across a board. The tip of the back edge of the blade is set at an angle with cutting teeth to allow cuts to be made right up to a skirting board without the handle fouling the wall.

A padsaw is useful for cutting timber in confined spaces and for making holes in ceilings to accept mounting boxes for light fittings.

Metal fittings and large cables, including the armoured variety, may be cut with an adjustable hacksaw, which will take 200 to 300mm (8 to 12in) long blades. Finally, small sawing jobs and shortening fixing screws can be carried out with a junior hacksaw.

Your tool box (above) should contain many general-purpose tools that will help you with your electrical jobs, as well as being useful for other repairs. Screwdrivers, chisels, drill bits and saws are all vital. In addition, it's a good idea to keep a number of spare electrical accessories in case of an emergency.

Drills
A hand drill should be available for light drilling of plastic or thin metal, and can also be used for drilling small holes in brickwork and masonry.

Alternatively, a power drill is a better bet providing, of course, that you already have a live circuit from which to operate it. Pick one with a large chuck capacity, and give serious consideration to buying a drill with an optional hammer action, which will be a great help when drilling into masonry.

Drill bits
A set of masonry drill bits is necessary for drilling brickwork. If you have a power drill with a hammer action make sure the drill bits are suitable for this; not all are.

For drilling holes in metal and plastic boxes, a selection of high-speed twist drills is a must.

Even if you're never likely to carry out any electrical installation work in your home, you're sure to have to cope with running repairs to your system when things go wrong. So you can find the tools and materials you will need when the lights go out, buy a small box and assemble an emergency tool kit you can keep near to the fuse board so you can always find it when you need it. Include a torch, a pair of pliers, a handyman's knife, a couple of screwdrivers, some PVC insulating tape and fuse wire or replacement fuses of appropriate types. It's also worth adding two or three spare light bulbs. Label the box, and always replace any components of the kit if they are used.

Emergency procedures

Before dealing with any repair, make sure that the circuit is safe to work on. If a fuse has blown, you should turn off the mainswitch and identify which circuit it is. Remove the fuse carrier and renew the wire or cartridge, or reset the MCB. Never undertake any work with wet hands and always make sure that you have sufficient light by which to see.

Hand brace and bits

Most general wood-drilling jobs can also be accomplished with a conventional carpenter's ratchet brace and a set of auger bits. However, drilling through joists often presents problems due to their close spacing. A special compact joist brace is made for this purpose and has a ratchet lever immediately behind the chuck.

Measuring tape

A retractable steel tape is essential for the accurate positioning of switches and other accessories. A 3m (10ft) one will do for installation work, but a longer one will be useful when estimating cable runs.

Plumb bob

The position of vertical runs of cable can be determined accurately with the aid of a plumb bob and line. It can also be used to carry a draw wire down into a hollow partition where it can be hooked out at the switch position.

Spirit level

Switch and accessory boxes need to be level, and a small spirit level is ideal for setting them correctly.

Soldering iron

For servicing and repairing electrical appliances, you will need a soldering iron to unsolder and remake connections. A range of sizes and wattages is available. You should keep a supply of flux and solder with it. FACTFINDER 57.

Testers

Two testers that every home electrician should have are a neon tester (usually in the form of a small screwdriver) and a continuity tester.

The neon tester is used to determine if a terminal is live. Place the tip of the tester blade on the terminal and a finger on the metal cap at the end of the tester's handle. This completes a circuit, causing a neon bulb in the handle to light if there is power. A built-in resistor prevents electric shocks.

Battery-powered testers are relatively cheap to buy. The most popular type has metal probes, and such a device will test cartridge fuses and other conductors of low resistance, continuity being indicated by a positive meter reading. Some models double as mains testers.

High resistance items, such as light bulbs and heating elements, should be checked with a special high-resistance tester.

Another useful tester takes the form of a 3-pin plug and is used for checking the cable connections at a socket. It has neon indicators to show whether the socket is wired correctly, has faulty earth, live or neutral connections, or reversed live and neutral connections.

hints

● *When lifting a floorboard, lever the end clear of the floor and lay a long cold chisel across the adjacent boards to support it in this raised position. Continue levering, moving the chisel as you go, until the board can be removed.*

● *A flooring saw with its specially shaped blade will allow you to cut through floorboards right up to skirting boards without the handle touching the wall. It may also be used for cutting through the tongues of T & G boarding.*

● *Right: A low-resistance continuity tester can be constructed using a 4.5V bell battery, a torch bulb, MES lampholder and insulated wire for leads.*

ELECTRICAL WIRING ACCESSORIES

Without electrical wiring accessories you could never make use of the power carried round your home by the various circuit cables. These accessories include such things as power sockets, light switches and much more besides. Here are some of the most useful.

It's a good idea to have a thorough knowlege of the available accessories when you plan a wiring job. That way you'll know what to use, and both when and where to use it. If you're fairly new to the world of home electrics then the chances are that you'll have to follow to the letter any guide that you're using. But instructions, however good, cannot cover every eventuality and a wide knowledge of what accessories are available will help you to prepare for the job and also save you extra work. Once you know what the various types of accessories do, and the special features that they have, you'll be

able to distinguish easily between those that will do a particular job and those that won't. Then you'll be able to work out exactly what you require before you go to the retailers and that way not risk making a fool of yourself. Before you go laying out a lot of money, it's important to understand a few technical terms that will help you to avoid making expensive mistakes.

Terms to know
Most accessories are rated at a certain number of amps, which indicates the amount of current the fitting can carry or control in complete safety. Under normal

354

circumstances, a rating of 13A means that the accessory is for use on a ring circuit or its spurs, and any other rating means the fitting is designed to form part of a purpose-made radial circuit.

In the latter case, the current rating you need depends on what the circuit feeds and should therefore match the current rating of the fuse in the consumer unit controlling that circuit. But there are exceptions. A shaver socket, for example, may overload above 2A, yet is quite safe if connected to a 5A lighting circuit. And fused connection units won't be rated at all as you decide their rating when the fuse is put into the carrier.

Next, there are a number of terms that classify switches. You'll find some described as SP (single-pole) and others as DP (double-pole). When a switch is described as SP it means that when it is turned off, it breaks only the live side of the circuit. A DP switch, on the other hand, breaks both the live and neutral sides, and so ensures total disconnection.

SP switches are used mainly in lighting circuits (because they have a low current rating), while DP switches are used in most power circuits (because these have a higher current rating). It's all a question of safety; obviously

the DP switch is the safer and is therefore used in most high rating circuits.

The other important expression you must understand is what is meant by a switch or socket having a certain number of gangs. This is, in fact, straightforward. Where switches are concerned, the number of gangs tells you how many separate switches you have built into a single face plate. With power sockets, the number of gangs refers to the number of plugs the socket will take without the need for an adaptor plug. An adaptor plug is not to be recommended as you can risk the danger of fire.

Decorative aspects

The days of all electrical accessories being finished in the same material are now, thankfully, long gone. The variety of different styles, colours and materials that are available make it possible for light switches, sockets and other accessories to be incorporated in the overall interior design.

That's really all you need to know if you're buying accessories for an electrics job in your home. You may well come across other odd expressions and terms but you'll find most of them explained satisfactorily in Chapter 1, pages 6-10.

POWER CIRCUIT ACCESSORIES

1 Ceiling switches with a higher current rating than a lighting ceiling switch are ideal for use in the bathroom to control appliances such as instantaneous electric showers.

2 Cooker control units are rated at 45A and incorporate a 13A power socket and two switches to control both cooker and socket.

3, 10, 14 DP switches are used to control permanently connected appliances such as water heaters and are rated at 20, 45, or 60A. Some 20A models have a flex outlet and many are fitted with pilot lamps.

4 Cooker switches are merely DP switches which control the power to the cooker. They are safer than a cooker control unit as you can't risk the danger of fire by trailing a kettle flex across a boiling ring.

5, 6 Shaver supply units are suitable only for electric shavers. A built-in transformer allows them to be connected to the power circuit, and an isolator provides complete safety for use in a bathroom. All have on/off switches and some a voltage selection switch for different models of shavers.

7 Shaver socket outlets don't have built-in transformers to lower the voltage which means that they must be wired into the lighting circuit and are not safe to be used in bathrooms.

8 Shaver adaptors will fit into any 13A plug and are protected by a fuse and a safety shuttered outlet.

9 Dual switches are used for controlling dual element immersion heaters – those with one element heating only the top part of the tank and another heating the entire tank. The unit has two switches, one controlling power, the other directing that power to one element or the other.

11-13 Fused connection units connect permanently the flex of an appliance, such as a freezer, to the power circuit. There is less risk of accidental disconnection than with a plug and socket, and a fused unit can be used to 'down-grade' the current for a spur off the ring circuit and so make it safe to use for a light. They are available with switches, lights and flex outlet holes.

15-20 13A socket outlets are for use with 13A square-pin plugs. One- and two-gang versions with switches and neon lights are available. They can be surface or flush-mounted or set in the floor – in which case they are fitted with a protective cover. There are versions fitted with earth leakage circuit breakers for extra protection and round-pin sockets are also available.

CABLE OUTLETS

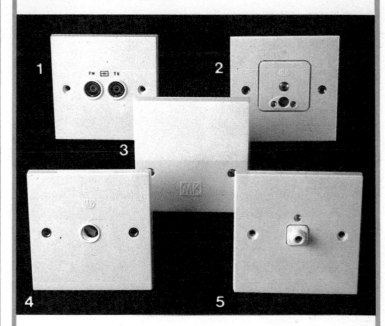

1 Aerial sockets can have either single or double outlets and allow you to use your outside aerial for both the television and the FM frequency of your radio.

2 Fused clock connectors are really specialised versions of the fused connection unit and were used to connect mains-operated clocks (now no longer made). They are also used in the installation of some extractor fans and can be flush or surface-mounted.

3 Cooker connection units are nothing more than purpose-built terminal blocks which allow you to connect the trailing cable of an electric cooker to a concealed, fixed cable run from the cooker control unit. They incorporate a clamp plate that protects the

cable and connections in case the cooker is moved.

4 Flex outlet plates are similar to blank plates but a hole in the face plate allows the flex of an appliance directly into the DP cable run. This set-up should really only be used on radial circuits designed for a specific job, such as providing power for a bathroom towel rail in conjunction with a fused connection unit. So, they are used in much the same way as a cooker connector – where it is impractical to pass the flex of the appliance directly into the DP switch or fused connection unit.

5 Telephone cord outlets have a moulded outlet designed to carry standard telephone cable. Double outlet models are available.

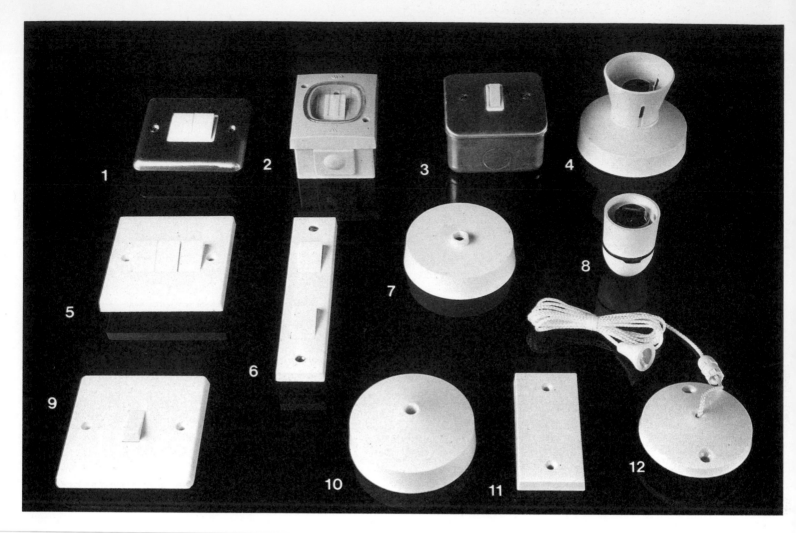

LIGHTING ACCESSORIES

1, 5, 9 Plate switches are rated at 5A, and are used in ordinary lighting circuits. They have up to six gangs and most can be connected for two-way switching.

2 Sealed switches are used where the switch is likely to be exposed to water or the elements.

3 Metal clad switches are surface-mounted and are used when the switch needs extra protection – such as in a garage or else where it is likely to get knocked.

4 Battenholders are for lights that are surface-mounted on a wall or ceiling. They can be used in a junction box lighting circuit, at the end of a fused spur from a power circuit, or wired into a loop-in lighting circuit.

6 Architrave switches, so-named because they can fit into the decorative surround of a doorway, are about 32mm (1¼in) wide.

7, 10 Ceiling roses connect the lighting circuit's cables to the pendant light flex. Most have their terminals arranged for the loop-in system, but two terminal versions for use in a junction circuit are also available. When used with a heavy pendant light, the rose should have a strain wire clamp which takes the weight off the conductor cores in the light flex.

8 Lampholders fit on a pendant light's flex and hold the bulb and lamp shade in position. They should be heat resistant and in bathrooms it's essential to use one with a deep protective shield for extra safety.

11 Blank plates allow you to seal off a mounting box when it is no longer in use so saving you the extra work of removing it.

12 Ceiling switches are rated at 5A for the lighting circuit and are the only sort of light switch permitted in a bathroom where stringent safety regulations apply.

MOUNTING BOXES

1 Accessories of all types can be fitted in surface-mounted boxes.

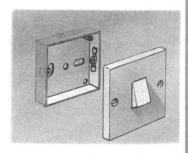

2 Light switches can be flush-mounted in plaster-depth boxes.

3 Power circuit accessories need deeper boxes than light switches – 35mm (1⅜in) is the commonest.

4 Extra-deep boxes are needed for flush-mounting some accessories. Fit with care in single-brick walls.

356

RUNNING CABLE UNDERGROUND

The most important part of taking power outside to a garden, a detached garage, or a workshop is running the electricity supply. An overhead cable run is a possibility, but taking it underground is the safer and more secure solution.

There are all sorts of reasons for taking a power supply out of doors. You may want to provide power to a garage so you can work on your car in light and warmth, or to transform your shed into an efficient workshop; you may require power sockets so you can use electrical appliances in the garden, or a circuit to light your pool or garden fountain. Whatever you do involves running cable out of doors and this is bound to be the major part of any outside installation. There are three ways of running cable: overhead (for further details of overhead cable runs see pages 361–365), along a wall or underground. Running the cable underground is probably best, even if it involves the most installation work. That way it is concealed, cannot be disturbed and presents no danger whatsoever. But before you run the power supply, you'll have to decide which type of cable you want to use.

Underground cables

Three sorts of cable are suitable for running underground, and two of them can be laid directly in the ground without the need for further protection. PVC-covered mineral-insulated copper-covered cable (MICC) has a very small diameter and will pass conveniently through an airbrick, so avoiding the necessity of chopping a hole through the house wall. However, as the mineral insulation tends to absorb moisture, the ends of the cable have to be fitted with a special seal to prevent this. It is a complicated job for the do-it-yourselfer to fit these seals and several special tools are required. The easiest thing to do is measure the cable run and ask your local electrical contractor for the length of cable with seals already fitted. This cable is usually two-core, as the copper sheathing provides adequate earth bonding and, as the cable run starts and ends in a metal conversion box (see below) which allows you to switch to ordinary PVC two-core and earth cable for indoor sections or for connection to accessories, each end should also be fitted with a screwed compression gland. These glands attach the cable to the box and provide the necessary earth continuity,. The cable usually has an outer

CABLE TYPES AND CONNECTIONS

Only PVC cable run in conduit (1) can be taken directly from the consumer unit to the switchfuse unit. If you use either PVC armoured cable (2) or mineral insulated copper cased cable (3) they must both be fitted with a gland and MICC with a seal and then run from a conversion box to another in the garage.

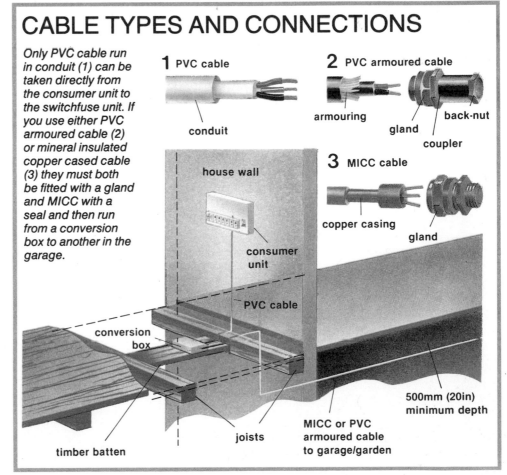

1 PVC cable

conduit

2 PVC armoured cable

armouring
gland
back-nut
coupler

3 MICC cable

copper casing
gland

house wall

consumer unit

PVC cable

conversion box

joists

timber batten

MICC or PVC armoured cable to garage/garden

500mm (20in) minimum depth

covering of PVC, often orange in colour, and is slim enough to be fairly unobtrusive – if run on the surface to wall-mounted light fittings, for example.

PVC-covered wire-armoured insulated and sheathed cable needs no seals, but has to have glands fitted at each end where it, too, enters the conversion box. This cable often comes with only two cores, in which case the armouring serves as an earth, but it may well be better to run three-core armoured cable. If you are using the three-core version, you'll find that the insulation colours will be slightly different to ordinary cable. Live is red, neutral blue, and earth yellow. The cable itself is usually black.

Both these types of cable are protected enough to allow them to be laid directly in the ground. But if you use PVC-sheathed two-core and earth cable then you'll have to run it in either heavy gauge galvanised steel or high impact rigid plastic conduit. You'll undoubtedly find it easier to use the plastic conduit as the steel sort requires stocks, dies and bending equipment that is not normally available to the householder. When using plastic conduit, however, do remember that it's likely to fracture in temperatures of –5°C or below, and also that fairly substantial holes will have to be cut in both the exterior wall and the garage wall to admit the cable.

The indoor section

All power supplies that are run outside are classified as sub-main cables and must originate from a spare fuseway in the consumer unit, or else from a new switchfuse unit. For further details on this and on the size of cable to use see pages 361–365. The section inside the home will normally be run in ordinary PVC-sheathed two-core and earth cable which will be taken to the exit point. Obstructions inside the home can alter the route of the indoor cable but there are a number of straightforward methods (for example, fishing cable through a ceiling void) which can be employed if you don't have access from above.

When the cable is being taken underground, the exit point is likely to be where the ditch in which it will run starts against the house wall. However, the presence of a concrete terrace or some other obstruction may mean you'll have to change the proposed exit point (although it may be possible to take other measures, such as chopping a chase to protect the cable). It is important to note that only if you're running the outdoor section in PVC two-core and earth cable will it run directly from the switchfuse unit to the outside installation. Otherwise the indoor section must be taken right inside the conversion box.

Laying cable underground

Having drilled the exit point in the house wall, if you are running the power to a garage in the outbuilding, you'll have to dig a ditch in which to lay the cable. This should be at least 500mm (20in) deep, and digging it will probably be the most tiring part of the job! Try to avoid taking the cable under vegetable plots and flower beds where it could be disturbed; and obviously you won't want to dig up your lawn. Probably the best place for a ditch is at the side of a concrete or gravel path; but if you're forced to run it at the edge of a flower bed, dig the ditch somewhat deeper to give the cable extra protection. If you're using either PVC-armoured cable or MICC cable, it's a good idea to place the cable on a layer of sand at the bottom of the trench and also to sift the soil before filling it in; that way you can avoid the slight risk of sharp stones damaging the cable. It's also wise to place a line of slates on top of the cable to give it extra protection, when you fill in the trench. If you're using PVC-sheathed two-core and earth cable, you should first lay the conduit in the trench and cut it to fit. You'll have to buy couplers for lengths that need to be joined; for vertical runs you'll have to fit elbows and you'll need a further elbow to take a short length of conduit into the wall so that the cable has complete protection. Do not use solvent-weld adhesive to assemble the conduit run at this stage, as you'll have to dismantle the fittings to thread in the cable. Start at the house end and, working in sections, thread through enough of the PVC cable to reach the mains switch in the garage to wherever you're running it. An alternative method is to attach the cable to a drawstring; thread it through the conduit and then pull the cable through after it. You can then start fixing the elbows and couplers permanently. Smear the solvent-weld adhesive over the end of the conduit and inside the elbows and couplers with the special brush provided before joining the sections together. Then place the assembled run into the trench, making sure that each elbow is correctly positioned. At the garage end push the end of the cable and the short length of conduit into the hole in the wall and then carefully fill in the trench. If you're using PVC-covered wire-armoured cable it should be laid directly in the trench and the ends passed directly into the house and garage. It will then be taken into a conversion box at each end.

Fitting a conversion box

Extending either PVC-armoured or MICC cable beyond the entry point to the house or garage is pointless. They are both relatively expensive cables, cannot usually be connected to a switchfuse unit and can be awkward to run. That is why you should fit what is called a conversion box. This allows

RUNNING CABLE UNDERGROUND

1 *After digging a ditch that is a minimum of 500mm (20in) deep, lay the conduit in it to give you an idea of what length you'll need.*

2 *Use a hacksaw to cut the conduit to length where necessary, and link it with special couplers; don't weld the joints yet.*

3 *Use an elbow fitting to join the vertical (above-ground) section of the conduit to the horizontal (underground) part next to the wall.*

4 *Fix a short section of conduit to the top elbow and check that it's long enough to take the cable completely through the garage wall.*

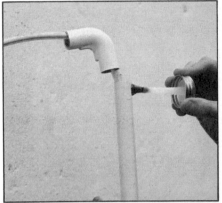

5 *Thread through the cable from the consumer unit. You can either dismantle the conduit or use a drawstring to pull through the cable.*

6 *With the cable in place, you should use special conduit adhesive to fix the couplers and elbows firmly in position. Then bury the conduit.*

you to change the type of cable in your sub-main circuit to ordinary PVC two-core and earth cable.

All that is required is a box containing three terminals and two entry holes. The correct one to use is an adaptable conversion box and lid or alternatively a standard one-gang metal mounting box fitted with a blanking-off plate as a cover. You can use a special three-way terminal block to make the connections, or else ordinary cable connectors. However, if you do use the cable connectors, you must make sure they are large enough for the current.

At the house end, the conversion box should either be fixed with wood screws to a timber batten fitted between the joists beneath the floor, or alternatively to the wall near the entry point of the cable. If you're running power to a garage or shed, the box at that end should be fitted to the wall near the cable entry point. You should remove two

knockout holes, one of which must be fitted with a PVC grommet while the other should be large enough to accommodate the PVC-armoured cable. Strip away the outer layer of PVC and slide a PVC sheath and gland nut onto the armoured cable. You should put a back-nut in the knockout hole without a grommet and then prepare the cable by clipping away the excess armouring, leaving enough to carry up to the end of the gland's thread. You can now slide on the gland which will screw into the gland nut and keep the armouring in place. It's a good idea to attach a coupler to the gland as this will allow you more room in the box for the connections. Then feed the cable into the box and attach the back-nut to the coupler. If you are using two-core cable the armouring will serve as the earth so the back-nut must be tightened by a spanner to provide good metal-to-metal contact. Then pull the PVC protective hood

over the whole assembly and remove the remaining PVC insulation to expose the red and black cores. If you are using two-core cable you'll now have to earth the box; it's a good idea to do this even if you're using three-core cable. You should link the earth screw on the box (which holds the earth connector) with a length of core that you have sleeved in green/yellow PVC. Feed in the PVC two-core and earth cable, which must be the same size as the sub-main cable, through the knockout hole previously fitted with a grommet, and prepare the ends of the cable in the usual way before joining the cores of the two cables together. From here the PVC cable will run to whatever appliance you want to supply. If it is a garage or workshop, it's likely to go to a switchfuse unit; if in the garden, it might be to well-protected sockets for lawnmowers, hedge trimmers, or lighting for an ornamental fountain.

FITTING A CONVERSION BOX

1 Use an adaptable mounting box to serve as a conversion box. Remove two opposite knockouts and fit a grommet to just one of them.

2 Remove two small knockouts at the back for the screws. Drill and plug holes in the corresponding spots on the wall, and position the box.

3 Fit a back-nut in the knockout hole. without a grommet, and then slide the PVC hood and gland nut onto the armoured cable.

4 Put on the gland and coupler and trim the armouring of the cable so that it ends at the bottom of the thread on the gland.

5 Feed the cable into the box and attach the back-nut to the coupler. Using a coupler allows you more room in the box for the connections.

6 The armouring serves as an earth but you should earth the box too by fitting an extra core to the box and connecting it to the terminal block.

7 Feed in the PVC two-core and earth cable that is to run to the switchfuse unit. Remember, this must be the same size as the armoured sub-main cable to which it is connected.

8 Using a block of three connectors, join the two cores of the armoured cable to their equivalents in the two-core and earth PVC cable and then connect the earth cores.

9 Finally screw on the lid of the conversion box. At the house end, the conversion box can be fitted safely to a timber batten that is fixed under the floorboards.

PROVIDING POWER IN THE GARAGE

If you add power and lighting to a garage, you can make it more than mere storage space for your car: your garage becomes a workshop. Connecting up the electricity supply is not difficult and sturdy accessories are produced specially.

Installing electricity in a garage can completely transform it. No more fumbling in the dark for car keys; or flat batteries on a winter's morning; and car repairs will be carried out in the relative comfort of a well-lit and pleasantly heated garage. Indeed, a garage equipped with a number of power sockets, some lights and a couple of work surfaces can double as an extremely efficient workshop. If your garage is attached to your home, it is likely that it will already have a power supply; if it's detached, it's possible you'll have to install the supply yourself. But running electricity to a garage, or indeed to any other outside building, is not that difficult. It should be done in three stages: work inside the house; work outdoors, and finally the new circuitry in the garage itself.

Inside the home

If you're going to run a power supply to your garage you should remember that the electricity supply to any outbuilding, even if only for a lighting circuit, must be independent of the house circuits. Tempting though it may be, you're not allowed to run the supply in the form of a spur from a ring circuit in the house. The basic requirements are: a separate mains switch and fuse unit in the home, and an isolating switch and fuse unit in the garage. The mains switch at the house end will usually be a switchfuse unit that should be linked to the mains by the electricity board. If there is a spare fuseway in the main consumer unit obviously you can make use of it. However, it's probably better to leave the spare fuseway for another circuit within the house and install a new switchfuse unit for the circuit to the garage or outhouse. Note that outdoor sockets should be RCCB protected – see pages 76-78. The cable running from the new switchfuse unit in the house to the garage is technically not a circuit cable and is classed as a sub-main cable. This is because it supplies a complete installation which has its own mains switch and fuse.

The section inside the house will normally be run in ordinary two-core and earth PVC

sheathed cable, the size of which depends upon the circuit requirements in the garage. The 2.5mm² size is suitable for a 20A supply; use 4mm² for a 30A supply, and 6mm² for a 45A supply. Do remember that if you are using the 4mm² cable for a 30A supply you must make sure that both switchfuse units are fitted with either a cartridge type fuse or MCB so that the circuit is uprated by one third. This is because 4mm² cable controlled by a rewirable fuse has a current-carrying capacity of only 27A and would consequently be a safety risk.

The outdoor section will either be in the same type of cable or else in special cable; which sort you use is determined by whether you run it overhead or underground, and, if run underground, whether or not it is to be in conduit. More details of underground cable runs are given in the previous section. It's best to make the outdoor section as short as possible, so the point at which the cable emerges from the house should be as near as practicable to the garage. This will obviously affect the section run in the home, as will obstructions inside.

Installing an overhead cable

Where the distance between the house and garage is no more than 5m (about 17ft), an overhead cable attached to a catenary wire is a practical alternative to an underground cable run. A catenary wire is merely a length of galvanised steel-stranded cable similar to that sometimes used for fencing and should be secured to an eye bolt or eye screw fixed into the wall of the house and of the garage. For spans larger than 5m, intermediate supports such as poles are required to prevent sagging. Apart from looking unattractive, there is always the risk of damage in high winds so you may find it better to take the cable underground for long runs.

In theory a span of less than 3.5m (11ft) need not be supported by a catenary wire. If you're running an overhead cable to your garage, you'll have to make sure that there is no danger of it being hit by anything passing underneath. For that very reason the regulation minimum height of an overhead cable run is 3.5m (11ft). However, when the cable is suspended across a driveway the minimum height is increased to 5.2m (17ft).

RUNNING CABLE OVERHEAD

Running power overhead keeps the cable out of harm's way provided you have the catenary wire at a minimum height of 3.5m (11ft). The cable should be taped and clipped and the catenary wire itself should be bonded to earth. To gain extra height at the garage end use a length of 100x50mm (4x2in) timber which should be bolted securely to the wall with 150mm (6in) coach screws.

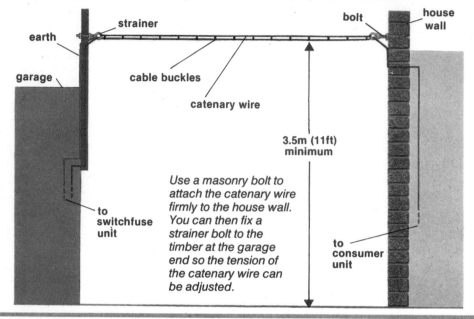

earth
strainer
bolt
house wall
garage
cable buckles
catenary wire
3.5m (11ft) minimum
to switchfuse unit
to consumer unit

Use a masonry bolt to attach the catenary wire firmly to the house wall. You can then fix a strainer bolt to the timber at the garage end so the tension of the catenary wire can be adjusted.

THE GARAGE CIRCUITS

The lighting circuit can be either a loop-in or junction box system; the power circuit is wired as a radial circuit. Metal-clad sockets and switches are more robust than plastic ones. Cable should be taken on the surface with vertical runs being clipped every 400mm (16in) and horizontal runs every 250mm (10in).

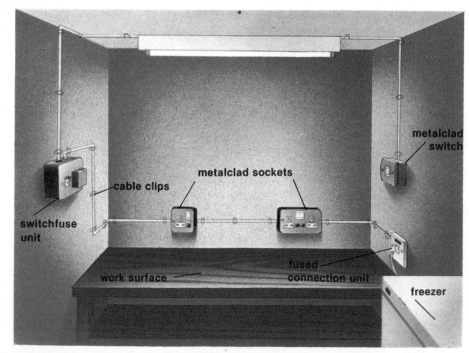

metalclad switch
metalclad sockets
cable clips
switchfuse unit
fused connection unit
work surface
freezer

ATTACHED GARAGES

If your garage is attached to your home you can safely run the power as a spur from a ring circuit.

DETACHED GARAGES

If your garage is detached from your home then it is deemed a separate building and must be:
● supplied by a sub-main cable
● controlled by an isolating switch and fuse unit at each end.

TEMPORARY POWER SUPPLY

The only other form of power supply allowed to a detached garage, other than a sub-main cable, is an extension cable. This can be linked up temporarily while the actual appliance that it supplies is in use.

PERMANENT POWER SUPPLY

Power can be supplied permanently to a detached garage in three ways:
● by an overhead cable
● by an underground cable
● by a cable fixed along a wall. Cable should never be taken along a fence for reasons of safety.

OVERHEAD CABLE RUNS

Points to note:
● the minimum height for an overhead cable run is 3.5m (about 11ft)
● if the cable crosses a driveway the minimum height is increased to 5.2m (17ft)
● with a span of under 3.5m (11ft) the cable need not be supported
● if the span is between 3.5m (11ft) and 5m (about 17ft) the cable should be attached to a catenary wire
● for spans over 5m (17ft) there should be intermediate supports in addition to a catenary wire.

TIP: TAPE THE CABLE

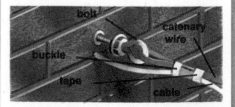

bolt
catenary wire
buckle
tape
cable

Attach the cable to the catenary wire with tape before fitting the buckle clips. That way the buckles will neither cut into the cable nor slide along it. It's also a good idea to leave a loop in the cable at each end to ease the strain and prevent water from entering the wall.

FITTING THE SWITCHFUSE UNIT

1 *If your garage is situated away from the house, it will need its own mains switch and fuses. Fix the unit to a sheet of treated chipboard.*

2 *Thread in the circuit cable and feed the red and black cores behind the switch so that they can connect to the unit's terminals.*

3 *Strip off some of the insulation from each core and make the connections. Sleeve the earth core in green/yellow PVC.*

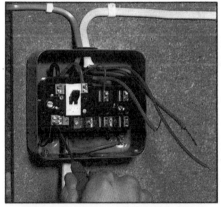

4 *Then feed in the cables for the two circuits to provide power in the garage. Connect the lighting circuit to the fuseway nearest the switch.*

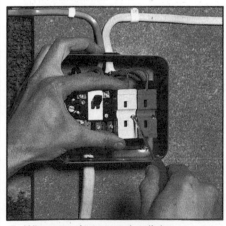

5 *When you have made all the connections fit the fuseway covers. Make sure you fit the correct one over each set of terminals.*

6 *Finally fit the cover and shield and slot in the two MCBs. You can then turn on the power in both the house and garage.*

Running the cable

It's a good idea to insert an adjusting device at one end so that the catenary wire can be tightened once the cable has been attached to it. You'll probably have to fix a length of 100x50mm (4x2in) timber to the garage wall to obtain the necessary minimum height at that end. To fix the timber to the garage wall you'll have to drill and plug two holes and use 150mm (6in) coach screws. You should drill a hole in the house wall to serve as an exit point for the cable. This should be at about first floor level in a two-storey house and at eaves level in a bungalow.

You'll also have to drill a hole in the garage wall to enable the cable to enter and run to the mains switch. In addition, it's wise to run a length of green/yellow PVC insulated cable from the catenary wire to the mains switch to bond the catenary to earth. Measure the length of cable required to run from the switch-fuse unit in the house to the mains switch in the garage. Having fixed and tightened the catenary wire to the two eye bolts, pass the end of the cable through the hole in the house and then pull through sufficient to reach the mains switch in the garage. You should connect the bared end of the catenary wire to the bonding earth core by using a cable connector. After temporarily attaching the cable to the catenary wire (so you can make sure that there is sufficient to reach the garage) you can make a permanent attachment by using cable buckles every 250mm (10in). Both the supply and the earth cable should be fixed to the post with plastic cable clips that should be no more than 400mm (16in) apart. Alternatively, you can run the vertical section in metal or plastic conduit that is attached to the timber. You can now make the connections to the switchfuse unit in the house and in the garage.

An alternative method of running cable overhead is to carry it in an unjointed length of heavy gauge steel conduit; in this case the minimum height is reduced to 3m (10ft). You could also run it in rigid plastic conduit, but this will sag and is also likely to fracture at temperatures below –5°C. If you don't want to run the cable either overhead or underground then you may be able to take it along a boundary wall to the garage. Under no circumstances, however, may the outdoor section be fixed to a fence.

Inside the garage

Running cable to the garage is probably the most important and also the most difficult part of installing electricity there. There are, to begin with, certain precautions you must take with the work inside the garage. Remember that a detached garage is classed as a completely separate building and therefore must be fitted with a double-pole isolating switch, enabling the electricity to all circuits

FITTING POWER POINTS IN A GARAGE

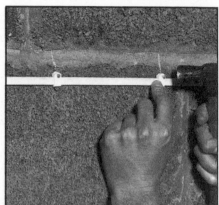

1 *To provide current for a garage power point you should use 2.5mm² two-core and earth cable clipped firmly to the wall every 150mm (6in).*

2 *Fit a grommet on a knockout hole and fix to the wall the special metal box for surface mounting in garages and workshops.*

3 *Make the connections after sleeving the earth core in green/yellow PVC. It's a good idea to add an extra earth to protect the box.*

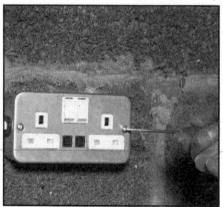

4 *Fit the faceplate with great care. This is necessary because its screws link the box into the earthing of the socket.*

Ready Reference

GARAGE ACCESSORIES

It's best to fit metal-clad switches and socket outlets in a garage or workshop. They are tougher than the plastic variety and last longer.

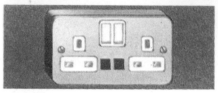

It's a good idea to choose versions which incorporate a neon indicator light. That way you can see at a glance if the power is on or off.

FIXING THE ACCESSORIES

These accessories are usually surface mounted. To install them:
● drill and plug the holes in the wall
● feed the cable into the surface mounting box
● fix the box to the wall with No 8 wood screws
● make the connections in the usual way
● attach the faceplate.

TIP: EARTH THE BOX

The circuit cable earth core protects the socket itself but it's wise to add extra protection for the mounting box. You can do this in two ways:

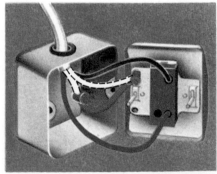

● loop the circuit earth core into the earth screw on the box and then take it onto the socket, or
● add an extra green/yellow sleeved earth core linking the box earth screw to the socket earth terminal.

and equipment to be completely cut off at the flick of a switch. If you're going to run more than one circuit within your garage, it's best to fit a switchfuse unit and the mains switch on this will serve as an isolating switch.

When you fit the new switchfuse unit, it's best to fix it as near as possible to the point where the incoming cable enters. It should be installed in the same way as inside the home and it's important to fit a sheet of fire-resistant material such as treated chipboard to the wall beforehand.

You can obviously install as many circuits as you like, but for most garages two – one for power and one for lighting – should prove ample. Generally, you should fit the new switchfuse unit with a 5A and 15A MCB. If, however, you plan to have a number of power sockets, heaters and appliances, it is wise to fit a 30A fuse for the power circuit. Cartridge fuses will also suffice but it's not advisable to

use rewirable fuses. You should run the lighting circuit in 1.0mm² or 1.5mm² two-core and earth PVC cable, fixed to the wall and roof surfaces, and you can install a loop-in or junction box system. The power circuit will have to be run in 2.5mm² two-core and earth cable and horizontal runs should be clipped every 250mm (10in), while vertical runs need to be clipped every 400mm (16in).

Although the standard plastic fittings can be used safely in a garage, it's probably best to use the special metal-clad versions. Although these are slightly more expensive, they are more robust and therefore safer in an environment where they could be subjected to the occasional knock or blow. It's also wise to choose versions with neon-indicators to show, at a glance, whether the socket is on or off. They are designed specifically for surface mounting and come complete with mounting boxes.

INSTALLING A LAMP AND SWITCH

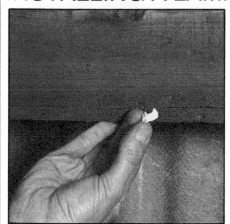

1 If you're fitting a lamp to a beam, clip the cable along the middle of the beam so it runs to the centre of the battenholder.

2 You'll have to nibble out some plastic knockouts on the pattress block before offering it up to the beam or ceiling.

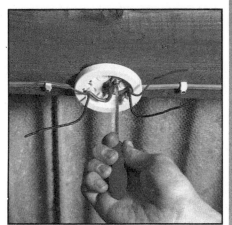

3 Clip the power and switch cables to the beam and run them into the pattress. Then sleeve and connect up the earth cores.

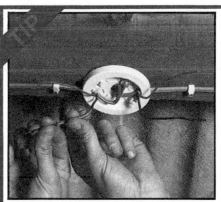

4 Before going any further make sure that you have flagged the black core of the switch cable with red PVC tape: this indicates that it's live.

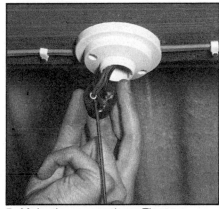

5 Make the connections. The two red cores go to one terminal; the flagged black core to another and the neutral to the third.

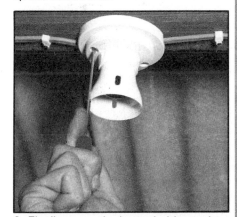

6 Finally screw the battenholder and pattress block to the beam after making holes with a bradawl. You can then connect up the switch.

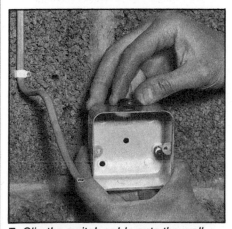

7 Clip the switch cable onto the wall and run it to the point where you'll mount the switch. Fit a grommet to the knockout hole.

8 Feed the cable into the box and make the connections. Remember to sleeve the earth in green/yellow PVC and also to earth the box itself.

9 Replace the switch in the mounting box and fit the faceplate. You can now switch on the power in the house and in the garage itself.

FITTING A POND PUMP & FOUNTAIN

A garden pond can add an extra dimension to any garden. By including a fountain, a waterfall and some lighting as well you can really bring your pond to life.

When it comes to adding interest to a pond, there's nothing to beat the splash and sparkle of moving water. It will turn the pond into the focal point of your garden, as well as giving soothing sounds of moving water. You can use an ornate fountain, a simple spout, a lively cascade or a full-blown waterfall, but first of all you have to get the water on the move.

It's not unknown for people merely to tap into the mains supply via a garden tap and a suitable length of hose. However, before you try this as an easy way to provide a waterfall, it's wise to realise the serious disadvantages associated with this method. While movement of the pond water will aerate it nicely, a continuous supply of tap water is not a good idea because it will reduce the temperature of the pond considerably and will also encourage the growth of algae. In addition, the local authority will probably object to the flagrant waste of water, as well as opposing this method on the grounds that dirty water from the pond could in theory find its way back along the hose to contaminate the mains water supply.

A more sensible method of moving the pond water will be simply to recirculate it, and to do this you're going to need some sort of electric pump. There are a great many on the market, available either from your local garden centre or else specialist suppliers. As their performance varies, with many being designed for a specific installation, you would do well to consult your supplier to make sure that the model you have in mind will actually do the job you want it to do. However, there are a couple of general points to consider before buying one.

Choosing a pump

One of the first things to think about is the pump's power. In simple terms, you'll have to find out how much water it will cope with and how much water you'll need to move in your pond. When it comes to fountains, the necessary calculations could hardly be simpler, as fountainheads and pumps are usually produced by the same manufacturer and a quick glance at the relevant sales literature should give you all the information

you need. You'll have to look at the amount of water the pump will move per hour; the height of the fountain produced and the diameter of the fountain or the falling circle (called the 'sill') of the water lifted into the air. So, for a small pond you're likely to need a pump that will produce a maximum output of about 680 litres (150 gallons) per hour with a maximum fountain height of 1.2m (45in) and a sill of 800mm (30in). It's still a good idea, though, to see the fountain in action before actually buying it. There are other factors, such as the thickness of the individual jets, which will have a marked effect on the way the fountain looks in use.

When it comes to creating waterfalls and cascades, things are not quite so straightforward. Again the volume of water is important, but relating the volume to the effect achieved is quite tricky. Most suppliers sell pre-fabricated waterfalls so they'll know exactly what works and what doesn't. If you want more than one effect – say, a number of waterfalls or fountains, or a combination of the two – then you'll have to make sure that the pump can cope with multiple applications. You'll then have to decide whether you want a surface or submersible one.

Types of pump

For all but the largest fountains and waterfalls, surface pumps mounted outside the pool and sucking in pond water to redistribute it through a series of pipes are now the

Ready Reference

TIP: A POOL HEATER

If you're worried about your fish surviving a cold winter the answer is to install a pool heater. This will keep an area of the pond surface ice-free and so allow vital oxygen into the water. Heaters are mains-powered and so can be simply plugged into the nearest socket outlet – in your home or an outbuilding.

TAKING POWER OUTSIDE

Extra care must be taken when running a circuit outside to provide power for your pool equipment. You should use:
● PVC-sheathed cable run in conduit and buried in the ground
● mineral-insulated copper-cased (MICC) cable, or
● PVC steel-armoured cable.
Only PVC-sheathed cable can run straight from a consumer unit to an outside socket. With other cables you'll have to
● fit both ends with glands, and the MICC cable with a special seal too
● run them from a conversion box located within the home to another in the outbuilding, and continue the circuit to a socket in PVC cable.

For further information see pages 357-363.

OBTAINING POWER

With a low voltage pump (below), house the transformer close to a socket outlet and run the low voltage cable outside to the pump. It's best to run it underground. With direct mains supply (right) the pump cable connects to flex run underground in conduit from the nearest socket outlet.

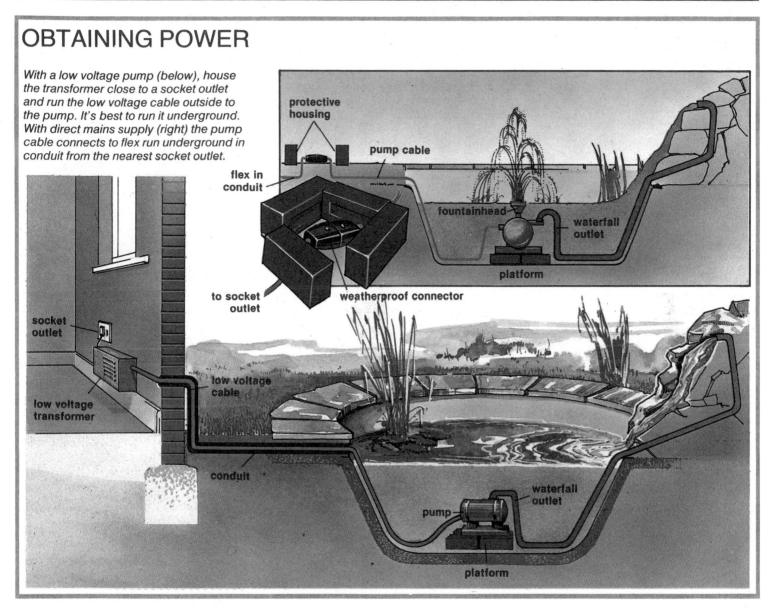

protective housing

pump cable

flex in conduit

to socket outlet

weatherproof connector

fountainhead

waterfall outlet

platform

socket outlet

low voltage transformer

low voltage cable

conduit

pump

waterfall outlet

platform

exception rather than the rule. This is because of the complications involved in installing and maintaining them: they cannot stand exposure to the weather and if they are deprived of water when they're in operation, they overheat and burn out.

In practical terms, ensuring an adequate water supply means installing the pump reasonably close to the pond. That way the inlet pipe is kept as short as possible. You can alter the size and length of the outlet pipe if you need, but you risk not achieving the full desired effect. The length and design of the inlet pipe is more critical. Of course, it needs to be the correct diameter, but most importantly it has to be sufficiently robust to resist collapse as the pump begins to suck. Even so, you might get problems if the pipe-work leaks, allowing air into the system, if the strainer fitted to the end of the inlet pipe becomes clogged or, worse, if the impeller

within the pump jams with ice or leaves. To avoid the danger of overheating, it's best to get a pump with a thermal cut-out.

Weatherproofing can create more difficulties. The pump must be housed in a weatherproof chamber where it'll be free from damp. At the same time, however, the chamber must be well-ventilated to stop the pump from overheating.

Finally, you'll have to decide where to position the pump in relation to the water level. If it's below the water level, so it's primed for use at all time, then there's always the risk of the pond overflowing and the chamber flooding. Conversely, if it's above the water level, you'll have to keep it primed – either by fitting a special kind of strainer to the inlet pipe, or by incorporating a header tank in the system. All things considered, a submersible pump is probably a better bet for most ponds. This type usually sits under-

water on the bottom of the pond and works silently, sucking in water and pushing it through a fountain jet or taking it to the top of the waterfall. With some models, however, you'll have to build a simple platform so they sit just below the surface. Most pumps come ready fitted with an integral fountain head so there is no plumbing to be done; all you have to do is connect it to the power source.

Pond lighting

No matter what type of pump, fountain or waterfall you choose, to make the most of moving water you need light. After all, it's really the sparkle of light on water that works the magic; not the water itself. During the daytime the surface will reflect light provided the pond is in a position where it'll catch the sun. However, in the evenings and at night you'll need some sort of artificial lighting.

Ordinary garden lighting certainly has a

MAKING A WATERFALL

1 *Test the flow of water down the waterfall where you want to install it. Make sure that it fills the pools and flows smoothly into the pond.*

2 *Make adjustments to the angle of the waterfall by removing or adding extra earth or sand. This will provide a stable base for the waterfall.*

3 *You'll have to run a hose from the pump position in the pond up to the top of the waterfall. Protect the hose by concealing it in the earth.*

4 *When you're happy with the waterfall's position, bed paving slabs or bricks in the earth to provide extra support for the waterfall pools.*

5 *Replace the waterfall and bed it securely in position. You can then pack round the edges with extra earth or build a rockery round it.*

6 *Pile up some rocks where the hose runs into the waterfall. These will conceal the water outlet and also disperse the water at its entry point.*

part to play (for further information on this, turn to pages 370–373). However, there are a number of attractive effects than can only be achieved by placing lights under the water. These fall into two categories; those that are general-purpose pond lights and those designed specially for use with fountains. The former normally consists of PAR lamps with a variety of coloured lenses that can either float on the surface or be tethered to the bottom of the pond. Fountain lights are more spectacular and the combination of a light and a fountain head, so the spray is illuminated from beneath, is quite striking. Alternatively, the lighting may be built into a submersible pump, complete with a fountain head. Some models even incorporate a rotating plastic filter which alters the lighting colour from red to amber to blue and on to green at a chosen speed – an effect you need to see working to appreciate.

Dealing with the electrics

Another factor to be borne in mind is the question of power supply. The choice is between a mains voltage system and a low voltage one. Mains voltage systems are obviously the more powerful of the two and will probably be necessary for the largest pumps and fountains. The cable supplied with the pumps can be fitted with an ordinary plug and linked to the nearest socket outlet in your home or in an outbuilding. However, it's not always the case that the pump will be sited close enough to the home or shed to do this. In this case you'll have to connect the pump cable to a length of flex run in conduit underground from the nearest socket outlet or else run an exclusive circuit for the pump. This will mean making use of a spare fuseway in your consumer unit or else installing a new switch-fuse unit. You'll then have to run special cable outside to the point where it can connect

to the pump cable. As an additional safety precaution, it's a good idea to equip your home with an earth leakage circuit breaker; that way if for some reason the cable gets cut, damaged or broken the power will cut off almost instantly; certainly before you have received more than a mild shock. Fuses and miniature circuit breakers are not fast or sensitive enough to prevent injury in this situation.

Low-voltage systems consist of a step-down transformer plugged into the ring main at a convenient socket outlet in your home or a spur to a shed. Keep the transformer inside, close to the socket in question. From here you merely run the special low-voltage cable to the pump. You can even leave the cable lying on the ground as long as you can be reasonably sure that no one will trip over it. Alternatively, it can be buried in the ground – ideally in plastic conduit.

INSTALLING A PUMP

1 *Before installing the pump, you'll have to assemble it. First of all fix on the plastic T-piece that incorporates the outlet for the waterfall.*

2 *You can then fit the fountainhead spray unit to the upper outlet of the T-piece. Turn the flow control nozzle so that it's fully open.*

3 *Before fitting the waterfall hose to the pump outlet, immerse its end in boiling water. This will soften it and make it that much easier to fit.*

4 *Slip the end of the hose on to the pump outlet on the T-piece. As the hose cools down it will contract and so give a tighter fit.*

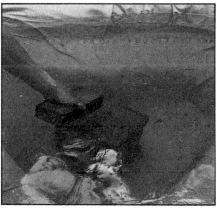

5 *You'll have to make a platform on which the pump should sit. Use bricks and then top them off with a paving slab to provide a level surface.*

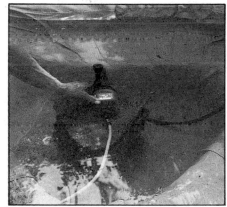

6 *You'll then be able to position the pump on the platform. Make sure that it sits about 150mm (6in) below the surface so the fountainhead just emerges.*

7 *Slip a length of plastic hosing over the submersed cable to give it extra protection, both from the water and from direct sunlight.*

8 *Connect this cable to the plug section of a weatherproof cable connector. The socket should be connected to a length of 0.5mm² two-core and earth flex.*

9 *House the connector in a special shelter. Run the flex in conduit underground to the nearest socket – see pages 357-361 for details.*

INSTALLING GARDEN LIGHTING

Apart from its functional value, being able to illuminate your garden after dark will extend the time you can enjoy it. Here's how to plan and install the fittings to get maximum effect.

The first thing to bear in mind when planning to install lighting in your garden is that in the dark, a little light goes a long way. In other words, a 40W lamp used outside will seem considerably brighter than, say a 100W lamp used in your home. This means that you won't have to floodlight the garden like a sports stadium merely to see and, with only a few lights, you'll be able to create some quite subtle effects. This is all due to the eye's ability to adapt to different lighting levels. However, as well as adapting to low light levels, the eye also adjusts to bright lights and if you install very bright lights then you'll view the rest of the garden as nothing more than shades of black.

While this will allow you to create attractive cocoons of light, in which you could enjoy an outdoor meal, for example, it can work against you. Stepping out of the spotlight, you'll effectively be blinded for several seconds, during which time you could easily miss your footing or walk straight into something. Further steps to prevent this happening should be taken by making sure you position the lights so that people can't look directly at them and by using lights with shades and diffusers. Better still, design your lighting scheme so that, where possible, illumination is provided by bouncing light off walls, shrubs or other surfaces.

The final thing to consider is the question of flexibility – whether you want to be able to adjust the level of lighting or even change the position of individual lights. The best guide for this is the thing you are illuminating. If it is a static structure, like a path or drive, then some sort of permanent light fitting giving a predetermined light level is best. Other structural garden features such as swimming pools and barbecues will also benefit from permanent lighting, but a more flexible approach to lighting levels will be required. After all, when you're using them you'll want lighting almost to indoor standards simply to be able to see what you're doing; when not in use, the lighting's role will change to showing off the structure as a feature of the garden as a whole and so won't have to be so bright. You might need a variety of lamps for this situation.

But when lighting foliage, though, with the exception of large, established, slow growing trees, mobility is the key. Install lights that you can move as plants come into bloom and fade or when you introduce new plants. After considering these design principles you'll have to decide just how you want to use the lighting in your garden. There are two categories, the practical and the pretty.

Lighting with a purpose

The main purpose of garden lighting is to allow you to see what you're doing and where you're going – in other words for safety and convenience. Lighting to see what you're doing applies mainly to such things as barbecues and swimming pools. With barbecues the ideal thing is to break the 'low level reflected light is best' rule and direct a couple of spotlights on the cooking or preparation area. However, you should keep this area as small as possible and keep the lights high up so that they shine down on what you're doing, reducing both glare and shadows. You'll have to arrange the lighting of the surrounding area very carefully so that its level gradually diminishes; you'll then avoid the risk of stepping out into pitch darkness. The same approach can be used for lighting a swimming pool, and you may find that by shining light down on the water, you don't need to light the poolside – the reflection could well be enough. Alternatively, you could consider lighting the pool from beneath the water – either with suitable lights built into the sides of the pool or merely with weighted lights lying on the bottom.

Lighting designed to help you see where you're going is more straightforward. With paths or drives, it's best merely to line them with bollards or mount lights on adjacent walls. For a subtler effect, consider lighting trees or shrubs near the path and use the light reflected back to illuminate the path itself. Do take extra care when lighting steps as for safety's sake they require stronger light, especially on the risers. Consider building lights into each riser or light the steps from the side to eliminate shadows. For further information on lighting paths see pages 374–378.

Lighting for looks

How you illuminate your garden to make it look more attractive after dark depends largely on its precise design and style and, of course, your personal taste. It's a good idea to build up a lighting scheme gradually, experimenting with cheap and mobile fittings before going to the expense of installing fixed lights. However, there are a few things to bear in mind. Firstly, aim for the lighting to look its best from a particular vantage point – the patio or a window, for example – that way planning will be a lot easier.

Secondly, remember that reflected light will always look best. Although lights can be expensive and quite attractive in their own right (when positioned within a flower bed, say,) it's the garden you really want to see. Thirdly, you should give thought to lighting levels. Varying the intensity will add interest, and by using progressively dimmer lights as you move away from your chosen vantage

IDEAS FOR GARDEN LIGHTING

Lighting your garden so it looks attractive after dark will require planning, combined with a certain amount of experimentation. Aim to design the lighting so that the garden will look its best from a particular vantage point – a patio or terrace, say. Consider, too, that you won't have to use particularly bright lamps – the light will go that much further in the dark and if parts of your garden are too brightly lit, then the rest is likely to appear just as a black hole.

As a rule, reflected light will look best. Aim to bounce it off walls, shrubs and trees. And, of course, try to conceal spotlights, which are not particularly attractive in their own right; either mount them high on a wall or else fix them within shrubs or a group of plants. When lighting foliage, think twice before using coloured lights as plants will probably turn out looking rather strange. Yellow will turn them pale and wan; red will make the leaves appear brown. Blue light will give plants a curious unearthly quality, while green will bring out the colour, but will make it look somewhat artificial. Coloured lamps could, however, be used to light a swimming pool or patio.

This low-voltage lamp, neatly concealed within the foliage at the side of a patio, gives a diffused light sufficient for any summer evening. Mounted on a spike, it can be easily moved.

Playing a couple of spotlights onto this mixed group of shrubs gives an attractive effect. Note how the illumination is in part produced by light reflected from the lawn in front.

For a really impressive effect spotlights can be positioned behind shrubs or bushes and then directed at a particular feature to give sharp, dramatic shadows.

Bollards on either side of these patio steps have the practical effect of lighting both treads and risers of the steps. And, of course, they highlight the foliage and plants too.

A couple of bollards driven into the soil on either side of this path not only serve to guide the feet but also lead the eye to the area on the other side of the tree arch.

point you can create an artificial perspective so making the garden seem larger.

Finally, think carefully before using coloured lights. They'll look fine when applied to water, statues, barbecues and a patio, lending a sort of party-like appearance. But most plants will look decidedly odd under coloured lights; yellow lights leave plants looking pale and sickly, for example.

Choosing the hardware

There is a tremendous selection of equipment available for installation in the garden. It falls into one of three basic categories. Perhaps the most useful are fittings that provide a general, diffuse light. If you're looking for a permanent fixture and there is a wall or similar structure close at hand then there's nothing to stop you using the same sort of lights as in a porch or a patio, see pages 374–378 for more details. However, these must, of course, be completely weatherproof.

Bollard lights vary considerably in design between the simple and highly decorative, and as a rule they are best suited to lighting paths, drives and other 'traffic' areas. Elsewhere in the garden lantern style fittings mounted on spikes that you drive in the ground are probably the best bet as they are quite attractive without being too obtrusive.

The second category worth considering is spotlights – essential if you want to highlight a particular feature or illuminate a small area very well. Again use spots that you might normally install on a patio or those mounted on spikes specially for fixing in the ground. Finally, there are lights designed to be decorative features in their own right and little else. The simplest type are fairy lights, strung through a tree, which lend themselves perfectly for the occasional party rather than anything more permanent. A host of other styles exist, however, ranging from ultra modern lights of almost every shape and size to full-size, old fashioned lamp posts.

Electricity outside

Finally, you must make sure that your outdoor lighting will be safe. After all, electricity and wet weather are a potentially lethal combination. That's why you must always use purpose-made, fully weatherproof lights and never make up your own from ordinary light fittings, however simple it might appear. Take extra care when running in the power. If your lights obtain their power directly from the mains then flexible cable must be run in conduit and buried at least 450mm (18in) below the soil. If you are using a low voltage system you can merely run the special cable along the ground, although you still need to be careful. Be sure you won't be able to cut through it accidentally when mowing the lawn and that people using the garden won't trip over it.

WIRING UP AND INSTALLING GARDEN

1 *Remove the cover of the terminal box by undoing the screws on the side. Work on a smooth surface to avoid the risk of losing small parts in the grass.*

2 *Next, unscrew the bush on the other side of the light body. Carefully lift out the rubber grommet and the nylon grab ring, and set them aside.*

5 *Trim back a short section of the flex sheathing. Then carefully remove enough insulation from the cores to allow their insertion into the connector terminals.*

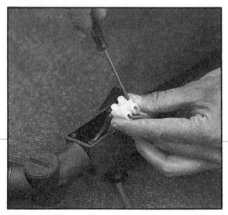

6 *Connect each core to its correct terminal. This is indicated by an equivalent coloured core of fixed wiring. Make sure each is securely held in place.*

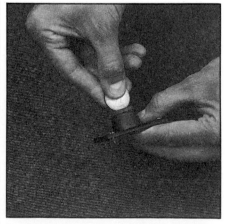

9 *You may want the cable to run on to another light connected in series. If so you'll have to remove the red blanking-off plate. Use a coin for this.*

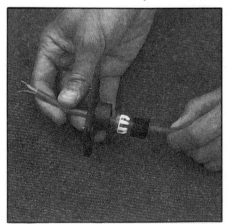

10 *Thread in the next section of flex, checking all the components are in the correct order. Strip the flex and make the connections.*

LIGHT FITTINGS

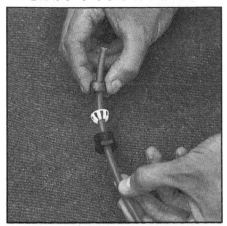

3 Use 0.75mm² two-core coloured flex to run power to the lamp directly from the mains. Thread on the bush, grab ring and grommet in the correct order.

4 Fix the bush into the flex entry hole without tightening it up too much. You can then pull through enough flex to allow you to make the connections.

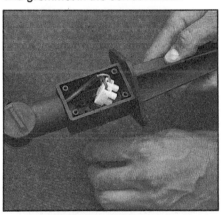

7 After making the connections you can then pull back the excess flex so that the connector sits comfortably in position within the terminal box.

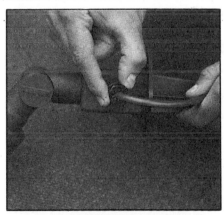

8 Then tighten the bush to hold the flex in place. Make sure the grommet and grab ring sit correctly in place, so guaranteeing a waterproof seal.

11 With the connections made, refit the cover plate. You can then screw in a PAR lamp, making sure that it sits tightly on the rubber gasket.

12 The flex is led to each light through conduit, buried 450mm (18in) underground. Spike the light into place and plug the cable into the nearest socket.

Ready Reference

TYPES OF GARDEN LIGHTING

spotlight

mini-bollard

bollard

globe light

low-voltage light

ALTERNATIVE GARDEN LIGHTING

If you don't want to have electric lighting in your garden, don't worry; there are alternative methods which can work almost as well. You might consider using
● candles or night lights in flower pots or glass jars
● a powerful weatherproof torch that can serve as a temporary spotlight
● garden flares, which provide a lot of light and burn for over two hours in all weather conditions. However, they tend to be a little too tall for some situations.

TIP: REPELLING INSECTS

Bright lights attract insects, especially outside. It's a good idea to use a special candle that not only provides light but also repels mosquitos and other insects.

WEATHERPROOF CONNECTIONS

If you are connecting any two lengths of cable together outside you must use a special waterproof rubber connector. Link the female section to the live side and the male one to the fitting's flex.

INSTALLING OUTDOOR LIGHTS

By installing outdoor lighting you can make your home that much more welcoming and secure as well as ensuring that it's easier and safer to approach.

Outdoor lighting can be divided into two groups; the largely decorative and the primarily functional. In the first group you'll find spotlights for various parts of the garden, festoon lights and underwater lights. Further information both on what decorative lighting is available and how to install it will be given in another article. Functional outdoor lighting is the most practical and also the most common. It's used to light front and back doors, patios, paths, drives and gateways.

The advantages of outdoor lighting
Outdoor lighting will make life a lot easier for any visitors arriving in the evening: no longer will they face the prospect of tripping down steps or stumbling blindly along paths to reach your front door. With a porch light installed you'll find that your home seems that much more welcoming and, of course, you'll no longer have to fumble in the dark for your keys. Equally importantly, would-be burglars will be deterred by a well-lit house. And, what's more, really efficient outdoor lighting will enable you to get that much more out of your patio or garden.

Outdoor lighting is usually simple to install and the circuit requirements are quite straightforward. When you are going to install one or perhaps two lights outside your home – in the porch or outside your back door, for example – you can normally run them off an existing lighting circuit. When you want to install a lot of lighting outdoors and away from the house you'll probably find it best to install a new circuit.

If your home has no outdoor lighting then the first areas you're most likely to consider will be the porch, walls and the back door.

Basic outdoor lighting
There are so many different types of lights that can be installed outdoors that the first thing you'll have to do is visit your local showroom and make your choice. For a porch light you could have a close-mounted ceiling fitting such as a globe or cube, a pendant lantern, a wall-mounted light with a bracket or bulkhead fitting or a period-style carriage light. Traditional fittings for a back door are bulkhead or bracket lights.

The former, usually containing either a tungsten halogen lamp or miniature fluorescent tube, is fixed directly to the wall surface. A bracket light is normally fixed to the wall by a backplate with the bracket – usually either a straight stub or what's referred to as a swan neck bracket – extending to the fitting itself. The bracket is likely either to be the type that can be fitted to a flat wall or to an external corner of the house, in which case the lamp will be able to throw light over a wider area – including part of the back and side of the house. The chances are that the light itself will consist of a well glass fitting available in various designs and containing a tungsten halogen lamp, which is particularly bright and long-lasting.

Lighting bricks are also available and are particularly suited to installation on side walls although, of course, they can easily be installed elsewhere. They consist of opal glass lights, normally rectangular or square although circular ones are also available, which are mounted on a die-cast aluminium backplate. The advantage of these lights is that they can either be flush or surface-mounted.

Wiring and controlling the lights
If your outdoor lights are being mounted directly on the external wall then running in the power is normally straightforward. It'll be a question of drilling a hole in the wall of the

374

WHERE TO SITE OUTSIDE LIGHTS

1 *Porch lights by the front door*
2 *External corner light to light two walls*
3 *Post top lights at the gateway*
4 *Patio lights above sitting areas*
5 *Bulkhead light above the back door*
6 *Bollard light on the path.*

porch, say, and bringing the power cable out at a point that coincides with the back-plate of the light fitting. Running in the cable for a roof or ceiling-mounted light may be slightly more involved but this depends largely upon the height of the porch and how easy it will be to drill through the wall.

You'll probably find it most convenient to mount the switch for a porch light in the hall, close to the front door. That way you'll be able to switch the light on and off as you wish. You might, of course, find it convenient to have a second switch actually in the porch, in which case it is a simple job to drill a hole through the wall, link the switches with a short length of three-core and earth cable and mount them back to back. Wiring in a back door light or wall-mounted light is much the same, although if you're going to install an outside switch you should make sure that it's thoroughly protected against the weather.

Patio lighting

If you're going to install lighting on your patio then you'll discover the range of lights available will be much wider. In addition to the types of fittings mentioned above, you could also fit spotlights, table lamps and standard lamps. While a single light could easily be wired from an existing lighting circuit it's probably best to run a separate circuit specifically for the new lighting. A socket outlet on your patio can obtain its power on a spur from the house ring circuit. However, you should always bear in mind that when added to the area in the house, the patio mustn't exceed the maximum area to be supplied by any one ring circuit. And, of course, you must take precautions to protect the socket from the weather. Probably your best bet is to twin-mount the socket and then fit a hinged plastic cover specially designed for outside sockets in relatively protected positions – such as a patio.

Probably the best way to supply power for patio lighting is to run a new radial circuit. Use a 20A circuit for a patio no larger than 20m^2 and a 30A one where the area is in excess of 20m^2. Once the circuit is installed, it's easy to supply fixed lights via switched fused connection units fitted with a 3A fuse.

Gateway lighting

If you want to install lighting on your gate to help people drive in at night then it must, of course, be visible from the road. Post top lamps are particularly suitable. They are robust and as they have only a small area of glass any damage that might be caused by high winds or vandals is likely to be minimal. Glass spheres look extremely attractive when mounted on top of gate posts and they provide considerably more light. However, they are also that much more fragile and shouldn't be installed if there is the slightest likelihood of them getting damaged. Possibly the best type of light to install would be a bulkhead fitting with a vandal-resistant acrylic diffuser in place of the more traditional glass. As your gateway is likely to be some way from the house the cable will have to be taken underground and must either be a specially protected cable or else run in PVC conduit – see pages 357–360.

Drive and path lighting

There's little point in lighting your gateway and then not providing sufficient illumination along the path or drive to your house. There is no reason why you shouldn't continue the style of the gate lighting along the drive.

Alternatively, you may find that small bollard-style lights are the most suitable for lighting your path. These shouldn't be confused with the bollards we find in the streets, as they are attractive, provide a useful amount of light and are available in numerous designs. The bollard is usually a

WIRING OPTIONS

There are several ways of obtaining power for outside lights.

1 For a porch light, break into an existing lighting circuit and run one cable to the light and one to a switch.

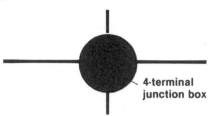

4-terminal junction box

2 If the light circuit isn't close by, run a spur cable from a 3-terminal junction box (A) and proceed as above.

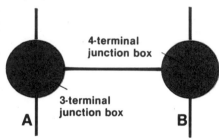

4-terminal junction box

3-terminal junction box

A   **B**

3 You can break into a circuit and run a spur. Take the cable to a fused connection unit and on to the lights and switch.

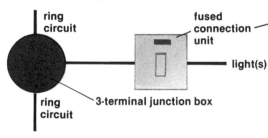

ring circuit

fused connection unit

light(s)

ring circuit

3-terminal junction box

4 If you are installing a number of outside lights, you might find it best to run in a completely new circuit.

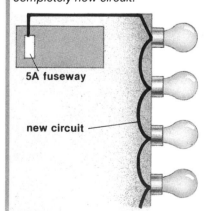

5A fuseway

new circuit

Sleeve earth cores with green/yellow PVC and flag the black cores of the cables.

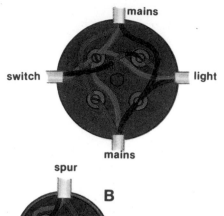

mains

switch   **light**

mains

spur

B

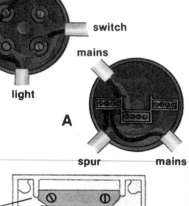

switch

mains

light

A

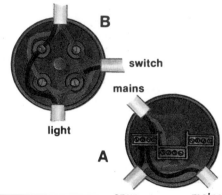

spur   **mains**

spur

to light/switch

Wiring a new circuit

The new circuit should originate at a spare fuseway in your consumer unit. There are several ways of wiring up the lights. You can:
● *install a 4-terminal junction box in the circuit before the first light (see 2B above) and link it to a master switch)*
● *use a junction-box system with individual switches and a branch cable to each light*
● *use a loop-in system with BESA boxes sunk in the house wall*

Ready Reference

TYPES OF OUTDOOR LIGHTING

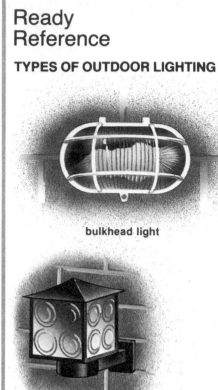

bulkhead light

porch light

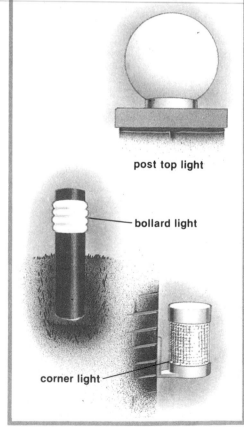

post top light

bollard light

corner light

FITTING AN OUTSIDE WALL LIGHT

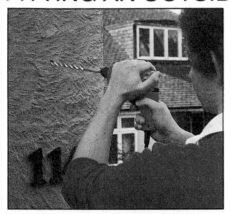

1 *Drill a hole for the cable or flex at an angle to prevent water penetration. Then mark the positions of the fixing holes, drill and plug them.*

2 *With this fitting the mains cable is linked to the fitting's flex via a connector block. Strip the cores and connect them; no earth is needed here.*

3 *The connector block will be concealed by the fitting's backplate. Wrap the block carefully with PVC tape to make it waterproof.*

4 *Mount the fitting using rust-proof screws, fit the lamp and add the glass dome, checking that it is secure. Then complete the connections indoors.*

5 *Where the cable runs directly into a terminal block within the fitting, feed it through a grommet to prevent chafing before making the connections.*

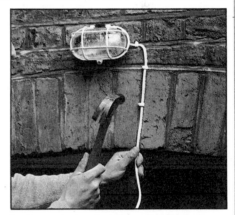

6 *If you don't mind the cable being on show, clip it neatly to the wall. You can, if you prefer, hide the cable run in surface-mounted conduit.*

black or green-finished aluminium or steel pole with a base plate for a secure fixing. They come in a variety of heights.

Taking power outdoors
The most important thing to remember when installing any outdoor lighting is that all fittings and cable runs must be protected against the weather.

If you're mounting a light on a porch wall or near the backdoor the easiest way of providing power is to break into an existing light circuit with a three-terminal junction box and extend a power cable to a four-terminal junction box near the lighting point. From here you'll have to run a length of 1.0mm² two-core and earth cable through the house wall and to the light's terminals. A similar-sized cable will be run from the junction box to a convenient point for the controlling switch to be mounted. If, however, supplying

an extra light will exceed the limits of the existing circuit then you could run in a new circuit and take it directly to a four-terminal junction box; from here you can run the cables to the light and switch respectively. Remember to sleeve all earth cores with green/yellow PVC sleeving and, at the junction boxes, to flag all switch neutrals with red tape as they're really live.

Wherever possible you should try to avoid running cable along an outside wall. However if this can't be avoided it's best to use PVC-covered mineral-insulated copper-covered (MICC) cable fixed directly to the wall. If you want to use MICC cable make sure you first measure the cable runs. That way you'll be able to get it cut to an exact length as well as having the correct seals and glands fitted to it. For further information on running cable out of doors, see pages 357–363. In fact for short lenghts that are unlikely to be

disturbed, PVC cable run in rigid high-impact plastic conduit will be acceptable. When cable is run on the surface to an outside light or switch the cable entry hole must be sealed with mastic to prevent moisture penetration.

Gate lights, drive lights and path lights are inevitably going to be some way from the house and will so obtain their power via cable run underground to them. Whichever cable you use will have to be buried in a trench that is at least 550mm (20in) deep.

Finally, if you want to control your outdoor lights with two-way switching then you'll have to link the switches with 1.0mm² three-core and earth cable. Should you want to provide two-way switching for your gate light, then rather than running two lengths of special cable it's easier and much cheaper to use PVC cable and run both cables in a single length of conduit.

INSTALLING LOW-VOLTAGE LIGHTING

1 *Low-voltage lighting kits contain all the necessary components. Lay them out and connect the brown low-voltage cable to the transformer's output terminals.*

2 *Assemble the lights by feeding the terminal lead in each one up through the extension pole. Then push the pole firmly into the spike base.*

3 *Unscrew the lampholder from the lamp housing. Then feed the terminal leads through the housing and push it onto the other end of the pole.*

4 *Connect the leads to the terminals on the lampholder by pushing them on firmly. Then screw the lampholder back into place in the lamp housing.*

5 *Next, fit the lamp into its holder by turning it in a clockwise direction. Add the translucent shade and snap on the green mushroom top.*

6 *Unscrew the spike base cover to expose the two metal terminal spikes. Decide where the light will go, and lay the cable over the terminals.*

7 *Press the flat side of the cable firmly onto the terminal spikes to drive them into the cable. That way you'll make the necessary connections. Then replace the terminal cover.*

8 *Stand each lamp in position in a hole 200mm (8in) deep and 150mm (6in) diameter, and replace the soil. You can bury the cable if you wish or run it along a conveniently-sited wall.*

9 *Unless the transformer is weatherproof, it must be installed under cover. Place it just inside your house or – if you have power there – in a garden shed. Plug it in and test the lights.*

IMPROVING LIGHT AND POWER IN THE KITCHEN

An old kitchen can be transformed and updated simply by adding extra socket outlets and additional lighting. Supplying the power is not complicated, and existing circuits can be easily adapted or completely rewired.

The kitchen is one of the most frequently used rooms in the home and as a result should be as efficient and streamlined as possible. A modern one ought really to be able to take full advantage of the growth in electrical appliances and the improvement in artificial lighting that has been seen over the past decade or so. If you cast a critical eye round your kitchen you'll probably find that the electrics certainly leave something to be desired. A couple of socket outlets and a central light are painfully inadequate in this day and age: if you were to equip your kitchen with many of the available labour-saving devices you certainly wouldn't be able to power them from individual socket outlets. And a single central light will mean that you're likely to have to prepare food and wash dishes in your own shadow.

If you're not satisfied with the electrics in your kitchen, to improve them you can either rewire the whole kitchen or else extend the existing circuits.

Planning your needs

Before you start work on your kitchen you must decide exactly what you want from it. You'll have to decide how many socket outlets you're going to need and just what sort of lighting you'll want. The best way of deciding on sockets is to make a list of electrical appliances and tick off those you own, or are likely to own. Then decide upon other things, such as a radio or television, which you might also want to use in the kitchen occasionally. In your calculations you shouldn't forget that some appliances, like a cooker hood or a waste disposal unit, are better connected to a fused connection unit rather than a socket outlet. However, it's still a good idea to allow more socket outlets than you think are necessary. That way you'll do away with the need for adaptors (never, in any case, to be recommended from a safety point of view) and the temptation of trailing flexes for long distances over worktops. And though you may think that you could use one socket for several different pieces of equipment, it's better, in fact, to have one per appliance so that you minimise the amount of plug changing. Moving appliances around is specially risky in a kitchen where you might be tempted to change plugs with wet hands and so risk getting a nasty shock.

There's only one electrical appliance used in the kitchen which can't get its power from an ordinary 13A socket outlet or fused connection unit and that's the cooker. Both freestanding and split-level cookers must be connected exclusively to their own radial circuits.

Planning your lighting needs is just as important, and you'll probably find that you'll need two sorts of artificial lighting to make your kitchen completely practical. It's a good idea to have some kind of general lighting and to complement that with more specific 'task' lighting on certain areas.

General lighting will be adequate for the kitchen as a whole, so you can eat and work in comfort, while the specific lighting will provide the more intense local light needed on worktops, sinks and sometimes the cooker. You might find that simply replacing your existing light with a fluorescent tube provides you with adequate lighting, and this will certainly be true if your kitchen is not very large. However, if you've a fairly sizeable kitchen you might well require spotlights or downlighters in addition to two or more fluorescent tubes on the ceiling. And if

Ready Reference

EXTENDING YOUR CIRCUITS

You can improve your electrics by:
● rewiring your kitchen completely
● adding new sockets and lights to existing circuits
● extending and modifying your existing circuits.

To extend a power circuit you should:
● remove the faceplate of the last socket outlet on the circuit
● connect a length of the equivalent-sized cable to the socket terminals
● run the new cable to any new outlets.

To split a power circuit you should:
● cut the circuit where it enters the kitchen
● use a junction box to connect new cable to the cut end, and run the new cable back to the consumer unit
● add extra sockets where needed
● link the cable from the second circuit to a spare fuse at the consumer unit.

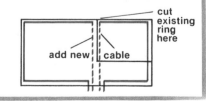

cut existing ring here

add new cable

you feel the light from fluorescent lights is too harsh, you might decide to fit an illuminated ceiling or recessed lights. None of this is beyond the ordinary do-it-yourselfer, and will all go towards transforming your kitchen into a modern one of which you can be proud.

Identifying the circuits

When you've decided exactly how you want to modify your kitchen you'll have to turn your attention to the existing circuitry. First of all you must establish whether the kitchen is supplied by its own ring circuit, whether it's part of a larger ring circuit serving a whole floor, or whether it's supplied by a radial circuit. The chances are that it'll be on a large downstairs ring circuit, but if you're not sure, it's quite easy to check. You'll have to switch on an appliance in the kitchen and then remove the fuse for the ring circuit from the consumer unit. Its fuse should be labelled but if it isn't, you can identify it by virtue of the two cables leaving the fuseway. If the appliance still doesn't work, you'll know it's on the ring and if the removal of the fuse doesn't affect electrical appliances in any other rooms you'll know the kitchen has its own ring circuit. If you find the kitchen circuit has only one cable leaving the consumer unit then that shows it is supplied by a radial circuit.

Remember that there are limitations imposed on both types of circuit. There is no limit to the number of sockets and fused connection units you can install on any new circuit, but you must make sure that the non-fused spurs do not outnumber them. However, there are limitations to the area which each new circuit can serve. A new ring circuit must on no account exceed 100sq m (1075sq ft), while an equivalent 30A radial circuit is limited to an area of 50sq m (540sq ft) – although this is still considerably larger than the average kitchen. A 20A radial circuit is restricted to an area of 20sq m (215sq ft). While those referring to the area each circuit supplies are unlikely to restrict you, they are worth bearing in mind, especially if you have a very large kitchen.

Adapting the circuitry

Once you've established exactly what kind of circuit you have you'll find that there are a number of options open to you. If your power needs are not going to be too demanding you simply fit new socket outlets onto your existing circuit. Alternatively you can modify it so you can provide new power outlets or, if you want, replace it completely with a new circuit for the kitchen's exclusive use.

Simply fitting new sockets onto an existing circuit is not difficult and the only inconvenience will involve disturbing the decorations in the kitchen.

PROVIDING POWER FOR APPLIANCES

Electrical appliances in the kitchen can obtain their power from the ring circuit, a spur or a radial circuit. Double socket outlets are best and switched fused connection units provide extra safety and convenience.

Instantaneous water heater

This is useful mounted close to a sink where there is no regular hot water supply. It should obtain its power through a fused connection unit.

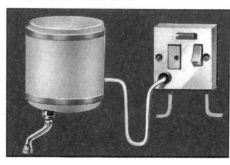

Double socket outlet

This kind of power point is specially suited to use in the kitchen because of the large number of electrical appliances. Switched sockets are safest.

Chest freezer

It's best to use an unswitched fused connection unit as the outlet. That way you avoid the risk of the freezer being accidentally switched off.

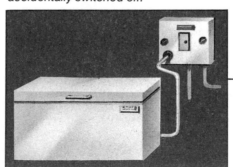

Washing machine

This can be supplied by a spur from the ring circuit. It's a good idea to use a switched fused connection unit so it can't be accidentally disconnected.

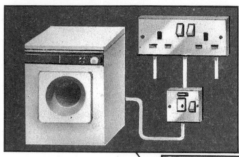

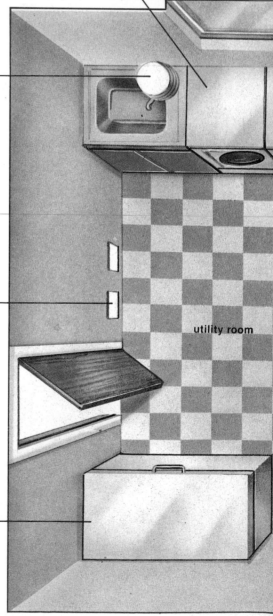

utility room

Dishwasher

A switched fused connection unit on a spur is the best way to provide the power. A neon indicator shows at a glance if the power is on or off.

Waste disposal unit

The switched fused connection unit can be sited under the worktop where it will be easily accessible if it is needed, but also neatly out of sight.

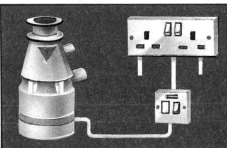

Extractor fan

A switched fused connection unit on a spur from the ring circuit lets you control the fan. A clock connector links the flex from the fan to the spur cable.

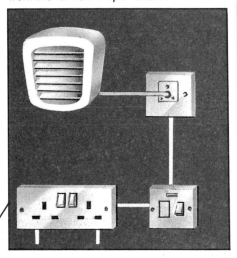

Cooker

This is the only appliance that requires an exclusive radial circuit. This should run from the consumer unit via a cooker switch and connector unit.

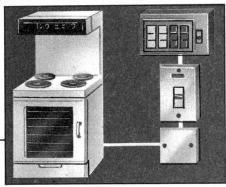

Refrigerator

This can be simply plugged into a socket outlet which should be below the worktop but where it can be easily reached without moving the appliance.

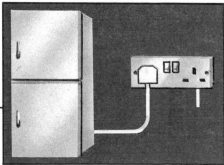

kitchen

IMPROVING YOUR KITCHEN LIGHTING

Adding new lights to your kitchen is not difficult. There is a wide variety available and you can provide overall or more specific illumination.

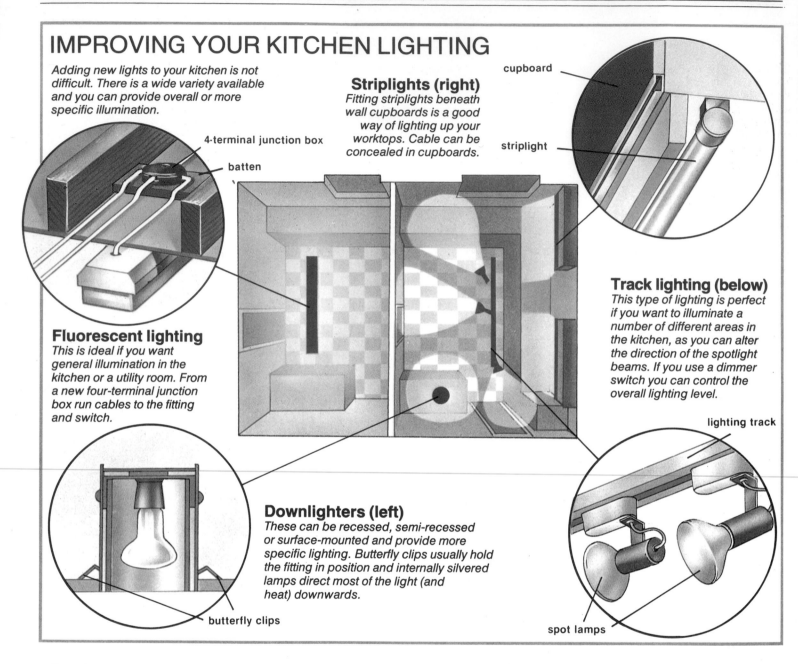

Striplights (right)
Fitting striplights beneath wall cupboards is a good way of lighting up your worktops. Cable can be concealed in cupboards.

cupboard

striplight

4-terminal junction box

batten

Fluorescent lighting
This is ideal if you want general illumination in the kitchen or a utility room. From a new four-terminal junction box run cables to the fitting and switch.

Track lighting (below)
This type of lighting is perfect if you want to illuminate a number of different areas in the kitchen, as you can alter the direction of the spotlight beams. If you use a dimmer switch you can control the overall lighting level.

lighting track

Downlighters (left)
These can be recessed, semi-recessed or surface-mounted and provide more specific lighting. Butterfly clips usually hold the fitting in position and internally silvered lamps direct most of the light (and heat) downwards.

butterfly clips

spot lamps

If you have a radial circuit in your kitchen this can easily be extended provided you don't exceed the limitations on area mentioned earlier. You'll have to break into the circuit at the last outlet. With the power off, you should then remove the outlet and connect the equivalent sized cable to it. Then extend the circuit's route so that it supplies as many extra sockets and fused connection units as you want to install. Otherwise you would install a new radial circuit to supplement an existing circuit.

A third option is to split a large ring circuit into two smaller ring circuits. That way you still use most of the existing cable and all of your existing power outlets. To do this sounds much more complicated than it actually is.

After you've switched off the power at the mains, you should trace the cable run of the existing circuit. At the point at which it leaves the adjacent room to enter the kitchen you'll have to break into it. Using 30A cable connectors you should then attach enough 2.5mm² two-core and earth cable to the cable in the adjacent room to enable you to run it back to the consumer unit. On the way, of course, you can add extra power outlets where you need them. You'll have to do exactly the same in the kitchen extending the existing cable so that it, too, returns to the consumer unit via whatever extra power outlets you wish to install. You'll probably find that you'll have to make a couple of alterations in the arrangements of fuses and cable in the

consumer unit. Each circuit will require its own 30A fuse where the circuit both starts and ends. Unless you already have a spare 30A fuseway, you'll probably have to fit a new MCB or fuse in your consumer unit. If there isn't enough room in the unit then you'll have to fit a new switchfuse unit close to the existing consumer unit.

The ultimate way to provide power for your new socket outlets and fixed appliances is to run in a completely new ring circuit. This is undoubtedly the best way, for not only does it satisfy all your power requirements but it also means that, should a fuse blow in the other circuit, you'll still have some power on the same floor.

Siting the sockets

The best position for the socket outlets in your kitchen will depend largely on how it is laid out. Sockets for portable appliances such as kettles, toasters, food mixers and so on should be on the wall above the work surfaces so flexes are not stretched and connections strained; switched fused connection units for fixed appliances such as refrigerators, freezers and washing machines and other appliances like cooker hoods or extractor fans can be fixed at a similar height or just below the work surface if you want them out of sight. But remember they should be accessible so they can be turned on and off without any trouble. If you fit them just above skirting board level, you'll conceal them neatly behind the appliance but they'll be extremely awkward to get at.

If the appliance is fitted with flex, you'll need a unit with a special flex outlet and it should be sited as near as possible to the appliance and fitted with the appropriate fuse – 3A for loads of up to 720W and 13A for loads up to 3kW.

There is a considerable choice of socket types available and for further details on the range of electrical accessories available see pages 354–356.

Rewiring your lights

Having considered the power circuits, you'll probably want to turn your attention to the lighting in your kitchen. It's no good getting all sorts of marvellous electrical gadgetry and then not being able to see to use it!

As a rule, you'll find there's one lighting circuit for each floor and each one supplies eight or nine lampholders. If there's any danger of overloading the circuit by adding new lights then you should install a new circuit. And an additional circuit means that should a fuse blow, the downstairs of the house won't be left in the dark!

However, you might find that modifying your existing lighting will be sufficient for your needs. For instance, replacing an existing tungsten filament lamp with a fluorescent fitting is simple and effective. If your lighting circuit is wired on the junction box system then all you have to do is remove the existing light, fit the new tube holder and make the connections. If, however, you've got loop-in wiring you'll have to modify the wiring a little as there are no loop-in facilities on a fluorescent fitting. With quite a large kitchen you can be more adventurous in your choice of lighting and there is a wide variety of fittings available, including conventional pendant or ceiling-mounted lights, illuminated ceilings, spotlights, downlighters and concealed striplights.

Choosing your lights

Pendant lights are probably not a particularly good idea in small kitchens. Not only do they cause more shadow than other types, but their flexes tend to get quickly covered in grime. However, a pendant light fitted on a rise-and-fall fitting is perfectly suited for use over an eating area in a larger kitchen.

Fluorescent lights are ideal for general lighting in a kitchen because they cast virtually no shadows. Although they don't give a particularly attractive sort of light, diffusers and coloured tubes make them much more acceptable, while their efficiency and relative cheapness are factors strongly in their favour.

If you find fluorescent lighting ugly and too 'cold' you could incorporate it in an illuminated ceiling. With this method two or more fluorescent lights are fitted to the original ceiling and a second 'ceiling' of translucent plastic panels is fitted below. This is not difficult to do. A lattice or grid of metal bars has to be fitted below the level of the existing ceiling and the panels are then laid on top. These panels can be of different colours to provide a slightly softer effect. A partly illuminated ceiling can be achieved by cutting out sections of the existing ceiling between a pair of joists and replacing them with translucent panels.

Spotlamps provide a concentrated light which is ideal for focussing on a particular area. They can be mounted on the ceiling, on the wall and singly or in groups on a track. Fitting track lighting is ideal for a kitchen as you can pick out a number of specific areas, as well as providing general lighting.

Downlighters are ideal for a kitchen as they will give a concentrated beam of light on a worktop. They are usually the recessed type and therefore lie flush with the ceiling. To fit one you'll have to cut a circular hole in the ceiling to take the tubular fitting. Remember it's a good idea to fit a heat-resisting pad to the underside of the floorboards above and that way you will avoid any possible risk from the rising heat of the bulb. However, semi-recessed and surface-mounted types are also available, and are rather easier to fit. For further details on recessed lighting see pages 58–61.

Finally, **striplights** provide a very effective method of lighting worktops that lie under wall cupboards and are therefore often poorly lit. The striplights are fitted to the underside of the cupboard along with a batten to cut out the glare.

Remember, the rewiring of a kitchen or the adapting of existing circuitry are not such daunting tasks as they first seem, and the results can be both rewarding and satisfying.

see pages 354–356. ... see pages 58–61.

Ready Reference

ENLARGING SOCKET OUTLETS

Changing a single socket outlet into a double one is easy. How you do it depends on how the existing socket is mounted.

For flush-mounted sockets
you should:
● remove the mounting box
● enlarge the hole
● fit the new double box.
If you don't want to chop out a larger hole you should:
● buy a surface-mounted double box
● attach it to the lugs of the existing single box.

For surface mounted sockets
you should:
● remove the existing single box
● fit a surface-mounted double box, or
● chop out a new hole
● fit a flush-mounted double box.

TYPES OF LAMP

Spotlights and downlighters can be fitted with a number of different lamps. The 'general service' lamp gives a wide spread of light.

The internally silvered lamp is silvered round the base and sides so the light is thrown forward. It gives a broad beam.

The crown silvered lamp controls the amount of glare and produces a narrow beam suited to lighting specific features in a room.

The parabolic aluminized reflector is made from armoured glass, lasts longer than most lamps and is mainly used outside.

TIP: RUNNING CABLE

Cable that is chased into the wall should never be run horizontally. This is only acceptable:
● if it is surface mounted, or
● if it is concealed in mini-trunking.
Remember, you can always hide cable runs behind kitchen units.

MISCELLANEOUS PROJECTS

Apart from ensuring that your home has adequate lighting and power supplies, there are a number of smaller but no less important projects you can carry out with your newly-found skills.

FITTING DOOR BELLS

If you have difficulty hearing visitors when they knock on your front door, the solution is to install a new bell, buzzer or set of chimes. Should one prove inadequate, you can always connect up an extension bell as well, so your system is even more efficient.

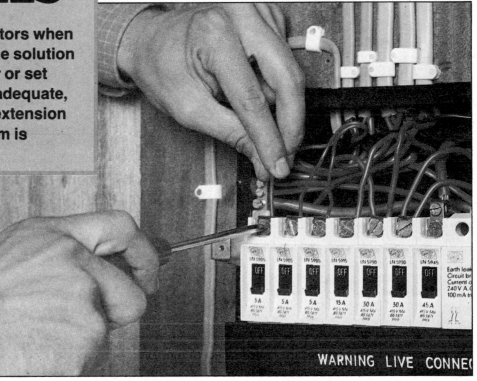

WARNING LIVE CONNE...

Imagine if someone was to knock on your front door while you were busy at the back of the house; the chances are you'd never hear them. Similarly, if you were in the garden and visitors called round, then the likelihood of them attracting your attention before they'd given up knocking on your door and gone home, is minimal. The obvious answer is to install a new bell, buzzer or set of chimes.

This needn't be a daunting job and in fact you'll find that even the most elaborate of the systems on the market is perfectly straightforward to install. Indeed, your most difficult task is likely to be deciding what sort of sound you want to announce the arrival of your visitors. The best thing to do is to visit an electrical shop where they're likely to have a display of what is available. Then all you have to do is listen to the various tones and decide which you like; but remember, whatever you install is likely to last for a long time, so you're going to have to pick a bell, buzzer or set of chimes which won't irritate you.

Making your choice

There are two principal types of electric bell, either of which you can install in your home. The most common is the trembler bell, which operates on what is called a make-and-break system. When an electric current is passed through the bell, the cores of an electromagnet are activated and they attract an arm, to which a striker and knob are attached; this then strikes a gong. At the same instant, the make-and-break contacts open, breaking the circuit and cutting off the current and causing the arm to return to its original position. When this happens, the circuit is reformed so the whole process is repeated – causing the arm to oscillate or 'tremble' to produce the familiar ringing of the bell – provided, of course, the bell push in the circuit is being depressed. The frequency of the trembling, and therefore the tone of the ring, can be altered simply by adjusting the contact screw. As soon as the finger is lifted off the bell push, the circuit is broken completely and the bell stops ringing. The big advantage of the trembler is that it will operate on both ordinary direct current (DC) from a battery or else on alternating current (AC)

CONNECTING BELLS TO BATTERIES

1 *If your bell has a separate battery you'll need two lengths of bell wire. The two floating cores should be joined and protected by insulating tape.*

2 *Connecting two bells in parallel is one way of installing an extension bell. Remember to use identical bells, otherwise the system won't work.*

join

extension bell

main bell

4½V battery

3 *Connecting two bells in series is better as there is no danger of one bell starving the other of power. But don't use two trembler bells together.*

trembler bell

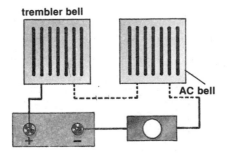

AC bell

4 *You can use an ordinary two-way switch as a changeover switch. That way you'll be able to select which bell you want working at a particular time.*

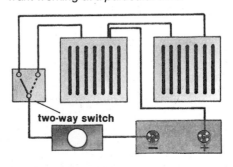

two-way switch

INSTALLING A BELL PUSH

1 *To make a hole in your door post, you'll probably have to drill through from both sides. Stick some tape right round the post to act as a guide.*

2 *Feed through the twin bell wire and check you have enough to make the connections. You can pull back the surplus after the push is fitted.*

3 *Connect the two cores to the two terminals on the bell push and then use a drill or bradawl to make pilot holes to fix the push to the post.*

4 *Finally use wood screws to fix the push securely in place. Bed the push on non-setting mastic if it will be exposed to rain.*

Ready Reference

TIP: POSITIONING THE UNIT

Bear these points in mind when siting a bell or buzzer:
● a single bell or buzzer should be mounted in the hall, from where it will probably be heard throughout the house
● the kitchen is a good place for an extension bell, but it should be sited away from a source of steam as the mechanism could easily get damaged
● chimes with long tubes should be mounted where they won't get easily knocked.

POWERING AN EXTENSION BELL

If your extension bell is connected in series to the main one, twice the voltage will be required. You can provide this,
● with a more powerful battery
● by connecting two 4½V batteries in series.

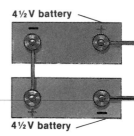

4½V battery

4½V battery

CHOOSING BELL PUSHES

A wide variety of bell pushes is available, including:
● illuminated pushes that can be used only when the circuit is powered by a transformer. This is because the bulb is continually alight, except when the push is used, and would quickly run down a battery
● small button pushes designed to take up as little room as possible on your door post
● pushes that have room for a name label. They should all be carefully positioned where they are easily accessible, clearly visible and not exposed to the weather.

MECHANICAL BELLS

As an alternative to electrical bells, you could choose a mechanical one. These work in one of three ways:
● by clockwork – they'll ring about 100 times before needing to be wound up
● by pulling a handle to cause a bell to rock on a pivot
● by pressure on a push that will make a mechanical chime sound.

Mechanical bells are usually mounted on the inner face of the front door and are extremely simple to fit.

from the mains, provided it comes via a low-voltage transformer.

An AC bell is similar in principle to the trembler bell, but has no make-and-break contact device. As a result it will only operate on AC current from the mains and must therefore be connected to a suitable transformer. It is the alternating pattern of the current itself that provides the required movement in the arm to make the bell ring.

A buzzer is basically an electric bell minus the striker and bell dome. That means that it's the arm hitting the electro-magnets that produces the buzzing noise. It, too, is made in DC versions for operation from a battery and in AC versions for use from the mains.

Chimes are more elaborate than simple bells and buzzers, and are, inevitably, more expensive. When the bell push is pressed, the current activates an electro-magnet, and a double-ended plunger is drawn across to strike one of the chime bars. When the bell push is released, it is sent back by the pressure of a spring to strike the second bar.

There is a wide range of models on the market and the most simple produces a two-note 'ding-dong' ring. Other models have special chimes playing more notes and some contain cassettes which produce familiar bars from popular tunes. Chimes can look rather ugly. This is because some models have long chime tubes that hang down underneath the casing. If you don't like the look of them, buy bar chimes which have all their apparatus concealed within the unit.

When choosing which type of bell, buzzer or chimes you want, it's well worth considering how it obtains its power, as well as what it sounds like. Where the power source is likely to be a mains transformer, either type of bell or buzzer may be used, but you'll probably find an AC bell or buzzer best. This is because

CONNECTING TO THE MAINS

1 *If you're going to connect your transformer to a spare fuseway, you'll have to fix it to the wall or back-board close to your consumer unit.*

2 *Run in the twin bell wire, fixing it to the wall with tacks or clips. Connect it to the secondary terminals that will provide the correct voltage.*

3 *Connect a length of 1.0mm² two-core and earth cable to the primary terminals. Ignore the earth core as most transformers don't need earthing.*

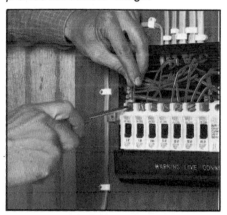

4 *Clip the cable to the wall and after switching off at the mains connect it to a spare 5A fuseway in the unit. Remember to label the fuseway.*

not only are they cheaper to buy, but with no make-and-break device there is the minimum of things that can go wrong: no contacts to corrode or burn and no adjusting screws to work loose and fall out.

Installing a bell

The simple circuit required for installing a bell is also suitable for the installation of a buzzer or a set of door chimes. You'll obviously require the new bell unit itself, a bell push, a length of twin bell wire, some tacks or insulated staples and a power source which will be either a 4½V battery or a special bell transformer. Bells, and all the necessary accessories and materials, are often available in kit form. You'll find that some bells have a special compartment in the unit for their battery; with others, the battery is housed separately. Remember, though, that circuit requirements are likely to vary between the different models of bells, buzzers and chimes that are on the market. Before starting any installation, do make sure that you read all of the manufacturer's instructions very carefully.

The first thing to do is to fix the bell to the wall with woodscrews. It's best to fit it high up in the hall, where it'll be audible throughout the home, yet out of harm's way. If you're fixing into masonry, remember that you should drill and plug the holes before screwing the unit to the wall. You should then drill a hole about 6mm (¼in) in diameter in the front door post at the height of the bell push, so that the bell wire will be able to run straight through and into its back. Do make sure that this is at an easily accessible height for visitors, and that its position will be clearly visible. Unless you have a long drill bit, you might find that you'll have to drill in from both faces of the post. To help the two holes meet up with each other in

the middle, it's a good idea to mark the line of the intended hole on the post with a pencil or a length of tape. Provided your bell contains its battery, a single twin wire is all that's needed to link the bell and its push. This should run along as unobtrusive a route as possible and if you've got a picture rail in the hall you'll probably find it ideal to fix the wire on top. In fact the wire is so small that it's rarely noticed and can be kept in place with bell wire tacks. All you do is press the point between the two insulated cores of the bell wire and then knock it into the timber. If you don't want to go to that trouble, however, you could use self-adhesive bell wire.

You can then pass the wire through the hole drilled in the door post and, after removing the cover from the bell push, connect it to the two terminals. The wire is then drawn back through the hole so no excess wire remains on the outside of the door post, and the push can then be fixed to the door post. This is simply done by drilling a couple of pilot holes and then fixing it with wood screws; once it's fixed you can then replace the cover. The other end of the wire should then be connected to the bell terminals and, with the battery fitted, it'll be ready for use.

If, however, your battery has to be mounted separately, or else you're using a transformer, the circuitry is altered slightly. Only one of the cores from the push is connected to the bell itself and you have to run another length of bell wire from the spare bell terminal to the battery. Both cores of this second wire are then connected to the battery, while at the bell end the core which remains unconnected is joined, by means of a small connector, to the floating core running from the bell push.

Installing a transformer

The function of a transformer is to reduce the mains voltage so that it's safe to use with bells, buzzers and chimes. It's important to make sure that it is a bell transformer and is therefore designed specifically for this purpose.

The transformer will have two sets of terminals. One set is for the cable linking it to the 240V mains supply, while the others are low voltage and commonly have outputs of 3, 5 and 8 volts. You can also get transformers which have outputs of 4, 8 and 12 volts. Bells and buzzers usually require only 3 or 5 volts, while chimes are normally connected to the 8V terminals, although some models require 12V.

You can connect the transformer to the mains simply by plugging it into a spare socket, in which case the plug should have its 13A fuse replaced with a 3A one. You could also run a fused spur from the mains to the transformer – in which case you'd use a fused connection unit, also fitted with a 3A fuse.

Another way of obtaining mains power for your bell, buzzer or set of chimes is to connect

FITTING THE COMPONENTS

1 Make up the speaker/receiver unit and fix it in a protected place near the front door. Ideally it should be recessed, but plastic surrounds are available.

2 Wire up the flexes to the unit, and screw the push-button panel over the top. Note that flexes run on the surface should be encased in PVC conduit.

3 Screw the backplate of the handset to the wall, about 1.5m (5ft) above the floor. Make the necessary wiring connections and then replace the cover.

4 Depending on whether your door has a rim or mortise lock, the electric latch either has to be set into the door frame (illustrated) or mounted on the architrave.

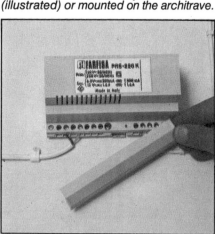

5 The transformer should be mounted where it can't be knocked accidentally. After wiring in all the flex cores, don't forget to replace the terminal cover.

THE ELECTRICAL CONNECTIONS

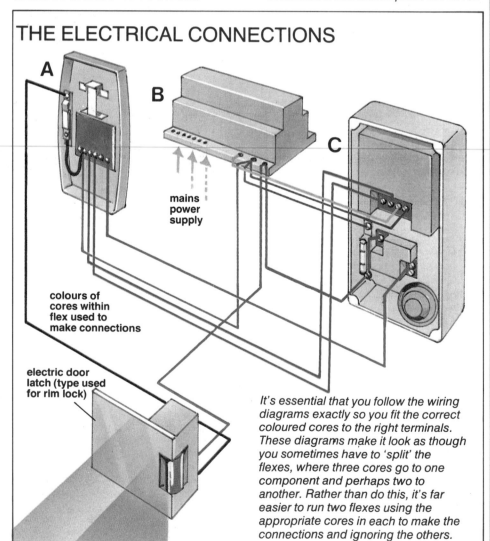

mains power supply

colours of cores within flex used to make connections

electric door latch (type used for rim lock)

It's essential that you follow the wiring diagrams exactly so you fit the correct coloured cores to the right terminals. These diagrams make it look as though you sometimes have to 'split' the flexes, where three cores go to one component and perhaps two to another. Rather than do this, it's far easier to run two flexes using the appropriate cores in each to make the connections and ignoring the others.

INSTALLING A BURGLAR ALARM

More and more people are choosing to protect their homes against intruders by fitting a burglar alarm. Here's how to install a typical kit system.

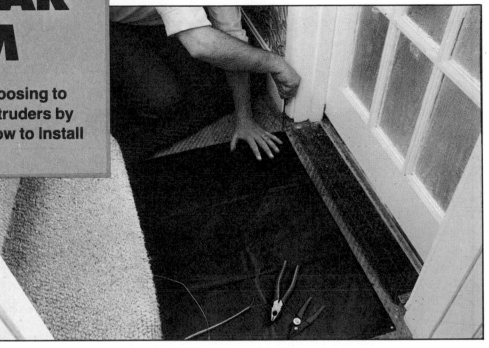

A typical domestic burglar alarm system serves two main purposes; to deter a burglar (either by warning him off when he sees the bell, or by scaring him off when it rings as he breaks in), and to alert you or your neighbours that a break-in is happening.

When you're thinking about fitting one to your home, there are several points to ponder. Firstly, even DIY kits are comparatively expensive, and you may feel that the money is better spent on locks and bolts for doors and windows all round the home – there's a very wide range to choose from. Secondly, false alarms can be a problem (and a nuisance), and the way you live may make having an alarm a distinct hindrance – for example, if you have children in and out all evening. Thirdly, if you live in a comparatively remote area, it's unlikely that anyone but the burglar will hear the bell anyway. However, if you feel that your home will be better protected (and your peace of mind guaranteed) with an alarm system fitted, the actual installation of a kit system is extremely straightforward.

What's in the kit

Most kits consist of the same ingredients. At the heart of the system is a control unit to which all the system components are linked by slim two-core cable. Most contain a battery, but with some models rechargeable batteries can be used. The main circuit cable runs out from and back to the control unit via magnetic contacts fitted to all windows and doors you want to protect (except for your main entry door, which is usually wired on a separate circuit to allow you a short time to leave the house when the system is on without activating the alarm). In addition, pressure-sensitive pads linked to the circuit can be laid under carpets to detect an intruder moving about the house, having bypassed the first line of defence. Another circuit runs from the control unit to the alarm bell, and on some systems there is also provision for a 'panic switch' which can be placed in the bedroom or by the front door; if it's pressed in an emergency, it sounds the alarm bell even if the rest of the system is switched off.

THE CIRCUITS

A typical burglar alarm system consists of circuits that link door and window sensors of various types to a central control unit. In this system there are five circuits in all.

1 *main loop to doors/windows*
2 *circuit to alarm bell*
3 *circuit to front door*
4 *circuit to warning buzzer*
5 *circuit to panic switch.*

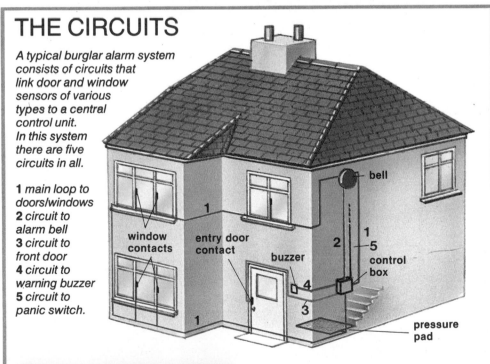

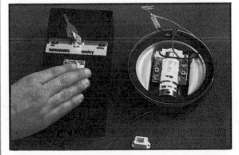

Testing the components

Before starting to install the various components of your kit, it's a good idea to carry out a bench test to familiarise yourself with the connections and to test that everything is working properly. In this case short lengths of wire are used to complete the various circuits. Have a cushion handy to smother the noise of the bell; it makes a very loud noise indoors.

INSTALLING WINDOW/DOOR CONTACTS

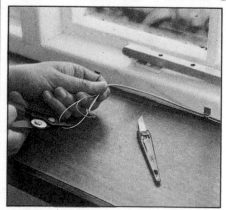

1 *Run the continuous circuit loop to each window or door to be protected, using cable clips to hold it in place. Then cut one core of the cable.*

2 *Mount the contacts using self-adhesive pads or small screws, or recess them neatly (see Ready Reference). Trim the pads to size first.*

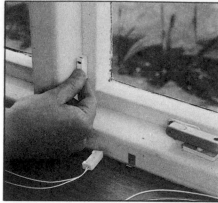

3 *Mount the magnetic part of the contact on the moving casement or door, making sure you fit it so that the magnets face the correct way.*

Testing the system

Your first step on unpacking the contents of the kit is to read the instructions carefully and to familiarise yourself with all the components. The manufacturers usually recommend setting up a bench test of the equipment (see box, page 167), which helps you to see how everything interconnects and to check that it is functioning correctly. Have a cushion handy to smother the sound of the bell when you're testing it indoors.

The next stage is to plan how the property will be protected and where the various components of the system will be sited. It is a good idea to draw a floor plan of the areas to be protected, and from this to work out the possible points of entry and the routes within the building that an intruder is likely to take. You also need to decide on your own main entry and exit route. This is probably the front door, and it is not a good idea to have pressure pads between this door and the control unit, which may be fitted with a timer that allows about 30 seconds only for opening and closing the final exit door once the control unit is switched on. This is not quite so important with a system that has a separate main exit/entry door switch which allows the keyholder free exit and entry whilst the system is in the 'alert' condition. In the latter case, a good position for the control unit is in a concealed position in an area to be protected by the alarm system, such as in an upstairs cupboard where the wire to the alarm bell can be kept as short as possible. When the control unit has a time delay, it should be sited in a convenient position for the front door, such as in a hall cupboard or cloakroom. The warning buzzer (which sounds on entry to remind you to switch off the system) should also be placed fairly near the front door.

FITTING PRESSURE PADS

1 *Position pressure pads in areas that an intruder cannot avoid, such as at the foot of the stairs. Fit them below carpet underlay, and secure with screws or tape.*

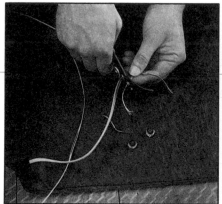

2 *Prepare the cores of the cable connected to the mat as described in the maker's instructions; this usually involves cutting away screening wires.*

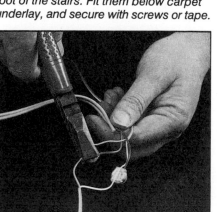

3 *Link the cores of the mat cable to the circuit cable (one core of which is cut as for fitting window contacts) using the special connectors provided.*

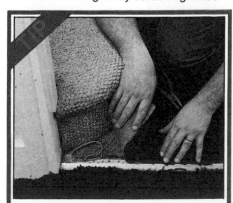

4 *Conceal the cable and connectors near the edge of the carpet. Avoid having the circuit cable visible – it could betray the mat's whereabouts.*

4 *Then mount the switch part of the contact on the window or door frame, checking that it is parallel to and in line with the magnetic contact.*

5 *Connect the leads from the contact switch to the cut ends of the circuit loop by inserting both into the connectors and squeezing them with pliers.*

6 *Fix the two connectors and the uncut part of the circuit loop to the frame with self-adhesive pads. Use conduit to conceal the cable if you prefer.*

INSTALLING THE CONTROL UNIT

1 *Screw the control unit to the wall in its chosen position, and then connect up the circuit cores and the links to the bell, the main entry door and so on.*

2 *Check all the connections carefully against the manufacturer's instructions, and then fit the battery. The red test light will light if the battery is sound.*

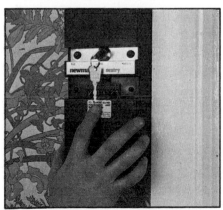

3 *Replace the battery compartment cover, checking that it is pushed fully home. The red test light should go out when the cover is completely closed.*

4 *Fit the entry/exit warning buzzer near to the front door so that you hear it clearly whenever you enter or leave the house and the system is switched on.*

Completing the installation

The alarm bell or siren should be fitted in a prominent position on the outside of the building, well out of reach of tampering. It should be as close as possible to the control unit and the cable connecting them should run through the wall immediately behind the alarm box so it is completely concealed.

Next, the control box is connected to the various sensors around the house with two-core cable which should be routed as unobtrusively as possible. Small cable clips are supplied, but where carpets are fitted the main loop cable can often be laid between carpet and skirting board. Exposed cable can, if you wish, be hidden in slim PVC electrical conduit – see *Ready Reference.*

The door and window contacts are magnetically-operated switches that are activated whenever a protected door or window is opened. Each sensor is in two parts. The switch section is fitted to the fixed frame, either on the surface or else neatly recessed into the frame – see *Ready Reference.* The magnetic section is fitted to the moving door or window, and you must ensure that both sections line up when the door or window is closed. The gap between them should not be greater than about 6mm (¼in).

Pressure pads are flat mats which in fact are electrical switches sensitive to the weight of a person through a carpet or rug. They can be used at any carpeted position where an intruder is likely to tread, such as at door thresholds between rooms, on stair treads, or beneath windows.

Once the wiring has been completed according to the installation instructions, it remains only to test the system before showing all members of the household how to use it.

Ready Reference

FITTING A PANIC SWITCH

If a panic switch is included in the kit, fit it by your bedside or near the front door, where it will be easy to reach in an emergency (A).

Run the cable from the control unit to the switch position, and connect the cores as per the manufacturer's instructions (B).

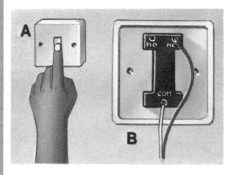

TIP: RECESS THE CONTACTS

You can make the window and door contacts far less obtrusive by recessing them into the woodwork. Mark up the positions of the recesses accurately.

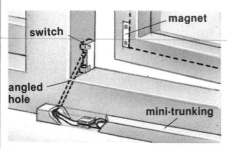

You can also conceal the circuit cable and the connectors if you wish by fitting lengths of slim PVC conduit along the rear edge of the window sill, and drilling an angled hole for the leads through the window frame.

TIP: SEAL THE BELL

The bell unit is usually fitted under the eaves, so it will get some protection from the weather. You can also seal the back of the bell housing with mastic to stop water running into the unit.

WARN YOUR NEIGHBOURS

When you install a burglar alarm
● tell your neighbours, so they'll know what's going on if the bell rings and can take appropriate action
● inform the local police, and leave a key with a neighbour so that the unit can be switched off in the event of a false alarm.
● make sure everyone in the house knows how to operate the system.

FITTING THE ALARM BELL

1 Fit the bell in a prominent position well out of reach of tampering. Put some non-setting mastic between backplate and wall to keep rain out.

2 Feed the cable from the control unit through a hole drilled in the wall behind the bell, and connect the cores to the two bell terminals.

3 Feed in the circuit loop cable, cut one core (as for windows) and use the connectors provided to link it to the leads from the anti-tamper switch.

4 Connect the flying leads from the gong to the bell terminals, by pushing the plug pins into the terminal sockets. Check that they are pushed fully home.

5 Hook the gong into position over the lugs on the backplate, tucking all the cables neatly away behind it, and secure it to the backplate by tightening the fixing screw.

6 Check that the magnet inside the bell cover lines up with the anti-tamper switch on the backplate, and then fix the cover in place. Now you can test the completed installation.

INSTALLING CONVENIENCE CONTROLS

You can make your life more comfortable and your home that much more secure by installing a variety of special controls for your lighting and electrical appliances.

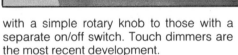

Special controls for electric appliances can be a real boon to the householder. They can make life much more comfortable by automatically switching appliances on and off, and more economic by preventing appliances from being left on to consume costly electricity. They can also help to make the home more secure by controlling lights, radios and curtains to give would-be burglars the impression that there's someone in.

But before you dash off to your local electrical supplies shop, pause for a moment's reflection. Are you being tempted by the sheer novelty of automatic controls? Remember, all automation is expensive, so it pays to take a slightly more hard-headed attitude towards making the decision. First of all, make sure that the equipment will actually do the job you have in mind. Read all the technical specifications carefully. You don't want to discover that your new dimmer light switch won't allow two-way switching or won't work on fluorescent lights. Secondly, do make sure that you know exactly what you're getting for your money. You may find out that the price quoted in the sales leaflet is just a basic 'starter kit' and that you'll have to spend more money to achieve the full performance suggested by the advertisement. Thirdly, consider whether it's actually worth automating a particular appliance; after all, many of the currently available devices perform only fairly menial tasks. Finally, remember that the development of home technology is advancing rapidly; buy now and you may well find that next year you can buy something that does more and does it cheaper.

Dimmer switches
Although dimmer switches offer no automatic form of control, they are considerably more versatile than the conventional rocker switch – allowing you greater flexibility in controlling the level of artificial lighting in the room where they are installed. They're usually used to control tungsten filament lights and spotlights. However, you can dim even a fluorescent lamp provided you have a special choke for the fitting. Various types of dimmer switches are available, ranging from those

with a simple rotary knob to those with a separate on/off switch. Touch dimmers are the most recent development.

Connecting a dimmer switch into your existing circuit is perfectly straightforward. Switch off at the mains and remove the fuse for the particular circuit you're working on; then you can switch the mains back on and have some light to work by. Unscrew the faceplate of your existing switch and pull it carefully away from the mounting box. This will give you enough room in which to disconnect the cable cores. Then simply connect up the cores to the dimmer switch according to the manufacturer's instructions and screw the faceplate to the box. If you want to put a dimmer into a two-way system then remember you can only replace one of the switches with a dimmer. Most one-gang dimmers will fit a standard plaster-depth or surface-mounted box, but some need a deeper box. Two-gang and multi-gang dimmers may need a double box.

Automatic light controls
The most basic automatic light switch is the time delay switch designed primarily for use on communal landings and stairwells. When you want light, all you do is switch on and leave the device to turn the light off again after a pre-set interval – usually anything from five to twenty minutes, depending on the model. Most versions allow you to adjust the timing to suit your needs. The most simple type works by means of a large spring-loaded button, while more sophisticated models use electronic timers and touch plate controls.

Time delay faders are a sort of cross between a dimmer and a time delay switch. They fade out the light gradually over a pre-set delay time and so are extremely handy for a child's bedroom, say. These are normally fitted with dual touch plate controls; the upper plate allows the switch to work like a conventional touch dimmer, the lower one triggers the dimming sequence. Time delay faders can be simply installed in the place of ordinary rocker switches, but, as a rule, they are not suitable for use with fluorescent lights.

Security switches
These switches are useful from a security point of view because lights are thereby turned on and off automatically to convince would-be burglars that you're at home. The basic switch incorporates a light-sensing device that will turn on the light at dusk and then off after a certain period of time (usually between two and ten hours). The faceplate carries a dial for selecting the time the light is on, and two switches, one to allow the switch to function as an ordinary on/off switch and the other to activate the light sensing device. It's not a good idea to fit this type of switch in unusually light or dark situations where the light-sensing device could get confused; avoid fixing it in a corner where there is little natural light or close to a window by a street light.

Photoelectric security switches don't, as a rule, incorporate on/off switches, so, if necessary, manual override will have to be provided separately. However, these switches are usually designed to be installed outside to control lights in exposed conditions. They

INSTALLING A DIMMER SWITCH

1 *Switch off at the mains and remove the lighting circuit fuse; then switch the power back on and unscrew the existing faceplate from its mounting box.*

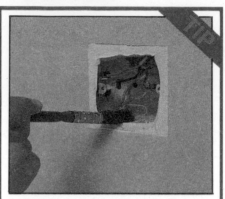

2 *Disconnect the old switch. Before fitting the dimmer switch brush away any plaster or debris that's fallen into the mounting box.*

3 *Make the connections to the new switch following the manufacturer's instructions. You may have to remove covers to get access to the terminals.*

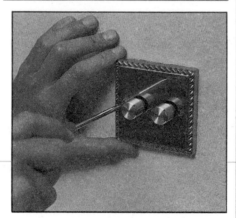

4 *If you're installing a metal switch, make sure the faceplate is earthed by linking it with the box earth terminal. Then screw the faceplate in place.*

USING A PLUG-IN DIMMER

1 *Plug-in dimmers can be easily moved, allowing you to dim any table lamps. They are not suitable for lamps below 40W or above 400W.*

2 *Simply plug the lamp into the dimmer socket. You'll then be able to control the brightness by moving the dial on the dimmer face.*

Ready Reference

INSTALLING DIMMER SWITCHES

Dimmer switches can easily replace one-way rocker switches and most two-way switches. However, in a two-way system only one switch need be replaced.

CONTROLLING THE LIGHT

There are three ways of switching lights controlled by a dimmer, depending on which model you fit;
● rotating an on/off knob
● flicking a separate rocker switch incorporated on the face plate
● tapping the touch plate.

MOUNTING BOXES

Most one-gang dimmer switches will fit into existing square plaster-depth (16mm/⅝in deep) mounting boxes (A), and have standard screw fixings.

Some dimmer switches will require deeper boxes – either 25mm (1in) or 35mm (1⅜in). If you're installing three – or four-gang switches, then you'll probably have to install rectangular mounting boxes (B). These are also available in various depths.

A   **B**

WATTAGE LIMITS

Dimmer switches operate between minimum and maximum wattage limits. Before buying one, check the light wattage of each lamp it will control. The minimum wattage is likely to be about 60W, so if you have a 40W lamp you won't be able to dim it successfully. On some switches the minimum can be as high as 120W, so a single 100W lamp would be too low.

The maximum wattage can be as low as 400W, which means that some switches would be unable to control a section of track lighting with, say, five 100W lamps.

DEALING WITH THE CORES

When replacing switches with dimmers, always follow the manufacturer's instructions. In particular
● take note of existing core connections
● apply the equivalent coloured insulation tape round cores with faded insulation so they'll be readily identifiable in the future
● don't separate cores that are joined together. Just fit them into the same terminal on the new dimmer.

INSTALLING A TIME-DELAY SWITCH

1 Switch off at the mains and remove the existing switch. Take off the front cover of the switch to gain access to the terminal screws.

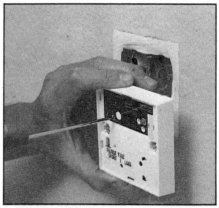

2 Connect the cores to the terminals as indicated on the switch. You can then fix the switch to the mounting box with the screws provided.

3 You can set the switch so the light will be switched off up to twenty minutes after being turned on. Use the special screwdriver to adjust the delay.

4 Finally, fit the touch plate back in position. Switch on at the mains and test the time setting. If necessary, adjust the setting again.

FITTING A SECURITY SWITCH

1 Switch off at the mains and remove your old switch. Make the connections to the security switch and screw it to the mounting box.

2 You can programme the light switch to turn interior and exterior lights on or off automatically. Programmes can be easily cleared and overidden.

can usually be mounted within plastic conduit systems and will switch outside lights on at dusk and off at dawn, so giving your home extra security when no one's in. And, of course, you'll have the lights on for you when you return from an evening out. Most exterior switches incorporate a designed time delay of 1 to 2 minutes so that car headlights won't cause the light to go off.

Automatic power control

Plug-in timers are merely a sort of sophisticated plug-in adaptor for ordinary power sockets. Once you have one in place, all you do is plug in whatever device you want the timer to control. This can be just about anything that can be powered from your home's ring circuit – standard lamps, radiators, blankets and radios. You programme the timer by using small pegs fixed in special holes on the dials or by moving small spring-loaded lugs; the timer will automatically turn the power on and off at these pre-set times.

The minimum period the power can be on for is thirty minutes, although you can control the timer to the nearest fifteen minutes. The on/off pegs are usually protected by a clear dust cover and spare pegs are normally provided with each timer so that more than one operation can be made in each cycle. Most basic versions will operate on a twenty-four hour cycle, although timers programmable for up to seven days are available. With these the setting intervals tend to be quite long – up to two hours in some cases. However, the timer with a longer cycle will obviously be more useful from a security point of view, since you can set it to turn lights on and off at different times each day.

Other control gear

Other devices on the market perform more specific tasks. An electric curtain controller, for example, will both open and close corded curtains provided the weight of pull on the cord required to do so is no greater than 8kg (17½lbs). The motor is controlled by a two-position switch and is simply plugged into the mains. As a safety precaution it will only operate for a period of five minutes before cutting out; that way any accidents in the event of a cord failure will be prevented.

Fan controllers are suitable for use with most electric extractor fans. They are basically specialised dimmer switches that allow you to vary the speed of the fan. They're normally fitted with a separate on/off switch and in some cases a switch for opening and closing the shutters found on very large fans. Other models also have reversing switches. Finally, immersion heater timers work in much the same way as plug-in timers, allowing a number of switching operations per day or per seven days.

FITTING A CEILING FAN

If any rooms in your home are difficult to ventilate – such as an internal WC or a bathroom – the answer could be to fit a ceiling fan, with ducting to the outside. Installing one is straightforward.

Installing an extractor fan is an ideal way of dealing with the problems of stale air, poor ventilation and condensation. But in some circumstances fitting the normal wall or window mounted fans could prove undesirable or even impossible. In these cases the answer is simple: install a ceiling fan.

When to use a ceiling fan
If either your bathroom or WC are internal rooms, then you'll be familiar with the problems of adequately ventilating them. With no outside wall, it will be impossible to fit either a wall or window fan, and merely opening a door will hardly suffice. In this type of situation a ceiling fan will really come into its own and will simplify the whole business of getting rid of stale air. If you want to ventilate a room beneath a flat roof then the fan can merely take the air straight out into the open. If there's loft space above it, then the air could be discharged directly here, but this is not recommended practice, and in these circumstances ducting should be installed to take the air to an exterior grille or out through the roof.

Choosing a fan
Choosing a ceiling fan is not that difficult as, apart from anything else, there aren't that many different models to choose from. However, the model you choose is likely to be decided by the exact job you want it to do. If you want to ventilate only one room – a bathroom, for example – then the chances are that you'll choose the simplest type of ceiling fan. You'll probably be able to choose between surface-mounted models, partially recessed models and those that are fully recessed so that only the louvred grille inlet is visible. As far as looks are concerned, most fans have rigid plastic casings finished in neutral tones of grey or off-white.

But what if your WC is separate from your bathroom and you want to provide adequate ventilation for both? In this case you'll have to get a fan that can cope with ventilating two or more rooms at the same time. The fan itself is fitted in one room or even in the loft, and linked to other rooms via a system of ducting.

Disposing of the air
Before you buy a fan you must consider how you're going to deal with the air it will expel. It is possible for a fan to release the stale air in the loft. However, in practice, there is a risk of causing condensation if you release a lot of warm and humid air there. Your best bet is to use some form of ducting to carry off air directly outside.

Most fans are designed to fit a PVC soil pipe, which is usually 100mm (4in) in diameter, and this is probably the simplest and best type of ducting to use. If your fan won't fit this the manufacturers might well be able to provide you with special adaptors. However, soil pipe is not suitable for every type of fan and it could prove awkward if your ducting run requires a number of corners. In this case purpose-made flexible ducting offers a better alternative. You'll have to extend the ducting run up through the roof, and finish it off with a special weatherproof collar and cowl that should be available from the manufacturers. Alternatively, you can extend the ducting out through the eaves, via a hole cut in the soffit and covered with a grille, or through a hole in a gable end wall.

With any type of ducting, however, you must always bear in mind the problem of condensation. This is a strong probability where ducting carrying warm, moisture laden air passes through a well insulated, and therefore cold, loft. You must insulate the ducting itself as efficiently as you would cold water pipes, otherwise you risk the condensation finding its way back to the fan. One way of avoiding this extra task is to use double-walled flue pipe in preference to soil pipe.

Controlling the fan
How you will actually control the fan is another important consideration. Some models have a simple on/off switch and this should be perfectly adequate if you're installing the fan in a kitchen, say. However, if the fan is to be installed in a bathroom this will have to be a cord-operated switch, otherwise the switch would have to be mounted outside the bathroom, safely out of reach of anyone in the bath or shower.

In fact, you'll probably find that some kind of automatic switching is your best bet and this is particularly suited to bathrooms and WCs. Two versions are available; one is

FITTING A ROOF VENT

1 *Lift off a few tiles from the roof to get at the felt. With a slate roof, you'll have to use a slater's ripper to remove the slates.*

2 *Cut a hole in the felt to let through the ducting. Use the rafters as a guide so the hole will be in line with a space between the joists.*

3 *Poke through the ducting and slip the weatherproof apron over it. Shape the apron with a piece of wood so it sits tightly on the tiles.*

4 *Replace some tiles so that little of the apron is visible. Finally, fit the cowl on top of the ducting so that the rain is kept out.*

connected to the door so that the fan will work whenever someone enters the room, the other is connected to a ceiling rose so that it works when you switch on the light. Both types of automatic switch should incorporate timers. That way the fan will stay on for a while after you've turned off the light or left the room. Normally, there's an adjustable screw to allow you to set the timer at almost any limit up to forty-five minutes.

Installing the fan

Once you've decided where you want the fan to go you'll have to get into the loft to check that there are no obstructions such as pipes and cables and that the position corresponds to a gap between the joists. After you've decided your ceiling is suitable, you'll have to make up a timber support for it. Use a piece of 12mm (½in) chipboard fixed to two battens. The template normally provided

by the manufacturers will help you cut out a hole in the timber for the fan exhaust spigot and also a suitable hole for the cables. You can use the timber as a template and make four holes through the ceiling to mark the diameter of the circle. Then return downstairs and use a padsaw to cut out the section of the ceiling.

Next, fix the support in position by screwing the battens to the joists. If the fan is to be surface-mounted, screw the chipboard to a couple of 50x25mm (2x1in) battens and then attach these to the sides of the joists so that the support timber is hard against the ceiling. If you want a recessed or partially recessed installation, then you'll have to fix the support to the top of the joists leaving a gap between the support and ceiling sufficiently deep to accommodate the body of the fan. If the fan is too large then you might be forced to accept only a partially recessed installation.

Ready Reference

ELECTRICAL CONNECTIONS

Fans must be connected to the mains via an isolating switch and you must use a switched fused connection unit. If you're taking power from the mains, run 2.5mm² two-core and earth cable to the feed side of the unit. With power from the lighting circuit use 1.0mm² or 1.5mm² two-core and earth cable.

DOOR SWITCH CONNECTIONS

From the connection unit run a length of 1.0mm² two-core and earth cable to the fan terminal block. You should then link the fan terminals and the door switch with 0.75mm² PVC sheathed two-core flex.

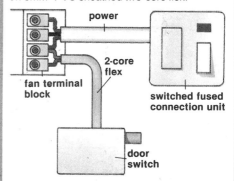

LIGHT SWITCH CONNECTIONS

From the fan's terminal block run 1.0mm² three-core and earth cable to the ceiling rose. That way the light will obtain its power via the fan, which works on its timer once the light has been switched off.

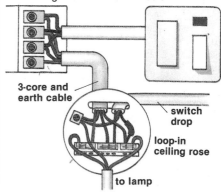

TIP: POSITIONING YOUR FAN

When positioning your fan on the ceiling you should:
● take into account a source of fresh air
● avoid direct water or spray
● avoid siting it so that someone in the bath or shower can touch it
● avoid siting it directly above a heat source producing a temperature above 40°C (104°F).

FITTING THE FAN

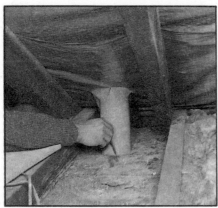

1 *Use the ducting to mark out the section of ceiling that will have to be cut away. Then pierce guide holes through the ceiling below.*

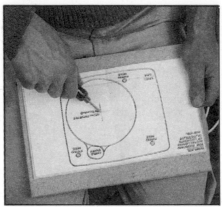

2 *You'll have to fit a timber support for the fan between the joists. Use 12mm (1/2in) chipboard and cut a hole in it with the help of a template.*

1 *Run in both the power cable from the fused connection unit (see Ready Reference) and the flex for the switch drop. Fit them under any cable clamps.*

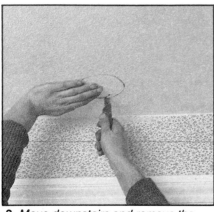

3 *Move downstairs and remove the section of ceiling marked out by the holes from above. Use a padsaw or jig saw to cut it away.*

4 *Return to the loft and screw the chipboard to two 50 x 25mm (2 x 1in) timber battens. Then fix the entire construction between the joists.*

5 *Finish off your work on the fan by fitting its cover. This will protect the fan's mechanism from water or humidity which would cause damage.*

5 *Now fix the fan backplate to the ceiling. Use dome-headed woodscrews long enough to make a secure fixing into the chipboard above.*

6 *Fix the ducting in place. Make sure it fits tightly over the fan spigot so that no humid air can escape. Seal the join with waterproof tape.*

Obtaining the power

Extractor fans can take their power from a lighting circuit or a power circuit. Irrespective of which method you use, however, the fan must be capable of being isolated from the mains. For this purpose all power cables must run to a switched fused connection unit fitted with a 3A cartridge fuse, before being connected to the fan itself. If you are going to get power from a lighting circuit, you have two options. You can either connect directly to a ceiling rose, or else break into the circuit with a new three-terminal junction box. But remember, before working on any of the circuits, switch off at the mains. To obtain power from a ring circuit you can run a spur from a nearby socket outlet, or break into the circuit with a new three-terminal junction box.

What happens now depends on the control arrangements you have chosen. Where the fan has an integral cord switch all you have

CONNECTING UP THE FAN

2 *Connect the cable and flex to the shrouded safety terminals. Make sure that you follow the manufacturer's instructions closely.*

3 *You can now attach the fan itself to the backplate. Hook it onto the special fixing screws and tighten them to hold it firmly in place.*

4 *With the fan fixed to the ceiling you can complete the electrical connections. Push the connector plug firmly into the terminal block.*

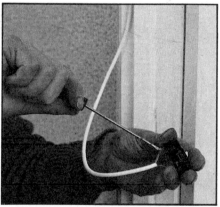

6 *Run the two-core flex in the loft and down to the door switch. Remove the terminal block from the switch and make the connections.*

7 *Mark the position of the door switch on the doorstop. Make sure that the plunger will be fully pushed in when the door is closed.*

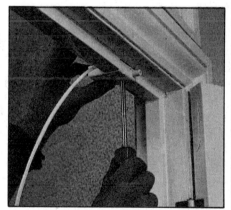

8 *Finally, refit the terminal block and screw the switch in place. You can now turn on at the mains and at the fused connection unit to the fan.*

to do is run the cable directly to the fan and connect it to the terminal block according to the manufacturer's instructions. However, when the fan is to be controlled by a remote switch – by a speed control unit or a door switch – a second cable has to be run between the switch and the fan's live and trigger terminals to complete the switching circuit. Fitting a doorswitch is straightforward. Run two-core flex in the ceiling void from the fan and then down to the switch position. The switch itself must be mounted in the door frame. Mark its position so that the plunger is completely depressed when the door is shut. You must then cut out a section of the frame. It's a good idea to chisel along the join between frame and surround so that the paint won't chip off and you'll be left with a neat edge. Then make the connections and fix the switch in place.

The wiring gets slightly complicated if you

wish to have the fan controlled by the room's light switch. In this case the room's lighting will still get its power from the normal circuitry, but it will have to be via the fan (see *Ready Reference*). In other words a length of three-core and earth cable will run from the fan's live, neutral and trigger terminals to the loop-in ceiling rose. The switch drop will then be wired up across the rose's live and switch terminals so that when the light is turned on, the fan will start to operate.

Fixing the ducting

Once you've installed all the cable runs you can secure the fan unit to the back of the spigot and then screw on the casing. You'll now have to install the ducting that will direct the stale air outside. Build up the run in the same way as you would a run of soil pipe, solvent-welding the joints where necessary. Make sure that the ducting is adequately

supported along its length, and take extra care where it passes through the roof and along horizontal sections; any sags could trap condensation.

Using flexible ducting is just as easy, only it should be linked to the fan's exhaust spigot and the PVC roof outlet with large worm clips.

Where the pipe is to pass through the roof, carefully lift off a few tiles. Then fit the weather apron by locating it beneath the surrounding tiles and poking the pipe through. With that done, you should complete the ducting's protection by fitting the weather cowl. Once the ducting is securely in place, make the final connections at the fan's terminal block, making sure that the cable is firmly held in any cable clamps. Ease the fan into the casing and secure it there before finishing off by fixing the grille plate to the fan body. Then you can switch on the power at the mains and test your fan.

PART 5

HOME PLUMBING

WATER SUPPLY AND DRAINAGE NETWORKS

Very few people are aware of what is involved in supplying clean, drinkable water to their homes, or indeed what happens to waste water when it disappears down a drain. Yet beyond the taps and the waste outlets is a vast network of underground pipes, drains and sewers, pumping stations, reservoirs, water towers and treatment works, all designed to ensure an efficient and constant supply of fresh water and the swift removal of waste.

TYPES OF PIPEWORK

Lead and iron are no longer used as plumbing materials, having been replaced by copper or stainless steel. Now plastic pipework is revolutionising domestic plumbing.

Virtually all **soil pipes** are now made from UPVC (1), which can be joined together using solvent welds or ring seals. Likewise, **overflow pipes** (2) are also made from UPVC, and lengths of these are connected with push-fit joins.

Waste pipes, made of UPVC and ABS plastic, are used for taking water away from baths, basins and sinks (3). Depending on the system they can be joined either by solvent welding or push-fit connections.

Plastic can also be used for water supply pipes. **Polybutylene pipes** (4) can take hot and cold water, the pipes being joined by compression fittings or special push-fit connectors. Similarly, **CPVC pipe** (5) can be used for hot and cold runs, but this is joined with solvent welds.

Black **polythene pipe** (6), the first plastic pipe to be used generally in domestic plumbing, is only suitable for cold water supplies, and consequently is mainly employed for garden and other outside water services.

Rainwater downpipes (7) are made from UPVC and have either circular or square profiles.

Half-hard temper **copper pipe** (8) is used for hot and cold distribution and central heating pipes, being easy to bend and join. **Stainless steel** (9) has also been used, mainly because it can be joined to copper and galvanised steel without causing electrolytic action.

Flexible copper pipe (10), which can be bent simply in the hands, is ideal for making the awkward connections between tap tails and the supply pipes without having to alter the existing runs.

UNDERSTANDING WATER SUPPLY

Each one of us uses about 160 litres (35 gallons) of water a day, and takes it for granted. Only in a long spell of dry weather comes an awareness that we should use it carefully. Our use is controlled by the supply system – this is how it works.

In the last 50 years the consumption of water has almost doubled. Rising standards of living have given rise to increased consumption, and a greater awareness of the need for hygiene has also played a large role in increasing the demand. Faced with this high demand, supply sources have been hard pressed to keep up.

Where it comes from

Water is supplied by the local water authority (or the 'Undertaking' as it is known in the plumbing trade). After falling as rain it is collected in reservoirs which are fed by streams and rivers, or is pumped from underground wells. Water varies a lot in its chemical makeup since it picks up minerals and gases as it flows. If it picks up calcium, magnesium and sodium salts it will be 'hard' – the menace of pipe systems. Before being distributed it is usually filtered through sand and pebble beds to remove solids and organisms, and may have chlorine added to it to ensure that it is 'potable' – drinkable. Fluoride is also sometimes added for the protection of teeth.

Distribution is carried out by a network of pipes starting with 'trunk mains' which may be as much as 610mm (24in) in diameter. These split into mains and sub-mains which run underneath streets and side streets. It is these sub-mains which are tapped by individual houses for their supply.

The house system may be 'direct' in which all cold water supplies are piped direct from the rising main, with the cistern only being used to supply the hot water tank. Or it may be an 'indirect' system in which all cold-water supplies are taken from the cistern, with the exception of a direct supply to the kitchen sink for drinking purposes.

For water to flow through the trunk mains – and eventually into your house – it must be under a certain amount of pressure. This pressure is assisted by pumps but it is vital that somewhere in the mains system the water should reach a height in a reservoir or water tower, higher than any domestic system it has to supply. The vertical distance through which the water 'falls' is known as the 'pressure head' and without it our

cisterns would never fill up without a lot of expensive additional pumping. The storage cistern also provides a pressure head inside the house, which is why it's preferable to have it in the roof space.

The house system

The sub-main underneath the road is tapped by the 'communication pipe' which ends at the authority's stop-valve. This is usually situated under the pavement about 300mm (1ft) outside the boundary of your property. The stop-valve is located at the bottom of a vertical 'guard' pipe – about 1 metre (39in) deep – which is covered at the surface by a hinged metal cover. It should only be operated by the water authority and requires a special key to turn it. But in a real emergency you may be able to turn it yourself. In old houses it may be the only way of turning off the water supply. After this stop-valve the water enters the service pipe and from then on all pipes become your responsibility.

The service pipe continues under the wall of the property at a depth of at least 750mm (2ft 6in) to protect it from frost – though some water authorities insist that it should be 900mm (3ft) deep. As it travels under the house wall or foundation it usually goes through an earthenware pipe to protect it

INDIRECT COLD SUPPLY

The most common system of water supply in the UK is called 'indirect' because most taps take water from the storage cistern in the roof and not direct from the mains. The cistern is fed by the rising main which in turn is fed by the distribution pipe from the mains.

Water input to the cistern is controlled by a high pressure ball-valve. If this valve jams open the water level rises to flow out of the overflow or 'warning' pipe which should stick well out from the wall.

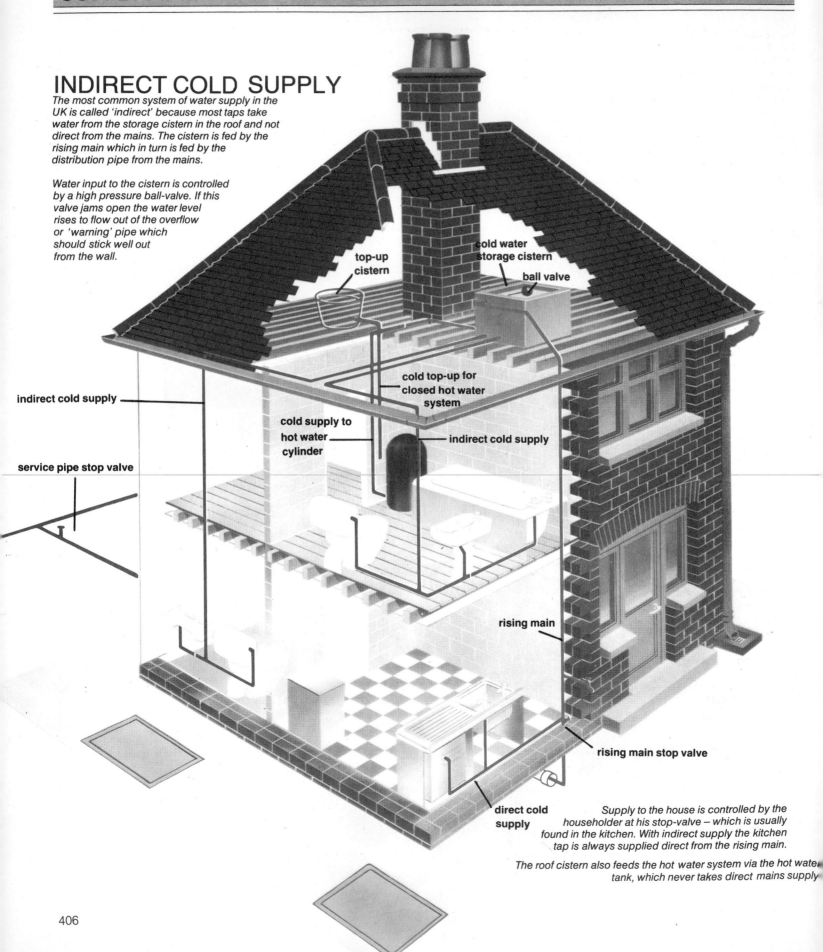

top-up cistern

cold water storage cistern

ball valve

indirect cold supply

cold top-up for closed hot water system

cold supply to hot water cylinder

indirect cold supply

service pipe stop valve

rising main

rising main stop valve

direct cold supply

Supply to the house is controlled by the householder at his stop-valve – which is usually found in the kitchen. With indirect supply the kitchen tap is always supplied direct from the rising main.

The roof cistern also feeds the hot water system via the hot water tank, which never takes direct mains supply.

from possible settlement which might cause it to fracture. To prevent any risk of freezing in cold weather the service pipe should not emerge above ground level until it is at least 600mm (2ft) inside the inside wall surface.

Up to about 40 years ago, service pipes were usually made of lead (in fact the word plumbing originally stemmed from the Latin word for lead – *plumbum)*. Today copper and polythene are used instead. The latter is particularly good as it is a poor conductor of heat and is less prone to freezing and fracture.

The service pipe

The service pipe continues under the wall near the kitchen sink, which means that it is often attached to the inner face of the outside wall. This is contrary to the recommendation that it should be attached to an inside wall, and so such a pipe should be lagged with insulation material. The pipe should also be insulated if it comes through any sub-ground floor cavity where it would be subjected to the icy blasts of winter from under-floor ventilation. Again these precautions are both intended to minimise the risk of frost damage.

When the service pipe rises above the ground floor it is called the 'rising main' and it eventually terminates in the supply cistern, which is usually in the roof cavity. The householder's main stop-valve is usually found on the rising main a little way above floor level. This is the most important 'tap' in the house. In any plumbing emergency – when bursts or leaks occur, for example, your first action should be to turn this tap off, thus isolating the house system from the mains water supply. The stop-valve should always be turned off when you go away if the house is going to be empty. In old houses the location of the stop-valve may vary considerably, it may be in the cellar, under the stairs, or even under a cover beneath the front path – or it may not exist at all, in which case the authority's stop-valve is the only control.

Branch supply pipes

At least one 'branch' supply pipe leaves the rising main close above the stop-valve and drain tap – this is to the tap over the kitchen sink. This tap must be supplied direct from the main supply as it is supposed to provide all drinking and cooking water. Water which has been in a storage cistern is no longer considered drinkable, sometimes termed 'potable', as it may be slightly contaminated by debris in the storage cistern.

Other branches may be taken at this point to an outside tap, or to a washing machine or dishwasher.

The rising main continues upwards and while its ultimate destination is the cold water storage cistern the pipework in between will vary from house to house, depending on

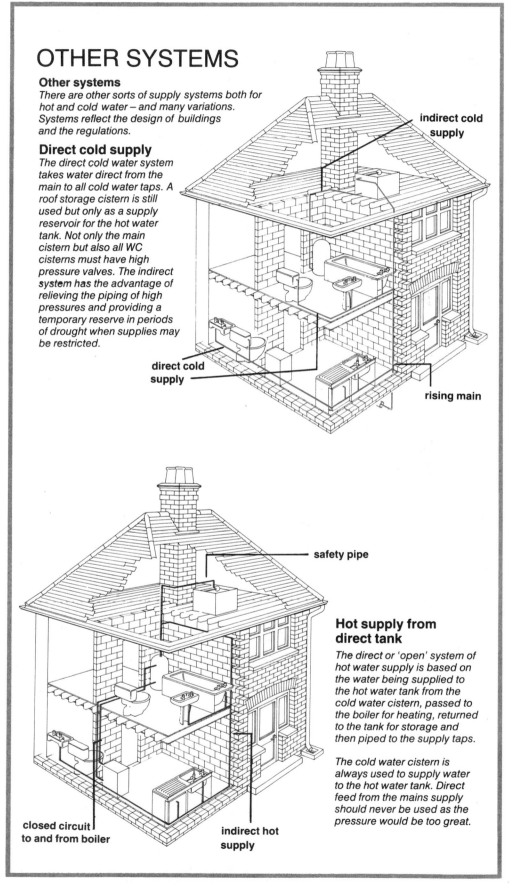

OTHER SYSTEMS

Other systems
There are other sorts of supply systems both for hot and cold water – and many variations. Systems reflect the design of buildings and the regulations.

Direct cold supply
The direct cold water system takes water direct from the main to all cold water taps. A roof storage cistern is still used but only as a supply reservoir for the hot water tank. Not only the main cistern but also all WC cisterns must have high pressure valves. The indirect system has the advantage of relieving the piping of high pressures and providing a temporary reserve in periods of drought when supplies may be restricted.

indirect cold supply

direct cold supply

rising main

safety pipe

Hot supply from direct tank

The direct or 'open' system of hot water supply is based on the water being supplied to the hot water tank from the cold water cistern, passed to the boiler for heating, returned to the tank for storage and then piped to the supply taps.

The cold water cistern is always used to supply water to the hot water tank. Direct feed from the mains supply should never be used as the pressure would be too great.

closed circuit to and from boiler

indirect hot supply

INDIRECT HOT WATER SUPPLY

In an indirect or 'closed' hot water system a closed pipe runs from the boiler, through a heat exchanger in the hot water tank and back to the boiler again. This closed system contains water which never comes into contact with the hot water used by the household. The closed circuit between boiler and hot water cylinder loses water very slowly, and is topped up automatically by water from a small reservoir cistern in the loft. A safety pipe returns over-heated water to this or the main cistern.

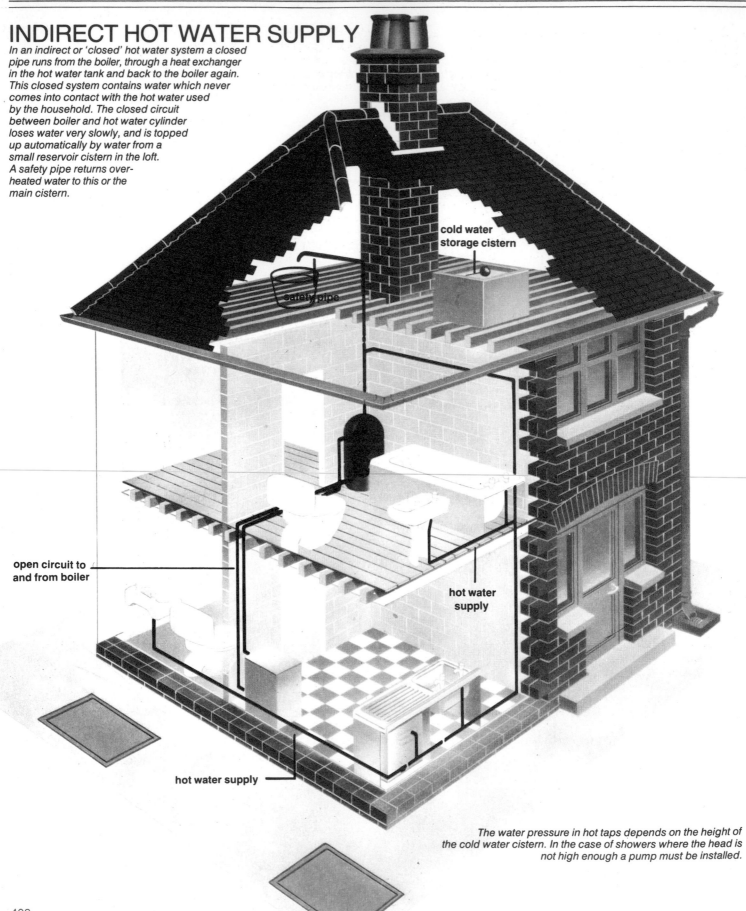

cold water storage cistern

safety pipe

open circuit to and from boiler

hot water supply

hot water supply

The water pressure in hot taps depends on the height of the cold water cistern. In the case of showers where the head is not high enough a pump must be installed.

408

whether a 'direct' or 'indirect' system has been installed.

In many areas indirect systems must be installed in new buildings, yet in Western Europe direct systems are the rule. Indirect systems have been encouraged because of the difficulty in maintaining constant mains pressure particularly at times of peak demand. Routing of most supplies through the storage cistern evens out fluctuations, and it also rules out the risk of 'back siphonage' whereby dirty water could be sucked back into the mains supply – though this rarely occurs. The 1976 drought in the UK provided good reason for indirect systems, since each house had an emergency supply in the storage cistern if the mains water had to be shut off.

Cisterns

The 'tank' in your loft or attic is in fact a 'cistern'. Cisterns are not sealed – though they should be covered – and so are subject to atmospheric pressure. Tanks are completely sealed – as with a hot water storage tank – and are not subject to atmospheric pressure.

Cold water cisterns have traditionally been made of galvanised mild steel and it is quite likely that you will find one like this in your loft. They are still available, but are not usually installed in new houses. Other materials used have been asbestos, cement, copper and glass fibre, but today the most common material is plastic, of which glass fibre reinforced polyester (GRP), polythene and polypropylene are the most common varieties.

The advantages plastics have over all other cistern materials are their lightness in weight, resistance to corrosion and flexibility. Galvanised steel is heavy and liable to corrode, while asbestos and cement are not only heavy but can become porous and are prone to accidental damage. Don't forget the capacity of a typical cistern is 227 litres (50 gallons), and this water alone weighs nearly 0.25 tonne (¼ ton), so all cisterns must be fully supported on the joists. With rigid materials such as steel the cistern can rest across the joists, but with plastic and glass fibre a platform should be installed to support the whole area of the bottom, otherwise the material may develop local weaknesses.

Cisterns should be covered to prevent any contamination of the water. Where the underside of the roof is exposed dust and dirt are liable to fall in. The top and sides should also be insulated to minimise the risk of freezing. The bottom is left uncovered to allow rising warm air from rooms below to keep the water above freezing point, and so you shouldn't insulate the roof space under the cistern.

Cisterns were often installed before the roof was put on and if you want to replace yours, perhaps because it's made of steel and is corroding, you may not be able to get it through the trap door. While it is sometimes suggested that a cistern should be cut up to get it out this is in fact a very heavy and arduous job in such a confined space and it would be better to manoeuvre it to one side and leave it in the loft, installing a new cistern alongside. Modern plastic cisterns can literally be folded up so they can be passed through small loft hatches.

Pipes and taps

Water leaves the storage cistern in distribution pipes which are usually 22mm (¾in) or 15mm (½in) in diameter. In a direct system, supply from the cistern will usually only be to the hot water tank, and in an indirect system this link must also be direct – but other distribution pipes are used with branches to supply the other appliances – basins, baths and WC cisterns. Distribution pipes usually end in taps but in the case of a WC a low pressure ball-valve controls the flow.

The WC in an indirect system has a low pressure ball-valve because when the water leaves the storage cistern it is no longer at mains pressure but at normal atmospheric pressure which is pressing down on the surface of the stored water. This means that the higher up the house a tap or other outlet is situated the lower will be the water pressure. In practice this means that you can't have a tap in an indirect system which is above the level of its distribution outlet from the cistern. Showers are particularly affected by this difference of pressure, and if there is not sufficient 'head' to 'drive' the shower a special pump may have to be installed.

Cold water supplied to the hot water tank is heated in two different ways again called indirect and direct systems – or, respectively, closed and open. In the latter the cold water is circulated through the boiler, where it is heated, and returned to the tank from where it flows to tapped outlets. In the indirect system the cold water supplied never actually goes to the boiler, instead it is heated in the tank by a coiled pipe or jacket containing hot water which is continuously circulating through the boiler. In either case a pump often helps the water flow through the boiler, and supplementary or alternative heat may come from an immersion heater. If there is no boiler but only an immersion heater in the tank the system is essentially direct with the heating of the water taking place in the tank rather than in the boiler.

Draining the system

Just above the rising main stop-valve should be a drain cock. With the stop-valve turned off the drain cock can be used to drain part of the cold water system when repairs are necessary – the hot water system has its own drain cock.

Ready Reference

PIPE SIZES AND THEIR USES

Distribution pipes
● 22mm (¾in) pipe – water supply to bath and hot water cylinder
● 15m (½in) pipe – WC, basin, bidet and shower supplies
● 28mm (1in) pipe – for use with multiple appliances, but usually unnecessary.

Warning pipes (Overflows)
● these must have a diameter greater than that of the inlet pipe to prevent cold water cisterns and WC cisterns from overflowing.

CONNECTIONS AT COLD WATER CISTERN

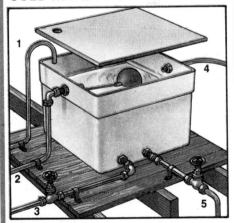

1 safety pipe   3 cold supply to taps
2 rising main   4 overflow
     5 cold supply to hot water tank

DRAINING THE SYSTEM

To drain the system from the mains stop-valve to cistern, turn off the stop-valve and attach one end of the hose to the drain cock, which should be just above the stop-valve, and run the other end to a drain. Then open the drain cock.
Drain remainder of system by turning off

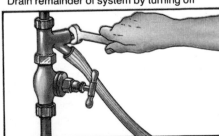

mains supply and opening cold water taps. The hot water system has its own drain cock, usually found close to the boiler.

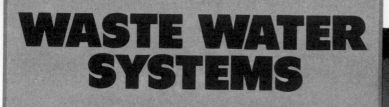

WASTE WATER SYSTEMS

A waste water system must be able to dispose of used water from the kitchen and bathroom efficiently and hygienically, and some also have to cater for rainwater falling on the roof. Here's how it's done.

The supply of hot and cold water to the taps in your house is really only half the domestic plumbing story. You also need a waste system to remove what you've used or don't want. And besides coping with the dirty water from the bath, basin and sink and the waste from the WC, the system also has to deal with the rainwater which falls on the roof.

The drainage system therefore has to be efficient and durable, and for obvious reasons of hygiene, self-cleansing. Waste matter mustn't be allowed to remain in the pipes and if blockages occur it should be possible to remove them easily.

How the drainage system works

There are several domestic drainage systems but each of them can be broken down into five separate sections. When waste water leaves an appliance of any sort, it will go immediately through a 'waste trap' – a 180° bend containing a water seal which fills the trap whenever the waste pipe empties. This keeps drain smells out of the room and prevents insects and the like from entering the home. With WCs it also makes self-cleansing easier. WC traps are cast as an integral part of the WC pan, but on other appliances they are separate, and are attached to the outlet pipe by a large retaining nut.

From the trap, waste water enters a branch pipe which leads to the main vertical drainage 'stack'. This takes it below ground level to the first underground section of the drainage system where it flows through at least one inspection chamber (covered with a manhole cover) and into the public sewer, which is usually situated underneath the road. The sewer is provided by the public health authority and it is their responsibility to remove all waste running into it.

Often rainwater from the roof is fed into the drainage system to flow into the public sewer. But some authorities provide a separate street drain for it or insist on the provision of soakaways (pits filled with rubble and gravel which allow the water to soak into the surrounding earth) near the house. Tanks and cisterns rarely overflow, but when they do they discharge clean water, so it's not necessary for the overflow pipes to be located over a drain.

The water can fall directly onto the ground.

The cost of laying public sewers in rural areas means that the waste from many houses in these parts flows into a cess pool or septic tank. These are specially constructed pits for storing effluent (and in the case of a septic tank, for breaking it down into harmless matter). Both of these require periodic pumping out, cess pools much more often as they store all the waste. If you're buying a house with one of these systems, check how often this has to be done, who does it and how much you may have to pay.

How it all began

Proper plumbing systems have only been around for about 100 years. The large urban expansion which took place during the Industrial Revolution lead to squalid housing conditions, and disease was rife. Eventually, enclosed sewers were introduced along with piped water supplies and pottery WC pans. By the 1870s many homes were equipped with a basin, a WC and a sink; but an acute shortage of qualified plumbers lead to ridiculous installations which often produced as great a health threat as before. The London County Council took the lead in sorting things out by laying out a set of rules in 1900, establishing the 'two-pipe' system – one stack for waste water from basins and sinks, another for 'soil water' from WCs.

The amount of pipework needed with the two-pipe system, and the increased siphonage problems on tall buildings, led to the introduction of the 'one-pipe' system. This system was the forerunner of the modern 'single stack' system and abandoned the distinction between the soil and the waste pipe stacks. It was only used extensively on multi-storey buildings.

On the one-pipe system all discharges flowed into a single stack which had an open-ended outlet at roof level. All traps had deep seals and each branch pipe was also connected to a vent pipe which rose to eaves level.

The single stack system was developed in the UK in the late 1940s to overcome the drawbacks and complications of the two-pipe systems, and to simplify the installation – everyone must be familiar with the untidy cluster of pipes on the outside walls of houses with these systems.

The advent of light plastic piping helped in this development, as it made the production of accurate mouldings easier, and cut down the installation time because plastic was quicker to join than the old metal piping.

The single stack system

This consists of a single waste stack into which all the branch pipes discharge. However, ground floor waste doesn't have to go

TWO-PIPE WASTE SYSTEM

The traditional two pipe system takes all soil to the underground drain by one pipe, and all the waste from baths, basins etc down another. It is found in most pre-war houses, and is still used, particularly in bungalows where the installation is spread out.

Roof drainage may flow into the same underground drainage system; it may go into a separate storm drain (out in the street) in areas of high rainfall; or it may drain into a soakaway in the garden.

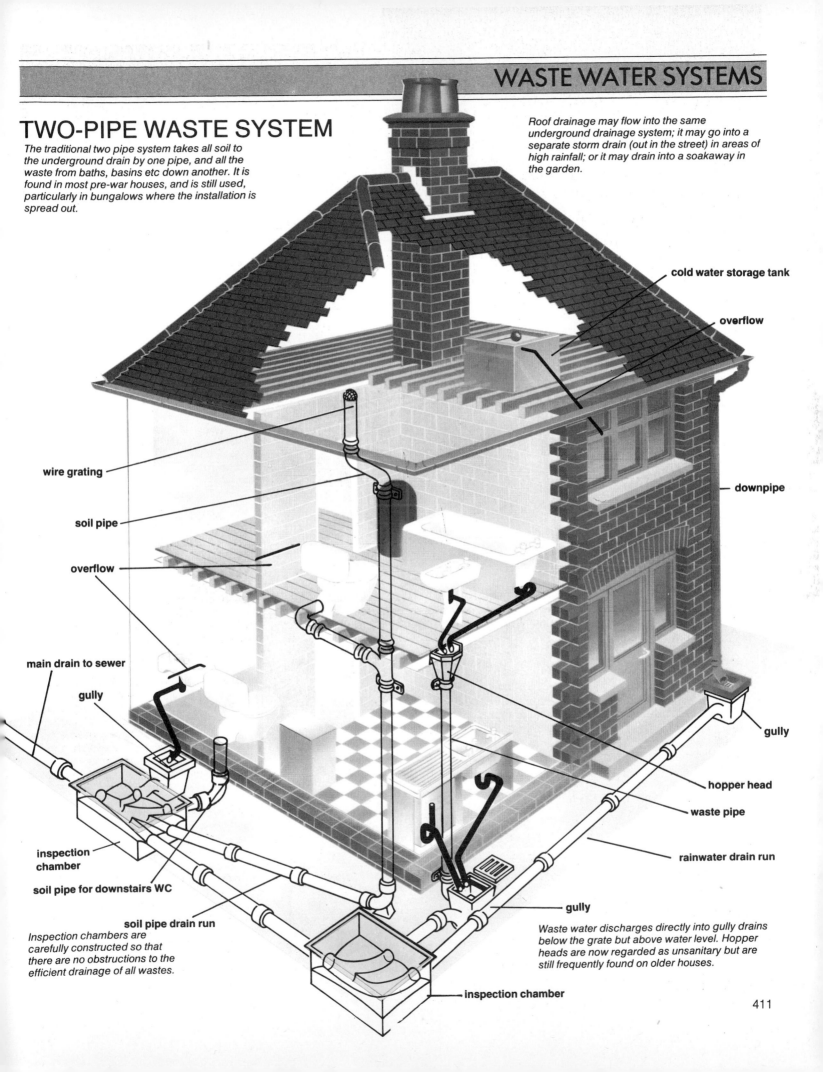

cold water storage tank

overflow

downpipe

wire grating

soil pipe

overflow

gully

main drain to sewer

gully

inspection chamber

soil pipe for downstairs WC

soil pipe drain run

hopper head

waste pipe

rainwater drain run

gully

Inspection chambers are carefully constructed so that there are no obstructions to the efficient drainage of all wastes.

Waste water discharges directly into gully drains below the grate but above water level. Hopper heads are now regarded as unsanitary but are still frequently found on older houses.

inspection chamber

411

SINGLE STACK WASTE SYSTEM

In most modern systems it is preferable to install a single stack system which involves less pipework provided that sources of waste are not too far from the stack itself.

In a single stack system the waste doesn't all have to go down the same stack – rainwater doesn't in any case. Ground floor waste and soil outlets can go direct into the underground drain. Waste outlets must discharge into trapped gullies. This arrangement is sometimes necessary where pipe runs get too long for the proper functioning of the single stack system or where the layout of appliances makes direct access to the drain more sensible.

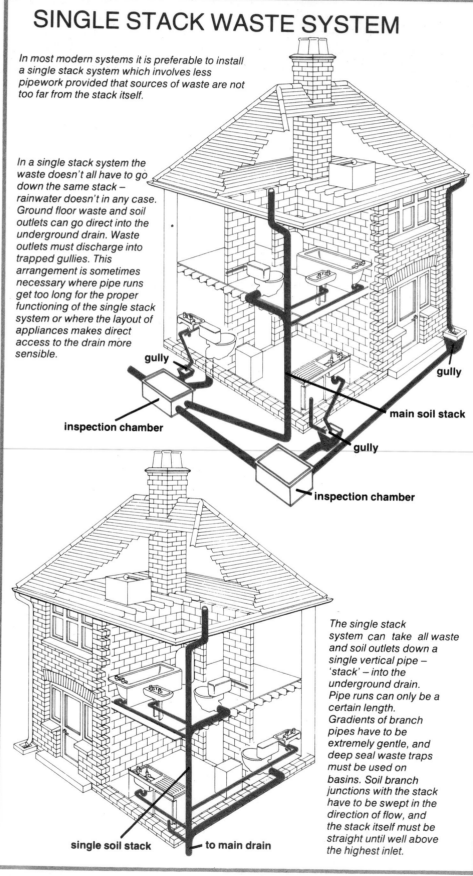

gully

inspection chamber

main soil stack

gully

inspection chamber

The single stack system can take all waste and soil outlets down a single vertical pipe – 'stack' – into the underground drain. Pipe runs can only be a certain length. Gradients of branch pipes have to be extremely gentle, and deep seal waste traps must be used on basins. Soil branch junctions with the stack have to be swept in the direction of flow, and the stack itself must be straight until well above the highest inlet.

single soil stack   **to main drain**

into the stack. Sink waste water may flow into a trapped gully and ground-floor WCs may be connected directly into the underground drain. This avoids any risk that a blockage at the base of the stack (where it bends to join the underground drain) could lead to waste water being forced back along the waste pipes to ground-floor appliances.

In appearance the single-stack system is the simplest waste system of all and the most economical to install. As a result it is incorporated in the majority of new houses. But because the branches have to be comparatively short, the system is less useful in bungalows where appliances are likely to be spread out. Usually all the pipework is sited indoors, which means a neater appearance for the house exterior; it also reduces the possibility of frost damage. All you'll see of the system is a tell-tale vent pipe poking up through the roof.

In order to make the system work properly a number of technical regulations have to be taken into account when it's being installed. These relate to the length, diameter, bend radii and angles of bend of the branch pipes, the use of P-traps and S-traps on waste pipes other than WCs (see *Traps for each appliance*), the positioning of the stack connectors, and the dimensions of the stack itself. While the system may look simple, considerable research has been done to ensure that problems of siphonage aren't likely to occur.

The two-pipe system

The principles of the two-pipe system were based on a belief that all kinds of disease were caused by the 'bad air' in drains, and the system aimed to keep this out of homes. The basic principle was that the 'soil' discharge from WCs went directly down one stack into the underground drain. All other discharges, termed 'waste', went down another stack which led into a trapped gully (a cast drain incorporating a water trap) at ground level and from there joined the soil discharge under-ground. Sometimes waste had to fall into a channel at ground level before running into the drain.

All waste and soil pipework had to be fixed to the outside of the building. The soil pipe was continued upwards to eaves level where it terminated open-ended in a wire cover to keep nesting birds from causing a blockage. This allowed free passage of air from the underground drain.

When the two-pipe system came into existence, most homes only had an outside WC (quite often shared) and a kitchen sink, so discharge was entirely at ground level, but when upstairs bathrooms became popular waste was directed into hoppers attached to stand-pipes, which caused new problems. Hoppers were not self-cleansing and soapy water drying on the inside could start to smell; draughts could also blow up the pipe to the hopper, bringing smells from the drain at the bottom. This led to some authorities banning hoppers and insisting on discharge direct into another stack which meant installing an eaves-level vent as with the soil stack.

On buildings over two storeys high this created another problem known as 'induced siphonage'. When water flowing down the waste stack from one outlet passed another outlet where it joined the stack, it could cause a partial vacuum in the second pipe which could suck out the contents of the water trap. To cure this problem the upper part of each trap had to be connected to a branch vent pipe which either connected to a separate vertical stack to eaves level, or joined the vented waste stack at least 900mm (3ft) above the level of the highest waste connection. If you live in a tall house you may have this system, and any repairs to vent pipes should follow the existing system. The alternative is to take out the entire system and replace it with a single stack arrangement.

Traps for each appliance

The traditional trap was a simple U-shaped bend attached to a horizontal branch outlet – today called a 'P' trap. If the branch outlet is vertical this trap bends round again into a double 'U' or 'S' outlet. In systems with lead pipes, the traps were often formed from lengths of pipe, while with modern plastic waste systems the traps are separate and easily detachable. The plastic bottle trap, which performs the same function, is also now widely used, and this is more compact and neater in appearance.

The depth of the water-filled part of the trap is known as the 'depth of seal'. Shallow traps have a seal depth of around 50mm (2in), 38mm (1½in) or 19mm (¾in), while 'deep-seal' traps have a 75mm (3in) seal.

Lead traps usually allow access for clearing blockages, and this is obtained by unscrewing an access cap or 'eye'. Modern plastic traps are connected by screwed collars at both ends and can be completely removed for cleaning if blocked. The lower part of bottle traps likewise completely unscrews. Adjustable plastic traps are available for fixing to existing pipework where access is difficult and special adaptors are used to link to copper and iron pipes.

Traps must remain filled with water and it is against the bye-laws if they don't. This is the most important and lasting principle handed down from the waste disposal thinking of the last century.

The water seal can be lost from traps for lots of reasons. Siphonage is the worst problem and where it occurs it's usually due to a badly designed system. Simply, if the air pressure beyond the trap is slightly less than the normal atmospheric pressure acting on the surface of the water in the trap, the water will drain away. This is more likely with 'S' traps than 'P' traps, and with shallow rather than deep traps. The problem of siphonage led to the introduction of venting systems and dictated the dimensions in the single stack system (and also excluded the use of 'S' traps).

Overflow pipes

There are two sorts of overflow pipes – those which are connected to storage cisterns and WC cisterns, and those which are attached to or form a part of appliances such as basins and baths. They are known in the trade as warning pipes. Both sorts should be fitted to avoid the risk of overflows damaging your home. This may be caused when you forget to turn off the bath, or by mechanical failure when the ball-valve on the water storage tank jams open.

In sinks, basins and baths the overflow must discharge into the branch waste pipe between the trap and the appliance, or into the trap above the water level of the seal, and must be able to cope with the flow of water from one tap turned full on.

Sink and basin overflows are usually built into the design of the appliance, while those for baths are supplied as part of the plumbing and connect to a slot in the waste outlet casting.

Overflows from tanks and cisterns consist of a length of pipe of a minimum 22mm (⅞in) internal diameter, capable of discharging water as quickly as any incoming flow. They usually emerge through the outside wall and stick out far enough to avoid any water flow sluicing down the wall surface, which could be a potential source of damp.

Pipe and trap materials

All waste and soil pipes are today mainly manufactured in plastic. Branch pipes were made of lead or copper, stack pipes of cast iron, traps of lead or brass and underground pipes of vitrified clay. Only the latter still predominantly utilize the traditional material.

Your legal position

Drainage regulations fall under the Public Health Acts as well as the Building Regulations, so it's important to know where you stand. The householder is responsible for the entire drainage system until it enters the public sewer – even though this is usually beyond the boundary of the property. While blockages beyond the lowest inspection chamber are rare, any clearance work can be very expensive – particularly if you use a '24-hour' plumbing service. The public sewer is provided by the public health authority and is their responsibility.

If your house was built as one of a group of houses, then it's quite possible that you'll have shared drainage facilities. This means there is one drainage pipe collecting the waste of several homes before it discharges into the public sewer. The system was adopted because it saved installation costs. If your house was built before 1937, it's still the responsibility of the local authorities to cleanse the shared drainage runs, although you're responsible for clearing blockages and for maintenance. But if you live in a post-1937 house then the responsibility for the shared drains rests collectively on all the owners concerned and if a blockage is caused by someone else you will have to pay a proportion of the bill. It is therefore important when moving house to check out the exact position. If this is difficult to ascertain, try the Environmental Health Officer for advice; he should also be consulted if you want to change the system.

PLASTIC WASTE TRAPS

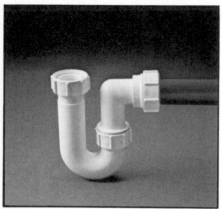

The modern U-bend *is made from one of several plastic materials.*

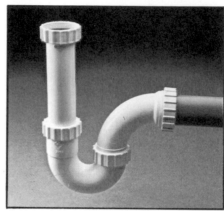

A U-bend with telescopic extension *can be adjusted to existing appliances.*

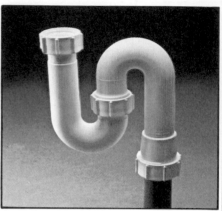

An S-bend *is designed for use where the outlet is vertical.*

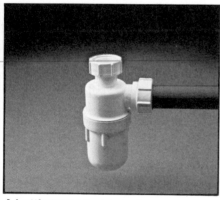

A bottle trap *gives a neater appearance, but is less efficient.*

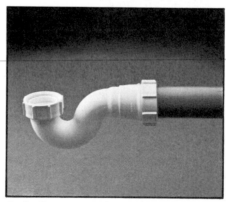

A shallow trap *is used beneath a bath or shower where space is crucial.*

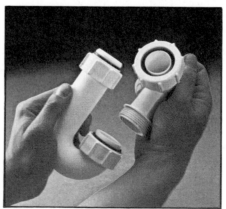

A running U-trap *handles two or more untrapped appliances piped together.*

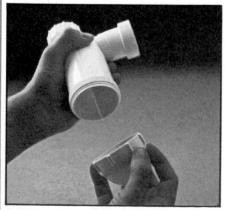

A dip partition bottle trap *has a base which unscrews.*

All modern traps come apart for easy cleaning and installation.

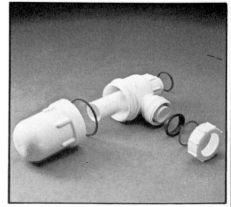

A dip tube trap taken apart to show the O rings and washers.

PLUMBING JOBS IN THE KITCHEN

Water is essential in the kitchen – for drinking, food preparation, washing cooking utensils and crockery and in many homes for washing clothes, too, unless there is a separate laundry room.

INSTALLING A SINK UNIT

The sink is a highly important item of kitchen equipment, and replacing an old model is usually one of the first priorities for anyone modernising their kitchen. In this article we consider the range available and how to fit them.

If your house was built in the 1930s or 1940s, and the kitchen has never been modernised, the chances are that it contains the original deep white glazed stoneware 'Belfast pattern' sink, supported by heavy cast-iron brackets built into the wall. It will incorporate a weir overflow and will probably have a detachable wooden draining board. A deep sink of this kind was regarded as the height of domestic luxury in the pre-war and early post-war years. An even older property might have a shallow yellow 'London pattern' sink, probably supported by brick pillars. In either case the water will very likely come from brass bib-taps (taps with horizontal inlets) projecting from a tiled splash-back fixed to the wall behind the sink. Old London pattern sinks were sometimes installed with an untrapped waste that passed through the kitchen wall to discharge over an outside gully drain. More recent sinks would have a lead or brass U-trap screwed to the waste outlet from which a branch waste pipe would discharge over the gully.

Sink units

Because these old stoneware sinks were certain death to crockery dropped into them, and looked increasingly dated, they were gradually replaced by sink units with one-piece sink tops. The sink tops were made of enamelled pressed steel or stainless steel, and the units into which they were fixed became the starting point for complete kitchen ranges incorporating continuous work surfaces. The early enamelled pressed steel sink tops had the disadvantage that the enamel was vulnerable to accidental damage. Dropping any hard object onto them could easily chip or crack the enamel. The stainless steel sink therefore became the most important innovation.

Taps and traps

It was usual, when replacing an old stoneware sink with a stainless steel or an enamelled pressed-steel sink, to get rid of the old bib-taps projecting from the wall, and to replace them with chromium-plated brass pillar taps or a mixer fitted into the

holes provided at the back of the sink and connected to the hot and cold water distribution pipes concealed within the unit.

Early sinks of this kind were provided with traps, also concealed within the unit. The trap might still be of brass with a copper waste pipe, but plastic was soon introduced, connected to a plastic waste pipe by means of ring-seal push-fit connectors. Bottle traps, as distinct from the traditional U-traps, became increasingly popular. They were neater in appearance, space saving and easy to dismantle in case of a blockage, although their discharge rate was not as great. Modern ground floor sinks often still discharge over a yard gully, but the waste pipe outlet should be taken to below the gully grid either through a slotted grid or by the use of a back or side-inlet gully.

Overflows

Early sink tops had a built-in overflow consisting of a unit welded to the back of the sink. But these inevitably leaked after a time, and nowadays they have been replaced by a flexible overflow pipe. This is like the overflow pipe from a bath which is taken from the sink's overflow outlet to connect, by means of a sleeve or 'banjo' fitting, to the slotted waste pipe, before its connection to the trap. Householders who possess a sink of the older pattern with a leaking built-in overflow, will find that if the sink is dismounted and turned upside down, the overflow unit can be sawn off and replaced with one of the more modern waste and overflow fittings. But, of course, it may be better to replace the the sink.

New developments

Nowadays, there is no question of being restricted to a single sink with either right or left-hand drainer. Double sinks, one for washing the crockery and cutlery and the other for a hot rinse before air drying, have become more and more popular. The two sinks may be of equal size, around 450mm (18in) in width, or one may be smaller than the other for use in food preparation. A second sink like this might be only 240mm (10in) in width. There are also sinks with double drainers, though these are rather less in demand as they take up a lot of space; they are usually around 2m (6ft 6in) long. Overall sizes of rectangular sinks and drainer units range from about 900mm (3ft) to 1500mm (5ft) in length, and usually measure 500 or 600mm (20 to 24in) deep, to fit metric base units. Some sink tops are still available in the 21in (533mm) size to match old imperial base units. There are also many intermediate sizes, and bowl depths may range between 130 and 180mm (5 and 7in).

Early glass-reinforced plastic sink tops and drainers proved to be a complete disaster. They were incapable of standing up to the very heavy use to which sinks are subjected, their colours faded and they cracked, and crazed. Considerable advances have since been made, and modern plastic sinks and sink tops seem well able to stand up to everything that is required of them.

Ceramic sinks are making a come back, though they are very different from the old Belfast and London pattern sinks. Modern ranges include tough inset sinks and tops in an attractive range of colours. There are inset round bowls 450mm (18in) in diameter with an accompanying but separate round drainer 380mm (15in) in diameter. Then there is a conventional rectangular double sink and drainer – all of ceramic ware – in an overall size of 1125 x 505mm (45 x 20in). There is also a conventional rectangular single sink and drainer and round double sinks and drainer in one unit. A feature of these new ceramic units is their extreme toughness.

The waste and overflow of the new ceramic sinks are arranged in exactly the same way as those of the old Belfast models. A built-in overflow connects to the slot in a slotted waste outlet that is bedded on mastic in the outlet hole. Stainless steel sinks are provided with the flexible overflow already referred to, which connects to the slotted waste below the sink but above the trap. Double sinks have only one trap. This is fitted into the outlet of the sink nearest to the drain outlet, the waste from the other sink being connected to it above the level of the single trap.

Mixers

Individual sink pillar taps are still freely available, but the choice nowadays is more likely to be a sink mixer. A mixer with a swivel spout is an essential where a double sink is installed.

Sink mixers differ from bath and basin mixers in one important respect. The latter are simply two taps with a single spout. The hot and cold streams of water mix within the body of the mixer unit. Sink mixers have separate channels for the hot and cold streams of water which mix in the air as they leave the spout. The reason for this is that the cold water supply to the kitchen sink (the household's supply of water for drinking and cooking) comes direct from the rising main. The hot supply usually comes from a cylinder storage hot water system, fed with water from a main cold water storage cistern. It is illegal to mix, in one fitting, water from the main and water from a storage cistern.

Everybody is familiar with the conventional sink mixer, made of chromium-plated brass with 'shrouded' cross-top handles of plastic and a long swivel spout. Nowadays, though, there are some exciting new designs available. With some the mixer unit is fitted into just one hole at the back of the sink. The other hole may be blanked off or may be used to accommodate a rinsing brush, supplied with hot water by a flexible tube connected to the hot water supply pipe.

Putting in the sink top

When you come to install your new sink it's a good idea to make the first job fitting the taps or mixer, waste and overflow to it. This will avoid unnecessary interruption to the rest of the plumbing services. Start by putting in the combined waste and overflow unit, then attach the taps or mixer. If the sink is made of stainless steel the shanks of the taps will protrude through the holes so you won't be able to screw up the back-nuts tight. Use 'top hat' washers or spacers to accommodate the shanks.

When the sink is in position the tap tails will usually be fairly inaccessible, so it may be a

Ready Reference

TRADITIONAL SINKS

The traditional Belfast sink, made of fireclay and enamelled after baking is still sometimes installed, fixed on cantilevered brackets or on leg supports.

Most modern sinks are made of stainless steel, stamped out of sheet metal, which gives a functional, streamlined finish and is easy to clean. Modern sinks come as either sink tops or as inset sinks.

SINK TOPS

Sink tops fit on top of a sink unit of the same size. While sink units started off as an alternative to the cantilevered support Belfast sink, they are now often made part of a work surface. As nearly all sink units are now designed on a modular basis, the sizes of sink tops correspond to the module sizes.

INSET SINKS

An inset sink is inset into a continuous work surface into which an aperture has been cut or built. As they are not required to form the top of a kitchen unit they can be positioned with greater flexibility provided that there is sufficient space underneath for a bowl and plumbing pipes.

good idea to attach purpose-made extension pieces to bring them to a level below the sink basin where they will be accessible.

When you've got the new sink top ready, you'll have to turn off the main stop-valve and drain the hot and cold water pipes which supply the existing sink. Then you can disconnect the waste outlet, and use a cold chisel and hammer to chip away any seal between the back of the sink and the wall. You can remove the old sink (remember, it's going to be very heavy) and saw off the heavy cantilevered brackets that supported the old sink flush with the wall.

The hot and cold water supply pipes to the bib-taps over the old sink will probably be chased (inset) into the wall, so you'll have to unscrew and remove the old taps, excavate the pipes from the wall and pull them forward so that they can be connected to the tails of new taps.

With the new sink unit in position, the next job is to cut the water supply pipes to the correct length to connect to the tails of the taps. The sink top simply rests on the sink unit, so the tails of the taps can now be connected to the water supply pipes. If the trap of the old sink will connect to the new waste it can be reused.

THE PLUMBING CONNECTIONS

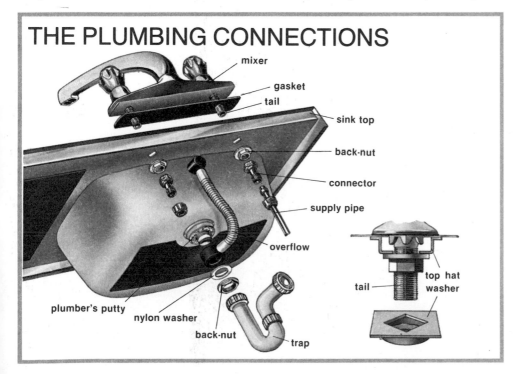

mixer
gasket
tail
sink top
back-nut
connector
supply pipe
overflow
plumber's putty
nylon washer
back-nut
trap
tail
top hat washer

INSTALLING A SINK TOP

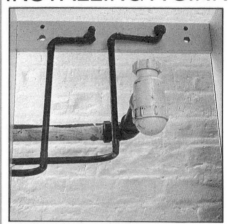

1 Take out your old sink top and check that the existing plumbing connections are undamaged. Replace as necessary.

2 Place your new sink top downwards on the floor. Take the waste outlet and press plumber's putty around the top of the screw.

3 Press the outlet firmly into position in the sink outlet aperture, at the same time squeezing out excess putty. Then put on the plastic washer.

6 Place the outlet collar of the banjo unit firmly on top of the plastic washer and support it with one hand before putting on the back-nut.

7 Put on the back-nut and screw it up tightly against the banjo unit collar, making sure it runs straight towards the sink outlet hole.

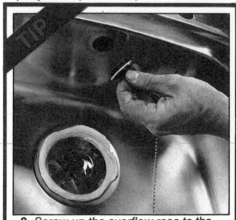

8 Screw up the overflow rose to the banjo unit overflow pipe. To help get it tight, hold the back of the outlet with a pair of pliers.

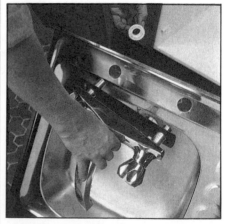

11 Take the mixer unit and ensure that the rubber gasket has no grit on it; then place the inlet tails into the holes and press the unit into position.

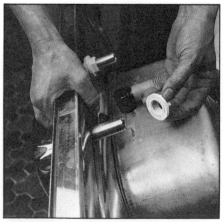

12 Screw on the inlet tail back-nuts and tighten them, making sure the gasket remains flat. You don't need to use any plumber's putty.

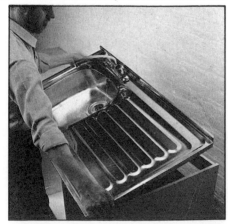

13 When the outlet and mixer installation is complete, lift the sink top into its correct position and screw it to the kitchen unit.

4 With the plastic washer pushed firmly home, take a roll of PTFE tape and run it around the thread right up to the end of the outlet.

5 Before putting on the banjo unit run a thick film of pipe-jointing compound around the uppermost surface of the plastic washer.

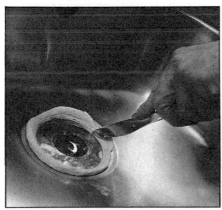

9 Run a knife around the edge of the plumber's putty squeezed out from around the outlet flange. Be careful not to score the metal.

10 Peel away the surplus putty and check that the outlet flange is tightly held into the sink. If not, tighten the back-nut further.

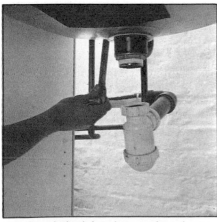

14 Attach the inlet pipes to the mixer tails and tighten the nuts with a crowsfoot spanner, which helps you reach them.

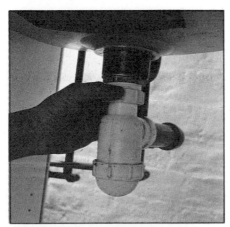

15 Check that the old trap is clear and screw it up tightly to the outlet pipe; then turn on the taps to check that there are no leaks.

Ready Reference

SINK DESIGNS

Sink designs come in several different variations particularly in the inset range. Think carefully about what you use your sink for, and what space you have available before deciding on size and design.

TYPICAL SINK SIZES

S=single, D=double, Si=sink, Dr=drainer

	Tops	Inset
SDrSSi	42x31in	37x19in
	1000x500mm	940x485mm
	1000x600mm	
	1200x600mm	
DDrSSi	63x21in	55x19in
	1500x500mm	1395x485mm
	1500x600mm	
SDrDSi	63x21in	55x19in
	1500x600mm	1395x485mm
DDrDSi	84x21in	74x19in
	2000x600mm	1850x485mm

TYPICAL DESIGNS

If you don't have a dishwasher a double bowl is useful – one for washing and one for rinsing.

double bowl

A double drainer will give you a greater working area at the sink but will cut down on the remainder of your work surface.

double drainer

If you're short of space you may dispense with the drainer altogether and use an inset bowl only. There are also units with small subsidiary bowls specially incorporated to house a waste disposal unit. These may also be supplied with trays which fit in or over the bowl, facilitating such tasks as salad preparation.

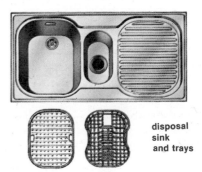

disposal sink and trays

INSTALLING AN INSET SINK

If you're fitting a new kitchen, or modernising an old one, one job you'll almost certainly have to carry out is to install an inset sink into a worktop.

Not so long ago, an assortment of cupboards, work surfaces and a kitchen sink unit formed the framework of the average kitchen. It was not a particularly efficient arrangement, but because few appliances had to be fitted in it didn't matter too much if a little space was wasted. However, as more and more homes acquired washing machines, tumble dryers, refrigerators and the like, some way had to be found of fitting these appliances into what was often a relatively small area.

What resulted from this was the 'integral' kitchen which housed all this equipment under roomy and well-lit worktops. And hand in hand with this development went the introduction of the inset sink.

The old enamelled and stainless steel sit-on sinks, with their single or double drainers, completely covered their base units. From a functional point of view they were ideal because the one-piece top meant that it was virtually impossible for water to seep into the cupboard below. Yet the kitchen sink remained a conspicuous, and somewhat unattractive, feature, divorced from other kitchen surfaces. And because of the space it took up, the unit was restricted to only one or two positions in the room. Consequently, many kitchens had to be planned around it, which naturally limited the ways in which they could be made more labour-saving and pleasant to work in.

However, once the move to creating uninterrupted work surfaces took hold, the benefits of installing a 'built-into-the-worktop' sink became readily apparent. For the first time it meant that a sink could be fitted into an overall design, which could still retain a clean, streamlined look. It didn't have to be fitted directly over a base unit, which gave far more flexibility as to where it could be positioned. However, there still had to be sufficient clearance under the worktop to take the bowl, and the plumbing supply and waste runs still had to make sense.

In fact, the idea for inset sinks stemmed from bathroom and bedroom vanity units, where a washbasin was let into the surface of a small cupboard. The surrounding melamine-finished surface was easy to clean and provided a standing area for bottles, cosmetics and the like. It was only a matter of time before the idea was adopted in the kitchen.

Choosing an inset sink

Whether you're revamping your kitchen, or just modernising the existing sink, there are a number of points to take into account before buying a new inset model.

The first is to decide what exactly the sink has to handle, because this will give you a fair guide as to the size you'll need, and whether two bowls would be better instead of just one. Indeed, there are a number of advantages in installing two or even two-and-a-half bowls (the 'half' being specifically for cutlery) not the least being that you'll still have access to the taps even if one bowl is occupied. And the amount of extra plumbing you'll have to carry out is quite small. All it entails is slightly extending the waste run. If you install a mixer tap with a swivel spout this can be used to fill both bowls so there's no additional work on the water supply side.

As with sit-on sinks, there is a wide range of bowl/drainer combinations. There are also individual round bowls which don't have an attached drainer, although there are separate drainers available that you have to let into the worktop nearby.

Round bowls do look attractive and they are increasing in popularity, but they have a couple of disadvantages. They tend to be shallower than the traditional rectangular shape – generally, the deeper the bowl the better – and their shape sometimes makes it awkward to submerge large pans and grill trays when they're being washed.

Which material to go for?

The other main consideration when choosing a sink is the material it's made of. Nowadays there is a far wider choice than ever before.

Stainless steel has retained its popularity, principally because it is relatively cheap and there is a wide range of styles available. Yet while it is heat-resistant and hard wearing, it can suffer at the hands of scourers and abrasive cleaners which leave minute surface scratches. You may also find this material somewhat clinical in appearance. However, if you do there are alternatives.

Don't shy away from plastic, for example. Admittedly the early glass-reinforced plastic tops proved to be a disaster: they simply weren't sturdy enough to cope with the use – and misuse – a kitchen sink is subjected to. But the ones on sale now are vastly different. These are made of impact-resistant modified polycarbonate in a range of attractive colours that extend right through the material. You can buy double as well as single sinks with round or rectangular bowls. As far as temperature resistance is concerned these sinks are very tough, and to prove it they are put through some remarkably nasty tests. One manufacturer, for example, has tested such sinks in hot water at up to 95°C for 40 days, in boiling water at five different levels of water hardness for 50 hours and by placing hot

THE PLUMBING CONNECTIONS

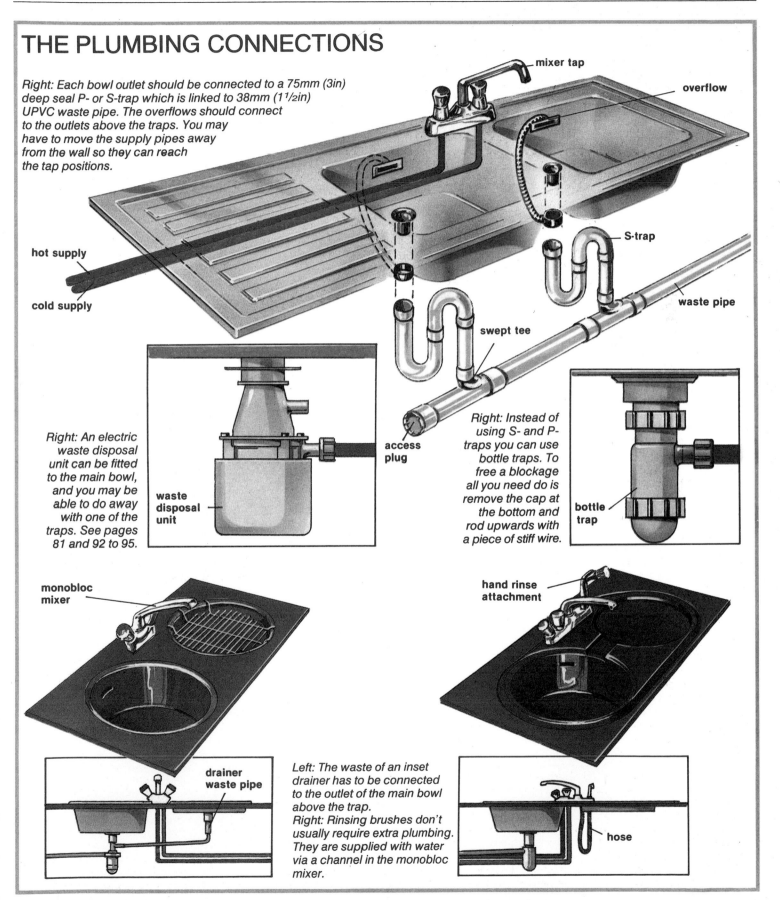

Right: Each bowl outlet should be connected to a 75mm (3in) deep seal P- or S-trap which is linked to 38mm (1½in) UPVC waste pipe. The overflows should connect to the outlets above the traps. You may have to move the supply pipes away from the wall so they can reach the tap positions.

mixer tap

overflow

hot supply

cold supply

S-trap

waste pipe

swept tee

access plug

Right: An electric waste disposal unit can be fitted to the main bowl, and you may be able to do away with one of the traps. See pages 81 and 92 to 95.

waste disposal unit

Right: Instead of using S- and P-traps you can use bottle traps. To free a blockage all you need do is remove the cap at the bottom and rod upwards with a piece of stiff wire.

bottle trap

monobloc mixer

hand rinse attachment

drainer waste pipe

Left: The waste of an inset drainer has to be connected to the outlet of the main bowl above the trap.
Right: Rinsing brushes don't usually require extra plumbing. They are supplied with water via a channel in the monobloc mixer.

hose

INSTALLING AN INSET SINK

1 If space is limited and the worktop is fixed in position, check underneath that there is clearance for the bowls and then mark round the template.

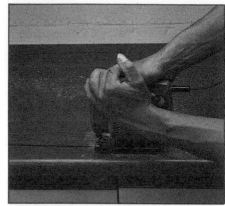

2 Drill a hole through the worktop on the waste side of the cut-out. Insert the jigsaw and cut out the hole, supporting the waste on the underside.

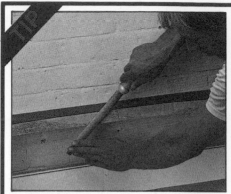

3 Test fit the sink in the hole, wriggling it a little to get it to drop down flush with the top. If it sticks, file back the area where it catches.

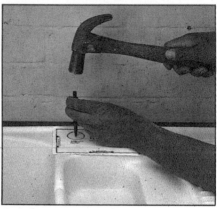

6 If the sink doesn't have a tap hole punched, place the special template over the knockout and gently use a hammer and punch to make one.

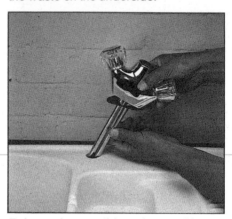

7 Insert the monobloc mixer, making sure that it sits on a rubber gasket. Then use a spanner to tighten the back-nut underneath the sink.

8 Make up the outlets for the main and half bowls and the overflow. Some outlets are bedded on plumber's putty while others sit on special plastic washers.

saucepans on them for short periods at temperatures up to 180°C. No domestic sink is likely to experience anything like that amount of misuse; even so the sinks weathered the punishment.

Ceramic sinks are once more on the market and are becoming increasingly popular. Again, they are very different from their early counterparts, but one thing hasn't changed. They spell certain death to any piece of crockery dropped into them. It's a point that should perhaps be borne in mind when choosing a sink top. Having said this, these sinks are available in an attractive range of colours (you can even get a mixer tap to match), and as with plastic and stainless steel models some versions have integral drainers. Once installed these sinks are highly resistant to being damaged. However, if you do plump for a ceramic sink and you want to install a waste disposal unit check

that the two are compatible, because it's impossible to widen the outlet as you can do with a stainless steel top.

Choosing the taps

Apart from all the other considerations it's important to choose an inset sink with the taps in mind.

If you go for a two or two-and-a-half bowl top then you're going to need some form of swivel mixer. Some sinks will only take a monobloc mixer because there is only one access hole for the hot and cold supply pipes. Others take conventional mixers. Alternatively, you could use separate pillar taps.

Some sink tops are reversible, in that depending on which way round you fit them they can have a left-hand or right-hand drainer. Obviously you can't have tap holes on both sides of the bowl, so to get round the problem usually there are knockouts in the

potential tap sites and you just remove those you want to use.

Sometimes no provision is made for taps. In this case you'll have to install bib taps coming out of the wall or drill holes through the worktop itself and fit the taps to these.

How to install an inset sink

Installing an inset sink presents no special difficulties. As with conventional sinks, and indeed most other plumbing fittings, it's best to carry out as much work as possible before putting the worktop in position. But if the worktop is fixed, rather than remove it work in situ instead. First, fit the taps. With a mixer you'll need a flat washer between the base and the sink top. And for a plastic or stainless steel sink, you'll probably need to use top hat or spacer washers over the tap tails to accommodate the protruding shanks before screwing on the back-nuts.

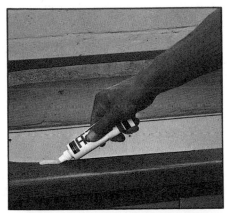

4 *Some sinks are bedded on a rubber or plastic seal. If not, run silicone rubber or non-setting mastic round the edge of the hole before fitting the sink.*

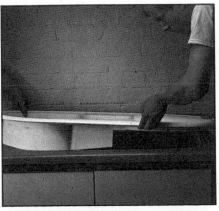

5 *Lower the inset sink into the hole and then fasten it in position underneath using the clips provided. Clean away any sealant that oozes from the edges.*

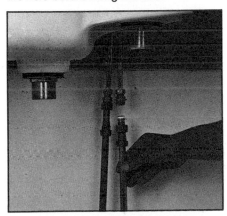

9 *Use tap connectors and special reducers to connect the 15mm (1/2in) hot and cold supply runs to the tap tails, which on this model are slightly narrower.*

10 *Use S-traps and swept tees to connect the 38mm (1 1/2in) wastes to a common waste run. An inspection eye at the end of the run aids blockage removal.*

The tap tails will be difficult to get to once the sink is in position, particularly if the unit you are fitting over has a back to it. Therefore it's best to fit a small run of pipe, or lengths of corrugated flexible pipe, to each of the tap tails at this stage.

The waste and overflow unit is usually supplied with the sink. Don't forget to bed the outlet on a layer of mastic, and as you tighten up the back-nut make sure the slot in the shank points in the direction of the overflow. Next, screw the overflow to the outlet point at the top of the sink bowl and then slip the 'banjo' connector at the other end of the flexible hose over the slotted waste. This is held in place by another back-nut.

As far as marking out the work surface is concerned, most sink manufacturers supply a template indicating the area of worktop to be removed. Needless to say this must be done with care and accuracy, and for this reason it's best to work on the top surface and not the underside so there's no risk of getting the sink in the wrong place.

Drill a hole through the waste side of the cut-out and then use a jigsaw to cut the hole. You can then fit the retaining brackets or rim round the underside edge. The fixing clips on the sink are secured to these when it's set in its final position.

Usually, inset sinks are provided with a rubber seal or gasket so that when fitted there's a watertight seal between the bowl and drainer and the worktop. If there isn't one, run a continuous bead of non-setting mastic round the perimeter and bed the top firmly onto this.

Once you've lowered the sink into position and clipped it in place all that then remains is to set the worktop in position on top of the unit and to connect the waste pipe and the hot and cold supply runs.

Ready Reference

CHECK UNDERSURFACE CLEARANCE

You've got considerable flexibility as to where you position an inset sink – it need not necessarily be directly over a base unit. But wherever you propose to site it make sure there is sufficient depth under the worktop to accommodate the bowls.

WHICH SINK TO CHOOSE

Inset sinks can have one, two or two and a half bowls. Some incorporate drainers, but with individual bowls separate drainers have to be installed alongside.

Many inset sinks are made of stainless steel, but if you choose a plastic or ceramic sink you have the added option of a wide range of colours.

TIP: CARE WITH HOT PANS

Whatever material your sink is made of it will withstand all likely treatment. If you've a plastic sink it's advisable not to put frying pans that have just been used for frying hot meat, dry cooked foods and hot oil directly in the sink. First allow the pan to cool briefly.

TIP: FITTING A WASTE DISPOSER

If you're installing a ceramic sink and you also want a waste disposal unit, make sure the outlet of the sink is compatible with the inlet on the disposer. Ceramic sinks can't be cut, so the two must match exactly.

BOWL ACCESSORIES

There are various accessories you can fit over the bowl of the sink such as a draining tray (A) and a chopping board (B). Ideally, use the chopping board over the sink with a waste disposer so that any vegetable matter can be hygienically flushed away.

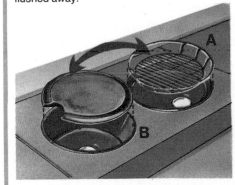

PLUMBING IN KITCHEN APPLIANCES

Washing machines and dishwashers can be a great boon in the house. They are best plumbed into a water supply and the waste outlet, otherwise you'll find they don't save as much time as they should.

These days you'll probably opt for an automatic washing machine that fills and empties itself according to a pre-set programme, and so can be left unattended. There is a choice between top loaders and front loaders, although the latter are by far the more common. Obviously top loaders can't fit under a work surface, but drum-type top loaders tend to be narrower and this may suit your particular space requirements.

Dishwashers are almost always automatic, except for some small, cheaper sink-top models. They, too, are available as top or front loaders, though again front loaders are by far the more popular. They are also easier to load and unload, as with top loaders it's easy for crockery and cutlery to slip to the bottom of the machines.

Washing machines have become almost a necessity in busy family homes, especially where there are young children. Dishwashers are far less common, but sales are developing rapidly as more and more people wake up to their advantages. It's a simple matter to stack a dishwasher with dirty crockery direct from the meal table and then turn it on before going to bed at night. Again, for a family the labour saving is considerable.

Some washing machines don't have to be plumbed in. The inlets can be attached to the kitchen taps when the sink isn't being used, and the outlet can be hooked over the edge of the sink. The same goes for dishwashers, which usually require only a cold water feed. But to keep things really neat and tidy as well as more practical, it is best to create permanent connections for both the water supply and the waste outlet. In most kitchens this should be a fairly easy task, provided you have room for the machines in the first place.

As far as the capacities of washing machines and dishwashers go, you don't really have much choice. Washing machines have a capacity of about 4-5kg (9-11lb) and dishwashers will function quite happily provided you stack them up within the obvious tray limitations. It's important to follow the manufacturers' instructions for day-to-day maintenance. Many washing machines need their outlet filter cleaned regularly, as do dishwashers. They may also need regular doses of salts, not to mention rinse aids.

Water supply

There are a number of ways in which you can arrange the water supply. One of them is sure to suit your plumbing system or the layout of your kitchen or utility room. A washing machine may need a hot and cold supply; dishwashers and some cheaper washing machines need only a cold supply.

Let's first consider the conventional means of plumbing in – the means that a professional plumber would almost certainly adopt if you called him in to do the job for you. It is likely to be most satisfactory where the machine is to be positioned in the immediate vicinity of the kitchen sink and the 15mm (½in) hot and cold supply pipes to the sink taps are readily accessible and in close proximity to each other.

The technique is to cut into these two pipes at a convenient level, after cutting off the water supply and draining the pipes, and to insert into them 15mm compression tees. From the outlets of the tees lengths of 15mm (½in) copper tube are run to terminate, against the wall, in a position immediately adjacent to the machine. Onto the ends of these lengths of pipe are fitted purpose-made stop-cocks. These are usually provided with back-plates that can be screwed to the wall after it has been drilled and plugged. The outlets of the stop-cocks are designed for connection to the machine's inlet hose or hoses.

As an alternative, which is best used where the hot and cold water pipes in the kitchen are in close proximity to the position of the machine, you can use a special patent valve. This is a 'tee' with a valve outlet designed for direct connection to the washing machine hose. There are compression joints at each end of the tee and the valve is particularly

PLUMBING IN A WASHING MACHINE

Plumbing in a washing machine shouldn't present too many problems. Normally it's sited next to an existing sink, so you'll know that the water supply pipes and drainage facilities are close at hand.

Most machines are run off separate 15mm (½in) hot and cold supplies (1 & 2) taken from tees (3) Inserted in the pipe runs to the sink. You should also insert some form of stop-valve (4) into the pipes so the machine can be isolated for repairs. You'll have to use female/male connections (5) to join the copper pipes to the machine's rubber inlet hoses (6).

When the water has been used, it's fed into a rubber drain hose (7) which should be loosely inserted into the top of the stand-pipe (8). This in turn connects to a 75mm (3in) trap and from here the waste water is taken in 38mm (1½in) pipe to discharge in the gully outside below the grille.

Dealing with single-stack drainage

From the trap at the bottom of the stand-pipe (11) the waste water is conducted to the main drainage stack (12) where the pipe is connected via a fitting known as a strap boss(13).

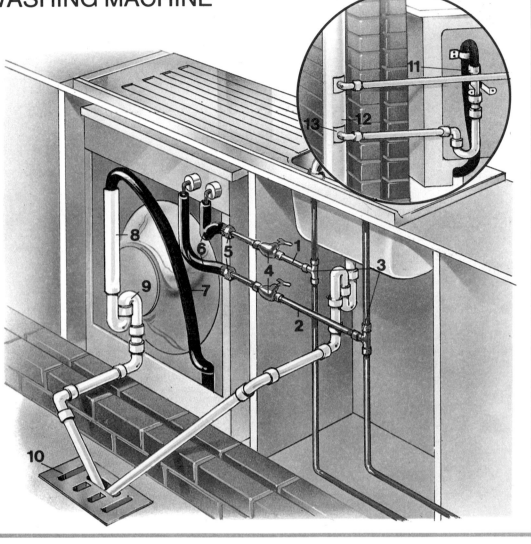

easily fitted because there is no tube-stop in one of these joints. This cuts out the difficult business of 'springing' the cut ends of the pipe into the tee.

Then there are valves which can be connected without cutting a section out of the water supply pipes. With one such valve the pipe is drained and is then drilled with a 8mm (⁵⁄₁₆in) bit. A back-plate is then fitted to the wall behind it and a front-plate, with a short projecting pipe and a rubber seal that fits into the hole in the pipe, is clamped to it. The washing machine valve then screws into this front-plate.

Yet another valve is self-tapping and screws its own hole in the water pipe. This, so the makers claim, can be done without cutting off the water supply and draining the pipe.

A valve which depends upon drilling the water supply pipe will not permit the same flow of water as one in which the pipe is cut and a tee inserted. It must be said, though,

that this seems to make very little difference in practice, but obviously in the former case the tightening of the connection must be more than sufficient for it to work properly.

Putting in drainage

The simplest method is undoubtedly to hook the machine's outlet hose over the rim of the kitchen or utility room sink when required. However, this method isn't always convenient and is certainly untidy. An alternative is to provide an open-ended stand-pipe fixed to the kitchen wall into which the outlet hose of the machine can be permanently hooked. The open end of the stand-pipe should be at least 600mm (24in) above floor level and should have an internal diameter of at least 35mm (1⅜in). A deep seal (75mm/3in) trap should be provided at its base and a branch waste pipe taken from its outlet to an exterior gully, if on the ground floor, or to the main soil and waste stack of a single stack

system if on an upper floor. As with all connections to a single soil and waste stack this should be done only under the supervision of the district or borough council's Building Control Officer. Manufacturers of plastic drainage systems include suitable drainage stand-pipes and accessories in their range of equipment (the trap and pipe being sold as one unit).

It is sometimes possible to deal with washing machine or dishwasher drainage by taking the waste pipe to connect directly to the trap of the kitchen sink and this course of action may be suggested at DIY centres and by builders' merchants staff. But it must be stressed that this is not recommended by the manufacturers of washing machines, who consider that it involves a considerable risk of back-siphonage. This could lead to waste water from the sink siphoning back into the machine. In the case of a washing machine this could mean considerable problems.

PLUMBING IN A DISHWASHER

1 Start by working out how to run the waste outlet. This will often mean making a hole in the wall using a club hammer and cold chisel.

2 Measure up the run on the inside, then cut a suitable length of 38mm (1½in) PVC plastic waste pipe and push it through the hole you have made.

3 Make up the outside pipe run dry, to ensure it all fits, then solvent weld it. It's useful to put in an inspection elbow in case of blockages.

6 Carry on assembling the run on the inside using standard waste pipe fittings. Try to keep the run close to the wall for a neat appearance.

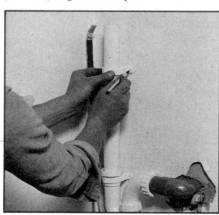

7 Take the trap and stand-pipe, which you can buy as a standard fitting or make up yourself, and mark the bracket positions on the wall.

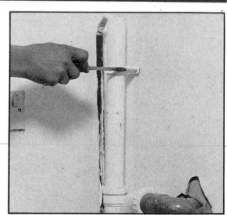

8 Drill and plug the wall, and fix the stand-pipe in position. Make sure that it is fully supported and vertical and the trap is screwed tight.

11 Make good the damage to the wall both on the inside and out; the plastic pipe will be held firmly in place by the mortar and plaster.

12 You can now move the machine into position and connect it up. The inlet hose has a female screwed connector, which must have a washer in it.

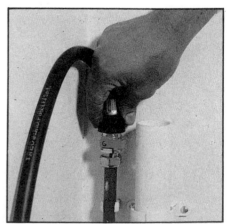

13 With the washer in place, screw up the connector to the tap on the inlet pipe; it's enough to hand-tighten this connection.

4 *If the run terminates in a gully drain, then make sure that you fit the pipe so that the end is situated below the level of the water.*

5 *When you have completed the outside waste run, replace the grid. Cut away as much of it as necessary to fit round the pipe, using a hacksaw.*

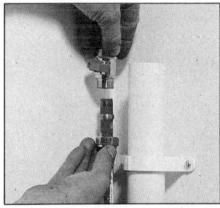

9 *Run the cold water supply using 15mm (¹/₂in) pipe via a tee cut into the domestic cold supply, and attach a running tap to the end.*

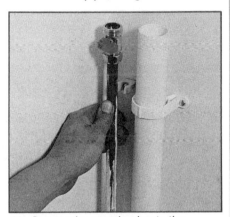

10 *Secure the supply pipe to the wall using pipe brackets, then go back and make sure that all your connections are sound.*

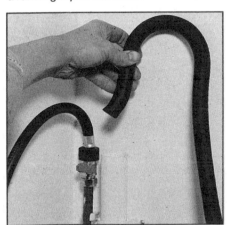

14 *Take the outlet hose from the machine and place it in the top of the stand-pipe.You should not attempt to make the connection airtight.*

15 *Move the machine exactly into position and check that it is level; if not, adjust the feet. Then turn on the water and test the machine.*

Ready Reference

INSTALLATION CHECKLIST

When installing a washing machine or dishwasher, remember that:
● it's usual to take the water supply from the domestic cold water system; if you want to use the mains you may need a pressure reducer, so check with the manufacturer's literature
● if the machine takes a hot and cold supply you will have to ensure that there is sufficient pressure in the hot supply and that this is the same as that from the cold
● to operate at maximum efficiency, the machine should stand on a level surface and this should be firm; washing machines in particular are extremely heavy when full of water.

BATHROOM REGULATIONS

If you want to put your washing machine in the bathroom then there are electrical rules that must be obeyed:
● it must be permanently wired in
● you must not be able to touch the controls when you're in the bath or shower.

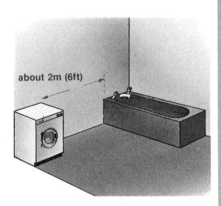

about 2m (6ft)

TIP: CHECK DIMENSIONS

If the machine is going to be put between existing units or under a work surface you'll have to measure up carefully before you buy. Make sure there is enough space behind for the plumbing work.

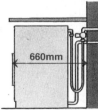

660mm

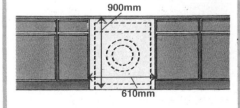

900mm

610mm

FITTING A WASTE DISPOSAL UNIT

Unwanted food — everything from potato peelings to leftovers — usually ends up in a smelly kitchen bin. It can be got rid of more quickly and hygienically with a waste disposal unit.

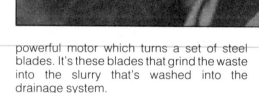

Waste disposal units are an excellent means of getting rid of waste food and the like. Potato and vegetable peelings, cabbage stalks and outer leaves, food scraps, apple cores, tea leaves, dead flowers and so on are simply washed down the kitchen sink, ground to a slurry and flushed into the drainage system. Disposal is instant and hygienic, so it removes the need for constantly emptying smelly bins of rotting food. Whether you live in a house, flat or apartment, one of these units can be a tremendous labour-saving device which makes keeping the kitchen clean that much easier.

Of course there are limitations to what a waste disposal unit can do: it can't deal with all household waste. Broken china, tin cans, bottle caps and large bones will only clog and possibly damage the appliance, so you must be careful not to put them in with other waste. Indeed, jamming is the most common problem with these units, and it usually occurs as a result of misuse. Many modern units have a reversible action motor which enables the jammed material to be cleared by flicking the reversing switch and restarting the motor. Jamming is likely to cause overheating and may operate a thermal cut-out, automatically turning off the motor. In a case like this, it may take some five minutes for the motor to cool sufficiently for it to be restarted. Models without a reversible motor are usually supplied with a key to free the jammed unit. But remember, the electricity supply must be cut off before using it.

When waste disposal units were first introduced, the sewage authorities were concerned that the slurry produced by them could result in sewers becoming choked with silt. Although these fears have proved unfounded, you must make sure that any sediment produced is flushed safely through the household drainage system. It's therefore important to leave the cold tap running while the unit is in operation. This will also help to prevent jamming.

Installation requirements

Waste disposal units have to be plumbed permanently into the waste outlet of the kitchen sink. They are driven by a relatively powerful motor which turns a set of steel blades. It's these blades that grind the waste into the slurry that's washed into the drainage system.

In order to operate effectively the unit needs to be connected to an 89mm (3½in) diameter sink waste outlet instead of the usual 38mm (1½in) hole, although some models can be adapted to fit this size. You can usually buy a sink with this larger sized opening, but if you already have a stainless steel sink the outlet can be enlarged using a special cutting tool which is rather like a hacksaw with a saw file as a blade.

If you have a sink top made of ceramic or plastic material, or enamelled pressed steel, you can't fit a waste disposal unit unless you're prepared to renew the sink top at the same time.

The outlet from the unit itself is 38mm (1½in) diameter and, like any other waste outlet, must be connected to a trap to prevent smells from the yard gully or the main soil and waste stack entering the kitchen. It's best to use a simple tubular P-trap which will allow the waste and slurry to pass through without leaving any sediment behind. Bottle traps should not be used as they are more likely to block and they also discharge more slowly.

Where the waste pipe from a waste disposal unit situated on the ground floor of a house is taken to a yard gully, it is particularly important that the waste pipe should discharge into the gully above the water level but below the level of the gully grid. In this way the grid will not become fouled by the slurry and, more importantly, the full force of the water discharged from the sink waste will be available to ensure that the slurry will be flushed through the gully and then out into the sewer.

Back or side inlet gullies are available and these are to be preferred when a new drainage system is being installed. However, there are also slotted gully grids on the market and these are highly suitable for converting existing drainage systems. The branch waste pipe from the kitchen sink is simply extended to discharge just below the slot in the gully.

Fitting a waste disposal unit

An existing stainless steel sink can be adapted by using a special cutting tool, after removing the existing waste outlet. When you are trying to remove the outlet, use a pair of pliers to hold the waste grid while turning the back-nut with a wrench. If this proves difficult, try heating it with a blow-torch. If this still doesn't do the trick, try burning out the washer between the base of the sink and the back-nut with your blow-torch and cutting through the old waste with a hacksaw. When

MAKING A NEW WASTE OUTLET

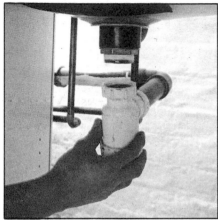

1 *Disconnect the waste trap from your waste outlet. If the trap is plastic this should be easy; for metal traps a little more effort may be required.*

2 *When you have detached the waste trap, use a wrench to unscrew the back-nut which holds the outlet in position. Remove it and the washer.*

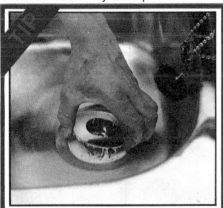

3 *Pull out the outlet when you have detached the back-nut. If the mastic or putty holds it tightly in position, lever it out with a screwdriver.*

4 *When you have removed the waste outlet, measure the hole you need, mark it out in the sink and cut it with a saw file cutting tool.*

5 *Lift out the metal section carefully as it will be ragged and sharp where you have cut it. Check that the hole is the right size.*

6 *Take the new outlet flange supplied with the unit and put a bead of plumber's putty underneath it before placing it in the opening.*

Ready Reference

OPERATING A DISPOSAL UNIT

ALWAYS
● grind food waste with a strong flow of cold water
● grind all soft waste including paper napkins, paper towels, cigar and cigarette butts, tea bags provided they don't have strings, and also small bones such as chicken bones
● flush the unit regularly to aid thorough cleaning
● turn the power switch off before attempting to clear a jam or remove an object from the disposer
● use a long piece of wood to clear jams
● leave the outlet cover in place to reduce the risk of objects falling into it when not in use
● make sure the unit is earthed.

NEVER
● put your fingers or hands into the unit to clear a jam
● let children operate the unit
● use hot water when grinding waste – but you can drain it out between grinding periods
● feed in large quantities of fibrous waste at once – instead, this should be well mixed with other waste and fed in gradually
● grind cans, bottles, bottle caps, glass, china, leather, cloth, rubber, string, feathers, newsprint, or large bones
● pour any drain-cleaning chemicals through the unit
● turn off the motor or water until grinding is completed (ie, only when you can hear the motor running freely).

FAULT FINDING
Problems may occur with your unit:
● if there is a water leak round the sink flange: the seal will have to be remade
● if the water drains slowly when the unit is in operation and the waste is clogging up the outlet: keep on grinding and flushing through
● if the disposer won't start. There may be an electrical fault or the motor may have been overloaded: check the cut-out and reset if necessary
● if the unit doesn't function properly immediately after installation. It is likely that the drain line is blocked or can't cope with the outlet discharge – unless there is a problem with the unit itself
● if there are loud noises from the unit when it's in operation: switch off and check for foreign bodies
● if the unit jams: turn it off and follow the manufacturer's instructions for clearing blockages.

INSTALLING THE WASTE DISPOSAL UNIT

1 Take the basic flange components supplied and check the assembly order. There will be a gasket ring, a spacer ring, and a protector ring.

2 Hold the sink flange down, slide the assembly into place, and tighten the screws evenly to make sure there is a watertight seal.

3 Lubricate the inner lip of the rubber flange on the top of the unit with a small amount of petroleum jelly or household oil.

4 Push the unit into place so that the rubber lip engages the sink flange and is held in place by it, leaving the unit hanging by itself.

5 Rotate the unit to align it with the waste outlet and tighten the screw clamp evenly all round to hold the whole assembly firmly in position.

6 Fix on the waste outlet elbow and attach a P-trap 38mm (1½in) in diameter. Check that the trap is tight and connect it to the waste pipe.

the outlet has been removed, check the size of the enlarged hole you need with the new outlet as a guide, then use the cutting tool to cut it out.

With your aperture cut, or with your new sink, bed down the new waste outlet with plumber's putty, and screw up the back-nut and washer. Then attach the suspension plate for the unit, and finally the unit itself. The manufacturer should provide full instructions for the whole operation; follow them carefully.

A tubular P-trap should be attached to the unit via pipe connections which will be supplied. If there is no convenient way of attaching a sink overflow to a disposal unit, you can either seal it off or pipe it down to a socket fitted above the trap in the waste outlet.

PARTS OF A WASTE DISPOSAL UNIT

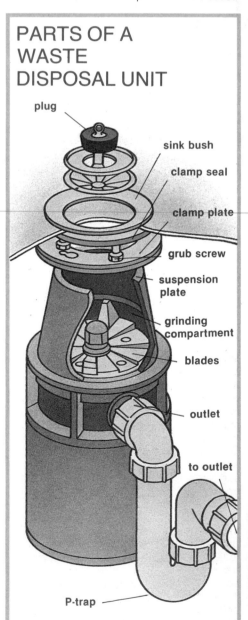

- plug
- sink bush
- clamp seal
- clamp plate
- grub screw
- suspension plate
- grinding compartment
- blades
- outlet
- to outlet
- P-trap

WIRING UP THE UNIT

Providing power for a waste disposal unit is simple. You can plug it directly into a 13A socket outlet, but it's better to run a spur and use a connection unit.

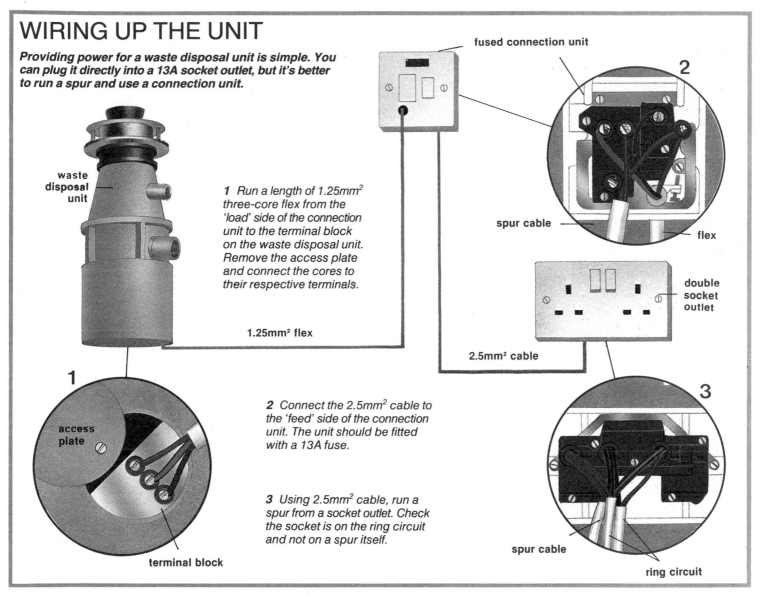

waste disposal unit

1 Run a length of 1.25mm² three-core flex from the 'load' side of the connection unit to the terminal block on the waste disposal unit. Remove the access plate and connect the cores to their respective terminals.

fused connection unit

2

spur cable

flex

1.25mm² flex

double socket outlet

2.5mm² cable

2 Connect the 2.5mm² cable to the 'feed' side of the connection unit. The unit should be fitted with a 13A fuse.

3 Using 2.5mm² cable, run a spur from a socket outlet. Check the socket is on the ring circuit and not on a spur itself.

3

1

access plate

terminal block

spur cable

ring circuit

Wiring up the unit

Most waste disposal units are powered by an electric induction motor. This sort of motor is constructed differently to the motor found in most other home electrical appliances. It starts immediately on full load, the starting current needed being much less than that of other types of electric motor. As a result a waste disposal unit needs only a 13A electricity supply, which can conveniently be provided from a nearby circuit.

There are a number of models on the market, and the differences between them can affect the electric wiring you have to provide. The principal difference is whether the unit has reversing facilities or not. The simplest type has no reversing facilities – it runs in one direction only. Should the unit become jammed the electricity supply must be switched off before a release key is inserted to engage the impeller and release the jam. Such one-way

motors are protected from the overloading a jam causes by a thermal cut-out; after clearing the jam you will have to reset this by depressing a button on the motor frame before the motor can be restarted.

Other versions have special switch-gear which reverses the direction of the electric motor every time it is switched on. With these types the reversing controller, which incorporates a double-pole switch and 13A fuse, is either mounted integral with the unit or fixed to the wall in the kitchen some 300mm (12in) above the work surface.

A waste disposal unit should ideally be connected to a 13A switched fused connection unit (once called a fused spur unit). This unit has the required double-pole isolating switch and 13A cartridge fuse; it might be best to choose the version with a neon indicator light.

A possible alternative outlet is a 13A fused plug and switched socket outlet, but as the

switch is only single-pole it is always necessary to remove the plug to isolate the unit and there is also a likelihood that the socket may be used temporarily for other appliances. The circuit wiring required to supply a waste disposal unit is simply a spur cable branching off the ring circuit cable. The connection at the ring circuit is usually more conveniently made at an existing 13A socket outlet than at a junction box inserted into the ring cable. You should use 2.5mm² two-core and earth cable and run it from the socket to the point where you intend to fix the switched fused connection unit or special reversing controller.

Connect a length of 1.25mm² three-core flex to the 'load' side of the connection unit and run it to the terminal block of the waste disposal unit. The brown core should then be connected to the 'L' terminal, the blue to the 'N' and finally the green/yellow to the 'E' terminal.

INSTALLING A WATER SOFTENER

Hard water is more than just a nuisance causing fur in kettles – scale can even affect the efficiency of a plumbing system. But if you install a water softener you can prevent most of these problems occurring.

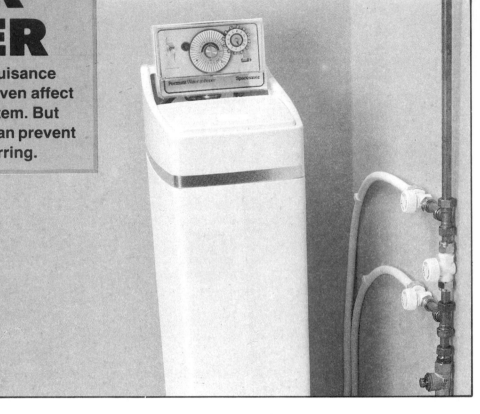

Wherever you are in the country, one glass of water looks virtually the same as a glass from another area. This may be stating the obvious – water is water – but there are important invisible differences which affect the chemical composition of water and therefore, in turn, its qualities. It's because of these differences that water can be described as being 'hard' or 'soft' (see below). And if you live in an area which has hard water you'll know all too well what that means. When you're washing, for example, the soap will form an insoluble curd – scum – instead of a cleansing lather. Woollens mat in the wash, hair washing becomes a misery, and a dirty tidemark is left round baths and basins which has to be laboriously wiped away. There are few things as unpleasant in a kitchen than 'fur' on the inside of a kettle (an instant sign of hard water). And if this is allowed to build up, eventually it will affect the taste of the water (as well as shortening the life of the heating element). Furthermore, hard water scale clogs ball-valves and taps, leaving an unsightly deposit round the spout.

As you can see, if the build up of scale is left unchecked it can seriously affect the efficiency of your plumbing system. A coating of scale on the element of an immersion heater, for instance, means the element has to become even hotter to get the water to the required temperature. Apart from using up expensive electricity to do this, it will soon burn itself out. The build-up of scale on the inside of pipes or a boiler will have a similar effect.

Causes of hard water

Most of our domestic water supply starts its life as rainfall. As each droplet falls, it absorbs gases in the atmosphere such as oxygen, sulphur dioxide and carbon dioxide. It is because of the absorption of the last gas in particular that rainwater is in fact very weakly acidic. This process of absorbing or carrying impurities in suspension continues once the rain reaches the ground, and it dramatically affects the overall qualities of the water.

For example, if rainwater falls on moorland peat or sandstone the water becomes more acidic and is said to be 'soft'. However, water

PLUMBING IN THE SOFTENER

Connect the softener to the rising main above the kitchen tap branch. The drain outlet can be fed into a stand-pipe or else run directly to a drain.

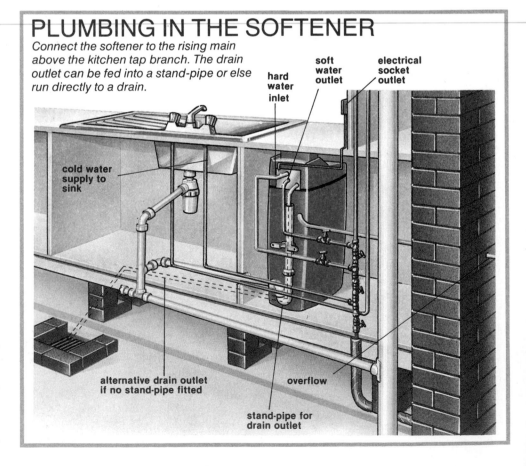

- cold water supply to sink
- hard water inlet
- soft water outlet
- electrical socket outlet
- alternative drain outlet if no stand-pipe fitted
- overflow
- stand-pipe for drain outlet

CONNECTING INTO THE MAINS

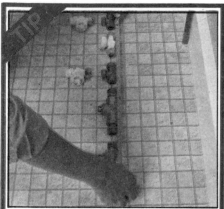

1 *Lay out the fittings in the order they have to be assembled (see* Ready Reference*). Remember to allow for short stubs of pipe linking the fittings.*

2 *Mark off the overall measurement of the length of fittings on the relevant section of rising main. Then turn off the water supply and drain the pipe.*

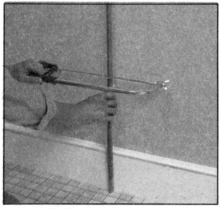

3 *Use a hacksaw to cut out this section of pipe. Make sure you support the rising main with your free hand to reduce damaging any joints on the run.*

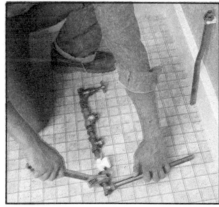

4 *Assemble the fittings in the correct order, but leave them finger-tight. The final tightening will be done when everything is in position.*

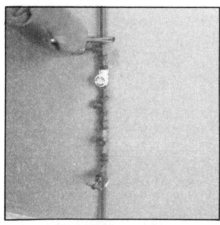

5 *Assemble the fittings in the rising main, making sure that the compression tees are parallel to the wall. Then tighten all the joins.*

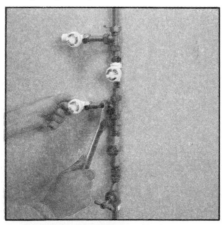

6 *Next, connect the inlet and outlet valves to the tees (the inlet valve goes at the bottom). Turn these valves 'off' and restore the water supply.*

Ready Reference

DO YOU NEED A SOFTENER?

If you live in the South or East of England, or in the Midlands, you'll almost certainly have a hard water supply. Elsewhere – in the Scottish Highlands, the West Country or Wales, for instance – the water supply may be soft, but there are also pockets of hard water in these areas.

TYPES OF HARD WATER

Hard water can either be 'temporary' or 'permanent':
● temporary hardness can be removed by boiling the water. This causes scale to be deposited which furs up kettles and hot water systems
● permanent hardness can't be removed by heating. It doesn't affect hot water systems but the other effects remain.

TIP: PREVENT SCALE

● Scale builds up when the water temperature exceeds 60°C, so in hard water areas turn boiler thermostats down to this level. In soft water areas it can be set at 70°C.
● Convert a direct to an indirect hot water system
● Add chemical softeners to the water to prevent scale building up.

HOW A SOFTENER WORKS

The softener has to be connected into the rising main. Water is passed through a resin where the chemicals which cause hardness – calcium and magnesium bicarbonates, sulphates and chlorides – are exchanged for sodium salts.

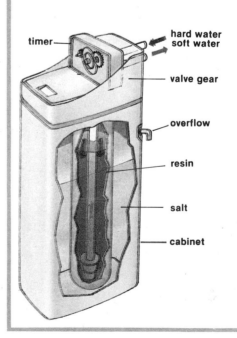

CONNECTING UP THE WATER SOFTENER

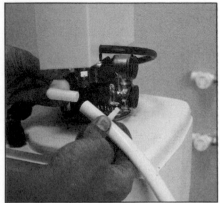

1 Measure the length of drain hose to run from the appliance to an outside drain. Push the end over the drain spigot and secure with a clip.

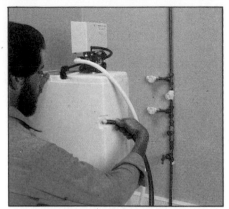

2 Similarly, fix a length of hose to the overflow spigot and then run it to an outside wall where you can easily see any water discharging from it.

3 Next connect the plastic nipples to the inlet and outlet of the appliance. First wind PTFE tape round the thread and screw in the outlet nipple.

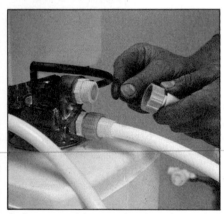

6 Insert a rubber washer into the end of the connector. Screw the outlet hose into position and then add the inlet hose above it.

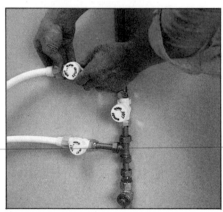

7 Repeat the operation to connect the hoses to the valves next to the rising main. You can use an adjustable spanner, but be careful not to overtighten the nuts.

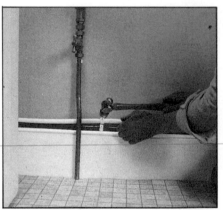

8 Once all the connections have been made, set the appliance in the correct position and clip the hoses neatly to the wall and skirting.

falling on limestone (or chalk) loses its dissolved carbon dioxide as it begins to erode the rock. Such water is also likely to contain bicarbonates, sulphates and chlorides of calcium and magnesium – the chemicals that produce hardness.

The problems of soft water
Despite the catalogue of problems associated with hard water, soft water also has some drawbacks. In particular, because soft water is acidic its corrosive properties are increased; some metals, notably iron, rust more quickly when they come into contact with it. So if you have iron pipes or tanks in a soft water area then you could expect problems as they start to corrode. The answer, obviously, is to use parts made from PVC, polythene, copper, asbestos cement or glass fibre – in other words materials not prone to this form of corrosive attack.

One other thing worth noting is that in areas where there is soft water more people are prone to cardio-vascular diseases – strokes and similar conditions – than in hard water areas. No one is really sure of the reason for this. It could be that the chemicals in hard water provide some form of natural protection. Another possible explanation is that soft water is much more likely to dissolve the metal of the pipes it flows through than hard water is – so the dissolved impurities could contribute to the diseases.

Dealing with hard water
There are a number of ways in which the annoying effects of hard water can be reduced. Boiler scale, for instance, may be reduced or eliminated by controlling the temperature of the water or by using a chemical scale inhibitor. The most disruptive solution is to install an indirect hot water

system, if you haven't already got one. Small quantities of hard water can be softened by the addition of water-softening chemicals (sold commercially as Calgon) which neutralise the dissolved salts causing the hardness. The most radical solution, though, is to install a mains water softener which can reduce to 'zero hardness' every drop of water that passes through it.

How a mains water softener works
Mains water softeners work on a chemical principle that used to be called 'base exchange' but is now more commonly known as 'ion exchange'. The principle was discovered by observing hard water as it filtered through beds of natural sand. The water became soft. So these sands were used in the early water softeners. Now synthetic resins are used to produce the same effect. The hard water is passed through the

4 *Cut the feed and return hoses to length. Then lubricate the ends with washing-up liquid to make it easier to slip them over the hose connectors.*

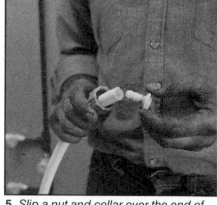

5 *Slip a nut and collar over the end of the hose, then push the end over the connector so that it butts against the shoulder.*

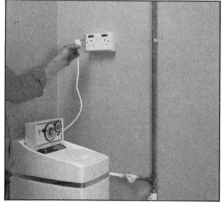

9 *The timing controls for the regeneration process have to be plugged into a convenient socket or linked to a fused connection unit.*

10 *Fill the appliance with salt and set the timer. The inlet and outlet valves can be opened and the bypass valve closed; the machine is then operational.*

Ready Reference

THE PLUMBING CONNECTIONS

Water softeners for DIY installation come with all the necessary fittings. You may also need to buy a new screw-down stop-valve. Arrange the fittings in the rising main in the following order:

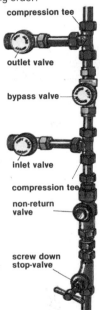

compression tee

outlet valve

bypass valve

inlet valve

compression tee

non-return valve

screw down stop-valve

TIP: CHECK THE STORAGE CISTERN

Fitting a water softener may reduce the pressure at the ball-valve supplying the cold water storage cistern. You may need to replace the valve with an equilibrium model.

---

appliance and the chemicals in the water literally 'exchange atoms' with the chemicals in the resin. The result is that dissolved *calcium* bicarbonate, for example, is replaced by dissolved *sodium* bicarbonate which does not cause hardness.

After a while, however, the softening qualities of the resin are exhausted, but they can be restored (regenerated) by passing a strong solution of sodium chloride (common salt) through the softener. The cycle of regeneration must be undertaken at regular intervals, perhaps once a week in a household with average water consumption. The resin is first backwashed to loosen up the resin bed and to remove any debris. The water is then run to waste. Next the salt solution is passed through the resin, followed by a final rinse of ordinary water to wash any surplus brine from the resin bed before the softener is brought back into use.

With early water softeners you had to carry out this regeneration process mechanically every week – a process which could become quite a chore. But now water softeners have a large salt reservoir capable of supplying brine for 25 or more regenerations. These take place automatically (usually at about 2 o'clock in the morning when everyone is asleep). The process can be started by a time clock, by a device that measures the volume of water that passes through the softener or by a sensor which can detect when the resin is beginning to lose its softening capacity. All you have to do is to replenish the salt reservoir perhaps once or twice a year.

Installing a water softener

A mains water softener has to be plumbed in to the rising main at any convenient point, and can be used to soften every drop of water flowing into the house. However, for health reasons it's best to retain a cold supply of hard water over the kitchen sink and there's no need to soften the water supplying an outside tap. Therefore hard water remains available for drinking and cooking while soft water is used for baths, laundry and (through the hot tap over the kitchen sink) for washing up.

Once you've decided on the make and capacity of the water softener, read the installation instructions carefully and consult your local water authority before you begin. You may have to install a pressure-reducing valve as part of the installation and the authority will almost certainly demand that a non-return valve is fitted to prevent any risk of contamination of the mains supply. The step-by-step photographs show how one of these appliances is plumbed in. The provision of inlet, outlet and bypass valves means the softeners can be isolated from the mains for any maintenance that's required.

REPLACING AN OUTSIDE SOIL STACK

You can't make new connections into an old cast iron soil pipe. So changing your indoor plumbing system will mean fitting a new soil stack too.

If your house was built before the mid-1950s it will almost certainly have a 'two-pipe' above-ground drainage system made of cast iron. This system was originally devised by Victorian sanitary engineers in a determined effort to keep 'drain air', which was believed by the public health experts of the time to be the cause of virtually all human disease, out of the home. The system made a distinction between 'soil appliances' – WCs – and 'waste appliances' – basins, sinks, baths, etc. Soil was sent down one pipe to the underground drain, and waste was sent down another (although it eventually reached the same drain). Drain smells were, and still are, prevented from spreading inside the house by the use of water traps at the outlet of each appliance.

Modern homes are provided with 'single stack' above-ground drainage systems using PVC or similar plastic waste pipes. In a single stack system no distinction is made between soil and waste appliances. All discharges go into one main stack which, as with the old soil pipe, terminates open-ended above eaves level. To make these systems safe they must be in strict accordance with the regulations. For more explanation of two-pipe and single stack systems see WASTE WATER SYSTEMS.

In most cases it is possible to replace an obsolete two-pipe system with a modern single stack one, but the local council's Building Inspector must be consulted about your plans in advance, and very careful attention should be paid to the design of the new system if it is to be both efficient and safe. In new houses the single stack is often located inside the house, in a boxed service duct, but this isn't a legal requirement and replacement of an existing external soil stack by a single stack in the same position is perfectly acceptable.

Single stack requirements

In order to prevent water from siphoning out of the traps of baths and basins which have pipe connections to a single stack, deep-seal 75mm (3in) traps must be used. For the same reason, branch waste pipes from baths and basins have to be laid with a very small angle of fall to the stack and should be as short as possible. This is particularly important with the basin waste, because, if the trap should siphon out, very little water is left after the main discharge to reseal it. The basin branch waste should preferably be no longer than 1.7m (5ft 7in). If a greater length is unavoidable, you should install a patent anti-siphon trap or use a branch waste-pipe 38mm (1½in) in diameter, instead of the usual 32mm (1¼in). This means that if an old system has shallow traps – often 50mm (2in) in depth – long pipe runs and steep angles, any replacement of the stack will mean considerable replumbing inside.

The branch soil pipe from the WC suite must be connected to the main soil and waste stack by a swept joint in the direction of the soil flow. To prevent waste outlets from baths, basins or bidets from being fouled or obstructed by discharges of soil from the WC, no connection may be made to the opposite side of the main stack within 200mm (8in) of the centre point of the connection of the soil branch. Special boss sockets are available which allow connections to be made at apparently the same level as the lavatory outlet. In fact, inside the boss the waste is deflected downwards to flow into the stack itself below the level of the soil pipe entry.

The main soil and waste stack, which must have an internal diameter of at least 100mm (4in), must connect to the underground drain with a bend of at least 200mm (8in) radius. In some cases this will mean that, as well as replacing the old soil pipe, it will be necessary to replace the – usually short – length of underground drain between the foot of the soil-pipe and the drain inspection chamber. This job is not too difficult but must be done with great precision to ensure efficient drainage.

Although the single stack is now the most popular system for the drainage of appliances on first floors and above, there is little, if anything, to be gained by converting ground floor drainage to a single stack system. Ground floor WCs may quite conveniently be connected direct to the nearest inspection chamber by means of a branch from the underground drain, and there is no objection to ground floor sinks, baths and basins discharging over a yard gully. These discharges should however enter the gully above the water level but below the level of the gully grid. Slotted grids are available to allow existing gullies to be adapted in this way.

Assembling the new system

Get an illustrated catalogue of plastic above-ground drainage components from your local builder's merchant, or send away for one. Using this, have a look at the existing

SOIL AND WASTE PIPE FITTINGS

The choice of modern plastic soil and waste pipes and fittings is quite bewildering. You will have to make a careful survey of the job to work out the individual components you will need. Try and get hold of a manufacturer's brochure which will show you the range available. Most soil fittings are made of unplasticised polyvinyl chloride (UPVC), but waste pipes may be of polypropylene (PP) and waste fittings of acrylonitrile butadiene styrene (ABS) or polyethylene. There are two systems for joining plastic pipes and fittings, push-fit and solvent welding (as described on pages 38 to 42). Push-fit fittings should be used where particularly hot water passes through the waste system, as they allow for expansion.

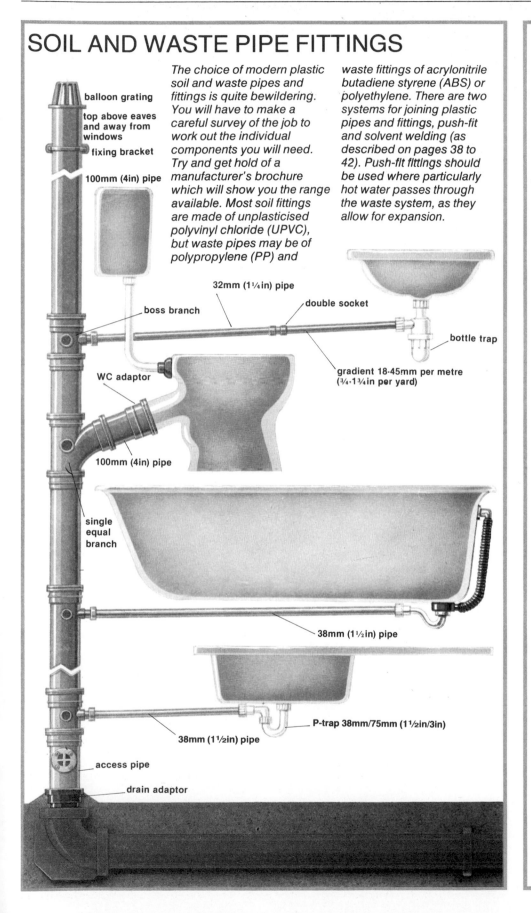

balloon grating
top above eaves and away from windows
fixing bracket
100mm (4in) pipe
boss branch
WC adaptor
100mm (4in) pipe
single equal branch
access pipe
drain adaptor

32mm (1¼in) pipe
double socket
bottle trap
gradient 18-45mm per metre (¾-1¾in per yard)

38mm (1½in) pipe

P-trap 38mm/75mm (1½in/3in)
38mm (1½in) pipe

Ready Reference

CHECKING REGULATIONS

Before you install a single drainage stack you should consult your local Building Inspector to ensure that your plans are in compliance with the Building Regulations. He may also want to inspect the work after you have finished it. Remember:

● basins, baths, showers, washing machines and dishwashing machine outlets need P-traps. The depth of trap seal, except on baths and showers should always be 75mm (3in). The exception is WC pans which can have integral S-traps (see WASTE WATER SYSTEMS)

● wash basins and bidets need a 32mm (1¼in) diameter trap and branch pipe, if the branch is up to 1.7m (5ft 7in) long. If it is more – up to a maximum of 2.3m (7ft 6in) – use a 38mm (1½in) trap and pipe

● baths, sinks and showers need a 38mm (1½in) diameter trap and branch pipe

● washing machines should have a vertical standpipe (usually about 600mm/24in high) with a 32mm (1¼in) diameter trap, at the bottom of which should be a P- or running P-trap. You need an air gap where the hose enters the stack pipe

● WC branch pipes should be 100mm (4in) in diameter with a maximum length of 6m (20ft) from stack to pan, though a shorter run is preferable

● branch pipe gradients should have an angle of between 1° and 2½° (18-45mm per metre/¾-1¾in per yard)

● ground floor WCs can connect directly into the underground drain as long as the top of the trap is less than 1.5m (5ft) above the point of entry into the main drain

● there should be no connection nearer than 200mm (8in) below the WC branch connection from the opposite side of the stack

● the lowest connection to the stack must be at least 450mm (18in) above the bottom of the bend at the base of the stack

● the bend at the base of the stack where the pipe turns to flow into the underground drain must have a radius of at least 200mm (8in)

● stack pipes must be at least the same diameter as the WC outlet

● the top of the stack pipe, capped with a grille, must be above the eaves and at least 0.9m (35in) above any window which is within 3m (10ft) of the pipe.

REMOVING THE OLD PIPEWORK

1 *Start on the old waste pipe; use a club hammer and chisel to loosen the brackets supporting the pipe and lever them out.*

2 *The pipe should now come free from the hopper head connection. If you can't move it easily, then tap gently downwards with a club hammer.*

3 *When you've got the waste pipe out of the way, remove any other inflows, including the old bath overflow pipe which is illustrated here.*

4 *The top part of the soil stack, with an eaves level vent, needs a lot of care. If you can't lift it free, try and break up the pipe.*

5 *When you have cracked the old pipe, lift the section clear. It will be quite heavy, so be careful how you lower it to the ground.*

6 *Move further down the stack and break each joint in turn. Lift each section clear and carry it carefully down to the ground.*

7 *When you get to the old outlet from the WC pan, lever it gently out through the wall. Try not to dislodge any bricks in the wall.*

8 *At the bottom of the stack, gently chip away the concrete round the base of the pipe, until it starts to loosen and come free.*

9 *Lift the pipe free of the drain socket connection. Ensure that no pieces of broken concrete and debris fall into the opening.*

ASSEMBLING THE STACK

1 Carefully clean out the old underground drain connection. It may need replacing if the bend is too tight; check the Regulations.

2 Install new outlet connections so that they emerge flush with the outside wall surface. Don't fix them rigidly in place yet.

3 Using a drain connector and access branch, start to make up the base of the stack. Use push-fit or solvent-weld fittings.

4 Mortar in the drain connector to the underground drain joint, using a quick-dry mortar. Check that the pipe is truly vertical.

5 When the mortar joint is firm, start to extend the stack upwards, using sockets according to the connections you want to make.

6 Support the stack with brackets about every 2m (6ft 6in). These are easily fixed by drilling into the wall and using wall plugs.

7 Make the lowermost connection to the stack using the appropriate plastic-pipe fitting technique. Here an inspection junction is being fitted.

8 Make sure the connections to the stack are firm, and don't finally fix the through-wall connections (see 2) until these are made.

9 In the case of solvent-weld jointing (as used here), further connections should only be made when the previous ones are completely firm.

ACKNOWLEDGEMENTS

Photographers: Jon Bouchier, Simon Butcher, Paul Forrester, Simon Gear, Jem Grischotti, Barry Jell, Keith Morris, Karen Norquay, Ian O'Leary, Roger Tuff
Artists: Roger Courthold Associates, Bernard Fallon, Nick Farmer, Val Hill, Trevor Lawrence, Linden Artists, David Pope, Peter Robinson, Mike Saunders, Ian Stephen, Ralph Stobart, Ed Stuart, Craig Warwick, Brian Watson, David Webb, Universal Studios